THE ENCYCLOPEDIA OF

WARSHIPS

THE ENCYCLOPEDIA OF
WARSHIPS

FROM WORLD WAR II TO THE PRESENT DAY

GENERAL EDITOR:
ROBERT JACKSON

THUNDER BAY
P·R·E·S·S

San Diego, California

Thunder Bay Press
An imprint of the Advantage Publishers Group
5880 Oberlin Drive, San Diego, CA 92121-4794
www.thunderbaybooks.com

All notations of errors or omissions should be addressed to Thunder Bay Press,
Editorial Department, at the above address. All other correspondence (author inquiries,
permissions) concerning the content of this book should be addressed to
Amber Books Ltd., Bradley's Close, 74–77 White Lion Street, London N1 9PF,
United Kingdom. www.amberbooks.co.uk.

ISBN-13: 978-1-59223-627-5
ISBN-10: 1-59223-627-8

Library of Congress Cataloging-in-Publication Data available upon request.

Printed in Singapore

1 2 3 4 5 10 09 08 07 06

PICTURE CREDITS
All photographs and illustrations provided by Art-Tech/Aerospace Publishing,
except the following:
8, 10–11: MARS
9, 286–287: U.S. Department of Defense

CONTENTS

The 'Los Angeles'-class attack submarine USS Louisville (SSN 724) surfaces off the coast of southern California, March 2005. Louisville was participating in a Joint Task Force Training Exercise with Carrier Strike Group Eleven (CSG-11).

Introduction

The types of warship that serve with today's navies are much the same as the types that served in World War II, albeit vastly different in terms of power and capability. Only the great battleships are gone, the last survivors turned into museum pieces after one final operational fling in the limited wars of the twentieth century's final decade.

LONG BEFORE, the battleships' place as the principal capital ships of a major navy had been usurped by the aircraft carrier, whose effectiveness as a weapon of war had first been demonstrated by Britain's Royal Navy in

A classic battleship of its type, the Royal Navy's HMS King George V was part of the group that chased and finally sunk the German battleship KMS Bismark in May 1941.

November 1940, when carrier-based, torpedo-armed aircraft crippled the Italian battle fleet at Taranto and assured British naval supremacy in the crucial Mediterranean theatre.

It was a lesson not lost on Japanese Admiral Isoroku Yamamoto, whose carrier aircraft repeated the exercise on a far greater scale at Pearl Harbor against the US Navy just over a year later.

Today, in addition to virtually unlimited high-speed

endurance, nuclear propulsion for aircraft carriers provides additional space for aviation fuel and ordnance. The mighty carriers of the US Navy's 'Nimitz' class, for example, displace over 96,000 tons at full load and are over 305 m (1,000 feet) in length, with accommodation for 6,000 personnel and more than 100 aircraft and helicopters. Such vessels, in their own right, provide a striking force of terrifying power.

Specialist roles

Cruisers, originally designed as fast warships with medium armament for shadowing enemy surface forces, are mainly used today in what is known as a 'Battle Force' role as part of an integrated naval task force. These ships are multi-mission Air Warfare (AW), Undersea Warfare (USW), and Surface Warfare (SUW) – surface combatants capable of supporting carrier battle groups, amphibious

forces, or of operating independently and as flagships of surface action groups. Cruisers are equipped with cruise missiles, giving them additional long-range strike mission capability.

Since World War II, the destroyer has evolved from a torpedo-armed, all-gun surface warfare vessel into a specialist anti-air or anti-submarine ship, capable either of independent operations for a short time or of operating as an escort in a task force. Perhaps the most capable modern destroyer design is the American 'Spruance' class, optimized for ASW. Modifying the design for the anti-air role produced the Kidd class, which at the time of commissioning were the most powerfully armed general purpose destroyers in the world.

Ever since the frigate was conceived in the eighteenth century – when it was used mainly for reconnaissance and commerce raiding – it has formed a very important element in the world's navies. Today, the name is applied to a wide variety of vessels, ranging from very expensive and highly specialized anti-submarine warfare ships like the Royal Navy's Type 22, to cheaper ships like the US Navy's 'Knox' class, designed to escort convoys and amphibious warfare task groups. At the heart of the latter is the assault ship. In 1940, the concept of amphibious warfare underwent a revolution with the formation of the first British Commando units and the development of the vessels that were to carry them into action.

Converted fast cargo ships became assault carrier ships, while assault landing craft were developed, some to carry troops, others to lift tanks and heavy support vehicles. The lessons of World War II, learned the hard way on the Normandy beaches and in the Pacific, gave birth to today's mighty amphibious task forces, with their huge weight of supporting airpower and firepower.

Submarine warfare

During World War II, the activities of Germany's U-boats brought Britain close to defeat, and turned the Atlantic Ocean into a crucial theatre of war. The lessons were not forgotten, and by the late 1950s the submarine was seen as an instrument that could decide the outcome of a war – perhaps even a non-nuclear war – fought on the high seas.

The United States could not match the USSR in terms of submarine production, but it could outstrip it technologically. In 1954 the US Navy commissioned its first nuclear-powered submarine, the USS *Nautilus*, and within three years was experimenting with submarine-launched ballistic missiles. So it was that the

The 'Nimitz' class aircraft carrier USS **Theodore Roosevelt** *(left) receives ammunition from the supply ship USS* **Santa Barbara** *off the coast of Virginia, December 1995. Today's aircraft carriers are so powerful as to constitute a strike force all on their own.*

ballistic missile submarine became the super-powers' new capital ship; and its deployment gave rise to a new generation of nuclear submarines, the hunter-killers, whose task was to track and destroy the former.

Including entries on all the main types and models, *The Encyclopedia of Warships* explains the development of the world's leading warships, from the grim days of World War II to the present, and provides a timely reminder that command of the seas is still a crucial factor in preserving world peace.

Robert Jackson, *Editor*

World War II

Aircraft carriers played a leading part in World War II, especially in the Pacific campaigns. By the mid-1930s, they featured prominently in the navies of the world's great maritime nations. Only Germany, preoccupied with the production of submarines and a new generation of battleships, was slow to realize the importance of the carrier, and although one was laid down prior to the war, it was never completed.

However, the U-boat weapon, in the hands of skilled and courageous crews, brought the Allies to the brink of disaster in the early years of the war, and generated a whole range of counter-measures to combat it. On the other hand, Germany's new battleships operated singly instead of at the heart of a task force, and were picked off one-by-one as the war progressed.

On the other side of the world, the Japanese also felt the overwhelming impact of air superiority, as their mightiest battleships were hunted to destruction by the US Navy, which rebuilt itself after Pearl Harbor to become the world's greatest maritime power.

Left: German U-boats undergo service checks in the docks at Krupp's Germania shipyard in Kiel, 1939. Krupp were Nazi Germany's largest steelmaker, and were consequently involved in the production of many of the Kriegsmarine's U-boats.

HMS *Warspite* Battleship

Like so many battleships that distinguished themselves in World War II, **HMS *Warspite*** was a veteran of the previous conflict. The fourth unit of the 'Queen Elizabeth' class, she was laid down in October 1912, launched in November 1913 and completed in March 1915. She served for most of World War I with the Grand Fleet, but at the Battle of Jutland in May 1916 her squadron was attached to Vice Admiral Beatty's battle-cruisers. When her steering gear broke down, she turned circles and came under fire from seven German battleships but was able to escape without suffering serious damage.

In the early 1920s the *Warspite* was modernized, with anti-torpedo bulges, more anti-aircraft guns and the forward funnel trunked backwards into the second one. In 1934, she was taken in hand for a much more comprehensive reconstruction, which was to be the prototype for all British capital ships. New steam turbines and new boilers were provided, with six modem boilers replacing 24 old boilers; this reduced their total weight from 3,690 tons to 2,300 tons. Subdivision was improved, more deck armour was added, and the elevation of the 15-in (381-mm) guns was increased from 20° to 30°, so increasing range from 21395 m (23,400 yards) to 29445 m (32,200 yards). The appearance of the ship was also transformed, with a single funnel and a massive tower superstructure enclosing all control positions.

Numerous honours

The *Warspite* added 13 battle honours to the one she had earned in 1916. In April 1940, her main armament helped to sink the German destroyers at Narvik. Then she became Admiral Cunningham's flagship in the Mediterranean Fleet, and was immediately in the forefront of the naval war.

During the Battle of Calabria in July 1940, she hit the Italian battleship *Giulio Cesare* with her first salvo at 23,775 m (26,000 yards), the greatest distance at which one ship ever hit another on the move. With HMS *Barham* and HMS *Valiant*, she sank three Italian heavy cruisers in the Battle of Matapan in March 1941, but two months later was badly damaged by air attack during the evacuation from Crete.

After repairs in the US she served in the Eastern Fleet in 1942, then returned to the Mediterranean in 1943. She was nearly sunk by glider bombs off Salerno in September 1943, but was repaired in time for the Normandy landings in June 1944. Despite mine damage she carried out a large number of bombardments until laid up in January 1945. She was sold for scrap in 1946, but ran aground on the Cornish coast.

SPECIFICATION	
HMS *Warspite*	decks 32–104 mm (1³⁄₄–4 in); turrets
Displacement: 31,372 tons standard; 36,450 tons full load	127–330 mm (5–13 in); conning tower 280 mm (11 in)
Dimensions: length 195.0 m (640 ft) overall; beam 31.7 m (104 ft) over bulges; draught 9.37 m (30 ft 9 in)	**Armament:** eight 15-in (381-mm), eight 6-in (152-mm), eight 4-in (102-mm) AA, 32 2-pdr 'pom-pom' and 16 0.5-in (12.7-mm) AA guns
Machinery: 4-shaft geared steam turbines delivering 59,656 kW (80,000 shp)	**Aircraft:** two Fairey Swordfish floatplanes
Speed: 23½ kt	**Complement:** 1,120 men
Armour: belt 102–330 mm (4–13 in);	

As the first British capital ship to be modernized in the 1930s, the Warspite *reflected changing ideas and technology. Her new machinery was much lighter, allowing more weight to be devoted to deck armour, AA armament and aircraft hangars.*

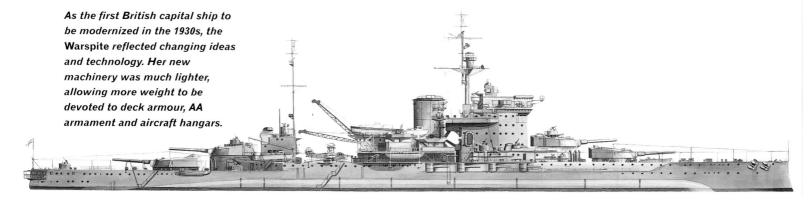

'R' class Battleships

Owing their creation to First Sea Lord John Fisher, following his return to the Admiralty, the **'R'-class** battleships were commissioned in 1916. In total, four 'R'-class battleships were constructed. These included the **HMS *Royal Sovereign***, **HMS *Revenge***, **HMS *Resolution*** and **HMS *Royal Oak***. A further three ships were also proposed during the initial design stage. These were **HMS *Resistance***, **HMS *Renown*** and **HMS *Repulse***.

While HMS *Resistance* never saw the light of day, HMS *Revenge* and *Renown* emerged as battlecruisers. HMS *Renown* and HMS *Repulse* were commissioned into the fleet in 1916. Interestingly, *Repulse* had the distinction of having served in both world wars. These ships carried six 15-inch (381-mm) guns and were also lightly armoured. However, their strength existed in their superior speed. Four-shaft Parsons geared turbines gave the vessel a top speed of over 30 knots. This was unlike their battleship counterparts, which were considered slow and obsolete on the eve of World War II. Although they were condemned as 'coffin ships', they saw extensive action during World War II.

While the R-class battleships recieved no major structural modifications, the battlecruisers recieved several extensive upgrades. One of the ships, HMS *Renown*, was rebuilt between 1923 and 1926. She was refitted with additional armour to improve her combat tolerance. A belt of 9-inch (229-mm) thick armour was mounted around the hull. This replaced the 6-inch (152-mm) armour orginally fitted to the ship. Furthermore, her secondary battery was also replaced. This had the added effect of increasing her overall displacement to 31,000 tonnes.

The *Renown* was upgraded yet again between 1936 and

1939, which improved her engines by fitting extra boilers and improved generators. Yet again, the secondary battery was also improved. The R-class boats were also fitted with an aircraft hanger and catapult, which gave the vessels a maritime patrol and reconaissance capability.

However, this capability was later withdrawn.

The R-class ships received extensive improvements to their Anti-Aircraft Artillery suites, a reaction to the ever present air threat from the Luftwaffe.

Several of the R-class suffered bad luck – for example, HMS *Royal Oak* was sunk after

being torpedoed off Scapa Flow, the home of the Royal Navy northern fleet, on 4 October 1939. HMS *Renown* survived

the war but her sister ship, HMS *Repulse*, was less fortunate. She was sunk in 1941.

HMS **Ramilies** *distinguished itself taking part in the bombardment of Bardia during August 1940.*

SPECIFICATION	
'R' class	254 mm (10 in); conning tower
Displacement: 29,150 tonnes	280 mm (11 in)
Dimensions: length 187 m	**Armament:** eight 15-in (381-mm), 12
(614 ft 5 in); beam 31.2 m	6-in (152-mm), eight 4-in (102-mm)
(102 ft 5 in); draft 9.2 m (30 ft 2 in)	AA, 16 2-pdr 'pom-pom' AA and
Speed: 23 kt	four 21-in (533-mm) torpedo tubes
Armour: belt 51 mm (12 in); main	**Complement:** 1,146 men
deck 76 mm (3 in); main barbette	

HMS *Renown* Battlecruiser

The battle-cruiser **HMS *Renown*** was a veteran of World War I but, unlike her sister **Repulse**, underwent full modernization. She emerged from Portsmouth Dockyard on 2 September 1939, just in time for the outbreak of World War II.

Refit

During her three-year refit she had been almost totally rebuilt, with new machinery and boilers, new superstructure and bridgework, and additional armour. The three gun turrets were taken out and modified to give the 15-in (381-mm) guns 30° elevation, and an entirely new anti-aircraft armament was provided: 10 twin 4.5-in (114-mm) gun mountings, three 8-barrelled pom-poms and four

quadruple 0.5-in (12.7-mm) machine-guns. The weight saved on machinery was used to strengthen deck armour, particularly by adding 102-mm (4-in) armour over the magazines and 51-mm (2-in) armour over the machinery. She was also given a cross-deck catapult and a large hangar capable of accommodating two Walrus amphibian aircraft.

Partnership

The new role for the ship was to act as a fast escort for aircraft-carriers, and when the *Renown* joined the Home Fleet she was teamed with the new carrier HMS *Ark Royal* in a partnership which continued for a long time.

After hunting for KMS *Graf Spee* in the South Atlantic in

November 1939, she returned to the Home Fleet as flagship of Vice Admiral Whitworth, and took part in the Norwegian campaign.

Early on 9 April 1940, the *Renown* was steaming 130 km (80 miles) west of the Lofoten Islands with nine destroyers when she sighted the battle-cruisers KMS *Scharnhorst* and

KMS *Gneisenau*. The British ship had the advantage of the light and at 04.17 scored a hit on *Gneisenau*'s main fire-control position. The German ships turned and escaped, but not before the *Renown* had scored two more hits. She was hit by two or three 280-mm (11-in) shells but suffered only slight damage.

SPECIFICATION	
HMS *Renown*	51–102 mm (2–4 in); turrets and
Displacement: 30,750 tons	barbettes 178–229 mm (7–9 in)
standard; 36,080 tons full load	**Armament:** (1944) six 15-in
Dimensions: length 242 m (794 ft)	(381-mm), 20 4.5-mm (114-mm) DP,
overall; beam 27.4 m (90 ft);	28 2-pdr 'pom-pom' and 64 20-mm
draught 14.4 m (30 ft 6 in)	AA guns, eight 21-in (533-mm)
Machinery: 4-shaft geared steam	torpedo tubes
turbines delivering 80,536 kW	**Aircraft:** two Supermarine Walrus
(108,000 shp)	amphibians
Speed: 29½ kt	**Complement:** 1,200 men
Armour: belt 229 mm (9 in); decks	

In August the *Renown* went to Gibraltar as part of Force 'H' with the *Ark Royal*, returning to home waters in October 1941. After covering the North African landings, she took Winston Churchill to Canada and was then sent to the Eastern Fleet, operating in the East Indies.

Three decades of service

On her return in March 1945, the *Renown* was laid up in reserve, and was sold for scrapping in 1948. Her career had spanned over 30 years, and she had served in every major theatre of the naval war.

The old battlecruiser HMS Renown was completely rebuilt for service in World War II as a fast carrier escort. She served in the Atlantic, Mediterranean and Far East.

HMS *Hood* Battlecruiser

A product of the escalating naval arms race during and after World War I, **HMS Hood** was one of the premier strategic platforms of its day. Prior to the aircraft carrier and the strategic bomber, ships like the *Hood* represented the sole means via which devastating firepower could be bought to bear on an adversary, and a means by which it could be deployed at comparatively short notice.

Completed in March 1920 on Clydebank, Scotland, the British Battlecruiser *HMS Hood* was, for two decades, the world's largest warship. She was said to have been the epitome of 'big gun' era sea power. Based on the previous 'Queen Elizabeth' battleships, the *Hood* was designed specifically to tackle the German *Mackensen*.

Between 1920 and 1939, HMS *Hood* undertook several voyages and patrols around Europe and beyond. Her first cruise was to Scandinavia in 1920, and she also visited ports in Brazil and the West Indies. In 1923, she undertook an eleven-month around-the-world voyage with the smaller battlecruiser HMS *Repulse* and a number of light cruisers, although from 1925, HMS *Hood* was assigned to the Atlantic and Home fleets. She was on patrol in the Mediterranean between 1936 and 1939 to protect British interests during the Spanish Civil War.

From 1939 onwards and for the first part of World War II, HMS *Hood* sailed with the Royal Navy Home Fleet in the North Atlantic and North Sea. Her first major mission was to defend the UK–Iceland–Faroes gap, an area of strategic importance to the UK. On 26 September 1939, she sustained minor damage following a German air attack. Between June and July 1940, HMS *Hood* was back in the Mediterranean, and was the flagship during the battle of Mers-el-Kebir, when the Royal Navy scuttled the French fleet to prevent it from falling into German hands.

However, she was to fight her last battle in May 1941. On the morning of 24 May, she was on patrol with two other Royal Navy vessels off the west coast of Ireland. There, HMS *Hood*

SPECIFICATION	
HMS *Hood*	127–305 mm (5–12 in); turrets
Displacement: 45,200 tonnes	279-381 mm (11–15 in); conning
(full load)	tower 229–279 mm (9–11 in);
Dimensions: length 262.3 m	bulkheads 102–127 mm (4–5 in);
(860 ft 7 in); beam 32 m (105 ft);	decks 26–76 mm (1–3 in)
draught 9.6 m (31 ft)	**Armament:** eight 15-in (381-mm),
Machinery: 4-shaft geared steam	12 5.5-in (140-mm), four 4-in
turbines delivering 107,381 kW	(102-mm), six 21-in (533-mm)
(144,000 shp)	torpedo tubes
Speed: 32 kt	**Crew:** 1,477 men
Armour: belt and barbettes	

was sunk during what would become known as the Battle of Denmark Strait. During vicious and bitter exchanges with the German battleship *Bismarck* and the cruiser *Prinz Eugen*, the *Hood* sustained hits from *Bismarck's* 15-inch (381-mm) shells. The *Hood's* aft magazines were hit, causing an explosion to tear through the ship. All but three of the crew perished.

*The **Hood** was, for a time, the largest warship in existence. She was sunk in 1941.*

'Nelson' class Battleship

At the outbreak of World War II, **HMS Nelson** and her sister **HMS Rodney** were the most modern British battleships in service. They had been completed in 1927, and were the only capital ships allowed to be built for the Royal Navy under the Washington Treaty. As such, they were severely constrained by the need to keep within a standard displacement of 35,000 tons while at the same time carrying 16-in (406-mm) guns and heavy protection.

Design features

Nelson and *Rodney* were greatly underrated. In 1939 they were among the most powerful battleships afloat, with many more advanced features than contemporary designs in other navies.

The designers adopted many unusual expedients to meet the specifications, including an 'all-or-nothing' scheme of armouring and the concentration of all three 16-in turrets forward of the bridge, and all 6-in (152-mm) guns aft. Another important innovation, not revealed until

Both of the 'Nelson'-class ships escorted the transatlantic convoys, protecting against German naval attack during the War in the Atlantic.

*HMS **Nelson** is shown here as it appeared while serving in the Indian Ocean in June 1942. Although slow, **Nelson** and **Rodney** were the most powerful battleships in the Royal Navy.*

SPECIFICATION	
HMS *Nelson*	(3.75–6.25 in); turrets and
Displacement: 33,313 tons standard;	barbettes 381–406 mm (15–16 in)
38,400 tons full load	**Armament:** nine 16-in (406-mm) and
Dimensions: length 216.40 m	12 6-in (152-mm) guns, six 120-mm
(709 ft); overall beam 32.30 m	(4.7-in) AA, 16 2-pdr 'pom-pom'
(106 ft); draught 8.50 m (28 ft)	and eight 12.7-mm (0.5 in) AA
Machinery: Geared steam turbines	guns, two 622-mm (24.5-in)
delivering 45,000 shp (33,556 kW)	torpedo tubes
to two shafts	**Aircraft:** normally none, though a
Speed: 23 kt	Walrus could be launched off a
Armour: belt 330–356 mm	catapult on top of C turret.
(13–14 in); decks 95–159 mm	**Complement:** 1,314 men

Above: The 16-inch Mk 1 guns used a light shell fired at high velocity, which reduced barrel life to only 180 charges.

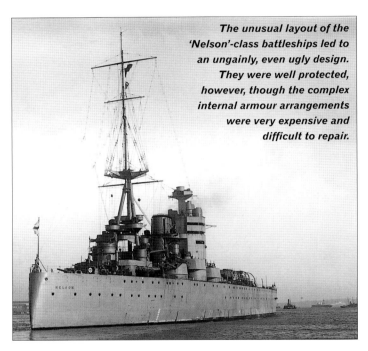

The unusual layout of the 'Nelson'-class battleships led to an ungainly, even ugly design. They were well protected, however, though the complex internal armour arrangements were very expensive and difficult to repair.

long after World War II was the provision of 'water protection', or liquid-loaded vertical bulkheads below the waterline.

Nelson was badly damaged by a magnetic mine while entering Loch Ewe in December 1939 and was under repair until

August 1940. In September 1941, she left the Home Fleet to join Force 'H' for a Malta convoy operation.

On 27 September she was hit forward by an Italian aircraft torpedo, but reached Gibraltar safely. *Nelson* provided covering

fire for the amphibious landings in North Africa, Sicily and Italy, and the armistice between Italy and the Allies was signed on board in Grand Harbour, Malta, on 29 September 1943.

Modernisation

Overhauled in the USA in 1944, *Nelson* sailed for the East Indies as flagship of the Eastern Fleet. On her return after the war, she replaced *Rodney* as flagship of the Home Fleet at Scapa Flow. In 1946 she joined the Training Squadron at Portland. Laid up alongside *Rodney* in the Firth of Forth in 1948, she was used as a target for aerial bombing before being scrapped.

Rodney spent most of the war with the home fleet, primarily escorting high-value

convoys. In May 1941, in company with HMS *King George V*, she battered the German *Bismark* battleship to destruction. After a period in the Mediterranean, the *Rodney* rejoined the Home Fleet as Flagship. Laid up at the end of the war, *Rodney* was scrapped in 1948.

The 16-inch guns carried by the 'Nelsons' were never as reliable or as accurate as the 15-inch guns on previous British battleships. The triple turrets with their complex shell handling arrangements also caused problems. The rate of fire was one shot every 45 seconds per barrel compared to one every 25 seconds for the earlier 15-inch weapons.

HMS *Prince of Wales* Battleship

The second ship of the **'King George V' class, HMS *Prince of Wales*** was laid down in January 1937, launched in May 1939 and completed by March 1941. It was still working up to operational efficiency on 23 May, when it was ordered to leave Scapa Flow, with HMS *Hood*, to engage the German battleship KMS *Bismarck*.

The *Prince of Wales* still had teething troubles: one of its 14-in (356-mm) turrets could handle only one shell at a time, the turrets were all subject to minor breakdowns, and the new Type 284 gunnery radar was not working. To make matters worse, the inexperienced crew of the aft quadruple 14-in turret made an error in loading drill, which jammed the turret.

Against the *Bismarck*

When *Hood* was blown up, the *Prince of Wales* was left to withstand the fire from two German ships. The Type 281 air-warning set radar used to provide ranges to the guns, enabling it to get 'straddles' on the *Bismarck*, resulting in two or three underwater hits. One of these hits contaminated the *Bismarck's* fuel oil and another reduced its speed by 2 kt.

Hit seven times, the *Prince of Wales* suffered comparatively

The doomed Prince of Wales *arriving at Singapore on 2 December 1941. In company with the battlecruiser HMS* Repulse, *the new battleship would be sunk only eight days later off the coast of Malaya by Japanese naval bombers.*

little damage, as only three of the shells detonated. The most serious damage was caused by a ricochet on the compass platform, which killed or wounded thirteen crew.

In August 1941, the ship took Churchill across the Atlantic to Newfoundland for the Atlantic Charter meeting with Roosevelt.

Sent to Singapore

Prince of Wales hoisted the flag of Sir Tom Phillips, Commander in Chief, Eastern Fleet in October, and left for Singapore on 25 October with HMS *Repulse*. Deploying as Force 'Z', the ships reached Singapore on 2 December, but were sunk eight days later by Japanese torpedo bombers. The *Prince of Wales* was crippled by a single torpedo, which struck the port

side abreast of the aftermost 5¼-in (133-mm) gun turret. The port outer propeller shaft was badly distorted, and gouged a hole in the after bulkheads. The shock-effect of near misses put five of the eight dynamos out of

Designed to the 35,000 ton limits of the Washington Treaty, the 'King George V' class, under construction at the outbreak of World War II, substituted rate of fire with ten 14-inch guns for the heavier but much slower 16-inch broadside of the preceding 'Nelson' class.

action, robbing the ship of power for the anti-aircraft gun.

Out of control, the *Prince of Wales* was unable to avoid further torpedoes and sank. Among those lost were Captain Leach and Admiral Phillips.

SPECIFICATION	
HMS *Prince of Wales*	(14–15 in); decks 127–152 mm
Displacement: 38,000 tons standard; 43,350 tons full load	(5–6 in); turrets and barbettes 305 mm (12 in)
Dimensions: length 227 m (745 ft); beam 31.40 m (103 ft); draught 8.50 m (28 ft) mean	**Armament:** 10 14-in (356-mm) main guns, 16 5¼-in (133-mm) dual-purpose anti-air/anti-surface guns, 32 2-pdr 'pom-pom' and 16 12.7-mm (0.5-in) AA guns
Machinery: geared steam turbines delivering 82,027 kW (110,000 shp) to four shafts	**Aircraft:** two Supermarine Walrus amphibians
Speed: 28 kt	**Complement:** 1,422 men
Armour: belt 356–281 mm	

KMS *Scharnhorst* Heavy Cruiser

KMS *Scharnhorst* was planned as the *Ersatz Elsass*, fourth of a class of six planned 'pocket battleships'. By 1933, however, the weaknesses of the 'pocket battleship', or Panzerschiffe, were so obvious that Hitler gave the German navy permission to expand the design to 26,000 tons as a reply to the French *Dunkerque*.

Undergunned

The initial plan was to arm the ship with three twin 380-mm (14.92-in) turrets, but three triple 280-mm (11.03-in) turrets were used to save time. The design was nominally of 26,000 tons, but reached 32,000 tons; to conceal this, the Kriegsmarine continued to quote the lower figure.

For most of her active life, the *Scharnhorst* operated with her sister KMS *Gneisenau*, and both ships made forays into the North Atlantic in 1940–41. The *Scharnhorst* was badly damaged by a torpedo fired by the destroyer HMS *Acasta* while attacking the carrier HMS *Glorious* in June 1940.

Although the two ships posed a threat to the British while lying at Brest in 1941, Hitler felt the two units were too exposed to air attack by units of the RAF, and ordered them to return to home waters. Operation 'Cerberus', the daylight dash through the English Channel in February 1942, was probably the Kriegsmarine's greatest success; it took the British by surprise, the two battle-cruisers and the heavy cruiser *Prinz Eugen* slipping past ineffectual air and sea attacks. Apart from slight damage to *Scharnhorst* from a magnetic mine during the final phase, this was a humiliation for the British and proof that audacity pays.

After repairs lasting until August 1942, the ship was sent to Norway. She took part in the raid on Spitzbergen in September 1943 but otherwise lay in a remote fjord until December 1943, when Admiral Dönitz ordered her to sea for an attack on a British convoy.

It was a badly planned operation, and the *Scharnhorst* failed in her attempt to brush aside the destroyers and cruisers escorting the convoy. Incompetent reconnaissance by the Luftwaffe left her with no idea that the battleship HMS *Duke of York* was closing on her fast, and she was taken by surprise when 356-mm (14-in) shells started to hit her.

Sunk by torpedoes

Scharnhorst then disengaged, but the British and Norwegian destroyers slowed her down with torpedoes, allowing the *Duke of York* to pound her again. She was finally sunk by torpedoes from HMS *Sheffield* and HMS *Jamaica*, and went down, with the loss of most of her crew.

The wreck of the *Scharnhorst* was located and photographed by a Norwegian Navy underwater exploration group during the year 2000.

Above: **Scharnhorst,** *before she was modified for Atlantic raiding. A new 'clipper bow' was fitted to improve her seakeeping.*

Above: For most of her active life, the **Scharnhorst** *operated with her sister KMS* **Gneisenau** *(background, right).*

SPECIFICATION	
KMS *Scharnhorst*	**Armour:** belt 330 mm (13 in); decks
Displacement: 32,000 tons standard,	50–110 mm (2–4.3 in); turrets 355
38,900 tons full load	mm (14 in)
Dimensions: length 234.90 m (770 ft	**Armament:** nine 280-mm (11-in), 12
8 in) overall; beam 30 m (98 ft 5 in);	150-mm (5.91-in), 14 105-mm (4-in)
draught 9.10 m (29 ft 10 in)	and 16 37-mm. AA guns and six
Machinery: 3-shaft geared steam	533-mm (21-in) torpedo tubes
turbines delivering 119,312 kW	**Aircraft:** two Arado floatplanes
(160,000 shp)	**Complement:** 1,840 men
Speed: 32 kt	

Scharnhorst, a 32,000-ton battlecruiser, was built at Wilhelmshaven, Germany. She was launched in October 1936 and commissioned in January 1939.

KMS *Tirpitz* Battleship

KMS *Tirpitz* was laid down in October 1936 as *Schlachtschiff G* and launched on 1 April 1939, starting sea trials in late February 1941. Identical to her sister *Bismarck* in most respects, she incorporated minor improvements, notably the addition of two sets of quadruple torpedo-tubes and improved aircraft-handling arrangements.

Long work-up

After a lengthy work-up in the Baltic, the *Tirpitz* was ready for operational service towards the end of September 1941 and her first operation was a cruise in the Gulf of Finland to prevent any breakout by the Soviet Baltic Fleet. She was then sent to Trondheim in Norway to disrupt Allied convoys to Murmansk, but on her first sortie she failed to find the convoy and narrowly escaped interception by Fairey

Albacore torpedo-bombers from HMS *Victorious* on 9 March. Her next move was much more successful, but inadvertent. A shift of berth led the British to think that she was putting to sea. As a result, the convoy PQ-17 was ordered to scatter, allowing U-boats and bombers to sink 24 merchant ships.

Although the *Tirpitz* never made another sortie, her presence could not be ignored. The Royal Navy was forced to keep two capital ships and a fleet carrier in home waters in case the *Tirpitz* should break out. The first of a long series of attempts to neutralize her was an air attack by 'Chariot' human torpedoes in October 1942, but this achieved nothing, as the Chariots were lost by accident. In September 1943, the *Tirpitz* put to sea once more but only to bombard Spitzbergen. Late that month two British X-craft,

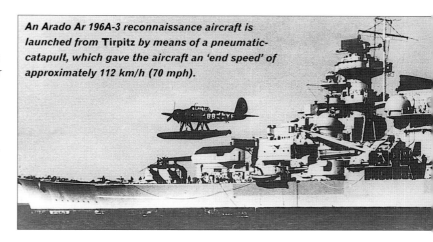

An Arado Ar 196A-3 reconnaissance aircraft is launched from **Tirpitz** *by means of a pneumatic-catapult, which gave the aircraft an 'end speed' of approximately 112 km/h (70 mph).*

or midget submarines, penetrated the defences of Altenfjord and laid two ton charges under the keel of *Tirpitz*, causing shock damage to the 380-mm (14.97-in) turrets and the main machinery.

Repairs lasted until the spring of 1944, and then on 3 April she was attacked by 40 Fairey Barracuda dive-bombers from British carriers. This Fleet Air Arm attack inflicted serious damage, but two later attacks in July and August had little effect,

for the steep sides of the fjord made accurate bombing almost impossible. Finally, on 15 September, RAF Avro Lancasters hit the *Tirpitz* with 5443-kg (12,000-lb) bombs, causing severe damage. *Tirpitz* then had to be moved south to Trondheim for repairs, where two more attacks by Lancasters resulted in her destruction. On 12 November, she was hit by three 5443-kg (12,000 lb) 'Tallboy' bombs and capsized with the loss of 1,000 crewmen.

SPECIFICATION

KMS *Tirpitz*
Displacement: 42,900 tons standard, 52,600 tons full load
Dimensions: length 250.50 m (821 ft 10 in) overall; beam 36 m (118 ft 1 in); draught 11 m (36 ft 1 in) maximum
Machinery: 3-shaft geared steam turbines delivering 102,907 kW (138,000 shp)
Speed: 29 kt

Armour: belt 320 mm (12.6 in); decks 50–120 mm (2–4.8 in), turrets and barbettes 230–355 mm (9–14 in)
Armament: eight 380-mm (15-in), 12 150-mm (5.91-in), 16 105-mm (4.14-in) AA, 16 37-mm AA and 70 20-mm AA guns, and eight 533-mm (21-in) torpedo tubes
Aircraft: four Arado floatplanes
Complement: 2,530 men

Tirpitz never actually came into contact with Allied shipping, and only fired her guns in anger during a September 1943 raid on Spitzbergen.

Above: Stationed in Norway, **Tirpitz** *tied down a significant amount of British warships in the Atlantic, which could have been better used in other theatres.*

Right: **Tirpitz** *was repeatedly attacked and damaged in her Norwegian lairs until she was finally sunk during Operation Catechism by RAF bombers on 19 November 1944.*

KMS *Bismarck*

Heavy battleship

Bismarck's eight 380-mm (15-in)/L47 guns were the most powerful weapons ever fitted to a German warship. A feature of the gun design was its high muzzle velocity, leading to a very flat shell trajectory. At their maximum elevation of 30°, the guns could fire an 800-kg (1,764-lb) shell out to a range of nearly 40000 m (131,234 ft). The two-gun turrets were exceptionally large, each weighing more than 1,000 tons.

The first German battleship to be built since the end of World War I, *Bismarck* was based on the final capital ship designs of the Imperial Navy. The first products of the Kriegsmarine's ambitious 'Z' plan of the 1930s, the *Bismarck* and its sister *Tirpitz* would have made a potent threat to Britain's Atlantic lifeline should they have ever served together. It is hardly surprising, therefore, that the British made every effort to sink the pride of Hitler's fleet, efforts which were ultimately to seal the *Bismarck's* fate.

KMS *Bismarck*

May 1941
1 Radar
2 Rangefinder
3 Armoured control tower
4 Admiral's bridge
5 Searchlight
6 Day bridge
7 37-mm gun
8 Rangefinder
9 Radar
10 Gimbal-mounted, gyro stabilized AA Director
11 AA command post
12 20-mm gun
13 Armoured conning tower
14 Navigation room
15 Wing of bridge
16 B Turret 15-in guns
17 A Turret 15-in guns
18 Exhaust trunking
19 Gunsight telescope
20 Breech mortice
21 Shell tray
22 Elevating gear
23 Training base on ball bearings
24 Elevating gear
25 Hydraulic pump
26 Machinery compartment
27 Auxiliary ammunition trunk
28 Barbette armour
29 Rammer
30 Crew quarters
31 Anchor gear
32 Battery deck
33 Stores
34 Forward armoured bulkhead
35 Armoured or lower deck
36 Honeycomb of bulkheads below armoured deck
37 B turret barbette
38 Machine shop
39 150-mm (6-in) gun barbette
40 Lifeboats
41 Catwalk
42 Motor boats
43 Crane
44 Funnel uptakes
45 Boat crane
46 Arado Ar 196 aircraft
47 Aircraft catapult gear
48 Lifeboats
49 Motor boats
50 Hangar
51 Machine shop
52 Stores
53 Crew
54 Engine gear room
55 Water hose reels
56 Engine and boiler rooms
57 Anti-aircraft control
58 Aft ensign mast
59 105-mm (4.1-in) gun barbette
60 C Turret 15-in guns
61 D Turret 15-in guns
62 Aft armoured bulkhead
63 Winch room
64 Stores
65 Anchor gear
66 Rudder
67 Propeller shafts (3)
68 Ship's double bottom
69 Radar
70 Aft superstructure
71 Armoured aft control positions
72 Boat stowage platform
73 Searchlight
74 AA control
75 Signalling lamp
76 Mainmast
77 Spotting positions
78 Rudder pointer
79 Remote control searchlight
80 Funnel
81 Searchlight (with cover in position)
82 Foremast
83 Radio aerials
84 Waterline
85 Gangways (2)
86 Boat sponsons

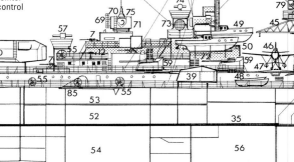

Below: HMS Dorsetshire's *torpedoes administered the finishing blow to sink* Bismarck. *However, British efforts to rescue survivors were aborted after a U-boat was reported to be in the area. Only about 100 of the battleship's crew of over 2,000 officers and men survived.*

Right: This view of Bismarck *photographed from astern in 1940-41, shows the stern anchor in its recessed well, folding propeller guards, armour belt and other details of the hull and superstructure.*

SPECIFICATION	
KMS *Bismarck*	50–120 mm (2–5 in); turrets and
Displacement: 41,676 tons	barbettes 228–356 mm (9–14 in)
standard, 50,153 tons full load	**Armament:** eight 380-mm (15-in),
Hull dimensions: length 251 m	12 150-mm (5.9-in), 16 105-mm
(823 ft 6 in); beam 36 m (118 ft);	(4.1-in) AA, 16 37-mm AA and 12
draught 9.30 m (30 ft 7 in)	20-mm AA guns
Machinery: 3-shaft, geared steam	**Fire control:** five 10.50-m (34 ft
turbines delivering 111,920 kW	5-in) base rangefinders, 1.70-m
(150,000 shp)	(5 ft 7-in) base rangefinder, two
Speed: 29 kt	6.50-m (21 ft 4-in) base
Range: 9,280 nm (17196 km;	rangefinders, four 40-m (13 ft 1-in)
10,686 miles) at 16 kt (29.5 km/h;	AA rangefinders
18.5 mph) and 4,500 nm (8338	**Armament:** four Arado Ar 196
km; 5,182 miles) at 28 kt	floatplanes
(52 km/h; 32 mph)	**Complement:** 2,192 men
Armour: belt 320 mm (13 in); decks	

Left: Ship builders at work during the fitting out of Bismarck *at the Blohm & Voss shipyard, Hamburg, Germany, between 10 and 15 December 1939. This view shows the port forward 150-mm (5.9-in) twin gun turret in the process of installation, with the ship's forward superstructure behind.*

Below: Bismarck, *photographed from* Prinz Eugen *on 24 May 1941, following the Battle of the Denmark Strait.* Bismarck *is down by the bow, the result of hits received in her engagement with* HMS *Prince of Wales and* HMS *Hood earlier in the day.*

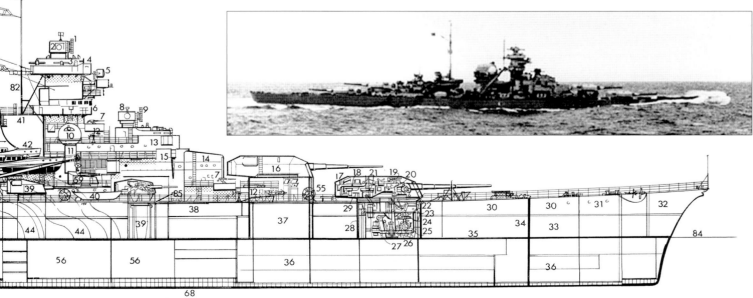

KMS *Bismarck*

As with most German warships of the 1930s, *Bismarck* was considerably heavier than dictated by the international treaty limits that she was supposed to meet. Under the Anglo-German naval agreement of 1935, any German battleships were supposed to be limited to 35,000 tons. In fact, *Bismarck* was almost 10,000 tons heavier, and at full load displaced more than 50,000 tons. Germany's first 'real' post-World War I battleship, the vessel had guns and protection on a similar scale to those of her best foreign contemporaries. She was commissioned in August 1940, and after working up in the Baltic, the batttleship attempted to break out into the Atlantic in May 1941. After sinking HMS *Hood*, *Bismarck* was hunted down and sunk by the British on 27 May 1941.

Bismarck is seen here in harbour, soon after commissioning in August 1940. The battleship has not yet finished fitting out, since she is still awaiting the installation of rangefinders atop her tower bridge and conning tower. This propaganda photograph appeared in a Spanish publication, early in 1941 before the Bismarck's final voyage.

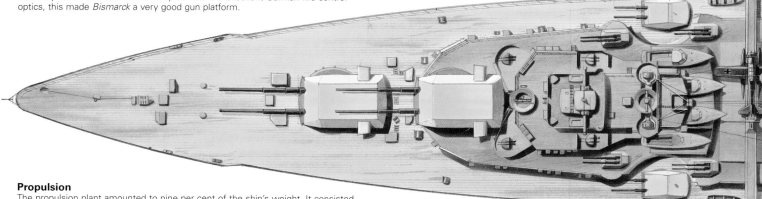

Beam
Bismarck's broad beam was a product of Admiral Tirpitz's dictum that any new battleships should be built to be stable and carry good internal protection rather than carry too heavy an armament. As a result, the Kriegsmarine's new battleship was very stable in all weathers. Coupled with the excellent German fire control optics, this made *Bismarck* a very good gun platform.

Propulsion
The propulsion plant amounted to nine per cent of the ship's weight. It consisted of three turbine sets manufactured by Blohm & Voss, which were housed in separated compartments. The steam power was produced by 12 Wagner high-pressure steam-heated boilers in six watertight compartments that were located amidships. The powerplant delivered 102,900 kW (138,000 shp) to the ship's three propellers, each of which was 4.80 m (15 ft 8 in) in diameter and had three blades.

Design

Bismarck's internal structure was a new design, based on experience with the 'Deutschland'-class pocket battleships and the 'Scharnhorst'-class battlecruisers. However, its internal protection reflected that of the last battleships of the Imperial navy, but considerably enlarged. As a result, its armour protection was not as sophisticated as that used by newer American and British battleships.

Radar

German advances in radar meant that *Bismarck* went to sea with three FuMo 23 radar sets, atop the bridge, in the foretop and on the aft control centre. Operating at a frequency of 368 MHz, FuMo 23 had an effective range under ideal conditions of about 25000 m (27,340 yards).

Fire control

German fire control was generally excellent. During the battle with HMS *Hood*, both *Bismarck* and the accompanying cruiser *Prinz Eugen* hit the British battlecruiser early on in the fight. *Hood* blew up soon afterwards.

Main armament

Bismarck's 380-mm (15-in) guns were designed in 1934, and were similar in capability to contemporary French and Italian designs. German armour-piercing shells were of poor quality, however. The guns were mounted in pairs, the turrets being identified alphabetically, bow to stern, as Anton, Bruno, Caesar and Dora.

Colour scheme

Originally painted grey, *Bismarck* sailed from the Baltic on her only operational sortie sporting a bright dazzle colour scheme. This was toned down considerably in Norway, before the huge battleship's unsuccessful attempt to break out unnoticed into the Atlantic.

Aircraft

Bismarck was equipped with aircraft for reconnaissance and patrol missions. Four Arado Ar 196 seaplanes were carried, though six could be embarked if necessary. Two of these robust and heavily armed single-engined aircraft were housed in the double hangar under the mainmast, and the other two in single hangars to both sides of the funnel amidships.

Armour

Battleships must be able to withstand repeated hits and continue fighting, so their armour expanse, its distribution and its thickness are extremely important. Forty per cent of the *Bismarck's* designed combat weight was devoted to belt, deck, turret, underwater and splinter armour.

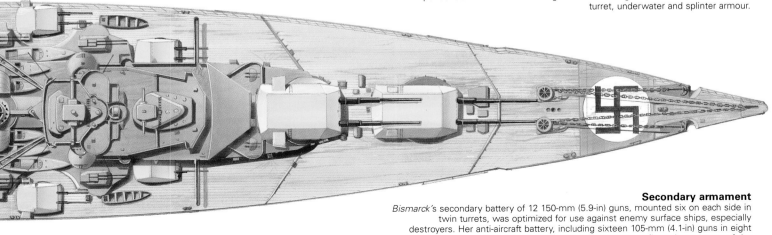

Secondary armament

Bismarck's secondary battery of 12 150-mm (5.9-in) guns, mounted six on each side in twin turrets, was optimized for use against enemy surface ships, especially destroyers. Her anti-aircraft battery, including sixteen 105-mm (4.1-in) guns in eight twin mounts and several 37-mm and 20-mm cannon, reflected even more of the prevailing pre-World War II underestimation of the threat from the air than was usual. In contemporary British and American designs, all secondary guns were dual-purpose.

USS *Arizona*

Battleship

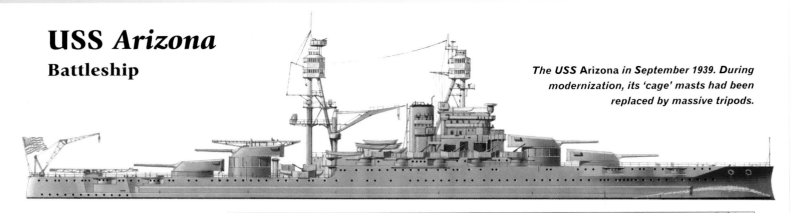

The USS Arizona in September 1939. During modernization, its 'cage' masts had been replaced by massive tripods.

The **USS *Arizona*** (**BB.39**) was laid down in March 1914, launched in June 1915 and commissioned in October 1916. She served with the 6th Squadron as part of the British Grand Fleet during World War I, and then helped to repatriate US soldiers from France. In 1929–31, she was modernized, and on 7 December 1941 became part of the US Pacific Fleet, lying at anchor in 'Battleship Row' at Pearl Harbor.

Peacetime service

Her peacetime service had been humdrum. After a trip to the Mediterranean in April–July 1919, she returned to the East coast, and 1921 transferred to the Pacific Fleet for eight years. In 1929, she returned to Norfolk for modernization, and on recommissioning took President Hoover to the West Indies before returning to the Pacific Fleet.

Pearl Harbor

The first Japanese aircraft to reach Pearl Harbor on 7 December easily identified their targets, for 'Battleship Row' contained seven ships: USS *Oklahoma*, USS *Virginia*

and the repair ship USS *Vestal* in the outer line, and USS *Maryland*, USS *Tennessee*, the *Arizona* and USS *Nevada* in the inner line. A torpedo and up to eight bombs hit the *Arizona*, setting her on fire and starting flooding. A 725-kg (1,600-lb) weapon did the most damage, striking at 08.10 and detonating in the forward magazine. The ship sank at her moorings, killing 1,104 of its crew, including Rear Admiral Kidd and Captain van Valkenburgh.

Salvage teams tried to raise the hull, but it was damaged

beyond repair. Two of the *Arizona*'s triple 14-in (356-mm) turrets were recovered and the guns installed in coast defence positions on land. The hull of the *Arizona* was later declared a national shrine to commemorate the men and ships lost in the attack. Today a concrete memorial stands over the *Arizona*'s remains, and an oil slick shows that oil is still leaking from its fuel tanks.

The sister of the *Arizona*, **USS *Pennsylvania*** (**BB.38**) was in dry dock at the time of the attack and suffered only

The Arizona's tripod masts sag slowly to port after the detonation of the forward 14-in (356-mm) magazine had wrecked the ship.

superficial damage from a single bomb hit. After repairs and modernization, she rejoined the Pacific Fleet and served across the Pacific until the Japanese surrender in August 1945.

At the end of the war, she was damaged by an aircraft-launched torpedo but survived and was used as a target in the Bikini nuclear tests in 1946.

Arizona (illustrated) and Pennsylvania were among the world's most powerful battleships when new. Both were modernized in the late 1920s.

SPECIFICATION	
USS *Arizona* (BB.39)	**Speed:** 21 kts
Displacement: 32,600 tons standard, 36,500 tons full load	**Armour:** belt 356 mm (14 in); deck 203 mm (8 in); turrets 229–457 mm (9–18 in)
Dimensions: length 185.32 m (608 ft); beam 29.56 m (97 ft); draught 8.76 m (28 ft 9 in)	**Armament:** 12 14-in (356-mm), 12 5-in (127-mm), 12 5-in (127-mm) AA and eight 0.5-in (12.7-mm) AA guns
Machinery: 4-shaft geared steam turbines delivering 24,980 kW (33,500 shp)	**Aircraft:** three floatplanes
	Complement: 2,290 men

USS *New Mexico* Battleship

The keel for the **USS New Mexico** (**BB.40**) was laid down at the New York Navy Yard, New York State, on 14 October 1915. She was launched on 13 April 1917, and was to be the lead ship in the three-vessel **'New Mexico' class**. **USS Mississippi** (**BB.41**) had been launched in January 1917 and **USS Idaho** (**BB.42**) was launched in June 1917.

The 'New Mexico' class incorporated many of the features seen on previous vessels. These included the 12 14-in (355-mm) main gun battery of the preceding 'Pennsylvania' class. 'New Mexico'-class vessels also had a 'clipper' style bow, which greatly improved their sea keeping. The secondary armament of the New Mexico class consisted of 14 5-in (127-mm) guns mounted on the superstructure rather than on the wet bow and stern positions.

New Mexico's first major voyage was to escort the *George Washington*, which was carrying US President Woodrow Wilson back from France to the United States after the Versailles Peace Conference in 1919. During July of that year, it became the flagship for the US Pacific Fleet. The next twelve years saw it undertaking several

voyages around the Pacific, Caribbean and South America.

New Mexico underwent an extensive refit in Philadelphia between March 1931 and January 1933, before returning to the Pacific Fleet. This modernization greatly altered the ship's appearance. The original 'cage' masts, positioned fore and aft of amidships, were removed and replaced by a more modern tower superstructure. Furthermore, the hull received extra torpedo protection, and the 'bulge' in the middle of its hull was widened to 32.3 m (106 ft), which increased the displacement by 1,000 tonnes.

Wartime service

As the political situation between the United States and the Japanese deteriorated during 1940, *New Mexico* was despatched to Pearl Harbor. However, as the Germans consolidated their gains across Europe, seizing several key European Atlantic ports, she was reassigned to neutrality patrol with the Atlantic Fleet, sailing from Norfolk, Virginia.

After the Japanese attack on Pearl Harbor in December 1941, she was reassigned to the Pacific Fleet, sailing from San Francisco on 1 August 1942 to

The primary armament of USS New Mexico *was its 12 enormous 14-in (356-mm) guns, a configuration previously seen on the 'Pennslyvania'-class of battleships.*

SPECIFICATION	
USS New Mexico (BB.40)	**Speed:** 21 kts
Displacement: 32,000 tonnes	**Armament:** 12 14-in (356-mm); 14
Dimensions: length 190 m (624 ft);	5-in (127-mm); four 3-in (76.2-mm)
beam 32.3 m (106 ft); draught	and two 21-in torpedo tubes.
9.1 m (30 ft)	**Complement:** 1,084 men

Hawaii, to begin patrols in the Pacific theatre. During 1942, she assisted the blockade of Attu Island and the bombardment of Kiska Island, both in the northern Pacific, before returning to Puget Sound Naval Yard, Washington, for a refit. From October 1943 onwards, she resumed patrols in the Pacific, having returned to Pearl Harbor. She protected transport convoys and carrier groups and

also provided air defence against Japanese attacks. On 19–20 June 1944, she participated in the Battle of the Philippine Sea and then, on 12 July, her guns bombarded Japanese positions before the invasion of Guam on 21 July. She continued to hit enemy positions there until 30 July.

Major overhaul

Between August and October 1944, she underwent a major overhaul at Bremerton, Washington. On 6 January 1945, during the invasion of Luzon, Philippines, she was hit by a kamikaze aircraft, which killed the commanding officer, Captain R. W. Fleming, together with 29 other crew members and injured 87. She suffered two more suicide attacks on 12 May 1945, while at anchorage at Hagushi on the southern Korean

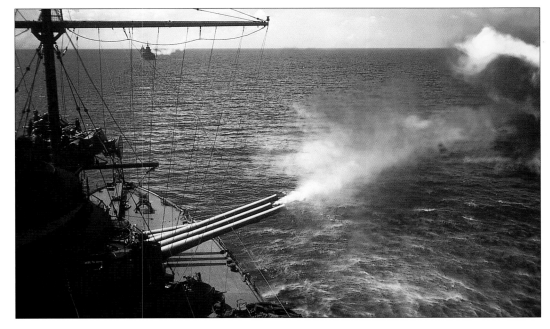

The forward guns of the **New Mexico** *point starboard and fire. All the ship's guns remained operational even after she was hit by kamikaze aircraft during the invasion of Luzon in January 1945.*

peninsula. She was set ablaze; 54 of its crew were killed and 119 were wounded. On 28 August 1945, She travelled from Saipan Island in the Philippine Sea to Tokyo Bay to witness the Japanese surrender on 2 September. She was decommissioned on 19 July 1946, and was sold for scrap to Lipsett Inc. of New York City. *New Mexico* received six battle stars for her service during World War II.

Lighting up a dark Pacific night, the guns of the **New Mexico** *supported the* **US bombardment of Kiska Island, and the US invasion of Guam.**

USS *Washington* Battleship

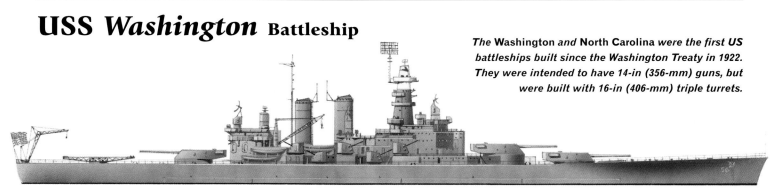

The **Washington** *and* **North Carolina** *were the first US battleships built since the Washington Treaty in 1922. They were intended to have 14-in (356-mm) guns, but were built with 16-in (406-mm) triple turrets.*

When the 15-year 'holiday' in battleship construction brought about by the Washington Treaty came to an end in 1937, the US Navy had plans to lay down two modern capital ships as soon as possible. The 35,000-ton limit was still in force, but the 1936 London Naval Treaty had reduced gun calibre from 16 in to 14 in (406 mm to 356 mm). The specification that emerged was very similar to the original design of HMS *King George V*, with three quadruple 14-in (356-mm) mountings and a speed of 28 kts. However, unlike the British, the Americans could afford to wait and when the Japanese refused to ratify the 1936 treaty, the USN announced that it would exercise its right to go back to 16-in (406-mm) guns. On the new design's dimensions, it was possible to have only three triple mountings, and nothing could be done to increase protection,

which had been planned to withstand 14-in (356-mm) hits.

'North Carolina' Class

USS *Washington* (**BB.56**) was the second of the two **'North Carolina'-class** ships. Laid down in June 1938 and commissioned in May 1941, she went to the Home Fleet in 1942. On 1 May she was damaged by the explosion of HMS *Punjabi's* depth charges after the destroyer had been rammed by HMS *King George V*. By September 1942 she was back in the Pacific, with Task Force 17 in the Solomons.

Then, on the night of 14/15 November, the *Washington* and USS *South Dakota* were stalking a Japanese task force attempting to bombard Henderson Field, but just before the US ships could open fire, the blast of a 5-in (127-mm) gun knocked out the *South Dakota's* electrical

system. Fortunately, *Washington* had not yet switched on her searchlights, and remained undetected while the Japanese concentrated their fire on the *South Dakota*.

Saving *South Dakota*

From a range of about 7,315 m (8,000 yards), the *Washington* closed the range to 1,830 m (2,000 yards) before opening fire; in seven minutes she fired 75 16-in (406-mm) and hundreds of 5-in (127-mm) shells, crippling the *Kirishima* with nine 16-in (406-mm) hits. Her intervention

saved the *South Dakota* from serious damage and not only sank the *Kirishima* but badly damaged two heavy cruisers as well and saved Henderson Field from attack.

On 1 February 1944 the *Washington* was badly damaged in a collision with the *Indiana*, but was repaired in time for the Battle of the Philippine Sea in June 1944 and the final onslaught on Okinawa and the Japanese Home Islands. USS *Washington* was decommissioned in June 1947 and was stricken in 1960.

SPECIFICATION	
USS *Washington* (BB.56)	**Armour belt:** 165–305 mm
Displacement: 36,900 tons standard; 44,800 tons full load	(6.5–12 in); decks 38–140 mm (1.5–5.5 in); turrets 178–406 mm (7–16 in)
Dimensions: length 222.12 m (728 ft 9 in) overall; beam 33 m (108 ft 3 in); draught 10.82 m (35 ft 6 in)	**Armament:** nine 16-in (406-mm), 20 5-in (127-mm) DP, 16 28-mm AA and 12 0.5-in (12.7-mm) AA guns
Machinery: 4-shaft geared steam turbines delivering 90,230 kW (121,000 shp)	**Aircraft:** three Vought Kingfisher floatplanes
Speed: 27 kts	**Complement:** 1,880 men

USS *South Dakota* Battleship

The 'South Dakota' design was shorter than that of the preceding 'Washington' class to permit heavier protection against 406-mm (16-in) shellfire without a major increase in tonnage.

The need for a class of battleships powerful enough to resist 406-mm (16-in) shellfire without infringing the 35,000-ton treaty limit was clear in 1931. To achieve this, however, was another matter, and the US Navy's designers were forced to make several compromises. Shortening the waterline length saved weight, but to support the additional weight of armour there had to be an increase in beam. This caused more drag, and to maintain a speed of 28 kts more power was needed, but in the shorter hull there was now less space for machinery. The problems were solved eventually by paying attention to the redesign of machinery, and

as a result the **'South Dakota' class** proved cost-effective.

The short hull was manoeuvrable, and protection against shellfire, bombs and torpedoes was as good as any contemporary built to the same limitations. In fact, like the British 'King George V' class, the 'South Dakota' class worked out at 38,000 tons, considerably lower than those of rival French, German or Italian designs.

Into service

The lead-ship, **USS *South Dakota* (BB.57)** was laid down in July 1939, launched in June 1941 and commissioned in March 1942. She headed for the Pacific after her shakedown

cruise, but damaged herself by running aground. Repairs were completed in time for the Battle of Santa Cruz, and on 26 October 1942 she claimed to have shot down 26 Japanese aircraft. This phenomenal performance can be explained by the fact that she was the first ship to use the new proximity-fused 127-mm (5-in) shells.

The next engagement was the Battle of Guadalcanal on the night of 14/15 November 1942, but this time the *South Dakota* was less successful. While approaching the Japanese battle line in company with USS *Washington,* she inadvertently blew the ring main and put her entire electrical supply out of

action. With no radar, fire control, lighting or navigation aids, she blundered towards the Japanese and got within 4,570 m (5,000 yards), at which range she was soon hit by a number of shells. She was hit by one 356-mm (14-in), 18 203-mm (8-in), six 152-mm (6-in) and one 127-mm (5-in) shells, plus one of unknown calibre, suffering extensive splinter damage which killed 38 men and wounded 60.

The USS South Dakota *was probably the best of the 35,000 ton 'Treaty' battleship designs, being relatively fast, with a powerful armament fit and an effective armour layout.*

SPECIFICATION	
USS *South Dakota* (BB.57)	**Speed:** 28 kts
Displacement: 38,000 tons standard, 44,374 tons full load	**Armour:** belt 311 mm (12.25 in); decks 38–127 mm (1.5–5 in); turrets 457 mm (18 in)
Dimensions: length 207.3 m (680 ft) overall; beam 33.0 m (108 ft 3 in); draught 11.1 m (36 ft 3 in) maximum	**Armament:** nine 406-mm (16-in), 16 127-mm (5-in) DP, 40 40-mm AA and 40 20-mm AA guns
Machinery: 4-shaft geared steam turbines delivering 130,000 shp (96,940 kW)	**Aircraft:** three Vought Kingfisher floatplanes
	Complement: 2,354 men

Across the Pacific

In 1943 the *South Dakota* joined the Home Fleet, serving alongside her sister USS *Alabama*, but she returned to the Pacific later in that year. With her three sisters, she took part in all the major amphibious operations that culminated in the surrender of Japan in

The USS South Dakota *engages a Japanese torpedo bomber during the Battle of Santa Cruz. Her proximity fused AA guns proved very effective, destroying 26 aircraft.*

August 1945. She was finally decommissioned in 1947 and stricken in 1962.

USS *Iowa* Battleship

Early in 1937, the US Navy began work on the design of 45,000-ton battleships as a contingency against any Japanese refusal to continue the international treaty limits on displacement. In January 1938, emphasis switched from ships with heavy armament and protection but modest speed (12 406-mm/16-in guns, 27 knots) to fast designs, capable of 30 kts or more. The new 'Essex' class carriers were being designed at this time, and there was a need to provide them with battleship escorts of similar performance.

Increased speed

The resulting **'Iowa' class** sacrificed gunpower (only nine 406-mm guns) and protection (310-mm belt armour) to permit the speed to be increased to 33 kts. Although intelligence sources suspected that the new Japanese battleships would have 45.7-mm (18-in) guns, it was hoped that the 'Iowa' class would not have to fight them, as carrier aircraft would keep the Japanese giants outside gun range. The 'Iowas' were primarily intended to keep heavy cruisers, rather than battleships, at bay, and as such they came close to the original concept of the battlecruiser, although they were never rated as such.

SPECIFICATION	
USS *Iowa* (BB.61)	**Armour:** belt 310 mm (12.2 in)~ decks 38–120 mm (1.5–4.7 in); turrets 457 mm (18 in)
Displacement: 48,500 tons standard, 57,450 tons full load	
Dimensions: length 270.43 m (887 ft 3 in) overall; beam 32.97 m (108 ft 2 in); draught 11.58 m (38 ft)	**Armament:** nine 406-mm (16 in), 20 127-mm (5-in) DR 60 40-mm AA and 60 20-mm AA guns
Machinery: 4-shaft geared steam turbines delivering 212,000 shp (158,088 kW)	**Aircraft:** three Vought Kingfisher floatplanes
Speed: 33 kts	**Complement:** 1,921 men

By the time the new 'Iowa' class battleships got into action, their main role was in shore bombardment and anti-aircraft defence. Here, one of the 'Iowas' opens fire on Japanese shore positions.

After the war, the battleship fell out of favour, but vessels of the 'Iowa' class were recalled to service in Korea and Vietnam. Here, the USS New Jersey is seen cruising in the Gulf of Tonkin at the beginning of 1969.

Into service

The **USS Iowa (BB.61)** was laid down in June 1940, launched in August 1942 and commissioned in February 1943. In August of that year she escorted convoys from Newfoundland and then took President Roosevelt to North Africa, before being sent to the Pacific to join the 5th Fleet. She took part in the Marshall Islands landing, and suffered slight damage from Japanese artillery.

At Leyte she was part of Vice Admiral William Halsey's Fast Carrier Force, and took part in the Okinawa landing; in July 1945 she bombarded targets on Hokkaido and Honshu, and was part of the enormous force anchored in Tokyo Bay for the Japanese surrender.

The *Iowa* was mothballed in 1949 but reactivated in 1951 for service in the Korean War. She carried out a large number of shore bombardments but was decommissioned once more in 1953. It was widely thought that she would be scrapped, but in 1981 she was towed to New Orleans to begin reactivation. In her new configuration she carried a large number of Harpoon anti-ship missiles and Tomahawk cruise missiles to enable her to function as the main unit of a Surface Action Group (SAG). Her 406-mm (16-in) guns were retained to provide gunfire support.

Right: Although the battleship's place as pride of the fleet had been taken by the aircraft carrier, it was aboard an 'Iowa' class battleship that World War II came to an end. General Douglas MacArthur accepted the surrender of the Japanese empire on the main deck of the USS Missouri.

IJN *Kirishima* Battlecruiser

IJN *Kirishima* was the third of four **'Kongo' class** battlecruisers built for the Imperial Japanese Navy between 1912 and 1915. Launched in December 1913, the *Kirishima* was completed in April 1915.

In common with her sisters, *Kirishima* was modernized twice, in 1927–31 and 1934–40. The second modernization transformed her into a fast battleship for escorting carriers, with speed raised from 26 to 30 kts by doubling the horsepower. The original three funnels were reduced to two in the first reconstruction, and the second gave her a typical 'pagoda' foremast.

When war broke out in December 1941, all four 'Kongo' class battlecruisers were serving with the 3rd Battle Division, and *Kirishima* and **Hiei** accompanied the force that attacked Pearl Harbor. In June 1942, the *Kirishima* suffered slight damage from air attacks during the Battle of Midway.

With *Hiei*, she attacked US forces on Guadalcanal on the night of 12–13 November 1942. The two fast battleships engaged a force of American cruisers, sinking **USS Atlanta**, damaging **USS San Francisco**, **Juneau**, **Helena** and **Portland** and sinking the destroyers **USS**

Barton and **Laffey** in a confused melée at short range.

Ambush

Two nights later, the Japanese tried again to get a troop convoy through to Guadalcanal and to bombard Henderson Field but ran into an American force. This time the battleships **USS South Dakota** and **USS Washington** were in support. Both modern ships had radar, but superior night-fighting techniques enabled the Japanese to plan an ambush in which the American destroyers came off worse. When the cruiser **Nagara** turned her searchlights on the *South Dakota*, the *Kirishima* opened fire with her 356-mm (14-in) battery, but in the confusion the Japanese lookouts failed to spot

the *Washington* closing from 7300 m (8,000 yards). Five minutes after midnight, her 406-mm (16-in) salvoes began to burst around the *Kirishima*, which was overwhelmed. Seven minutes later she was ablaze, unable to steer and taking on water from underwater damage.

Admiral Kondo ordered the destroyers **IJN Asagumo**, **IJN Teruzuki**, and **IJN Samidare** to

The horsepower of the Kirishima and her three sisters was doubled during reconstruction to add five knots to their speed.

take off survivors, but no attempt was made to save the ship. *Kirishima*'s sea cocks were opened and she sank at 03.23, about 11 km (7 miles) north-west of Savo Island.

SPECIFICATION	
IJN Kirishima (after second reconstruction) **Displacement:** 31,980 tons standard, 36,600 tons full load **Dimensions:** length 222.0 m (728 ft 6 in) overall; beam 31.0 m (102 ft 4 in); draught 9.7 m (31 ft 9 in) **Machinery:** four-shaft geared steam turbines delivering 101,415 kW (136,000 shp)	**Speed:** 30.5 knots **Armour:** belt 76–203 mm (3–8 in); deck 121 mm (4.75 in); turrets 280 mm (11 in) **Armament:** eight 356-mm (14-in), 14 152-mm (6-in), eight 127-mm (5-in) AA, and 20 25-mm (1-in) AA guns **Aircraft:** three floatplanes **Complement:** 1,437 men

The Japanese Kirishima, built as a battle cruiser in 1915, was rebuilt as a fast battleship in the 1930s.

IJN 'Fuso' class Japan's first dreadnought

Japan's first true dreadnoughts were powerful vessels capable of matching the best in the world. They were based on the design of the 'Kongo' class, but enlarged and given true battleship protection. They had

about 25 per cent more armour and carried six twin turrets armed with 14-inch guns, compared with the four turrets of the 'Kongos'. Driven by four-shaft turbines, these **'Fusos'** had considerably less power

than the battlecruisers, giving them a lower maximum speed.

Fuso was built at the Kure Naval Yard. Laid down in 1912, the new battleship was launched in 1914 and was commissioned in November

1915. **Yamashiro** was launched at Yokosuka Naval Yard in 1915, entering service in 1917.

Extra platforms

After World War I, both received extra platforms to their

foremasts. The *Yamashiro* conducted the first trials using aircraft, and from 1927 both battleships added three aircraft to their equipment.

The planes were launched from flying-off platforms, located atop 'C' turret amidships on the *Fuso* and mounted on the quarterdeck aboard the *Yamashiro*.

The 'Fuso' class were completely rebuilt in the 1930s. The hulls were lengthened and anti-torpedo bulges were installed. To cope with the extra weight (up from just over 30,000 tons in 1915 to more than 38,000 tons in 1936), they were fitted with new boilers and new geared steam turbines. The most obvious change was in the

fitting of a 'pagoda' foremast.

Neither warship saw much action during World War II. They were sent through the Surigao Strait during the Battle of Leyte Gulf in October 1944, where they ran a gauntlet of torpedo

attacks from American PT-boats and destroyers, followed by a line of old American battleships – survivors of Pearl Harbor. Neither of the Japanese battleships survived this concentrated action.

The use of twin turrets made the 'Fuso'-class dreadnought longer than its American triple-turreted contemporaries, allowing it to achieve a higher speed than the Japanese required.

SPECIFICATION		
IJN *Fuso*	(six boilers powering four Kampon geared steam turbines delivering 75,000 shp/55,930 kW after reconstruction) to four shafts	**Armament:** 12 356-mm (14-in), sixteen 152-mm (6-in) (reduced to 14 after reconstruction), four 140-mm (5½-in) replaced by eight 127-mm (5-in) after reconstruction, four 76-mm (3-in) AA added in 1920s, 16 25-mm (1-in) AA added after reconstruction, rising to more than 38 25-mm in wartime, six 533-mm (21-inch) submerged torpedo tubes
Displacement: 30,600 tons (34,700 tons after 1930s reconstruction); full load 35,900 tons (38,530 tons after reconstruction)		
Dimensions: overall length 202.7 m/665 ft (212.7 m/698 ft after reconstruction); beam 28.7 m/94 ft (30.8 m/101 ft after bulges added in 1930s); draught 8.6 m/28 ft 3 in (9.4 m/31 ft after reconstruction)	**Speed:** 22.9 knots ((24.7 knots after reconstruction)	
	Endurance: 8,000 nm (14,820 km/9,206 miles) at 14 knots	
	Armour: side 305-mm; bow and stern 89 mm; deck 33 mm minimum, 76 mm maximum (increased to 119/165 mm after reconstruction); turrets 305 mm face, 152 mm sides; barbettes 292 mm; conning tower 330 mm	**Aircraft:** 3 Nakajima 95 floatplanes
Propulsion: 24 boilers powering four Brown Curtis geared turbines delivering 40,000 shp/29,830 kW		**Complement:** 1,193 as built, 1,400 in wartime

IJN 'Ise' class Battleship and battleship/carrier

The **'Ise' class** was a modified version of the preceding **'Fusos'**, the major difference being the re-arrangement of the main 356-mm (14-in) armament into pairs of turrets, which simplified both fire control and damage control.

Ise was built by Kawasaki at Kobe. Laid down in 1915, *Ise* was launched at the end of

1916, and completed a year later. **Hyuga** was built at Nagasaki by Mitsubishi. Launched in January 1917, she entered service in the spring of 1918.

Radical change

Secondary armament was changed from 152.4-mm (6-in) guns to 140-mm

(5.5-in) weapons – apparently this was because the new lighter shells were easier for the generally short-statured Japanese seaman of the time to handle.

Main armour protection was similar to the preceding type, but about 1,000 tons of additional armour was added to the ship to provide extra

protection. More efficient boilers delivered extra power, giving the 'Ise' class about a knot speed advantage over the 'Fusos'.

A more radical change came in 1942, following Japan's catastrophic defeat at Midway. Both *Ise* and *Hyuga* were rebuilt as hybrid battleship/carriers, with a hangar and aircraft deck

replacing the aft gun turrets. A wing of 22 seaplanes was intended to be shipped, being launched by catapult and then recovered from the sea by crane.

Completed late in 1943, neither ship carried any aircraft operationally. Both were used as decoys during the Battle of Leyte Gulf in October 1944.

Japan's crippling loss of carriers at Midway inspired the navy to convert the 'Ises' into hybrid carrier/battleships. However, the concept was never tested in action.

Lack of fuel left them helpless at the end of the war, and both were sunk in shallow water at Kure by US Navy carrier aircraft.

The 'Ise' class battleships were follow-ons to Japan's first true dreadnoughts. As with all Japanese battleships of the period, they were extensively rebuilt in the 1930s, receiving extra armour and more power.

SPECIFICATION

IJN *Ise*
Displacement: 29,900 tons (33,800 tons after carrier conversion); full load 35,900 tons (39,680 tons after carrier conversion)
Dimensions: overall length 206 m/675 ft (220 m/721 ft after conversion); beam 28.7 m/94 ft (31.6 m/104 ft after conversion); draught 8.8 m/29 ft (9.5 m/31 ft 2 in after reconstruction)
Propulsion: 24 boilers powering four geared turbines delivering 45,000

shp/33,560 kW (8 boilers powering four Kampon geared steam turbines delivering 81,000 shp/60,400 kW after 1930s reconstruction) to four shafts
Speed: 23 knots (25.6 knots after reconstruction)
Endurance: 9,680 nm (17,900 km/11,140 miles) at 14 knots
Armour: similar to *Fuso*
Armament: 12 35-mm (14-in) (four guns removed during carrier conversion), 20 140-mm (5½-in) (reduced to 16 after reconstruction);

eight 127-mm (5-in) added during 1930s reconstruction; four 76-mm (3-in) AA added in 1920s; 20 25-mm (1-in) AA added after reconstruction, rising to 57 in 1942 and 104 by late 1944; six 533-mm (21-inch) submerged torpedo tubes
Aircraft: 3 Nakajima 95 floatplanes as battleship; 22 floatplane dive bombers as hybrid carrier
Complement: 1,360 as built, up to 1,476 in wartime

IJN *Nagato* Battleship

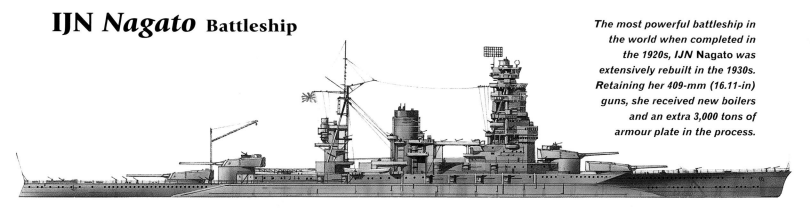

*The most powerful battleship in the world when completed in the 1920s, IJN **Nagato** was extensively rebuilt in the 1930s. Retaining her 409-mm (16.11-in) guns, she received new boilers and an extra 3,000 tons of armour plate in the process.*

Japanese naval expansion in the early years of the 20th Century saw the Imperial Navy grow from a young coastal force into one of the world's major fleets. During World War I, an ambitious building programme was initiated, with the aim of fielding eight powerful new battleships and eight equally powerful battlecruisers by the middle of the 1920s. The Washington Naval Treaty of 1922 brought all such naval expansion to an end, before more than two ships could be completed.

These two vessels, the **Nagato** and the *Mutsu*, were the world's most powerful battleships when launched in 1919 and 1920 from the Kure and Yokosuka navy yards respectively. Fast by contemporary standards, they were heavily armoured and were the world's first capital ships to carry 16-inch guns in their main batteries.

Modified in the mid-1920s, the two vessels underwent extensive modification between 1934 and 1936. Lengthened and fitted with hull bulges for stability, the forward funnel was removed and a large 'pagoda' bridge structure and mast was fitted. Extra armour was added throughout, taking the total armour weight from 10,400 tons to over 13,000 tons. The increased displacement meant a slower speed, since although more efficient boilers were fitted, the main turbines were not replaced.

Nagato served for many years as flagship of the Combined Fleet. The high point of her ceremonial career came on 11 October 1940: flying the flag of Vice-Admiral Isoroku Yamamoto, the battleship led the Imperial review in celebration of the 2,600th anniversary of the enthronement of Emperor Jimmu. A year later, Yamamoto

commanded the attack on Pearl Harbor from her decks.

Both *Mutsu* and *Nagato* were used throughout World War II.

War service

They served alongside the new superbattleship *Yamato* as Battle

Division One during the Battle of Midway, before transferring to BatDiv 2 alongside the *Fuso* and the *Yamashiro*. In August 1942, they formed a support group during the battle off the Solomon Islands that preceded the American landings on

SPECIFICATION
IJN *Nagato*

Displacement: 33,900 tons (39,250 tons after 1930s reconstruction); full load 38,625 tons (43,580 tons after reconstruction)
Dimensions: overall length 213.40 m/700 ft (225 m/739 ft after reconstruction); beam 29 m/95 ft 4 in (33 m/108 ft after bulges added in 1930s); draught 9 m (29 ft 7 in) (9.60 m/31 ft 6 in after reconstruction)
Propulsion: 21 Kanpon boilers (reboilered with 10 boilers in 1930s) powering four Brown Curtis geared turbines delivering 59,656 kW (80,000 shp) (67859 kW/91,000 shp after reconstruction) to four shafts
Speed: 26.5 kt (25 kt after reconstruction)
Armour: side 305 mm (12 in); bow and stern 89 mm (3.5 in);

deck 41 mm (1.5 in) minimum, 76 mm (3 in) maximum (increased to 119 mm/ 5 in); (185 mm/7.2 in after reconstruction); turrets 356 mm (14.03 in) face, 203 mm (8 in) sides; barbettes 292 mm (11.5 in); conning tower 356 mm (14 in)
Armament: Eight 409-mm (16-in); 20 140-mm (5.5-in) (reduced to 18 in 1930s reconstruction); eight 127-mm (5-in) AA added in 1930s; four 76-mm (3-in) AA; 20 25-mm (1-in) AA added in 1930s, increased to 98 during World War II; eight 13-mm (0-.5-in) MG removed April 1944; eight 610-mm (24-in) torpedo tubes, four above water, four submerged
Aircraft: 3 floatplanes
Complement: 1,350 as built, 1,480 in wartime

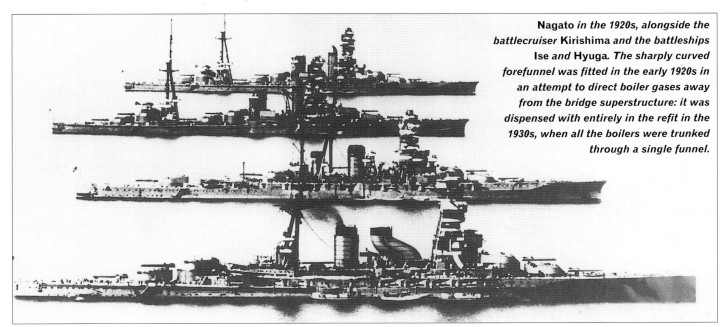

Nagato in the 1920s, alongside the battlecruiser Kirishima and the battleships Ise and Hyuga. The sharply curved forefunnel was fitted in the early 1920s in an attempt to direct boiler gases away from the bridge superstructure: it was dispensed with entirely in the refit in the 1930s, when all the boilers were trunked through a single funnel.

Guadalcanal. *Mutsu* was destroyed by an internal magazine explosion that split the ship into two while anchoring in Hiroshima Bay on 8 June 1942. After an accident investigation, the Imperial Navy blamed the loss on a disgruntled seaman who had brooded over theft charges and was killed in the explosion, though the true cause may never be known.

Through 1943 the *Nagato* served in the Southwest Pacific, moving on to Singapore early in 1944. The battleship escorted elements of Admiral Ozawa's Mobile Fleet during the Battle of the Philippine Sea, and formed part of Admiral Kurita's 1st Mobile Striking Force during the Leyte Gulf campaign.

Severely damaged by carrier aircraft in the Sibuyan Sea,

Nagato nevertheless took part in the action off Samar, alongside the *Yamato*. Again attacked and damaged by carrier aircraft, *Nagato* eventually returned to Japan, serving as a floating AA battery at Yokosuka.

The *Nagato* was the only major surface combatant of the IJF to survive the war. She was later used as a target by the United States when undertaking the Bikini Atoll atom bomb tests.

Nagato *in 1936, after the completion of her major rebuild. Her anti-aircraft armament was increased, with the addition of eight 127-mm (5-in) and twenty 25-mm (1-in) guns. By 1944* **Nagato** *also carried nearly 100 light anti-aircraft guns.*

IJN *Yamato* Battleship

The Imperial Japanese Navy, pursuing a goal of quality to offset the numerical advantage of the US Navy, started work in 1934 on a design of battleship to outclass any opponent. The ships were to be faster, better armoured and have longer-range guns, but the only way in which these qualities could be achieved was by contravening existing international arms limitation treaties.

Superbattleship
The design evolved to meet the requirement produced the biggest, most powerful battleships ever built. They

displaced 64,000 tons and were armed with nine 460-mm (18-in) guns capable of hitting targets at 48 km (30 miles). The protection was on an equally massive scale, with 410-mm (16-in) belt armour and 650-mm (25½-in) face plates on the turrets.

To get the ships built without alarming the Americans and British required total secrecy, the theory being that if Japan refused to ratify the next naval treaty in 1936 and had the ships ready by 1940 (when all tonnage limits expired) nobody could accuse the Japanese of cheating. It was also assumed

that if the new ships were longer and wider than the locks of the Panama Canal, the US Navy would be unable to build battleships of equivalent power. In that case, the Americans would be unable to oppose the Japanese Fleet in the Pacific without the enormous expense (and delay) of widening the Panama Canal.

Two ships, **IJN *Yamato*** and IJN *Musashi* were ordered

under the 3rd Reinforcement Programme of 1937. *Yamato* was laid down in November 1937, launched in August 1940 and completed in December 1941, just over a week after Pearl Harbor. *Musashi* was completed in August 1942. Two more were ordered in 1939, but the IJN *Shinano* was completed as a massive carrier, and the fourth was broken up incomplete in 1942.

Far and away the largest and most powerful battleships ever built, the 'Yamato' class were never to achieve the destiny hoped for by their designers. The day of the big-gun ship was done; instead of engaging the British and American battlefleets gun to gun, these mighty vessels were to succumb to the gnatlike attacks of carrierborne aircraft.

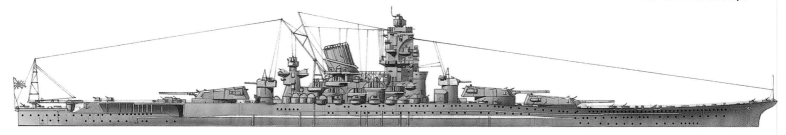

In combat

Yamato was Admiral Yamamoto's flagship at the Battle of Midway, but turned back before getting within gun range of the American carriers. *Yamato* was torpedoed by the USS *Skate* in February 1944, but repairs were completed in time for her to take part in the Battle of the Philippine Sea in June 1944, in Vanguard Force of the 1st Mobile Fleet.

The *Yamato, Musashi* and *Nagato* formed the main strength of Vice-Admiral Kurita's Force A in the Battle of Leyte Gulf, and *Yamato* fired her main armament for the first and last time at surface targets when she engaged American light carriers and escorts. However, poor visibility prevented her from using her monster guns to good effect. As the Japanese retreated, they came under ferocious attack by US Navy carrier aircraft, and *Musashi* was sunk, being hit by as many as 19 torpedoes and 17 bombs.

Yamato's last sortie was a suicide mission from the Home Islands to Okinawa. She only had enough fuel for a one-way trip, the aim being to beach her as a massive artillery battery close to the invasion fleet. On 7 April 1945, long before she could reach the island, she was sunk by massive air strikes, taking 13 torpedo hits and six bombs before blowing up.

Yamato in the Sibuyan Sea, during the Battle of Leyte Gulf. Yamato *escaped with minor damage from a bomb hit on the forecastle:* Musashi *was not so lucky, being sunk by overwhelming air attack.*

SPECIFICATION	
IJN *Yamato*	barbettes 380–560 mm (15–22 in);
Displacement: 64,000 tons standard,	turrets 190–650 mm (7½ in–25½ in);
69,988 tons full load	conning tower 75–500 mm
Dimensions: length 263 m (863 ft)	(3 in-19½ in)
overall; beam 38.90 m (127 ft 9 in)	**Armament:** nine 460-mm (18-in);
draught 10.45 m (34 ft 3 in)	12 155-mm (6-in) DP (reduced to
Machinery: 4-shaft geared steam	six in 1943); 12 127-mm (5-in) AA
turbines delivering 111895 kW	(increased to 24 in 1943); 24
(150,000 shp)	25-mm (1-in) AA (increased to 130
Speed: 27 kt (50 km/h; 31 mph)	by 1944)
Armour: belt 100–410 mm (4–16 in);	**Aircraft:** six floatplanes
bulkheads 300–350 mm (12–13½	**Complement:** 2,500 men
in); decks 200–230 mm (8–9 in);	

Left: Yamato *takes a bomb hit on the foredeck as Admiral Kurita's Force A traverses the Sibuyan Sea in October 1944.* Musashi *was sunk in the same action.*

Below: Fast by pre-war battleship standards, Yamato *was too slow to keep up with the 30-kt (56-km/h; 35-mph) carrier task forces that dominated the Pacific War.*

'Richelieu' class Battleships

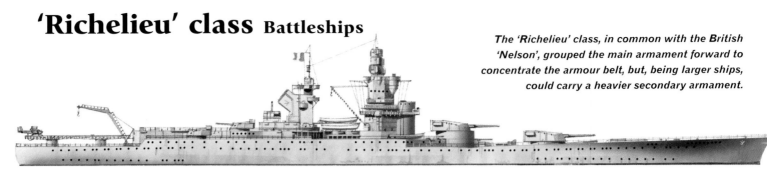

The 'Richelieu' class, in common with the British 'Nelson', grouped the main armament forward to concentrate the armour belt, but, being larger ships, could carry a heavier secondary armament.

Richelieu escaped from Brest to Dakar in June 1940, where she was damaged by a British attack. Placed in reserve following the war, Richelieu was finally scrapped in Italy in 1968.

In 1942 the incomplete Jean Bart was damaged by air attack and by gunfire from the veteran American battleship USS Massachusetts. The vessel was not completed until ten years after the end of the war.

To compete with other navies, the French navy authorized two 35,000-ton battleships in 1935, **Richelieu** and **Jean Bart**. Larger versions of the 26,000-ton battlecruisers *Dunkerque* and *Strasbourg*, they had heavier armament and protection.

The design was unique, with two large quadruple turrets well forward and widely spaced, and a backward-angled funnel forming part of the after superstructure. Their only drawback was low endurance, a result of being intended for operations in the Mediterranean.

In combat

The *Richelieu* escaped to North Africa when France fell in June 1940 and then survived several British attacks made to prevent her falling into German hands. A torpedo attack on the morning of 8 July struck the stern, and the *Richelieu* flooded, settling on the bottom of the harbour.

However, her 15-in (380-mm) guns were still functioning, and helped to defeat an attack by British and Free French forces in September. Fleeing the German occupation of Vichy France in 1942, *Richelieu* went over to the Allies. She joined the British Home Fleet at Scapa Flow, escorting convoys. In March 1944, *Richelieu* was sent to Trincomalee to serve with the Eastern Fleet. Taking part in a number of bombardments, she came under air attack several times. Apart from a short refit at Casablanca from October 1944 to January 1945, the *Richelieu* remained in the East Indies until October 1945, when she sailed for Indo-China. Decommissioned in 1956, the *Richelieu* was finally scrapped in 1964.

Jean Bart was incomplete when France fell, and was then damaged by Allied gunfire during the 1942 landings in North Africa.

Construction was not completed until 1955. She took part in the Anglo-French Suez operation a year later, and continued to serve into the 1960s. She was finally scrapped in 1970.

SPECIFICATION	
Richelieu	**Armour:** belt 343 mm (13.5 in); decks 50–170 mm (2–6¾ in); turrets 170–445 mm (6¾–17½ in)
Displacement: 41,000 tons standard; 47,500 tons full load	**Armament:** eight 380-mm (15-in), nine 152-mm (6-in) DP, 12 100-mm (3.9-in) AA, 16 37-mm AA and eight 13.2-mm (0.52-in) AA guns
Dimensions: length 247.9 m (813 ft 4 in) overall; beam 33.0 m (108 ft 3 in); draught 9.7 m (31 ft 10 in)	
Machinery: 4-shaft geared steam turbines delivering 111855 kW (150,000 shp)	**Aircraft:** three Loire-Nieuport floatplanes
Speed: 30 kts	**Complement:** 1,550 men

'Dunkerque' class Fast battleships

The rearmament of Germany after Hitler became Chancellor created considerable unease in French government circles. The Marine Nationale's fears focused on the 'Deutschland'-class 'pocket battleships', which posed a threat to France's large mercantile fleet.

To deal with the German commerce-raiders, the Minister

of Marine approved the construction of two fast battleships, the **Dunkerque** and **Strasbourg**. They were given an ample margin of speed, but armour protection was relatively light, being intended only to defeat the German 280-mm (11-in) guns of the 'Deutschland' class. In fact, they were the first of a new generation of fast

battleships, close to the original idea of the battlecruiser.

The *Dunkerque* was funded in the 1931 Programme and built at Brest. It was a handsome ship, and the designers had adopted the same disposition of the main armament as the Royal Navy's 'Nelson' class. The eight 330-mm (13-in) Modéle 33 guns were mounted in two quadruple

turrets, well spaced to avoid both being knocked out by a single hit. Most of the secondary armament of 130-mm (5.1-inch) dual-purpose guns was situated aft, and a large tower bridge structure also reflected the influence of the 'Nelson' class. Design speed was an impressive 29 kts, easily exceeded on trials.

The outbreak of war in 1939 offered an opportunity to show the *Dunkerque*'s qualities, and together with the *Strasbourg*, the two operated in the Atlantic, protecting convoys and hunting the *Admiral Graf Spee*. Unfortunately, *Dunkerque* was badly damaged by Royal Navy gunfire at Mers-el-Kebir, and later by aerial torpedoes.

After temporary repairs the vessel withdrew to Toulon, and on 27 November 1942 was scuttled in dry dock when German troops tried to capture the fleet.

The wreck was removed in 1945 when the French Navy reoccupied Toulon, and was eventually scrapped in 1958, a sad end to a fine capital ship.

SPECIFICATION	
Dunkerque	**Armour:** belt 248–146 mm
Displacement: 26,500 tons	(9¾–5¾ in); decks 127–38 mm
(standard); 35,500 tons (full load)	(5–1½ in); turrets 336–152 mm
Dimensions: length 209.0 m (685 ft	(13¼–6 in)
3 in) overall; beam 31.08 m (102 ft);	**Armament:** eight 330-mm (13-in),
draught 8.70 m (28 ft 6 in)	12 130-mm (5.1-in) DP, 10 37-mm
Machinery: 4-shaft geared steam	AA and 32 13.2-mm (0.52-in)
turbines delivering 83891 kW	machine-guns
(112,500 shp)	**Aircraft:** 2 floatplanes
Speed: 29.5 kts	**Complement:** 1,431
Range: 500 nm at full speed	

Conte di Cavour Modernized battleship

A World War I battleship, the **Conte di Cavour** was rebuilt and refitted in October 1933 at Trieste, and recommissioned in June 1937. She first saw action off Punta Stilo in July 1940 against the Royal Navy ships *Warspite*, *Malaya* and *Royal Sovereign*. During August and September, the vessel operated against convoys to Malta. In November, she was attacked by aircraft from the British carrier *Illustrious* at Taranto, and sank in shallow water. However, the vessel was raised in July 1941, and towed back for repairs. Work began in 1943, but in October she was scuttled. A German salvage commando

*The **Conte di Cavour** is pictured together with her sister ship **Guilio Cesare** at Crete in July 1940. The **Guilio Cesare** maintains the dubious record of being struck from the greatest distance by another warship while steaming; being damaged by **HMS** Warspite off **Calabria** in 1940, from a range of some 24,140 m (79,200 ft).*

team raised her, but she was sunk again on 15 February 1945 by a US air attack. Other ships in the class included **Leonardo da Vinci** (decomissioned after

World War I) and **Guilio Cesare**. The latter survived in Soviet hands as **Novorossiysk**, before being sunk by an explosion at Sevastopol in 1955.

SPECIFICATION	
Conte di Cavour	**Armament:** 10 320-mm (12.6-in),
Displacement 23,619 tons standard;	12 120-mm (4.7-in), eight 100-mm
29,100 tons full load	(3.93-in) AA, 16 37-mm AA, 12
Dimensions: length 186 m (611 ft	20-mm AA
5 in); beam 28 m (91 ft 9 in);	**Armour:** belt 248–102 mm (9¾–4 in);
draught (maximum) 10.4 m (34 ft)	deck 279 mm (11 in); turrets
Speed: 28 kts	119 mm (4¾ in)
Range: 3,100 nm at 20 kts	**Complement:** 1,236

Vittorio Veneto Battleship

*The **Vittorio Veneto** saw more action than any other Italian battleship, and was hit twice by torpedoes and once by bombs. On 28 March 1941, the vessel was the target of six Albacore torpedo bombers and a pair of Fairey Fulmar fighters from **HMS** Formidable, which managed to get one torpedo hit.*

At the outbreak of World War II, it was hoped that the high speed and heavy armament of the **Littorio,** the **Vittorio Veneto** and the **Roma** would deter the British Mediterranean Fleet.

However, the *Vittorio Veneto* was the cause of a disaster that overtook the Italian navy, the Battle of Matapan. On 28 March 1941, she was attacking British convoys evacuating troops from Greece to Crete and Alexandria, when she was hit by a torpedo

from one of HMS *Formidable*'s Fairey Albacores. The torpedo hit abaft 'Y' turret on the port side at 15.21. The vessel flooded, losing power, but escaped.

Dusk brought more British attacks. Though hit, the *Vittorio Veneto* made her way back to Taranto, leaving the cruiser *Pola* and two sisters to be destroyed.

She was damaged several more times and then, in September 1943, steamed for Malta to surrender. Her crew

could only watch as the *Roma* was sunk by a German guided bomb.

She was forbidden to be used by the post-war Italian Navy, and was sold for scrap in 1951.

SPECIFICATION	
Vittorio Veneto	**Armour:** belt 60–345 mm
Displacement: 41,700 tons	(2½–13½ in); decks 165 mm (6½ in);
standard; 45,460 tons full load	turrets and barbettes 200–280 mm
Dimensions: 237.8 m (780 ft) overall;	(8–11 in)
beam 32.9 m (108 ft); draught	**Armament:** nine 381-mm (15-in), 12
10.5 m (34 ft 5 in)	152-mm (6-in), 12 90-mm (3.5-in)
Machinery: 4-shaft geared steam	AA, 20 37-mm AA and 16 20-mm
turbines delivering 95450 kW	AA guns
(128,000 shp)	**Aircraft:** three floatplanes
Speed: 30 kts	**Complement:** 1,872

USS *Lexington* Aircraft carrier

The terms of the Washington Treaty allowed the US Navy to convert two of four incomplete 33,000-ton battlecruisers into aircraft carriers. The ships chosen were the *Lexington* and *Saratoga*, under construction by Fore River at Quincy and New York Shipbuilding at Camden, and the opportunity was sensibly taken to incorporate many ideas from a cancelled aircraft carrier design of 1919.

The **USS *Lexington*** (**CV-2**) was launched in October 1925, and when completed was a remarkable ship with an 'island' superstructure on the starboard side, flanked by two twin 8-in (203-mm) gun turrets forward and two aft. Other key features were a hull that was plated right up to the flight deck but with an

Above: The USS Lexington (pictured), together with her sister ship USS Saratoga, helped to build the experience upon which the US Navy based its World War II carrier operations. The ships boasted a 137-m (450-ft) long hangar, as well as a 36.6-m (120-ft) hold for knocked-down aircraft. Additional aircraft could be suspended from the hangar roof.

Lexington really begin to flex her muscles.

Counter-strike

After a short refit at Pearl Harbor, the *Lexington* returned to the Coral Sea, where the Japanese carriers were supporting an attack on Port Moresby, New Guinea. On 8 May *Lexington*'s SBD

Above: Lexington's distinctive funnel provided a useful mounting point for some of the advanced radar equipment that was added during 1941.

opening for the launch and recovery of boats, a two-storied hangar arrangement, two centreline elevators for the movement of aircraft between the flight deck and the hangar decks, and one forward-located catapult. A feature retained from the ship's origins was the turbo-electric propulsion, with four turbo-generators supplying power to eight electric motors coupled two to a shaft.

Escape from Midway

At the time of the Japanese raid on Pearl Harbor, the ship was delivering aircraft to the US Marines holding Midway Island, and so escaped the disaster. *Lexington* was hurriedly refitted, losing her cumbersome 8-in (203-mm) guns and four 5-in (127-mm) guns, and receiving a few single 20-mm Oerlikon guns to supplement her otherwise very meagre close-range anti-aircraft armament.

The *Lexington*'s first operation was an attempt to relieve Wake Island immediately after Pearl Harbor, an operation that ended in failure. At the end of January

1942 the carrier provided cover for a raid on the Marshall Islands and thereafter saw limited action in the South West Pacific. Not until she was joined by the newer aircraft carrier *Yorktown* in March 1942 did the

SPECIFICATION	
USS *Lexington* (CV-2) **Displacement:** 36,000 tons standard; 47,700 tons full load **Dimensions:** length 270.66 m (888 ft) overall; beam 39.62 m (130 ft) over flight deck; draught 9.75 m (32 ft) **Propulsion:** four turbo-generators delivering 156,660 kW (210,000 shp) to four shafts **Speed:** 34 kts	**Armour:** belt 152 mm (6 in); flight deck 25 mm (1 in); main deck 51 mm (2 in); lower deck 25–76 mm (1–3 in); turrets 38–76 mm (1.5–3 in); barbettes 152 mm (6 in) **Armament:** (in 1942) eight 5-in (127-mm) AA, 30 20-mm AA and six quadruple 1.1-in (27.9-mm) AA guns **Aircraft:** (1942) 22 fighters, 36 dive-bombers and 12 torpedo-bombers **Complement:** 2,951

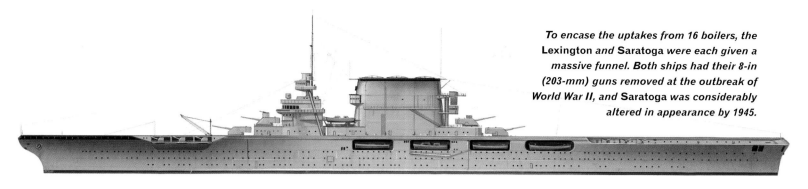

To encase the uptakes from 16 boilers, the Lexington and Saratoga were each given a massive funnel. Both ships had their 8-in (203-mm) guns removed at the outbreak of World War II, and Saratoga was considerably altered in appearance by 1945.

Dauntless dive-bombers attacked the Imperial Japanese navy's aircraft carriers *Shokaku* and *Zuikaku*, but without scoring any hits. Unfortunately while this attack was in progress a Japanese counter-strike hit the *Lexington* with two torpedoes on the port side, and the ship

also suffered two bomb hits and several near misses. The 'whip' of the hull from the explosions ruptured the aviation gasoline tanks, so that even after the fires had been extinguished the lethal vapour continued to seep through the ship. About an hour after the attack, a chance spark

ignited this vapour, and the ship suffered a series of explosions. Six hours after the first hit the order was given to abandon ship, and after escorting destroyers had rescued as many men as possible, the wreck was torpedoed – 216 men from a crew of 2,951 were killed.

In a short war career, the *Lexington* failed to inflict any significant damage on the enemy, largely as a result of the inexperience of her air group and faulty US Navy tactical doctrine. The loss of a big carrier was a heavy price for the Coral Sea victory.

USS *Saratoga* Aircraft carrier

Like her sister ship, the USS *Lexington* – which was laid down in January 1921 at Bethlehem (Fore River), launched in October 1925 and commissioned on 14 December 1927 – the aircraft carrier **USS Saratoga** (**CV-3**) was launched, in April 1925, after conversion

from an incomplete battlecruiser hull that had been laid down at New York Shipbuilding, and was commissioned on 16 November 1927. The two ships played a major role in developing the US Navy's important concept of the fast carrier task force, and from 1928 they took part in the

annual 'Fleet Problem' wargame of the Pacific Fleet. This organization was the ideal parent for the two large aircraft carriers, which had the size, range and aircraft strength (by 1936 reduced from 90 aircraft to 18 fighters, 40 bombers and five utility aircraft) to play a decisive part in any future operations in the Pacific Ocean.

As completed, both of the ships have a primary gun armament of eight 8-in (203-mm) guns in four twin turrets grouped ahead and abaft the ships' massive island and funnel combination. The armament had originally been schemed on the basis of 6-in (152-mm) guns, the change to larger-calibre weapons probably

being spurred by the probability of encountering 'treaty' cruisers with an armament of 8-in guns.

At the time of Pearl Harbor, the 'Sara' was back at San Diego on the US west coast undergoing a short refit, but she sailed shortly after this time and took part with the 'Lex' in an abortive attempt to relieve the garrison of Wake Island. During the ship's refit the four twin 8-in turrets were removed, and in their place *Saratoga* received four twin 5-in (127-mm) L/38 dual-purpose mountings controlled by two combined high/low-angle director control towers. At the same time, the original secondary armament of 12 5-in (127-mm) L/25 low-angle guns was replaced by eight 5-in L/38 dual-purpose guns. The *Lexington*, it should be noted, had been stripped of her 8-in (203-mm) guns but had not been fitted with the 5-in replacement weapons.

SPECIFICATION	
USS *Saratoga* (CV-3) **Displacement:** 36,000 tons standard; 47,700 tons full load **Dimensions:** length 270.66 m (888 ft) overall; beam 32.2 m (105 ft 6 in) hull; draught 9.75 m (32 ft) **Propulsion:** four General Electric turbo-generators delivering 156597 kW (210,000 shp) to four shafts **Speed:** 34 kts **Armour:** belt 152 mm (6 in); flight deck 25 mm (1 in); main deck	51 mm (2 in); lower deck 25–76 mm (1–3 in); barbettes 152 mm (6 in) **Armament:** (in 1945) four twin and eight single 5-in (127-mm) dual-purpose, 24 quadruple 40-mm Bofors AA, two twin 40-mm Bofors AA, and 16 20-mm AA guns **Aircraft:** (1945) 57 fighters and 18 torpedo-bombers **Complement:** (1945) 3,373 men

'Sara' in September 1944, painted in Camouflage Measure 32/11A. Twin 5-in (127-mm) and light AA guns had by this time replaced the original 8-in (203-mm) guns. Despite her age, the ship was still the largest US carrier, if not the most capacious.

The *Saratoga* was torpedoed by a Japanese submarine off Hawaii on 11 January 1942, and needed four months of repairs. At this time the flight deck was enlarged from its original length of 270.66 m (888 ft) to 274.7 m (901 ft 3 in), with width increased to 39.62 m (130 ft). The *Saratoga* was also fitted with a deep port-side bulge to help restore the ship's buoyancy, which had been degraded from commissioning standard by the addition of extra equipment, including a greater number of light AA weapons. The light AA armament was increased by the grouping of 100 40-mm guns in quadruple mountings along the sides of the flight deck and 16 single 20-mm guns at the flight deck's after end. Other changes to affect the ship included the heightening of the bridge, the replacement of the original tripod mast by a pole mast, and the addition of both warning and gunnery-control radar.

Guadalcanal action

The 'Sara' was used to ferry fresh aircraft out to the Central Pacific, and so missed the decisive Battle of Midway, but was a welcome reinforcement by 8 June, the day after the sinking of the USS *Yorktown*. *Saratoga*'s fighters and dive-bombers were given the task of softening up the defences of Guadalcanal on 7 August 1942 before the big amphibious landing by the US Marine Corps. The Japanese responded vigorously to this challenge, and by 20 August a powerful carrier task force was nearing the Eastern Solomons.

The *Saratoga*, the USS *Enterprise* and the USS *Wasp* were heavily engaged in the Battle of the Eastern Solomons, but the 'Sara' escaped lightly. Not until 31 August did she sustain damage, when she took a torpedo hit from the submarine *I-68* after dawn. The carrier was not badly damaged by the hit, in spite of having one boiler room flooded and another partly flooded, but an electrical failure soon put her machinery out of action. Two hours later the carrier got back limited power, and reached Pearl Harbor six days later, where she underwent six weeks of repairs.

In 1943–44, the *Saratoga* took part in the 'island-hopping' drive across the Pacific, and in 1944 was detached to the East Indies, co-operating with the British and Free French to attack Japanese positions in Java and Sumatra. On 21 February 1945, she was hit by a kamikaze while supporting the landings on Iwo Jima. Although repaired, she was restricted to training duties at Pearl Harbor: it is indicative of the *Saratoga*'s battlecruiser origins that though larger than an 'Essex'-class carrier, she carried fewer aircraft.

On 25 July 1946, the *Saratoga*'s stripped hull was finally sunk in Bikini Atoll during the United States' early atomic bomb tests.

*Above: The USS **S**aratoga (CV-3) in March 1932 with a large part of its air group at the forward end of the flight deck. The ship and its sister 'fought' each other in annual manoeuvres.*

*Left: The USS **S**aratoga in World War II. This aircraft carrier played a major role in the Pacific, but despite her size was slowly relegated to less important tasks as the arrival of modern carriers revealed its limitations.*

USS *Yorktown* Aircraft carrier

The Yorktown (CV-5) and her sister carriers were prototypes for the successful 'Essex' class. Although much smaller than the 'Lexington'-class carriers, they could actually carry more aircraft.

The **USS *Yorktown*** (**CV-5**) was the lead ship of a new class of aircraft carrier authorized out of President Roosevelt's Public Works Administration, the Federal Unemployment Relief Agency. The vessel and its sister USS *Enterprise* (CV-6) were authorized in 1933, and were followed by the USS *Hornet* (CV-8) five years later.

The design was a development of that of the *Ranger*, with an 'open' hangar rather than the 'closed' type of the *Lexington* and *Saratoga*, to allow up to 80 aircraft to be carried. This arrangement proved highly successful, and formed the basis for the even more successful 'Essex' class.

Battle of Coral Sea

The ship was commissioned in September 1937, and was hurriedly transferred to the

Above: The Yorktown's Curtiss SB2C Helldiver dive-bombers were eventually replaced by Douglas SBD-5 Dauntless dive-bombers, due to the unsatisfactory performance of the former.

SPECIFICATION	
USS *Yorktown* (CV-5) **Displacement:** 19,800 tons standard; 27,500 tons with a full combat load **Dimensions:** length 246.7 m (809 ft 6 in) overall; beam 25.3 m (83 ft); draught 8.53 m (28 ft) **Machinery:** 4-shaft geared steam turbines delivering 89520 kW (120,000 shp) **Speed:** 33 kts	**Armour:** belt 102 mm (4 in); main deck 76 mm (3 in); lower deck 25-76 mm (1–3 in) **Armament:** (1942) eight 5-in (127-mm) AA, four quadruple 1.1-in (27.94-mm) AA and 16 0.5-in (12.7-mm) machine-guns **Aircraft:** (1942) 20 fighters, 38 dive-bombers and 13 torpedo-bombers **Complement:** 2,919 men

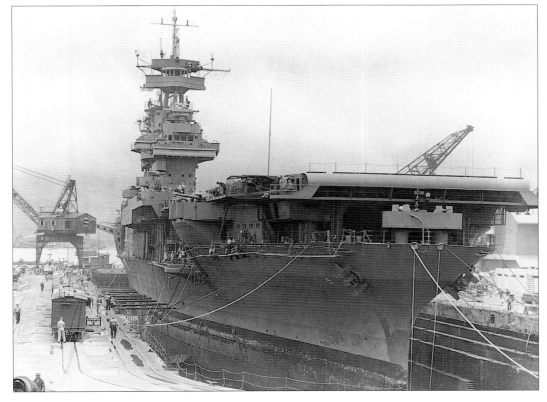

Below: USS Yorktown preparing to sail from Pearl Harbor. The vessel was later lost at the battle of the Coral Sea.

Pacific after Pearl Harbor. Under Rear Admiral Frank J. Fletcher, she was sent to the South West Pacific in the spring of 1942, and took part in the Battle of the Coral Sea. Her Air Group 5, comprising 20 Grumman F4F Wildcat fighters, 38 Douglas SBD-5 Dauntless dive-bombers and 13 Douglas TBD Devastator torpedo-bombers, played a major role in the battle, sinking the light carrier *Shoho* in a brilliant attack lasting only 10 minutes. On the next day, 8 May, her dive-bombers inflicted damage on the carrier *Zuikaku*, but in return a force of Nakajima B5N 'Kate' torpedo-bombers and Aichi D3A 'Val' dive-bombers penetrated a dense screen of fighters and gunfire to

score a devastating hit on the flight deck.

The bomb went through three decks before exploding, and numerous fires were started. The damage control parties brought the fires under control, and the ship was able to return to Pearl Harbor for repairs.

Battle of Midway

Working around the clock, the repair teams were able to get Yorktown back in action in only four days, just in time for the Battle of Midway in June 1942. At a crucial point in the battle, Yorktown's dive-bombers took part in the attack on the Japanese carriers, and her aircraft were the only ones able to mount a search for the surviving Japanese carrier Hiryu. Even after the Yorktown was hit by three 250-kg (551-lb) bombs she was able to operate its aircraft, and was finally put out of action only after being hit by two torpedoes.

Although the carrier had already taken considerable punishment during the Battle of the Coral Sea, the Yorktown might have survived even this heavy damage, for by first light on 6 June salvage parties had put out the fires and had started to pump out the ship's flooded compartments. However, the Japanese submarine I-168 put two more torpedoes into her, and early the next morning she capsized and sank.

USS *Enterprise* Aircraft carrier

Easily the most distinguished carrier of the Pacific War, the 'Big E' played a major role in the US Navy's victory and epitomized the new type of warfare.

The **USS *Enterprise*** (CV-6) was the second of the

Attended by tug-boats, the USS Enterprise (CV-6) is seen at harbour in New York. Attempts to preserve the 'Big E' were unsuccessful, but the the impressive ships of the 'Yorktown'-class formed the basis of the subsequent 'Essex'-class aircraft carriers.

'Yorktown' class, and joined the Pacific Fleet in 1938. Fortunately, it and the other two carriers of the Pacific Fleet were away from Pearl Harbor on 7 December 1941 when the Japanese attacked.

Warship *Enterprise*

When they returned to Oahu, they were immediately put into the front line, for the battle fleet no longer existed. Three days afterwards the *Enterprise's* aircraft sank the submarine *I-170*, the first Japanese submarine to be destroyed.

The *Enterprise* escorted her sister *Hornet* on the Tokyo Raid in April 1942, but did not embark B-25 bombers, as her aircraft were to be used to sink the Japanese early warning picket line. Neither carrier was back in time for the Battle of the Coral Sea in the following month, but they joined the

The much larger hulls of **Enterprise** *and* **Yorktown** *conferred superior seaworthiness than their predecessor* **Ranger,** *and increased speed by 4 kts.*

Yorktown in time for Midway in June. Here, the Douglas SBD Dauntlesses from the *Enterprise* sank the carriers *Kaga* and *Akagi*, and *Yorktown's* Dauntlesses flying off *Enterprise's* deck joined the group which sank the *Hiryu*. Two days later the *Enterprise's* dive-bombers sank the heavy cruiser *Mikuma* and damaged the cruiser *Mogami* and two destroyers.

The *Enterprise* covered the Guadalcanal landings in August 1942, and her aircraft shot down 17 Japanese aircraft in two days. During the Battle of the Eastern Solomons on 24 August, the vessel was hit by three bombs,

and returned to Pearl Harbor, where repairs continued for about two months. In the Battle of Santa Cruz on 26 October, *Enterprise* again took three hits, but was able to operate her aircraft, and as she was now the only US carrier left, she had to remain in the forward area. On 13 November her Grumman TBF Avenger torpedo-bombers finished off the damaged battleship *Hiei*, and next day devastated a troop convoy of 11 ships with no fewer than 26 bomb and six torpedo hits.

'Turkey Shoot'

Enterprise was given lengthy repairs in the United States and did not return to the Pacific until mid-1943. On 25 November 1943, one of her Avengers achieved the world's first night 'kill' at sea. She took part in the

strike on Truk in February 1944, and in the 'Marianas Turkey Shoot' during the Battle of the Philippine Sea that June. She continued in action into 1945, surviving two kamikaze attacks. A third kamikaze strike on 14 May ended her career, for she had to return to the United States for major repairs.

At the end of the war, the *Enterprise* had one of the most impressive combat records of any allied ship, having participated in and survived several of the major Pacific naval battles. As the holder of 19 Battle Stars, the 'Big E' was a candidate for preservation as a memorial, but efforts to save her came to nothing and in 1958 she was sold for scrap, releasing the name for the first nuclear carrier.

SPECIFICATION	
USS *Enterprise* (CV-6)	**Armour:** belt 102 mm (4 in); main
Displacement: 19,800 tons standard;	deck 76 mm (3 in); lower deck
25,500 tons full load	25–76 mm (1–3 in)
Dimensions: length 246.74 m (809 ft	**Armament:** (1942) eight 127-mm
6 in); beam 34.75 m (114 ft) over	(5-in) AA, four quadruple 1.1-in
flight deck; draught 8.84 m (29 ft)	(27.94-mm) AA and 16 0.5-in
Machinery: 4-shaft geared steam	(12.7-mm) machine-guns
turbines delivering 89,520 kW	**Aircraft:** (1942) 27 fighters, 37 dive-
(120,000 shp)	bombers and 15 torpedo-bombers
Speed: 33 kts	**Complement:** 2,919 men

Left: **Enterprise,** *seen with aircraft ranged on the rear of the flightdeck, fought in most of the great Pacific carrier battles, from Midway to the Philippine Sea.*

USS *Ranger* Light fleet aircraft carrier

USS *Ranger* (**CV-4**) was the first US aircraft carrier. She was conceived to a tonnage well below the limit imposed by the terms of the Washington Naval to extract the maximum air fleet out of its allocated tonnage. In the *Ranger*, therefore, basic ship requirements came second to carrier requirements, meaning she was slower, with less gun armament and less protection than other carriers, but carried more aircraft.

Construction

She was designed with a flush deck, although an island was constructed, partly for control of flightdeck operations. A feature was the use of six hinged funnels, three on each side, which could be turned to the horizontal position for flight deck operations. The ship's original air group comprised 36 bombers, 36 fighters and four utility aircraft, and aircraft handling features included one elevator between the hangars and the flight deck, a catapult at the forward end of the flight deck, and cranes on each side for hoisting seaplanes in and out.

Performance

She was commissioned in July 1934, but in 1939 her captain reported that the ship pitched too much for flight deck operations. *Ranger* was too poorly protected and armed for first-line service during World War II, taking part only in the North African operation of November 1942 and a carrier raid on Norway in 1943. After this, she was used as a training carrier.

AEW trials

In 1945, *Ranger* was involved in the first trials of AEW (Airborne Early Warning) aircraft. She was finally sold for spare parts in January 1947.

Above: The USS Ranger *(CV-4) pictured in 1942. Designed as a flush-deck carrier,* Ranger *added a small island during construction.*

Below: Three SB2C Helldivers provide air cover for the Ranger *in the Pacific in June 1945. The vessel proved incapable of operating aircraft under heavy weather conditions.*

SPECIFICATION	
USS *Ranger* (CV-4) **Displacement:** 14,575 tons standard, 17,577 tons full load **Dimensions:** length 234.39 m (769 ft) overall; beam 33.37 m (109 ft 6 in) over flight deck; draught 6.83 m (29 ft) **Machinery:** 2-shaft steam turbines delivering 39,890 kW (39890 shp) **Speed:** 29.25 kts	**Armour:** 25 mm (1 in) decks and 51 mm (2 in) sides and bulkheads **Armament:** (1941) eight 5-in (127-mm) AA, 24 1.1-in (27.94-in) AA and 24 0.5-in (12.7-mm) AA; (1943) eight 5-in AA, 24 40-mm AA and 46 20-mm AA **Aircraft:** 76, 86 as aircraft transport **Complement:** 1,788 men (2,000 in war)

USS *Hornet* Fleet aircraft carrier

The third member of the 'Yorktown' class, the **USS *Hornet*** (**CV-8**) was commissioned on 20 October 1940, shortly before Pearl Harbor. After a shakedown cruise with her air group in the Caribbean in January 1942, the ship embarked the first twin-engine North American B-25 bombers for the Doolittle Raid on Tokyo. After two months of trials and training, the *Hornet*

The new carrier Hornet *on trials in 1941. The vessel was commissioned seven weeks before Pearl Harbor and left for the Pacific in March 1942.*

left for the Pacific on 2 April, with 16 B-25 Mitchell bombers.

Surprise raid

The raid on 18 April surprised the Japanese, and most of the bombers reached China safely. The *Hornet*'s next assignment was the Battle of Midway, on 4–6 June 1942. Although her air group lost all her Douglas TBD Devastator torpedo-bombers and five Grumman TBF

Avengers, and failed to hit the Japanese carrier *Hiryu* in a second strike, she sank the heavy cruiser *Mikuma* and inflicted severe damage on her sister *Mogami*.

The *Hornet* was ferrying US Marine Corps fighters at the time of the Guadalcanal landings in August 1942, but after landing her aircraft she joined the *Wasp* and *Saratoga* in the covering force. Although withdrawn to Espiritu Santo to submarines, she sortied early in October to attack Japanese targets, and on 25 October met the Japanese carriers once more, in the Battle of Santa Cruz.

Fatal attack

On 26 October, the two American carriers launched an air strike (a total of 158 aircraft), while the four Japanese carriers launched most of their 207 aircraft. But while the *Hornet*'s torpedo-bombers and dive-bombers were on their way, 27 Japanese strike aircraft broke through the fighter screen and scored six bomb and two torpedo hits on the *Hornet*. Four hours later another Japanese strike scored a torpedo hit and two more bomb hits. By now the US destroyers screening the *Hornet* were dangerously exposed, and the decision was taken to scuttle the *Hornet*.

To the Americans' dismay, several torpedoes failed to detonate, and a total of 430 5-in (127-mm) shells fired at the carrier's waterline had no effect.

The waterlogged hulk was abandoned, and finally two Japanese destroyers gave the *Hornet* her death-blow in the early hours of 27 October.

SPECIFICATION	
USS *Hornet* (CV-8) **Displacement:** 19,000 tons standard, 29,100 tons full load **Dimensions:** length 252.2 m (827 ft 5 in) overall; beam 34.8 m (114 ft 2 in) over flight deck; draught 8.84 m (29 ft) **Machinery:** 4-shaft geared steam turbine's delivering 89,520 kW (120,000 shp) **Speed:** 33 kts	**Armour:** belt 64–102 mm (2½-4in); main deck 76 mm (3 in); lower deck 25–76 mm (1–3 in) **Armament:** (1942) eight 5-in (127-mm) AA, four quadruple 1.1-in (27.94-mm) AA, 30 20-mm AA and nine 0.5-in (12.7-mm) machine-guns **Aircraft:** (1942) 36 fighters, 36 dive-bombers and 15 torpedo-bombers **Complement:** 2,919 men

USS *Wasp*
Light fleet aircraft carrier

A port profile of the Wasp*. The tall funnel made the vessel unique among US carriers. A small carrier,* Wasp *was designed to use up the remaining carrier tonnage allowed under the Washington Treaty.*

The **USS *Wasp* (CV-7)** was an improved version of the *Ranger* was ordered, also with modest speed and light armour but big aircraft capacity. Commissioned in April 1941, she was training in the Atlantic from the autumn of that year. In March 1942 she went to the Mediterranean to ferry RAF Spitfires to Malta. In July she left for the Pacific and took part in the Guadalcanal landings. She missed the Battle of the Eastern Solomons as she

had been detached to refuel, and she returned to Noumea to take on board fighter aircraft for the US Marines on Guadalcanal.

Substantial damage

Early in the afternoon of 15 September 1942 the *Wasp* flew off its fighters, but shortly afterwards was hit by three torpedoes fired by the Japanese submarine *I-19*. Two of the torpedoes struck her on the port side near the aviation gasoline

tanks, while the third struck higher up and damaged the refuelling system.

The ship was gutted, and the order to abandon ship followed. The destroyer USS *Lansdowne* was then ordered to sink her.

The loss of *Wasp* provided lessons for the future. A board of enquiry showed that most of the damage was caused by the third torpedo-hit, the 'whip' of the hull knocking out the damage control organization.

SPECIFICATION	
USS *Wasp* (CV-7) **Displacement:** 14,700 tons standard, 20,500 tons full load **Dimensions:** length 225.93 m (741 ft 3 in) overall; beam 24.61 m (80 ft 9 in); draught 8.53 m (28 ft) **Machinery:** 2-shaft geared steam turbines delivering 55950 kW (75,000 shp) **Speed:** 29.5 kts	**Armour:** belt 102 mm (4 in); main and lower decks 38 mm (1½ in) **Armament:** (1942) eight 5-in (127-mm) AA, four quadruple 1.1-in (27.94-mm) AA and 30 20-mm AA guns. **Aircraft:** (1942) 29 fighters, 36 dive-bombers and 15 torpedo-bombers **Complement:** 2,367 men

The USS Wasp *(CV-7) at Pearl Harbor on 8 August 1942, a month before it was sunk. The vessel offered even less underwater protection than the 'Yorktowns'.*

USS *Essex* Aircraft carrier

The units of the 'Essex' class can claim to be the most cost-effective and successful aircraft carriers ever built. The specification, issued in June 1939, was for an improved 'Yorktown' class type but with the displacement increased by 7,000 tons to provide stronger defensive armament, thicker armour, more power and, above all, more aviation fuel. With more than 6,300 tons of oil fuel, the endurance was 27360 km (17,000 miles) at 20 kts, while 690 tons of gasoline and 220 tons of ammunition pushed up the number of sorties that could be flown by the carrier's embarked squadrons before these essential supplies had to be replenished. In addition, the same number of aircraft could be carried, although in practice many more could be carried: the nominal strength was 82, but by 1945 a total of 108 latest-generation aircraft could be embarked.

Eleven units of the class were ordered in 1940 and a further 13 were built during World War II. Building times were extremely short: **USS *Essex* (CV-9)** was built in 20 months, and the wartime average building time was cut to just 17 months.

Into battle

The lead ship of its class, the *Essex* reached the Pacific in May 1943, by which time the US Navy's worst problems were

over, but the vessel saw considerable and indeed heavy fighting with the Fast Carrier Task Force, in which she served with the USS *Enterprise* and USS *Saratoga* as well as the light fleet carriers of the 'Independence' class. In the spring of 1944, the *Essex* was withdrawn for a short refit, but returned to join Task Group 12.1 for the raid on the Marcus Islands. Later the *Essex* formed part of the famous Task Group 38.3 within Task Force 38. On 25 November 1944, while supporting the Leyte Gulf landings, the ship was hit on the port side by a kamikaze, suffering 15 dead and 44 wounded, and had to be withdrawn for repairs. The carrier was back in action,

however, after only three weeks.

In 1945 the *Essex* returned to TF 38 and took part in the attacks on Lingayen, Formosa, the Sakishima Gunto, and Okinawa. With TF 58, the *Essex* took part in the final assault on Japan, and was one of the enormous fleet mustered in Tokyo Bay for the Japanese surrender in August 1945. On her return, the battered carrier received its first full repairs and was put into reserve.

Capable and rugged

In retrospect, the design of the 'Essex' class proved to be ideal for the US Navy's operations in the Pacific. It was seaworthy and had the endurance needed to cover the enormous

Large, sturdy, fast and able to carry large quantities of aircraft fuel and munitions in addition to its own considerable bunkerage, the USS **Essex** *was ideally suited to the fast carrier operations characteristic of the US Navy's carrier operations later in World War II.*

distances involved, not only for itself but for its aircraft. Despite its 'open' hangars, the class in general proved surprisingly rugged, and during the first 14 months in action only three units of the class were damaged by enemy action; apart from the USS *Franklin* (CV-13), which reappeared after the war, all returned to active service after sustaining severe battle damage.

Seen in 1943, USS **Essex***, could handle every type of US Navy carrierborne warplane to enter service in World War II, but before the squadrons started to take-off on a mission, the flight deck could look very crowded.*

SPECIFICATION	
USS *Essex* (CV-9)	**Armament:** (1943) 12 5-in (127-mm)
Displacement: 27,100 tons standard	AA, 11 quadruple 40-mm Bofors
and 33,000 tons full load	AA, and 44 20-mm AA guns
Dimensions: length 267.21 m (876 ft	**Armour:** belt 64–102 mm (2.5–4 in);
8 in); beam 45 m (147 ft 8 in) over	flight deck 38 mm (1.5 in); hangar
flight deck; draught 8.69 m (28 ft	deck 76 mm (3 in); main deck
6 in)	38 mm (1.5 in); turrets and
Propulsion: geared steam turbines	barbettes 38 mm (1.5 in)
delivering 111,900 kW (150,000	**Aircraft:** (1943) six fighters, 36 dive-
shp) to four shafts	bombers and 18 torpedo-bombers
Speed: 33 kts	**Complement:** 3,240

USS *Princeton* and 'Independence' class Light carriers

To meet its acute shortage of carriers after Pearl Harbor, the US Navy decided to complete nine 'Cleveland' class light cruisers as carriers. In consequence, the *Amsterdam* (CL-59), *Tallahassee* (CL-61), *New Haven* (CL-76), *Huntington* (CL-77), *Dayton* (CL-78), *Fargo* (CL-85), *Wilmington* (CL-79), *Buffalo* (CL-99) and *Newark* (CL-100) were completed as the **Independence (CVL-22)**, **Princeton (CVL-23)**, **Belleau Wood (CVL-24)**, **Cowpens (CVL-25)**, **Monterey (CVL-26)**, **Langley (CVL-27)**, **Cabot (CVL-28)**, **Bataan (CVL-29)** and **San Jacinto (CVL-30)**.

'Independence' class

It was an ingenious but disappointing conversion, for the small hangar, measuring 65.5 m (215 ft) by 17.7 m (58 ft), could accommodate fewer aircraft than that of the 'Sangamon'-class escort carriers: just 33 instead of the 45 planned. However, this **'Independence' class** did have the speed to keep up with the fast carriers, and this kept its members in the front line.

The *Princeton* was commissioned late in February 1943, just over a month after the lead ship *Independence*, and arrived at Pearl Harbor in August 1943 to begin exercising with the new *Essex* and *Yorktown*. They launched their first strike on 1 September against Marcus Island. Five weeks later, the *Princeton* and two other CVLs joined in a successful raid on Wake Island.

Battle of Leyte Gulf

During the Battle of Leyte Gulf, the *Princeton* was part of Task Group 38.3, in the main Fast Carrier Group. On the morning of 24 October 1944, a lone D4Y dive-bomber came out of cloud cover and dropped two 250-kg (551-lb) bombs on the flight deck of the *Princeton*. The bombs passed through three decks before exploding, and the blast started fierce fires in the hangar. Six armed Avengers caught fire, and their torpedoes exploded, adding to the carnage. At 10.10 hours, about half an hour after the attack, other ships were ordered alongside to take off all but

essential firefighters and damage-control personnel.

The light cruisers *Birmingham* and *Reno* lay alongside, pumping water and providing power for the carrier's own pumps, and all the while ships and friendly aircraft fought off Japanese air attacks. At 14.45, it appeared that all fires were out, but at 15.23 the *Princeton* blew up in a huge explosion. The blast swept the crowded decks of the

Birmingham, killing 229 men and wounding 420; the carrier itself had over 100 men killed and 190 injured. Surprisingly the shattered hulk of the *Princeton* was still afloat, but wrecked beyond any hope of salvage. At 16.00, the carrier was abandoned and the cruiser USS *Reno* was ordered to sink the hulk with two torpedoes after the destroyer USS *Irwin* had missed it with four.

Left: An 'Independence'-class carrier rides at anchor. The class made a vital contribution at a time when 'Essex'-class ships were not available in numbers.

Below: As seen from the USS **Independence (CVL-22)**, the USS **Langley (CVL-27)** pitches in heavy seas en route to attack targets on the Japanese mainland during March 1945. In the background are escorting light cruisers ready to help ward off air attacks.

SPECIFICATION	
USS *Princeton* (CVL-23)	(127-mm) AA, two quadruple
Displacement: 11,000 tons standard and 14,300 tons full load	40-mm Bofors AA, nine twin 40-mm Bofors AA and 12 20-mm AA guns
Dimensions: length 189.74 m (622 ft 6 in); beam 33.3 in (109 ft 3 in) over flight deck; draught 7.92 m (26 ft)	**Armour:** belt 38–127 mm (1.5–5 in); main deck 76 mm (3 in); lower deck 51 mm (2 in)
Propulsion: geared steam turbines delivering 74,600 kW (100,000 shp) to four shafts	**Aircraft:** (1943) 24 F4F Wildcat fighters and nine TBF Avenger torpedo-bombers
Speed: 31.5 kts	**Complement:** 1,569 officers and men
Armament: (1943) two 5-in	

The **Princeton (CVL-23)** was converted on the stocks from the hull of the light cruiser **Tallahassee**. Although cramped, the CVLs were fast and could keep up with the Fast Carrier Groups. Later they operated night fighters.

USS *Intrepid*

The USS *Intrepid* (CV-11) was the third ship of the 'Essex' class, not only the largest class of major warships ever built but also the most effective. The ship and four of her sisters were ordered under Fiscal Year 1940 programmes, while the remaining six of the first group were ordered under FY 1941. A further 15 were laid down during the war, and 17 of them entered service before VJ-Day. The *Intrepid* was floated out of her building dock on 26 April 1943, and such was the speed of wartime construction that she was commissioned on 16 August, less than four months later, and only 20 months after being laid down. The carrier's first task was to finish sea trials and allow the raw crew to 'shake down', and when the ship's organization was ready the time came to embark the air group. By late 1943, the flying schools had expanded enormously and there was no shortage of well-trained aircrew to make good the losses in battle, but they still needed a period of intense training at sea. Combat experience had shown the need for new tactics, particularly in air defence, and these tactics could only be exercised with an embarked air group.

Flight deck
The *Intrepid* had an overall length of 267 m (876 ft) and a hull beam of 28.35 m (93 ft) although the flight deck was 44.96 m (147 ft 6 in) wide.The design of the 'Essex' class was schemed with three catapults installed as two longitudinal units on the flight deck and one double athwartships unit on the hangar deck. Weight considerations meant that the first ships were completed with only one flight-deck catapult, but the athwartships unit proved effectively useless and was soon discarded, allowing a second catapult to be added on the flight deck.

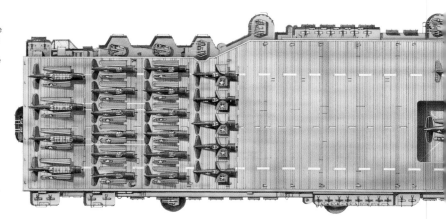

Air group
The air group of the 'Essex'-class aircraft carrier was a nominal 80 aircraft. In 1943 the air group was somewhat larger, and the 91 aircraft comprised 36 Grumman F4F Wildcat fighters, 37 Douglas SBD Dauntless dive-bombers and 18 Grumman TBF Avenger torpedo-bombers. The capability of these aircraft to undertake sustained operations was ensured by the provision of magazines for a large quantity of ordnance and also tankage for 908500 litres (240,000 US gal) of aviation fuel.

Secondary armament
As completed, the *Intrepid* had a secondary armament of eight quadruple mountings for 40-mm Bofors guns, but the intensity of Japanese air attacks in the war's later stages dictated a radical enhancement of the secondary armament. In the case of the *Intrepid*, this amounted to 17 quadruple Bofors mountings by the end of the war.

Propulsion
The propulsion arrangement of the 'Essex'-class aircraft carriers was based on an arrangement of four propellers driven by four sets of Westinghouse steam turbines driven by steam from eight Babcock & Wilcox oil-fired boilers. In the early ships, including the *Intrepid*, the turbines were geared, but in the others they were of the direct-drive type. In the ships of the first group as well as the *Hancock* and *Ticonderoga*, the oil bunkerage was 6,161 tons, rising to 6,331 tons in all of the others of the 13-strong second group except the *Randolph*, which carried 6,251 tons of oil.

Tertiary armament
The dictates of high-intensity Japanese air attacks in the Pacific theatre led to the introduction of a steadily enlarged complement of 20-mm Oerlikon cannon in single mountings placed wherever there was sufficient deck area. By the end of World War II, the *Intrepid* carried 52 such cannon, which supplemented the efforts of the 40-mm Bofors guns in putting up a veritable wall of HE projectiles through which Japanese kamikaze aircraft had to penetrate before reaching the ship.

Basic design
Despite the fact that it was designed without any treaty-imposed restrictions and was therefore fully optimized for the US Navy concept of carrier warfare, the 'Essex' class avoided the British concept of the flight deck being built as part of the hull. Thus the hangars and flight deck were built as superstructure, and as such made no real contribution to the strength of the hull.

The vessel is painted in Camouflage Measure 32/A, which she carried from June 1944, when she returned to the Pacific after repairs. During her three months in dock, *Intrepid* received three additional quadruple 40-mm Bofors gun mountings below the island, and two more were resited to improve their sky arcs.

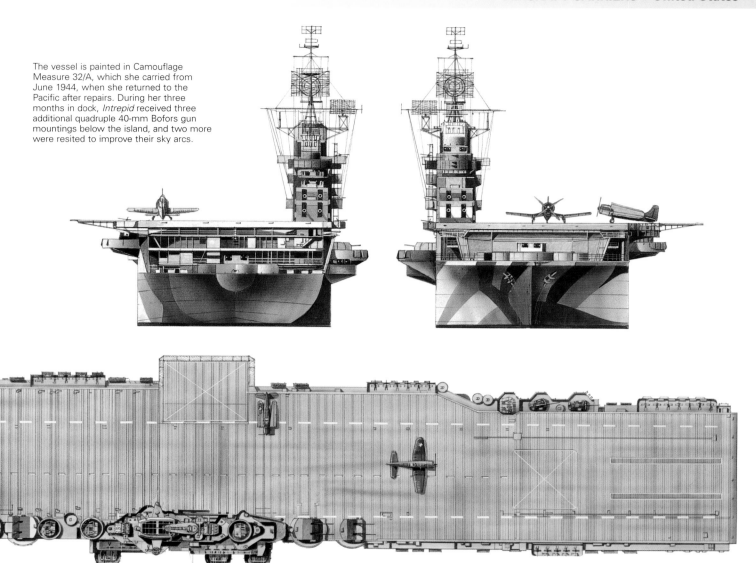

Aircraft elevators
The wooden-planked rather than steel flight deck of the *Intrepid* and the other 'Essex'-class aircraft carriers was connected to the hangar deck by three aircraft elevators. Two of these were in the 'standard' positions in the flight deck fore and aft of the island superstructure, while the third was installed, as had been pioneered in the *Wasp*, on the port side of the flight deck. This last proved so successful that many senior carrierborne aviation officers requested later in the war that the forward elevator be revised to a similar configuration.

Protection
The ships of the 'Essex' class proved themselves to be very well built and excellently protected. Despite heavy damage, none of the ships was lost, and damage was generally repaired quickly. The main belt of armour was 63.5 and 102 mm (2.5 and 4 in) thick along its lower and upper edges respectively, and other thicknesses included 51-76 mm (2–3 in) for the bulkheads, 38 mm (1.5 in) for the flight and main decks as well as the turrets, and 76 mm (3 in) for the hangar deck.

Island
Command and control of the *Intrepid* was exercised from the bridge and other compartments in the island superstructure, which located, as always on American aircraft carriers, on the starboard side of the flight deck with the stacks from the boiler rooms trunked through its after part. Fore and aft were eight of the ship's 5-in (127-mm) L/38 DP main guns in four twin mountings, the other four being located in single mountings below the port edge of the flight deck. The island carried search radar antennae and two radar-equipped directors for the 5-in gun mountings.

Radio equipment
The arrangement of two lattice masts and horizontal wires, located right forward and off the starboard side of the flight deck was the antenna group for the ship's long-range radio equipment. Also evident is the location, over virtually every other available patch of deck with any type of sky arc, of the ship's secondary and tertiary anti-aircraft guns of 40-mm Bofors and 20-mm Oerlikon cannon.

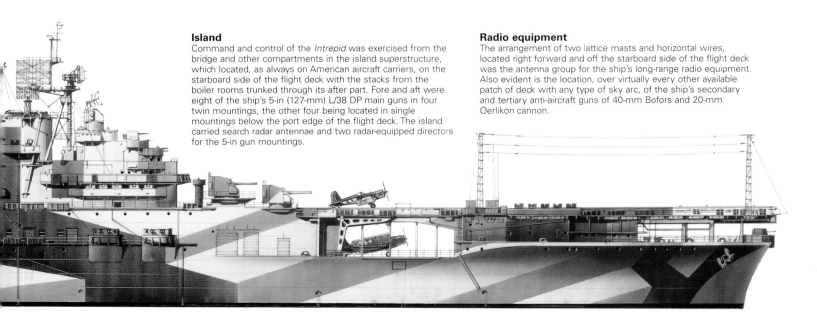

*The **USS** Intrepid trails smoke after a kamikaze hit. In all, the vessel was hit three times by kamikazes and was also torpedoed once, but survived.*

USS *Intrepid*
In action

Possessing a maximum speed of 32.7 kts and a range of 27,800 km (17,275 miles) at 15 kts, the *Intrepid* was also excellently protected and carried a large air group of advanced aircraft flown by skilled crews. In combination with large quantities of ordnance and aviation fuel, the ship was thus a potent fighting machine well able to take the war to the Japanese across the expanses of the Pacific Ocean. Many times the *Intrepid*'s warplanes devastated Japanese naval and air bases, sank and crippled ships, and supported US amphibious forces. Kamikaze aircraft hit *Intrepid*, making necessary repair visits to the US west coast, but the well-built ship survived to return for more.

*The **USS** Intrepid launches an attack on targets in the Japanese home islands, an Avenger torpedo-bomber being caught by the camera as it leaves the ship's port catapult, while three Helldivers wait with wings folded. The date was 19 March 1945.*

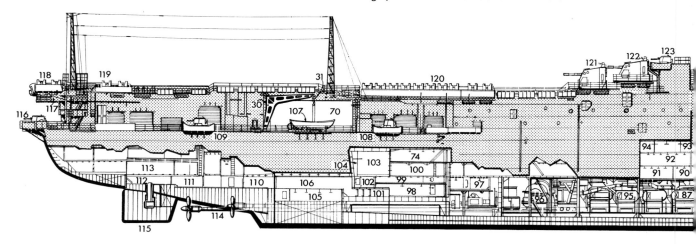

CVS-11: THE 'NEW' *INTREPID*

Decommissioned in 1947, the *Intrepid* was taken in hand for a major upgrade between 1952 and 1954 to re-emerge as the CVA-11 attack carrier with more powerful catapults, a strengthened flight deck and a new island. The ship was then revised with an enclosed bow and angled flight deck before being reclassified in 1962 as the CVS-11 for the anti-submarine role. After service mainly in European waters, the ship was revised for the embarkation of a group of light attack warplanes as a 'special attack carrier' for service off Vietnam, where the vessel is seen in the South China Sea during 1968. The *Intrepid* was finally decommissioned in 1974 and is now a museum.

Above: The USS Intrepid *in the Pacific in the spring of 1945. Visible here are two of the four 5-in (127-mm)* L/38 *DP gun mountings that constituted the heaviest element of the ship's gun armament.*

USS *Intrepid*

1 YE antenna
2 SG surface warning radar antenna
3 SK air warning radar antenna
4 Repair platform
5 SM radar antenna
6 Mast head platform
7 Mk 4 fire control radar antenna
8 Mk 37 director for 5-in guns
9 Target designator, port and starboard
10 40-mm Bofors mounting
11 Mk 51 director
12 Navigating bridge
13 Flag bridge
14 5-in handling room and ready service ammunition
15 5-in L/38 DP twin gun mounting

16 Mk 51 director
17 Six single 20-mm Oerlikon AA gun mountings
18 Three 40-mm Bofors quadruple mountings (three aft)
19 36-in searchlight
20 Single 20-mm Oerlikon AA gun
21 Three single 20-mm Oerlikon AA gun mountings
22 Trash burner smoke pipe
23 Stack hood
24 24-in searchlight
25 Trunnion
26 Mount captain's blast hood
27 Trainer's telescope
28 Side access door
29 Barbette (fixed to ship)
30 Crane jib
31 Main lift hook
32 Life rafts
33 Life net rack
34 Antenna down-leads screen
35 Wireless mast
36 Long-range wireless rig
37 Ladder (inside mast)
38 Five single 20-mm Oerlikon mountings

39 Flight deck
40 Galley deck
41 Forward quadruple 40-mm mounting
42 Forecastle deck
43 30,000-lb stockless bower anchor
44 Main deck
45 Second deck
46 Third deck
47 Fourth deck
48 First platform
49 Second platform
50 Hold
51 Store
52 Chain locker
53 Sump tank
54 Watertight trunk
55 Pump room
56 Incendiary bombs stowage
57 Pyrotechnics stowage
58 Torpedo exercise heads stowage
59 Bilge water machinery and pump room
60 Alcohol stowage
61 Inflammable liquid store
62 Aviation fuel tank
63 5-in handling and projectile stowage

64 Small arms magazine
65 Detention cells
66 Aviation lubricating oil tank pump room
67 40-mm and 20-mm AA ammunition stowage
68 Bomb stowage
69 Bomb vanes stowage
70 Roller curtain openings in hangar sides
71 Aviation lubricating oil
72 40-mm AA ammunition stowage
73 Rocket motor stowage
74 Crew's berthing
75 Damage control HQ
76 Crew's mess
77 CIC (Combat Information Centre)
78 Plotting room
79 Bomb fuse magazine
80 Forward auxiliary machine room
81 Generator platform
82 Medical stores
83 No. 1 boiler room
84 Boiler uptake space
85 No. 2 boiler room
86 No. 1 machinery room
87 No. 3 boiler room

88 Clothes and small stores
89 Fire brick stowage
90 Barber's shop
91 Athletic gear stowage
92 General workshop
93 Crew's toilet
94 Crew's washroom and showers
95 No. 4 boiler room
96 No. 2 machinery room
97 Aft auxiliary machinery room
98 Bomb stowage
99 Rocket motor stowage
100 Aviation stores
101 Plotting room
102 Air flask stowage
103 Torpedo stowage
104 Gas trunk
105 Pump rooms
106 Fruit and vegetable stowage
107 26-ft motor whaleboat
108 40-mm Bofors gun mounting sponson
109 40-mm Bofors gun mounting sponson
110 Blue uniform and coat stowage
111 Motor control room

112 Steering gear room
113 Aviation engine stowage
114 Four-blade propeller and shaft units
115 Rudder
116 Stern 40-mm quadruple mounting
117 Walkway
118 Two single 20-mm Oerlikon AA gun mountings
119 Two single 20-mm Oerlikon AA gun mountings
120 10 single 20-mm Oerlikon AA gun mountings
121 5-in L/38 DP Mk 32 twin mounting
122 5-in L/38 DP Mk 32 twin mounting
123 40-mm Bofors mounting
124 40-mm Bofors mounting
125 Ensign staff
126 Mk 4 radar antenna
127 SC antenna
128 Mast
129 Vertical ladder
130 Radar platform
131 Battle gaff
132 YJ antenna

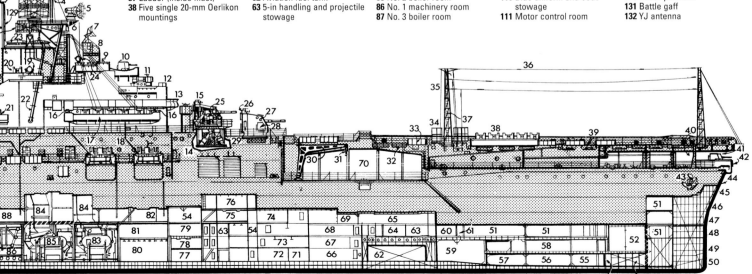

USS *Bogue* Escort carrier

To provide air cover for convoys in the Atlantic, mercantile hulls were converted into small aircraft carriers. When the first 'escort carriers', or CVEs, proved their worth, orders went out for the first production class of 21 CVEs from US shipyards. Eleven went to the UK as the 'Attacker' class, while the remainder became the US Navy's **'Bogue' class**. The **USS Bogue** (**CVE-9**) was launched in January 1942 and carried 28 aircraft. With radar and more space than the destroyers and frigates, escort carriers made good flagships for the 'hunter-killer', or anti-submarine, support groups established in the autumn of 1942. The *Bogue* and her support group sank 13 U-boats.

The USS *Bogue* joined the Atlantic Fleet in February 1943, and on the vessel's fourth Atlantic crossing, her aircraft sank her first U-boat. She accounted for two more on the next trip and another on seventh cruise, in July 1943.

The worst point of the battle was now over, and in late 1943 the *Bogue* and its group accounted for three U-boats. After a break in 1944 to ferry aircraft to the UK, *Bogue* returned to submarine-hunting, and in March helped to sink *U-575*. Three more U-boats were sunk by September 1944, and on her last hunter-killer mission in April 1945, the *Bogue* took out the last of 13 U-boats.

Towards the end of the war *Bogue* was sent to the Pacific, ferrying aircraft and stores to outlying garrisons. When Japan surrendered, *Bogue* continued to serve, ferrying PoWs and servicemen to the US.

The escort carrier Bogue *(CVE-9) with Avenger torpedo-bombers on the wooden flight deck.*

SPECIFICATION	
USS Bogue (CVE-9)	**Speed:** 18 kts
Displacement: 11,000 tons standard; 15,400 tons full load	**Armour:** none
Dimensions: length 151.1 m (495 ft 8 in) overall; beam 34 m (111 ft 6 in) over flight deck; draught 7.92 m (26 ft)	**Armament:** two 5-in (127-mm) AA, four twin 40-mm Bofors AA and 12 20-mm AA guns
Machinery: 1-shaft geared steam turbine delivering 6,340 kW (8,500 shp)	**Aircraft:** (1943) 12 F4F Wildcat fighters and 12 TBF Avenger torpedo-bombers
	Complement: 890 men

'Sangamon' class Escort carrier

Converting escort carriers got top priority in 1942, but the rate at which they could be brought into service was limited by the number of hulls available. So in January 1942 four new US Navy oilers, the *Sangamon* (AO-28), *Santee* (AO-29), *Chenango* (AO-31) and *Suwannee* (AO-33), were reclassified as AVGs (Aircraft Escort Vessels). The **'Sangamon' class** was more successful than the earlier escort carriers, being larger and faster. They had their machinery right aft, so the small smoke-ducts interfered less with flying operations.

The **Sangamon's** *port profile shows her tanker origin, with the original well deck marked by large openings in the sides. Being fast and capacious, they were the most successful of all the* **CVE** *conversions.*

The **Santee** (**AVG-29**, later **CVE-29**) was the first to be commissioned, on 24 August 1942, followed a day later by the **Sangamon** (**CVE-26**); the **Suwannee** (**CVE-27**) was commissioned on 24 September, five days after the **Chenango** (**CVE-28**). The shortage of carriers in late 1942 and early 1943, combined with their good turn of speed and aircraft capacity meant that they were used with the main fleet more than other CVEs, and frequently operated together.

All four supported the landings in North Africa in 1942, and then transferred to the Pacific, operating with CarDiv 22 in the South Pacific. The *Santee* returned to the Atlantic in March 1943, operating south of the Azores and off the coast of Brazil with a hunter-killer group, but returned to the Pacific in February 1944, as the great 'island-hopping' drive across the Pacific got underway.

Battle of Leyte Gulf

All four took part in the Battle of Leyte Gulf, forming 'Taffy One' as part of Task Group 77.4. On 25 October, the *Santee* was badly damaged, first by a kamikaze attack and then by a torpedo hit from the submarine *I-56*. Next a kamikaze hit the *Suwannee*. Despite this, both were operational by the spring of 1945. The *Sangamon* was badly damaged by a kamikaze hit off Okinawa on 4 May 1945, but also proved rugged enough to be returned to service.

SPECIFICATION	
USS Sangamon (CVE-26)	**Armour:** none
Displacement: 10,500 tons standard; 23,875 tons full load	**Armament:** two 5-in (127-mm) AA, two quadruple 40-mm Bofors AA, seven twin 40-mm Bofors AA and 21 20-mm AA guns
Dimensions: length 168.71 m (553 ft 6 in) overall; beam 34.82 m (114 ft 3 in) over flight deck; draught 9.32 m (30 ft 7 in)	**Aircraft:** (1942) 12 F4F Wildcat fighters, nine SBD Dauntless dive-bombers and nine TBF Avenger torpedo-bombers
Machinery: 2-shaft geared steam turbines delivering 10070 kW (13,500 shp)	**Complement:** 1,100 men
Speed: 18 kts	

USS *St Lô* Escort carrier

After the success of the converted CVEs came the 'Casablanca' class (CVE–55 to 104), in 1942. Its design took the best of the 'Sangamon', 'Bogue' and 'Prince William' classes, and was a success. The flight deck was short (152.4 m/ 500 ft by 32.9 m/ 108 ft), but two lifts and a catapult were provided, while two propeller shafts gave greater manoeuvrability than one.

Service entry

The **USS *St Lô*** (**CVE-63**) was

The port profile of the 'Casablanca' class; these ships were an improved version of the 'Bogue' design, tailored for faster construction.

laid down as the **Chapin Bay** (**AVG-63**) at Henry Kaiser's Vancouver shipyard in January 1943, but in April the ship was renamed **Midway** in honour of the recent battle, and entered service under that name in October 1943. The name was then allocated to a much bigger carrier, so on 15 September 1944 CVE-63 became the USS *St Lô*. She had already made two ferry trips out to the Pacific and had supported the amphibious landings in Saipan, Eniwetok, Tinian and Morotai. In

October 1944 *St Lô* formed part of 'Taffy Three' (under Rear Admiral Thomas L. Sprague), part of the vast armada that fought the Battle of Leyte Gulf. On 25 October 1994, 'Taffy Three', the most northern group of escort carriers covering the amphibious landing, suffered a gruelling bombardment from Japanese surface warships, followed by a kamikaze attack. *St Lô* sank, losing 100 men.

The new escort carrier USS **Midway** *(CVE-63) was subsequently renamed* St Lô *to release the name for a larger and more prestigious carrier. The* St Lô *was the first US ship lost to a kamikaze attack.*

SPECIFICATION	
USS *St Lô* (CVE-63)	**Speed:** 19 kts
Displacement: 7,800 tons standard; 10,400 tons full load	**Armour:** none
Dimensions: length 156.13 m (512 ft 3 in) overall; beam 39.92 m (108 ft) over flight deck; draught 6.86 m (22 ft 6 in)	**Armament:** one 5-in (127-mm) AA, eight twin 40-mm Bofors AA and 20 AA guns
Machinery: 2-shaft vertical triple expansion delivering 6715 kW (9,000 shp)	**Aircraft:** (October 1944) 17 F4F Wildcat fighters and 12 TBF Avenger torpedo-bombers
	Complement: 860 men

USS *Langley* Aircraft transport

In April 1920, to gain experience of building an aircraft carrier, the US Navy converted the fleet collier *Jupiter* (AC-3). Renamed **USS *Langley*** (**CV-1**), she began trials in July 1922. The biggest drawback was a low speed, for the turbo-electric machinery was underpowered. In service, the *Langley* could make only 14 kts, well below the speed of the fleet. Nonetheless, she served with the fleet for five years.

She was designed to operate 24 aircraft, but 33 could be accommodated. *Langley* operated aircraft until 1936, when she was converted to a seaplane carrier. Redesignated **AV-3**, she reappeared in April 1937 with a short flight deck.

Trials vessel

It was on the *Langley* that a proper hydraulic arrester system was developed, which is the basis of modern carrier landings.

Another innovation was a pair of flush-mounted pneumatic catapults on the flight deck; intended for seaplanes, they were shown to speed up the launching of conventional aircraft, and this procedure is still standard today.

On 27 February 1942, Japanese naval bombers caught *Langley* en route for Tjilatjap in Java and the carrier was sunk by five bombs.

The old **Langley**, *with the forward part of her flight deck removed, served as a seaplane carrier from 1936. In her short wartime career, the first US carrier acted as an aircraft transport until sunk by Japanese bombers in February 1942.*

SPECIFICATION	
USS *Langley* (CV-1)	turbo-electric delivering 5,335 kW (7,150 shp)
Displacement: 11,050 tons standard; 14,700 tons full load	**Speed:** 14 kts
Dimensions: length 165.3 m (542 ft 4 in) overall; beam 19.96 m (65 ft 6 in); draught 7.32 m (24 ft)	**Armour:** none
Machinery: 1-shaft steam	**Armament:** four 5-in (127-mm) guns
	Aircraft: (1923) 30 fighters
	Complement: 410 men

HMS *Furious* Fleet carrier

The World War II camouflage does not conceal the battlecruiser origins of HMS Furious. The island was not added until 1939.

The several guises of **HMS Furious** represented the transitional stages between what might be termed 'air capable' ships and the true aircraft carrier. As the third of Admiral Fisher's 'tin-clad' light battlecruisers (laid down in 1915), *Furious* was launched in August 1916 but her completion was delayed to allow her to ship the navy's largest gun, an 18-in (457-mm) weapon, in single mounts at each end. Although virtually complete in March 1917, she then had her forward gun removed in favour of a sloping flying-off deck some 69.5 m (228 ft) long. Beneath this, a hangar accommodated up to 10 aircraft (some seaplanes and

some wheeled). Completed thus in July 1917, *Furious* rapidly showed the limitations of carrying aircraft that could not (officially at least) be recovered after a flight. In November 1917, therefore, the after gun mounting was removed to make way for a 86.5-m (284-ft) flying-on deck over a second hangar. Much of the superstructure still remained, however, and the high speeds at which *Furious* steamed to create the necessary wind-over-deck resulted in severe turbulence, causing an unacceptable accident rate among would-be landers-on. Relegated again to flying-off only, the *Furious* still had the distinction of mounting

The first ship to launch an air strike, HMS Furious was originally designed for Admiral Fisher's plan to attack Germany's Baltic coast during World War I.

Landing on the forward deck of HMS Furious was very dangerous: Squadron Commander E. H. Dunning was killed when his Sopwith Pup overshot and stalled during trials in August 1917. In November 1917, the after 18-in gun was removed in favour of a flying-on deck.

the first real carrier-based air strike when, on 19 July 1918, seven of its Sopwith Camels destroyed two Zeppelins and their sheds at Tondern. A through-deck was obviously required, as provided on the new *Argus*, and *Furious* was thus modified between 1921 and 1925. Even following this, the ship was still of interim design, having no island. Not until a final prewar refit did she acquire a vestigial super-structure, topped-off by a

diminutive mast that supported a distinctive homing beacon.

Service

Despite her age and infirmities, the *Furious* saw service in Atlantic hunting groups and convoy escorts, the Norwegian campaign, and the North African landings. Her last action was against the *Tirpitz*, immured in a Norwegian fjord, before going into reserve during September 1944. *Furious* was finally scrapped in 1948.

SPECIFICATION	
HMS *Furious*	**Speed:** 31.5 kts
Displacement: 22,500 tons standard and 28,500 tons full load	**Armour:** belt 51–76 mm (2–3 in); hangar deck 38 mm (1.5 in)
Dimensions: length 239.5 m (785 ft 9 in); beam 27.4 m (90 ft); draught 7.3 m (24 ft)	**Armament:** six twin 4-in (102-mm) AA, three octuple 2-pdr AA, and several smaller-calibre guns
Propulsion: 4-shaft geared steam turbines delivering 67,113 kW (90,000 shp)	**Aircraft:** 33
	Complement: 750 excluding aircrew

HMS *Eagle* Fleet carrier

Before World War I, Chile ordered two 'Iron Duke'-class battleships from Armstrong's Elswick yard. Only one, the *Almirante Latorre*, was well advanced by August 1914; compulsorily purchased by the Admiralty, she was completed in 1915 as HMS *Canada*. Work on an unlaunched sister, the

Almirante Cochrane (laid down in 1913), ceased with hostilities but post-Jutland, the ship was completed as an aircraft carrier. Like the *Hermes*, she was too late for the war, launched in June 1918 and commissioning for trials in 1920. Several versions of the pioneering island superstructure were tried, which

SPECIFICATION	
HMS *Eagle*	**Armour:** belt 102–178 mm (4-7 in); flight deck 25 mm (1 in); hangar deck 102 mm (4 in), shields 25 mm (1 in)
Displacement: 22,600 tons standard and 26,500 tons full load	
Dimensions: length 203.3 m (667 ft); beam 32.1 m (105 ft 3 in); draught 7.3 m (24 ft)	**Armament:** nine 6-in (152-mm), four 4-in (102-mm) AA, and eight 2-pdr AA guns
Propulsion: 4-shaft geared steam turbines delivering 37,285 kW (50,000 shp)	**Aircraft:** 21
Speed: 24 kts	**Complement:** 750 excluding aircrew

kept the vessel in dockyard hands for much of the period between 1920 and 1923. The final version of the island was long and low, topped-off by two funnel casings. The ship's more ample battleship proportions made her slower than the large cruiser conversions, but she had better stability. Despite the fact that she introduced the two-level hangar, the ship still had only modest aircraft capacity.

Inter-war service

Much of the **Eagle's** pre-World War II service was in the Far East, but the carrier moved into the Indian Ocean in September 1939, thence to the Mediterranean to replace the *Glorious*. Following air strikes against Italian shipping at Tobruk, *Eagle* was badly shaken by bombing during the action off Calabria, suffering damage that caused her to miss

the Taranto raid. Before *Eagle* could refit in the UK, she saw further action in the Red Sea and the South Atlantic. Arriving back in the Mediterranean early in 1942, *Eagle* was then involved in the famous August

convoy (Operation Pedestal) when 41 warships fought to bring through just five out of 14 merchantmen to lift the Malta siege. The *Eagle* was a major casualty, sunk by four torpedoes from *U-73* on 11 August 1942.

HMS Eagle spent the bulk of her service career on the China station, returning to the Mediterranean in spring 1940. When the carrier was finally sunk by a U-boat north of Algiers, it was with the loss of 260 lives.

HMS *Hermes* Light carrier

The first British carrier designed as such, HMS Hermes was built along the lines of a light cruiser. The ship carried six 5.5-in (140-mm) guns, as it was not believed that aircraft could repel enemy surface attack.

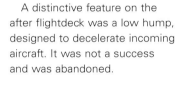

With the *Argus* concept deemed sound, the keel was laid down for **HMS Hermes** early in 1918. However, without a precedent that had seen service, her designers made the ship too small. With the end of World War I, construction was leisurely, the ship being launched in September 1919 and its completion delayed until 1923. As a result *Hermes* entered service after the much larger but converted HMS *Eagle*, which had proved the idea of

the island superstructure. On both, the island seemed too large, with a massive battleship-style tripod and fighting top, bearing rangefinders for the unusual armament of six 5.5-in (140-mm) guns: early carriers were meant to be able to repel light surface attack, the potential of their aircraft not having been fully evaluated. A light armour belt was also worked in. An improvement on the *Argus* was a doubling of installed power to increase speed to over 4 kts.

A distinctive feature on the after flightdeck was a low hump, designed to decelerate incoming aircraft. It was not a success and was abandoned.

Valuable contribution

Though obsolete by World War II, the *Hermes* made a valuable contribution, hunting for raiders in the Atlantic; undertaking spotting and reconnaissance

missions in operations against the Vichy French in West Africa and the Italians in the Red Sea; giving shore support during the suppression of the Iraqi rebellion of 1941; and escorting Indian ocean convoys. *Hermes* was sunk in April 1942 off Ceylon, but had demonstrated the value of even a small flightdeck in areas where no other aviation support existed.

SPECIFICATION	
HMS Hermes **Displacement:** 10,850 tons standard and 12,950 tons full load **Dimensions:** length 182.3 m (598 ft); beam 21.4 m (70 ft 3 in); draught 6.9 m (22 ft 7 in) **Propulsion:** 2-shaft geared steam turbines delivering 29828 kW (40,000 shp)	**Speed:** 25 kts **Armour:** belt 51–76 mm (2–3 in); hangar deck 25 mm (1 in); shields 25 mm (1 in) **Armament:** six 5.5-in (140-mm), and three 4-in (102-mm) AA guns **Aircraft:** about 20 **Complement:** 660 excluding aircrew

HMS Hermes served in the Far East for most of its career. This photograph clearly shows the unusually large island superstructure. Purpose-built, the vessel carried almost as many aircraft as Eagle, a ship of twice its displacement. Hermes was finally claimed by aircraft from the Soryu, Akagi and Hiryu.

'Courageous' class Fleet carrier

Admiral of the Fleet 'Jackie' Fisher had a strategy for landing an army on the Baltic coast of north-eastern Germany, only 130 km (80 miles) from Berlin. This famous trio of light battlecruisers – known, for political reasons, as large light cruisers – were supposed to be the largest units of a 600-strong, shallow-draught armada that would realize this vision. The plan died with Fisher's departure from the Admiralty in 1915, but his strange ships were completed as a legacy of this extraordinary but deeply flawed concept.

Both commissioned in January 1917, the first two of these light battlecruisers were **HMS *Courageous*** and **HMS *Glorious*** (laid down in March and May 1915, and launched in February and April 1916 respectively), and were found to be virtually unemployable in the active fleet because they were essentially unprotected. They had a belt only 76 mm (3 in) thick and were slow to get onto a target, with a primary armament of only four 15-in (381-mm) guns in two twin turrets; the secondary armament was 18 4-in (102-mm) guns in six triple mountings. They saw serious action only once, against conventional light cruisers of the German High Seas fleet in the Heligoland Bight on 17 November 1917, suffering more damage than they inflicted.

Though lacking in armament and protection, the two ships were notably fast, achieving 32 kts on the 67,104 kW (90,000 shp) delivered to their four

HMS Glorious *could be distinguished from HMS* Courageous *by her longer flight deck aft. Her aircraft gave sterling service over Norway in 1940, but she was caught and sunk during the withdrawal by the German battlecruisers KMS* Scharnhorst *and KMS* Gneisenau.

shafts by four sets of Parsons geared turbines driven by the steam generated by 18 oil-fired Yarrow small-tube boilers. Under the terms of the Washington Treaty, the two ships were eligible for conversion into aircraft carriers. The process of rebuilding both of the ships started in 1924, the *Courageous* completing in 1928 and the *Glorious* in 1930. The two ships' half-sister *Furious*, which had been completed with two single 18-in (457-mm) rather than four 15-in guns, had been similarly adapted from 1922 to a standard that included no island and the boiler uptakes led well aft, detracting from its hangar space. The two later conversions had the benefit of developments on HMS *Hermes* and HMS *Eagle*, and their combined funnel and bridge structure had the effect of boosting their air complement considerably.

Twin flight decks

The *Courageous* and *Glorious* had similar forward flight decks, which terminated about 20 per cent of the ship's length back from the bows. The hangar deck was extended forward at forecastle level, allowing smaller and lighter aircraft to take off from the lower level in favourable circumstances. Both ships were extensively bulged to improve stability. In 1935–36 the short forward flight decks were removed, and the main flight deck was fitted with two catapults to launch a 3629-kg (8,000-lb) aircraft at 56 kts or a 4536-kg (10,000-lb) aircraft at 52 kts. The ships each had two

hangar decks 167.64 m (550 ft) long, and the hangars and the flight deck were connected by two centreline elevators each measuring 14.02 x 14.63 m (46 x 48 ft). The aircraft fuel storage comprised a total of 156,835 litres (34,500 Imp gal) in each vessel.

The *Courageous* was the Royal Navy's first major casualty of World War II, being sunk only a fortnight after hostilities had started in September 1939. Its loss brought the *Glorious* back from the Mediterranean as a replacement and this, too, was lost only nine months later during the evacuation of Norway in June 1940.

SPECIFICATION	
'Courageous' class	**Speed:** 30 kts
Displacement: 22,500 tons standard and 26,500 tons full load	**Armour:** belt 38–76 mm (1.5–3 in); hangar deck 25–76 mm (1–3 in)
Dimensions: length 239.5 m (785 ft 9 in); beam 27.6 m (90 ft 6 in); draught 7.3 m (24 ft)	**Armament:** 16 120-mm (4.7-in) AA guns and four 2-pdr AA
Propulsion: geared steam turbines delivering 67104 kW (90,000 shp) to four shafts	**Aircraft:** about 48
	Complement: 1,215 including aircrew

HMS Courageous *and HMS* Glorious *each carried an air group of 16 Fairey Flycatcher fighters, 16 Fairey IIIF reconnaissance aircraft and 16 Blackburn Ripon torpedo-bombers.*

HMS *Ark Royal* Fleet carrier

Completed in 1938, **HMS *Ark Royal*** was the Royal Navy's first 'modern' carrier. A combination of meagre naval budgets and the lowly status of the Fleet Air Arm meant that she was the first carrier to join the fleet since the remodelled HMS *Glorious* in 1930. Plenty of time had thus been available to plan the ship, resulting in a thoroughly workmanlike and influential design laid down in 1935 and launched in April 1937. Though similar in size and displacement to the *Glorious*, the new carrier seemed considerably larger, having two levels of hangars with adequate headroom. Three elevators were incorporated, but these were small and, had the ship enjoyed a longer career, would have had to be replaced to cater for the increasing size of aircraft. Two catapults (or 'accelerators') were fitted to the vessel from the outset.

The *Ark Royal*'s most innovatory feature was her strength, for the ship introduced armoured flight and hangar decks, with the hangar walls being an integral part of the

HMS Ark Royal, the battlecruiser HMS Renown and the cruiser HMS Sheffield. During the hunt for the Bismarck, Ark Royal's Swordfish aircraft attacked Sheffield by mistake but made up for their error by crippling Bismarck's steering with a daring torpedo attack in appalling weather.

main hull girder. Despite this configuration's space-consuming aspects, the ship could stow a far greater number of aircraft than the *Glorious*. Capable of 31 kts, *Ark Royal* was also as fast as the earlier ships.

Though the earlier conversions had 16 medium-calibre guns, these were poorly sited, mainly with a view to defence against surface attack. The *Ark Royal* carried eight twin 4.5-in (114-mm) destroyer-type mountings, with high elevations conferring a true dual-purpose capability. The mountings were sited four on each beam at the flight deck edges to give good firing arcs. Designers were, at last, alive to the dangers of air

HMS Ark Royal *fights off German air attack in the Mediterranean. In the face of heavy bomb and torpedo attacks, the ship flew off about 170 Hurricane fighters to reinforce Malta in 1941. It was while returning from one such mission that she was sunk by* **U-81.**

attack and a comprehensive fit of smaller automatic weapons was also incorporated. Though aircraft were, indeed, to prove the main hazard to both American and Japanese carriers during the war, the Royal Navy

was pitted primarily against fleets without carriers, and therefore suffered most of its carrier casualties to submarine attack: the *Ark Royal* succumbed to a torpedo hit from the *U-81* on 14 November 1941.

SPECIFICATION	
HMS *Ark Royal*	**Armour:** belt 114 mm (4.5 in); deck 64 mm (2.5 in)
Displacement: 22,000 tons standard and 27,720 tons deep load	**Armament:** eight twin 4.5-in (114-mm) AA, four octuple 2-pdr AA, and eight quadruple 0.5-in (12.7-mm) AA guns
Dimensions: length 243.8 m (800 ft); beam 28.9 m (94 ft 9 in); draught 6.9 m (22 ft 8 in)	
Propulsion: geared steam turbines delivering 76,051 kW (102,000 shp) to three shafts	**Aircraft:** about 65
Speed: 31 kts	**Complement:** 1,580 including aircrew

Returning to Gibraltar after ferrying aircraft to Malta, **Ark Royal** *was attacked by the German submarine* **U-81** *and hit on the starboard side by a single torpedo.*

Below: HMS **Ark Royal** *was as long as dry docking facilities would allow, and was protected by a 114-mm (4.5-in) armour belt. The flight deck had 63-mm (2.5-in) armour and the lifts were offset and rather narrow to maximize deck strength. The positioning of the twin 4.5-in (114-mm) AA guns alongside the flight deck gave them excellent fields of fire.*

'Illustrious' class Aircraft carrier

Above: HMS **Formidable**, *seen here from HMS* **Warspite**, *fought for most of the war in the Mediterranean. An attack by her aircraft on the Italian fleet on 28 March 1941 damaged the battleship* **Vittorio Veneto** *and crippled the cruiser* **Pola**, *which was subsequently sunk.*

SPECIFICATION	
'Illustrious' class	**Armour:** belt and hangar wall
Type: fleet aircraft carrier	114 mm (4½ in) except *Indomitable*
Displacement: 23,000 tons standard	38 mm (1½ in); deck 76 mm (3 in)
and 25,500 tons full load	**Armament:** eight twin 4.5-in
Dimensions: length 229.7 m (753 ft	(114-mm) DP, six octuple 2-pdr AA,
6 in); beam 29.2 m (95 ft 9 in);	and eight 20-mm AA guns
draught 7.3 m (24 ft)	**Aircraft:** about 45, except
Propulsion: geared steam turbines	*Indomitable* about 65
delivering 82,027 kW (110,000 shp)	**Complement:** 1,400 including
to three shafts	aircrew
Speed: 31 kts	

Joining the fleet in August 1940, **HMS** Illustrious *steamed to the Mediterranean, where her air group sank two Italian destroyers and raided North Africa.*

HMS *Ark Royal* was very much a prototype, combining speed with increased capacity and new standards of protection. She had hardly been launched when a new **'Illustrious' class** of four aircraft carriers was laid down in 1937 in response to the increasing threat of war.

Despite having rather lighter protection than its sister ships, **HMS** Indomitable *absorbed a great deal of punishment. She survived two hits from 500-kg (1,102-lb) bombs during Operation Pedestal, a torpedo hit off Sicily in 1943 and several kamikaze attacks in the Far East.*

Operational experience was, therefore, not a part of the later concept, which added a 114-mm (4.5-in) hangar wall to the *Ark Royal*'s vertical and horizontal protection. The entire vulnerable aircraft thus accommodation

became an armoured box, but so much weight high in the ship limited the protection to only one hangar. So while **HMS Illustrious**, **HMS Victorious**

and **HMS Formidable** – all launched in 1939 – were not significantly smaller than the *Ark Royal*, they carried far fewer aircraft. There must have been

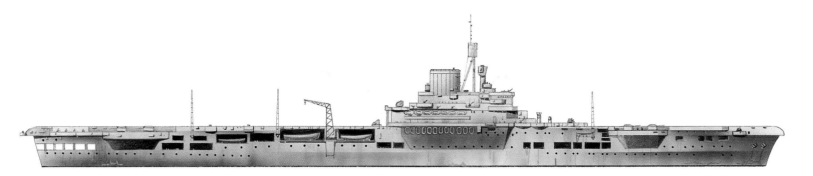

second thoughts on reducing the ships' primary arm so drastically, for **HMS Indomitable** was launched in 1940 as the last of the four, and the following two 'Implacable'-class ships reverted to lighter protection and an extra half-length hangar.

The immense strength of the ships stood them in good stead, for their war turned out to be one of air, rather than

submarine, attack. Soon after Taranto, the *Illustrious* was dive-bombed but survived the type of punishment that would have sunk any other carrier afloat, a performance echoed by the *Formidable* after Matapan. In the Pacific War, most of the ships withstood one or even two kamikaze strikes without having to leave station. But all these immense blows were absorbed mainly by the ships'

The 'Illustrious'-class ships were probably the toughest aircraft carriers of World War II, but although their thick armour enabled them to withstand heavy blows, this level of protection was achieved only by a large reduction in aircraft strength.

horizontal protection. It would seem in retrospect that the vertical armour was bought at an excessive price in operational efficiency even though, in the Pacific, the class worked with something like 60 per cent more than its designed aircraft

complement. When the Americans copied the armoured deck concept, it was not at the cost of capacity, so carrier sizes began their inevitable escalation. The ships were scrapped in 1956, 1969, 1955 and 1963 respectively.

'Implacable' class Aircraft carrier

Completed 30 months after the four 'Illustrious' class ships, the two **'Implacable' class** aircraft-carriers were more closely related to the prototype *Ark Royal*, their hangar walls slimmed down to only 38 mm (1.5 in). This allowed a better weight distribution for the ships' increased displacement, including the all-important lower hangar. The ships were slightly longer but appeared much bulkier than their half-sisters, their larger hull also containing a fourth set of propulsion machinery. This gave them the extra speed that enabled them to pace an American 'Essex'-class unit in the Pacific War, although smaller in terms of size and aircraft capacity.

Delayed completion
Though laid down in 1939, **HMS Implacable** and **HMS Indefatigable** were both

HMS Implacable was faster and carried more aircraft than the ships of the 'Illustrious' class. She is seen here as she returns to Sydney, Australia, during 1945.

launched only in December 1942 and completed in August and May 1944 respectively, their completions having been delayed by altered shipyard priorities. When the ships were most needed, they were still on the stocks, a fact that underlines

the truth that the navy fights a war largely with what it has available at the beginning of that conflict.

Once completed, the two ships were active for a comparatively short period. In March 1944, while still a new

ship, the *Indefatigable* achieved a 'first' in the first-ever deck landing by a twin-engined aeroplane, a de Havilland Mosquito. Before heading east to join the rapidly expanding British Pacific Fleet, she participated in some of the

many carrier strikes against the *Tirpitz*, holed up in Norwegian waters. Though damaging the target sufficiently to keep it almost permanently under repair, her aircraft proved the ship's weakest operational link until they were replaced by more advanced types. These became cornerstones of the BPF's offensive capability, but by then the ships were engaged in a war that had in reality already been won, and in which the British participation was not welcomed in all quarters.

After World War II, the ships were employed mainly in the training role before being scrapped in 1955 and 1956 after hardly a decade of service. This was the result of the official decision that it was not worth the vast expense of rebuilding the ships along the lines of HMS *Victorious*.

Hangarage

The 'Implacable' class aircraft carriers had a flight deck with an effective length of 231.65 m (760 ft), located some 15.2 m (50 ft) above the deep-load waterline. The deck carried a single catapult capable of launching 7258 kg (16,000 lb) at 66 kts or 9072 kg (20,000 lb) at 56 kts, and was served by two aircraft lifts. Each of these could lift a 9072-kg aircraft, and while the forward lift measured 13.72 x 10.06 m (45 x 33 ft), the after unit measured 13.72 x 6.71 m (45 x 22 ft). There were two hangars, one above the other, and while the lower unit in the after part of the ship measured 63.4 x 18.9 m (208 x 62 ft) with a height of 4.27 m (14 ft), the upper unit had the same width and height but was considerably longer at 139.6 m (458 ft). The height was just too little for the ships to embark the powerful Corsair multi-role fighter. Another deficiency was in the aircraft fuel carried: a mere 430280 litres (94,650 Imp gal).

SPECIFICATION	
'Implacable' class	**Speed:** 32.5 kts
Type: fleet aircraft carrier	**Armour:** belt 114 mm (4.5 in);
Displacement: 26,000 tons standard	hangar wall 38 mm (1.5 in); deck
and 31,100 tons full load	76 mm (3 in)
Dimensions: length 233.4 m (765 ft	**Armament:** eight twin 4.5-in
9 in); beam 29.2 m (95 ft 9 in);	(114-mm) DP, six octuple 2-pdr AA
draught 7.9 m (26 ft)	and about 38 20-mm AA guns
Propulsion: geared steam turbines	**Aircraft:** about 70
delivering 82,027 kW (110,000 shp)	**Complement:** 1,800 including
to four shafts	aircrew

HMS Implacable is seen while passing though the Suez Canal to join the growing strength of the British Pacific Fleet for the final stages of the war against Japan.

HMS *Argus* Aircraft carrier

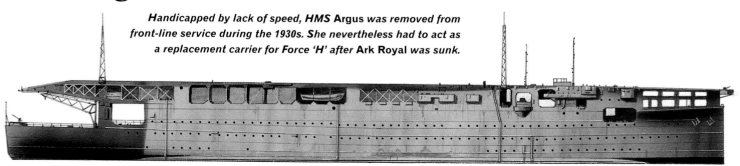

Handicapped by lack of speed, HMS Argus was removed from front-line service during the 1930s. She nevertheless had to act as a replacement carrier for Force 'H' after Ark Royal was sunk.

SPECIFICATION	
HMS *Argus*	turbines delivering 15,660 kW
Type: training, aircraft-ferry and	(21,000 shp)
second-line aircraft-carrier	**Speed:** 20.5 kts
Displacement: 14,000 tons standard	**Armour:** none
and 15,750 tons full load	**Armament:** six 102-mm (4-in) AA,
Dimensions: length 172.2 m (565 ft),	and several smaller-calibre guns
beam 20.7 m (68 ft); draught 7.3 m	**Aircraft:** about 20
(24 ft)	**Complement:** 370 excluding aircrew
Propulsion: 4-shaft geared steam	

Proposals were made before World War I for an aircraft-carrier with a straight-through flight deck capable of handling the launch and recovery of wheeled aircraft, but the Royal Navy had to make do with improvised seaplane carriers. It was not until 1916 that the proposer, the Beardmore commercial yard, was given the contract to complete a half-finished Italian liner as a prototype carrier. The ship, the *Conte Rosso*, had been laid down in 1914 and had suitable dimensions plus the high freeboard necessary for the job. No superstructure was planned to interrupt the flight deck which, like those of all pioneering carriers, was pointed at the forward end. A single hangar was provided and the necessary small charthouse retracted into the flightdeck. As full of character as she was devoid of grace, **HMS *Argus***, the world's first 'flat-top', was understandably known as 'The Flatiron'.

Recce duties

In Greek mythology, Argus was an all-seeing giant with 100 eyes, so the name suggests that she was designed for reconnaissance. This was an asset that had been much

Argus off the North African coast in November 1942. Argus participated in Operation Torch, but by 1943 had been relegated to the role of training carrier.

needed at Jutland, a victory lost for want of good intelligence. *Argus* was commissioned only weeks before the Armistice of November 1918, carrying a squadron of the unpopular Sopwith Cuckoo torpedo aircraft.

In the 1920s *Argus* was bulged to improve stability and protect against torpedo attack. After the larger fleet carriers were completed, she acted as a training and target ship, but was recalled to active service in 1939.

Small and slow by World War II standards, *Argus* nonetheless gave valuable service, ferrying fighter aircraft to Gibraltar, Malta and Takoradi (for onward staged flights to Egypt). The lack of carriers meant that she also took part in operational roles from time to time, notably on an Arctic convoy and at the North African landings. From mid-1943, she was used only for training in home waters, being paid off in 1944. HMS *Argus* was scrapped in 1947.

HMS *Audacity* Escort carrier

Though contingency plans existed before the war to convert merchant ships to auxiliary aircraft carriers, the production of the first such ship seems, in retrospect, to have been surprisingly leisurely. The hull selected for conversion was that of the fire-damaged *Hannover*, a Hamburg-Amerika cargo liner seized by the Royal Navy off San Domingo in February 1940. The new carrier was commissioned as **HMS *Audacity*** in June 1941 to carry fighters to curb the menace of the long-range German maritime aircraft and, if possible, Fairey Swordfish to provide a measure of anti-submarine protection.

Her facilities were basic, a 140-m (460-ft) flight deck being laid from the raised forecastle over a lowered bridge structure to a built-up poop. There were just two arrester wires and a barrier; the six aircraft were stowed and serviced on deck, flight operations involving much manual rearrangement. Because of a shortage of Hawker Sea Hurricanes, she took Grumman Martlets to sea for the first time in the Royal Navy.

Initial journey

September 1941 saw the carrier's first trip, with the UK-Gibraltar convoy OG41. Attacks from both submarine and

aircraft sank six ships but greater losses were prevented by the *Audacity*'s aircraft, which caused several U-boats to dive and lose contact. They also shot down a Focke-Wulf Fw 200C and chased off other intruders. The *Audacity* returned with the next convoy, HG76, in mid-December 1941. During a four-day non-stop battle, the

enemy lost five submarines for two merchantmen. With radar direction, the carrier had downed two more 'snoopers' and spoiled the attacks of various U-boats. On 21 December, she herself fell victim to three submarine torpedoes but had succeeded in proving the value of the escort carrier.

SPECIFICATION	
HMS *Audacity*	kW (4,750 shp) to two shafts
Type: escort aircraft-carrier	**Speed:** 15 kts
Displacement: 5,540 tons standard	**Armour:** none
Dimensions: length 144.7 m (474 ft	**Armament:** one 102-mm (4-in) and
9 in); beam 17.1 m (56 ft); draught	some smaller guns
8.3 m (27 ft 3 in)	**Aircraft:** six
Propulsion: diesels delivering 3542	**Complement:** not known

HMS Audacity's handful of fighters meant the difference between life or death for a convoy. Employed in protection duties to and from Gibraltar, Audacity was destroyed off Portugal by torpedoes from U-751 in December 1941.

British-built escort carriers

British yards produced few escort carriers, working on more specialized ships and leaving series production to US yards. There was also a reluctance to release mercantile tonnage for conversion when ships were needed for convoys. As a result, only five British-built CVEs saw service, HMS *Vindex*, HMS *Nairana*, HMS *Activity*, HMS *Campania* and the former passenger liner HMS *Pretoria Castle*.

The British escort carriers all differed from each other, with longer but narrower flight decks. In addition, the hangar of each ship was served by only one elevator, which made for much manhandling of aircraft. They were solidly built, however, with steelsided hangars and steel flight decks. Each ship accommodated between 15 and 18 aircraft, with two Swordfish attack aircraft for one fighter (Sea Hurricane, Martlet/Wildcat or Fulmar). The *Activity* stowed fewer aircraft, while the *Pretoria Castle* spent most of her career in the trials and training roles. The four smaller ships were converted from fast cargo liners of the Blue Funnel and Port Lines with a diesel propulsion arrangement and two propellers, and the ships were taken up for wartime service with a view to a return them to mercantile use after the end of hostilities.

The *Vindex* and *Nairana* were converted from fast merchant ship hulls, and were completed in December 1943. The ships had deep-load displacements of 17,000 tons and a flight deck 150.88 m (495 ft) in effective length. This was served by a lift measuring 13.72 x 10.36 m (45 x 34 ft), and 18 aircraft were embarked. The other armament was two 4-in (102-mm), 16 2-pdr 'pom-pom' and 16 20-mm AA guns.

Convoy work

The CVEs ran with convoys to and from Gibraltar. Working in pairs, they became potent anti-submarine ships. The Swordfish aircraft were equipped with search radar and they themselves with Asdic (sonar), allowing for co-operation with dedicated hunter-killer groups. Later in the war, the ships were used on the Arctic convoy route, the significance of their efforts on this hazardous service being recognized by their wearing the flag of the senior naval officer. However, they proved less successful in the severe northern conditions, their lack of length making them extremely lively in pitch, restricted flight operations for much of the time.

SPECIFICATION	
HMS *Pretoria Castle*	to two shafts
Displacement: 17,400 tons standard and 23,450 tons deep load	**Speed:** 16 kts
Dimensions: length 180.44 m (592 ft); beam 23.27 m (76 ft 4 in); draught 8.89 m (29 ft 2 in)	**Armament:** two twin 102-mm (4-in) AA, four quadruple 2-pdr AA, and 10 twin 20-mm AA guns
Propulsion: diesel engines delivering 11,930 kW (16,000 shp)	**Aircraft:** 15
	Complement: not known

SPECIFICATION	
HMS *Activity*	delivering 8950 kW (12,000 shp) to two shafts
Displacement: 11,800 tons standard and 14,250 tons full load	**Speed:** 18 kts
Dimensions: length 156.06 m (512 ft); beam 20.24 m (66 ft 5 in); draught 7.65 m (25 ft 1 in)	**Armament:** two 4-in (102-mm) AA and 10 twin 20-mm AA guns
Propulsion: diesel engines	**Aircraft:** 11
	Complement: 700

HMS Nairana *is seen here in her 1943 colour scheme as completed.* Nairana's *wartime service focused on convoy escort duties, embarking No. 835 Sqn's Sea Hurricane Mk IIc aircraft in summer 1944. One of these later claimed a Ju 290. Following the war, the vessel was transferred to the Netherlands to become* Karel Doorman.

American-built escort carriers

Like the British, the Americans converted mercantile hulls to auxiliary aircraft carriers. Early in 1941, two C3 hulls were thus earmarked, the first commissioning as the USS *Long Island* (AVG-1). She had both a hangar and an elevator, but made poor use of available space, the hangar occupying only the after quarter or so of the underdeck space, a similar volume ahead of it being used for accommodation. What she did have was a catapult.

The *Long Island*'s first sister was completed in November 1941, then transferred to the British as HMS *Archer*, being joined later by three more 'Archer'-class ships. As the American escort carrier

HMS Avenger *and* Biter, *pictured here in heavy seas, were both 'Archer'-class escort carriers.*

SPECIFICATION	
'Archer' class	6,338 kW (8,500 shp) (except *Archer* 6,711 kW; 9,000 shp) to one shaft
Displacement: 10,366 tons (except *Archer* 10,220 tons) standard and 15,125 tons (except *Archer* 12,860 tons) deep load	**Speed:** 16.5 kts (except *Archer* 17 kts)
Dimensions: length 150 m (492 ft 3 in); beam 20.2 m (66 ft 3 in); draught 7.1 m (23 ft 3 in)	**Armament:** three 4-in (102-mm) AA, and 15 20-mm AA guns
Propulsion: diesel engine delivering	**Aircraft:** 15
	Complement: 555

construction programme got into its stride the Royal Navy received eight units of the **'Attacker' class** and 26 units of the similar **'Ruler' class**. Both had full-length hangars, the later class having improved stowage factors. The British required higher standards of fuel and fire protection than the Americans, promoting some criticism. The earlier ships from American yards were powered by diesel engines, but later units switched to steam plants, releasing the of diesel engines for the US Navy's

expanding submarine arm.

With limited capacity for flexibility, CVEs were in general outfitted for a specific role, either in convoy escort or in assault support. Once available in larger numbers, they were often integrated directly with anti-submarine groups. They often worked in larger groups (five for the Allied landing in Italy at Salerno and nine for the landing in the south of France), but some saw no action at all, being engaged on aircraft-ferrying rather than operational

SPECIFICATION	
'Attacker' class	one shaft
Displacement: 10,200 tons standard and 14,170 deep load	**Speed:** 17 kts
Dimensions: length 150 m (492 ft 3 in); beam 21.2 m (69 ft 6 in); draught 7.3 m (24 ft)	**Armament:** two 4-in (102-mm) AA, four twin 40-mm AA, and 10 to 35 20-mm AA guns
Propulsion: geared steam turbines delivering 6,972 kW (9,350 shp) to	**Aircraft:** 18 to 24
	Complement: 646

SPECIFICATION	
'Ruler' class	one shaft
Displacement: 11,400 tons standard and 15,390 tons deep load	**Speed:** 17 kts
Dimensions: length 150 m (492 ft 3 in); beam 21.2 m (69 ft 6 in); draught 7.7 m (25 ft 3 in)	**Armament:** two 4-in (102-mm) AA, eight twin 40-mm AA, and 27 to 35 20-mm AA guns
Propulsion: geared steam turbines delivering 6,972 kW (9,350 shp) to	**Aircraft:** 18 to 24
	Complement: 646

The UK received eight 'Attacker'-class and 26 'Ruler'-class escort carriers from the US. They were used for both convoy escort and anti-submarine warfare, and also provided air support during several of the amphibious assault landings in the Mediterranean.

HMS *Perseus* and HMS *Pioneer* Aircraft maintenance ships

The British soon found that they had to undertake their naval operations against the Japanese in the Far Eastern campaigns on the basis of long-range sweeps far removed from bases and maintenance facilities.

These operations were also characterized by high attrition rates in aircraft, and 'repair by replacement' was the best means of keeping the front-line carrier force fully operational. Experience showed that escort carriers were well suited to the task of aircraft ferrying, and therefore operated extensively in the exchange process.

Lightly damaged aircraft and routine maintenance could be carried out on the carrier itself. Lack of space and time meant that anything more complex had to be shipped out for repair and, by the very nature of a war fought in a region without shore establishments, the repair facilities had to be afloat.

Replacements

With the only specialist maintenance carrier *Unicorn*

used permanently in an operational role, two of the new light fleet carriers of the 'Colossus' class were earmarked as replacements.

HMS *Perseus* and **HMS *Pioneer***, which had been laid down in June and December 1942 for launch in March and May 1944 respectively, were completed in October and February 1945 respectively, and thus only the *Pioneer* reached an operational theatre, arriving with the 11th Aircraft Carrier Squadron in the Far East just in time for the Japanese surrender.

Paradoxically, earlier in the war when they could have been of use, they would almost certainly have been pressed into an operational role, leaving CVEs to be used as auxiliaries. In time of peace, too few active flight decks were maintained to warrant their existence. With little post-war application, the *Pioneer*, which was originally to have been named **Mars**, was scrapped as early as 1954. It had been intented to convert the ships into passenger liners,

but this was not pursued, due to cost and the rise in air travel. The *Perseus*, originally to have been named **Edgar**, was nearly recommissioned for the Suez affair of 1956, but was then scrapped in 1958.

The other eight 'Colossus'-class light fleet aircraft carriers were the *Colossus*, *Glory*, *Ocean*, *Venerable*, *Vengeance*, *Theseus*, *Triumph* and *Warrior*. These were laid down at seven yards (Harland & Wolff building two units) between June 1942 and January 1943. All of the ships were launched in 1944, but only three were completed in time for operational service. The other five were completed after the war, and of the eight ships, four (*Warrior*, *Vengeance*, *Colossus* and *Venerable*) were

transferred or sold respectively to Argentina as the *Independencia* in 1958, Brazil as the *Minas Gerais* in 1956, France as the *Arromanches* in 1946 and the Netherlands as the second *Karel Doorman* in 1948. The other four units were kept in British service or loaned to Australia (*Vengeance* between 1952 and 1955) and Canada (*Warrior* between 1946 and 1948). The *Glory*, *Ocean* and *Theseus* were broken up in the early 1960s, and the *Triumph* was converted into a repair ship for further service.

The 'Colossus'-class ships had a flight deck offering an effective size of 210.31 m x 24.38 m (690 ft x 80 ft), one large hangar, one catapult and two lifts, with 37 aircraft.

SPECIFICATION	
HMS *Perseus* and HMS *Pioneer*	to two shafts
Displacement: 13,300 tons standard and 18,040 tons deep load	**Speed:** 25 kts
Dimensions: length 211.84 m (695 ft); beam 24.38 m (80 ft); draught 5.59 m (18 ft 4 in)	**Armour:** minimal
	Armament: three quadruple 2-pdr AA and 10 20-mm AA guns
Propulsion: geared steam turbines delivering 31,319 kW (42,000 shp)	**Aircraft:** none
	Complement: not known

IJN *Hosho* Light carrier

As with most early Japanese carriers, **Hosho** *spent most of her career as a flush-decked design.*

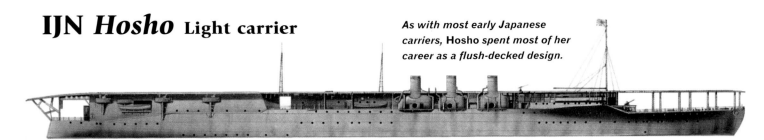

SPECIFICATION

Hosho
Type: Light carrier
Displacement: 7,470 tons standard, 10,000 tons full load
Dimensions: length 168.1 m (551 ft 6 in) overall; beam 18 m (59 ft); draught 6.2 m (20 ft 4 in)
Machinery: two-shaft geared steam turbines delivering 22,370 kW

(30,000 shp)
Speed: 25 kt
Armour: not known
Armament: 4 x 140-mm (5.5-in), 2 x 80-mm (3.2-in) AA (1941), eight twin 25-mm (0.985-in) AA guns
Aircraft: (1942) 11 'Kate' torpedo bombers
Complement: 550

The first carrier of the Imperial Japanese Navy was the *Hiryu*. Laid down in 1919 as a naval oiler, she was taken over in 1921 to emerge as **Hosho** a year later. The design owed much to a British technical mission that had details of the carrier *Hermes* and the Sopwith Cuckoo torpedo-bomber.

Turbine power

The original triple-expansion steam engines were replaced by destroyer-type turbines for a speed of 25 kt, and smoke was vented through triple folding funnels, which hinged downwards when flying was in progress. At first the ship had an 'island' navigating bridge, but this was removed in 1923.

As with many of the early carriers, the *Hosho* lacked a sufficient margin of stability to carry her full armament and complement of aircraft. By the outbreak of World War II, her air group had shrunk from 21 to 12 aircraft, and all of the original guns had been replaced.

Even so, the *Hosho* provided invaluable experience for the conversion of *Akagi* and *Kaga*, as well as the design of *Ryujo*, the first Japanese carrier built as such from the keel up. She saw action off the China coast in the 1930s, and ferried aircraft during the Sino-Japanese War, By the late 1930s, however, the *Hosho* was relegated to training duties.

Into combat

Despite this, the carrier served with Carrier Division 3 from December 1941, alongside the *Zuiho*, but after four months in the Palau Islands she was returned to training duties. Operational again for the Midway campaign, she carried 11 Nakajima B5N 'Kate' bombers, offering reconnaissance for Admiral Yamamoto's battleships.

Withdrawn from the front line in June 1942, she was damaged by grounding in 1944 and hit twice by American bombs at Kure, but was still afloat when the war ended.

Survivor

She was then recommissioned as a transport to repatriate Japanese servicemen from all over the Far East. *Hosho* continued in this job until August 1946, but was finally scrapped in 1947 after nearly 25 years of service.

IJN *Akagi* Fleet carrier

The Washington Naval Disarmament Treaty after World War I left the Imperial Japanese Navy with several incomplete capital ships destined for the scrapyard. In the light of the success of the *Hosho*, the naval staff decided instead to press ahead with two carrier conversions. Two battlecruisers, to be known as **Akagi** and

Akagi was one of the few aircraft carriers to have had her navigating 'island' on the port side. This was to allow her to operate in tandem with the **Kaga***, which had a starboard island, but it caused accidents.*

Amagi, were chosen, projected as 40,000-ton ships capable of 30 kt (55 km/h; 34 mph).

SPECIFICATION

Akagi
Type: Fleet carrier
Displacement: (1941) 36,500 tons standard, 42,000 tons full load
Dimensions: length 260.6 m (855 ft) overall; beam 31.3 m (102 ft 8 in); draught 8.6 m (28 ft 3 in)
Machinery: 4-shaft geared steam turbines delivering 99,180 kW (133,000 shp)
Speed: 31 kt (57 km/h; 36 mph)
Armour: 15-cm (6-in) waterline belt; 7.9-cm (3.1-in) armoured deck (main

deck, beneath double hangar decks)
Armament: six 200-mm (7.9-in), six twin 120-mm (4.7-in) AA; 14 twin 25-mm (0.985-in) AA guns added between 1935 and 1938
Aircraft: (June 1942) 21 Mitsubishi A6M Zero fighters, 21 Aichi D3A 'Val' dive bombers and 21 Nakajima B5N 'Kate' torpedo bombers
Complement: 1,340 men

Earthquake

Work began in 1923 but the hull of the *Amagi* was damaged during the Tokyo earthquake in September and she was scrapped. The *Akagi* was completed in March 1927. She was a flush-decked ship with two funnels at the starboard edge of the flight deck, a triple flight deck forward, and ten 200-mm (7.9-in) guns, six of them in old-fashioned casemates. In 1937, she was rebuilt, with an island superstructure on the port side and a full length flight deck.

Flagship

With her half-sister *Kaga* she formed Carrier Division 1 as Vice Admiral Nagumo's flagship and led the attack on Pearl Harbor. She then led the other carriers on raids through the East Indies and Indian Ocean; the force sank the British carrier *Hermes* and drove the Allies out of Java. At the Battle of Midway on 4 June 1942, *Akagi* was attacked by aircraft from the USS *Enterprise* and hit twice. She was abandoned, and a destroyer ordered to sink her.

IJN *Kaga* Fleet carrier

Like her half-sister Akagi, Kaga was completed with a short flight deck and two flying-off decks forwards. This was needlessly complex, and in a mid-1930s refit she acquired a full-length flight deck and a navigation island.

The Japanese battleship **Kaga** was laid down in 1918 and launched in November 1921, but as a result of the Washington Naval Disarmament Treaty of 1922, the incomplete hull was scheduled to be scrapped.

In September 1923, however, an earthquake struck the Tokyo area. The docked battlecruiser *Amagi*, which was about to start her conversion to an aircraft-carrier, was damaged, so the hull of the slightly smaller *Kaga* was substituted.

The conversion produced a carrier with a flush deck and two short flying-off decks forward and smoke-ducts trunked on the starboard side.

She became operational only after more than two years of trials. Then, in 1934, she was taken in hand for modernization. *Kaga* was greatly improved, with more aircraft (90 instead of 60) and an 'island' superstructure.

Wartime Service

The *Kaga* was one of the six carriers to attack Pearl Harbor on 7 December 1941. She and her half-sister *Akagi*, as Carrier Division 1, then took part in the strikes in the East Indies, South Pacific and Indian Ocean which destroyed Allied military power in the first half of 1942.

At Midway on 4 June 1942, she was attacked by Douglas SBD Dauntless dive bombers from the USS *Enterprise*. The carrier had to be abandoned, for the loss of over 800 men.

SPECIFICATION	
Kaga	**Armour:** 15.2-cm (6-in) armour belt; 3.8-cm (1.5-in) armour deck (main deck, beneath hangars)
Type: Fleet carrier	
Displacement: (1941) 38,200 tons standard, 43,650 tons full load	**Armament:** 10 200-mm (7.9-in), 12 11.9-cm (4.7-in) AA; AA fit later upgraded to 16 127-mm (5-in) DP and 11 twin 25-mm (0.985-in) AA guns
Dimensions: length 247.6 m (812 ft 4 in) overall; beam 32.5 m (106 ft 7 in) over flight deck; draught 9.5 m (31 ft 2 in)	
Machinery: 4-shaft geared steam turbines delivering 95,020 kW (127,400 shp)	**Aircraft:** 90 fighters, dive-bombers and torpedo-bombers
Speed: 28 kt	**Complement:** 2,016 officers and men

IJN *Ryujo* Light fleet carrier

The Washington Treaty limited Japan to 80,000 tons of carriers, but vessels under 10,000 tons were exempted, so the naval staff decided to build an extra carrier inside the limit.

The design was for an 8,000-ton ship carrying 24 aircraft, but a second hangar was added to double the aircraft capacity. This pushed the displacement 150 tons over the limit – the first major breach of the treaty.

Bad reputation

Even with the extra tonnage, the new carrier, called **Ryujo**, was found to be top-heavy on completion in 1933. She was twice rebuilt, with bulges added, guns removed and the forecastle raised, increasing her displacement to 12,000 tons. As may be imagined, the *Ryujo*

Ryujo's double hangar looks much too large for the carrier's sleek cruiser hull. Indeed, topweight was always to be a problem for this compromised light carrier design.

was not popular in the fleet. Apart from her topweight problems, her flight deck was too small and she carried too few aircraft to be effective, while congestion on the deck meant that she took longer than other carriers to launch and recover aircraft.

The *Ryujo* was not part of the force that attacked Pearl Harbor, but supported the amphibious landings in the Philippines. In April 1942 she attacked Allied merchant shipping and later she joined in operations against the Aleutian Islands, but her only major (and last) action was the Battle of the Eastern Solomons.

Guadalcanal

Ryujo was chosen to spearhead an operation to reinforce the defenders of Guadalcanal. Escorted by a heavy cruiser and two destroyers, she was used to lure the American carriers away from the main force. At 09.05 on 24 August 1942 she was attacked by aircraft from the *Enterprise* and *Saratoga*. In a brilliant attack, US Navy dive bombers and torpedo-bombers smothered the carrier, and the ship was doomed. There were only 300 survivors.

SPECIFICATION	
Ryujo	**Speed:** 29 kt
Type: Light carrier	**Armour:** virtually none
Displacement: 10,600 tons standard, 14,000 tons full load	**Armament:** six twin 127-mm (5-in) AA; later modified to four twin 127-mm, two twin 25-mm (0.985-in) and six triple 25-mm mounts
Dimensions: length 180 m (590 ft 6 in) overall; beam 20.8 m (68 ft 3 in); draught 7.1 m (23 ft 4 in)	
Machinery: two-shaft geared steam turbines delivering 48470 kW (65,000 shp)	**Aircraft:** 24 Mitsubishi A6M Zero fighters and 12 Nakajima B5N 'Kate' bombers
	Complement: 924 men

Hiryu Fleet carrier

Hiryu differed from Soryu in having an increased beam to allow more bunkerage (giving an extra 4828 km/3,000 miles in endurance), an increased level of protection and a higher (by one deck) forecastle in the interests of seaworthiness.

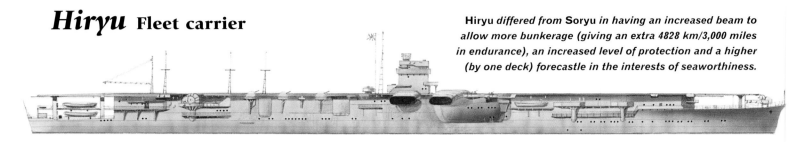

Launched in 1941, the **Hiryu** aircraft carrier was built to take account of lessons learnt during the construction of the 10,150-ton light aircraft carrier *Ryujo* and the 18,800-ton carrier *Soryu*. A wider hull permitted additional bunkerage on the vessel, increasing her range by almost 4,790 km (3,000 miles).

Hiryu had several interesting design features. These included a port-side island superstructure, to allow *Hiryu* to operate alongside the larger carrier *Akagi*. *Hiryu's* aircraft would fly an anti-clockwise circuit, while the *Akagi*, with its traditional starboard island, would operate a clockwise circuit, thus increasing air cover for the rest of the fleet. However, this practice was never used.

Airflow disturbance

Hiryu did have disadvantages. The airflow over the flight deck was disturbed by the funnel uptakes, which were located on the starboard side of the vessel. This caused the hot exhaust gases from the ship's engines to mix with the air flowing across the flight deck causing dangerous turbulence for the aircraft during landing and take-off from the vessel.

Hiryu was deployed as part of the Second Carrier Division of the 1st Air Fleet. She took part in the attacks on Pearl Harbor, along with the carriers *Kaga*, *Soryu*, *Shokaku* and *Zuikaku* on 7 December 1941. During the

attack, *Hiryu* launched 18 Nakajima B5N 'Kate' torpedo-bombers and nine Mitsubishi A6M Zero fighters during the first wave of attacks at 06.00.

The *Hiryu* continued the onslaught. During the second wave of strikes, the vessel launched 18 Aichi D3A 'Val' dive-bombers and another nine Zeros. Despite deploying 54 aircraft throughout the assault, *Hiryu* lost only five aircraft.

From Pearl Harbor, *Hiryu* steamed towards Wake Island in the central Pacific, and later that helped to attack the US garrison. The ship then took part in the invasion of Palau in January 1942, and provided air cover for the invasion of the Moluccas Islands.

In March 1942, *Hiryu* undertook intercepts of Allied shipping around Java, and during an attack on Christmas Island sank the Dutch freighter *Poelau Bras*.

Operation C

In April 1942, *Hiryu* took part in a devastatomg attack against the Royal Navy fleet. Code-named Operation C, the

*The last survivor of four Japanese fleet carriers at Midway, **Hiryu** was struck by SBD Dauntless dive-bombers late on 4 June 1942. Burning fiercely and with its flight deck shattered, the carrier was abandoned and scuttled, sinking some 12 hours later on 5 June.*

Japanese attacked the navy base at Colombo in Ceylon (Sri Lanka). During the attack, aircraft from *Hiryu* helped to sink the heavy cruisers HMS *Cornwall* and *Dorsetshire*.

As at Pearl Harbor, the Japanese struck on a Sunday morning before breakfast. Shore-based radar tracked the incoming Japanese air armada. RAF aircraft were scrambled and intercepted the Japanese strike package, but their efforts were largely unsuccessful. For instance, some 40 RAF fighters engaging the Japanese attack were unable to break up the hostile formation, and the RAF force lost half of its aircraft, whereas the Japanese lost only seven.

At this point, the port still functioned, but Vice-Admiral Chuichi Nagumo had organized a second strike force, centred around the *Ryujo*, which was too slow to participate in the

initial attacks. The follow-up attack force included the *Hiryu*.

Utter confusion

The second attack was meant to exploit the confusion triggered by the initial strike. One of the biggest successes of the day occurred when the *Hiryu* helped to destroy the Royal Navy aircraft carrier HMS *Hermes*, which had sailed from the harbour during the initial attacks and was particularly vulnerable. *Hermes* carried no fighters, as its air wing had been deployed elsewhere. Furthermore, the British carrier experienced communication problems when requesting shore-based air support. *Hermes* was devastated by a raid of 85 dive-bombers and absorbed 40 250-kg (551-lb) munitions. She capsized, and sank within minutes. Following the attacks, the force sank over 145,000 tons of merchant shipping.

SPECIFICATION	
Hiryu	(152,000 shp)
Displacement: 17,300 tons standard; 21,900 tons full load	**Speed:** 34.4 kts
	Armament: six twin 127-mm (5-in),
Dimensions: length 227.4 m (746 ft) overall; beam 22.3 m (73 ft 2 in); draught 7.8 m (25 ft 7 in)	seven triple 25-mm AA and five twin 25-mm AA guns
	Aircraft: 64 aircraft
Machinery: 4-shaft geared steam turbines delivering 113350 kW	**Complement:** 1,100 men (including air wing).

*Dawn on 7 December 1941, and a B5N 'Kate' loaded with an 800-kg (1,764-lb) torpedo takes off from the **Hiryu**. The attack on Pearl Harbor was timed to cause maximum confusion to US forces, with the first waves over target when the Americans were breakfasting.*

Hiryu was to meet its fate at the Battle of Midway on 4 June 1942. The carrier was organized into Nagumo's 1st Carrier Striking Force, alongside the *Akagi*, *Soryu* and *Kaga*; plus an additional two battleships and a three cruisers.

The force was scheduled to arrive off the coast of Midway Island on 4 June to begin a heavy bombardment of the American airfield. This would be done to facilitate the arrival of airborne troops and a transport group by the 6 June.

Hiryu launched 18 'Kate' torpedo-bombers and nine Zeros for the dawn attack. Fortune was on the ship's side, and *Hiryu* managed to avoid the bomb damage suffered by the other three Japanese carriers, which was unleashed by the American counter-attack.

By 10.30, three of the four carriers were suffering major fires. *Hiryu* had lost eight 'Kates' and two Zeros. However, at around midday, waves of *Hiryu*'s aircraft had helped disable the USS *Yorktown* with three direct hits.

Hiryu followed up this attack at 14.45, when a torpedo attack struck a mortal blow against the *Yorktown*. *Hiryu* lost most of its aircraft during this second attack, yet enough were able to return to the carrier to prepare to conduct a third strike.

The Japanese carrier's luck was short-lived. While the second wave of attacks against the *Yorktown* was underway, the American carrier launched 10 SBD Dauntless dive-bombers to find and sink the *Hiryu*. Two aircraft, piloted by Lieutenants Samuel Adams and Harlan R. Dickson flying from the USS *Enterprise,* located the Japanese carrier. By 16.00, 24 dive-bombers, including 10 refugees from the *Yorktown* were in the air.

They found the *Hiryu* shortly after 17.00, preparing to launch a third strike against the *Yorktown*, with its remaining air wing of four torpedo- and five dive-bombers.

US Marine Corps aircraft dropped four bombs along the centreline of the *Hiryu*'s flight deck, all of which were closely spaced at the forward area of the flight deck. *Hiryu* was then strafed with machine-gun fire by B-17s that had flown from airfields at Midway and Hawaii.

The attacks set fire to the forward part of the ship, yet this did not prevent *Hiryu* from withdrawing to the west. Eventually, the fires spread out of control, and for all intents and purposes the vessel was dead in the water.

Japanese destroyers picked up the survivors from the ship and *Hiryu* was torpedoed. However, the carrier stubbornly refused to sink, and remained afloat until 09.00 on 5 June. The vessel was photographed by an aircraft from the carrier *Hosho*, which was accompanying Admiral Yamamoto's force of battleships. The aircraft noted that the carrier still had some survivors aboard, and the destroyer *Tanikaze* was sent to investigate, and if possible rescue the survivors. The ship found nothing. Steaming back to the force following its investigations, *Tanikaze* came under heavy fire from the US Navy, when 50 aircraft attacked the vessel. In a miraculous display of ship-handling, the destroyer escaped.

Hiryu's legacy

Hiryu may have had a curious design, but many of its features were carried over into future designs.

The design for the carrier *Unryu* closely followed that of the *Hiryu*, except the position of the island superstructure was changed to the starboard. The design could be produced quickly and cheaply, but of the six carriers started by Japan after the Battle of Midway, all were either destroyed outright or severely damaged. The main point of vulnerability proved to be the ease with which bombs could penetrate the flight deck, causing major damage when they exploded in the hangars below.

Hiryu		
1 Flight deck	12 Access doors for stores etc	24 Bulkhead dividing boiler rooms
2 Hangar	13 Twin 127-mm (5-in) 40-calibre dual-purpose guns	25 Ventilating doors to hangar
3 Boat deck	14 Ammunition hoist	26 Fire screen
4 Crew quarters, canteens	15 Machine shop	27 Lift
5 Stores	16 Auxiliary engine room	28 Lift machinery
6 Wireless aerials	17 Thin side armour	29 Funnel casing
7 Boat crane	18 Turbine reduction gear	30 Funnel uptake
8 Balanced rudder	19 Turbine	31 Bridge
9 Screws	20 Boiler room	32 Command centre
10 Shaft	21 Pair of Kampon boilers (4x2)	33 Main rangefinder
11 Safety net	22 Water tubes inside boiler	34 Rangefinder for aft guns
	23 Bulkhead dividing engine rooms	35 AA gun rangefinder
		36 Navigating bridge

37 Flight control bridge	43 Fuel
38 Aircraft stores	44 Flight deck crew shelters
39 25-mm AA guns	45 Anchor
40 Main mast	46 Waterline
41 Officers' quarters/offices	47 Double bottom
42 Aviation fuel	

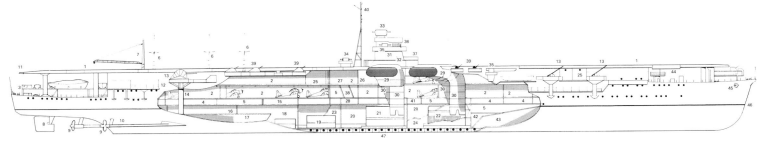

IJN *Soryu* Fleet carrier

Soryu, designed as a carrier, as opposed to being an adaptation, integrated the lower hangar within the hull structure, rather than having it superimposed on top of the hull.

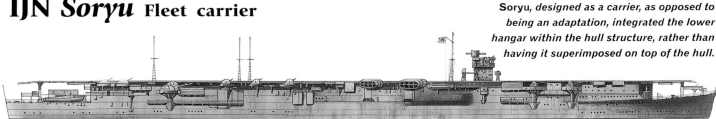

With the experience gained from operating two large carriers and one small, as well as the *Hosho*, the Imperial Japanese Navy staff now drew up a standard design for future carriers. Under the Second Reinforcement Programme of 1934 the first of this series, the **Soryu**, was laid down in that year, and she went to sea at the end of 1937. The designers were, however, still constrained by the Washington disarmament treaties that limited any class of military shipping to a maximum tonnage. After subtracting the overweight *Ryujo*, there was only a total of 20,000 tons left. The new carrier was accordingly notified as a 16,000 tonner despite displacing 2,000 tons more; the problem of how to accommodate a second carrier was solved by withdrawing from the treaty after December 1936.

Long low hull

The *Soryu* had a starboard island, and smoke was discharged through a pair of downward-curved funnels below the flight deck. The hull was a light structure for a ship of her size. Powerful machinery made the carrier exceptionally fast. Protection was sacrificed in favour of aircraft capacity. However, the excessively long but low hull resulted in very low clearance in the two hangars: 4.60 m (15 ft) in the upper and 4.30 m (14 ft) in the lower hangar. Three centre-line lifts served these hangars, and 63 aircraft could be stowed.

Soryu served as a model for most succeeding Japanese carrier designs. With an excellent power-to-weight ratio, she was fast and agile and had a large complement of aircraft but, carrying the minimum of armour, she was not built to take punishment.

SPECIFICATION	
Soryu	**Speed:** 34.5 kt
Type: fleet carrier	**Armour:** uncertain
Displacement:: 15,900 tons standard, 19,800 tons full load	**Armament:** six twin 127-mm (5-in) and 14 twin 25-mm AA guns
Dimensions: length 227.50 m (746 ft 6 in) overall; beam 21.30 m (69 ft 11 in); draught 7.60 m (25 ft)	**Aircraft:** 21 Mitsubishi A6M 'Zero' fighters, 21 Aichi D3A 'Val' dive-bombers and 21 Nakajima B5N 'Kate' torpedo bombers
Machinery: 4-shaft geared steam turbines delivering 113350 kW (152,000 shp)	**Complement:** 1,100 men

IJN *Zuikaku* Fleet carrier

Zuikaku, the second ship of the 'Shokaku' class, entered service in September 1941. She joined her sister in Carrier Division 5, and for the next three years the two were inseparable. The inexperience of CarDiv 5's aircrews meant the ships had a supporting role during the Pearl Harbor attack, but they were fully worked up by the time CarDiv 5 began its destructive raids on the British in Ceylon. They then went to Truk, from where they covered the invasion of Port Moresby on 1 May 1942.

Coral Sea

In the ensuing Battle of the Coral Sea, CarDiv 5 scored a tactical victory by sinking the *Lexington*, in exchange for the light carrier *Shoho*. The Japanese carriers wasted their efforts on sinking a destroyer and a fleet oiler, which they misidentified as a cruiser and a carrier. A strike by 24 B5N 'Kate' and 36 D3A 'Val' bombers failed to penetrate the US carriers' screen, but on 8 May a similar strike failed to find the *Zuikaku* in a rain squall. However, her highly trained aircrew had suffered serious attrition, so she had to return to Japan to retrain her air group. As a result, CarDiv 5 missed the Battle of Midway, and was then incorporated into a new CarDiv 1.

In the Battle of the Eastern Solomons, on 24 August 1942, *Zuikaku* damaged *Enterprise* but at considerable cost. She was also mauled at the Battle of the Philippine Sea in June 1944. In October 1944 she formed part

Wartime modification of the Zuikaku, as with American and British carriers, included an upgrade of her AA defences. In 1943 she was also fitted out with Type 13 air-warning and Type 21 air/surface-warning radar systems.

Zuikaku was lost off Cape Engano during the Battle of Leyte Gulf. As she sank, her crew saluted the naval ensign while it was lowered.

of CarDiv 3, drawing the US carriers supporting the Leyte Gulf landings.

On 24 October *Zuikaku* launched her last air strike.

All the aircraft were shot down, and next day US Navy pilots sank all four Japanese carriers, including the *Zuikaku*, in the Battle of Cape Engano.

SPECIFICATION	
IJN *Zuikaku*	**Speed:** 34.2 kt
Type: fleet carrier	**Armour:** 215 mm (8½ in) armour
Displacement: 25,675 tons	belt; deck 170 mm (6¾ in)
standard, 32,000 tons full load	**Armament:** eight twin 127-mm (5-in)
Dimensions: length 257.50 m (844 ft	dual-purpose and 12 triple 25-mm
9 in) overall; beam 26 m (85 ft 4	(0.99-in) AA guns
in); draught 8.90 m (29 ft 2 in)	**Aircraft:** 27 fighters, 27 dive-
Machinery: 4-shaft geared steam	bombers and 18 torpedo-bombers
turbines delivering 119,310 kW	**Complement:** 1,600 men
(160,000 shp)	

IJN *Shokaku* Fleet carrier

The best carriers extant, at the time of their introduction, the 'Shokakus' had strong AA armament but suffered from a vulnerable fuel system.

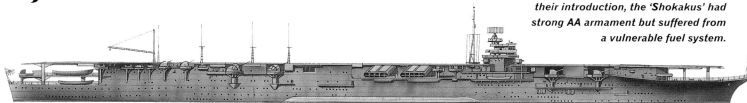

Japan's withdrawal from the treaties limiting warship size enabled the design of carriers that suited requirements. Under the 1937 Reinforcement Programme two carriers were to be built, similar to the *Hiryu* but large enough to accommodate all that was required.

Lessons learned

In the **'Shokaku' class** all the earlier faults were remedied. Two catapults were provided, and a much larger hangar enabled aircraft capacity to be increased from 63 to 75. With a considerable increase in power (the most powerful machinery ever fitted in a Japanese warship), the two ships had a range of nearly 16,000 km (10,000 miles), as they carried 5,000 tons of fuel. Equally important, they were well armoured and carried a heavier anti-aircraft armament than their predecessors. Their defect was the light construction of the flight deck, aggravated by enclosed yet unprotected double hangars. In addition, their fuel systems were vulnerable. Not only were the fuel lines to the hangars and flight deck liable to be ruptured by explosions some distance away, but the fuel storage tanks were inadequately protected against shock.

Into action

Shokaku went to sea in August 1941, just two months before Pearl Harbor. She took part in the attack, bombing the airfields on Oahu. With her sister *Zuikaku* she formed Carrier Division 5, and after their work-up early in 1942 they operated off Ceylon and New Guinea.

During the Battle of the Coral Sea, *Shokaku* was damaged by a strike from the *Yorktown*; she was saved with some difficulty, and had to return to Japan for repairs. The worst casualties were, however, the loss of 86 aircraft and most of their aircrews, so that neither carrier could take part in the Battle of Midway. On 14 July they joined the new Carrier Division 1, with the light carrier *Zuiho*. In the Battle of the Eastern Solomons. they damaged the *Enterprise* but again lost precious aircrew and aircraft. On 26 October, the *Shokaku* was severely damaged by a dive-bomber strike from the *Hornet*.

During the Battle of the Philippine Sea on 19 June 1944, she was hit by three torpedoes from the submarine USS *Cavalla*, and an explosion from ruptured aviation fuel tanks subsequently sank her.

SPECIFICATION	
IJN *Shokaku*	**Speed:** 34.2 kt (63 km/h; 39 mph)
Type: fleet carrier	**Armour:** belt 215 mm (8½ in); deck
Displacement: 25,675 tons	170 mm (6¾ in)
standard, 32,000 tons full load	**Armament:** eight twin 127-mm (5-in)
Dimensions: length 257.50 m (844 ft	dual-purpose and 12 triple 25-mm
9 in) overall; beam 26 m (85 ft 4 in);	(0.99-in) AA guns
draught 8.90 m (29 ft 2 in)	**Aircraft:** 27 fighters, 27 dive-
Machinery: 4-shaft geared steam	bombers and 18 torpedo-bombers
turbines delivering 119,310 kW	**Complement:** 1,600 men
(160,000 shp)	

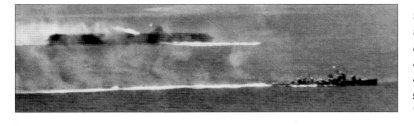

Shokaku *during the Battle of the Philippines on 19 June 1944. Her design incorporated the lessons learned from the* **Hiryu** *and* **Soryu***. She had much greater armour protection without sacrificing her speed.*

Zuiho Light carrier

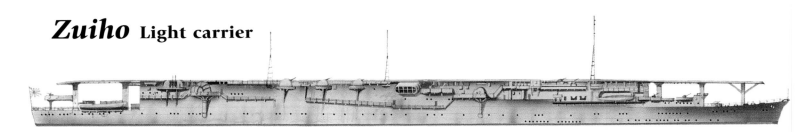

*Originally diesel-powered submarine support ships, **Zuiho** and its sister **Shoho** were fitted with steam turbines during conversion. With single hangars, aircraft capacity was 30.*

To remedy the shortage of aircraft carriers, the Japanese naval staff decided that certain large fleet auxiliaries should be designed for rapid conversion to carriers in wartime. One such class was the 'Tsurigizaki' class of high-speed oilers, which were ordered under the 1934 Second Reinforcement Programme with strengthened hulls. The design was then altered to submarine tenders, and the lead-ship entered service early in 1939. Her sister ship *Takasaki*, however, was not completed, and was laid up for nearly four years. Work to convert her to a carrier began in January 1940, under the name **Zuiho**.

Zuiho conversion

Apart from the replacement of the diesels with geared steam turbines, as much of the original hull was retained as possible. A single hangar was provided, accommodating a maximum of 30 aircraft, with two centreline lifts; there were two catapults but no island superstructure. To retain speed and endurance, all planned armouring was deleted. The conversion was carried out in a year, and the *Zuiho* joined the Combined Fleet in January 1941. With the old *Hosho* (Carrier Division 3), she was sent to the Palaus in the late autumn of that year and took part in the attack on the Philippines. She then returned to Japan for repairs before taking part in the conquest of the East Indies in the spring.

Surprise attack

Fortunately for the carrier, she was with the Support Force at Midway and therefore escaped the destruction of the main carrier force. In the Battle of the Santa Cruz Islands, she formed part of Admiral Nagumo's Carrier Strike Force. At 07.40 on 25 October 1942, a divebomber from the USS *Enterprise* made a surprise attack out of low cloud, dropping its bomb in the centre of the flight deck.

With a 15-m (50-ft) crater in her flight deck, the *Zuiho* was no longer able to operate aircraft, and so after launching her aircraft, she had no choice but to return to her base.

Decoy

In February 1944, *Zuiho* rejoined Carrier Division 3, and took part in the Battle of the Philippine Sea, when her aircraft hit the battleship USS *South Dakota*. In the fighting around Leyte Gulf, she was one of the doomed carriers that attempted to decoy the Americans: in the Battle of Cape Engano, she was hit by two bombs on the flight deck and was near-missed six times. In spite of a fire and flooding, *Zuiho* was under way for another six hours, as the other carriers were picked off. Finally it was *Zuiho*'s turn: three waves of attackers finished her off.

SPECIFICATION	
Zuiho	(52,000 shp)
Displacement: 11,262 tons standard; 14,200 tons full load	**Speed:** 28.2 kts
	Armour: none
Dimensions: length 204.8 m (672 ft) overall; beam 18.2 m (59 ft 8 in); draught 6.6 m (21 ft 8 in)	**Armament:** four twin 127-mm (5-in) dual-purpose and four twin 25-mm AA guns
Machinery: 2-shaft geared steam turbines delivering 38,770 kW	**Aircraft:** 30
	Complement: 785 men

Shoho Light carrier

The submarine tender *Tsurigizaki* had been serving with the Combined Fleet in 1939–40, but as soon as the conversion of its sister *Takasaki* into a carrier was completed in December 1940 she was taken in hand, re-emerging in January 1942 as the light carrier **Shoho**. *Shoho* did not see any action until the spring of 1942, when she covered the Port Moresby invasion, in the Support Force commanded by Rear-Admiral Aritomo Goto. It was this move by the Japanese which led to the Battle of the Coral Sea, the first carrier versus carrier battle in history.

Bombing attack

The *Shoho* was heading for Port Moresby on 6 May 1942, and at 10.30 she was sighted 100 km

Shoho *entered service in January 1942, but unlike* **Zuiho** *its operational career was brief.* **Shoho** *had the unhappy distinction of being Japan's first aircraft carrier loss, sunk by aircraft from USS* **Yorktown** *on 7 May 1942 in the Coral Sea.*

(60 miles) south of Bougainville by four B-17 bombers. The four aircraft attempted a high-level bombing attack on the carrier, causing little damage. The two sides were largely ignorant of each other's whereabouts. In an attempt to find the American carriers, *Takagi* flew off reconnaissance planes for a dawn sweep on the next day. At 07.30 they reported a carrier and a cruiser, and the *Shokaku* and *Zuikaku* flew off a strike. Unfortunately, the 'task force' turned out to be the US Navy oiler *Neosho* and her escorting destroyer, the USS *Sims*. It was a fatal error, for while the Japanese were sinking these

ships they missed the chance of finding Task Force 17, leaving the Americans time to discover the *Shoho*'s carrier group.

Brutal assault

The luckless *Shoho* had been ordered to launch all available aircraft for an attack on the US carriers, and when at 09.50 the *Lexington*'s strike spotted her turning into wind, they encountered no resistance to their attack.

The first strike scored no hits, but a near-miss blew five aircraft off its deck. At 10.25 a second strike arrived, from the USS *Yorktown* this time. This strike scored two hits with

1,000-lb (454-kg) bombs on the flight deck, in spite of anti-aircraft fire from the *Shoho*'s escorts. The carrier reeled under the blows, and as she began to lose speed, more bombs and torpedoes found their mark.

According to Japanese records as many as 11 more bombs and seven

torpedoes hit, and the *Shoho* aircraft carrier burst into flames. Approximately six minutes after the last US aircraft had left, the order was given to abandon ship, and at 10.35 the burning carrier rolled over and sank. Only 255 men out of an estimated total of 800 on board were saved. The Japanese had lost their first aircraft carrier.

SPECIFICATION	
Shoho	(52,000 shp)
Displacement: 11,262 tons standard; 14,200 tons full load	**Speed:** 28.2 kts
	Armour: none
Dimensions: length 204.8 m (672 ft) overall; beam 18.2 m (59 ft 8 in); draught 6.6 m (21 ft 8 in)	**Armament:** four twin 127-mm (5-in) dual-purpose and four twin 25-mm AA guns
Machinery: 2-shaft geared steam turbines delivering 38770 kW	**Aircraft:** 30
	Complement: 785 men

'Junyo' class Aircraft carrier conversions

Like the trio of 'Taiyo'-class ships that preceded them, the **Junyo** and its sister **Hiyo** of the 'Junyo' class were useful conversions from Nippon Yusen Kaisha liners that had been designed from the outset with this procedure in mind. Where the earlier ships had undergone rebuilding at a late stage, the larger 'Taiyo'-class ships were taken in hand before launching, both being in the water by June 1941 (over five months before the Pacific War began) and completed in mid-1942.

As they had been designed as passenger liners, they had

considerable freeboard and could accommodate two hangars, albeit of restricted headroom. They also had respectably sized flight decks, measuring 210.2 x 27.3 m (689ft 7in x 89ft 7in), and two centreline elevators, but suffered badly from the combination of their low mercantile speed and lack of catapults.

Additional equipment

The two ships were the first Japanese carriers to incorporate a funnel as part of the island, though it was of strange aspect,

While their capacious liner hulls had room for two hangars, the 'Junyo'-class vessels suffered from a lack of speed, and without catapults aircraft operations were hampered. Both were at the Battle of the Philippine Sea, Junyo being damaged and Hiyo sinking.

canted outward at a sharp angle. Except for the never completed Italian *Aquila*, this pair of carriers were the largest ever converted from mercantile hulls.

Junyo's 53 aircraft could have had a decisive effect at Midway but the ship was engaged in the rather fruitless Aleutians diversion. At Santa Cruz in October 1942, her aircraft damaged the battleship USS *South Dakota* and a cruiser, playing also a significant role in the sinking of the carrier USS *Hornet*.

The two sisters operated together as Kakuta's Carrier Division Two but, at the battle of the Philippine Sea, where

Ozawa took on the vastly superior force of Mitscher's TF 58, the partnership was broken, the *Junyo* being heavily damaged by bombing and *Hiyo* sunk after blowing up. The *Hiyo* had been struck by two torpedoes and was probably lost from the detonation of a build-up of vapour from leaking Avgas tanks.

Out of service

The *Junyo*, newly repaired, was torpedoed in December 1944 and, though she was not sunk, she never re-entered service, and survived to be one of the very few Japanese naval ships of any size to fall eventually into US hands.

SPECIFICATION	
'Junyo' class	to two shafts
Displacement: 24,500 tons standard and 26,960 tons full load	**Speed:** 25 kts
	Armour: none
Dimensions: length 219.2 m (719 ft 2 in); beam 26.7 m (87 ft 7 in); draught 8.2 m (26 ft 11 in)	**Armament:** 12 127-mm (5-in) DP and 24 25-mm AA guns
	Aircraft: 53
Propulsion: geared steam turbines delivering 41760 kW (56,000 shp)	**Complement:** 1,220 men

Taiho Fleet carrier

Technically the most advanced of the Japanese carriers, the **Taiho** was unique. In 1939, a new type of armoured carrier was planned under the Fourth Reinforcement Programme, and two more units were ordered in 1942.

The flight deck was protected by 75-mm (3-in) armour, but only between the lifts. There were two hangars, the lower hangar being protected by 35-mm (1-in) armour as well. Waterline armour was provided, with 150-mm (6-in) of protection abreast of the magazines and 55-mm (2-in) over the machinery.

Weight penalty

All this armour involved a colossal topweight penalty, and

to preserve stability the designers were forced to allow one less deck above the waterline. This meant that the lower hangar deck was just above the waterline, while the bottom of the liftwells were below the waterline.

The opportunity was taken to use the latest defensive guns: a new high velocity 100-mm (3.9-in) Type 98 twin mounting. For the first time an air warning radar was included.

Torpedo strike

The new carrier, *Taiho*, went to sea in March 1944. Joining Carrier Division 1 (CarDiv 1), she was sent with the *Shokaku* and *Zuikaku* to Singapore. As soon as the air group was trained,

Probably the most advanced of all Japanese carriers, Taiho had an armoured flight deck, enclosed bow and the latest in AA defences (including an air warning radar for the first time). Taiho was lost just before the Battle of the Philippine Sea.

SPECIFICATION	
Taiho	**Speed:** 33 kts
Displacement: 29,300 tons standard; 37,270 tons full load	**Armour:** see text
	Armament: six twin 100-mm (3.9-in) AA and 15 triple 25-mm AA guns
Dimensions: length 260.5 m (854 ft 8 in); beam 27.7 m (90 ft 10 in); draught 9.6 m (31 ft 6 in)	**Aircraft:** 30 Yokosuka D4Y 'Judy' dive-bombers; 27 Mitsubishi A6M Zero fighters and 18 Nakajima B6N 'Jill' torpedo-bombers
Machinery: 4-shaft geared steam turbines delivering 134225 kW (180,000 shp)	**Complement:** 2,150 men

CarDiv 1 was sent to join the First Mobile Fleet. On 19 June, during the Battle of the Philippine Sea, the *Taiho* had just launched her aircraft when the American submarine *Albacore* fired six 21-in (533-

mm) torpedoes, one of which hit. Her fuel tanks were ruptured, and about 5 hours later, some mischance (probably the switch on an electric pump) sparked an explosion. About 90 minutes later, *Taiho* sank.

'Unryu' class Fleet carrier

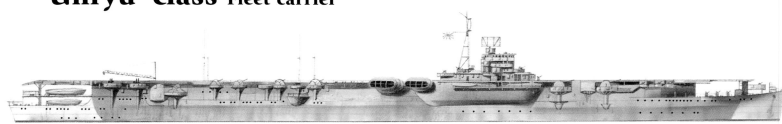

Series production of a standard design was the only way to commission enough quality carriers in time for them to be of any use. To this end the basic 'Hiryu' design was simplified. Seventeen units of this **'Unryu' class** were planned initially, but after the losses at Midway,

priorities changed and the programme slowed, eventually halting. In the event, only three were ever completed and three more launched.

Production

The three completed were the **Amagi** (August 1944), the

The 'Unryu' class were to have been a standard design, produced in quantity. Although 17 were planned, only three of the modified, simplified 'Hiryu' design were built, with only Unryu being completed in time for war service.

Katsuragi (October 1944) and **Unryu** (August 1944); the three others launched were the **Aso**, **Ikoma** and **Kasagi**. The main differences between the 'Unryu' and the 'Hiryu' designs was one less elevator less and an altered layout of main armament. The 'Unryu'-class ships gained stability through a greater beam yet had a smaller aircraft capacity.

For their size, they were well protected over vitals, and like all larger 'regular' Japanese

carriers, the 'Unryu'-class units had a good speed. With shortages biting, however, two of those launched had to take a couple of sets of destroyer machinery.

Despite a one-third reduction in power, the speed penalty was only a couple of knots. The *Amagi* was lost to air attack in Kure during July 1945, the *Katsuragi* survived and was surrendered, and the *Unryu* was sunk in December 1944 by a US submarine.

SPECIFICATION	
'Unryu' class	to four shafts
Displacement: 17,250 tons standard and 22,550 tons full load	**Speed:** 34 kts for *Unryu* and 32 kts for *Aso* and *Katsuragi*
Dimensions: length 227.2 m (745 ft 5 in); beam 22 m (72 ft 2 in); draught 7.8 m (25 ft 7 in)	**Armour:** belt 25–150 mm (1–5.9 in); deck 55 mm (2.17 in)
	Armament: 12 127-mm (5-in) DP and between 51 and 89 25-mm AA guns
Machinery: geared steam turbines delivering 113345 kW (152,000 shp) in *Unryu* and 77555 kW (104,000 shp) in *Aso* and *Katsuragi*	**Aircraft:** 64
	Complement: 1,450 men

Shinano Fleet carrier

By far the largest carrier of the war, Shinano *was to have been the third 'Yamato'-class battleship. The small aircraft capacity and slow speed pointed to its eventual role as repair and resupply vessel to front-line carriers, a role it was destined never to fulfil.*

The loss of four carriers at Midway, solely to aircraft from US carriers, convinced the Japanese to increase the number of carriers.

Most of their programme of conversions date from this point, none of them more impressive than the **Shinano**. Created from the incomplete third 'Yamato'-class battleship, it displaced nearly 72,000 tons full load, a figure not eclipsed until the US post-war supercarriers. The hull was already fitted with a 200-mm (7.87-in) armoured deck and vertical protection of the same order, and the ship's great beam (increased further by bulging) allowed for a flight deck of 80-mm (3.15-in) thickness over most of its area.

Despite the ship's size, the flight deck was over 1 m (3 ft 4 in) shorter than that of the *Taiho* of less than half the displacement, although it was far wider.

Viewed as too slow to act as an attack carrier, *Shinano* was not even fitted with catapults and carried an undersized complement of 47. The ship's considerable stowage was looked upon mainly as a repair and re-supply facility for the front-line carriers.

Brief career

Like the *Taiho*, the *Shinano* had an integral funnel and island, but lacked the smaller ship's British-style 'hurricane bow'. Not quite complete in time for the Japanese fleet's self-immolation at Leyte Gulf in October 1944, it transferred from Yokosuka to Kure for a final fitting-out. On the way it was hit by six torpedoes from a US sub-marine: its watertight subdivision still incomplete, it foundered from flooding on 29 November and sank.

SPECIFICATION	
'Shinano' class	shp) to four shafts
Displacement: 64,000 tons standard and 71,900 tons full load	**Speed:** 27 kts
Dimensions: length 265.8 m (872 ft); beam 36.3 m (119 ft); draught 10.3 m (33 ft 10 in); flight deck 255.9 x 40.1 m (839 ft 7 in x 131 ft 7 in)	**Armour:** belt 205 mm (8.07 in); flight deck 80 mm (3.15 in); hangar deck 200 mm (7.87 in)
	Armament: 16 127-mm (5-in) DP and 145 25-mm AA guns, and 12 28-barrel AA rocket-launchers
Machinery: geared steam turbines delivering 111,855 kW (150,000	**Aircraft:** 18 (later 47)
	Complement: 2,400 men

'Taiyo' class Escort carrier

Carriers were required by the Japanese for other than fleet purposes. Firstly, for the defence of trade, a function that had been badly neglected pre-war due to a lack of hard experience and the belief that the war would be short. Secondly, for the training of large numbers of aircrew for carrier operations, a task for which first-line units could not be spared. Thirdly, for the ferrying of aircraft, a task made essential by the sheer size of the newly-acquired empire, which had airfields thousands of miles from the homeland itself.

Like Western fleets, the Japanese navy rebuilt good-class mercantile tonnage into auxiliary carriers, particularly NYK ships, which had government-subsidized features built into them. The **Taiyo** was the first such example, converted from the *Kasuga Maru* in 1941 as the lead ship of the **'Taiyo' class**, before the outbreak of the Pacific War.

Auxiliary tasks

After a few months of evaluation, the similar *Yawata Maru* and *Nitta Maru* were rebuilt into the **Unyo** and **Chuyo** respectively. Though of a larger size than Western escort carriers, none of them was equipped with arrester gear or catapults which, combined with their low speed, made aircraft launch and recovery difficult. All were lost to submarine torpedo attack within a space of 10 months between December 1943 and September 1944 having spent their lives engaged in auxiliary tasks.

Probably for reasons of weapons availability, the first of the class, the *Taiyo*, was armed with 120-mm (4.7-in) guns. These were probably spare weapons obtained from older destroyers.

SPECIFICATION	
'Taiyo' class	to two shafts
Displacement: 17,850 tons standard	**Speed:** 27 kts
Dimensions: length 180.1 m (590 ft 11 in); beam 22.5 m (73 ft 10 in); draught 8 m (26 ft 3 in); flight deck 171.9 x 23.5 m (564 ft x 77 ft 1 in)	**Armour:** none
	Armament: eight 127-mm (5-in) DP (except *Taiyo*, see text) and eight (later 22) 25-mm AA guns
Machinery: geared steam turbines delivering 18,790 kW (25,200 shp)	**Aircraft:** 27
	Complement: 800 men

The three 'Taiyo'-class vessels were largely used for aircraft transport and training. Their heavy AA armament was to no avail, all three succumbing to submarine attacks from USS **Rasher** *(which sank* Taiyo*),* **Barb** *(*Unyo*) and* **Sailfish** *(*Chuyo*).*

'RO-100' and 'RO-35' classes Coastal submarines

Directly comparable in performance and size to the British 'U'-class boats, the 'RO-100s' should have been equally successful, but were to prove less able to cope with operational limitations.

Small- to medium-sized submarines in the Imperial Japanese Navy (IJN) were designated 'RO'. In the case of the **'RO-100' class**, the term **'Kaisho'** or **Type KS** was also used, denoting 'small'. Constructed at the Kure Naval Yard, between 1941 and 1943, these vessels were designed as limited endurance boats for use in the waters off the Japanese home islands. For this reason operational depth was reduced to only 75 m (245 ft). However, the function of the boats was extended to protection of the numerous islands that were acquired to defend the outer perimeter of the new empire. These were often surrounded by deep water, giving the 'RO-100' boats an instant disadvantage. Once submerged, the boats'

small sonar profile did not compensate for their poor performance and all 18 vessels in the class were sunk, only two by aircraft. No less than five of the class were sunk by the destroyer escort USS *England* in the space of just eight days.

Endurance

The fact that one was sunk off the coast of eastern India says much for the endurance of its crew. The design was smaller than the earlier 'RO-33', and similar to the British 'U'-class. They were unsuitable for attacking the warships that were designated their prime targets. Yet, while they could have operated effectively against mercantile targets, the Japanese submarine command showed a lack of imagination,

and it was this that was primarily responsible for the submarine's poor results.

Parallel class

The class of 18 was ordered pre-war but were being completed up to May 1944. Nine more units were cancelled.

The parallel 'RO' type, the **'RO-35' class** ('**Kaichu**' or '**Type K6**') was larger and comprised

the last medium-sized boats built by the IJN. Of the 18 completed only one survived the war. Between them, the combined 'RO-35' and 'R-100' classes are credited with sinking just four minor warships and six merchantmen, a catastrophically poor rate of exchange that led also to the cancellation of 60 further 'RO-35' boats.

SPECIFICATION	
'RO-100' class	**Speed:** surfaced 14 kts and
Displacement: 601 tons surfaced and 782 tons submerged	submerged 8 kts
Dimensions: length 60.9 m (199 ft 10 in); beam 6.1 m (20 ft); draught 3.5 m (11 ft 6 in)	**Range:** surfaced 6,500 km (4,040 miles) at 12 kts and submerged 110 km (68 miles) at 3 kts
Propulsion: surfaced diesels delivering 820 kW (1,100 shp) and submerged electric motors delivering 570 kW (760 shp) to two shafts	**Armament:** one 76-mm (3-in) gun (often removed), and four 533-mm (21-in) torpedo tubes (all forward) with eight torpedoes
	Complement: 38 men

'I-15' class
Ocean-going submarine

The 'I-15'-class boats were designed to put aircraft into submarines. A couple of the class, with the similar 'Type B2' and 'Type B3' variants, were modified to carry Kaiten suicide midget submarines.

An 'I' prefix, equivalent to the Western 'A' prefix, denoted a larger submarine designed for fleet and cruising work. These two functions had merged in this class, for the 'fleet' concept was a hangover from earlier ideas of using large boats with a good surface performance to act

in close support to the surface fleet, a concept that proved unsuccessful at the time.

Design influences

The **'I-15' class** was influenced by two previous designs. The first was the 'Type KD' fleet submarine of the mid-1930s,

capable of a surface speed of 23 kts and a range suitable for a coast-to-coast return trip across the Pacific. The other design was the 'Junsen', or cruiser submarine, of a slightly later date, which incorporated floatplanes in a pressure-tight hangar that formed part of the

superstructure. One of the class, **I-25**, deployed a Yokosuka E14Y1 for the first ever aircraft attack on the American mainland. On 9 September 1942, Warrant Officer Fujita took off from the submarine and dropped four 77-kg (168-lb) phosphoros bombs in a bid to set the Oregon woodland on fire. The attack failed. Despite Fujita's bombing raid, it would appear that these aircraft were principally used to increase the boat's reconnaissance capabilities rather than for offensive purposes.

The first 'I-15' class, the **'Type B1'** was 20 strong. The hangar was placed in a low, streamlined structure protruding (usually forward) from the tower. The freeboard was positioned high to improve aircraft handling in a seaway, and was made higher still by a sloping catapult track. A folding crane was also

incorporated for recovery purposes. A 140-mm (5.5-in) gun was set on a substantial bandstand. In practice, the aircraft and its equipment proved more trouble than it was worth, and several boats had this provision removed in favour of a second gun to augment their attack role. As such, the boats were among the more successful of the Japanese submarines, and were credited with the sinking of eight warships (including the carrier USS *Wasp* by **I-19**) and 59 merchantmen of around 400,000 gross tons.

The losses of the 'I-15' boats were disastrously high, a result of their poor submerged performance and the fact that only three full salvoes of torpedoes were carried. Only

one boat of the 20 built survived when Japan surrendered. The similar **'Type B2'** was the **'I-40' class** (six completed) and the **'Type B3'** was the **'I-45' class** (three completed).

'I-361', 'I-373' and 'I-351' classes Supply submarines

The exploits of the 'Tokyo Express' to Guadalcanal tend to overshadow the fact that the Japanese had other island garrisons that needed support and resupply. Once the American counteroffensive began to make progress in 1943, many of these were bypassed as having a low strategic significance. With the enemy firmly across their lines of supply, Japanese surface forces (even if available) would have had little chance of survival in such a role, so the

supplementary 1942 building programme included a dozen specialist cargo-carrying submarines, known as the **'Type D1'** or **'I-361' class**, named after the first unit. Though not large, the boats were ungainly, their high casing acting as a stowage for two 13-m (42-ft 8½-in) landing craft abaft of the fin. These were built to resist diving to 60 m (197 ft) and could be floated on and off by trimming the depth of the submarine. Twenty tons of stores could also be carried externally, with a

Similar in size to the 'I-361' class, some of the 'KD6a' class of attack submarine were converted to transports, the gun being removed and a 13-m landing craft carried in place of spare torpedoes. I-68 (re-numbered I-168) was sunk in May 1943.

further 60 tons and two large rubber boats inside the hull. Alternatively 110 equipped men could be carried on short hauls.

By Japanese standards, the boats' submerged endurance was good. However, their numbers were insufficient, as resupply over the radius of which the boats were capable would have required many more of the class. Though they boasted a 140-mm (5.5-in) gun, the boats had no torpedo tubes, the two fitted in early units being removed in an effort to improve the boat's poor handling characteristics.

Suicide submarine

Once detected, therefore, the boats were vulnerable and nine

were lost. The **'Type D2'** or **'I-373' class** exchanged endurance for stowage, but this class included only two boats. Five of the 'Type D1' boats were converted to *Kaiten* (suicide midget submarine) carriers.

More ambitious were the three **'I-351' class** boats, known as the **'Type SH'** for **'Sen Ho'** or 'submarine replenisher'. Some 111 m (364 ft 2½ in) in length, these were the equivalent of the German Type XIV *Milchkühe*. They had triple hulls, between two of which could be stowed about 600 tons of aviation spirit for refuelling long-range flying-boats. Inboard was stowed a comprehensive range of stores, ordnance and even spare crews. Only one was ever completed.

'I-400' class Aircraft-carrying submarine

Unable to strike at targets on the US west coast, the Imperial Japanese Navy conceived the idea of submarines carrying a pair of bomber floatplanes. To accommodate these, the resultant boat would need to be large, with considerable beam as well as length to minimize ship motion during aircraft operations. It was expected that the aircraft would also be used as scouts. Thus the **'I-400 class** design, known as the **'Type STo'** for **'Sen-Toku'** or 'special submarine', was to combine several functions: control, attack and reconnaissance. The length was about 122 m (400 ft). A satisfactory length to beam ratio would have meant too deep a hull if constructed as a single cylinder; it was, therefore, built as a horizontal figure eight in section, reinforced for an diving depth of 100 m (328 ft).

Like most Japanese submarines, submerged performance was not very good and, with operations on the American seaboard in mind, the boats were equipped with a crude, fixed snorkel device.

The hangar was a separate pressure cylinder, accessible from within the hull, tilted slightly to the slope of the catapult track running the length of the foredeck. As completed,

the boats had an aircraft complement of three. The hangar was sited on the centreline, and the long bridge structure on top needed to be offset to port.

Large and unwieldy

The beam of the boats allowed for two diesels on each shaft driving through a common gearbox, but the 'I-400' class

Like a number of projects designed to have universal capabilities, the Japanese 'I-400'-class submarines fell short in almost every sense. Outsized, highly vulnerable and with only a vaguely defined role, only four of these aircraft-carrying submarines were ever completed.

were so big they must have been a problem to dive. Handling once submerged was clumsy.

In the event, like the 'I-13' class boats, their priority lapsed and only three were ever completed. They were never used and all were scuttled after the war. Like so many special-purpose warships, their need passed with their promoters.

Two 'I-400s', together with one example of the smaller 'I-15' class, are seen being prepared for scuttling after Japan's surrender. The hangars, tracks and offset towers are all clearly visible.

SPECIFICATION		
'I-400' class		**Speed:** speed surfaced 19 kts; speed submerged 7 kts; range surfaced 7,000 km (4,350 miles) at 14 kts; range submerged 110 km (68 miles) at 3 kts
Type: ocean-going submarine		
Displacement: 5,223 tons and 6,560 tons submerged		
Dimensions: length 121.90 m (400 ft); beam 12 m (39 ft 4 in); draught 7 m (23 ft)		**Armament:** one 140-mm (5.5-in) gun, 10 25-mm AA guns, three Aichi M6A1 aircraft (with torpedoes and bombs), and eight 533-mm (21-in) torpedo tubes (all forward) with 20 torpedoes
Propulsion: surfaced diesels delivering 5,780 kW (7,750 shp) and submerged electric motors delivering 1790 kW (2,400 shp) to two shafts		
		Complement: 140 men

'Ha-201' class
Fast coastal submarine

Like the German Type XXIIIs, the 'Ha-201'-class boats were small, fast and versatile. However, in spite of their prefabricated construction, they also appeared too late in the war to be of genuine use. Larger than their German equivalents, they had superior endurance.

Technically the most interesting of Japan's submarine designs, the small **'Ha-201'-class** boats, complemented by the 78-m

(256-ft) long 'I-201'-class boats, were the equivalent of the German Types XXIII and XXI respectively. In 1943, as the

Americans pressed ever closer to the home islands, the Japanese realized that they had the wrong types of submarine

to tackle the warships that were their chosen targets. Japan's strategy would best have been served by concentrating its existing boats on mercantile targets. However, persevering to the end, the Japanese developed the 'Ha-201' class or **'Type STS'** as a fast, manoeuvrable design to protect the home islands against warships. In common with similar German boats, however, these arrived too late to be of use, their enemy having achieved absolute superiority.

Using data derived from pre-war experiments with the 43-m (141-ft) long evaluation boat, *No. 71*, the Japanese planned the rapid production of 90 boats. Even with extensive prefabrication and the use of five separate yards, they managed to complete only

about ten, none of which completed an offensive patrol. A further 28 were in an advanced state of construction at the surrender.

Streamlined hull

The Japanese prefix 'Ha' corresponded to the letter 'C', denoting a small boat. The exterior was kept as clean of protuberances as possible. The boats were capable of 'grouping-up' for limited bursts of high submerged speed, necessary as they had only two torpedo tubes and attacks needed to be carried out from close range to guarantee success. Interestingly, they were propelled by a single,

centreline propeller, set abaft a cruciform control surface assembly, remarkably similar to modern arrangements. They possessed only limited endurance and their crew of 22 could be supported for about 15 days. A type of snorkel was fitted to allow prolonged periods

of submersion, necessary for the vessels to survive at a time when American air power was virtually unchallenged. Together with advanced German submarine types, these vessels yielded the Americans much valuable post-war data to apply to their 'Guppy' programmes.

SPECIFICATION	
'Ha-201' class **Type:** coastal submarine **Displacement:** 377 tons and 440 tons submerged **Dimensions:** length 53 m (173 ft 11 in); beam 4 m (13 ft 1 in); draught 3.40 m (11 ft 2 in) **Propulsion:** surfaced diesels delivering 298 kW (400 shp) and submerged electric motors delivering 930 kW (1,250 shp) to two shafts	**Performance:** speed surfaced 10.5 kts; speed submerged 13 kts; range surfaced 5,600 km (3,480 miles) at 10.5 kts; range submerged 185 km (115 miles) at 2 kts (3.7 km/h; 2.3 mph) **Armament:** one 7.7-mm (0.303-in) machine-gun, and two 533-mm (21-in) torpedo tubes (both forward) with four torpedoes **Complement:** 22 men

Type II
German coastal submarine

*The Type II coastal boats were not built after 1941. Shown here is **U-3**, an early command of the U-boat 'ace' Joachim Schepke. He sank two ships (totalling 2,348 tons) with **U-3** before January 1940, when he took command of **U-19**.*

In 1935 Germany repudiated the treaty that prevented her from operating submarines, forcing an Anglo-German agreement that allowed direct construction up to a total tonnage equivalent to 45 per cent of that operated by the British. A major task for the submarine supremo Karl Dönitz, was to break this figure down into numbers and types of boat that would fulfil a wartime strategy. One requirement was for a coastal submarine roughly equivalent to the UB series that operated successfully in UK waters during World War I. During the fallow years of the treaty, German design expertise was maintained through work for export, and the prototype for the **Type IIA** can thus be found in the **Vesikko**, which was

based on an amalgam of data from the UBII and the later UF. This boat was built in Finland in 1933 to German design.

Production

The Type IIAs went quickly into production and proved to be highly manoeuvrable, able to crash-dive in 25 seconds. Though the small displacement of the Type IIA favoured larger numbers in a restricted ceiling, the design was limited in terms of endurance, requiring progressive 'stretching' through the **Type IIB**, **Type IIC** and **Type IID** sub-types. The Type IIB had greater bunkerage and radius, the Type IIC was modelled on the Type IIB with more powerful engines, and the Type IID had saddle tanks.

The design encompassed a single hull with a trim tank at each end of the pressure hull, and an internal 'rapid dive' tank amidships. As only three torpedo tubes and limited reloads were carried, a load of mines was an alternative weapon rather than an addition.

As the sea war moved into the open ocean, construction of the Type IIs ceased in 1941 and the boats were used for training and trials purposes, including experimentation with snorkel gear. In total, six Type IIAs, 20 Type IIBs, eight Type IICs and 16 Type IIDs were built.

SPECIFICATION	
Type IID **Type:** coastal submarine **Displacement:** 314 tons surfaced and 364 tons submerged **Dimensions:** length 43.95 m (144 ft 2 in); beam 4.87 m (16 ft); draught 3.90 m (12 ft 9 in) **Propulsion:** surfaced diesels delivering 522 kW (700 shp) and submerged electric motors delivering 306 kW (410 shp) to two shafts	**Performance:** speed surfaced 13 kts; speed submerged 7.5 kts; range surfaced 6,500 km (4,040 miles) at 12 kts (22 km/h; 13.7 mph); range submerged 105 km (65 miles) at 4 kts (7.4 km/h; 4.6 mph) **Armament:** one (later four) 20-mm AA guns and three 533-mm (21-in) torpedo tubes (all forward) with six torpedoes **Complement:** 25 men

Type VII U-boat

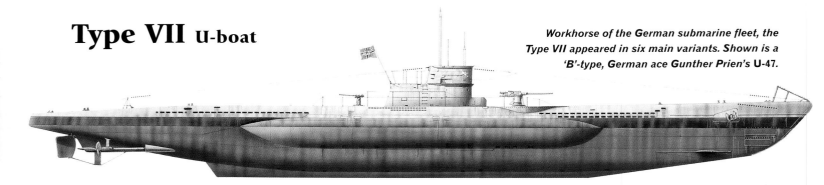

Workhorse of the German submarine fleet, the Type VII appeared in six main variants. Shown is a 'B'-type, German ace Gunther Prien's U-47.

Like that of the Type II, the design of the **Type VII** sea-going boat had its origins in a Finnish-built series of 1930–31 (the 'Vetehinen' class) and, beyond that, in the earlier UB III of 1918.

To permit the greatest number of hulls to be built within the ceiling tonnage agreed, size was severely limited in the 10 **Type VIIA** boats (626/745 tons). With performance and offensive capacity optimized, conditions aboard were somewhat spartan even with internal space saved by mounting the after tube in the casing (where it could be reloaded only with difficulty and then on the surface) and by the external stowage of spare torpedoes.

Bunkerage

The only real drawback of the VIIA was the small fuel storage for its intended role. To counter this, the **Type VIIB** carried an additional 33 tons of fuel in external saddle tanks, which gave it an additional range of about 2,500 nm (4,633 km; 2,879 miles) at 10 kt (18.5 km/h; 11.5 mph). The Type was also considerably more powerful and slightly faster than the VIIA. These boats (and all following the design) had two rudders instead of the one found on the VIIA, and this gave them even more agility.

Extra volume

External stowage of fuel rendered the Type VII vulnerable to depth-charging and the **Type VIIC** was therefore stretched to increase internal volume. This also allowed more powerful diesels to be fitted, a significant

factor in surface operations. The modified boat was highly successful and nearly 700 units were built, in various sub-variants, until the war's end. Later improvements included greater operational depths, reinforced towers, enhanced AA armament and snorts, all features reflecting developing Allied anti-submarine procedures. Significantly, most lacked a deck gun as surface operations became impossible.

While mines configured to the standard 21-in (533-mm) torpedo tube could be laid by all German submarines, these weapons were more likely to disable a target rather than sink it. To lay the largest moored mines, therefore, six Type VIIs were stretched by the addition of an extra 10-m (32-ft 9½-in) section amidships, containing five vertical free-flooding tubes, each containing three complete mine assemblies. These tubes protruded upward to 01 level into an extended tower. Designed in 1939–40, the class was known as the **Type VIID**. It can be considered the forefather of the big ballistic submarines of today's navies.

A further four boats, the **Type VIIF** sub-class, were similarly lengthened. In the additional space up to 25 spare torpedoes could be stowed for transfer, thereby extending the operational duration of other boats. But transfer operations, during which both boats were temporarily immobilized on the surface, became increasingly unpopular and were eventually abandoned. The **Type VIIE**, a study in improved propulsion, never progressed beyond the drawing board.

SPECIFICATION

Type VIIC
Type: sea-going submarine
Displacement: 769 tons surfaced and 871 tons submerged
Dimensions: length 66.50 m (218 ft 2 in); beam 6.20 m (20 ft 4 in); draught 4.75 m (15 ft 7 in)
Propulsion: surfaced diesels delivering 2089 kW (2,800 bhp) and submerged electric motors delivering 559 kW (750 hp) to two shafts
Speed: surfaced 17.5 kt (32.4 km/h; 20 mph) and submerged 7.5 kt (14 km/h; 8.6 mph)
Range: surfaced 15,750 km (9,785 miles) at 10 kt (18.5 km/h; 11.5 mph) and submerged 150 km (93 miles) at 4 kt (7.4 km/h; 4.6 mph)
Armament: one 88-mm (3.46-in) gun, one 37-mm AA gun, two (later eight) 20-mm AA guns, and five 533-mm (21-in) torpedo tubes (four forward and one aft) with 14 torpedoes
Complement: 44 men

The majority of U-boats that fought the Battle of the Atlantic were Type VIIs. Only 10 of the original Type VIIA were built before production switched to the VIIB submarine.

Type IX U-boat

The **'Type IX' class** was designed for ocean warfare. Loosely based on the smaller Type II, it differed in having a double hull. This increased internal volume by enabling fuel and ballast tanks to be sited externally. In turn, the extra hull improved survivability by cushioning the inner (pressure) hull from explosive shock, and gave the boats improved ability on the surface. Habitability was improved for operations of longer duration and the number of torpedoes carried, at 22, was about 50 per cent more than those of a Type VIIC. The deck gun was increased in calibre from 88 mm to 105 mm (3.46 in to 4.13 in). Diving depth was designed as 100 m (330 ft) operational and 200 m (660 ft) crush depth, although many boats went deeper. They had the same hydroplane and rudder layout as the Type VIIC. There was one periscope in the control room (deleted from Type IXC onwards) and two in the tower.

Developments

To give an idea of how designs developed during the war, the **Type IXA** and Type VIIA boats were, respectively, 76.50 m and 64.50 m (251 ft and 211 ft 7¼ in) long, while the final **Type IXD** and Type VIIF marks were 87.50 and 77.60 m (287 and 254 ft 7¼ in) long.

The objective with the Type IX variants was to improve range. Thus the eight Type IXA boats could achieve 19,500 km (12,120 miles) on the surface at 10 kt (18.5 km/h; 11.5 mph) yet, even before September 1939, were complemented by the first of 14 **Type IXB** boats capable of 22,250 km (13,825 miles). This type was the most successful overall, with each boat averaging over 100,000 tons of sinking. They had 23 torpedoes stored, which gave a determined U-boat commander a serious striking power that could be used night after night against the same convoy, as was often the case.

Minelayers

These were followed by the largest group, the **Type IXC**. This had storage for an additional 43 tons of fuel, giving it increased range of up to 25,000 km (15,535 miles) at 10 kt. This series omitted the control room periscope, leaving the boats with two tower scopes.

As mine-layers, they could carry 44 TMA or 66 TMB mines. There was also a **Type IXC-40** which was virtually identical to the IXC but had provision for extra bunkerage and was accordingly slightly heavier.

From the opening of hostilities, the Type IX worked the western and southern Atlantic. After Hitler declared war on the USA, it was supplemented by Type VIICs for the 'Happy Time', then ravaging shipping down the USA's eastern seaboard to the Caribbean.

As early as 1940, the **Type IXD** was on the board, with an extra 10.80-m (35-ft 4¾-in) section worked in. Two examples of the **Type IXD1**

*Commissioned in February 1944, **U**-805 carried out only one, fruitless patrol from March 1945. It surrendered on 14 May 1945 off New Hampshire, USA.*

U-boat crews lived in conditions of almost unspeakable squalor – cramped, crowded, damp, unhygienic and often too hot or too cold for comfort.

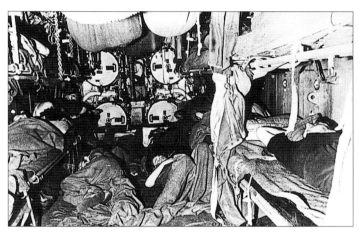

U-38 was commissioned in October 1938, and survived combat to be scuttled on 5 May 1945. It is pictured here returning from a two-month patrol.

were built, with no armament, but capable of stowing over 250 tons of fuel for the topping-up of other boats. The 29 **Type IXD2** boats were operational boats with a range of 58,400 km (36,290 miles), enabling them to work the Indian Ocean and even reach Japan. Some included a small single-seat towed gyro kite to increase their visual search radius. The **Type IXD2** was further refined to the Type IXD2–42, but only one of this variant was ever completed. Advanced diesels in the Type IXD1s gave a 21-kt (40-km/h; 24-mph) surface speed, but were found unreliable and not not repeated.

SPECIFICATION	
Type IXC	submerged 7.5 kt
Type: ocean-going submarine	**Range:** surfaced 25000 km
Displacement: 1,120 tons surfaced and 1,232 tons submerged	(15,535 miles) at 10 kt (18.5 km/h; 11.5 mph) and submerged 115 km
Dimensions: length 76.70 m (251 ft 8 in); beam 6.75 m (22 ft 2 in); draught 4.70 m (15 ft 5 in)	(71 miles) at 4 kt (7.5 km/h; 4.5 mph)
Propulsion: surfaced diesels delivering 3281 kW (4,400 hp) and submerged electric motors delivering 746 kW (1,000 hp) to two shafts	**Armament:** one 105-mm gun, one 37-mm AA gun, one 20-mm AA gun, and six 533-mm (21-in) torpedo tubes (four forward and two aft) with 22 torpedoes
Speed: surfaced 18.2 kt and	**Complement:** 48 men

Type X and Type XI Minelayer and long-range cruiser submarines

Planned at a time when the larger cruiser submarine idea was still in vogue, only three Type XIs were built, due to changing priorities. With a length of 115 m (377 ft), the four boats (U-112/-115) would have had a range of 25430 km (15,800 miles) at 12 kts.

Of the five types of U-boat identified by pre-war staff requirements, the patrol submarines of short-, medium- and long-endurance capabilities became the Type II, Type VII and Type IX respectively. The others were a 'small' minelayer and a long-range cruiser submarine; these became the **Type X** and **Type XI**.

Main variants

Only three Type XIs were ever built, these being large boats with a length of 115 m (377 ft) and a surface displacement of 3140 tons. Submersible surface raiders, they had a useful surface speed of 23 kts, and a superstructure that included stowage for a small scout seaplane and paired 127-mm (5-in) guns at each end.

Minelayer design

The **Type XA** was, in fact, a minelayer design, but never progressed beyond the drawing board, being superseded by the **Type XB**. These eight boats were smaller, with a circular-section pressure hull flanked by a slab-sided outer hull. On the centreline forward, six mine storages projected from keel to the top of a hump in the casing, each accommodating three mine assemblies. On each side, in the space between the hulls, were fitted 12 shorter stowages, each containing two mines.

The total load was, therefore, 66 large mines. Built to avoid action if possible, the Type XBs had only two torpedo tubes.

SPECIFICATION	
Type XB	submerged 7 kts
Type: minelaying submarine	**Range:** surfaced 344,00 km
Displacement: 1,763 tons surfaced and 2,177 tons submerged	(21,375 miles) at 10 kts; submerged 175 km (109 miles) at 4 kts
Dimensions: length 89.8 m (294 ft 7 in); beam 9.2 m (30 ft 2 in); draught 4.1 m (13 ft 6 in)	**Armament:** one 105-mm gun (later removed), one 37-mm AA gun, one (later four) 20-mm AA guns, two 533-mm (21-in) torpedo tubes (both aft) with 15 torpedoes, and 66 mines
Propulsion: surfaced diesels delivering 3,131 kW (4,200 shp) and submerged electric motors delivering 820 kW (1,100 hp) to two shafts	**Complement:** 52 men
Speed: surfaced 16.5 kts and	

Type XVII Coastal submarine

A combination of anti-submarine aircraft and radar gradually made it impossible for U-boats to use their high surface speed as a basis for attack and, to ensure their survival as a viable attack platform, submarines had to be optimized for submerged performance. Only a machinery system independent of surface air in combination with a cleaned-up, high-speed hull would suffice, and the **Type XVII** marked this step forward.

Radical powerplant

The key to the concept was the Walter closed-cycle propulsion system, which relied on the near-explosive decomposition of concentrated hydrogen peroxide in the presence of a catalyst. The reaction produced a high-temperature mix of steam and free oxygen, into which fuel oil was injected and fired, resulting in high-pressure gases that drove a conventional turbine. Unfortunately, almost any impurity could act as a catalyst to initiate the process at a disastrously early stage.

Prototype boats

Two prototype boats proved the machinery feasible, and the system was used for the Type XVIIs. A drawback was the extreme thirst of the system, dictating a small boat with a single propeller. For cruise purposes, this was driven by a conventional diesel/electric combination, with the Walter coupled up only to force or decline an engagement.

The hull was cleaned up, with no guns and few protuberances. It was of figure-eight section, formed of two overlapping circular pressure hulls of unequal diameter. In practice, the length to beam ratio was too high, resulting in too much drag, so the **Type XVIIA** never realized its theoretical top speed of 25 kts, possible with two turbines on a common shaft. As a result, only four boats were built, the modified **Type XVIIB** (three completed) having only one turbine. Space was available for only two torpedo tubes, with one reload for each, a deficiency offset by the increasing lethality of the weapon.

A projected **Type XVIIK** would have abandoned the volatile Walter for conventional diesels aspirated with pure oxygen stored aboard.

Type XVII potential

Development of the Type XVII had begun at a time when the balance of naval power had shifted in favour of the Allies. But for a lack of resources, it is possible that this class, together with the Types XXI and XXIII, could have helped return naval control to Germany.

SPECIFICATION	
Type XVIIB	shaft
Type: coastal submarine	**Speed:** surfaced 9 kts and submerged 21.5 kts on Walter engine or 5 kts on electric motor
Displacement: 312 tons surfaced and 357 tons submerged	
Dimensions: length 41.5 m (136 ft 2 in); beam 3.4 m (11 ft 2 in); draught 4.3 m (14 ft)	**Range:** surfaced 5550 km (3,450 miles) at 9 kts and submerged 210 km (131 miles) on Walter engine or 75 km (47 miles) on electric motor
Propulsion: surfaced diesel delivering 157 kW (210 shp) and submerged Walter closed-cycle engine delivering 1,865 kW (2,500 hp) or electric motor delivering 57 kW (77 shp) to one	**Armament:** two 533-mm (21-in) torpedo tubes (both forward) with four torpedoes
	Complement: 19 men

Type XXI
Ocean-going submarine

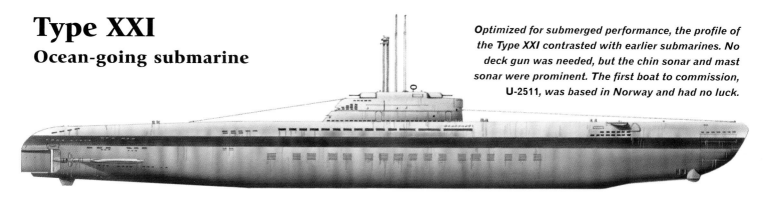

Optimized for submerged performance, the profile of the Type XXI contrasted with earlier submarines. No deck gun was needed, but the chin sonar and mast sonar were prominent. The first boat to commission, U-2511, was based in Norway and had no luck.

One of the most influential designs in the history of the submarine, the **Type XXI** was to set standards until the introduction of the nuclear boat a decade later. With the lower pressure hull packed with high-power density cells, the Type XXIs could, for the first time, develop more power submerged than surfaced. Their main propulsion motors were supplemented by low-power units for silent manoeuvring.

'Double-bubble' hull

Like that in the Type XVII, the pressure hull of the Type XXI was of 'double-bubble' cross section, though externally framed. It was prefabricated in eight sections at varous sites,

being brought together for final assembly at the Blohm und Voss shipyard in Hamburg. The external framing increased volume and facilitated the addition of a hydrodynamically clean outer skin. Construction was all-welded for a target of three boats per week in a programme to produce an eventual 1,500 units (**U-2500** to **U-4000**). Most other submarine programmes were curtailed or cancelled to this end.

The Type XXIs were designed to spend their full patrol time submerged, so the snort was used mainly to run diesels for battery recharge. Habitability was greatly improved, with air-conditioning and air-regeneration apparatus.

The only guns were paired automatic weapons set into the forward and after profiles of the elongated fin. A combination of active and passive sonars gave a full torpedo-firing solution without using the periscope.

Two proposed variants, the **Type XXIB** and **Type XXIC**,

would have increased the number of torpedo tubes from six to 12 and 18 respectively by the insertion of extra sections into the hull. Fortunately for the Allies, the type never became fully operational. Several were sunk, however, all by Allied aircraft and in home waters.

SPECIFICATION	
Type XXIA	
Type: ocean-going submarine	**Speed:** surfaced 15.5 kts and submerged 16 kts on main electric motor or 3.5 kts on creeping electric motors
Displacement: 1,621 tons surfaced and 1,819 tons submerged	
Dimensions: length 76.7 m (251 ft 8 in); beam 6.6 m (21 ft 9 in); draught 6.2 m (20 ft 4 in)	**Range:** surfaced 28,800 km (17,895 miles) and submerged 525 km (325 miles) at 6 kts
Propulsion: surfaced diesels delivering 2,985 kW (4,000 shp) and submerged electric motors delivering 3,730 kW (5,000 shp) or electric motors delivering 169 kW (226 shp) to two shafts	**Armament:** four 30-mm or 20-mm AA guns and six 533-mm (21-in) torpedo tubes (all forward) with 23 torpedoes
	Complement: 57 men

Type XXIII High-speed coastal submarine

The **Type XXIII** was small and agile for shallow water operations and, like its larger cousin the Type XXI, packed with high-capacity battery cells for maximum underwater speed. Its hull had the 'double-bubble' cross section over the forward half but was internally framed and prefabricated in four sections. The partial length

lower hull contained both batteries and some ballast and fuel capacity.

Rapid diver

A departure was the near abandonment of outer casing except in the transitional zones and this, together with a low reserve buoyancy, made for rapid crash-dive times, less than

10 seconds being recorded.

No guns were carried and only two torpedo tubes were fitted. With no space inboard for orthodox loading, the boat needed to be trimmed by the stern to expose the bow caps. Attacks had to be carried out positively, from close range and with very fast or very stealthy disengagements.

Final confrontation

That this was possible was shown by the last U-boat attack in European waters, which occurred on 7 May 1945, well inside the Firth of Forth, when the **U-2336** sank two British merchantmen of an escorted convoy. By this time, a total of 62 Type XXIII submarines had entered service and their only losses had been to aircraft.

The small size of the German Type XXIII is apparent from this view of U-2326 alongside a Dundee quay in May 1945. Few fittings protrude to spoil the flow over the very clean hull and tower. Surprisingly, only two bow torpedo tubes were fitted to the boat.

SPECIFICATION	
Type XXIII	
Type: coastal submarine	shp) to one shaft
Displacement: 232 tons surfaced and 256 tons submerged	**Speed:** surfaced 10 kts and submerged 12.5 kts on main electric motor or 2 kts on creeping electric motor
Dimensions: length 34.1 m (112 ft); beam 3 m (9 ft 10 in); draught 3.8 m (12 ft 3 in)	**Range:** surfaced 2,500 km (1,555 miles) and submerged 325 km (202 miles) at 4 kts
Propulsion: surfaced diesel delivering 433 kW (580 shp) and submerged electric motor delivering 447 kW (600 shp) or electric motor delivering 26 kW (35	**Armament:** two 533-mm (21-in) torpedo tubes (both forward) with two torpedoes
	Complement: 14 men

'Sirena', 'Perla', 'Adua' and 'Acciaio' classes
Sea-going submarines

Dating from a period of great expansion for the Italian navy's submarine arm, the 12 **'Sirena'-class** submarines were also known as the **'600'-class** boats. This figure was indicative of their standard surface displacement and, though the final design exceeded it by a considerable margin, they proved very useful boats for the constricted conditions of the Mediterranean. Their detail design was greatly influenced by that of the preceding 'Argonauta' class, but, as they were laid down before the latter's entry into service, they did not benefit from working experience. Simple and robust, they were heavily used and suffered accordingly, only one surviving beyond the armistice of September 1943.

'Perla' class
Ten almost identical derivatives, the **'Perla' class**, followed on.

Above: A more powerful 'Adua'/'Perla' with reduced tower, 'Acciaio' was lead boat of a class of 13. The submarine was sunk by HM Submarine Unruly on 13 July 1943.

The Italian submarine Perla at Beirut after capture in 1942. The shadow accentuates the unusual tumblehome of the casing.

SPECIFICATION	
'Sirena' class	submerged 8 kts
Displacement: between 679 and 701 tons surfaced and between 842 and 860 tons submerged	**Range:** surfaced 9,000 km (5,590 miles) at 8 kts and submerged 135 km (84 miles) at 4 kts
Dimensions: length 60.18 m (197 ft 6 in); beam 6.45 m (21 ft 2 in); draught 4.7 m (15 ft 5 in)	**Armament:** one 100-mm (3.9-in) gun, two (later four) 13.2-mm (0.52-in) machine-guns, and six 533-mm (21-in) torpedo tubes (four forward and two aft) with 12 torpedoes
Propulsion: surfaced diesels delivering 895 kW (1,200 shp) and submerged electric motors delivering 597 kW (800 shp) to two shafts	**Complement:** 45
Speed: surfaced 14 kts and	

Two of these, **Iride** and **Onice**, served – controversially – under Spanish Nationalist colours during the Spanish Civil War. During World War II, the *Iride*, together with the **Ambra**, were converted to carry SLC human torpedoes. The latter boat had already distinguished itself when, two days after the Battle of Cape Matapan, she sunk the British cruiser HMS *Bonaventure*.

After conversion, *Ambra* attacked the harbour at Algiers in December 1942, heavily damaging four ships totalling 20,000 gross registered tons.

Yet another virtual repeat class had followed in the

Usefully sized 'Mediterranean' boats, the 17-strong 'Adua' class were named after places in Italian North Africa. Boats of the class were modified for use as carriers for the SLC human torpedo.

17 **'Adua'-class** boats, launched during 1936–38. Two of these were converted to carry SLCs and one of these, the **Scirè**, was particularly successful. Scirè attacked Gibraltar on no less than four occasions, the raid of September 1941 accounting for two ships, including the auxiliary tanker Denbydale. The vessel's greatest coup, however, was in December 1941, when its three SLCs put the battleships HMS Queen Elizabeth and HMS Valiant, together with a tanker, on the bottom of Alexandria harbour. Scirè was itself sunk by the anti-submarine trawler Islay outside Haifa in August 1942,

The final expression of the '600' type was in the enlarged 13-boat **'Acciaio' class** of 1941–42.

'Cagni' class Ocean-going submarine

It is not clear how the Italian navy, with few commitments outside the Mediterranean, could justify investment in submarines for ocean warfare. Italy's merchant marine was of reasonable size, but could not be protected on a worldwide basis by Italy's surface fleet, which was geared to short-endurance, high-speed undertakings, so coherent operations in the defence of trade were out of the question, even against the rival neighbour France. Despite this, the four **'Cagni'-class** submarines were all laid down in September and October 1939 at the outbreak of hostilities between Germany and the Anglo-French alliance. As these submarines were aimed specifically at long-range commerce raiding, one can only speculate that Italy, as yet uninvolved, saw involvement against the maritime powers as only a matter of time.

Large-scale boats

The 'Cagnis' were the largest attack boats yet built for the Italian navy and armed with light 450-mm (17.7-in) torpedoes. Though longer than the standard 450-mm weapons and enabling them to carry a warhead of 200 kg (441 lb) in place of the more usual 110 kg (243 lb), this payload was still much less than the 270 kg (595 lb) of the larger 533-mm (21-in) torpedoes. The torpedoes were to be used primarily against 'soft' targets,

Ammiraglio Cagni *returns from sea with a damaged after casing. The heavy armament of two 100-mm and four 13.2-mm guns can be seen, also the generally bulky appearance typical of most Italian ocean-going boats.*

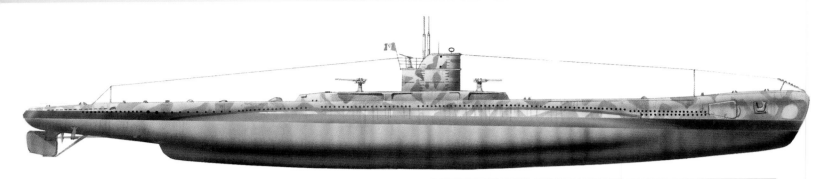

Name ship and sole survivor of its class, **Ammiraglio Cagni** *is seen here with a modified and rather Germanic-style tower, reducing the vessel's radar profile.*

SPECIFICATION	
'Cagni' class **Displacement:** 1,680 tons surfaced and 2,170 tons submerged **Dimensions:** length 87.9 m (288 ft 5 in); beam 7.76 m (25 ft 6 in); draught 5.72 m (18 ft 9 in) **Propulsion:** surfaced diesels delivering 3260 kW (4,370 shp) and submerged electric motors delivering 1,345 kW (1,800 shp) to two shafts	**Speed:** surfaced 17 kts and submerged 8.5 kts **Range:** surfaced 20,000 km (12,425 miles) at 12 kts; submerged 200 km (124 miles) at 3.5 kts **Armament:** two 100-mm (3.9-in) guns, four 13.2-mm (0.52-in) machine-guns, and 14 450-mm (17.7-in) torpedo tubes (eight forward and six aft) with 36 torpedoes **Complement:** 82 men

so this was judged acceptable, as was their lack of range. The advantage it brought was the ability to carry 36 torpedoes, the eight tubes forward and six aft permitting large spreads to enhance chances of success. An unusual feature was that the torpedoes could be transferred from one end of the boat to the other. Two large deck guns were also carried to conserve torpedoes.

Unfortunately for Italian plans, the Mediterranean sea war required the keeping open of the vital North Africa supply route. Following heavy surface losses, the navy pressed large submarines into this service. In completing 15 trips, three of the four boats in the class were sunk in only three months. Only the name boat **Ammiraglio Cagni** worked as designed, but unsuccessfully, sinking less than 10,000 gross registered tons in two long patrols.

'Archimede' class Ocean-going submarine

The four **'Archimede'-class** submarines were enlargements of the preceding 'Settembrini' design, its ballasting rearranged to improve bunker capacity. An extra gun was also fitted, in keeping with the boats' 'ocean' role. All were launched in 1934 and, as part of their covert support of the Nationalist cause during the Spanish Civil War, the Italians transferred two to Spanish colours. These were the **Archimede** and the **Torricelli** and, to conceal their transfer, two of the follow-on 'Brins' assumed their names. The three classes of boat formed a closely related group, used extensively in colonial work.

Wartime action

That part of the Italian navy stationed in the Red Sea in June 1940 was cut off from the homeland and severely handled by the British as a threat astride the route from the Suez Canal eastward. The *Galilei* sank a Norwegian tanker less than a week after the outbreak of hostilities and then, only two days later, stopped a neutral for examination. On the following day, the vessel was intercepted by the British anti-submarine trawler *Moonstone*, which inflicted damage that caused the boat to fill with noxious fumes. Unable to dive, *Galilei* fought it out on the surface. Far larger, faster and more heavily armed than its opponent, *Galilei* should have been successful had not the *Moonstone* shot up every gun's crew that emerged topside. With most officers dead, the demoralized crew surrendered. Captured, the boat assumed the British pennant *P711* until its disposal in 1946.

Replacement

The replacement for *Galilei*, *Torricelli* was also apprehended by British forces. Forced to the surface near Perim Island, the boat engaged in a gun action with three 'K'-class destroyers and a sloop. *Torricelli* was, inevitably, sunk but not before hitting both the sloop and the destroyer HMS *Khartoum*. The hit on the latter was on one of the banks of torpedo tubes and it seems that this caused a compressed air explosion followed by the detonation of a torpedo warhead. The ship was destroyed.

SPECIFICATION	
'Archimede' class **Displacement:** 985 tons surfaced and 1,259 tons submerged **Dimensions:** length 70.5 m (231 ft 4 in); beam 6.83 m (22 ft 5 in); draught 4.1 m (13 ft 6 in) **Propulsion:** surfaced diesels delivering 2,235 kW (3,000 shp) and submerged electric motors delivering 970 kW (1,300 shp) to two shafts	**Speed:** surfaced 17 kts and submerged 8 kts **Range:** surfaced 19,000 km (11,805 miles) at 8 kts; submerged 195 km (121 miles) at 3 kts **Armament:** two 100-mm (3.9-in) guns, two 13.2-mm (0.52-in) machine-guns, and eight 533-mm (21-in) torpedo tubes (four forward and four aft) with 16 torpedoes **Complement:** 55 men

The 'Archimede'-class submarine **Galilei** *is seen about to be taken in tow by the destroyer* **Kandahar***. Noxious gas filled the submarine, forcing its surrender.*

'Saphir' class Minelayer

Like the Royal Navy, the French had a six-strong class of minelaying submarines, the **'Saphir' class** of 1925–29. These were smaller than the British boats and geared to Mediterranean operations. As a mine capable of being launched through a standard torpedo tube had not been developed, the hull design was dominated by the mine stowage. The design for this had been produced by a well-known submarine builder, Normand, but was based on the British 'E'-class minelayers of 1914–18: 16 vertical chutes were built into the space between the widely separated double hulls, in four groups of four, and each chute could accommodate two mines. These were of special manufacture, which proved a disadvantage. The British had abandoned the system in favour of laying over the stern with the mines stowed within the upper casing.

Stretched 'Emeraude'

Four stretched versions, continuing the 'jewel' names as the **'Emeraude' class**, were due to follow in 1937–38. Lengthened by almost 7 m (23 ft), they would have carried 25 per cent more mines, but only the nameship was ever laid down and this was destroyed on the slip at the occupation.

Of the 'Saphirs', three (**Nautilus**, **Saphir** and **Turquoise**) were taken by the enemy at Bizerta and one (**Le Diamant**) was scuttled at Toulon. The **Rubis** and **Perle** operated throughout the war under the Free French flag (though tthe latter was sunk in error by British aircraft in July 1944). The *Rubis* operated with the British Home Fleet from April 1940, laying mines in Norwegian waters. Between then and the end of 1944, she carried out 22 successful minelaying operations, most to interrupt the enemy's coast-hugging mercantile routes. The total of 15 ships destroyed on her mines included several Scandinavians carrying German ore cargoes, a minesweeper and four small anti-submarine vessels. *Rubis* also torpedoed and sank a Finnish vessel.

*The most successful minelaying submarine of the war, **Rubis** was responsible in its 22 minelaying patrols for the sinking of at least 15 vessels. These included five warships as well as vessels running iron ore in coastal convoys to Germany.*

SPECIFICATION	
'Saphir' class	submerged
Displacement: 761 tons surfaced; 925 tons submerged	**Endurance:** 12,970 km (8,059 miles) at 7.5 kts surfaced; 148 km (92 miles) at 4 kts submerged
Dimensions: length 65.9 m (216 ft 2½ in); beam 7.12 m (23 ft 5 in); draught 4.3 m (14 ft 1 in)	**Armament:** one 75-mm (2.95-in) gun, three 550-mm (21.65-in) torpedo tubes (two bow and one stern), two 400-mm (15.75-in) torpedo tubes in a trainable mounting, and 32 mines
Propulsion: two diesels delivering 969.4 kW (1,300 shp) and two electric motors delivering 820.3 kW (1,100 shp) to two shafts	
Speed: 12 kts surfaced; 9 kts	**Complement:** 42 men

'Surcouf' class
Cruiser submarine

Most of the major maritime nations at some time or other experimented with the idea of the cruiser submarine. All were larger than usual, with an exceptional surface armament and good endurance. Some carried an aircraft to increase their effective search radius. The only design to combine all these features, reasonably successfully, in one hull was the **Surcouf**. Ordered under the 1926 programme as the first in a class of three, it was destined to be the only unit of the **'Surcouf' class**, and the largest submarine in the world in terms of displacement, though it was shorter than both the American 'Narwhal' and the Japanese 'A' boats.

At the time of the Washington Treaty, the British *M1* to *M3* had 12-in (304.8-mm) guns and, to prevent further escalation in this direction (though even these were over large and totally unwieldy), the treaty limited future submarines to 8-in (203.2-mm) weapons. Only the French ever fitted the latter, and these to the *Surcouf*, paired in a complex pressure-tight turret.

*Among the largest submarines of its time, **Surcouf** was unique in possessing twin 203.2-mm (8-in) guns. The boat was also fitted with a specially designed Besson floatplane, which was hangared immediately behind the conning tower.*

This structure was faired into a pressure-tight 'hangar' abaft it and containing a specially-designed Besson M.B.411 floatplane. This had to be taken out and the wings attached before it could be lowered into the water, a time-consuming

Surcouf, seen here in the Clyde estuary, was a product of the inter-war concept of the 'cruiser submarine', espoused by many navies. The vessel was the closest of all such designs to being a success, without ever having the chance to be employed against enemy merchant shipping.

and highly risky business which, while acceptable in 1926, was certainly not in 1939–45.

The torpedo tube fit featured four 550-mm (21.65-in) tubes set in an orthodox bow arrangement, with six reloads; one quadruple 550-mm trainable mounting in the casing three-quarters aft; and a quadruple 400-mm (15.75-in) trainable mounting in the casing right aft, with four reloads.

The suggested mode of operation of submarines such as these was always rather uncertain and the Surcouf, like the rest of its kind, was never to

find a proper role. Seized in Plymouth in July 1940, the vessel was operated by a Free French crew on several Atlantic patrols. In December 1941, Surcouf participated with three French corvettes in the seizure of the Vichy islands of St Pierre and Miquelon, in the St Lawrence estuary. In February 1942, the boat finally sank in the Caribbean after a collision.

SPECIFICATION	
'Surcouf' class	**Endurance:** 18,531 km (11,515 miles) at 10 kts surfaced; 111 km (69 miles) at 5 kts submerged
Displacement: 3,270 tons surfaced; 4,250 tons submerged	
Dimensions: length 110 m (360 ft 11 in); beam 9 m (29 ft 6 in); draught 9.07 m (29 ft 9 in)	**Armament:** two 203.2-mm (8-in) guns, two 37-mm guns, eight 550-mm (21.65-in) torpedo tubes (four bow and four in a trainable mounting), and four 400-mm (15.75-in) torpedo tubes (in a trainable mounting aft)
Propulsion: two diesels delivering 5667.3 kW (7,600 shp) and two electric motors delivering 2535.4 kW (3,400 shp) to two shafts	
Speed: 18 kts surfaced; 8.5 kts submerged	**Complement:** 118 men

Old 'S' class Coastal submarine

S28 as it appeared in 1943. One of the Holland-designed boats, this vessel, along with its sisters, saw action early in the war, and at that time was not devoid of success. While most of the class was replaced by 1943, S28 was lost in 1944.

Like the 'O' and 'R' classes, the World War I-designed **'S'-class** (or **'Sugar'**) boats were well represented in the US Navy in December 1941, when the US found itself in World War II. Sixty-four of these boats were

still available, though many had for years been involved only in training. All suffered from having been designed at a time when the submarine was regarded by the US Navy as a weapon for use in the defence of home

territory. None, therefore, had adequate endurance for the Pacific operations that had not been foreseen, since Japan was an ally in 1914–18.

The 'O' and 'R' boats were fitted with 18-in (457-mm) torpedo tubes and had poor endurance, and the general specification for the improved 'S' class had been put out to competition. At this time, US submarine practice was dominated by the companies

owned by Holland and Lake; each tendered, together with the Portsmouth Navy Yard. Three prototypes were built, but the *S2* by Lake was considered unsatisfactory. In total, 25 Holland-designed boats, the **'S' class Group 1**, were launched between 1918 and 1922, followed by six of an improved version known as the **'S' class Group 3**. The 15 boats of the **'S' class Group 2** were to the naval design (some built by Lake's

SPECIFICATION	
Old 'S' class	**Speed:** 14.5 kts surfaced; 11 kts submerged
Displacement: 854 tons surfaced; 1,065 tons submerged	
Dimensions: length 66.83 m (219 ft 3 in); beam 6.3 m (20 ft 8½ in); draught 4.72 m (15 ft 6 in)	**Endurance:** 9,270 km (5,760 miles) at 10 kts surfaced
	Armament: one 4- or 3-in (102- or 76.2-mm) gun and four or five 533-mm (21-in) torpedo tubes (all bow or four bow and one stern) for 12 torpedoes
Propulsion: two diesels delivering 894.8 kW (1,200 shp) and two electric motors delivering 1118.6 kW (1,500 shp) to two shafts	
	Complement: 42 men

yard), and these were followed by four improved boats, the **'S' class Group 4**. All had about the same speed, armament and complement, but varied greatly in size and, somewhat, in endurance. All were of double-hulled design, one carried a

seaplane for an experimental period, and four were fitted with an extra tube aft.

Six were transferred to the Royal Navy early in the war, one then being passed on to Poland. As the **Jastrzab,** this was sunk in error by the British during a

convoy action in 1942; one of the escorts concerned was also ex-American, the 'four-piper' HMS *St Albans*. Most of the American 'S'-class boats in the Far East had been replaced by newer boats by late 1943, but some had success. Before the

Savo Island action, for instance, Mikawa's approach was reported by the **S38**, and the **S44** exacted a toll on the victors by sinking the *Kako*. In October 1943 this old veteran's luck ran out and she was sunk near the Kamchatka peninsula.

'Narwhal' class
Cruiser submarine

SPECIFICATION	
'Narwhal' class	**Speed:** 17 kts surfaced; 8 kts
Displacement: 2,730 tons surfaced;	submerged
3,900 tons submerged	**Endurance:** 33354 km (20,725 miles)
Dimensions: length 112.95 m (370 ft	at 10 kts surfaced; 93 km (58 miles)
7 in); beam 10.13 m (33 ft 3 in);	at 5 kts submerged
draught 4.8 m (15 ft 9 in)	**Armament:** two single 6-in (152-mm)
Propulsion: combination drive with	guns and six 21-in (533-mm)
four diesels delivering 4026.8 kW	torpedo tubes (four bow and two
(5,400 shp) and two electric motors	stern) later increased to 10 tubes
delivering 1894.1 kW (2,540 shp) to	for 40 torpedoes
two shafts	**Complement:** 89 men

USS **Nautilus** *in pre-war trim. The two 'Narwhals' were thought to be too slow for fleet submarine work during the war, and were often used for clandestine operations, although it was* **Nautilus** *that finished off the stricken* **Soryu** *after Midway.*

The two **'Narwhal'-class** units **USS** *Narwhal* and **USS** *Nautilus* must be classed as a group with the **USS** *Argonaut* that preceded them. The large German transport submarines that worked the eastern US seaboard during World War I made a great impression on the navy, and in the early 1920s

designs were produced for a minelayer (**V-4**, later **Argonaut**) and two cruiser submarines *Narwhal* (**V-5**) and *Nautilus* (**V-6**). All were large, and all longer than the monstrous French *Surcouf*. As a minelayer, the *V-4* could load 60 mines, which were laid through two tubes exiting beneath the counter.

Forward of the after bulkhead of the engine room, the 'Narwhals' were nearly identical, mounting two torpedo tubes aft in place of the mine stowage, a smaller demand on space that allowed for their shorter length. Upwards of 36 torpedoes could be carried, both within the hull and the casing topside. To stretch them further, two 6-in (152-mm) deck guns were mounted, the largest in any American submarine.

All were considered slow by US standards, and though due to be re-engined, only the

Nautilus was so modified by the outbreak of war. The latter was fitted with two extra tubes in the after casing and the other two gained four, all in the amidships casing, two firing forward and two aft.

Clandestine work

Despite the US fleet's shortage of submarines in 1942, these boats were considered too slow and vulnerable for combat patrols and were modified for clandestine operations, running personnel and supplies. The *Nautilus* had facilities to refuel long-range seaplanes, but was never so used during hostilities. All operated between their bases in west Australia and the Philippines. The *Nautilus* finished off the Japanese carrier *Soryu* after Midway, and landed personnel on an unoccupied island near Tarawa to build a secret airstrip. The *Argonaut* was lost in 1943.

Narwhal *and its sisters were the largest submarines in* **US** *service until the arrival of the nuclear submarines of the 1950s. In a scene from the happier pre-war days,* **Narwhal** *is seen towing a seaplane with engine trouble back to Pearl Harbor.*

New 'S' class Fleet submarine

Known as the **New 'S' class** because the early units confusingly took pendants of the Old 'S'-class boats still in service, 16 boats were built in two very similar groups. They were also referred to as the **'Salmon'** or **'Sargo' class**. Their design was based closely upon that of the preceding 1,320-ton 'R' class, but differed particularly in having a deeper stern to accommodate an increase in the after torpedo tube complement from two to four tubes.

The 'R'- and 'S'-class boats were the first all-welded submarines in the US Navy and, though techniques were still being developed, workmanship was sound, as evinced by the survival of the **USS Salmon (SS-182)**, lead boat of the **New 'S'-class Group 1**, which was severely depth-charged in October 1944 by four Japanese escorts after torpedoing a tanker off Kyushu. The combination of

concussion and the effects of overpressures through being driven far below design depth left the hull dished between frames, but the boat made it home. Irreparable, *Salmon* was eventually scrapped. The double hull of the American boats was a protective feature, provided that the ballast and fuel tanks within retained an ullage space over the liquid contents.

Composite propulsion systems were fitted in some, arrangements whereby the two forward diesels drove generators directly and the two after units were geared to the shafts, the gearing being shared also by two propulsion motors on each shaft. Though complex, the system proved satisfactory.

Torpedo armament

Twelve reload torpedoes were located within the pressure hull and four more in external stowage in the casing, an

arrangement vulnerable to the effects of depth charge attack. Two mines could be carried for each internal torpedo and laid through the tubes. The original 3-in (76.2-mm) gun fitted was changed to a 4-in (102-mm) weapon in most of the boats. Wartime modifications saw the bulky 'sails' cut down to a profile similar to later classes.

The launch of USS Swordfish on 1 April 1941. Few of those present could have foreseen that in nine months, within a week of Pearl Harbor, Swordfish would sink the first of 1,113 Japanese merchant ships to fall victim to the US submarine fleet.

The **New 'S' class Group 2** included the **USS Squalus (SS-192)**, which foundered through an induction valve failure while on trials in May 1939. Salvaged and refitted, the boat survived the war as the **USS Sailfish**. The **USS Swordfish (SS-193)** was credited with the first Japanese merchantman sunk, a week after the outbreak of war.

SPECIFICATION	
New 'S' class ('Salmon' group)	submerged
Displacement: 1,440 tons surfaced and 2,200 tons submerged	**Endurance:** 18532 km (11,515 miles) at 10 kts surfaced; 158 km (98 miles) at 5 kts submerged
Dimensions: length 93.88 m (308 ft); beam 7.98 m (26 ft 2½ in); draught 4.34 m (14 ft 3 in)	**Armament:** one 3-in (76.2-mm) gun (upgraded to one 4-in/102-mm gun in most units) and eight 21-in (533-mm) torpedo tubes (four bow, four stern) for 24 (later 20) torpedoes
Propulsion: composite drive with four 4101.4 kW (5,500 shp) diesels and four 1983.6 kW (2,660 shp) electric motors driving two shafts	
Speed: 21 kts surfaced; 9 kts	**Complement:** 75 men

'Gato' class Fleet submarine

From the New 'S' class design the Americans developed the 'T' class submarine, a dozen of which were launched in barely

13 months, mostly in 1940. They differed primarily in receiving two extra tubes forward (10 in all) and later substituting a

specially modified 5-in (127-mm) deck gun for the earlier 4-in (102-mm) gun, or 3-in (76.2-mm) gun in some cases. This gradual

evolutionary process was successful and produced at the right time a submarine with acceptable characteristics for

the Pacific War. What was needed was a long endurance and self-sufficiency. Because of the distances involved, patrols were much longer than those in the European theatre and more boats were needed to maintain numbers on station.

Improved 'T' class

Thus the **'Gato' class** was an improved 'T' and went into volume production, the first of class, the **USS *Drum* (SS-228)**, being completed shortly before hostilities commenced. Officially capable of operating down to 91 m (300 ft), they often went deeper. The earlier boats had a large, solid looking sail, similar to pre-war designs. These were soon reduced as boats came in for repair but, although the structure could be lowered, the very high standards ('shears') demanded by the long periscopes remained a lofty feature. Operating on the

*USS **Darter** aground on Bombay Shoal during the Battle of Leyte Gulf. After the triumph of the previous day when the submarine sank the cruiser **Atago** and also damaged the cruiser **Takao**, **Darter** was badly damaged and finally scuttled on 24 October.*

surface more than would have been possible in European waters, they began also to accumulate varied outfits of automatic weapons, regular and non-regular, the structures gaining various platforms to support them. Even extra main-calibre deck guns appeared, all in the cause of making the 24 torpedoes aboard last longer.

After 73 boats, the hull was improved by the adoption of HT steels and advanced sections, increasing their official limit to 122-m (400-ft) depths. Some 256 were ordered and known as the **'Balao' class**, but only 122 were completed, a further 10 unfinished hulls being scrapped.

The combined group formed the backbone of the US Navy's wartime submarine strength,

A 'Gato'-class boat of late 1942. By this time, production was approaching three per month from three separate yards, and operational experience was being incorporated through the adoption of a smaller sail and more weapons for surface work.

achieved much and suffered 29 losses. Operations in European waters were limited; early in 1943, a few boats carried out beach reconnaissance and support missions off North Africa. Post-war, with the

example of German developments, many were modernized under the GUPPY programmes, remaining the greater part of the fleet's underwater arm until the introduction of nuclear boats.

SPECIFICATION	
'Gato' class **Displacement:** 1,525 tons surfaced and 2,415 tons submerged **Dimensions:** length 95.02 m (311 ft 9 in); beam 8.31 m (27 ft 3 in); draught 4.65 m (15 ft 3 in) **Propulsion:** four diesels delivering 4026.8 kW (5,400 shp) and four electric motors delivering 2043.2 kW (2,740 shp) to two shafts	**Speed:** 20 kts surfaced; 8.5 kts submerged **Endurance:** 21,316 km (13,245 miles) at 10 kts surfaced and 175 km (109 miles) at 5 kts submerged **Armament:** one 5-in (127-mm) gun and 10 21-in (533-mm) torpedo tubes (six bow, four stern) for 24 torpedoes **Complement:** 80 men

'Tench' class Fleet submarine

The **'Tench' class** marked the ultimate refinement in the basic design that could be traced back to the 'P' class. Externally they were virtually identical with the 'Balao' class, and so closely related was the design that some later 'Balao' contracts were converted to 'Tenches'. Although 25 boats had been completed by the end of

hostilities, most were still working up in home waters; less than a dozen saw operational duty and none were lost. Total production was 33 boats between 1944 and 1946, with another 101 cancelled or scrapped incomplete.

New machinery

Differences, though not obvious,

were important. The first concerned machinery. In the 'Balao' class, the four diesels each ran a direct-coupled generator, which served both to charge batteries and power the electric propulsion motors when surfaced. Each shaft had two motors, coupled to it via reduction gearing. Both the high-speed motors and the

reduction gear were noisy (to the extent where it was fortunate that Japanese ASW techniques and equipment were so backward). Reduction gears were also expensive, temperamental, easy to damage and, traditionally, a slow delivery item in the US (as was the turbo-electric propulsion in battleships). It made sense,

A 'Tench'-class submarine in its natural environment, on the surface. By the time that this photo was taken, in June/July 1945, there were very few targets for the highly successful sub skippers, Japanese vessels having been all but swept from the seas.

SPECIFICATION	
'Tench' class	**Speed:** 20 kts surfaced and 9 kts
Displacement: 1,570 tons surfaced	submerged
and 2,415 tons submerged	**Endurance:** 21316 km (13,245 miles)
Dimensions: length 95 m (311 ft 8½	at 10 kts surfaced and 204 km
in); beam 8.31 m (27 ft 3 in);	(127 miles) at 4 kts
draught 4.65 m (15 ft 3 in)	**Armament:** one or two 5-in
Propulsion: four diesels delivering	(127-mm) guns and 10 21-in
4026.8 kW (5,400 shp) and two	(533-mm) torpedo tubes (six bow
electric motors delivering	and four stern) for 28 torpedoes
2043.2 kW (2,740 shp) to two	**Complement:** 81 men
shafts	

therefore, to develop a large and slow-turning motor that could be direct-coupled. Two of these larger units, with no associated gear housings, could be accommodated without the earlier awkward crank in the hull, illustrating some of the problems facing submarine designers.

Internal capacity

Fuel and ballast tanks were better organized, firstly to obviate the need to lead the vents of the ballast tanks through the pressure hull (where they constituted a flooding hazard) and, secondly, the better to compensate for the considerable change in weight and trim as stores were consumed during a long patrol. Even a further four torpedo reloads were squeezed in, and this, combined with radar and efficient mechanical fire-control

computers, put the 'Tenches' far ahead of the opposition. In order to improve on the average, but slow, diving times of 55–60 seconds, the casings were pierced with many more lightening holes.

USS Pickerel, one of the later war-built fleet submarines, caught during one of the most dramatic methods of surfacing. Transferred to Italy in 1972 after extensive updating, the submarine served under the name Gianfranco Gazzana Priaroggia until 1981.

'O', 'P' and 'R' class Ocean-going submarine

HMS Odin as it appeared at the start of World War II. Completed in the late 1920s, the 'O'-class boats were large vessels designed to operate down to 90 m (300 ft). Odin was sunk in June 1940 by Italian destroyers.

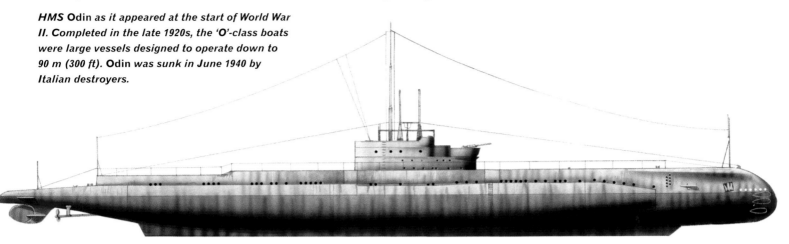

The British **'O' class**, later redesignated as the **'Oberon' class**, was developed as a replacement for the 'L' class of ocean-going submarines designed in World War I. They were officially categorized as overseas patrol submarines, and it is worth noting that, even as early as the concept stage in 1922, there was a requirement for long range, with an eye to possible future operations against the Japanese, despite the fact that they had been allies during World War I. The lead boat, **HMS Oberon**, was laid down by Chatham Dockyard in 1924 and was closely followed by two others, **HMS Otway** and **HMS Oxley**. A basic element of the design was the incorporation of six bow and two stern tubes, each with a reload torpedo. Together with extensive bunker spaces, these made for a large hull, soon proved by service deployment to be unwieldly, and a plethora of external fittings served to

reduce speed. Even after the introduction of fairings and other drag-reducing features, the boats barely achieved their designed surface speed, and failed altogether to reach the required submerged speed.

Weeping oil

The hull was fitted with saddle tanks, which contained most of the ballast capacity. Some of these spaces could double as extra fuel tanks, but were unpopular, as they emitted tell-tale oil traces through leaky rivet heads. As with the 'L' class boats, a 4-in (101.6-mm) gun was fitted in the tower to provide the above-water height to permit the gun to be worked in heavy seas.

Because of the limitations of the 'Oberon' class, an improved **'Odin' class** was evolved: this was longer to permit the accommodation of more powerful machinery, and had greater beam to improve stability in the surfaced

condition. Completed in 1928–29, these boats were **Odin**, **Olympus**, **Orpheus**, **Osiris**, **Oswald** and **Otus**. They were still plagued by weeping oil, but their outsides were marked by a clean-up of general clutter. An interesting idea, fortunately not pursued, was to install auxiliary accommodation in the upper casing to ease the confines of the crew on extended patrols. The **'Parthian' class** and **'Rainbow' class** were essentially 'Odin' repeats; six of each were ordered, differing only in detail. Two 'Rainbows' were ultimately cancelled, and the units completed in 1929–30

were **Parthian**, **Perseus**, **Phoenix**, **Poseidon**, **Proteus**, **Pandora**, **Rainbow**, **Regent**, **Regulus** and **Rover**.

Most of the 'O'-class boats were in the Far East in September 1939 but one of those in home waters, the *Oxley*, gained the melancholy distinction of becoming the first British submarine lost when torpedoed in error by another British submarine, HMS *Triton*. Of the joint class total of 18 boats, 12 were lost, most by the end of 1940 and many while serving in the Mediterranean, for whose confines they were totally unsuited.

SPECIFICATION	
'Odin' class	**Speed:** 17.5 kts surfaced and 9 kts submerged
Displacement: 1,781 tons surfaced and 2,038 tons submerged	**Endurance:** 21123 km (13,125 miles) at 8 kts surfaced and 97 km (60 miles) at 4 kts submerged
Dimensions: length 86.41 m (283 ft 6 in); beam 9.12 m (29 ft 11 in); draught 4.17 m (13 ft 8 in)	**Armament:** one 4-in (101.6-mm) gun, and eight 21-in (533-mm) torpedo tubes (six bow and two stern) with 16 torpedoes
Propulsion: two diesels delivering 3281 kW (4,400 shp) and two electric motors delivering 984 kW (1,320 shp) to two shafts	**Complement:** 53 men

---

'Porpoise' class Minelaying submarine

Based on the design of the six recently completed boats of the 'Parthian' class, the **'Porpoise'-class** submarines were purpose-built for the minelaying role. German practice tended to near-vertical mine chutes located within the envelope of the pressure hull, but the British preferred external stowage,

despite the risk of damage from overpressures or depth-charging.

Practical British experience with the concept of submarine minelayers had begun in World War I, when the first boats to be used for the task had been six units of the 'E' class. This experience allowed the update

SPECIFICATION	
'Grampus' class	**Speed:** 15.75 kts surfaced and 8.75 kts submerged
Displacement: 1,810 tons surfaced and 2,157 tons submerged	**Endurance:** 21308 km (13,240 miles) at 8 kts surfaced and 122 km (76 miles) at 4 kts submerged
Dimensions: length 89.3 m (293 ft); beam 7.77 m (25 ft 6 in); draught 5.13 m (16 ft 10 in)	**Armament:** one 4-in (101.6-mm) gun, six 21-in (533-mm) torpedo tubes (all bow) with 12 torpedoes, and 50 mines
Propulsion: two diesels delivering 2461 kW (3,300 shp) and two electric motors delivering 1215 kW (1,630 shp) to two shafts	**Complement:** 59 men

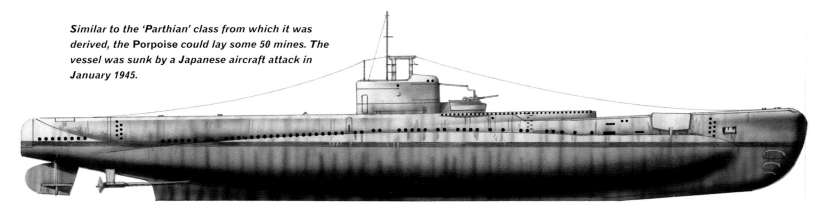

Similar to the 'Parthian' class from which it was derived, the **Porpoise** *could lay some 50 mines. The vessel was sunk by a Japanese aircraft attack in January 1945.*

of the basic design, and the first two of the new type were initially designated *E57* and *E58* before officially becoming *L1* and *L2* of the new 'L' class. There were eventually four major subgroups: *L1* to *L8* each had four 18-in (457-mm) tubes in the bow and two more amidships; *L9* to *L33* were lengthened by 2.3 m (7 ft 6 in) to carry four 21-in (533-mm) tubes forward and two 18-in tubes amidships except in the six minelaying boats with mine chutes in place of the 18-in tubes; and the subgroups from *L52* had a heavier battery of tubes all forward. Earlier classes had tended to disappoint with their poor surface speed, and the 'L'-class boats were generally capable of better than 17 kts. Like the 'E'-class units, they were of saddle tank construction but nominally capable of diving to 76 m (250 ft) as opposed to 61 m (200 ft), but in service they exceeded this depth by at least 40 per cent.

Revised mine carriage

The minelayers of the 'E' and 'L' classes had stowages in the saddle tanks on each side but in the experimental conversion of the *M3* in 1927, tracks were laid atop the hull over the greater part of the boat's length and inside the free-flooding space

contained within an extra-deep casing. An endless-chain mechanism fed the mines through doors right aft as the submarine moved slowly ahead. In essence this was the system that was incorporated in the 'Porpoises': in the name boat it extended over about three-quarters of the length, but in the remaining boats it was longer. All this gear added about 54 tons of topweight, making the boats very tender when first surfaced with a full load in a heavy sea. Extra lightening holes improved both draining and flooding time, the latter allowing the boats to dive more quickly.

HMS *Porpoise* was laid down by Vickers-Armstrongs at Barrow and launched in August 1932. The boat was completed with a 4.7-in (119.4-mm) QF Mk IX gun, which was an L/45 weapon, but in 1934 this was replaced by a 4-in (101.6-mm) QF Mk XII gun. There were 12 torpedoes for the six tubes, and later in the boat's career the torpedoes could be replaced on a one-for-one basis by M2 tube-launched mines.

Modest changes

Launched between August 1935 and September 1938, the other five 'Porpoise'- type boats are often characterized as the units of the **'Grampus' class**. These boats were: **HMS *Grampus*,**

built by Chatham Dockyard; **HMS *Narwhal*,** built by Vickers-Armstrongs at Barrow; **HMS *Rorqual*,** built by Vickers-Armstrongs and at Barrow; **HMS *Cachalot*,** built by Scotts; and **HMS *Seal*,** built by Chatham Dockyard. Three other units, initially known as **P411-413** and ordered from Scotts in 1941 with a circular-section pressure hull, were cancelled in September the same year.

Being weight-critical, the 'Porpoise'- and 'Grampus'- class boats took rather small diesel engines, resulting in a modest surface speed. To avoid detection from fuel leaks, the boats of the 'Grampus' class had bunkerage that was wholly internal, and it was necessary to extend the pressure hull downwards like a box keelson to meet the saddle tanks. In overall terms, the bunkerage of the 'Grampus'- class boats was less than that of the single 'Porpoise'- class unit. This oddly shaped and therefore weaker cross-section undoubtedly contributed to the designed depth being limited to 91 m (300 ft) compared with the 152 m (500 ft) of the 'Parthian'-class boats. The diving depth was in fact the same as that for the *Porpoise*, and the test depth for the boats of both classes was just 61 m (200 ft).

Most lost

The main function of the 'Porpoise'-class boats was, officially at least, superseded by the development of a mine capable of being laid through a conventional torpedo tube. Despite this, though, the boats of the class were still to lay some 2,600 mines operationally. The boats proved themselves invaluable during the height of the siege of Malta. Working in concert with the available 'O'-class boats, the 'Porpoise'-class submarines delivered personnel and supplies to the island.

The *Seal*, after being damaged by a mine in the Kattegat and unable to dive, had to surrender to two Arado floatplanes. Repaired, the vessel was recommissioned as the **UB-A** in German service, but was not used operationally.

The *Grampus* and *Cachalot* were sunk by Italian destroyers in June 1940 and July 1941 respectively, while the *Narwhal* was lost in July 1940, possibly to German air attack. Thus the only survivor of the class was the *Rorqual*, with armament bolstered by the addition of a single 20-mm cannon in an effort to provide greater protection against air attack, survived to the end of World War II in 1945, but was by then obsolete and therefore broken up in 1946.

'Thames' class Ocean-going submarine

With the steam-driven 'K'-class boats and the experimental *X1*, the Royal Navy had attempted to produce submarines with the

characteristics required for operations in concert with the service's surface fleet. Unfortunately, the 'K'-class

boats were disastrously problem-prone and the *X1* remained a one-off type. There still existed, therefore, the

requirement for a boat able to fulfil the desired role while avoiding the technical and operational weaknesses of the

'O'-class boats. The UK was bound by the limitations imposed by the Geneva Conference, and the Admiralty decided to build a class of 20 boats, each of the maximum allowable surface displacement of 1,800 tons, to provide both a fleet co-operation and a long-range oceanic patrol capability.

In the event, with the ships of the surface fleet becoming steadily faster, the basic policy was changed and only three units of the **'Thames' class** were completed between 1932 and 1934 as HMS *Thames*, HMS *Severn* and HMS *Clyde*. The boats were only 1.83 m (6 ft) shorter overall than the monstrous 'K'-class boats and were actually beamier overall, despite a narrower pressure hull. In cross-section the hull was carried downward at the keel to meet the line of the outer hull. Little oil fuel was

carried inboard, most of it instead being stowed in spaces above the main ballast tanks. Weepage was apt to be into the main hull through started rivet-heads.

Only now were there becoming available the diesel engines of the size and power to allow the new boats to match the 'K'-class boats' legend speed of 23.5 kts on their geared steam turbines. The design of the new engine was by the Admiralty, and the resulting engines turned out to be lighter than forecast. This was fortunate, as the boats were highly weight-critical. For their extended patrols, for instance, 41 tons of fresh and distilled water were carried, some two per cent of surface displacement. The general policy in submarine armament of replacing 4.7-in (119.4-mm) guns with 4-in (101.6-mm) weapons

resulted in a saving of 6 tons in topweight, while a further 8 tons was gained by burning fuel of a lower specific gravity.

Operational success

In the Norwegian campaign of 1940, the *Thames* was lost on a mine, while the *Clyde* damaged the German navy's battlecruiser KMS *Gneisenau* by torpedo. The

Clyde also ran an invaluable 1,200 tons of supplies to a beleaguered Malta and sank several enemy merchantmen while working out of Gibraltar. The *Severn* was active for a time in the little-known Levant operations.

The *Clyde* and the *Severn* both survived World War II, but were scrapped in 1946.

The 'Thames'-class submarine HMS **Clyde** *is seen acting as escort while the tanker* **Dingledale** *refuels the 'Dido'-class cruiser* **Hermione**. *These large boats were very capable and a class of 20 such boats had been planned in the early 1930s.*

SPECIFICATION	
'Thames' class	**Speed:** 22.5 kts surfaced and
Displacement: 2,206 tons surfaced	10.5 kts submerged
and 2,723 tons submerged	**Endurance:** 18532 km (11,515 miles)
Dimensions: length 105.16 m	at 8 kts surfaced and 219 km (136
(345 ft); beam 8.61 m (28 ft 3 in);	miles) at 4 kts submerged
draught 4.76 m (15 ft 11 in)	**Armament:** one 4-in (101.6-mm) gun,
Propulsion: two diesels delivering	and six 21-in (533-mm) torpedo
7,456 kW (10,000 bhp) and two	tubes (all bow) with 12 torpedoes
electric motors delivering	**Complement:** 61 men
1,864 kW (2,500 hp) to two shafts	

'S' class Long-range submarine

Although its origins went back to 1928, the **'S'-class** submarine was successful during World War II and, with 62 completions, was the Royal Navy's most prolific submarine class. Ostensibly replacements for the 'H' class, the 'S'-class boats required a performance better than their predecessors to allow service in the Mediterranean and Baltic. A tight, 600-ton surfaced displacement target was set to pave the way for a small submarine which, nevertheless, had to be able to transit 805 km (500 miles) to and from its patrol area, where it was expected to remain up to 10 days. Any increase in the 805-km (500-mile) radius meant having to find space for very much larger radio equipment. The specification was later to be altered drastically, calling for 1930-km (1,200-mile) passages at not less than 9 kts and eight days on station.

Increased building

Initially, a class of four ('**Swordfish' type**) boats was built; launched between 1931

HMS Storm returns to the UK in 1945. During its Far East commission, the submarine sank 20 Japanese supply vessels, 19 of them by gunfire, together with a destroyer and four escorts. On its most successful patrol the submarine sank 11 vessels, nine on a single day. Note that torpedoes were reserved for warships, gunfire sufficing to despatch cargo ships.

and 1933 by Chatham Dockyard, these displaced 640 tons despite every effort at weight control. The design was really too tight and was relaxed to 670 tons for the eight lengthened '**Shark' type** boats of 1934–37. Though it was planned to terminate the class at 12, the advent of war saw the design stretched further and constructed in series.

Gun armament

To save on topweight, a 3-in

(76.2-mm) gun was fitted but, with the extra hull length, a further torpedo tube was worked-in aft on some boats. Others traded both of these for a single 4-in (10.6-mm) gun. With only 12 or 13 torpedoes aboard, the gun was a useful means of disposing of 'soft' targets which, while not warranting the expenditure of a torpedo, were often reluctant to sink. Earlier boats had fuel tanks within the pressure hull, but later units supplemented these

with external capacity, which allowed them to work even in the Far East.

Interestingly, eight units were lost from the original 12, the same number as were lost from the following 50. All of the first group's losses occurred before February 1941, while the first hull of succeeding groups was not launched until October 1941. Submarine operations in European waters during the war's early months were clearly very hazardous.

HMS Sibyl enters Algiers harbour in May 1943. Intended originally for operations in the Mediterranean and Baltic, the 'S' class boats also found themselves in the East Indies. Sixty-two were produced, making them the largest submarine class in the Royal Navy.

SPECIFICATION	
'S' class (later boats)	(1,300 shp) to two shafts
Displacement: 860 tons surfaced and 990 tons submerged	**Speed:** 15 kts surfaced and 9 kts submerged
Dimensions: length 66.14 m (217 ft); beam 7.16 m (23 ft 6 in); draught 3.2 m (10 ft 6 in)	**Endurance:** 13,896 km (8,635 miles) at 10 kts surfaced
Propulsion: two diesels delivering 1416.8 kW (1,900 shp) and two electric motors delivering 969 kW	**Armament:** one 4-in (101.6-mm) or 3-in (76.2-mm) gun; six or seven 21-in (533-mm) torpedo tubes
	Complement: 44 men

'T' class Patrol submarine

Instantly recognizable by their oddly cranked profiles, the '**T'-class** boats were the Royal Navy's standard patrol submarines of World War II. Between **HMS Triton** and **HMS Tabard**, launched in October 1937 and November 1945

respectively, the class reached a respectable 54 in number. With the 'Thames' class abandoned and a replacement required for the unsatisfactory 'O' class, design of the 'T' class needed not only to rectify shortcomings but also to conform to the treaty

agreements that bedevilled inter-war planning. The London Naval Treaty limited total (rather than individual) displacement so, to obtain maximum numbers of boats, a 1,000-ton target was set. Into this a 42-day endurance was to be packed.

That the final result was only some 9 per cent heavy, while being highly reliable, was a credit to the design team.

Low surface speed

Because of their limiting parameters, the 'T'-class boats

SPECIFICATION	
'T' class	**Speed:** 15.25 kts surfaced and 9 kts submerged
Displacement: 1,325 tons surfaced and 1,570 tons submerged	**Endurance:** 20,382 km (12,665 miles) at 10 kts surfaced
Dimensions: length 83.82 m (275 ft); beam 8.1 m (26 ft 7 in); draught 4.5 m (14 ft 9 in)	**Armament:** one 4-in (101.6-mm) gun and 10 or 11 21-in (533-mm) torpedo tubes (in first group 10 bow and in second group eight bow and three stern)
Propulsion: two diesels delivering 1864.3 kW (2,500 shp) and two electric motors delivering 1081.3 kW (1,450 shp) to two shafts	**Complement:** 56 (first group) or 61 (second group)

*Above: HMS **Tally-ho** is seen in transit to the Far East. Such passages of the Bitter Lakes of the Suez Canal had become more common by January 1945, with any German naval threat extinct and additional British resources being released for service against the Japanese.*

could ship only small-sized diesels and their surface speed was thus modest. In contrast, they carried a large punch, the six forward tubes within the pressure hull being augmented by a pair in the bulged bow casing and a further pair in the casing, one on each side of the tower. Thus, a 10-torpedo forward salvo could be fired, albeit at the cost of a highly individual profile.

This arrangement applied to all 22 submarines built before World War II, later units having the amidships tubes moved farther aft and reversed, and a single tube added in the casing right aft.

War-built boats also had their bows altered to set the external tubes higher, and some external ballast tanks converted to bunker space. Oil fuel capacity was almost doubled and the endurance of the boat became more than that of her crew and their supplies.

Fourteen of the pre-war boats were lost, mainly in the Mediterranean. Those from the wartime programmes were completed largely after the end of the war in the Mediterranean and only one of the boats was lost at sea.

After the end of World War II, many of the submarines were sold, while others were stretched and streamlined for greater underwater speed, serving alongside their successors, the boats of the 'A' class, until late into the 1960s. Four units were cancelled and another boat was only projected but not laid down.

*Left: HMS **Tigris** is seen at a depot ship just before its final patrol. It was one of the original 'T' class, launched in October 1939, but was lost in March 1943, probably to mines. Note the external tubes at the bow and amidships, and the unusual hull profile.*

Below: The submarines of the 1940 'T' class design were slow but durable, although their limited size meant they were not capable of supporting their crews for such a length of time.

'U' and 'V' classes Coastal submarines

The highly successful single-hulled boats of the **'U' class** were designed originally as unarmed targets to replace the elderly boats of the 'H' class, and were a little larger. Three were laid down as such but, as the Royal Navy did not possess a modern 'coastal' submarine, it seemed advantageous to modify the bow to take torpedo tubes. The after hull had a sharp taper and the casing ended short of the stern, so all armament was set forward. There were four tubes in the pressure hull and the bow casing was bulged to take two more (reflecting the doubtful accuracy of the torpedo salvoes of the day). This was not a good feature, as the restricted height of the design meant a shallow periscope depth, and the oversize bow casing made it both difficult to maintain constant depth and also caused a distinctive 'pressure hump' in the water above. With the outbreak of World War II, a further group of 12 boats was ordered, 1.6-m (5-ft 3-in) longer

The straightforward 'U'-class submarines proved remarkably successful. Seen in Mediterranean colours, and with the original bow form, boats like this, operating out of Malta, put a stranglehold on supplies for the German and Italian armies operating in North Africa.

HMS Utmost alongside a depot ship and the 'S'-class boat Seawolf. Utmost had recently returned from the Mediterranean, where she had torpedoed and damaged the heavy cruiser Trieste, as well as sinking supply vessels and undertaking clandestine missions.

SPECIFICATION	
'V' class	**Speed:** 12.5 kts surfaced and 9 kts
Displacement: 670 tons surfaced	submerged
and 740 tons submerged	**Endurance:** 8,715 km (5,415 miles)
Dimensions: length 62.79 m (206 ft);	at 10 kts surfaced and 113 km
beam 4.88 m (16 ft); draught 4.72	(70 miles) at 7 kts submerged
m (15 ft 6 in)	**Armament:** one 3-in (76.2-mm) gun
Propulsion: two diesels delivering	and four 21-in (533-mm) torpedo
596.6 kW (800 shp) and two	tubes (all bow) for eight torpedoes
electric motors delivering 566.7	**Complement:** 37 men
kW (760 shp) to two shafts	

Upgraded design

Again, therefore, the design was updated. An extra midbody section was inserted to house uprated machinery, and the hull was redesigned to permit submergence to 91 m (300 ft) rather than the 60 m (200 ft) of the earlier boats, and to facilitate all-welded construction in modules, producing faster building times. This later type was known as the **'V' class**, of which 33 were ordered but only 21 completed. It is a noteworthy fact that, except for two early units built in Chatham Dockyard, all 81 boats were built in the two Vickers Armstrongs yards at Barrow and on Tyneside.

The submarines of the 'U' and 'V' classes were particularly suited to the shallow and confined waters of the Mediterranean and North Sea but though successful, they suffered the loss of 19 of their numbers. After the effective end of the Mediterranean war in 1943, they had little use and many were either transferred or used for the unglamorous but important training role.

to improve the lines and ease the cramped internals; most of these boats had only four tubes. Thirty-four more boats of this type followed, with improved lines and increased bunker space. Though extremely useful, the 'U' class boats were rather limited in diving depth and had a low surface speed.

HMS Uproar demonstrates the small size of these boats. In a short-range war, such as those fought in the North Sea and Mediterranean, endurance was less important than manoeuvrability, and the 'U'-class boats proved very useful, in spite of having been designed for training rather than operations.

'X' craft British midget submarines

Though popular with some foreign fleets, the midget submarine concept had no part in the Royal Navy's pre-war plans. Only in 1942 did it become apparent that no orthodox method existed to strike at enemy ships that menaced the northern convoy route from safe, protected anchorages. Two prototype **'X'-type** midgets (**X3** and **X4**), based on a private design, were quickly built and tested, then followed by a production run of six (**X5** to **X10**). The design avoided the snare of over-miniaturization and the craft could support a volunteer crew of four for several days. A distinctive feature was the armament, not torpedoes but two large explosive charges conformal with the hull. These could be deposited on the seabed below a stationary target or if the water was too deep, slung beneath it. A key member of the crew was the diver, who could leave and re-enter the craft by a floodable forward compartment. It was he who secured the lines for the neutrally buoyant charges or placed limpet mines on the target's hull.

Twelve production 'X' craft were built (including the training units **XT1** to **XT6**), of which seven were lost. They were followed by a slightly larger **'XE'** type for use in the Far East and equipped with a rudimentary air-conditioning system. Eleven of the 12 ordered (**XE1** to **XE12**) were completed, and one of these was lost. The job for which the 'X' craft was designed succeeded magnificently. The Japanese cruiser *Takao* was

sunk by a single 'X' craft in the Johore Strait in water so shallow that the submarine was in danger of being trapped between the cruiser and seabed as the tide receded. 'X' craft reconnoitred and provided navigational aids for the D-Day beaches, sank a floating dock in Bergen and cut underwater cables in the Far East.

Attack on the *Tirpitz*

From January 1942, until its eventual destruction by bombing in November 1944, the battleship *Tirpitz* remained in Norwegian waters almost continuously, rarely moving yet posing a real threat to the precarious northern convoy route, a threat too distant to easily eradicate. The concern that *Tirpitz* was at sea prompted the scattering of PQ17, and the raid on St Nazaire was mounted to deny it a graving dock on the Atlantic coast. What could not be achieved by frontal assault the British chose to accomplish through guile, developing the 'X' craft primarily for this purpose.

In April 1943, six of these craft, with base facilities, were installed in a remote western Scottish loch to exercise intensively in penetrating net and boom defences, in using divers and in the accurate placement of the two-ton explosive charges that constituted their main weapon. Simultaneous attacks were planned on the *Tirpitz*, *Scharnhorst* and *Lützow*, all of which were using protected anchorages around the Altenfjord, hard by North Cape.

Eventually, on the night of 11/12 September 1943, six patrol

submarines left the loch, each towing an 'X' craft manned by a passage crew for the long haul northward. Broken towlines were all too common, and one led to the disappearance of **X9**. Leaks in **X8** obliged its scuttling to avoid delay to the enterprise, while **X7** was fortunate to actually impale a floating mine with its bows without causing its detonation.

After a nine-day passage and having embarked their attack crews, the four surviving craft left their parent submarines on the night of 20/21 September, crossed the offshore minefield on the surface and entered the long fjord. Not until the day after did the three craft tasked with attacking the *Tirpitz* arrive at her Kaafjord anchorage. With some difficulty, they forced the nets,

Above: Though capable of an independent range of 2,776 km (1,725 miles), this involved a long and endurance-sapping test for the 'X' craft's crew and it was, therefore, customary to tow them with large submarines to the area of their attack.

Rear Admiral C. B. Barry, Flag Officer Submarines, lowers himself into the hatch of a late model 'X' craft, moored alongside the depot ship HMS Forth at Holy Loch in February 1944.

SPECIFICATION	
'X' class	to one shaft
Displacement: 27 tons surfaced and 29.5 tons submerged	**Speed:** 6.5 kts surfaced and 5 kts submerged
Dimensions: length 15.62 m (51 ft 3 in); beam 1.75 m (5 ft 9 in); draught 2.26 m (7 ft 4¾ in)	**Endurance:** 2,776 km (1,725 miles) at 4 kts; surfaced and 148 km (92 miles) at 2 kts submerged
Propulsion: one diesel delivering 31.3 kW (42 shp) and one electric motor delivering 22.4 kW (30 shp)	**Armament:** two 2-ton explosive charges and limpet mines
	Complement: 4 men

but **X6** had a faulty compass and a virtually jammed periscope. Effectively blinded, its skipper inadvertently broached while forcing the battleship's inner net defence. Though sighted, *X6* was too close to be engaged by other than grenades and small-arms fire. Blundering into their target, the crew released its charges, surfaced, scuttled and baled out. All aboard were captured.

X5, *depicted showing one of the two conformal 2-ton explosive charges, was one of the unfortunate boats of the six-strong* **Tirpitz** *'X' class attack force, not being heard of again after setting off.*

Explosion

The Germans made rapid preparations to get under way but then sighted *X7* and decided to stay within the anti-torpedo nets, compromising by veering anchor cable to shift position. *X7*, however, had managed to plant a charge under each end of its adversary. When the first detonated, it countermined the remainder in one enormous explosion.

At the time, *X7* was still negotiating the inner net on its way out and was heavily damaged as a result. *X7* broke clear but then foundered, two of the four crew being lost. *X5* was not seen after the initial approach: there is no evidence that she was able to launch an

Right: The 'X' craft of the **Tirpitz** *attack were towed by larger submarines to the northern tip of Norway, were passage crews were exchanged with combat crews.*

attack and so the German claim to have sunk the boat with gunfire about 30 minutes after the main action may well be true.

The fourth craft, *X10*, scheduled to attack the *Scharnhorst*, also suffered compass and periscope failure. After trying unsuccessfully to rectify this, its skipper aborted plans and sailed to meet its parent submarine offshore. The craft eventually had to be scuttled in a gale.

For the cost of six 'X' craft and 10 lives, the *Tirpitz* was sorely damaged. Much machinery was unseated and misaligned by the shock of the explosion and, though partially repaired, the ship was never again fully battleworthy.

Axis midget submarines Italian, Japanese and German craft

By their very nature, midget submarines possessed a 'cloak and dagger' aura that has tended to cause their true potential to be overrated. The fleets of all the major Axis powers operated them but, despite their odd success, they really did not repay the considerable effort expended on them in both design and construction. Philosophies regarding their use varied from fleet to fleet.

Italian craft

Like the British, the Italians saw them as the means of attacking targets in difficult anchorages or for deploying specialist swimming teams. If the British 'X' craft are taken as a yardstick,

they corresponded to the most used of the Italian types, the four-man **CB**. Several of these were transported overland to the Black Sea in 1942 during the Axis blockade of the Soviet naval base at Sevastapol and accounted for a pair of Soviet submarines, but little other activity is recorded. The smaller, 10-m (32-ft 10-in) **CA** could carry torpedoes or swimmers, depending on type. Prototypes for much larger, 33-m (108-ft 3-in) **CC** and **CM** types were built but never saw production.

The Japanese had a far more ambitious use for midget submarines, seeing their role as being carried by surface ships and fleet submarines for launching in the course of a

fleet action. However, with the speeds and ranges at which these were likely to be fought, this idea became manifestly impracticable and the midget boats were viewed more in the context of specialist attack and defence against enemy landings. About 400 were built

to various designs, but only the 24-m (78-ft 6-in) **Ko-gata** (**Type A**) was used at all effectively, although their debut during the Pearl Harbor attack was far from auspicious. In 1941 the Imperial Japanese navy had more than 40 of these two-man 46-ton midget submarines. The five

This Japanese Type A two-man midget submarine is seen off Oahu, Hawaii, in December 1941, after being forced to beach and surrender by the destroyer USS **Helms**, *the only US vessel that was underway at the start of the Japanese attack on Pearl Harbor.*

used in the attack on Pearl Harbor attack were lost.

Following the occupation of Madagascar by the British some six months later, however, naval forces were reconnoitred by a Japanese seaplane. Despite this warning, the battleship HMS *Ramillies* and a tanker were afterwards torpedoed in sheltered waters off Diego Suarez. The battleship survived but was considerably damaged. The attack had been carried out by Type As which, with the seaplane, had been carried on three Japanese submarines. This well integrated operation was followed a day later by an unsuccessful attempt on Sydney Harbour. The three-man 25-m (82-ft) 50-ton **Hei-gata (Type C)** was also employed alongside the Type A during the Philippines campaigns but this met with little success.

As the war swung against them, the Japanese produced a suicide torpedo, the **Kaiten**. These were to be used in large numbers, launched from submarines and surface ships. Fortunately, their steering was as suspect as the dedication of many of their pilots. There were also the 17-m (56-ft) 19-ton two-man **Kairyu** (sea dragon) and the larger, faster 26.2-m (86-ft) 60-ton two- or five-man **Koryu** (scaly dragon), which had explosive charges in the bows or carried torpedoes.

German designs

Germany built a wide range of torpedo-carrying midgets for use against amphibious landing fleets. The **Neger** and **Marder** each had one, and the **Biber** two, 533-mm (21-in) torpedoes, the latter being able to carry them for 240 km (149 miles) at 6 kts. The one-man 9-m (19-ft 6-in) Biber displaced only 6.5 tons. Its scalloped hull could also carry two mines. At the forward end was a towing point that allowed the craft to be towed to a point near its operational area. The Biber was an unsatisfactory design since the carbon monoxide from the petrol engine could asphyxiate the crewman, but it was used off the mouth of the Scheldt estuary in 1944 to harass Allied shipping. Built in quantity and transported overland, they were also in action off Anzio and Normandy, but found the Allied escorts plentiful, aggressive and more than able to cope. Many of the craft went missing.

Effective vessels

Potentially more effective were the true submarines of the **Type XXVIIA Hecht** and **Type XXVIIB Seehund** classes. These were 10.5 and 12 m (34 ft 5 in and 39 ft 5 in) long respectively, and the latter had two torpedoes and a 560-km (342-mile) range. The diesel-engined two-man 15-ton

Seehund was capable of 6–7 kts. It entered service in 1944, and was used in the Channel, Thames Estuary and the Scheldt. Its range was sufficient to reach the British east coast but, again, could do little more than sink the odd one or two merchantmen. Kept well in check by the anti-submarine

forces, their challenge finally died with the liberation of the Channel Coasts by Allied forces.

The 10-m (33-ft) 11-ton **Molch** (newt) also carried two torpedoes and was used to attack Allied shipping off the Normandy beaches following D-Day in June 1944, and was also used in the Scheldt estuary.

Above: An Sdkfz 7 halftrack tows a Biber. The combination was caught in an Allied air strike during the retreat from Normandy in August 1944.

Below: A Japanese Type C midget submarine is seen on a launching cradle aboard a transport submarine outside Kure harbour in August 1944.

Below: A CB type midget submarine at Taranto in November 1943. Italian plans to attack shipping in New York harbour with midget submarines came to nothing after Italy's surrender in 1943.

Above: A Kaiten is launched from a converted light cruiser. The pilot was housed within a remodelled Type 93 torpedo, which had a speed of 30 kts.

'Deutschland' class 'Pocket battleships'

Above: **Lützow** *(formerly Deutschland) as it appeared in 1945. The curved bow was fitted in 1940, and the tall funnel cap in 1941. It was scuttled in May 1945 after being damaged by near misses from RAF 'Tallboy' 12,000-lb (5443-kg) bombs.*

Until 1934 Germany was bound by the terms of the Treaty of Versailles, which stipulated that no warship exceeding 10,000 tons could be built. To extract the maximum potency within this general limitation, designers had to balance the conflicting requirements of speed, armament and protection. Long endurance was required to conduct an extensive *guerre de course* against France and the UK, and the three **'Deutschland' class** ships were given the quite novel machinery of eight diesels driving two shafts, allowing for flexible and economical propulsion.

Electric welding saved 15 per cent on weight as compared with riveting, allowing for extra weight to be allocated to both armament and protection. Despite the overt weight saving, however, the ships all exceeded their stated displacement. When constructed, they continued the

concept of the armoured cruiser, being faster than any battleship and more powerful than any cruiser. But like armoured cruisers, they were vulnerable to battlecruisers. And by the outbreak of World War II, 'fast battleships' were coming into service that were also able to intercept these 26-knot cruisers.

Official classification

Until 1940, the ships were officially classified as *Panzerschiffe* (armoured ships), but were popularly known to the Allies as 'pocket battleships'. After the destruction of the **Admiral Graf Spee**, subsequent to the River Plate action, the surviving pair were recategorized as heavy cruisers. The **Admiral Scheer** had a brief but successful career as a raider, gaining particular

Graf Spee, *pictured off the coast of Norway (above) and in the English Channel in April 1939 (below), spent the beginning of the war engaged in commerce raiding. The vessel was finally scuttled by its crew off Montevideo on 13 December 1939, after sustaining damage from the Royal Navy cruisers* **Ajax, Achilles** *and* **Exeter** *during the Battle of River Plate.*

SPECIFICATION	
'Deutschland' class (*Admiral Graf Spee***)**	to two shafts
Ships in class (launched): *Deutschland* (1931), *Admiral Scheer* (1933) and *Admiral Graf Spee* (1934)	**Speed:** 28.5 kts
	Armour: belt 80 mm (3.1 in); deck 45 mm (1.8 in); turrets 85-140 mm (3.3–5.5 in); barbettes 100 mm (3.9 in)
Displacement: 12,100 tons standard and 16,200 tons full load	
Dimensions: length 186 m (610 ft 3 in); beam 21.3 m (69 ft 11 in); draught 5.8 m (19 ft)	**Armament:** six 280-mm (11-in), eight 150-mm (5.9-in), six 105-mm (4.1-in) AA, eight 37-mm AA and 10 20-mm AA guns, plus eight 533-mm (21-in) torpedo tubes
Propulsion: eight MAN diesels delivering 41760 kW (56,000 shp)	**Aircraft:** two floatplanes
	Complement: 1,150 men

Above: **Deutschland,** *seen in January 1940, and renamed* **Lützow** *the following month, was severely damaged on 9 April 1940, during the invasion of Norway.*

Right: **Graf Spee** *and the other 'Deutschland'-class vessels combined diesel engines and light electric welded hulls in the quest for long endurance.*

notoriety with the sinking of the armed merchant cruiser *Jervis Bay*. She cruised as far as the Indian Ocean and tied down large numbers of British warships in the hunt for her, as well as delaying vital convoys. The **Deutschland** herself was politically renamed **Lützow** after the *Admiral Graf Spee* affair and, until early 1942, spent much time in dock after being torpedoed on two separate occasions. Her major action was the tactical defeat off North Cape on 30/31 December 1942. Both ships were eventually sunk by British heavy bombers in the closing days of the European war.

'Hipper' class Heavy cruiser

When Germany finally built heavy cruisers in the late 1930s, they were of orthodox design showing no influence from the 'Deutschland'-class *Panzerschiff*. The nameship of the **'Hipper' class**, the **Admiral Hipper**, was launched in February 1937 after various treaties had lapsed, and was comparable in displacement to the big Japanese cruisers. By shipping only an eight-gun main battery, however, the Germans had scope for improved protection.

Active service
The *Admiral Hipper* was the best known of the class. Active in the Norwegian campaign of 1940, she was rammed by an intended victim, the British destroyer HMS *Glowworm*. In 1940/1941, she acted as a raider in the Atlantic, but these cruisers were built as 'sprinters' and lacked endurance for prolonged operations. She was moved to Norway, where her presence was partly responsible for the PQ 17 convoy disaster in July 1942. On the last day of the year, in company with the 'pocket battleship' *Lützow* and a

Prinz Eugen *at Brest in May 1941, after accompanying* **Bismarck** *into the Atlantic and participating in the sinking of HMS* **Hood.**

Supposedly built to the Washington Treaty limit of 10,000 tons, the 'Hipper' class varied in tonnage from 14,000 to 17,000 tons, and up to 20,000 tons when deeply loaded. **Prinz Eugen** *is shown as it was at Bergen in April 1941. The dazzle stripes were later painted over.*

SPECIFICATION	
'Hipper'-class (*Prinz Eugen*)	(132,000 shp) to three shafts
Ships in class (launched): *Admiral Hipper* (1937), *Blücher* (1937) and *Prinz Eugen* (1938)	**Speed:** 33.4 kts
	Armour: belt 70-80 mm (2.75-3.1 in); deck 12-50 mm (0.5-2 in); turrets 70-105 mm. (2.75-4.1 in)
Displacement: 14,475 tons standard and 18,400 tons full load	
Dimensions: length 210.4 m (690 ft 4 in); beam 21.9 m (71 ft 10 in); draught 7.9 m (25 ft 10 in)	**Armament:** eight 203-mm (8-in), 12 105-mm (4.1-in) DP, 12 37-mm AA and 24 20-mm AA guns, plus 12 533-mm (21-in) torpedo tubes
Propulsion: Brown Boveri geared turbines delivering 98,430 kW	**Complement:** 1,450 men

destroyer force, she attacked the JW 51B convoy off North Cape. The outclassed British destroyer escort kept the Germans at bay for three hours until relieved by a cruiser force; Hitler's reaction at this inept operation was an order to decommission all heavy units. The *Hipper* thus survived to be taken in 1945. Also captured was the **Prinz Eugen**, best known for being in company with the *Bismarck* in May 1941, and then accompanying the battle cruisers *Scharnhorst* and

Gneisenau in their dash up the English Channel from Brest back to Germany.

The **Blücher** went down in April 1940 with a heavy loss of life, overwhelmed by Norwegian shore defences while carrying an invasion force. The partially complete **Lützow** was sold to the Soviets in 1940 (freeing the name to be transferred to *Deutschland* later) and the **Seydlitz**, earmarked for conversion into an aircraft carrier, was never completed. Oversized and plagued by overly complex, unreliable machinery, the 'Hipper' class was one of the less successful cruiser designs of the war.

Left: **Hipper** *took part in only two major actions, the invasion of Norway and the raid on the convoy JW 51B, before being decommissioned in 1943.*

Below: After avoiding the fate of **Bismark** *in the Atlantic in 1941,* **Prinz Eugen** *was finally expended during A-bomb trials in the Pacific after the war.*

'Zara' class
Heavy cruiser

In contrast to the preceding 'Trento' class, the 'Zara' class sacrificed high speed in the interests of much improved protection. Zara and two of the vessels in the class met their end at the hands of ships of the British Mediterranean Fleet off Cape Matapan in the course of March 1941.

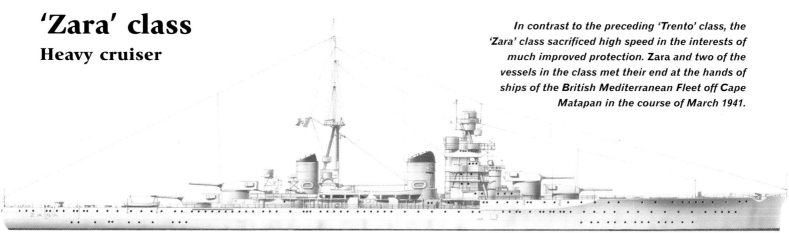

Franco-Italian naval rivalry broke out after the Washington Treaty, the two French 'Duquesne'-class cruisers being immediately trumped by the Italian 'Trento' class with superior protection. This had not been completed, however, before the French embarked on the four 'Suffren'-class cruisers. Italy then took three years to reply, with the four **'Zara'-class** cruisers, suggesting that the French design was acquired and digested beforehand. In any case, the Italian ships were excellent, with reduced power on only two shafts but with a high level of protection, whose weight in fact took the ships beyond treaty limits.

Three of the class formed the 1st Cruiser Division at the Battle of Calabria, a month after the outbreak of the Mediterranean war. The action was an anti-climax, the Italians disengaging as soon as the flagship was hit.

Last action

The next significant action was also their last. At the end of March 1941, a complex set of fleet movements was undertaken to intercept a British convoy near Crete. The British, aware of what was afoot, set a trap. Sensing danger, the Italians made for home. Anxious to bring the Italian battleship to

'Zara'-class cruisers on patrol in the Mediterranean. Built in the early 1930s in response to the new French vessels then entering service, the units of the 'Zara' class were fine, well-balanced ships, somewhat larger than the size set down in the Washington Treaty.

SPECIFICATION	
'Zara' class	to two shafts
Ships in class (launched): *Zara* (1930), *Fiume* (1930), *Gorizia* (1930) and *Pola* (1931)	**Speed:** 32 kts
	Armour: belt 100-150 mm (3.9-5.9 in); deck 70 mm (2.75 in); turrets 120–140 mm (4.7–5.5 in); barbettes 140–150 mm (5.5–5.9 in)
Displacement: 11,545–11,680 tons standard and 13,945–14,330 tons full load	
Dimensions: length 182.8 m (599 ft 9 in); beam 20.62 m (67 ft 7 in); draught 5.9 m (19 ft 4 in)	**Armament:** four twin 203-mm (8-in), eight twin 100-mm (3.94-in) DP and eight 37-mm AA guns
Propulsion: Parsons geared turbines delivering 80535 kW (108,000 shp)	**Aircraft:** two floatplanes
	Complement: 841

account, the British used carrier air strikes to slow her and allow their heavy ships to close. Only the 1st Division's **Pola** was thus stopped, however, and her two running mates, **Zara** and **Fiume,** with two destroyers then stayed to assist. Admiral Sir Andrew Cunningham's battleships despatched them with close-range 15-in (381-mm) salvoes at what become known as the night Battle of Matapan. With the American 'Astoria' and British 'Cressy' classes, the 'Zara' class thus shares the record of losing three of its type in a single engagement.

The final ship of the class was the **Gorizia**, which the Germans seized after Italy's armistice with the Allies. Italian-manned human torpedo 'chariots' sank her at La Spezia in June 1944.

'Condottieri' class Light cruiser

The Italians built many fine cruisers, but lack of an offensive policy in war meant that few were tested in action. The 12 **'Condottieri'-class** ships formed the backbone of their light cruiser strength, a quartet and four pairs constituting a logical development sequence over a five-year period. The **Garibaldi** and its sister ship were the ultimate pair, and very close to the 10,000-ton limit.

As a yardstick for the **'Giussano' class** – which made up the four-strong first group of 'Condottieri', laid down in 1928 – the French 'Duguay-Trouin' class had been completed less than two years earlier. Both classes

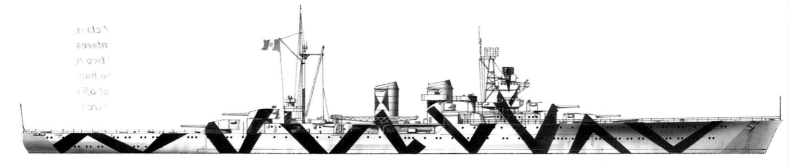

Above: The final 'Condottieri'-class vessels were increased in size and reduced in performance in the interests of protection. The **Luigi di Savoia Duca degli Abruzzi,** *seen here in 1942-pattern dazzle camouflage, survived World War II to remain in service until 1961.*

SPECIFICATION	
'Condottieri' class (Group 5) Ships in class (launched): Group 1 *Alberto di Giussano* (1930), *Giovanni delle Bande Nere* (1930), *Alberico da Barbiano* (1930) and *Bartolomeo Colleoni* (1930); Group 2 *Armando Diaz* (1930) and *Luigi Cadorna* (1930); Group 3 *Raimondo Montecuccoli* (1931) and *Muzio Attendolo* (1933); Group 4 *Emanuele Filiberto Duca d'Aosta* (1932) and *Eugenio di Savoia* (1933); and Group 5 *Luigi di Savoia Duca degli Abruzzi* (1933) and *Giuseppe Garibaldi* (1933) **Displacement:** 9,440 tons standard and 11,575 tons full load	**Dimensions:** length 187 m (612 ft 6 in); beam 18.9 m (61 ft 11 in); draught 5.2 m (17 ft) **Machinery:** Parsons geared turbines delivering 76,060 kW (102,000 shp) to two shafts **Speed:** 33.5 kts **Armour:** belt 130 mm (5.1 in); deck 40 mm (1.6 in); turrets 135 mm (5.3 in) **Armament:** two triple and two twin 152-mm (6-in), four twin 100-mm (3.94-in) AA, four twin 37-mm AA and 10 20-mm AA guns, plus six 533-mm (21-in) torpedo tubes **Aircraft:** two floatplanes **Complement:** 640 men

The 'Condottieri'-class cruisers, represented by **Duca d'Aosta,** *was built in five groups, as a response to the steady evolution of French light cruiser design.*

carried four twin turrets and, though the Italian ships were rather faster, neither type was more than minimally protected. An immediate response in the French 'La Galissonnière' class

was paralleled by the remaining 'Condottieri' over the same period. With the French ships incorporating a measure of protection, the Italians increased power and dimensions to

The greater size and displacement of the last two units of the 'Condottieri' subclasses of light cruisers allowed two additional 152-mm (6-in) guns to be worked in through the adoption of triple rather than twin turrets in the foremost and aftermost positions. **Guiseppe Garibaldi** *was one of the last two 'Condottieri'-class cruisers built, surviving wartime damage to serve the Italian navy into the 1970s.*

maintain speed while improving survivability in the two-ship **'Cadorna'**, **'Montecuccoli'** and **'Duca d'Aosta'** and **'Abruzzi' classes**. The last was the final iteration of the concept with significant increases in beam, draught and displacement to allow the incorporation of two extra guns (in A and Y triple turrets) and an upgrading of protection. A fundamental shift in policy was the acceptance of a lower speed, but this still represented a margin over the equivalent French ships.

The *Garibaldi*'s war was concerned mainly with the distant cover of the supply and troop convoys to North Africa. In July 1941 she was torpedoed and heavily damaged by the submarine HMS *Upholder*.

Both sisters were incorporated into the post-war fleet. The *Garibaldi* lasted until the 1970s and was then converted to a prototype guided-missile cruiser with Terrier surface-to-air missiles. The **Duca degli Abruzzi** was deleted in 1961.

'Capitani Romani' class Light cruiser

The British concept of the small cruiser as used in World War I was followed by the Japanese in the 1920s, but development then lapsed for a decade until the French embarked on the creation of the 'Mogador' class.

Super-destroyers

The 'Mogador' class looked like, and in fact were, super-destroyers. However, on a deep-load displacement of barely 4,000 tons, they could outgun a light cruiser such as the British 'Dido'-class units. With 68,605 kW (92,000 shp) they could also make 40 kts. The Italians, stung by the appearance of this French class and feeling themselves vulnerable within the context of Mediterranean operations, therefore acted with considerable speed to produce the **'Capitani Romani' class** of light cruisers, laying down no fewer than 12 keels in the space of just six months. As a result of Italy's varying fortunes of war, however, only four were completed.

Less than 5 m (16 ft 5 in) longer than the 'Mogador'-class ships, the 'Capitani Romani'-class units looked like small cruisers, their extra beam allowing space for machinery developing an astonishing 93,250 kW (125,000 shp) – equivalent to that of a US 'Salem'-class heavy cruiser of four times the displacement. At this power, the Italian ships were good for 43 kts and, while they were virtually unprotected, they also shipped a very respectable main battery. In addition, eight torpedo tubes were fitted and mines could be carried, though probably in place of other topweight. The ships' Roman names were splendidly euphoric, belying the headache

The Italian light cruiser **Scipione Africano**. *Although 12 units of the 'Capitani Romani' class were laid down, by September 1943 only three had entered service.*

that they could have caused any convoy escort commander not blessed with air support. As it was, four were demolished on the ways, five were sunk through various agencies whilst fitting out, and three were completed in 1942–3. One other was eventually salvaged and fitted out, the four being the **Attilio Regolo**, **Pompeo Magno**, **Giulio Germanico** and **Scipione Africano**.

One pair served post-war with each of the French and Italian fleets. Of the Italian ships, the **San Giorgio** (ex-*Giulio Germanico*) served, albeit re-engined, until 1971. None of the four mounted its original armament, however, supply considerations dictating American 127-mm (5-in) L/38 guns in the Italian ships and ex-German 105-mm (4.13-in) weapons in the French units.

SPECIFICATION	
Ships in class (launched): *Attilio Regolo* (1940), *Pompeo Magno* (1911), *Giulio Germanico* (1941) and *Scipione Africano* (1941) **Displacement:** 3,685 tons standard and 5,335 tons full load **Dimensions:** length 142.9 m (468 ft 10 in); beam 14.4 m (47 ft 3 in); draught 4.1 m (13 ft 5 in)	**Propulsion:** geared steam turbines delivering 82,015 kW (110,000 shp) to two shafts **Speed:** 40 kts **Armament:** four twin 135-mm (5.31-in), eight 37-mm AA and eight 20-mm AA guns, plus eight 533-mm (21-in) torpedo tubes **Complement:** 418 men

'Nachi' class Heavy cruiser

While clearly related to the preceding 'Aoba' class, the four **'Nachi'-class** cruisers were some 10 per cent longer and introduced the fearsomely massive aspect characteristic of the next decade of Japanese cruiser construction.

Powerful units

Proportionately more 'beamy' than earlier classes, the 'Nachi'-class ships mounted ten 203-mm (8-in) guns and had improved protection worked in. Like most of their kind, they looked odd to Western eyes but

Above: **IJN** Myoko, *the second of the four 'Nachi'-class heavy cruisers, accelerates to her full speed of more than 33 kt (61 km/h; 38 mph) off Ukuru Island in the summer of 1941.*

Below: **Myoko** *in late-war camouflage with two submarines alongside. Torpedoed at Leyte Gulf in October 1944 and again two months later,* **Myoko** *managed to reach Singapore where it remained, unrepaired, until the end of the war.*

Below: Japanese cruisers originally carried limited air defences. However, the eight 25-mm anti-aircraft guns of 1941 soon grew to match the threat of US Navy carrier aircraft, and by the end of the war surviving cruisers were carrying more than 50 such guns.

*The heavy cruiser **Nachi** manoeuvres violently in Manila Bay on 5 November 1944. It is trying to escape the attentions of US Navy dive bombers, but to no avail: soon afterwards, **Nachi** was hit repeatedly and sunk.*

SPECIFICATION	
'Nachi' class	**Speed:** 33.5 kt
Ships in class (launched): *Nachi* (1927), *Myoko* (1927), *Haguro* (1928) *Ashigara* (1928)	**Armour:** belt 100 mm (4 in); deck 65-125 mm (2½-5 in); turrets 40 mm (1½ in)
Displacement: 13,380 tons full load	**Armament (as built):** Ten 203-mm (8-in), eight 127-mm (5-in) DP and eight 25-mm AA guns, plus 16 610-mm (24-in) torpedo tubes
Dimensions: length 201.7 m (661 ft 9 in) waterline; beam 20.7 m (68 ft); draught 6.3 m (20 ft 9 in)	**Aircraft:** three floatplanes
Propulsion: geared steam turbines delivering 96,940 kW (130,000 shp) to four shafts	**Complement:** 780 men

were powerfully built and proved to be extraordinarily difficult to sink.

More torpedoes

Immediately before the outbreak of World War II, their torpedo armament was increased to 16 610-mm (24-in) tubes in keeping with the aggressive tactical doctrine that was to pay such handsome dividends for the Imperial Japanese Navy – in the early years, at least. Their topweight reserves must have been pushed to the limit, however, for

when AA armament was urgently enhanced later in the war, some had the torpedo armament reduced again.

Like most of the hard worked Japanese cruiser classes, the 'Nachi' class suffered badly at enemy hands. Unusually, two of the four were accounted for by the Royal Navy, the **Ashigara** being sunk by submarine torpedo in the Bangka Strait and the **Haguro** falling to a classically executed night destroyer attack in May 1945. **Nachi**, which with the *Haguro* had smashed the ABDA cruiser

force in the Java Sea early in 1942, was destroyed by US Navy carrier aircraft off Leyte in November 1944. **Myoko** was surrendered in a totally unserviceable state.

Combat losses

The *Haguro* had fought at the Java Sea, Sunda Strait and the action off Samar. She had survived Midway, Empress Augusta Bay and the second

battle of the Solomons. It was, therefore, particularly gratifying for the renascent British Pacific Fleet to intercept her as she passed through the Malacca Strait in May 1945 en route to evacuate the garrison of the Andamans. Five destroyers of the 26th Flotilla attacked in divisions so that, in avoiding the torpedoes of the first, the *Haguro* ran foul of those of the second.

'Mogami' class Light/heavy cruisers

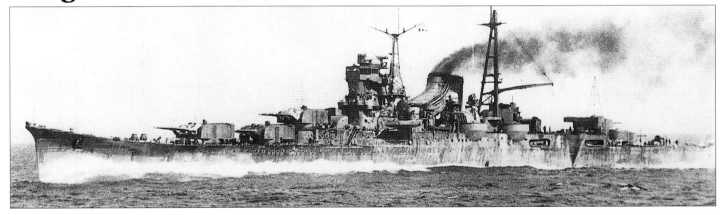

Japan took to the 203-mm (8-in) cruiser enthusiastically, her only light cruisers being 140-mm (5½-in) gunned 'scouts' such as the 'Sendai' class. But because of the restrictions of the 1930 London Treaty, four large 155-mm (6-in) gunned ships were built as the 'Mogami' class, stimulating the Americans

to build the 'Brooklyn' class. Each class had a powerful 15-gun main battery.

To achieve their designed speeds of 37 kt (68 km/h; 42 mph), the Japanese ships were very slender, and proved to be dangerously vulnerable. They were, therefore, bulged externally in 1937.

*Top: Seen on trials in 1933, **Mogami** was built as a large 'light' cruiser armed with fifteen 152-mm (6-in) guns. With the end of the Washington Treaty, she and her sisters were converted to heavy cruisers, being refitted with ten 203-mm (8-in) guns.*

Re-armed

Less than two years later, all treaties having lapsed, they were again modified, their triple 155-mm (6-in) turrets being

exchanged for twin 203-mm (8-in) turrets and the bulge being increased in size. Their speed was now barely 34 kt (63 km/h; 39 mph), the same as that of

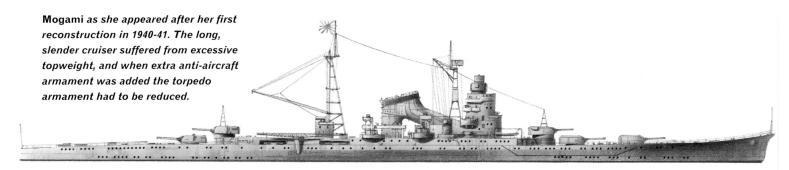

Mogami *as she appeared after her first reconstruction in 1940-41. The long, slender cruiser suffered from excessive topweight, and when extra anti-aircraft armament was added the torpedo armament had to be reduced.*

Right: **Suzuya**, *the third of the 'Mogami' class, accelerates to 37 kt (68 km/h; 42 mph). Although nominally a light cruiser at this time, her exceptionally heavy armament of fifteen 152-mm (6-in) guns made her a force to be reckoned with in surface combat.*

the 'Brooklyn' class but with 50 per cent extra power.

During World War II the class formed the coherent 7th Cruiser Squadron under the redoubtable Rear Admiral Kurita, and was continuously active. The **Mogami**, in company with the **Mikuma**, took part in the destruction of the USS *Houston* and HMAS *Perth* after the Java Sea battle. Later, as part of the diversionary force at Midway, the two cruisers collided heavily before being attacked by carrier aircraft; the *Mikuma* was sunk but *Mogami*, with 300 dead, survived to fight another day.

Damaged

In November 1943 the *Mogami* was part of a large Japanese fleet caught unawares by air attack at Rabaul. Hit heavily, blazing and down by the bows from flooded magazines, she again escaped sinking.

She then survived the Battle of the Philippine Sea, only to meet her end at the night action in the Surigao Strait. Battered by gunfire, she collided with the heavy cruiser *Nachi* but, typically, continued into action.

Mogami *lies a battered wreck after collision damage and air attack at Midway. The cruiser was back in action by the end of 1943, with the two rear turrets removed to make room for up to 11 seaplanes.*

Attacked next day by aircraft, she was scuttled by a Japanese torpedo.

The other two units were also lost in the war, **Suzuya** being sunk by carrier aircraft off Samar. **Kumano** was damaged in the same action, before being hit by a submarine torpedo. The disabled cruiser was finished off by aircraft a month later.

SPECIFICATION	
'Mogami' class	**Speed:** 37 kt (68 km/h; 42 mph)/
Ships in class (launched): *Mogami* (1934), *Mikuma* (1934), *Suzuya* (1934) and *Kumano* (1936)	34 kt (63 km/h; 39 mph) post-rebuild
	Armour: belt 100 mm (4 in); deck 35 mm (1½ in); turrets 25 mm (1 in)
Displacement: 12,400 tons	**Armament:** Fifteen 155-mm
Dimensions: length 203.9 m (669 ft); beam 20.2 m (66 ft 3 in); draught 5.8 m (19 ft)	(6-in) later replaced by ten 203-mm (8-in); eight 127-mm (5-in) DP and eight 25-mm AA guns, plus 12
Propulsion: geared turbines delivering 111855 kW (150,000 shp) to four shafts	610-mm (24-in) torpedo tubes
	Aircraft: three floatplanes
	Complement: 780 men

'Takao' class Heavy cruiser

SPECIFICATION

'Takao' class
Ships in class (launched): *Takao* (1930), *Atago* (1930), *Maya* (1930), and *Chokai* (1931)
Displacement: 9,850 tons standard and 12,781 tons trial; *Takao/Atago* 13,400/14,600 tons after refit
Dimensions: length 203.76 m (661 ft 8 in); beam 18.03 m (59 ft 2 in); draught 6.11 m (20 ft 1 in)
Propulsion: geared turbines delivering 96,941 kW (130,000 shp) to four shafts
Speed: 35.5 kts

Armour: belt 100 mm (3.9 in); magazines 127 mm (4.9 in); deck 35 mm (1.5 in); turrets 25 mm (1 in)
Armament: 10 203-mm (8-in) guns, four 120-mm (4.7-in) guns (from 1942, and eight 127-mm/5-in DP guns) but see text for *Maya* in 1944; all units had 26 or more 25-mm AA guns in 1944; as built, eight 610-mm (24-in) torpedoes, *Takao* and *Atago* 16 610-mm torpedoes from 1941
Aircraft: 3
Complement: 773 men

*The cruiser **Takao** outside Tokyo Bay. Modernized between 1938 and 1940, the **Takao** was struck and damaged by torpedoes from the submarine USS **Dace** on 23 October 1944 north-west of Palawan in the Philippines, and was finally claimed by a British 'X'-craft midget submarine in the Johore Strait.*

The most imposing heavy cruisers of World War II, the ships of the **'Takao' class** were similar to the 'Myoko' class but with an even more massive – and armoured – bridge structure. Their other distinguishing feature was that the second funnel was upright rather than raked back. The 'Takaos' were intended to be of slightly lower displacement than the 'Myokos', but the designers strove to add more armour and improved gun mounts. The magazines received 125 mm (4.9 in) of protection, and the 203-mm (8-in) gun mountings allowed elevation of up to 70° like those of the British 'County'-class ships. The 203-mm guns were never seriously capable of anti-aircraft use, however, and the mountings on **Maya** allowed only 55°. Although US heavy cruisers were built with heavily armoured turrets, the Japanese followed British practice and provided a scant 25 mm (1 in) of armour to protect them.

Like the earlier 'Myoko' class, the 'Takao' class required

extensive alterations within a few years of their completion. The **Takao** and **Atago** were in dockyard hands during 1939–40, receiving double-layer bulges and a doubling of their torpedo armament. They swapped their 120-mm (4.7-in) secondary guns

for 127-mm (5-in) dual-purpose weapons in 1942. Their displacement increased to 13,400 tons (of which 18 per cent was protection) and their speed reduced to 34.25 kts. The outbreak of war prevented *Maya* and **Chokai** undergoing such substantial reworking. They

landed their old 120-mm secondary armament in favour of more capable 127-mm dual-purpose weapons, but they may have spent the early war without their 610-mm (24-in) 'Long Lance' torpedoes being fitted. The *Maya* was severely damaged by US bombers at

*Pictured at Yokosuka in June 1938, the massive superstructure of the **Chokai** typifies Japanese cruiser design before the war. American vessels of the same period were much less effectively armoured, their vulnerability to Japanese shells contributing to heavy early losses in the Solomons.*

Rabaul in November 1943, 'C' turret being destroyed and not replaced. Instead, the vessel was rebuilt as an anti-aircraft cruiser with an additional four 127-mm dual-purpose guns and some 30 25-mm AA guns. The *Maya* ran across the submarine USS *Dace* in the early stages of the Leyte Gulf operations in October 1944, took four torpedo

hits and sank.

The *Chokai* was also earmarked for conversion to anti-aircraft cruiser standard, but in this instance the work was never undertaken. Closing the US escort carriers at the Battle off Samar, the ship was sunk by repeated bomb hits from aircraft defending their own ships. The *Atago* ran into four torpedoes

from the USS *Darter* in the preliminary stages of the Battle of Leyte Gulf and sank. The *Takao* was hit by two torpedoes from the same submarine but limped back to Singapore. There

it was sunk at its moorings on 31 July 1945 by the British midget submarine *XE-3* – the wreck was refloated after the war and scuttled in the Straits of Malacca.

*The **Atago** is seen cruising at a speed of 34.12 kts off Tateyama in August 1939 after its modernization. The heavy armament of the 'Takao' class was crucial to the Japanese victory in the Battle of Savo Island in August 1942.*

'Tone' class Light/heavy cruiser

The **'Tone' class** attempted to combine the armament of a 'Mogami'-class cruiser – 12 155-mm (6.1-in) guns in four triple turrets – with a hull displacing only 8,500 tons. This compared to the 'Mogami'-class ships' designed displacement of 9,500 tons, which rose to over 11,000 tons during construction. This policy stemmed from Japan's determination to extract

maximum value from the tonnage limitations imposed on her by treaty. The renunciation of those treaty limits came in time to save the 'Tone' design from mutually incompatible specifications and the ships were changed to 'scout cruisers', intended to carry eight reconnaissance floatplanes.

Just as the 'Mogami' class traded their 155-mm guns for

203-mm (8-in) weapons, the 'Tone' class were completed with 203-mm guns. Japan failed to develop a triple turret for these, so the 'Tone' class had eight guns in four twin turrets. This devotion to surface firepower in a design intended for aerial reconnaissance was typically Japanese: a lighter battery would have freed weight and space for more anti-aircraft weapons. The guns were concentrated forward in an arrangement calculated to tighten the grouping of their salvoes while requiring less armour for a similar level of protection.

With no barbettes at the stern, the 'Tone'-class ships had roomier accommodation than other Japanese cruisers and were popular with their crews. However, the Imperial naval high

command regarded them as failures and abandoned the 'scout cruiser' concept. In the event, the ships never carried the eight aircraft planned: six was the maximum operational number but five was the usual quantity, and by 1944 they were reduced to two or three – no more than a standard cruiser.

Ironically, given their intended role, it was the failure of the **Tone**'s aircraft that shaped the opening moves at the Battle of Midway. The **Chikuma** survived a heavy bombing attack off the Solomons but was disabled by an aerial torpedo during the Battle of Leyte Gulf and was scuttled by the Japanese destroyer *Nowake* on 25 October 1944.

The *Tone* was sunk on 24 July 1945, caught near Kure by a US air attack.

SPECIFICATION	
'Tone' class	**Armour:** belt 100 mm (3.9 in);
Ships in class (launched): *Tone*	magazines 145 mm (5.7 in); deck
(1937), and *Chikuma* (1938)	31 mm (1.2 in); turrets 25 mm (1 in)
Displacement: 10,500 tons standard;	**Armament:** 15 155-mm (6.1-in) guns
15,000 tons maximum	as designed but eight 203-mm (8-in)
Dimensions: length 201.5 m (661 ft 1	guns after modernization, eight 127-
in); beam 19.4 m (63 ft 7 in);	mm (5-in) DP guns, eight to 12
draught 10.9 m (35 ft 10 in)	25-mm AA guns, and 12 610-mm
Propulsion: geared turbines	(24-in) torpedo tubes
delivering 97113 kW (90,000 shp) to	**Aircraft:** 5 (but see text)
four shafts	**Complement:** 850 men
Speed: 33 kts	

Japanese light cruisers

The Imperial Japanese navy built a few light cruisers in the 1920s before concentrating on heavy cruisers armed with 203-mm (8-in) guns. Before World War II,

it ordered four **'Katori'-class** training ships/submarine flotilla flagships, which served as light cruisers, but there were no equivalents of the US and

British 6-in 152-mm) cruisers that made up a high proportion of the Allies' cruiser squadrons.

The four units of the **'Sendai' class** laid down in 1922 were

similar to the light cruisers completed by the British at the end of World War I. The **Kako** was cancelled to comply with the terms of the Washington

The 'Agano'-class cruiser **Noshiro** *is pictured in June 1943. These vessels had thin armour plating and proved to be underarmed. It is likely that a turret was planned in the 'X' position, but this was replaced by more torpedo tubes (the six tubes planned being eight tubes upon completion), as well as facilities for aircraft.*

Naval Treaty and the hull dismantled on the slipway. The surviving three ships' seven 140-mm (5.5-in) guns were mounted in single turrets and the 5 per cent of displacement allocated to armour protection was enough to keep out the 4-in (102-mm) shells of US destroyers of the time. By World War II, US destroyers were better armed and the **Sendai** and **Jintsu** were sunk in gun actions with US light cruisers and destroyers. The **Naka** succumbed to air attack.

Three classes of light cruiser built during World War I were still in first-line service in 1941: the **'Tenryu' class** (two units), the **'Kuma' class** (five units), and the **'Nagara' class** (six units). The 'Tenryus' were 3,200-ton flotilla leaders armed with four 140-mm guns and six 533-mm (21-in) torpedo tubes.

Short-ranged for Pacific operations, both were sunk by US submarines. The 5,500-ton 'Kumas' had the same gun armament as the 'Sendais'. They were rearmed with 'Long Lance' torpedoes in 1940 but the **Kitakami** and **Oi** were rebuilt as torpedo-cruisers, carrying 40 610-mm (24-in) torpedoes. Neither had a chance to use its armament: the Kitakami was converted into a fast transport in 1943, and the Oi was sunk by the submarine USS *Flasher*. The 5,570-ton 'Nagaras' were again armed with seven 140-mm guns but equipped with 'Long Lance' torpedoes during the war. The **Yuri** was crippled by US Marine aircraft off Guadalcanal in October 1942 and scuttled; two sister ships were lost at Leyte Gulf and three to submarine attack in 1944–45.

Four modern light cruisers

SPECIFICATION	
'Sendai' class	delivering 97,113 kW (90,000 shp) to four shafts
Ships in class (launched): *Sendai* (1923), *Jintsu* (1923) and *Naka* (1925)	**Speed:** 35 kts
	Armour: belt 63 mm (2.5 in); deck 28 mm (1.1 in)
Displacement: 5,195 tons standard; 7,100 full load	**Armament:** seven 140-mm (5.5-in) guns, two 76-mm (3-in) guns, eight 610-mm (24-in) torpedo tubes, and 80 mines
Dimensions: length 163 m (534 ft 9 in); beam 14.17 m (48 ft 5 in); draught 4.91 m (16 ft 1 in)	
Propulsion: geared turbines	**Aircraft:** 1

were laid down in 1939. The 6,652-ton **'Agano' class** had six 152-mm guns in three twin turrets and eight 610-mm torpedo tubes. Conceived as destroyer leaders, they were capable of 35 kts but their protection was effective only against shells of 127-mm (5-in) calibre or less, The **Yahagi** accompanied the super battleship *Yamato* on its suicide sortie in April 1945.

The single **'Oyodo'-class** vessel was an enlarged and

improved version of the 'Agano' class and was intended to be used as a flagship for attack groups of submarines and aircraft. The after 152-mm gun position was discarded in favour of a large hangar to accommodate six large high-speed reconnaissance bombers. The aircraft were never built, however, and instead **Oyodo** carried two standard scout aircraft and served as a fleet flagship, taking no real part in combat operations.

Left: The 'Nagara'-class cruiser **Yura** *is seen during Sino-Japanese hostilities off Shanghai in August 1937. The class were originally fitted with hangars.*

Below: An enlarged and improved 'Agano', the **Oyodo** *was intended to serve as a flagship for attack groups comprised of submarines and aircraft.*

'County' class Heavy cruiser

It was because of the new British 'Hawkins'-class ships – nearly 10,000 tons displacement and armed with 7.5-in (190.5-mm) guns – that the Washington Treaty limits on cruisers were set as they were. In keeping with the remainder of the signatories, who built up to these limits, the British produced the **'A'** or **'County' class**. Their designers eschewed, however, the current competitions for optimal armament or speed, producing instead a compromise well-suited to duties on imperial trade routes. Even so they were well armed, had an adequate turn of speed, and were reasonably protected. They were notable for their considerable freeboard and three funnels,

recognizable anywhere. Excellent endurance and good standards of habitability made them both effective and popular. The London Treaty came into force before the construction programme was complete and some five planned units were cancelled.

Though built in three separate groups as the **'Kent' class** (seven ships), **'London' class** (four ships) and **'Norfolk' class** (two ships), the 'County'-class ships were originally similar, but modernization during the 1930s produced variations. On four, the after superstructure was enlarged as an aircraft hangar, two of them being cut down a deck aft to compensate as the hull had a reputation for hard rolling. **HMS London** (only)

*HMS **Norfolk** as it appeared in 1943. The 'County'-class heavy cruisers were a compromise designed to operate effectively in the protection of long trade routes. They had excellent endurance and were popular with their crews.*

SPECIFICATION	
'County' class ('London' sub-class) **Ships in class (launched):** *Berwick* (1926), *Cornwall* (1926), *Cumberland* (1926), *Kent* (1926), *Suffolk* (1926), *Australia* (1927), *Canberra* (1927), *Devonshire* (1927), *London* (1927), *Shropshire* (1928), *Sussex* (1928), *Dorsetshire* (1929) and *Norfolk* (1928) **Displacement:** 9,8250 tons standard and 14,000 tons full load **Dimensions:** length 193.3 m (633 ft); beam 20.2 m (66 ft); draught 6.6 m (21 ft 6 in)	**Propulsion:** Parsons or Brown Curtis geared turbines delivering 59655 kW (80,000 shp) to four shafts **Speed:** 32 kts **Armour:** belt 76–127 mm (3–5 in); deck 38–102 mm (1.5–4 in); turrets 38–mm (1.5–2 in); barbettes 25 mm (1 in) **Armament:** eight 8-in (203-mm), eight 4-in (102-mm) AA and eight or 16 2-pdr AA guns, plus eight 21-in (533-mm) torpedo tubes **Aircraft:** one or three flying-boats **Complement:** 660 men

*The 'County'-class cruiser HMS **Devonshire** draws alongside HMS **Mauritius** in the Indian Ocean. The two ships are about to effect a transfer of either stores or personnel, with a line being passed from one ship to the other by means of a small rocket.*

emerged in 1941 from a rebuilding that left it looking like an enlarged 'Fiji'-class cruiser with improved AA armament, the war preventing further such exercises. In surface action, the ships proved effective but fell victim to air attack as readily as any other of their vintage. Their main contribution to the war at sea lay in the unspectacular but vital tasks of convoy protection and operations against raiders. Losses were **HMAS** *Canberra*, **HMS** *Dorsetshire* and **HMS** *Cornwall*.

Instrumental in the hunt for the Bismarck in May 1941, when using its primitive radar, HMS Suffolk, seen with a Walrus floatplane embarked, was part of the initial group of seven 'County'-class cruisers, also known as the 'Kent' class.

'Arethusa' class Light cruiser

Three generations of light cruiser are seen heading to join the naval bombardment of Normandy in June 1944. Beyond HMS Arethusa can be seen HMS Danae, dating from 1918, and the 'Fiji'-class cruiser HMS Mauritius, completed in 1941.

At the time of the London Treaty of 1930, the UK was building the first 6-in (152-mm) cruisers designed since World War I. Ostensibly replacements for the smaller 'C'- and 'D'-class cruisers, these were the five eight-gun 'Leander'-class ships designed around a twin-gun mounting tried experimentally on HMS *Enterprise*. A three-ship derivative, the 'Amphion' class differed mainly in having widely spaced funnels through the improved layout of machinery spaces.

Once ratified, the treaty imposed limits on the total replacement 6-in tonnage that the British were permitted to build, and the Admiralty experimented with a cut-down six-gunned version known as the **'Arethusa' class**. In tonnage terms, four could be built for three 'Leanders', but they were considered too small and only four were built.

Despite their lack of size, the 'Arethusa'-class cruisers found their ideal slot in the Mediterranean war. Best known were **HMS** *Aurora* and **HMS** *Penelope* which, while forming the core of Force K working out of Malta in 1941, destroyed

Built within Washington Treaty limits, the six-gun 'Arethusa'-class cruisers were considered too small, but gave fine service in the Mediterranean. Here an 'Arethusa' is photographed from HMS King George V.

convoyed Italian shipping at a rate that caused the Axis armies in North Africa acute supply problems. Both were damaged on the night when Force K was very nearly destroyed in a minefield.

The *Penelope* was repaired and went on to take part in the most hard-fought of the Malta convoys, including Admiral Vian's superb defence at the 2nd Battle of Sirte in March 1942. Docked again in Malta, *Penelope*

was so riddled with splinters as to earn the soubriquet 'HMS Pepperpot'.

Together once again with the *Aurora* in Force Q, the *Penelope* saw the end of Axis ambitions in North Africa, going on to the Sicilian and Salerno landings. Bombed and damaged in the Aegean, the ship saw its last action at Anzio, being sunk by a torpedo from the German submarine *U-410* while returning to Naples in February 1944. Also

sunk in the war was **HMS *Galatea***, which was lost to a

torpedo from *U-577* west of Alexandria in December 1941.

SPECIFICATION	
'Arethusa' class	**Speed:** 32.25 kts
Ships in class (launched): *Arethusa* (1934), *Galatea* (1934), *Penelope* (1935), *Aurora* (1936)	**Armour:** belt 51 mm (2 in); deck 51 mm (2 in); turrets 25 mm (1 in); conning tower 25 mm (1 in)
Displacement: 5,250 tons standard	**Armament:** six 6-in (152-mm), eight 4-in (102-mm) AA, and eight 2-pdr AA guns, plus six 21-in (533-mm) torpedo tubes
Dimensions: length 154.2 m (506 ft); beam 15.5 m (51 ft); draught 4.2 m (13 ft 9 in)	
Propulsion: geared turbines delivering 47725 kW (64,000 shp) to four shafts	**Aircraft:** one flying-boat (not in *Aurora*)
	Complement: 470 men

'York' class Heavy cruiser

In the mid-1920s, the Admiralty became increasingly wedded to the idea that the Royal Navy required a large number of small, heavy cruisers.

The **'York'-class** cruisers were ostensibly designed for convoy escort missions. The amount of armour covering their machinery was reduced, as naval architects assumed that the class would be more at risk from attack from an oblique angle rather than at a right angle to the broadside. **HMS *Exeter*** and **HMS *York*** were of a similar design, except the *Exeter*'s bridge was lower. This vessel also had a slightly wider beam to improve its stability, and a catapult amidships.

Launched on 18 July 1929, the *Exeter* was commissioned into the Second Cruiser Squadron, and from October 1933 to August 1939 joined the America and West Indies Squadron.

Battle of River Plate

However, on 25 August 1939, *Exeter* sailed towards Latin America on the eve of the Battle of River Plate. By 7 December, the German pocket battleship, *Admiral Graf Spee*, had sunk nine ships totalling over 50,000 tons and was hunted prey. *Exeter* led a task force of the light cruiser *Achilles* of the Royal New Zealand Navy and HMS *Ajax*. At 06.08, on 13 December, *Graf Spee* was sighted and intercepted by the

Allied ships. Trapped between *Exeter*, *Achilles* and *Ajax*, *Graf Spee* was bombarded from both sides. However, *Graf Spee* had a technical advantage, its surface warning radar locating *Exeter* to begin a bombardment lasting for 35 minutes. *Exeter* took hits from *Graf Spee*'s 208-mm (11-in) shells. *Exeter* retaliated, her 8-in (203-mm) guns raining damage on the German pocket battleship. *Graf Spee* ran for the safety of neutral Montevideo, to be scuttled there on 17 December. Three days later, *Graf Spee*'s captain, Hans Langsdorf, committed suicide.

Exeter spent the next month undergoing emergency repairs in the Falkland Islands, and then returned to the UK, to undergo an extended refit and modernization. *Exeter* then swapped the western

hemisphere for the eastern, and on March 1941, after a short spell in the hunt for the *Bismarck*, sailed for Singapore.

In February 1942, *Exeter* was damaged during the Battle of Java Sea. Between 27 and 28 February, the ship underwent repairs in Surabaya, Java. However, she was forced to flee as the Japanese approached. Pounced on by the heavy cruisers *Nachi*, *Haguro*, *Ashigara*

Designed as a cut-down 'County'-class cruiser, HMS Exeter saw a great deal of action, ranging from an engagement with the pocket battleship Graf Spee through convoy protection and patrol duty to its final action in the East Indies.

and *Myoko*, she was severally damaged and was scuttled on 1 March 1942.

SPECIFICATION	
'Exeter' cruiser	**Speed:** 32 kts
Ships in class (launched): *York* (1928); *Exeter* (1929)	**Armour:** belt 51–76 mm (2–3 in); deck 51 mm (2 in); turrets 38-51 mm (1.5-2 in)
Displacement: *Exeter* 8390 tons standard; *York* 8250 tons standard	**Armament:** *Exeter* six 8-in (203-mm), eight 4-in (102-mm), and 16 40-mm AA guns, plus six 21-in (533-mm) torpedo tubes; *York* six 8-in (203-mm), and eight 4-in (102-mm) guns, plus six 21-in (533-mm) torpedo tubes
Dimensions: *Exeter* length 164.9 m (540 ft); beam 18 m (58 ft); draught 6.2 m (20 ft); *York* length 164.9 m (540 ft); beam 17.4 m (57 ft); draught 6.2 m (20 ft)	
Propulsion: geared turbines delivering 59656 kW (80,000 shp) to four shafts	**Aircraft:** two flying-boats
	Complement: 630 men

'Town' class Heavy cruiser

The eight **'Southampton'-** or **'Town'-class** cruisers represented the end of British involvement with treaty-imposed limitations. With their 'Brooklyn' class, the Americans had matched the Japanese 'Mogami' class, and the Admiralty felt obliged to respond with a powerful 6-in (152-mm) cruiser aimed at fleet work rather than commerce protection, as had been the case with the 'Leander' class and its successors.

Launched in 1936–37, the class was completed for the outbreak of World War II. Though designed on a smaller scale than the units of the classes which had led to their construction, the ships carried 12 reliable guns in a new-pattern triple turret, and could maintain more than 32 kts in a seaway. They were used mainly in the European theatre. Three of the ships (**Southampton**, **Manchester** and **Gloucester**) were lost to enemy action in the Mediterranean, two of them in 1941 and one in 1942, but none of the ships was sunk through conventional surface action.

For the ship's size and scale of protection, the main battery was ambitious, and the last three units of the 'Southampton' class (**Liverpool**, *Manchester* and *Gloucester*) were completed to a revised standard typified by a 0.15-m (6-in) increase in beam and a 300-ton increase in displacement. Further modernizations saw the removal of the X turret and the enhancement of the AA armament.

In 1938, two examples of an improved version were launched. While carrying the same armament as their predecessors, **Belfast** and **Edinburgh** were larger and better protected and also had more powerful machinery. All of the 'Town'-class ships were well built, giving in some cases more than 30 years of useful service. Indeed the *Belfast* is

Above: Developed from the 'Town' class ships, the cruisers of the 'Crown Colony' class such as HMS Kenya reflected wartime experience. The ships were shorter but faster than their predecessors, and had a much improved secondary ammunition supply.

Seen on escort duty, HMS Sheffield was a Type I 'Town'-class cruiser. The 'Town' class was intended to match the vessels of the Japanese 'Mogami' class.

still afloat as the sole remaining example of a long line of British cruisers.

Developed from the 'Town' class was the **'Fiji'** or **'Crown Colony'** class (11 ships), and its first derivative, the **'Swiftsure'** class (six ships). Smaller but slightly faster, these were emergency programme ships and, while they did prove effective in service, the inferior quality of their construction was reflected in shorter lives.

SPECIFICATION	
'Town' class (Type III)	draught 5.3 m (17 ft 6 in)
Ships in class (launched): Type I or 'Southampton' class *Newcastle* (1936), *Southampton* (1936), *Birmingham* (1936), *Glasgow* (1936) and *Sheffield* (1936); Type II or 'Liverpool' class *Liverpool* (1937), *Manchester* (1937) and *Gloucester* (1937); Type III or 'Belfast' class *Belfast* (1938) and *Edinburgh* (1938)	**Propulsion:** Parsons geared turbines delivering 61520 kW (82,500 shp) to four shafts
	Speed: 32 kts
	Armour: belt 114 mm (4.5 in); deck 51 mm (2 in); turrets 25–63.5 mm (1–2.5 in); conning tower 102 mm (4 in)
Displacement: 10,550 tons standard and 13,175 tons full load	**Armament:** 12 6-in (152-mm), eight 4-in (102-mm) AA and eight or 16 2-pdr guns, plus six 21-in (533-mm) torpedo tubes
Dimensions: length 187 m (613 ft 6 in); beam 19.3 m (63 ft 3 in);	**Aircraft:** three seaplanes
	Complement: 850 men

The heavy cruisers of the 'Town' and immediately following classes were well balanced ships offering a good combination of capabilities. Seen returning from patrol, HMS Belfast was one of two Type III 'Town'-class vessels.

'Dido' class Light cruiser

An increasing awareness of the threat from aerial attack was apparent in the warship design programmes just before World War II. Besides rebuilding some of its older cruisers as AA ships, the Royal Navy acquired the 16-strong **'Dido' class** in two groups for close defence work. A little larger than the 'Arethusa'-class cruisers, the original 11 ships had a lean, elegant appearance. They had no secondary armament, the main battery being 10 5.25-in (133-mm) dual-purpose (DP) guns in the twin mountings developed as a secondary weapon for the 'King George V'-class battleships. These turrets were light enough to permit three superimposed mountings forward, though in later years the proliferation of tophamper resulted in the landing of the uppermost, or Q, mounting.

The last five ships were of the **'Improved Dido' class** with eight-gun fits from the start, shorter vertical funnels and sturdier masts. These modifications did nothing for their looks, but these ships served farther afield, even for Arctic convoy escort, whereas the earlier ships were used mainly in the Mediterranean. There they were superb and though one was sunk by a glide bomb attack off Anzio, none was lost to direct air attack.

HMS Dido on fire-support duty off Gaeta during the final Allied drive up the length of Italy. The dual-purpose twin turrets had been designed for use in the secondary armament of the 'King George V'-class battleships.

Despite their limitations in both the anti-ship and anti-aircraft roles, the light cruisers of the 'Dido' class were well balanced vessels. HMS Black Prince was a cruiser of the improved Type II 'Dido' class.

The 5.25-in gun was not an ideal dual-purpose weapon; it was light for surface use against the protected ships of the day, yet too heavy for effective use against aircraft, with too slow a

SPECIFICATION

'Dido' class (Type II)
Ships in class (launched): Type I *Dido* (1939), *Euryalus* (1939), *Naiad* (1939), *Phoebe* (1939), *Sirius* (1940), *Bonaventure* (1939), *Hermione* (1939), *Charybdis* (1940), *Cleopatra* (1940), *Scylla* (1940) and *Argonaut* (1941); Type II *Bellona* (1942), *Black Prince* (1942), *Diadem* (1942), *Royalist* (1942) and *Spartan* (1942)
Displacement: 5,710 tons standard and 6,970 tons full load
Dimensions: length 156.3 m (512 ft); beam 15.4 m (50 ft 6 in); draught

5.3 m (17 ft 3 in)
Propulsion: Parsons geared turbines delivering 47725 kW (64,000 shp) to four shafts
Speed: 32.25 kts
Armour: belt 76 mm (3 in); deck 51 mm (2 in); turrets 25–38 mm (1–1.5 in); barbettes 13–19 mm (0.5–0.75 in); conning tower 25 mm (1 in)
Armament: eight 5.25-in (133-mm) DP, eight or 12 2-pdr AA, and 12 20-mm AA guns, plus six 21-in (533-mm) torpedo tubes
Complement: 535 men

rate of fire and reaction. After the war, the 'Dido'-class ships proved of little more use to the Royal Navy than the 'Atlanta' class to the US Navy, and most had been scrapped by the end of the 1950s. Wartime losses were the **Charybdis** (torpedoed off the north coast of France, 1943), **Hermione** (torpedoed Eastern Mediterranean, 1942), **Bonaventure** (torpedoed Eastern Mediterranean, 1941), **Naiad** (torpedoed north east of Egyptian coast, 1942) and **Spartan** (glide bomb, Anzio 1944).

The primary AA role of the 'Dido' class was evident in the their main armament, which comprised 10 5.25-in (133-mm) DP guns in five superfiring turrets. The Type I ship HMS Argonaut is seen here at speed.

'La Galissonnière' class Light cruiser

Contemporary with the penultimate pair of Italian 'Condottieri'-class light cruisers, the French 'La Galissonnière'-class light cruisers had a distinct edge in the overall capability of their design. By adopting a triple 152-mm (6-in) turret, the designers managed an excellent balance on the low standard displacement of 7,600 tons. Three mountings conferred a one-gun advantage over the eight guns of their rivals while economizing on weight, length of hull, and the area to be protected. Thus, vertical protection of up to 120 mm (4.62 in) could be worked into the basic design, with a 50-mm (1.97-in) protective deck. While the Italians could dispose of 89485 kW (120,000 shp), the French had only 62640 kW (84,000 shp) available to them,

yet the effective speed of the two classes in a seaway were little different at 33 to 34 kts.

Interestingly, the French hulls incorporated wide transom sterns of the type that is today virtually universal in modern warship design, reducing resistance through the suppression of the stern wave. Another interesting feature was the method of aircraft recovery: a sloping steel mesh mat was lowered out of the stern onto which the aircraft was taxied, before being hoisted aboard by a stern crane.

Machinery problems

Six ships of the type were built, but they fared badly with the changing fortunes of the French state. After France's June 1940 armistice with Germany, the loyalties of French Senegal

were not known to the British, who mounted an operation against Dakar: the **Gloire**, together with the **Montcalm** and **Georges Leygues**, sailed from Toulon to assist. Suffering from machinery problems, the *Gloire* went into Casablanca but the other two light cruisers reached Dakar. This port, though effectively neutralized, passed to Allied control only

when Axis forces finally occupied Vichy France in November 1942, the three cruisers coming over to the Allied cause. With the occupation, the remaining major ships of the French fleet, which were still inactive at Toulon, were scuttled, including the three surviving ships of the class. Of these, two were salvaged by the Italians, only to be sunk finally by Allied bombing in 1943. The *Gloire* was present at Anzio, and the *Montcalm* at Normandy.

Pictured in the bold markings designed to make an enemy's optical ranging of the ship very difficult, the Gloire was a unit of France's most successful pre-war cruiser design. By this time, the ship had been refitted in the US with radar and much enhanced AA armament. Two other vessels in the class were similarly refitted.

SPECIFICATION	
'La Galissonnière' class	63640 kW (84,000 shp) to two shafts
Ships in class (launched): *La Galissonnière* (1933), *Jean de Vienne* (1935), *Marseillaise* (1935), *Gloire* (1935), *Montcalm* (1935) and *Georges Leygues* (1936)	**Speed:** 35.7 kts
	Armour: belt 75-120 mm (3-4.7 in); deck 50 mm (2 in); turrets 75–130 mm (3–5.1 in)
Displacement: 7,600 tons standard and 9,120 tons full load	**Armament:** nine 152-mm (6-in), eight 90-mm (3.5-in) DP and eight 13.2-mm (0.52-in) AA guns, plus four 550-mm (21.7-in) torpedo tubes
Dimensions: length 179 m (586 ft 3 in); beam 17.5 m (57 ft 4 in); draught 5.3 m (17 ft 5 in)	
Propulsion: Rateau-Bretagne or Parsons geared turbines delivering	**Aircraft:** two floatplanes
	Complement: 540 men

'Northampton' class Heavy cruiser

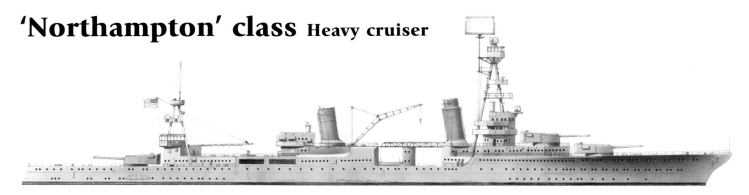

An improvement on the preceding 'Pensacola' class, the 'Northampton'-class cruisers were found to be dangerously vulnerable to Japanese 203-mm (8-in) shells even at long ranges. USS Northampton is depicted as it was in mid-1942, before its final campaign around Guadalcanal.

SPECIFICATION	
'Northampton' class	to four shafts
Ships in class (launched):	**Speed:** 32.5 kts
Northampton (1929), *Chester*	**Armour:** belt 76 mm (3 in); deck
(1929), *Louisville* (1930), *Chicago*	51 mm (2 in); turrets 38–64 mm
(1930), *Houston* (1929) and	(1.5–2.5 in); barbettes 38 mm
Augusta (1930)	(1.5 in); conning tower 203 mm
Displacement: 9,050-9,300 tons	(8 in)
standard and 12,350 tons full load	**Armament:** nine 8-in (203-mm),
Dimensions: length 183 m (600 ft 3	eight 5-in (127-mm) AA, two 3-pdr
in); beam 20.1 m (66 ft); draught	and eight 0.5-in (12.7-mm) AA guns
4.95 m (16 ft 3 in)	**Aircraft:** four floatplanes
Propulsion: Parsons geared turbines	**Complement:** 1,200 men
delivering 79790 kW (107,000 shp)	

America's first pair of Washington Treaty cruisers were the two 'Pensacola'- class heavy cruisers of 1929. Both had very active lives in World War II, but in basic design the ships were not successful, being cramped and having an extremely low freeboard. Their 10-gun 8-in (203-mm) armament (set, unusually, in two triple and two twin turrets) was overambitious to the point at which the ships became extremely tender.

Even before their completion, the design of a much improved **'Northampton'-class** heavy cruiser, was well advanced. These regrouped the main battery into a homogeneous nine guns set in three triple turrets, and had a hull 4.4 m (14 ft 6 in) greater in length plus a raised forecastle to improve seaworthiness.

Of the six ships of the 'Northampton' class, the **USS Houston** was lost in March 1942 in the aftermath of the Java Sea debacle. The **USS Chicago** survived the Savo Island battle in August 1942 with most of her bows removed by a Japanese torpedo. Guadalcanal still claimed her, however, for after repairs she returned to cover a resupply trip to the island and, near Rennell Island, she was sunk by air-launched torpedoes. The **USS**

Northampton also went down in the area, in the night action of Tassafaronga. An American force of five cruisers and six destroyers fell foul of the so-called 'Tokyo Express'. The latter were surprised, but acted with great resolution and speed, using their specialized night-fighting training to good advantage. Despite being encumbered with embarked troops and stores, they split into

subdivisions and launched a devastating torpedo attack.

Four of the five American cruisers were hit, although only the *Northampton* was lost. The surviving trio of the class, known as the **'Chester' class**, lasted until 1960. By 1945, the light AA armament had been boosted by the addition of 16 40-mm guns in quadruple mountings and some 27 20-mm guns in single mountings.

'New Orleans', 'Wichita' and 'Baltimore' classes
Heavy cruisers

Launched between 1933 and 1936, the seven cruisers of the **'New Orleans' class** constitute the primary link between the 'Wichita' and later World War II American heavy cruisers with the lightly protected ships that preceded them. By the late 1920s, concern as growing about the light protection being built into the large cruisers then under construction. It was conceded that the director-controlled 8-in (203-mm) guns of these ships might well prove highly capable, even at high speed and considerable range, but the Bureau of Construction

and Repair was adamant that a high-speed ship of 10,000-ton displacement and armed with 8-in guns could not also be well protected. The completion of the first US cruisers to Washington Treaty limits then revealed that they were some 1,000 tons under the treaty limit.

New cruisers
In 1929, therefore, the US Navy launched a programme of 15 new cruisers to be built in three groups as **CL-** (later **CA-**) **32** to **-36**, **-37** to **-41** and **-42** to **-46**. The programme was later disrupted by the design effects

of the London Treaty of 1930 and the ramifications of the 'Great Depression', but in 1929 came approval of a design like the earlier 'Northampton' class for CA-32 to -36, and the recommendation that the ships of the next group be built to the same design to save time and cost. There was pressure inside the US Navy at this time for a better-protected cruiser, and the Bureau of Construction and Repair conceded that a measure of internal cramping might offer better protection.

At this time the Bureau of Ordnance convinced the

General Board to shift from a specification written in terms of armour thickness to one written in terms of an immune zone: for the new cruiser this was to be 10,975–21,945 m (12,000–24,000 yards) at an impact angle of 60° against the 260-lb (118-kg) 8-in shell.

At first, the new design was to apply only to CA-37 to -41, but of the five previous ships, three (CA-32, -34 and -36) were to be built in Navy yards and so, as the cost of a new design would thus be minimized, they too were built to the new design. CA-33 and -35 were

built as planned but with additional armour on the basis of weight savings discovered in the earlier ships. Of the next group, CA-37 and -38 were modified to incorporate a new and lighter 8-in gun. By the time they had been laid down, it was clear that the 'New Orleans' class design was uncomfortably close to the treaty tonnage limit, and when quadruple 1.1-in (27.9-mm) AA gun mountings were requested for the next ship, CA-39, a programme of

weight reduction, including less protection, was undertaken. The last ship of the class was CA-44, which was a repeat of the CA-39 design. On trials, the name ship made 32.47 kts at 11,179 tons on 82,391 kW (110,503 shp).

Combat survivability

For a class intended for high survivability, the sinking of the **USS Astoria**, **Quincy** and **Vincennes** within a short time in the Battle of Savo Island on

8 August 1942 off Guadalcanal was a great worry, but other members of the class showed great combat survivability. Modification of the ships in World War II was undertaken on a small scale, and included a reduction in the bridgework, elimination of the conning tower, installation of an open bridge, landing one crane and, much later, one of the two

The 'New Orleans' class cruisers had the unhappy distinction, shared with the Italian 'Zara' class, of losing three vessels in a single action. USS Minneapolis, not present at Savo Island, was one of the type.

catapults, and boosting of the light AA armament. By August 1945, the four surviving ships had six quadruple 40-mm and a variety of 20-mm batteries: 14 twin in CA-32, eight twin in CA-36, 28 single in CA-37, and 26 single in CA-38. The four ships were scrapped in the late 1950s/early 1960s.

The **USS Wichita** (CA-45), sole unit of the **'Wichita' class**,

SPECIFICATION
'Baltimore' class **Ships in class (launched):** CA-68 *Baltimore* (1942), CA-69 *Boston* (1942), CA-70 *Canberra* (ex-*Pittsburgh*) (1943), CA-71 *Quincy* (ex-*St Paul*) (1943), CA-72 *Pittsburgh* (ex-*Albany*) (1944), CA-73 *St Paul* (ex-*Rochester*) (1944), CA-74 *Columbus* (1944), CA-75 *Helena* (ex-*Des Moines*) (1945), CA-122 *Oregon City* (1945), CA-123 *Albany* (1945), CA-124 *Rochester* (1945), CA-125 *Northampton* (1951), CA-130 *Bremerton* (1944), CA-131 *Fall River* (1944), CA-132 *Macon* (1944), CA-133 *Toledo* (1945), CA-135 *Los Angeles* (1944), and CA-136 *Chicago* (1944) **Displacement:** 14,472 tons standard	and 17,031 tons full load **Dimensions:** length 205.26 m (673 ft 5 in); beam 21.59 m (70 ft 10 in); draught 7.32 m (24 ft) **Propulsion:** General Electric geared turbines delivering 89,400 kW (120,000 shp) to four shafts **Speed:** 33 kts **Armour:** belt 152–102 mm (6–4 in); deck 64 mm (2.5 in); barbettes 160 mm (6.3 in); turret 203 mm (8 in) face, 76 mm (3 in) roof, 95–51 mm (3.75–2 in) sides and 38 mm (1.5 in) rear; conning tower 152 mm (6 in) **Armament:** nine 8-in (203-mm), 12 5-in (127-mm) DP, 48 40-mm AA, 24 20-mm AA, and four aircraft **Complement:** 1,142 men

*Captured by the camera in 1942, the **USS** Vincennes (CA-44) was the last unit of the US Navy's 'New Orleans' class of heavy cruisers.*

The 'Baltimore' class cruiser USS Chicago (CA-136). In 1958, the ship was converted into a missile cruiser. Five of the class were so configured, and the ships were deleted in the 1970s and early 1980s.

SPECIFICATION

'New Orleans' class
Ships in class (launched): CA-32 *New Orleans* (1933), CA-34 *Astoria* (1933), CA-36 *Minneapolis* (1933), CA-37 *Tuscaloosa* (1933), CA-38 *San Francisco* (1933), CA-39 *Quincy* (1935) and CA-44 *Vincennes* (1936)
Displacement: 10,136 tons standard and 12,463 tons full load
Dimensions: length 179.22 m (588 ft); beam 18.82 m (61 ft 9 in); draught 6.93 m (22 ft 9 in)
Propulsion: Westinghouse geared turbines delivering 79,780 kW
(107,000 shp) to four shafts
Speed: 32.7 kts
Armour: belt 127–83 mm (5–3.25 in); deck 57 mm (2.25 in) over magazines; barbettes 127 mm (5 in) except 152 mm (6 in) in CA-37 and CA-38, and 140 m (5.5 in) in CA-39 and CA-44; turrets 152 mm (6 in) face, 57 mm (2.25 in) roof and 38 mm (1.5 in) side
Armament: nine 8-in (203-mm), eight 5-in (127-mm) AA, eight 0.5-in (12.7-mm) AA, and four aircraft
Complement: 868 men

was a heavy cruiser version of the 'Brooklyn' light cruiser, and as such the precursor of the 'Baltimore' class cruiser.

London treaty

By the terms of the London Treaty, the US was permitted to lay down single heavy cruisers in 1934 and 1935. The 1934 ship was the *Vincennes*, but for 1935 there was proposed a new design based on the USS *Brooklyn* and possessing the superior aft rather than midships aircraft arrangement to allow the incorporation of an improved secondary battery arrangement, better stability and freeboard, increased radius, and better protection since it could possess the same 76-mm (3-in) deck protection as the *Quincy* and still have 200 tons for additional protection. The use of 'spare' tonnage brought the ship close to the 10,000-ton treaty limit, and the *Wichita* was commissioned in February 1939 without two of her 5-in (127-mm) secondary guns. However, the ship had improved protection and the new triple turret with the 8-in guns farther apart to cure a serious

A view of the damaged USS San Francisco (CA-38) heavy cruiser of the 'New Orleans' class off Guadalcanal in December 1942.

dispersion problem. The 5-in L/38 gun was specified during construction, but the *Wichita* was too far advanced in construction for a twin mounting to be used, so the original six guns were installed in open single mountings. The weight of the last two of these mountings had to be balanced by inserting of 200 tons of iron in her hull. The secondary armament disposition was retained in the 'Baltimore' class cruisers, which had twin gunhouses in place of the *Wichita*'s original six single weapons. There were also two aircraft catapults.

Armour

Wichita used 163-mm (6.4-in) 'Class A' side armour rather than the 140-mm (5.5-in) 'Class B' protection of the *Vincennes*, which gave protection against 8-in armour-piercing shells at 90° at 9,145 m (10,000 yards) rather

than 14,995 m (16,400 yards), and the decks of both ships could be pierced at ranges above 20,115 m (22,000 yards). In 1939 the Bureau of Ordnance introduced a new, longer AP shell which was expected to penetrate the *Wichita*'s belt at 14,355 m (15,700 yards) and that of the *Vincennes* at 16,460 m (18,000 yards), but also had a flatter trajectory and would not penetrate the ships' deck armour at less than 20,390 m (22,300 yards). The new shell was also fired at a lower muzzle

velocity, a fact that enhanced barrel life. The ship's enhanced AA armament in August 1945 comprised four quadruple and four twin 40-mm guns, and 18 single 20-mm guns. Little modified during the war, *Wichita* was finally broken up in 1959.

The **'Baltimore' class** of heavy cruisers was in effect the US Navy's standard class of such ships in World War II, and shared much with the earlier 'Cleveland' class light cruiser despite 19.8 m (65 ft) greater length, 1.2 m (4 ft) more beam

and a triple-turret armament of 8-in rather than 6-in (152-mm) guns. The 'Baltimore' class was initially conceived as an **'Improved Wichita' class**, but evolution during the design process resulted in enlargement of the hull. The level of armour protection was improved slightly over that of the *Wichita*, most of the design's greater tonnage being used for hull strength, stability, and extra dual-purpose and AA armament. As a result the 'Baltimore' class was credited with an immune zone, at 90° impact angle, of 14,355–21,945 m (15,700–

24,000 yards) against a 228-kg (503-lb) shell. As the design progressed, the Bureau of Ordnance introduced heavier shells, the one for the 8-in gun weighing 152 kg (335 lb): the immune zone against this was calculated at 17,920–19,295 m (19,600–21,100 yards). A larger ship would have been needed to restore the original immune zone, but this was rejected in 1940 as the US Navy's requirement for new ships was now more than urgent.

As with the 'Cleveland' class, a modified design was prepared and adopted in 1942 as the

'Oregon City' subclass. The first group of ships comprised **CA-68** to **-75**, and then **CA-130** to **-136** were repeats of the first ships, as design of the 'Oregon City' subclass was behind schedule and further delay unacceptable. CA-134 was later re-ordered as the first of the new 'Newport News' class with fast-firing 8-in guns. **CA 122** to **-124** became the 'Oregon City' subclass units, and **CA-126** to **129**, **CA-137** and **-138** were cancelled at the end of the war. The **USS *Northampton*** (**CA-125**) became a prototype fleet flagship.

On trials the **USS *Boston*** recorded 32.85 kts at 16,570 tons on 88,380 kW (118,536 shp). There were differences in the AA armament, CA-68 to -71 carrying 12 quadruple 40-mm, while 20-mm cannon amounted to 22 in CA-72 to -75, 28 in CA-130 to -133, CA-135 and CA-136 as 14 twin mountings, and 20 in CA-122 to -124 as 10 twin mountings. There were two catapults, and only two aircraft were carried in all but CA-68 to -71.

The units of the 'Baltimore' class served after World War II, some in Vietnam.

'Atlanta' class Light cruiser

The four cruisers of the **'Atlanta' class** (**CL-51** to **CL-54**) laid down in the spring of 1940 were designed as true multi-role vessels. Under the terms of the 1936 London Naval Treaty, the United States agreed to strict limits on additional heavy cruisers. This certainly influenced the attempt to

squeeze so much firepower into the modest dimensions of the 'Atlanta' class.

The main armament was unprecedented: 16 5-in (127-mm) dual purpose guns in eight turrets, six on the centreline (three forward, three aft) and two wing turrets. The large number of barrels was intended

USS Atlanta underway. Originally classified as light cruisers (CL), two of the 'Atlanta' class survived the war and were reclassified as light anti-aircraft cruisers (CLAA). The two war losses comprised the name ship and Juneau, both lost to Japanese warships at the Battle of Guadalcanal in November 1942.

to deliver sufficient weight of fire to engage both aircraft and destroyers. However, there were only two Mk 37 fire-

control systems, and this restricted the number of targets that could be engaged simultaneously.

A full length bow view of the 'Atlanta'-class anti-aircraft cruiser USS Juneau (CL-52) seen in February 1942, and lost nine months later. A second ship of the same name and class, CL-119, was launched in 1945. This vessel was leadship of a three-strong subclass, and was not decommissioned until 1956.

ASW firepower

The 'Atlantas' also carried a powerful torpedo armament, two quadruple 21-in (533-mm) tubes and, uniquely among US cruisers, a sonar set and depth charges. The fact that the 'Atlantas' were not sufficiently manoeuvrable to prosecute a sonar contact against a submarine handled with any competence should not detract from this far-seeing design. Before the US had even gone to war, it had developed a cruiser designed to deal with the main threats to aircraft carriers: aircraft and submarines.

The design proved to be top-heavy, especially for the later units that shipped so many additional anti-aircraft guns. The **USS Reno** had 16 40-mm and 16 20-mm anti-aircraft guns by the time it was torpedoed by a Japanese submarine in November 1944 – and nearly capsized. In 1945 some of the class landed their torpedoes to improve their stability.

CL-95 to **CL-98** were ordered as part of the massive naval programme launched in 1940 as war became inevitable. At this date, the series production of existing designs was preferred in order to maximize production, so criticisms that the 'Atlantas' were cramped and subject to vibration were ignored. However, these four units, sometimes called the **'Oakland' class**, were built with open bridges and incorporated additional splinter protection. They also swapped additional light anti-aircraft weapons for the two wing turrets.

CL-119 to **CL-121** were ordered in 1944, for reasons that remain unclear. They were completed without torpedo tubes and with the second and fifth gun mounts at deck level.

USS Fresno and **USS Spokane** were commissioned in 1946 but paid off in 1949 and 1950 respectively. All apart from **USS Juneau II** were decommissioned by 1950 and this last ship was struck off in 1956 as the advent of the surface-to-air missile made a gun-armed anti-aircraft cruiser obsolete.

'Atlanta' losses

Two were war losses. **USS Atlanta** was hit by 49 shells during a night action off Guadalcanal on 13 November

SPECIFICATION	
'Atlanta' class	55,950 kW (75,000 shp) to two shafts
Ships in class: ('Atlanta' class) *Atlanta, Juneau, San Diego, San Juan*; ('Oakland' subclass) *Oakland, Reno, Flint* (ex-*Spokane*), *Tuscon*; ('Juneau' subclass) *Juneau II, Spokane, Fresno*	**Speed:** 32 kts
	Armour: 95 mm (3.75 in) belt and bulkheads; 32 mm (1.25 in) deck and gunhouses
Displacement: 6,718 tons standard; 8,340 tons full load	**Armament:** 16 5-in (127-mm) guns, 16 1.1-in (28-mm) guns (replaced 1943 by six 40-mm guns and 14 20-mm guns); eight 21-in (533-mm) torpedo tubes in quadruple deck mountings (but see text)
Dimensions: length 165 m (541 ft 6 in); beam 16.21 m (53 ft 2 1/2 in); draught 6.25 m (20 ft 6 in)	
Propulsion: two turbines delivering	**Complement:** 623 men

USS Juneau fights back during the Battle of Santa Cruz on 26 October 1942. The two surviving 'Atlantas' were decommissioned in 1946, while the vessels of the 'Juneau' subclass remained in service into the 1950s.

1942 (19, including seven from a single salvo, were 8-in/203-mm rounds from USS *San Francisco*) as well as a Long Lance torpedo. Six gun mounts were knocked out and flooding cut all power after 20 minutes. However, the crew managed to keep the vessel afloat another 12 hours before it had to be scuttled. The **USS Juneau** was less fortunate: in the same action, the cruiser was struck by a Long Lance torpedo that cut its speed to 13 kts, then a Japanese submarine put a second torpedo into exactly the same place. *Juneau* sank in a matter of seconds taking all but ten of the crew with it.

'Cleveland' class Light cruiser

Stimulated by the Japanese 152-mm (6-in) 'Mogami' class, the Americans built the nine 15-gun 'Brooklyn'-class cruisers during the 1930s. For the war programmes, however, a more practical 12-gun layout was adopted, with enhanced secondary and AA batteries. While obviously derivatives of the 'Brooklyn' class, these new cruisers of the **'Cleveland' class** were beamier on about the same length, and were better protected. The name ship was laid down in July 1940 and five years later the class stood

at 26 units, with a further nine hulls converted to fast light carriers (CVL) of the 'Independence' class. Three more were cancelled and a fourth completed as a guided-missile cruiser, making a total of 39, the largest cruiser programme ever.

As with the heavy cruisers, layout was improved by development of a single-funnelled version, the **'Fargo' class**. Only two of these were completed because of the war's end and introduced a fully automatic 6-in gun mounting. As

Developed from the 'Brooklyn' class but with a wider hull, the 'Cleveland' class carried 12 6-in (152-mm) guns in four triple turrets. The two-tone scheme depicted is typical of post-war colour schemes. The 'Cleveland' was the most numerous class of cruiser ever laid down, amounting to 39 vessels.

a result of the extra bulk of its loading gear, this weapon was accommodated in a new twin mounting and, with its higher rate of fire fewer barrels per ship could have been expected. Even so, the US Navy still demanded 12 guns and the resultant six-turret ships, the **'Worcester' class** needed to be 21.7 m (69 ft 3 in) longer, with 20 per cent greater power.

Like all guns of its generation, the automatic 6-in (152-mm)

weapon arrived too late to avoid being overtaken by the guided missile. Only two 'Worcester'-class ships were completed, being rebuilt aft as interim CLGs with the long-range Talos surface-to-air missile. These survived in service until 1958, largely because their unfashionably spacious accommodation made them popular as peacetime flagships. No 'Cleveland'-class ships were lost in World War II.

Twenty-six 'Cleveland'-class vessels entered service during World War II. USS Biloxi *was commissioned in August 1943 and broken up in 1962.*

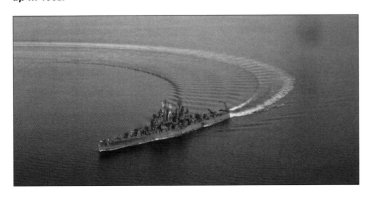

SPECIFICATION	
'Cleveland' class	deck 76 mm (3 in); turrets
Displacement: 10,000 tons standard and 13,775 tons full load	76-127 mm (3–5 in); barbettes 127 mm (5 in); conning tower
Dimensions: length 185.9 m (610 ft); beam 20.3 m (66 ft 6 in); draught 7.6 m (25 ft)	165 mm (6.5 in) **Armament:** 12 6-in (152-mm), 12 5-in (127-mm) DP, eight (first two) or 24
Propulsion: General Electric geared turbines delivering 74570 kW (100,000 shp) to four shafts	(eight ships) or 28 (others) 40-mm AA, and between 10 and 21 20-mm AA guns
Speed: 33 kts	**Aircraft:** four floatplanes
Armour: belt 38–127 mm (1.5–5 in);	**Complement:** 1,425 men

'Le Fantasque' and 'Mogador' classes Fast light cruiser

The **'Le Fantasque' class** was the penultimate class of a series that set new 'top-end' destroyer standards, yet which had little real influence on construction abroad as they stemmed largely from local naval rivalry between France and Italy.

It was with the three 'Leone'-class ships of 1921–22 that the Italians first stimulated the French, who replied with the six destroyers of the 'Chacal' class, significantly with similar names. The impressive 37,285 kW (50,000 shp) of these ships was increased to 47,725 kW (64,000 shp) in the six ships of the 'Guépard' class of 1927, the larger number of boilers also producing an imposing four-funnel profile. The Italians answered with the 12 1,950-ton ships of the 'Navigatori' class but, by their completion in 1931, the French had embarked on the 12-ship 'Aigle' class and 'Vauquelin' class group. From

these came the 'le Fantasque'-class ships (**L'Audacieux**, **Le Fantasque**, **Le Malin**, **Le Terrible**, **Le Triomphant** and **L'Indomptable**).

These six destroyers were of magnificent appearance with an imposing freeboard and an extra 3 m (9 ft 10 in) in overall length to allow the incorporation of a fifth gun and three triple sets of torpedo tubes. The four boilers were split into two pairs, separated by a machinery space

Le Fantasque as the vessel appeared after its 1939 refit. This fine-looking vessel typified the kind of super-destroyer that emerged out of Franco-Italian rivalry in the Mediterranean. These large destroyers were ultimately designated as light cruisers.

and with a squat funnel exhausting each pair. Their installed power was officially 55182 kW (74,000 shp), but this would appear to have been exceeded by at least 10 per cent, for all could produce 43 kts on occasion and, more importantly, could maintain 37 kts in a seaway.

Only the two 2,885-ton destroyers of the **'Mogador' class** pushed the specification further, their 137.5-m (451-ft) hulls carrying eight 139-mm (5.5-in) guns and 10 tubes. Although still very much super-destroyers in concept and

appearance, they were a direct response to the Italian 'Capitani Romani' which, while having very similar major parameters, were more scout cruisers in approach.

Both latter groups of French destroyers were, in fact, later to be termed 'light cruisers', although their original label of *contretorpilleur* better defined their primary task in breaking up enemy destroyer attacks. Half a dozen of them survived World War II and, after being well modified, went on to serve the French fleet through to the 1950s.

SPECIFICATION	
'Le Fantasque' class (as built)	55182 kW (74,000 shp) to two
Displacement: 2,570 tons standard;	shafts
3,350 tons full load	**Speed:** 37 kts
Dimensions: length 132.4 m (434 ft	**Armament:** five 139-mm (5.5-in) and
4 in); beam 12.45 m (40 ft 6 in);	two twin 37-mm (1.46-in) AA guns,
draught 5.01 m (16 ft 5 in)	and three triple 550-mm (21.65-in)
Propulsion: two sets of geared	torpedo tube mountings
steam turbines delivering	**Complement:** 210

'Bourrasque', 'L'Adroit' and 'Le Hardi' classes
Torpedo boat destroyers

Corresponding to British fleet destroyers, the French *torpilleurs d'escadre* ranked between the light 'Mediterranean' boats and the super-destroyers. By 1940, there were 34 in commission, of three separate classes. Of these the 1,320-ton **'Bourrasque' class** dated from the 1922 programme. Named after winds, these 12 ships were 105.77 m (347 ft) long and had an unusual arrangement of three funnels (one for each of the three boilers) that were unequally spaced and of unequal height as

they had to be cut down as a stability measure soon after completion. Even so, with four 130-mm (5.1-in) guns (potent but slow-firing) and only six torpedo tubes, they were still quite modestly armed in comparison with, for example, a later American 'Gridley', which had 16 tubes on a hull of very similar dimensions.

The 'Bourrasque' class ships were the **Bourrasque**, **Cyclone**, **Mistral**, **Orage**, **Ouragan**, **Simoun**, **Sirocco**, **Tempète**, **Tornade**, **Tramontane**, **Trombe** and **Typhon**.

Even before the completion of the 'Bourrasques' in 1928, the first of 14 1,389-ton destroyers of the **'L'Adroit' class** were being constructed to an improved design with heavier but still slow-firing guns. Marginally larger in both dimensions and displacement, slightly higher powered and faster, they retained the individual funnel arrangement. The ships were **L'Adroit**, **L'Alcyon**, **Basque**, **Bordelais**, **Boulonnais**, **Brestois**, **Forbin**, **Le Fortuné**, **Foudroyant**, **Fougueux**, **Frondeur**, **Le Mars**,

La Palme and **La Railleuse**.

Completion of this second group in 1931 was followed by a five-year 'holiday', construction being resumed with the planned 12-strong **'Le Hardi' class**, though these were more scaled-down *contretorpilleurs* than related to the 'L'Adroits'. Much larger at 1,770 tons standard, they carried half as many guns again in twin mountings as well as more torpedo tubes and, more importantly, had greater endurance. The ships were the **Casque**, **Le Corsaire**, **Epée**, **Le Flibustier**, **Fleuret**, **Le Hardi**,

Lansquenet, *Mameluck*, *L'Aventurier*, *L'Intrepide*, *L'Opiniâtre* and *Le Téméraire*.

The pattern of losses among the medium-sized French destroyers reflected the divided nature of their country's loyalties. Of the 'Bourrasques', the evacuation from Dunkirk in 1940 accounted for four; three more were lost when the British landed at Oran in 1942 and another was scuttled at Toulon in November 1942 as the Germans occupied Vichy France. In the case of the 'L'Adroits', two were lost to German action at Dunkirk, four more through Allied action at Casablanca in 1942 and three scuttled at Toulon.

Of the 'Le Hardi' class, only the lead unit was ready in time to be of use, but was Vichy-manned at Dakar. Later units were completed by both the Germans and Italians, serving without much note.

SPECIFICATION

'L'Adroit' class (as built)
Displacement: 1,378 tons standard; 1,900 tons full load
Dimensions: length 107.2 m (351 ft 8 in); beam 9.84 m (32 ft 3 in); draught 4.3 m (14 ft 1 in)
Propulsion: two sets of geared steam turbines delivering 24980 kW (33,500 shp) to two shafts
Performance: maximum speed 33 kts; endurance 2125 km (1,320 miles) at 15 kts
Armament: four 130-mm (5.1-in) and one 75-mm (2.95-in) AA guns, and two triple 550-mm (21.65-in) torpedo tube mountings
Complement: 140 men

Improved versions of **Bourrasque**, *the first French destroyer design after 1918,* **L'Adroit** *and the 13 vessels in its class were completed in the late 1920s.* **L'Adroit** *was sunk in 1940.*

'Tromp' class destroyer

The **Tromp** and the **Jacob van Heemskerck** of the **'Tromp' class** were interesting in being more 'pocket cruisers' than destroyers and demonstrate how, at the top of the size scale, the distinction between the two could be less than clear cut. They both possessed a solid angularity that belied their small size and which was typical of Dutch practice. The French 'Le Fantasques' were as large as the 'Tromps', but the latters' armament equalled that of the planned German *Spahkreuzer* (scout cruiser) concept; they were also designed to carry more torpedoes than many destroyers, but what really set them apart was their lack of speed. Even so, their excellent seakeeping enabled them to maintain their modest 32.5 kts long after 'faster' ships had been obliged to ease back.

Destroyer leaders

The pair had true destroyer ancestry, being planned as leaders. Their design was enlarged, however, and welding and aluminium were employed to save weight. Reflecting their use in the vast Dutch East Indies was the incorporation of a Fokker C.XI-W floatplane and facilities. These would also have been included on the destroyers of the 'Callenburgh' class had they ever been built as planned.

The *Tromp* was completed in August 1938, the same builders immediately laying down *Jacob van Heemskerck*. At the invasion of 1940, the latter came to the UK for completion with a very different armament. A stir was caused in British naval circles by the advanced Hazemeyer fire-control for the AA armament, and even the 150-mm (5.9-in) main battery could be elevated to 60°.

Though part of the hard pressed ABDA force at the opening of the war with Japan, the *Tromp* escaped after being damaged disputing the invasion of Bali. Sent to Australia for repairs, the lengthy nature of which was its salvation, *Tromp* re-entered service in time for the new Allied naval build-up in the Far East. During the counter-offensive *Tromp* took part in operations against Sabang and Balikpapan in Borneo.

SPECIFICATION

Tromp' class (as designed)
Displacement: 4,200 tons standard; 4,900 tons full load
Dimensions: length 132 m (433 ft); beam 12.4 m (40 ft 8 in); draught 4.2 m (13 ft 9 in)
Propulsion: two sets of geared steam turbines delivering 41759 kW (56,000 shp) to two shafts
Speed: 32.5 kts
Armament: three twin 150-mm (5.9-in), four 75-mm (2.95-in) AA, and two twin and four single 40-mm AA guns, and two triple 533-mm (21-in) torpedo tube mountings (12 torpedoes)
Armour: deck 35 mm (1.38 in); belt 25 mm (0.98 in)
Complement: 295 (*Tromp*) men

The **Tromp** *escaped the capitulation of the Netherlands to serve with the Allies, with whom the vessel saw extensive action. Damaged in the Far East,* **Tromp** *survived to form the nucleus of the Netherlands' navy after World War II.*

'V' and 'W' classes Destroyers

Recognizable by their two 'thick and thin' funnels of unequal height, the original **'V'** and **'W' class** destroyers served for over a quarter of a century. Derived from five flotilla leaders ordered in 1916 to provide command capability for the new 'R' class destroyers, the class introduced superimposed guns both forward and aft, and featured extra length and freeboard for improved seaworthiness. Their limitations were in shipping only four torpedo tubes and in needing to take the machinery of the smaller Admiralty 'R' class design but, though a little underpowered, the first of the initial five units, **HMS Valkyrie,** still made nearly 35 kts on trials in June 1917. As still larger flotilla leaders were now beginning to appear, the first five 'V' class ships (**Vampire, Valentine, Valhalla** and **Valorous** in addition to the *Valkyrie*) were used as divisional (or 'half') leaders.

*HMS **Venomous** as seen from the captain's bridge of HMS **Formidable**.*

Increased production

Once proved, and in response to suggestions that the Germans were building a new class of large destroyers, the design was extended by 25 more 'V' and then by 23 'W' class destroyers, the latter differing mainly in adopting two triple torpedo tube mountings. Stability proving no problem, the **'Modified V and W' class** then followed (an order for 54 ships being placed in early 1918) with the usefully heavier armament of 4.7-in (119-mm) guns in place of the earlier classes' 4-in (102-mm) weapons, their projectiles weighing 50 lb (22.7 kg) instead of 35 lb (15.9 kg). With the Armistice of November 1918, most of the ships were cancelled, only **Vansittart, Venomous, Verity, Veteran, Volunteer, Wanderer, Whitehall, Whitshed, Wild Swan, Wishart, Witch, Witherington, Wivern, Wolverine, Worcester** and **Wren** being built. One of the ships was lost during World War I, and two more in the Baltic in 1919 during the Allied

*In 1945, HMS **Watchman** was serving as a long-range escort, with her forward boiler and funnel removed to allow for extra fuel, and the 'A' gun replaced by an ahead-firing Hedgehog anti-submarine mortar unit. With the extra fuel the ship had transatlantic range.*

intervention against the Bolshevik revolutionary regime in Russia.

The surviving units of the classes formed the backbone of the Royal Navy's fleet destroyer strength into the 1930s and, except for five, then embarked for service in their second war during 1939.

Conversions

Between 1938 and 1941, 16 of the ships, from various groups, were converted to **'Wair' class** AA escort standard by the substitution of two twin 4-in high-angle guns and a quadruple 2-pdr mounting for the original armament. Another 20 were

adapted to the long-range escort (LRE) standard by removing the forward boiler and funnel to give enhanced bunker capacity. The original armament was cut back in favour of an ahead-firing Hedgehog projector and extra depth charges, and though now capable of a speed of only 25 kts or less, the ships were able to cross the Atlantic without refueling.

Most of the remainder, unsuitable for similar conversion, were adapted to the short-range escort (SRE) standard with a wide variety of armament but retaining their original machinery. Three of the ships were lost in World War II.

SPECIFICATION	
'Modified V and W' class (as built)	to two shafts
Displacement: 1,120 tons standard; 1,505 tons full load	**Performance:** maximum speed 34 kts; endurance 6437 km (4,000 miles) at 15 kts
Dimensions: length 95.1 m (312 ft); beam 8.99 m (29 ft 6 in); draught 3.28 m (10 ft 9 in)	**Armament:** four 4.7-in (119-mm) and one 3-in (76-mm) guns, and two triple 21-in (533-mm) torpedo tube mountings
Propulsion: geared steam turbines delivering 20,134 kW (27,000 shp)	**Complement:** 134 men

*This is HMS **Walker** as it appeared before her conversion to long-range escort standard. One of the most successful of U-boat hunters, the ship sank both Kretschmer's **U-99** and Schepke's **U-100** (in company with HMS **Vaux**).*

'A' class Destroyer

Not until the mid-1920s did the Admiralty order a pair of prototype destroyers with a view to replacing tonnage built in World War I. These, **HMS Amazon** and **HMS Ambuscade**, were heavily based on the 'Modified V and W' class but with a contract speed of 37 kts. This was made possible by the extra power developed by the new Admiralty three-drum boiler and steam superheat. With modifications, the design of this pair formed the basis of a full **'A' class** of eight and a leader (**HMS Codrington**, lost in 1940), ordered in the 1927 programme for completion in 1929 and 1930. These were followed, alphabetically, by a flotilla per year, with surprisingly few 'improvements' up to the **'I' class** vessels of 1935. It was an excellent design: simple yet robust, with an elegance that influenced foreign construction.

Destroyers, now larger and more capable, worked in smaller groups than before, each flotilla having a leader, enlarged for the captain's staff and carrying an extra gun, largely of prestige value, between the funnels. The armament of the 'A' class destroyers was improved over that of their prototypes by the provision of extra elevation to the guns and quadruple in place of triple torpedo tube banks. To improve wartime topweight margins, the 'Y' gun was landed, more than 2 m (6ft 7in) were lopped from the after funnel, and the tall mainmast was replaced by a short jigger.

In June 1940, **Ardent** and **Acasta** perished gallantly off the Norwegian coast in an inevitably vain attempt to defend the aircraft carrier HMS Glorious from the German battle cruisers KMS Scharnhorst and Gneisenau, of which the former was torpedoed. **HMS Achates** was also mined off Norway, her whole forward section needing to be rebuilt. She, too, was lost in valiant circumstances during the desperate action off the North Cape on the last day of 1942: while Captain R. Sherbrooke and four 'A' class destroyers kept at bay a German 'pocket battleship', a heavy cruiser and six large destroyers, the Achates shielded their convoy with smoke, virtually until going under from the effects of 203-mm (8-in) shell damage. The convoy was saved by the timely arrival of two British 6-in (152-mm) cruisers. The other 'A' class destroyers were **Acheron** (lost in 1940), **Active**, **Antelope**, **Anthony** and **Arrow**.

SPECIFICATION	
'A' class (as built)	**Performance:** maximum speed
Displacement: 1,330 (leader 1,520) tons standard; 1,770 tons full load	35 kts; endurance 8,851 km (5,500 miles) at 15 kts
Dimensions: length 98.45 m (323 ft); beam 9.83 m (32 ft 3 in); draught 2.16 m (7 ft 1 in)	**Armament:** four (leader five) 4.7-in (119-mm) and two 2-pdr pom-pom AA guns, and two quadruple 21-in (533-mm) torpedo tube mountings
Propulsion: geared steam turbines delivering 25,354 kW (34,000 shp) to two shafts	**Complement:** 138 men

'J', 'K' and 'N' classes Destroyers

The 16 'Tribals' of the later 1930s were a class apart but, in answering to the increasing size and power of foreign destroyers, were also an acknowledgement of the Royal Navy's need for a larger general-purpose fleet destroyer. Following the extended 'A' to 'I' series of classes came a new design.

Design departure

Visually, it departed considerably from earlier practice. Two boilers replaced the earlier three, allowing for a single funnel. Three of the twin 4.7-in (119-mm) gunhouses used in the 'Tribals' were shipped, allowing space for a second bank of torpedo tubes of the quintuple pattern introduced with the 'I' class. This heavy torpedo armament showed a continuing commitment to a form of attack that, in the event, was used seldom. To improve the firing arc of the after gun mounting a mainmast was not stepped, the W/T aerials being strung from the tripod foremast to a braced ensign staff.

HMS Javelin rejoins her flotilla after a special mission. Although severely damaged on more than one occasion, the Javelin was one of only two 'J' class destroyers to survive the war. Altogether 13 of 24 'J', 'K' and 'N' class destroyers were lost.

Despite the improved angles of elevation on the main battery, the primary AA weapon was still the quadruple 2-pdr 'pom-pom'. Sited abaft the funnel, it had a better field of fire than on the preceding two-funnel ships yet still had a wide blind sector forward. As in most British destroyers, there was a constant struggle to keep topweight within acceptable bounds. Eight **'J' class** and eight identical **'K' class** destroyers were ordered in 1937, followed by eight similar **'N' class** ships in 1939, the 'L' and 'M' classes already under construction. Of the total of 24 ships, no less than 13 were sunk during World War II, eight of them to air attack due to their indifferent AA armament.

Five of the 'N' class were Australian-manned, two Dutch and one Polish. The ships proved to be of remarkably tough construction: **HMS Javelin**, for instance, survived both a major collision and, at a later date, being parted from both bow and stern sections by a salvo of enemy torpedoes. The leaders were **Jervis**, **Kelly** and **Napier**, the other units being **Jackal**, **Jaguar**, **Janus**, **Jersey**, **Juno**, **Jupiter**, **Kan-dahar**, **Kashmir**, **Kelvin**, **Khartoum**, **Kimberley**, **Kingston**, **Kipling**, **Nerissa**, **Nestor**, **Nizam**, **Noble**, **Nonpareil**, **Norman** and **Nepal**.

SPECIFICATION	
'J', 'K' & 'N' classes (as built)	**Performance:** maximum speed
Displacement: 1,690 (leaders 1,695) tons standard; 2,330 tons full load	36 kts; endurance 10,139 km (6,300 miles) at 15 kts
Dimensions: length 108.66 m (356 ft 6 in); beam 10.87 m (35 ft 8 in); draught 2.74 m (9 ft)	**Armament:** three twin 4.7-in (119-mm) and one quadruple 2-pdr pom-pom AA guns, and two quintuple 21-in (533-mm) torpedo tube mountings
Propulsion: geared steam turbines delivering 29,828 kW (40,000 shp) to two shafts	**Complement:** 183 men

'O' to 'Z' class Fleet destroyers

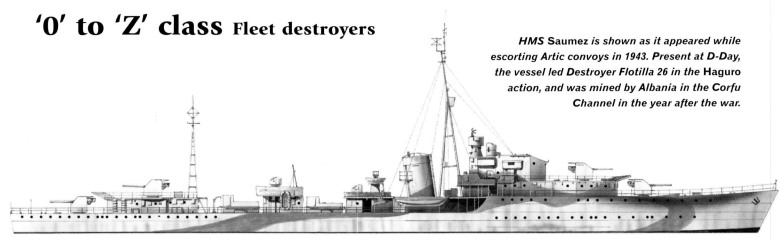

*HMS **Saumez** is shown as it appeared while escorting Artic convoys in 1943. Present at D-Day, the vessel led Destroyer Flotilla 26 in the Haguro action, and was mined by Albania in the Corfu Channel in the year after the war.*

War emergency programmes produced 112 fleet destroyers, but only through a degree of standardization and reduction of minimum peacetime standards. Two 'intermediate' classes, the **'O' class** and **'P' class**, came first, with eight units apiece. These 1,540-tonners were influenced by the thinking that produced the 'Hunt'-class escort destroyers and were armed only with 4-in (102-mm) guns. The modern twin HA mountings were not available, so obsolete single mountings were used. Four of the 'O' class were fitted for minelaying, and war losses were five 'P'-class ships.

With the **'Q' class** came the first of a line of standard groups, whose 1,705-ton design was

based on the 'J' class, its heavy twin 4.7-in (119-mm) gun mountings replaced by singles. Savings in topweight were made by reverting to quadruple torpedo tubes. The return to the 4 7-in gun may have been decided by the availability of the excellent 20-mm Oerlikon. Of the eight units, two were lost.

'R' class

The 'Q' class was well received, so the eight **'R'-class** destroyers were almost identical except for the quartering of officers and crew both forward and aft. This arrangement facilitated coming to action stations in all weather conditions, but was not judged successful. None of the class was lost.

*HMS **Raider** is shown as part of the group of an escort carrier in East Indian waters in early 1945. Among the most stable of destroyers, the 'Q' and 'R' classes were the first to have a transom stern. Raider became INS **Rajput** in the Indian Navy, to which it was transferred in 1949.*

SPECIFICATION	
'Q' class (as built)	shafts
Displacement: 1,705 (leader 1,725) tons standard and 2,425 tons full load	**Performance:** maximum speed 36.5 kts; endurance 8,690 km (5,400 miles) at 20 kts
Dimensions: 109.19 in (358 ft 3 in); beam 10.87 in (35 ft 8 in); draught 2.9 m (9 ft 6 in)	**Armament:** four single 4.7-in (119-mm), one quadruple 2-pdr 'pom-pom' and three twin 20-mm AA guns, and two quadruple 21-in (533-mm) torpedo tube mountings
Propulsion: two sets of geared steam turbines delivering 29,828 kW (40,000 shp) to two	**Complement:** 175

With the **'S' class** (also eight ships) came a modification to the forward lines to reduce the spray wetness that had provoked complaint as far back as the 'J' class. They were also first with 40-mm Bofors guns and a full complement of Oerlikons, while the main battery haf an improved elevation for AA purposes. Two of the class were war losses.

Tripod mast

Radar and other antennae proliferated to the point where the standard tripod mast was subject to severe stress and

vibration so, with the eight-strong **'T' class**, the lattice mast was introduced. **'U'**, **'V'** (of which one unit was lost) and **'W'** classes, each of eight ships, followed to the same design, the eight-strong **'Z' class** then arriving with the 4.5-in (114-mm) gun. Finally, came the four eight-ship groups of **'C'-class** destroyers, with 'Ca', 'Ch', 'Cr', and 'Co' names. Many war emergencies were built of poor materials and had short lives, but others were rebuilt into Type 15 and Type 16 frigates, acting as a link with frigate-dominated fleets of modern times.

*HMS **Zebra** in 1945. Developed from the 'J' class, with similar machinery in a smaller hull, the war emergency classes were produced in large numbers, and to a largely standard design. HMS Zebra was armed with the new 4.5-in (114-mm) gun, in addition to AA cannon.*

'Tribal' class Fleet destroyer

Quite unlike any previous British destroyer design, the 'Tribals' were an answer to heavily armed contemporaries such as the Japanese 'Fubuki' class. Superb sea boats, the 'Tribals' were always in the thick of the action, losing 12 out of the 16 built.

Among the finest destroyers ever built for the Royal Navy, the 16 **'Tribal'-class** ships appear, nevertheless, to have been produced as an answer to those being built by potential enemies rather than to fill any role in the fleet. The long series of flotillas then culminating in the 'T' class had been armed with four single 4.7-in (119-mm) guns and, in order to uprate these to twin mountings, the 'Tribals' needed to increase tonnage by 36 per cent. Despite having only one set of torpedo tubes, they were also one-sixth longer. They were seen as gun-armed 'super-destroyers', and there was much disagreement over their correct classification. Indeed, one casting of the original design had provided for a fifth gunhouse on the forward side of the larger after deck house, but this was abandoned in favour of

a quadruple 'pom-pom'. Even so, five of their number were sunk by aircraft attack.

New guns

By any standards they were magnificent-looking ships, their well balanced profile in harmony with the high-freeboard hull that was introduced to improve their fighting qualities in poor weather. Wartime modifications included the exchange of 'X' mounting for a more useful twin 4-in (102-mm) HA mounting, and the suppression of the main-mast to improve firing arcs. The class was launched in 1937, but only four of the 16 were still afloat at the end of 1942, and these all eventually received lattice masts that did nothing for their appearance.

'Tribal' exports

'Tribals' were built also for the

Royal Australian Navy (three ships) and Royal Canadian Navy (eight ships), and all saw a great deal of action. Notable exploits include the '*Altmark* incident', where **HMS *Cossack*** rescued a large number of British merchant seamen from inside Norwegian territorial waters just before the German invasion, and the harrying of the *Bismarck* by four 'Tribals' and a Polish destroyer for the whole night before it was eventually sunk. Of those lost, **HMS *Sikh*** and

HMS *Zulu* were sunk when a commando raid near Tobruk went badly wrong, and **HMS *Punjabi***, sunk in collision with the battleship HMS *King George V*, seriously damaged the latter in turn when its full outfit of depth charges exploded. The other units were **HMS *Afridi*, HMS *Ashanti*, HMS *Bedouin*, HMS *Eskimo*, HMS *Gurkha*, HMS *Mashona*, HMS *Maori*, HMS *Matabele*, HMS *Mohawk*, HMS *Nubian*, HMS *Somali*** and **HMS *Tartar***.

SPECIFICATION	
'Tribal' class (as built) **Displacement:** 1,870 tons standard and 1,975 tons full load **Dimensions:** length 115.1 m (377 ft 6 in); beam 11.13 m (36 ft 6 in); draught 2.74 m (9 ft) **Propulsion:** two sets of geared steam turbines delivering 32,811 kW (44,000 shp) to two shafts	**Performance:** maximum speed 36 kts; endurance 10,541 km (6,550 miles) at 15 kts **Armament:** four twin 4.7-in (119-mm) and one quadruple 2-pdr 'pom-pom' guns, and one quadruple 21-in (533-mm) torpedo tube mounting **Complement:** 190 men

'Tribal' class (1940)

1 Aft navigation light
2 Twin 4.7-in (119-mm) guns
3 Blast screen
4 Steering compartment
5 Provision room
6 Ammunition hoist
7 Waterline
8 Balanced rudder
9 Twin screws
10 Shaft
11 Wardroom
12 Store
13 CO's bathroom
14 CO's sleeping cabin
15 CO's day cabin
16 CO's pantry
17 Sick bay
18 Engineer's workshop
19 Aft superstructure deck
20 Mainmast
21 40-in (102-cm) searchlight
22 Searchlight platform

23 Ventilator
24 2-pdr Mk 4 'pom-pom'
25 Upper deck
26 21-in (533-mm) quadruple torpedo tubes
27 Officers' cabins
28 Upper ammunition handling area
29 Gunner's office
30 Shell room
31 4.7-in magazine
32 Ship's office
33 Torpedo store
34 Engineer officer's cabin
35 Oil fuel tanks

36 Gearing room
37 Main circulating inlet
38 Engine room
39 Torpedo tube turntable machinery space
40 Reserve feed tanks
41 Double bottom
42 No. 1 boiler room
43 No. 2 boiler room
44 No. 3 boiler room
45 Funnel easing
46 Torpedo handling crane
47 7.62-m (25-ft) motor launch

48 8.22-m (27-ft) whaler
49 Boiler room vent
50 Wireless aerials
51 Foremast
52 Spotting top/lookout
53 Combined RF and AA control
54 Director control

55 Bridge
56 Compass platform
57 Signal platform
58 20-in (51-cm) searchlight
59 2-pdr 'pom-pom' director
60 CO's sea cabin
61 Asdic room
62 Wheelhouse
63 Remote control station
64 Chart house
65 Drying room
66 Galley
67 PO's scullery
68 Engineer's office
69 Crew mess
70 Signal deck
71 Torpedo store
72 Toilets
73 CPO's washroom
74 Potato store

75 Canteen
76 Transmitting station
77 Crew space
78 Forecastle deck
79 Paint room
80 Capstan
81 Anchor
82 Bow
83 Breakwater
84 Cable room
85 Dry stores/provisions
86 Asdic office
87 Lower deck
88 Hold
89 Generating room
90 Diesel tank
91 Keel
92 Forefoot
93 Signal office
94 Admiralty drum boiler

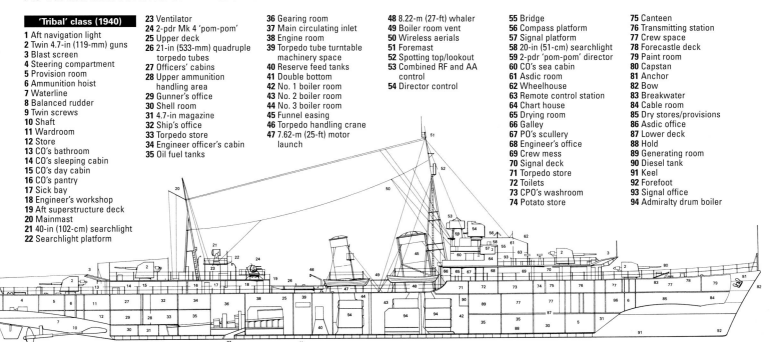

'Battle' class Destroyer

SPECIFICATION	
'Battle' (1943 type) class (as built)	**Performance:** maximum speed 35.5 kts; endurance 8047 km (5,000 miles) at 20 kts
Displacement: 2,380 tons standard; 3,290 tons full load	
Dimensions: length 115.52 m (379 ft); beam 12.34 m (40 ft 6 in); draught 4.67 m (15 ft 4 in)	**Armament:** two twin and one single 4.5-in (114-mm) DP plus two twin and two single 40-mm AA guns, and two quintuple 21-in (533-mm) torpedo tube mountings
Propulsion: two sets of geared steam turbines delivering 37,285 kW (50,000 shp) to two shafts	**Complement:** 232 men

Designed with the early lessons of the war very much in mind, the 'Battles' were the first British destroyers to have a main armament of 85° elevation, together with radar direction. This gave a very effective anti-aircraft armament, when added to the six 40-mm weapons also mounted.

As they served into the 1960s, it is sometimes forgotten that the **'Battle'-class** destroyers were built in World War II. In fact, the class had its genesis about the time of the Battle of Matapan in March 1941, when the Royal Navy was still seeking ways of combatting the aerial threat that had been so underestimated in the 1930s. Hard experience showed that the dive-bomber needed to be countered by plenty of metal yet, while the 'pom-pom' was an excellent weapon, main battery guns were capable of only 40° or 55° maximum elevation. The specification for the new destroyer called for 85° elevation and a high rate of fire, while the ship itself was to be stabilized for higher accuracies and designed for rapid rudder response. By the time that the specification had been finalized there was also a Pacific war to be taken into account, together with the fact that the ships might not be completed in time to be of use.

Formidable vessel

The result was a large ship with considerable endurance and twin gunhouses, sited forward. A single 4-in (102-mm) gun was added abaft the stack, good for little more than firing illuminants. The large after structure supported two twin 40-mm mountings, which had their own directors and were fully stabilized, so active fins were not incorporated into the hull. A prominent feature was the Mk 6 'greenhouse' director control for the main armament, with the twin nacelles of the American-built Type 275 radar. Right aft, the initial large outfits of depth charges were soon superseded by the ahead-firing Squid mortar.

Sixteen of these ships, the **'1942' type**, were ordered, followed by three eight-ship flotillas of a modified **'1943' type**. In the latter, the main battery was increased by the substitution of an extra 4.5-in (114-mm) for the amidships 4-in gun, the torpedo tubes were increased from eight to 10 (no doubt as a result of lessons from Japanese expertise) and the gunnery radar was revamped into a new-style Mk 37 tower.

In the event, only a few 'Battles' were finished before the war's end and, while 24 were completed, 16 hulls were dismantled.

'Weapon' class Destroyer

Complementing the heavily AAW-optimized 'Battle'-class destroyers, the 'Weapon'-class vessels were designed as fleet ASW escorts.

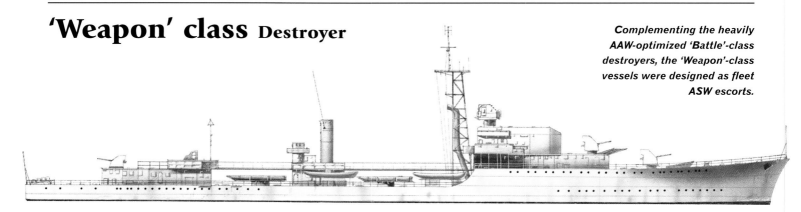

Hard experience during World War II had exposed the limitations of fleet destroyers as anti-submarine platforms. Nevertheless, the fleet still required a screen of fast anti-submarine ships that could not only protect themselves but also contribute to the AA defences of a task group, allowing the carrier's aircraft complement to be devoted to the greatest extent to offensive rather than defensive operations. In European waters a full outfit of torpedo tubes had become superfluous, but this was not yet true of the Far Eastern theatre. It was these changed priorities which dominated the design of the destroyers of the **'Weapon'** **class**, whose departure from the accepted idea of destroyers was radical enough to attract a large measure of often unfair criticism.

The choice of the high-angle 4-in (102-mm) gun for the main battery was logical, its 14-kg (31-lb) projectile enabling fast hand-working even up to the maximum elevation of 80°. Only two twin mountings could be shipped, however, as the hull length was limited by available building berths. A third planned mounting was, therefore, abandoned in favour of the newly introduced Squid three-barrel anti-submarine mortar, which could be sited either forward or aft. Close-in AA protection was afforded, as in the 'Battles', by two stabilized twin 40-mm mountings aft, with single 40-mm guns flanking the bridge structure. With an eye to Pacific operations, two quintuple torpedo tube banks were fitted, although this was at a time when US contemporaries were having to shed tubes in favour of enhanced AA armament. In a torpedo attack against surface targets, unsupported 'Weapons' would have suffered badly with their small-calibre main battery,

and to redress this deficiency, a follow-on 'G' class of eight ships was planned, largely similar but with twin 4.5-in (114-mm) DP mountings. As with all but four of the 20 'Weapons', however, the end of hostilities saw the 'G'-class ships cancelled. The four ships completed in 1947–48 were **Battleaxe**, **Broadsword**, **Crossbow** and **Scorpion**. Three other hulls were scrapped after launching.

To improve damage control,

SPECIFICATION	
'Weapon' class (as built)	shafts
Displacement: 1,980 tons standard; 2,825 tons full load	**Performance:** maximum speed 35 kts
Dimensions: length 111.25 m (365 ft); beam 11.58 m (38 ft); draught 4.47 m (14 ft 8 in)	**Armament:** two twin 4-in (102-mm) DP plus two twin and two single 40-mm AA guns, and two quintuple 21-in (533-mm) torpedo tube mountings
Propulsion: two sets of geared steam turbines delivering 29828 kW (40,000 shp) to two	**Complement:** 255 men

the boiler and machinery spaces were sited alternately, requiring two funnels. It was the supporting of the forward funnel within

the lattice foremast (copied also in the following 'Darings') that appeared particularly to offend the critics.

'Four-piper' type Destroyers

HMS Churchill *was the former USS* Herndon, *a 'Clemson'-class destroyer of 1918. Transferred to the Soviet navy in 1944 and renamed* Deyatelnyi, *the vessel was sunk by* U-997 *off Kola in January 1945.*

SPECIFICATION	
'Clemson' class (as built)	**Performance:** maximum speed 35 kts; range 6,435 km (4,000 miles)
Displacement: 1,190 tons standard; 1,308 tons full load	
Dimensions: length 95.8 m (314 ft 4 in); beam 9.4 m (30 ft 10 in); draught 3 m (9 ft 10 in)	**Armament:** four 4-in (102-mm) and one 3-in (76-mm) AA guns, and four triple 21-in (533-mm) torpedo tube mountings
Propulsion: two sets of geared steam turbines delive 20,507 kW (27,500 shp) to two shafts	**Complement:** 135 men

Known as **'four-pipers'**, or **'flush-deckers'**, the survivors of this large group of American destroyers fought, like the British 'V' and 'W' classes, in two world wars. Resulting from the expansion of the US Navy as it moved towards war in 1917, the design was derived directly from the 12-ship **'Tucker' class**. With the same displacement and major dimensions, the latter differed in having the European type of raised forecastle. With two waist-mounted 4-in (102-mm) guns, which needed forward arcs, this meant facetting the ships' sides. Six **'Caldwell'-class** prototype ships changed the hull form to a long, easy sheerline with the amidships guns resited on a house.

Any improvement must have been marginal as the forward arcs were still restricted, blast effects were significant, and weight was moved upward on an already tender hull. Some 12 torpedo tubes were fitted, mainly because the quantity of tophamper precluded centreline mounting: thus there were two triple mountings on each beam.

The main series, which were the 111 **'Wickes'-class** and 156 **'Clemson'-class** units, retained these features but were given higher installed power for 35 kts when launched in 1918–21.

Under the terms of the London Naval Treaty, 93 of these ships were scrapped in the early 1930s. In July 1940, only weeks after the Dunkirk

HMS Wells, *a 'Wickes'-class destroyer, is seen making smoke in 1942. These old ships gave valuable service after their hand-over to the Royal Navy following Dunkirk.*

evacuation that had cost the British many light warships, the Royal Navy was short of escorts and took over 50 of the old vessels in the famous exchange for a 99-year US lease on British air and naval bases in the western hemisphere. Many of the ships were in dubious condition but were very useful, generally in cut-down form.

The **USS Reuben James** was one of two US destroyers torpedoed in October 1941 while covering convoys before

the US's entry into the war. In December 1941, a dozen four-pipers were the only US destroyers in the Far Eastern theatre, five being lost during the unequal struggle of the ABDA multi-national force. Many worked throughout the war, converted to escorts, minelayers, minesweepers or small auxiliaries. Typical armament in 1945 was one 4-in, one 12-pdr AA, three or four 20-mm AA, three 21-in torpedo tubes and 60 to 80 depth charges.

'Farragut', 'Mahan', 'Porter' & 'Somers' classes Destroyers

With adequate war-built destroyer tonnage available, the US Navy did not undertake any new construction until the 1930s. The eight-strong **'Farragut' class** launched in 1934 and 1935 was influenced by the series of British flotillas then being built, and featured both superimposed guns and a reintroduced raised forecastle.

With more compact modern machinery, only two funnels were required, releasing centre-line deck space for two quadruple torpedo tubes. Thus, though only eight torpedoes were carried, the full number could be launched on each beam, compared with 12 and six respectively in the earlier

classes. The 'Farraguts' carried the newly standardized 5-in (127-mm) gun and any top-weight saved by fewer tubes was offset by an extra, fifth gun.

Typhoon losses

Despite these modifications, two of the three lost capsized when the American 3rd Fleet was caught in a Pacific typhoon in December 1944. Units were the **USS Farragut (DD-348)**, **USS Dewey (DD-349)**, **USS Hull (DD-350)**, **USS MacDonough (DD-351)**, **USS Worden (DD-352)**, **USS Dale (DD-353)**, **USS Monaghan (DD-354)** and **USS Aylwin (DD-355)**.

Closely related were the follow-on 1,500-ton **'Mahan'**

The massive bulk of USS **South Dakota** *dwarfs the 'Mahan'-class destroyers USS* **Dunlap** *and* **Fanning**, *recognizable by their shielded gun mounts forward and unshielded guns aft. Note that the inner of the two appears to have lost its bow in an accident.*

class, which added another 38.1 cm (15 in) on the beam and increased installed power. The main battery was retained and a third quadruple torpedo tube mount was added, the forward one now being on the centreline and the others sided. Of the 18 'Mahans' at Pearl Harbor, the **USS Shaw (DD-373)** exploded and the **USS Cassin (DD-372)** and **USS Downes (DD-375)** were left in ruins.

Built at the same time in 1934 and 1935 were the eight enlarged 1,800-ton destroyers of

the **'Porter' class**. Though these British-style leaders were some 12.2 m (40 ft) longer, their beam was scarcely increased and they could not accommodate four of the new twinned gunhouses, so two were usually landed. The designers followed on with the five 1,850-ton destroyers of the **'Somers' class** of 1937 and 1938, which had eight guns and a third quadruple torpedo tube mounting. With an eye to Pacific operations, US destroyers were larger than British equivalents and with more endurance.

SPECIFICATION	
'Farragut' class (as built)	shafts
Displacement: 1,395 tons standard	**Performance:** maximum speed 36.5 kts
Dimensions: length 104.01 m (341 ft 3 in); beam 10.41 m (34 ft 2 in); draught 2.69 m (8 ft 10 in)	**Armament:** five single 5-in (127-mm) DP and four machine-guns, and two quadruple 21-in (533-mm) torpedo tube mountings
Propulsion: two sets of geared steam turbines delivering 31,916 kW (42,800 shp) to two	**Complement:** 250 men

'Gridley' and 'Sims' classes Destroyers

Concurrent with the 'Somers', the US Navy built 22 destroyers of the **'Gridley' class**, smaller ships but better balanced. The main battery was halved, four single 5-in (127-mm) L/38 guns saving topweight for investment in an unprecedented 16-tube torpedo armament. The four quadruple mountings were placed sensibly low, at upper deck level, two per side.

A feature of both the 'Gridleys' and their derivatives, the 12 1,570-ton destroyers of the **'Sims' class**, was the single enormous funnel casing, trunked to serve two adjacent boiler spaces. In the variant, one set of tubes was traded for an extra 5-in gun. Length was also increased by 1.98 m (6 ft 6 in) to allow for increased bunkerage but even with the extra size and

displacement, the wartime 'Sims' ended one gun and a set of tubes lighter. Both classes were high-powered, the extra length of the 'Sims' allowing for better lines and an extra knot of speed over the 'Gridleys'. Wartime losses were five 'Gridleys' and five 'Sims'.

Savo Island

Six 'Gridleys' were present at the debacle of Savo Island, their potential being wasted by faulty tactics. For example, there were

some 96 nominal torpedoes between them, but only eight were launched. **USS Blue (DD-387)** and **USS Ralph Talbot (DD-390)** were the two radar pickets whose lack of attention allowed Mikawa's cruiser force to penetrate the strait.

Of the follow-ons, the **USS Sims (DD-409)** was sunk before at Coral Sea.

All destroyers built pre-war were written off after August 1945, with 11 being expended at the Bikini nuclear site.

SPECIFICATION	
'Gridley' class (as built)	to two shafts
Displacement: 1,500 tons standard	**Performance:** maximum speed 36.5 kts
Dimensions: length 104.11 m (341 ft 7 in); beam 10.97 m (36 ft); draught 2.97 m (9 ft 9 in)	**Armament:** four single 5-in (127-mm) DP and five machine-guns, and four quadruple 21-in (533-mm) torpedo tube mountings
Propulsion: two sets of geared steam turbines delivering 36,539 kW (49,000 shp)	**Complement:** 250 men

USS **Trippe**, *a destroyer of the 'Benham' class, leaves Pearl Harbor in 1940. The 'Benhams' were derivatives of the 'Bagley' class, which were 'Gridleys' built by the Navy Yards. USS* **Trippe** *ended its days at Bikini in 1948, as another atom bomb target.*

'Benson' and 'Livermore' classes Destroyers

USS **Benson** *as the ship appeared prior to Pearl Harbor. Officially 1,600-ton destroyers, the class were usually displacing nearly 2,400 tons at full load by the end of the war.* **Benson** *was transferred to Taiwan as* **Lo Yang** *in 1954, serving until 1975.*

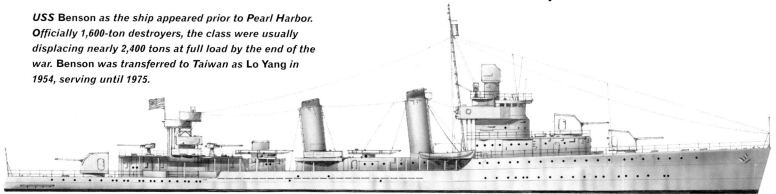

USS **Farenholt** *(DD-491) is seen from the carrier* **USS** **W**asp *(CV-8) as the destroyer comes alongside to re-supply.* **Farenholt** *was to survive the fierce fighting in the* **S**olomons, *but the carrier was not so lucky. Within three weeks of the photo being taken, it was torpedoed to the south of Guadalcanal.*

On the same day in October 1939, the Boston Navy Yard launched four destroyers, the last pair of the 'Sims' series and the first two destroyers of the **'Benson' class**. Though the same hull and machinery were used, the later ships had the boiler spaces divided for improved damage control, necessitating a return to two funnels. A realistic armament was fitted in five 5-in (127-mm) guns and two quintuple sets of torpedo tubes, but for wartime conditions, one gun and a set of tubes being landed. Only the first 24 hulls were completed with the full designed armament. The reduced fit was the most modest since the American destroyer adopted the 5-in gun.

'Livermore' subclass

This design was used for the first major series in the rapid expansion of the US Navy as it headed toward another war: 96 'Bensons' were built between 1939 and 1943, and though the last 64 were officially the separate **'Livermore' class**, there were marginal differences only, the latter type having a slightly greater displacement.

Right: USS **Buchanan** *(DD-484) replenishes from USS* **W**asp *in June 1942.* **Buchanan** *survived the war to be sold to Turkey, where it served under the name* **Gelibolu.** *One of the main guns was removed, and the light AA replaced by four 3-in (76-mm) guns.*

They were the last American destroyers to have the European type of raised forecastle, with its characteristic rounded sheerstrake. This feature took a high freeboard farther aft and increased enclosed volume, but introduced a high stress concentration at the hance. Amidships, where British destroyers tended to be wet, the Americans had bulwarks with continuous freeing ports running to a point abaft the after funnel. This was possible because the continuous topside casing required that torpedo tubes were set on one level higher than the upper deck. This arrangement alone accounted for many American destroyers not being able to carry their full designed armament.

SPECIFICATION	
'Benson' and 'Livermore' classes (as built)	37,285 kW (50,000 shp) to two shafts
Displacement: 1,620 tons	**Performance:** maximum speed 37 kts
Standard dimensions: length 105.99 m (347 ft 9 in); beam 11.05 m (36 ft 3 in); draught 3.12 m (10 ft 3 in)	**Armament:** five single 5-in (127-mm) DP and four machine-guns, and two quintuple 21-in (533-mm) torpedo tube mountings
Propulsion: two sets of geared steam turbines delivering	**Complement:** 250 men

On 10 April 1941, near Iceland, the **USS Niblack** (**DD-424**) became the first US destroyer during World War II to prosecute a submarine contact by depth charging. And the following October, while covering convoy SC 48, the

USS Kearny (**DD-432**), it became the first US warship to be torpedoed.

Many of the later 'Bensons' were converted to high-speed destroyer/minesweeper (DMS) at the expense of a further gun and the remaining tubes.

'Fletcher' class Destroyer

Backbone of the US destroyer force in the Pacific, the 'Fletchers' displayed strong surface warfare armament typical of that theatre, where clashes with Japanese destroyers could often be expected.

Though the extensive 'Benson' class achieved its aim of putting the US destroyer-building industry onto a war footing, the design had limitations for a Pacific war, both in terms of endurance and its curtailed weapons fit. So even before the end of the programme, the first of an improved class were going into the water. The first two of this **'Fletcher' class** went down the slipways in February 1942 and the last four of 175 ships were launched in September 1944 at Puget Sound Navy Yard.

The designed armament of the 'Bensons' was carried by the new ships on a hull some 8.53 m (28 ft) longer and 0.91 m (3 ft) beamier. An improvement was the substitution of licence-built 20-mm and 40-mm AA guns in place of the earlier

0.5-in (12.7-mm) machine-guns. No mainmast was fitted, and a further lowering of the centre of gravity was achieved through reversion to the flush-decked hull, also considered stronger. Funnels were shorter and, as a result, fitted with pronounced caps. Four units, in an unsuccessful experiment, had their No. 3 gunhouse and after tubes replaced by a catapult and scout aircraft.

Though the 'Fletchers' were generally sent quickly to the Pacific on completion, those built on the Atlantic seaboard saw some service there. Two of the earliest, for instance, the **USS Fletcher** and **USS O'Bannon**, were diverted to the Windward Passage where two crossing convoys were being simultaneously assailed by

U-boats. The existing escort was led by an ex-US flush-decker, HMS *Churchill* but, even reinforced, was unable to prevent the loss of five merchantmen. The *O'Bannon* also fought in the night action off Vella Lavella, where three of six US destroyers, including four early 'Fletchers', tangled unwisely with six Japanese destroyers involved in a garrison withdrawal. Attacked by torpedoes and gunfire, the **USS Chevalier** was torn in two, the *O'Bannon* then ploughing into the vessel. The enemy *Yagumo* was immediately torpedoed itself, but the sole American still under way,

seeking still to close the enemy transports, was also hit by one of 16 torpedoes launched towards the Japanese warship. Though only the *Chevalier* was actually lost, the Japanese had succeeded in their aim.

Post-war operators

Following the war, 'Fletchers' were transferred to Argentina (five), Brazil (eight), Chile (two), Columbia (one), West Germany (five), Greece (seven), Italy (three), Japan (two), South Korea (three), Mexico (two), Peru (two), Spain (five), Taiwan (four) and Turkey (five). Surviving US Navy vessels paid off by the early 1970s.

SPECIFICATION	
'Fletcher' class (as built)	**Performance:** maximum speed 37 kts
Displacement: 2,050 tons standard	**Armament:** five single 5-in (127-mm) DP, three twin 40-mm AA and four single 20-mm AA guns, and two quintuple 21-in (533-mm) torpedo tube mountings
Dimensions: length 114.76 m (376 ft 6 in); beam 12.04 m (39 ft 6 in); draught 5.41 m (17 ft 9 in)	
Propulsion: two sets of geared steam turbines delivering 44,742 kW (60,000 shp) to two shafts	**Complement:** 295 men

---

*USS **Stevens (DD-479)** leaves Charleston in December 1942 after completing its trials. By this time, a year after Pearl Harbor, American industry was becoming increasingly geared up for war and 'Fletcher'-class destroyers were coming off the slips at a rate of four per month.*

'Allen M. Sumner' and 'Gearing' classes Destroyers

*USS **G**earing as it appeared on completion in May 1945. Lengthened versions of the 'Allen M. Sumner' class, the large 'Gearings' were the ultimate US wartime destroyer class and some remained in service into the 1980s with the **US R**eserve Fleet.*

To squeeze in more AA armament, the later 'Fletchers' needed to have their director tower lowered by way of compensation. The next design step was to give the hull an extra 45.7 cm (18 in) of beam and to adopt the new twinned 5-in (127-mm) L/38 gunhouse. Three of these occupied less axial length than the five singles of the 'Fletcher' class and enabled a six-gun main battery to be shipped with very little weight penalty. Less demand on space at the after end enabled the

*USS **P**erkins, in common with many of the 'Gearing' class, received extensive modification post-war, serving as a high-speed **ASW** carrier escort. Seen off **O**ahu in 1966, **P**erkins was transferred to the Argentine navy as the **C**ommodoro **P**y in 1973. The vessel served during the Falklands War.*

Rio Grande De Norte (ex-USS Strong) was sold to Brazil in 1973 and is seen here on joint Brazilian/US exercises. In Brazilian service, the 'Sumner' vessel carried a single Wasp helicopter. Five 'Sumners', two 'Gearings' and three 'Fletchers' remained in Brazilian service in the early 1980s.

rearmost tubes to be brought well aft, improving weight distribution and freeing the area abaft the stacks for three quadruple 40-mm AA mountings. These effective weapons, used here for the first time in destroyers, thus enjoyed wide arcs and, being closer to amidships, reduced the ship motion that degraded accuracies. The result was the **'Allen M. Sumner' class**.

Twelve of this 58-strong class were converted to destroyer-minelayers during construction, sacrificing both sets of tubes for a 100-mine capacity. Some were further modified for radar picket duty but, in warning the main body of the fleet against the approach of the kamikaze, they often tended to become victims themselves. The **USS Aaron Ward** became a constructive total loss off Okinawa after being struck by five, while the **USS Laffey** somehow survived

six such hits.

Yet more space and endurance requirements stretched the basic 'Sumner' hull by a further 4.27 m (14 ft) to produce the **'Gearing' class**, which was to prove the ultimate stage in this long series of closely related classes. Externally these larger ships were distinguishable through their more widely-spaced funnels. With the threat from the rump of the Japanese surface fleet by 1945 less than that posed by aircraft, it was also common to sacrifice a set of tubes for a braced tripod bearing a surveillance radar antenna, or even for an extra quadruple 40-mm gun mounting.

FRAM updates

Only with peacetime did the new 3-in (76-mm) automatic guns, which could disintegrate a suicide aircraft, become generally available. These were usually fitted during the extensive FRAM modernizations that converted 'Gearing' destroyers to fast anti-submarine escorts, a primary function for which they were not intended. The FRAM programme also saw the addition of the DASH unmanned helicopter, new Mk 32 torpedo tubes, and ASROC launchers.

SPECIFICATION	
'Allen M. Sumner' class (as built)	shafts
Displacement: 2,200 tons standard	**Performance:** maximum speed 36.5 kts
Dimensions: length 114.8 m (376 ft 6 in); beam 12.5 m (41 ft); draught 5.79 m (19 ft)	**Armament:** three twin 5-in (127-mm) DP and three quadruple 40-mm AA guns, and two quintuple 21-in (533-mm) torpedo tube mountings
Propulsion: two sets of geared steam turbines delivering 44,742 kW (60,000 shp) to two	**Complement:** 350 men

Typ 34 or 'Maass' class Destroyer

*The **Leberecht Maass** is seen in a disruptive camouflage that includes a false bow wave and wash. Soon after completion the vessel had its hull strengthened by additional plating and its bow extended slightly.*

When the keels of the first destroyers of the **Typ 34 class** (or later **'Maass' class**) were laid from late in 1934, Germany had had virtually no destroyer design experience since the end of World War I. This lack of continuity resulted in the use of much that was untried, particularly with respect to boilers and machinery, and the ships gained a reputation for unreliability. They were of a conventional layout and more than a little influenced by British fleet destroyers of the time. Advantage was conferred by extra length, though this was offset by a poorly designed forward end which, lacking sufficient freeboard and flare, left them very wet ships in any sea. A new 127-mm (5-in) gun was selected rather than the better-tried 105-mm (4.13-in)

weapon in order to match the weight of standard French shells. The new gun was reliable but not dual-purpose, and was carried as three singles aft and two singles forward, each group having a separate rangefinder and control.

Two quadruple banks of 533-mm (21-in) torpedo tubes were shipped. Like the Japanese, the Germans believed in these weapons, trained in them and used them to good effect when allowed. Four reloads could be carried. The ships also had two upper-deck tracks for 60 mines.

Homogeneous design

In all, there were 22 destroyers of fairly homogeneous design but, of these, only the first four were Typ 34. Officially, the next 16 ships were of the **Typ 34A**

class and the remaining units were of the **Typ 36 class**. There were few differences externally and these went across type boundaries, as did the several small changes in hull length, though it is noteworthy that the final group of four featured a hull some 6 m (19 ft 8 in) longer than that of the original quartet. This increase partly offset the type's poor range, which resulted from the fact that their stability range did not allow running at below 30 per cent bunker capacity.

It was the misfortune of the group to lose 10 of its number at Narvik, mainly through poor leadership. Another five were lost later.

During the first couple of months of the war, these ships had contributed greatly to the mining campaign off the east coast that cost the Royal Navy heavily.

Originally named **Z1** to **Z22**, the ships in the class were the **Leberecht Maass, Georg Thiele, Max Schultz, Richard Beitzen, Paul Jacobi, Theodor Riedel, Hermann Schömann, Bruno Heinemann, Wolfgang Zenker, Hans Lody, Bernd von Arnim, Erich Giese, Erich Köllner, Friedrich Ihn, Erich Steinbrinck, Friedrich Eckoldt, Diether von Röder, Hans Lüdemann, Hermann Küne, Karl Galster, Wilhelm Heidkamp** and **Anton Schmitt**.

*The **Karl Galster** was the fourth of six destroyers of the Typ 36 class, which were slightly modified Typ 34s. All five of **Galster's** sister-ships were sunk at Narvik, but **Z20** survived the war and ended its days in Soviet service in the Baltic, renamed the **Protshnyi**. The ship was finally broken up in the 1950s.*

SPECIFICATION	
Typ 34 class (as built) **Displacement:** 2,230 tons standard; 3,160 tons full load **Dimensions:** length 119.3 m (391 ft 5 in); beam 11.3 m (37 ft); draught 4 m (13 ft 1 in) **Propulsion:** geared steam turbines delivering 52,199 kW (70,000 shp) to two shafts	**Performance:** maximum speed 38 kts; range 8,150 km (5,064 miles) at 19 kts **Armament:** five 127-mm (5-in), two twin 37-mm (1.46-in) AA and six 20-mm AA guns, two quadruple 533-mm (21-in) torpedo tube mountings and up to 60 mines **Complement:** 315

Typ 36A or 'Z23' class Destroyer

Laid down between November 1938 and April 1940, the Typ 36A vessels were more manoeuvrable than their predecessors but still mediocre.

The destroyers of the **Typ 36A class** were war-built and launched in 1940–42. The fleet would have preferred a ship enlarged from the Typ 34 and capable of long-range operation, but received another slight stretch of the original design with the major difference of an increase in main battery calibre to 150 mm (5.9 in). This had 60 per cent greater weight of shot and a better range, but was difficult and slow for hand-working. The weight of the two forward superimposed guns was cut by substituting a twin turret, but this was long in development and trouble-prone when it finally entered service, and most of the class started their lives with only one single mounting forward, which at least improved their seakeeping. Those that were retrofitted with

the twin turret experienced severe green water effects forward in heavy weather. A problem with the earlier class – poor manoeuvrability – was met by a redesign of the area of the cut-up and the provision of twin rudders but, overall, the Typ 36A did not appeal to a seaman.

Initial order

The initial order for the Typ 36A comprised **Z23** to **Z30**, to which seven more, **Z31** to **Z34** and **Z37** to **Z39** (to a modified design) were later added. These ships, though unnamed, were popularly known as the **'Narvik' class**, the name originating with the Germans themselves, their Norwegian-based units adopting something of the earlier ships that had been destroyed there in April 1940.

Perhaps surprisingly, only six

*The **Z25** cruises purposefully off the Norwegian coast before conversion to 'Barbara' standard, which gave the ship an impressive AA capacity of 12 37-mm (1.46-in) and 18 20-mm automatic weapons. Transferred to the French navy at the end of World War II, the ship served as the **Hoche** until 1956.*

of the 15 Typ 36A ships were lost during the war. Two of the survivors gave the French fleet over a decade of post-war use while another, the **Z38**, was actually commissioned into the post-war Royal Navy as **HMS Nonsuch** for machinery evaluation and 'special trials'. The **Z26** was lost in March 1942

during the destroyer attack on convoy PQ13. While launching a salvo of torpedoes to finish off this ship, the British cruiser HMS *Trinidad* hit itself with a 'rogue' runner: the three German ships involved had already launched about 20 torpedoes in a fruitless attempt to secure the same result!

Z39 was taken over by the Royal Navy in 1945, but transferred to the US. Whereas many other contemporaries were scuttled in the Skagerrak loaded with poison gas shells, the Z39 was finally handed to France and cannibalized to help maintain the ex-German destroyers in French service.

SPECIFICATION	
Typ 36A class	36 kts; range 10,935 km
Displacement: 2,600 tons standard;	(6,795 miles) at 19 kts
3,600 tons full load	**Armament:** three single and one
Dimensions: length 127 m (416 ft	twin 150-mm (5.9-in), two twin
8 in); beam 12 m (39 ft 4 in);	37-mm (1.46-in) AA and five 20-mm
draught 3.92 m (12 ft 10 in)	AA guns, two quadruple 533-mm
Propulsion: geared steam turbines	(21-in) torpedo tube mountings,
delivering 52,199 kW (70,000 shp)	and up to 60 mines
to two shafts	**Complement:** 321 men
Performance: maximum speed	

'SP1' or 'Z41' class
Scout cruiser/heavy destroyer

Z40 according to the final plan. Z40 to Z42 were Type 36A class destroyers, cancelled but reinstated in 1941 as an enlarged threesome known as 'Zerstörer 1941'. Their larger hulls would have made a steady platform for the 150-mm (5.9-in) guns. Torpedo armament was also increased.

The Germans were concerned at the potential firepower of the big French destroyers and initiated the **Spähkreuzer** (scout cruiser) or **SP** concept. However, at the beginning of World War II, the number of destroyers was trimmed in view of other priorities. Of the five stricken from the Type 36A programme, three (**Z40** to **Z42**) were reinstated early in 1941.

The SPs would have had better endurance conferred by a three-shaft layout, with steam turbines on the wing shafts and cruising-diesel drive on a centre-line shaft. They would have been nearly 10 m (32 ft 9½ in) longer than the comparable 'Capitani Romani' of the Italian fleet. Their extra size would have made for steadier gun platforms and justified the 150-mm (5.9-in) main battery. Final innovations were the uprated torpedo tube battery and mine stowage.

Diesel power

Beyond the SPs the Germans worked on a couple of all-diesel designs. The multi-diesel layout was a popular concept as lighter distillate fuels were more readily available in Germany by synthesis than heavy bunker oils, which had to be imported. The Type 42 class embraced one prototype, Z51, a small (114-m/374-ft) ship of only 2,050 tons standard displacement and a four 127-mm (5-in) gun arma-ment. Lack of supply caused the six-diesel/three-shaft layout to be truncated to a four-diesel/sin-gle-shaft arrangement, but this was wrecked by bombing while fitting out in 1945.

SPECIFICATION	
'SP1' class	**Speed:** 36 kts on steam power
Displacement: 4,540 tons standard	**Endurance:** 22250 km (13,826 miles) at 19 kts
Dimensions: length 152 m (498 ft 8 in); beam 14.6 m (47 ft 11 in); draught 4.6 m (15 ft 1 in)	**Armament:** three twin 150-mm (5.9-in), one twin 88-mm (3.46-in) DP, four twin 37-mm AA and three quadruple 20-mm AA guns, two quintuple 533-mm (21-in) torpedo tube mountings, and up to 140 mines
Propulsion: two sets of geared steam turbines delivering 5,7792 kW (77,500 shp) to the two wing shafts and one diesel delivering 10,813 kW (14,500 shp) to one centreline shaft	
	Complement: 538 men

'T22' or 'Elbing' class Light destroyers

In both world wars the German navy operated so-called 'torpedo boats'. Similar to destroyers, they were spared the need to operate as units of the main fleet and could be considerably smaller while able to carry the same scale of weapons.

Reborn Kriegsmarine

During the 1920s, the dozen 'Albatros'- and 'Iltis'-class units were built. These carried not only their torpedoes but three 105-mm (4.13-in) guns. These were followed by 21 numbered ships of the Type 35 and Type 37 classes. The size of the craft and their armament was shrunk, leaving the ships with the weak-nesses of the smaller 'S'-boats and few of their virtues.

Effective and popular

These were followed by the **Type 39 class**, in which a 15-ship group (**T22** to **T36**) was built at Elbing, becoming known as the **'Elbing' class**.

They readopted the two-funnelled layout and, despite their lack of raised forecastle, were often mistaken for destroyers. Launched in 1942–44, they had 17 m (55 ft 9¼ in) of extra length, accommodating four 105-mm guns along the centreline and two triple banks of torpedo tubes.

The 'Elbings' were used widely in French waters. The **T27** and **T29** were both sunk in April 1944, while the **T24** sank HMCS *Athabaskan*. The **T25** and **T26** were sunk in the daylight action of December 1943 when 11 German ships, hampered by heavy seas, were savaged by two British cruisers in the Bay of Biscay.

Smoke pours from the side of T24 (foreground) as the ship reels from a rocket salvo fired from RAF Beaufighters at the mouth of the Girond, August 1944. T24 sank; its companion, the destroyer Z24, managed to reach its berth but capsized shortly afterwards.

SPECIFICATION	
'T22' class	**Speed:** 33.5 kts
Displacement: 1,295 tons standard and 1,755 tons full load	**Endurance:** 9300 km (5,789 miles) at 19 kts
Dimensions: length 102 m (334 ft 7 in); beam 10 m (32 ft 9½ in); draught 2.6 m (8 ft 6 in)	**Armament:** four single 105-mm (4.13-in), two twin 37-mm AA and six single 20-mm AA guns, two triple 533-mm (21-in) torpedo tube mountings and up to 50 mines
Propulsion: two sets of geared steam turbines delivering 23862 kW (32,000 shp) to two shafts	**Complement:** 198 men

'Generale' class Light Destroyers

Like the Germans, the Italians operated a large force of light destroyers alongside their main fleet units. Both navies referred to these as torpedo boats, a term that can confuse some readers, who may think of them in terms of the British MTBs. The nearest thing to such ships in the Royal Navy were the 'Hunt' classes, which were more robust but slower; the equivalent to the older enemy boats were the few Admiralty 'S'-class units still serving. The six **'Generale'-class** ships

were the last of four very similar 73-m (239-ft 6-in) classes that commenced with the eight-strong 'Pilo' class of 1914–15. These were narrow-gutted three-stackers, typical destroyers of their time, which were downgraded to torpedo boat status between the wars as larger ships commissioned. For their size they were quite ambitiously armed, with five single 102-mm (4-in) guns and two twin 440-mm (17.3-in) torpedo tube mountings. The gun layout was hardly satisfactory,

with one mounting on the raised forecastle, two sided amidships and two on the quarterdeck, no more than three being effective on either beam. The four 'Sirtori'-class ships squeezed in an extra gun on an already tight topweight reserve. Dating from 1916–17, these were followed by the eight 'La Masa'-class ships of 1917–19, which had their armament reduced to only four guns. In 1919–20 came four 'Palestro'-class ships, slightly larger at 82 m (269 ft) to accommodate a near 50 per cent increase in power.

Though these were to have a follow-on in the 'Curtatone' class of 1922–23, these two groups were separated by one last 73-m (239-ft 6-in) class, the 'Generali', all six of which were launched in 1921–22 by the single yard of Odero, at Sestri

Ponente. The ships were the **Generale Antonio Cantore**, **Generale Antonio Cascino**, **Generale Antonio Chinotto**, **Generale Carlo Montanari**, **Generale Achille Papa** and **Generale Marcello Prestinari**. Of similar size to the earlier ships, they carried only three guns, a complement to which most were eventually reduced by wartime demands. None of these small and elderly ships was employed in front-line operations, but all became war casualties. Three were mined, one of them the *Chinotto*, sinking in a field laid by the British submarine HMS *Rorqual* during a particularly fruitful patrol. These mines, off western Sicily, also claimed two merchantmen, while the submarine also sank another ship and an Italian submarine by torpedo.

SPECIFICATION	
'Generale' class (as built)	(15,000 shp) to two shafts
Displacement: 635 tons standard and 890 tons full load	**Speed:** 30 kts
Dimensions: length 73.5 m (241 ft 1 in); beam 7.33 m (24 ft); draught 2.5 m (8 ft 2½ in)	**Armament:** three single 102-mm (4-in) and two 76-mm (3-in) AA guns, two twin 450-mm (17.7-in) torpedo tube mountings and up to 18 mines
Propulsion: two sets of steam turbines delivering 11,186 kW	**Complement:** 105 men

'Turbine' class Destroyers

Dating from 1927–8, the eight **'Turbine'-class** destroyers (**Aquilone, Borea, Espero, Euro, Nembo, Ostro, Turbine** and **Zeffiro**) were almost identical to the 'Sauro'-class units that preceded them, the major difference being an extra 3 m (9 ft 10 in) of length to accommodate an 11 per cent increase in power. A feature of both types was the armoured

'pillbox' of a conning tower that topped-off the enclosed bridge. They were the last Italian destroyers to have the low-velocity 45-calibre 120-mm (4.72-in) guns but the first to mount a second director for the after guns.

The four 'Sauro'-class ships were destroyed as part of the Red Sea squadron, while no less than six of the 'Turbine'

class were sunk in 1940. Each of the class could carry over 50 mines, and four of them mined the waters off Tobruk. The Axis garrison there was as much a problem to support as later it proved for the British, and on 28 June 1940 the *Espero* became the first casualty when caught by the Australian cruiser HMAS *Sydney*, the ship that sank the cruiser *Bartolomeo Colleoni* off Cape Spada three weeks later. 'Stringbags' from the carrier HMS *Eagle* disposed of the *Zeffiro* and a freighter, then damaged the *Euro* in Tobruk harbour in early July, and a

fortnight later sank the *Ostro* and *Nembo* as well as a freighter in the adjacent Gulf of Bomba. It was these same aircraft, working from a shore base near Port Sudan, that sank two of the 'Sauros' in the Red Sea in the following April. Carrier-based air attack accounted for another pair on the night of 16/17 September when HMS *Illustrious* blitzed Benghazi. The *Euro* was sunk by German bombers after the Italian capitulation while the *Turbine* itself, captured by the Germans, was finally sunk by American aircraft in September 1944.

SPECIFICATION	
'Turbine' class	29,828 kW (40,000 shp)
Displacement: 1,090 tons standard and 1,700 tons full load	**Speed:** 33 kts (operational)
Dimensions: length 92 65 m (304 ft); beam 9.2 m (30 ft 2½ in); draught 2.9 m (9 ft 6 in)	**Armament:** two twin 120-mm (4.72-in) and two single 40-mm AA guns, two triple 533-mm (21-in) torpedo tube mountings and up to 52 mines
Propulsion: two sets of geared steam turbines delivering	**Complement:** 180 men

Turbine, *in the scheme it adopted at Piraeus in 1942, was taken over by the Germans after the Italian surrender and destroyed by American aircraft off Salamis in 1944.*

'Navigatore' class Destroyer

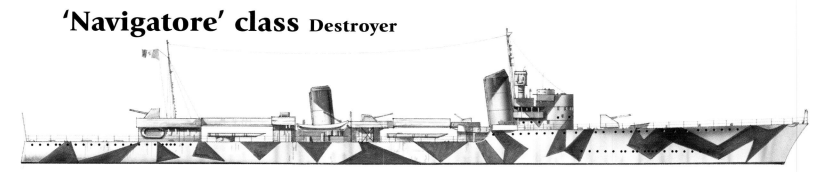

Four years after completing the scouts of the 'Leone' class, the Italians launched between 1928 and 1930 the **'Navigatore' class** of destroyers, namely the **Alvise da Mosto, Antonio da Noli, Antonio Pigafetta, Antoniotto Usodimare, Emanuelle Pessagno, Giovanni da Verazzano, Lanzerotto Malocello, Leone Pancaldo, Luca Tarigo, Nicoloso da Recco, Nicolo Zeno** and **Ugolino Vivaldi**. They were of smaller dimensions but of greater displacement than the 'Leone' class. Much of this was accounted for by machinery that produced up to 44,742 kW (60,000 shp) and a third twin 120-mm (4.72-in) gun mounting between the two groups of torpedo tubes.

SPECIFICATION	
'Navigatore' class	shafts
Displacement: 1,945 tons standard and 2,580 tons full load	**Speed:** 38 kts
Dimensions: length 107.75 m (353 ft 6 in); beam 10.2 m (33 ft 6 in); draught 3.5 m (11 ft 6 in)	**Armament:** three twin 120-mm (4.72-in) and three single 37-mm AA guns, two twin or triple 533-mm (21-in) torpedo tube mountings and up to 54 mines
Propulsion: two sets of geared steam turbines delivering 37,285 kW (50,000 shp) to two	**Complement:** 225 men

High speed

The 'Navigatore' were produced when speed was an obsession with the Italians. The ships were therefore very lightly built, and their seakeeping left something to be desired. A futile gesture towards weight-saving was the provision of torpedo tubes of 450-mm (17.72-in) calibre. In the event, however, the vessels shipped 533-mm (21-in) mountings.

Wartime action

The fate of the 'Navigatore' was a reflection of the conflicting loyalties of Italians during the war. Eleven of the 12 were sunk – six from direct action by the British and another by a mine; two sunk in action by the Germans; one scuttled; and the last sunk in error by an Italian submarine. The *Pancaldo* was an early loss, sunk by aircraft from HMS *Eagle* outside Augusta

The 'Navigatore' class was designed above all to achieve high speed, and sacrificed both armament and seakeeping for this end. They were constructed to counter the threat posed by the French 'Jaguar' and 'Guepard' destroyer classes, but found themselves fighting a very different war.

after returning from the Battle of Calabria. The vessel was later salvaged and recommissioned, only to be sunk again by aircraft off Cape Bon in April 1943. Another, the *Pigafetta*, was also sunk twice, being scuttled at Fiume at the Italian surrender, but refloated and put back into service by the Germans, only to be destroyed by British air attack on Trieste in February 1945.

'Ariete' class Torpedo boat

Ariete was the only vessel of the class to serve with the Italian navy, the others being seized by the Germans in September 1943. The 'Arietes' were improved 'Spica'-class ships intended primarily to protect convoys from a surface threat. The 'Spicas' themselves became very active minelayers during the war.

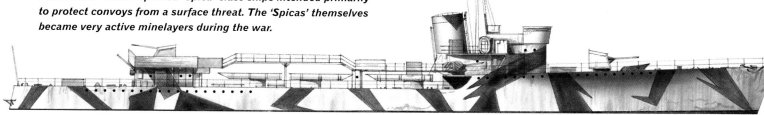

With the 32 torpedo boats of the 'Spica' class launched between 1936 and 1938, the Italians were able to adopt a single-funnel arrangement, the more efficient hull being driven at the same speed as the preceding 'Curtatoni' for power.

SPECIFICATION	
'Ariete' class	16,405 kW (22,000 shp) to two shafts
Displacement: 800 tons standard and 1,125 tons full load	**Speed:** 31 kts
Dimensions: length 82.25 m (269 ft 9 in); beam 8.6 m (28 ft); draught 2.8 m (9 ft)	**Armament:** two single 100-mm (4-in) and 37-mm AA guns, two triple 450-mm (17.72-in) torpedo tube mountings and up to 28 mines
Propulsion: two sets of geared steam turbines delivering	**Complement:** 155 men

Their profile was similar to that of the contemporary class of 'Oriani' fleet destroyers, the major difference being the much bulkier funnel casing of the latter, necessary because of extensive trunking from the two separate boiler spaces. These ships also lacked the funnel cap of the torpedo boats. With the 'Spicas' the 100-mm (3.9-in) gun was introduced; only three were carried and these were

essentially for use against ships, having an elevation of only 45° and a rate of fire of about eight rounds per minute. Surprisingly, considering their category, they adhered to only four of the small 450-mm (17.72-in) torpedo tubes, and these were largely wasted by initially installing them as singles. This meant that only two tubes were bearing on either broadside. Centreline twin mountings were thus later substituted. The design of the **'Ariete' class** was only that of an improved 'Spica', whose extra beam demanded about 15 per cent more installed power, but allowed greater topweight. This extra weight was taken up by the two extra torpedo tubes (these were never uprated to the far more useful 533-mm/ 21-in size). Furthermore, it

allowed for an increase in mine capacity from 20 to 28 and an equivalent increase in depth charge capacity. The Italians used their torpedo boats extensively and effectively for minelaying.

Not until 1942–43 were the 'Ariete' laid down, the fleet having by then the benefit of combat experience. Over 40

units were planned in an extended programme but, though spread among three yards, only 16 (namely the **Alabarda**, **Ariete**, **Arturo**, **Auriga**, **Balestra**, **Daga**, **Dragone**, **Eridano**, **Fionda**, **Gladio**, **Lancia**, **Pugnale**, **Rigel**, **Spada**, **Spica** and **Stella Polare**) were actually laid down. Of these only the nameship was

actually delivered to the Italian fleet, a month before the armistice.

The remainder, in various stages of completion eventually fell into German hands, only 13 of them actually seeing service at sea. Only two (*Ariete* and *Balestra*) survived to serve post-war, both under the Yugoslav flag.

'Soldato', 'Folgore', 'Maestrale' and 'Oriani' classes
Destroyers

The most numerous class ever ordered by the Italian navy, the 'Soldato' class trunked all their boiler uptakes into a single large funnel casing, which created a very distinctive silhouette. Once again they were highly powered and capable of up to 39 kts.

The extensive **'Soldato' class** was the ultimate development of a sequence that began with the four-ship 'Dardo' class of 1930–32. They used deck space very effectively by combining all of the boiler uptakes into one substantial funnel casing. Four 120-mm (4.72-in) guns were carried, sited in two twin mountings, one on the forecastle deck and one on the same level atop a house set well aft, saving both deck space and topweight.

The ships were highly powered, eficient only in their torpedo complement, weapons that the Italians never valued

highly. Their distinctive profile was repeated in the similar **'Folgore' class** quartet built in parallel. One feature was a separate director for each pair of guns, allowing two targets to be engaged simultaneously.

Increased power
To improve seaworthiness and fighting qualities, the four ships of the **'Maestrale' class** of 1934 were lengthened by nearly 10 m (32 ft 9½ in), and the beam increased proportionately. Otherwise, they and the four ships of the **'Oriani' class** of 1936 were essentially repeats, the latter with increased power.

SPECIFICATION	
'Soldato' class (first series) **Displacement:** 1,830 tons standard and 2,460 tons full load **Dimensions:** length 106.75 m (350 ft 2 in); beam 10.15 m (33 ft 4 in); draught 3.6 m (11 ft 9 in) **Propulsion:** two sets of geared steam turbines delivering	35,794 kW (48,000 shp) to two shafts **Speed:** 39 kts **Armament:** four or five 120-mm (4.7-in) and one 37-mm AA guns, two triple 533-mm (21-in) torpedo tube mountings and up to 48 **Complement:** 219 men

Repeat order
With war in Europe looming, the Italian navy expanded, placing a 12-ship repeat 'Oriani' order. All were launched 1937–38 as the first group of 'Soldati', and were the **Alpino**, **Artigliere**, **Ascari**, **Aviere**, **Bersagliere**, **Camicia Nera**, **Carabiniere**, **Corazziere**, **Fucillere**, **Geniere**, **Granatiere**

and **Lanciere**. Four of these took a fifth 120-mm gun in a single mounting between the torpedo tube groups. The arrangement was kept in all but one of a further series of seven, only five of which were completed. The *Lanciere* of the first group and the **Scirocco** of the 'Maestrale' class were lost in a gale. Four of the first group survived the war, two then being ceded to the Soviet Union. Three of the second were ceded to France.

Like many Italian destroyers, the 'Soldato' class emphasised speed at the expense of armament and strength, and the Lanciere, seen here, also went down in the storm that overwhelmed Scirocco. The 'Maestrales' were the basis for the extensive 'Soldato' class.

'Minekaze' and 'Kamikaze' classes
Destroyers

SPECIFICATION	
'Minekaze' class	shafts
Displacement: 1,215 tons standard and 1,650 tons full load	**Speed:** 39 kts
Dimensions: length 102.5 m (336 ft); beam 9 m (29 ft 6 in); draught 2.89 m (9 ft 6 in)	**Endurance:** 6670 km (4,145 miles) at 14 kts
	Armament: four single 120-mm (5-in) guns, two machine-guns, two triple 533-mm (21-in) torpedo tube mountings and up to 20 mines
Propulsion: two sets of geared steam turbines delivering 28,709 kW (38,500 shp) to two	**Complement:** 148 men

The 21 'Momi'-class and 15 **'Minekaze'-class** destroyers were the first original designs of the Japanese navy. The 'Minekazes' all launched between 1919 and 1922.

The classes introduced the 533-mm (21-in) torpedo tube to Japanese destroyers, twins in the 'Momis' and triples in the'Minekazes'. Both carried their 120-mm (4.72-in) guns high on deckhouses and forecastle.

During World War II, when the shortage of escorts was

exploited by American submarines, most of the 'Minekazes' shed their minesweeping gear, half their main-calibre guns and all but a pair of torpedo tubes to mount depth charge throwers and ammunition. Four units were converted to convoy escorts. One, the *Sawakaze*, was fitted with an ahead-firing nine-barrelled AS rocket launcher. By the end of the war, nine of the class had fallen victim to US Navy submarine attacks.

Above: The venerable 'Minekazes' were launched between 1919 and 1922 but served throughout the war. Many had their original weapon fit altered to include depth charge throwers and light AA guns, as the enemy was no longer likely to be another destroyer. The name ship was lost to the submarine USS Pogy in early 1944.

Top: The 'Kamikaze'-class destroyers, follow-ons to the 'Minekazes', represented a departure for the Japanese navy, which had hitherto followed Royal Navy designs, although the choice of 120-mm (4.72-in) guns as main armament reflected British naval policy.

Below: This is a 'Minekaze' as it appeared in late 1944 after being converted to carry Kaiten suicide torpedo craft. This desperate expedient failed to achieve success on a scale to rival that of the kamikaze aircraft, which had begun to launch their attacks earlier in the year.

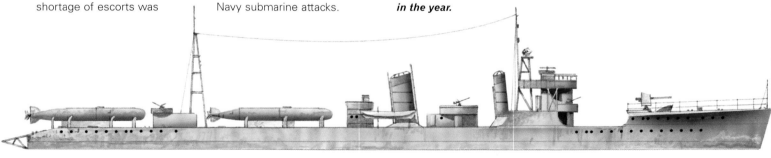

'Fubuki' class Destroyers

At their construction, the 20 **'Fubuki'-class** destroyers (launched in 1927–31) were trend-setters. They had been preceded by the 12 'Mutsuki'-class destroyers, which had

refined the 'Kamikazes' with their strong Anglo-German influences. Only then did the Japanese designers go their own way and produce a type of destroyer so advanced that it

The 'Fubuki' class revolutionized destroyer design by substantially increasing the size of the vessel. This reduced the vulnerability to heavy seas and enabled them to carry a formidable armament of six 127-mm (5-in) guns and nine 610-mm (24-in) torpedo tubes.

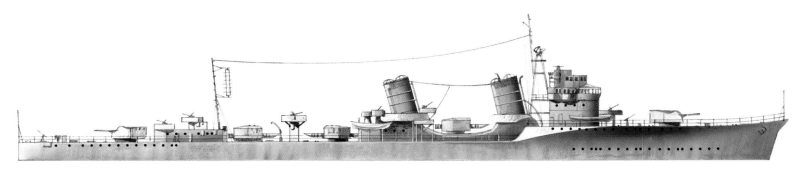

was formidable 15 years later at the end of World War II, besides influencing all the classes that followed it. An increase in size was accepted to accommodate additional topweight. The awkward forward well was replaced by a continuous forecastle, the freeboard was increased, and the bridgework was strengthened and raised to reduce water impact damage. In the preceding class, the 610-mm (24-in) torpedoes had been introduced and the 'Fubukis' carried three triple mountings, with stowage for nine spare torpedoes. This early commitment to the torpedo was obvious, yet Allied forces were surprised by the bold manner in which the Japanese used them in World War II.

A further innovation was the uprating of the main calibre guns to 127 mm (5 in) and mounting these in fully enclosed twin gunhouses, one forward and two aft to lower their combined centre of gravity. In those units launched from 1929, the elevation of the main battery was increased to 70°, an angle unmatched in their day to give a dual-purpose capacity. This class was also of high power, the 37285 kW (50,000 shp) being good for 37 kts.

Hull weakness

Unfortunately, this was bought at the expense of hull strength, and a degree of tenderness. Service during the 1930s highlighted these failings, and the ships were strengthened and given extra ballast. This added another 400 tons to the displacement, slowing them by 4 kts. Further topweight was

From 1943, the 'X' turret was removed from surviving 'Fubuki'-class destroyers in favour of more light AA guns. The original AA armament of two 13-mm machine-guns was changed to four 13-mm and 14 25-mm weapons as US aircraft were recognized as a major threat.

saved later by not carrying spare torpedoes and exchanging the superfiring after mountings in favour of an enhancement to the AA defences. The class served in all theatres, only one unit surviving the war. The ships were the **Akebono**, **Amagiri**, **Asagiri**, **Ayanami**, **Fubuki**,

Hatsuyuki, **Isonami**, **Miyuki**, **Murakumo**, **Oboro**, **Sagiri**, **Sazanami**, **Shikinami**, **Shinonome**, **Shirakumo**, **Shirayuki**, **Uranami**, **Ushio**, **Usugumo** and **Yugiri**.

Fubuki was lost during the battles in the Solomon Islands in 1942.

SPECIFICATION	
'Fubuki' class (as built) Displacement: 2,090 tons standard **Dimensions:** length 118.35 m (388 ft 4 in); beam 10.36 m (34 ft); draught 3.2 m (10 ft 6 in) **Propulsion:** two sets of geared steam turbines delivering 37,285 kW (50,000 shp) to two shafts	**Speed:** 37 kts **Endurance:** 8700 km (5,406 miles) at 15 kts **Armament:** three twin 127-mm (5-in) guns, two machine-guns, three triple 610-mm (24-in) torpedo tube mountings with nine reloads, and up to 18 mines **Complement:** 197 men

'Tomodzura' and 'Ootori' classes Coastal destroyers

Warship design rarely profits from attempting an ambitious fit on a limited displacement, yet this is just what the inter-war treaties brought about.

The Japanese operated a class of first-class torpedo boat up to the mid-1920s, but did not repeat the type until the four-ship **'Tomodzura' class**, ordered in 1931. At 650-ton standard displacement, these ships carried an ambitious armament of a single and a twin 127-mm (5-in) gunhouse and two pairs of 533-mm (21-in) torpedo tubes, all on a fine hull able to achieve 30 kts on a modest 8,203 kW (11,000 shp).

Slender proportions

The weakness of this design was revealed when the nameship capsized in heavy weather in 1943. It was recovered, heavily modified (as were the remainder of the class) and recommissioned.

The lesson was also timely as regards the **'Ootori'-class** boats, then about to be ordered. The navy eventually had to accept a reduced armament of two 120-mm (5-in) guns, and only one pair of torpedo tubes.

Eight of the 16 units projected were cancelled, but those completed were reportedly good AS ships (the **Hato**, **Hayabusa**, **Hiyodori**, **Kari**, **Kasasagi**, **Kiji**, **Ootori** and **Sagi**, all launched in 1935–7). The *Sagi* and *Hiyodon* were sunk by the submarine USS *Gunnel* and the nameship was sunk off Saipan in June 1944.

Chitori, *second ship of the 'Tomodzura' class, is seen here off Maizuru in 1934, the year the nameship capsized while on running trials due to the designers' attempt to cram an excessive armament on to a vessel of modest displacement.*

SPECIFICATION	
'Ootori' class (as built) **Displacement:** 840 tons standard and 1,050 tons full load **Dimensions:** length 88.35 m (289 ft 11 in); beam 8.2 m (26 ft 11 in); draught 2.84 m (9 ft 4 in) **Propulsion:** two sets of geared steam turbines delivering 14168 kW (19,000 shp)	to two shafts **Speed:** 30 kts **Endurance:** 7400 km (4,598 miles) at 14 kts **Armament:** three single 120-mm (5-in) and one 40-mm AA guns, and one triple 533-mm (21-in) torpedo tube mounting **Complement:** 112 men

'Akatsuki' and 'Kagero' classes
Special-type and cruiser-type destroyers

The **Hibiki** *was Japan's first welded warship, and was the only destroyer of the 'Akatsuki' class to survive World War II. The ship's 'X' turret was replaced with more light AA weapons in 1942.*

In the 'Fubuki' class, the Japanese had destroyers of a specification superior to that of the British 'J' class of a decade later. This sudden leap in capability brought problems, as succeeding classes revealed.

The four ships of the **'Akatsuki' class** of 1931–33

The **Shiranuki** *in less happy circumstances, berthed in Maizuru dock after narrowly surviving a torpedo hit from a* **US** *submarine off the Aleutians. The Japanese destroyer fleet was designed for surface action and had to be hastily modified for* **AA** *and* **ASW** *operations.*

kept the same arrangement on a slightly shorter hull but reduced the forward funnel to a thick pipe to save topweight, with lightweight masting and a reduction in depth charges. The *Hibiki* of this group was the first all-welded Japanese destroyer.

In the six ships of the 'Hatsuhara' class that followed, length was again cut, along with one 127-mm (5-in) gun and a set of torpedo tubes with reloads; power and speed were also reduced to comply with London Treaty restrictions. They were largely repeated with the 10 ships of the 'Shiratsuyu' class, which were reduced in length yet had the torpedo armament increased to eight 610-mm (24-in) weapons with a set of reloads. The 10 ships of the 'Asashio' class of 1937 were late enough to bypass treaties and returned to a size and armament almost identical with the 'Fubukis' of nearly a decade

before. This basic design was the basis of the necessary expansion in destroyers in the lead-up to war. Thus 18 more destroyers, nearly identical but proportionately beamier and known as the **'Kagero' class**, were launched in 1938–41. These were similar to the 'Fubukis', with superfiring twin gunhouses aft and one forward, the latter separated from the bridge by a distinctive gap, which allowed very wide arcs. A 20-ship repeat class, the 'Yugumo' class, followed in 1941–43.

Of the 'Kagero' ships, only one survived the war.

SPECIFICATION	
'Kagero' class (as built)	shafts
Displacement: 2,035 tons standard; 2,490 tons full load	**Performance:** maximum speed 35 kts; range 9,250 km (5,748 miles) at 15 kts
Dimensions: length 118.5 m (388 ft 9 in); beam 10.8 m (35 ft 5 in); draught 3.76 m (12 ft 4 in)	**Armament:** three twin 127-mm (5-in) and two twin 25-mm AA guns, and two quadruple 610-mm (24-in) torpedo tube mountings
Propulsion: two sets of geared steam turbines delivering 38,776 kW (52,000 shp) to two	**Complement:** 240 men

'Akitsuki' class Fleet escort/ASW destroyer

By far the largest series-built Japanese destroyers, the ships of the **'Akitsuki' class** were conceived originally as AA escorts comparable with the British 'Dido' and US 'Atlanta' cruiser classes, but offering a cheaper solution to the problem.

The choice of a 100-mm (3.9-in) gun was probably better than that of the slower-firing 5.25-in (133.4-mm) and 5-in (127-mm) weapons of the Western ships, though the lively hull of a destroyer must have presented problems. These were the only

eight-gun Japanese destroyers, and the quadruple torpedo tube mounting was probably an afterthought.

The Japanese had underestimated the devastating effect of a determined air attack and only four 25-mm light

automatic guns were originally shipped. War experience demanded the addition of more at every opportunity, and by the end of the war, those still afloat (six were sunk) had up to 50 such weapons. Launched in 1941–44, the ships were the

The destroyers of the 'Akitsuki' class were fast AA escorts built to operate with carrier groups.

Akitsuki, Fuyutsuki, Hanatsuki, Harutsuki, Hatsutsuki, Natsusuki, Niitsuki, Shimotsuki, Suzutsuki, Terutsuki, Wakatsuki and **Yoitsuki**.

The most distinctive feature of the class was the complex casing of the single stack; extensive trunking enabled the funnel to be sited far enough abaft the bridge to cut the smoke problem and greatly improve visibility, while placing it sufficiently far forward to permit extra AA platforms to be located where there would have otherwise been an after stack.

A feature of preceding classes had been their extremely light masts, but the 'Akitsukis' were among the first to have their masts strengthened for the support of the considerable bulk

Carrying only a light gun armament and four torpedo tubes, the ships of the 'Akitsuki' class could accommodate a substantial number of depth charges. Their large hulls soon bristled with light AA weapons, 40 to 50 25-mm guns being fitted to the units that were still operational in 1945.

of the Type 22 surveillance radar antenna. The size of the hull, combined with a comparatively light gun armament and few torpedoes, allowed more generous topweight margins than was customary with Japanese destroyers, one result being a large depth-charge capacity. Nearly 40 more hulls to two improved designs were planned but never completed.

'Matsu' class Escort destroyer

Japan's commitment to a short war was nowhere more evident than in her lack of plans for rapid fleet expansion. Convoy escorts were virtually non-existent (as, indeed, were plans for the convoy system itself), and pre-war fleet destroyers, which were being lost at an alarming rate, were being replaced by ships of equal quality. Though the notion was laudable, Japan lacked the time and the capacity to produce such ships, and a utility design had therefore to be developed rapidly. In profile, this **'Matsu' class** looked large by virtue of the two spindly and widely spaced funnels, but it was the smallest – in terms of both size and displacement – to be built since World War I.

The correct scale was given by the gun mountings, which appeared over-large. These were

simple in the extreme, a single hand-worked 127-mm (5-in) weapon in a shield forward and a twin in a open structure aft. Installed power was little more than one-third that of the fleet destroyers, but the 'Matsus' could still manage about 28 kts, more than adequate for convoy work.

AA weaponry

A respectable two dozen 25-mm automatic AA weapons

Designed for rapid production, the ships of the 'Matsu' class were powered by turbines providing only about a third of the power available to a fleet destroyer, but they were capable of a respectable 28 kts. The ships of the 'Matsu' class had their two sets of machinery arranged in separate units for better damage control.

were carried, though many of these were single-barrel mountings sited in very exposed positions along the edges of the hull. Right amidships was a quadruple 610-mm (24-in) torpedo tube bank; a new pattern sextuple unit had been planned but not completed. In a ship of this capacity and speed, the tubes were mainly of defensive value but still had the splinter-proof house from which this weapon could be worked in some comfort.

This and the enclosed bridge contrasted with the spartan appointments on British ships, where it was not appreciated

that a comfortable crew performed better, without the tendency to 'go soft'.

Only 17 of the planned 28 'Matsu'-class escort destroyers were completed in 1944–45, by which time the design had been even further simplified into the 1,290-ton 'Tachibana' class variant, of which 30 were laid down (13 of them to a further simplified design) and another 90 planned.

Because they were completed very late in World War II and then used only for second-line duties, an unusual number survived, with losses amounting to 11 ships.

Axis assault vessels Landing craft

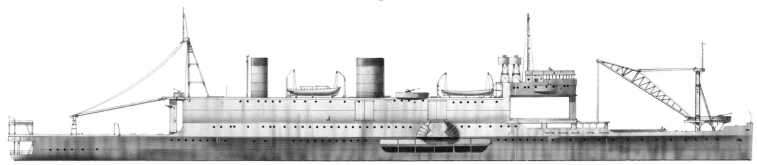

Although the prospect of an invasion of the UK loomed large in their minds during the summer of 1940, the Germans never came to grips with the problems of large-scale amphibious operations. The Japanese, by contrast, had from the very beginning realized the importance of amphibious warfare in any future acquisition of territory among the myriad islands of the Pacific Ocean.

Norwegian campaign

Both the Germans and Japanese developed a variety of vessels capable of being used in amphibious warfare, and these make interesting contrasts with equivalent British and American craft. Only one major landing was made by the Germans over any distance, and this was the assault on Norway in April 1940. As the country was neutral, and had very weak defences, it was possible to conduct a surprise landing of troop detachments from warships, simultaneously in each major port.

Once seized, these ports could immediately handle orthodox transports carrying reinforcements, transport and equipment.

Following the seizure of beach-heads, the follow-up wave of troops depended upon about 2,000 inland waterway barges. While good for their designed purpose, these barges were not fit for an opposed short-sea crossing. They had low freeboards, enormous hatches with weak wooden covers, and cavernous, unobstructed holds with no double bottom or cellular hull sides.

While brows could be fitted for offloading troops, a bow door was a different matter. The bow door would open into a 'tank deck' that was well below waterline. Once holed, they would have rapidly foundered.

Any assault depending upon such craft would have required total air superiority. Moreover, any assault on the UK would have required the Royal Navy's absence, and given the mass of bases close to all threatened British shores this was a virtual impossibility. Once the Operation Sealion invasion had been abandoned, the Germans had no obvious need to mount any further assault landings. The only true landing craft developed was based closely on the Allied design of LCM. In place of the slow LCA, the Germans preferred to put their spearhead troops ashore from wooden-built **Sturmboote** with a length of 6 or 14.5 m (19 ft 6 in or 47 ft 6 in). Of these, the larger was capable of carrying 40 equipped men at 25 kts.

The F-lighter

There were two types of vehicle carriers, used widely as general-

The **Shinshu Maru** *was designed and built for the Japanese army, and has the distinction of having been the world's first purpose-built landing ship. Twenty landing craft could be carried for launch through stern doors.*

purpose utility craft. The sea-going type was the **MFP**, or **Marine Fahrprahm**. This was known to the Allies as the **F-lighter**, and was often met in the Mediterranean. The MFP was transported in sections for assembly in its operating theatre. At 50 m (164 ft) long, it drew only 1.5 m (4 ft 9 in). It had a miniscule superstructure aft, forward of which was a long well flanked by comparatively high coamings and accessible via a bow ramp. The MFP could carry a gun as powerful as an 88-mm (3.46-in) Flak weapon, together with numerous light automatic weapons. Doubling as a cargo carrier and escort, it was regularly encountered in the Aegean and the Adriatic, being greatly respected by Allied coastal craft as its firepower was complemented by a virtual immunity to torpedo attack largely because of its shallow draught. Though strictly speaking a riverine type, the **Siebel ferry** was also met in sheltered open waters. It was a simple vessel comprising two

T149 *is seen on trials in March 1944. These landing ships are reputed to have been based on photographs taken by the Germans of early Allied amphibious landing operations in the Mediterranean.*

A disabled German infantry landing craft abandoned in the wake of the German 14th Army's rapid retreat north through Italy. This craft was encountered by the Allies at Civitaveccia, near Rome, its bow jammed on the rocks outside the harbour.

powered pontoons bridged, catamaran-style, by a rectangular vehicle deck measuring 27 x 14.5 m (88 ft 6 in x 47 ft 6 in). Very effective but also very slow, it could carry up to 100 tons at 9 kts in favourable conditions. Its typical armament of two quadruple 20-mm cannon mountings was usually considerably augmented by the heavier weapons of vehicles in transit and, like the F-lighter, it could give an MGB a hard time.

Before World War II, Japan, a maritime power with wide-ranging ambitions, had devoted considerable thought to the problems of transporting an army by sea. An early success was the ubiquitous **Daihatsu**, a flatbottomed barge with a bow ramp and a sheerline obviously derived from fishing craft. It came in various lengths between 10 and 17 m (32 ft 9 in and 55 ft 9 in), which was equivalent to the Allied LCA and LCM. With 1,140 built, the workhorse was the type 14 m (45 ft 10 in) long, large enough to lift a light armoured vehicle, 10 tons of cargo or 70 equipped men. There were 163 of the 17-m model. Powered by a

variety of diesel and petrol engines, these barges were good for 7 or 8 kts, their patient plodding becoming essential to the survival of Japanese island garrisons. Their 'milk runs' involved lying concealed by day and running by dark, an endless flow that was fiercely contested by the US but never fully suppressed.

As early as 1935 the Japanese had produced, in the odd-looking **Shinshu Maru** and its derivatives, the world's first examples of seagoing ships designed to carry landing craft in numbers. Twenty Daihatsus could be stowed inboard to be launched over a stern ramp and loaded through cargo doors amidships. Though of highly original concept, they would have been of little use in an opposed landing; their success in China and during the early days of World War II was due to Japan's total local superiority.

On 13 December 1941, the Japanese sailed from Cam Ranh Bay in present-day Vietnam to invade British Borneo. A force of 10 transport ships carried the Japanese 35th Infantry Brigade headquarters, the 124th Infantry Regiment from the 18th

Division, the 2nd Yokosuka Naval Landing Force and the 4th Naval Construction Unit. During this operation, the Japanese navy used landing barges. However, these proved to be problematic in rough weather, when troops and supplies were having to be transferred from transport ships to the barges. When occupying islands around the Pacific during their southern expansion, the Imperial Japanese navy was often notably resourceful: upon capturing one island, they would commandeer local fishing boats or small river craft, which could then be used to land troops in future operations. This was done as the Japanese sought to consolidate their gains on the islands that surrounded British Borneo.

Tank transports

Early Japanese attempts at an LST resulted in the 22-strong **'SS'** or **'Koryu Maru' class**, similar to 63 m (206 ft 6 in) aft-engined coasters but equipped with bow doors to handle up to four medium tanks and a troop detachment. Designed along conventional ship lines, however, they drew far too much water and gave way to the rakish-looking **'T101'**- and **'T103'-class** LSTs with diesel and steam machinery respectively. At 80.5 m (264 ft), these were shorter than their

Allied equivalents while devoting proportionately more space to machinery and superstructure. Some were run by the army, others by the navy, but the 1944–45 building programme was too late in the war to be of assistance in any significant amphibious operation; by this time, both air and sea superiority had been lost. Their speed of 16 kts made the vessels useful in the endless transport of supplies and replacements around the island maze of the new Japanese empire, and it was while engaged on these missions that the majority were sunk by US aircraft and surface ships.

A fast transport with no real Allied peer was the **'T1' class**, of which 22 of a planned 46 were completed. These 1,800-tonners were 96 m (315 ft) in overall length and were unusual in having wide side decks amidships, linked to a clear afterdeck that ran in a curved slope to the water, there being no conventional transom. Daihatsus, amphibious tanks and midget submarines, carried as deck cargo, were simply rolled into the sea, even with the ship under way. Again, it was a design suitable for the small-scale operations to which the Japanese were reduced once they had lost the strategic initiative.

LSH and AGC Landing Ship, Headquarters and Amphibious Force Flagship

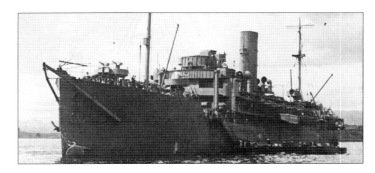

HMS Hilary, *built in 1931 as a cargo liner, spent the first part of the war as an ocean boarding vessel. The vessel was converted into a headquarters ship in 1943, being fitted with the complex communication systems required to control an amphibious landing.*

Amphibious operations are exceedingly complex and, despite meticulous planning and allowance for apparently adequate contingencies, everything that can go wrong will try to go wrong. Headquarters ships were devised to lie off the beach and control operations until a proper HQ could be set up ashore, after which they could probably stay on as long as there was any requirement for naval support. Early practice was to employ a major warship in the role, but suitably equipped ships were rare, never had sufficient accommodation and were liable to be called out to do some

fighting. Not until 1942 were dedicated ships introduced: medium-sized merchantmen (with plenty of space for conversion) were selected, and these were instantly recognizable by the variety of communications antennas that were added. These ships handled a tremendous volume of signal traffic, the embarked staff being able to make rapid decisions on the spot to counter any problem as it arose. On occasion the **Landing Ship, Headquarters** (**LSH**) even acted as an aircraft-direction ship, a complex enough task in itself and usually undertaken by a specialist Landing Ship, Fighter

Direction (LSF), with which it worked closely. For major landings, more than one LSH might be required and, in any case, a replacement was a wise precaution, particularly when the enemy recognized their importance and singled them out for attention.

LSH conversions

HMS *Bulolo* was a typical British conversion, starting as an armed merchant cruiser before doing a spell as an LSI. As an LSH the vessel saw service at Algiers, in the Levant, at Anzio

and, finally, at Normandy, where it was damaged by bombing. Other large British conversions were **HMS *Hilary***, **HMS *Largs*** and **HMS *Lothian***. The American equivalent was the **Amphibious Force Flagship** (**AGC**), converted C2 and C3 hulls, the former going to 17 units. For smaller operations, the British modified eight assorted frigates and gunboats, the Americans preferring the more suitable long-endurance coastguard cutters, which became available for regular naval use in time of war.

SPECIFICATION	
HMS *Bulolo*	**Performance:** maximum speed
Displacement: 9,110 tons standard	15 kts
Dimensions: length 125.7 m	**Armament:** two twin 4-in (102-mm)
(412 ft 6 in); beam 17.8 m	AA, five single 40-mm AA and 14
(58 ft 3 in); draught 6.6 m	single 20-mm AA guns
(21 ft 8½ in)	**Capacity:** as an LSI(L) six LCP(L)s
Propulsion: two diesels delivering	and 258 troops
4698 kW (6,300 shp) to two shafts	**Complement:** 264 men

LSI(L) and AP Landing Ship, Infantry (Large) and Transport

The **Landing Ship, Infantry (Large)** or **LSI(L)** delivered troops over distances too great for their embarkation and support in landing craft. Many were conversions of cargo/passenger liners, others were rebuilt for specific purposes. Such were the trio of Glen Line ships (***Glenearn***, ***Glengyle*** and ***Glenroy***) converted in 1941 after service as stores carriers and commando ships. Extra davits were installed to stow 12

LCAs, and two heavier LCMs were carried on deck. The ships were well armed, initially with eight 2-pdr 'pom-poms' but later with six 4-in (102-mm) AA guns, four 2-pdr guns and up to eight 20-mm Oerlikons. Despite heavy involvement, in Crete, Syria, Malta and Dieppe, none was lost.

Siege of Malta

There were three further sisters; of these ***Breconshire*** became

famous for runs to Malta during the siege before it was sunk. ***Glengarry*** was a fourth Glen ship, building in Denmark when the Germans invaded. This was converted to the auxiliary cruiser *Meersburg* and survived the war. Last was the Blue Funneler ***Telemachus***, converted to the

escort carrier HMS *Activity*.

AP was the general category for American troop transports, modified to **APA** for the more specialist **Attack Transport** category. Notable classes designed to purpose were the 11,500-ton **'Generals'** and 12,700-ton **'Admirals'**.

The **Empire Arquebus,** *built in the US under a massive maritime commission programme and supplied under Lend-Lease. It was similar in many respects to the US Navy's 'General' and 'Admiral' classes, and like them was used as an infantry transport.*

SPECIFICATION	
'Glen' class	18 kts; range 22250 km
Displacement: 9,800 tons gross	(13,825 miles) at 14 kts
Dimensions: length 155.7 m (511 ft);	**Armament:** three twin 4-in (102-mm)
beam 20.3 m (66 ft 8½ in); draught	AA, four single or twin 2-pdr AA,
8.5 m (27 ft 9 in)	and eight to 12 single 20-mm AA
Propulsion: two diesels delivering	guns
8948 kW (12,000 shp) to two	**Capacity:** two LCMs, 12 LCAs, 232
shafts	landing craft crew and 1,087 troops
Performance: maximum speed	**Complement:** 291 men

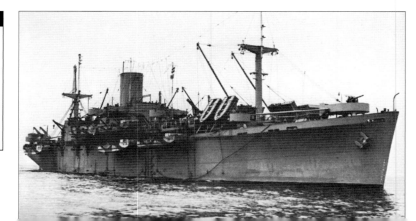

LSI(M) and APD Landing Ship, Infantry (Medium) and High-Speed Transport

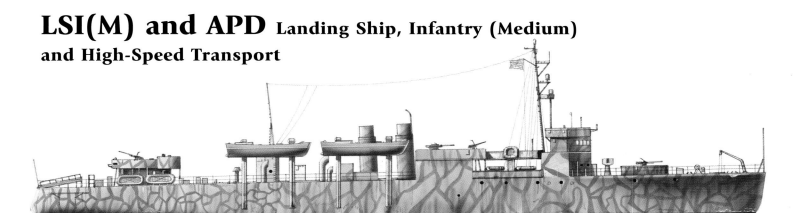

Cross-channel packets were fast and showed great potential for conversion, and the German invasion of the Low Countries provided many fine Belgian and Dutch ships as well as British and French vessels. **Queen Emma** (ex-**Kaningen Emma**) and **Princess Beatrix** (ex-**Prinses Beatrix**) had been completed by only months before hostilities and had the advantage of small machinery spaces and great economy. They were converted for small-scale assault as **Landing Ship, Infantry (Medium)** or **LSI(M)**, able to carry of a complement of 600. The troops were put ashore by six LCAs, stowed under davits. Two LCMs were also davit-carried but had to be pre-loaded with vehicles by crane. Both ships carried the bulk of the force on the Dieppe raid, all returning safely.

High-speed assault

Not similar in designed function but often used as such were the American **APD**, or **High-Speed Transport** ships. The first group comprised 32 flush-decked destroyers (the 'four-pipers').

By stripping out the forward machinery spaces, it was possible to accommodate 150 troops.

Topside, the two forward funnels and all torpedo tubes were landed and four LCP(R) added in davits. These craft could each land up to 36 troops. These destroyer conversions were followed by nearly 10 rebuildings of destroyer escorts (DE) with similar size and speed. These carried four LCVPs. The APD proved useful in the island war of the western Pacific.

SPECIFICATION	
'Queen Emma' class **Displacement:** 4,140 tons gross **Dimensions:** length 115.8 m (380 ft); beam 14.4 m (47 ft 3 in); draught 4.6 m (15 ft) **Propulsion:** two diesels delivering 9694 kW (13,000 shp) to two shafts **Performance:** maximum speed	22 kts; range 12,979 km (8,065 miles) at 13 kts **Armament:** two single 3-in (76-mm) AA, two single 2-pdr AA and six single 20-mm AA guns **Capacity:** two LCMs, six LCAs, 60 landing craft crew and 372 troops **Complement:** 167 men

LST(1) Landing Ship, Tank Mk 1, 'Maracaibo' type

As early as 1940 Winston Churchill's mind was turned to matters offensive and he perceived the need for a vessel able to put armour and vehicles ashore 'over beaches' and 'anywhere in the world'. Ships could be designed and built for this purpose but, at the time, only conversions were feasible to prove the concept. The problem was a nice one, for a beach of a gradient kind enough for the operation would have shallow approaches. This required a ship large enough both for ocean passage and to accommodate the designed load, yet of shallow enough draught to put its bows ashore. Even then it was likely that a considerable width of water would exist between the ship and the beach, so a bow door with ramps of considerable length were needed.

The ships identified for conversion were the **Bachaquero**, **Misoa** and **Tasajera**, launched in 1937–38 and used in British operations to shuttle oil from Venezuela's shallow Lake Maracaibo and therefore designed with a mean draught of only 3 m (9 ft 9½ in). Their original design was that of a turret-decker, the weather decks at the side flanking a deep centreline trunk.

Bow ramp design

As the ships' length:beam ratio was only about 6:1, they had plenty of deck space once the side decks were plated over. The drawback was that the resultant tank deck was well above the waterline, making even more acute the design of the bow ramp. In the event, the already bluff bows were modified with a flat rectangular door which hinged from its lower edge. This allowed a two-stage ramp to be run down an internal slope, under the control of several winches. The first 21.6-m (71-ft) long stage supported a 16.5-m (54-ft) extension. While these permitted the dry landing of a 30-ton tank, they were very greedy of internal space. The **'Maracaibos'** can claim to be the first LSTs and though far from ideal, particularly in terms of speed, these **Landing Ship, Tank Mk 1** or **LST(1)** vessels demonstrated the practicality of working on and off a beach in a controlled manner, the value of good subdivision and the need for well-distributed ballast space. Interestingly, even the eventual last word in LSTs never claimed to be able to work more than 17 per cent of the world's beaches, with the American LCAC air cushion landing craft not extending this beyond a reported 70 per cent.

SPECIFICATION	
LST(1) 'Maracaibo' type **Displacement:** 4,890 tons gross **Dimensions:** length 116.5 m (382 ft 6 in); beam 19.5 m (64 ft); draught 4.6 m (15 ft); beaching draught 1.3 m (4 ft 3 in) forward **Propulsion:** two sets of reciprocating steam engines delivering 2,237 kW (3,000 shp) to two shafts **Performance:** maximum speed	11 kts; range 12,045 km (7,845 miles) at 10 kts **Armament:** two 4-in (102-mm) smoke mortars, and four single 2-pdr AA and six single 20-mm AA guns **Capacity:** two LCMs, 20 25-ton tanks and 207 supernumeraries **Complement:** 98 (NB: the *Tasajera* was slightly smaller)

Landing Ship, Tank Mks 2 and 3 LST(2) and LST(3)

Even while the three LST(1)s were in the early stages of construction, before the entry of the US into the war, it was realized that a great number of large landing craft would be required for the assault that would have to precede the reconquest of Europe. Only construction in the US under Lend-Lease terms could produce these numbers, but the resulting ships would need to be capable of Atlantic crossings. The conception of the **Landing Ship, Tank Mk 2** or **LST(2)**, despite claims to the contrary, was British and was worked out in detail by a British mission in Washington in the winter of 1941–42, the first order being placed in February 1942.

Major differences

The major differences from the LST(1) were the adoption of an engines-aft layout, a smaller length–beam ratio and an acceptance of a maximum speed of 10 kts. A suitable locomotive-type diesel was available, and two of these gave sufficient power while having only a limited height, enabling the tank deck to be continued over the machinery space, and thus run the full length of the ship. By adopting a bluff, beamy form, the loaded draught was reduced; for sea passages the ship could be ballasted down and, for beaching, trimmed by the stern to give a small forward draught. This enabled the vessel to ground closer to the tideline and only a short ramp was fitted inside the vertically hinged bow doors. On beaches with the minimum declivity of 1 in 50, this still meant a lot of water for vehicles to traverse, and research began into their waterproofing. Only with the adoption in 1943 of sectioned pontoons for the rapid construction of ship-to-shore causeways was the problem solved.

A spacious upper deck was served by hatch and elevator (or ramp in later versions). It could be used for stowage of light vehicles or an LCT(5) or LCT(6). Heavy gravity davits could accommodate up to six LCVPs for use as lifeboats or utility craft.

The LST(2) became the standard assault ship and played a role in all theatres, 1,077 of these ships being built between 1942 and 1945.

Anglo-Canadian LST

So well did the LST(2) suit the needs of the US that the UK had difficulty in being allocated suitable numbers from the construction programme that it had itself initiated. Eighty were needed, and it was decided to improvise on the LST(2) design, with 45 to be built in the UK and the remainder in Canada.

The **Landing Ship, Tank Mk 3** or **LST(3)** took more time to build and used the steam-reciprocating engines used in frigates, which were bulky and heavy. The resulting low-efficiency hull was significantly longer to accommodate the steam machinery and disposing of over three times the power, the LCT(3) was only 3 kts faster than the diesel-driven LST(2)s.

With their deeper draught, the LST(3)s tended to ground farther from the dry beach and a double-section bow ramp was incorporated as compensation. The LST(3)s were well built, having LCAs under their gravity davits and the capacity for up to seven LCM(7)s on the upper deck. These were offloaded via a 30-ton SWL derrick set on a portside kingpost forward of the bridge. A 15-ton derrick was stepped on the other post.

Though a few of the programme were eventually cancelled, the 44 British and 28 Canadian ships completed gave 20 years and more of post-war service.

SPECIFICATION	
LST(2)	**Armament:** one 5-in (127-mm) or 3-in (76-mm) DP gun, which was usually omitted when the full secondary battery of two twin and four single 40-mm AA and six to 12 single 20-mm AA guns was carried
Displacement: 1,490 tons standard; 2,160 tons full load	
Dimensions: length 100 m (328 ft); beam 15.2 m (50 ft); draught 0.9/2.9 m (3 ft 1 in/9 ft 6 in)	
Propulsion: two diesels delivering 1341 kW (1,800 shp) to two shafts	**Capacity:** two LCVPs, 18 heavy tanks, 27 lorries or one LCT(5), and 163 troops
Performance: speed 10.5 kts; range 11,120 km (6,910 miles) at 9 kts	**Complement:** 211 men

Unloading equipment from LST(2)s at the Allied beach-head at Anzio, 1944.

Landing Ship, Dock LSD

So many examples of the **Landing Ship, Dock** (**LSD**) and its derivatives have been constructed by the US that one could be forgiven for assuming that the concept stemmed from the US Navy. In fact, the draft was prepared in the UK as a

*USS **Belle Grove** was the second vessel of the first class of US LSDs, and had Skinner Uniflow reciprocating engines which were replaced by steam turbines in subsequent classes. The wartime LSDs provided the basis for the 'ro-ro' cargo vessels of today.*

carrier for the largest LCTs then envisaged. This was September 1941, when the sea-going LST had not yet been developed. The LCT was not regarded as sea-going, yet, loaded, was far too heavy to be handled by the likes of the LSS or LSG, hence the idea of floating them in and out of a self-propelled floating dock. The draft was put to the US for completion and execution under the terms of Lend-Lease. Seven were requested but, in the event, the Americans completed another 20 to their own account. The 27 ships were launched between 1942 and 1946.

They were designed around a pontoon deck (or dockfloor) large enough to stow two LCTs.

This was enclosed by the dock walls and a full-width stern gate pivoted at the lower edge. From the forward end of the dock well the craft was an orthodox ship. All were steam-propelled, the first eight having Uniflow reciprocating engines and the last seven conventional steam turbines. The latter were preferred as all machinery and boilers were sited below the pontoon deck and height was limited. Uptakes and funnels were sided to avoid impeding the clear dock space.

A later addition was temporary decking spanning the dock for the stowage of motor vehicles and stores, which could be trans-shipped by crane.

Flooding down

In the event, the LSDs proved stable and the sides below the deep waterline were flared-in, reducing the amount of ballast needed to trim the ship down. An apparently enormous volume was available for ballast space, but proved scarcely adequate in

practice. Flooding down usually took 1½ hours and pumping dry 2½ hours, even at a pumping rate of 69,650 litres (18,400 US gal) per minute. Initially dividing gates were provided on the pontoon deck, but the expected surge (or 'bath water effect') did not materialize.

SPECIFICATION	
LSD	**Performance:** speed (LSD-1 to LSD-8) 17 kts or (others) 15.5 kts; range 14,830 km (9,215 miles) at 15 kts
Displacement: 4,270 tons standard; 7,950 tons full load	
Dimensions: length 139.5 m (457 ft 9 in); beam 22 m (72 ft 3 in); draught 5.3 m (17 ft 6 in)	**Armament:** one 5-in (127-mm) or (British ships) 3-in (76-mm) DP, and six twin 40-mm AA or 16 single 20-mm AA guns
Propulsion: (LSD-1 to LSD-8) two reciprocating steam engines delivering 8,203 kW (11,000 shp) to two shafts, or (others) two geared steam turbines delivering 5593 kW (7,500 shp) to two shafts	**Capacity:** two LCT(3)s or LCT(4)s, or three LCT(5)s, or 36 LCMs, landing craft crew (varying with landing craft carried) and 263 troops
	Complement: 254 men

Landing Craft, Tank Mks 1 to 4 LCT(1–4)

*Only 30 two-shaft **LCT(1)**s were constructed before the three-shaft **LCT(2)** was introduced. Beside and below the tank deck, the double skin of the vessel was heavily compartmented into ballast and trim tanks as well as bunkerage and stowage.*

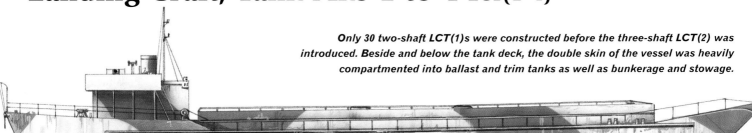

Little work had been done before World War II with respect to putting wheeled and tracked vehicles over a beach, simply because no application was seen for it, but Dunkirk and Churchill changed all that. It was decided that a craft should be created for the carriage of three 40-ton tanks, which could be landed in less than 1 m (3 ft 4 in) of water on a 1/35 beach. The resulting **Landing Craft, Tank Mk 1**, or **LCT(1)**, was the first of its type anywhere. The reinforced tank deck was over and between heavily compartmented double skins that provided ballast and trim tanks, together with bunkers and stowage. The cargo was screened by high coamings on the inboard edges of the side decks, and could be covered with light tarpaulins spread over hatch beams. The single-

element bow ramp was not watertight, so it was backed by a pair of low watertight doors. Most LCT(1)s were built during 1940–41 in four sections that could be broken down for shipment to distant parts.

Thirty LCT(1)s were built before being superseded by the **LCT(2)**. With small increases in dimensions, two rows of smaller tanks could be accommodated, while endurance increased from 1665 to 5000 km (1,035 to 3,110 miles). Three engines were fitted, petrol or diesel as available. To increase capacity, a fifth mid-body section was inserted to create the **LCT(3)**, allowing for the carriage of five heavy or 11 medium tanks.

New type

The LCT(1), (2) and (3) were too deep-draughted for use on

French beache. The result from October 1941 was the **LCT(4)** based on light scantlings. The new type was shorter but beamier than the LCT(3) and of shallower draught and, propelled by the same machinery, was slower. The tank deck carried six heavy tanks in two rows of three or nine medium tanks in three rows. Once loaded, the craft could beach successfully on a 1/150 slope, putting vehicles down in a depth of only 76 cm (30 in) of water.

The craft entered service in the autumn of 1942 and lacked

longitudinal stiffness. So for later Far Eastern service involving sea passages, the shell plating was brought up to the height of the coaming, creating a box section of maximum depth. These measures allowed the craft to proceed to the Indian Ocean on their own bottoms. Some were converted to **Landing Craft, Flak Mk 4** or **LCF(4)** by the addition of four 2-pdr 'pompoms' and eight 20-mm Oerlikons, or **Landing Craft, Gun Mk 4** or **LCG(4)** with two 4.7-in (119-mm) guns and up to 12 20-mm cannon.

SPECIFICATION	
LCT(4)	**Propulsion:** two diesels delivering 686 kW (920 bhp) to two shafts
Displacement: 200 tons light; 586 tons (or 611 tons when stiffened) loaded	
Dimensions: length 57.07 m (187 ft 3 in); beam 11.79 m (38 ft 8 in); draught 1.07/1.42 m (3 ft 6 in/ 4 ft 8 in)	**Performance:** speed 9 kts; range 2,035 km (1,265 miles) at 8 kts
	Armament: two 20-mm cannon
	Capacity: six heavy or nine medium tanks
	Complement: 12 men

Landing Craft, Tank Mks 5 to 8 LCT(5–8)

A short, beamy, drive-through craft, the LCT(6) series was designed to ferry vehicles ashore from an LST if the latter's draught was too great for the beach or alternatively to make an improvised bridge.

As World War II proceeded, it became apparent that draught problems would inhibit the use of LSTs in some instances, so the British proposed a short, drive-through craft that could either ferry the LSTs' vehicles ashore or act as a temporary bridge to link the vessel to the beach. The result was the **Landing Craft, Tank Mk 5** or **LCT(5)**, which could either be transported in sections and assembled afloat, or transported complete on an LST's upper deck and launched by sliding it over the side. The LCT(5) was a slow short-haul craft and nearly 500 were built in the US before

the **Landing Craft, Tank Mk 6** or **LCT(6)** was introduced, on similar dimensions but with the bridge on the starboard side to permit the drive-through operation proposed earlier. Triple-screw propulsion improved the craft's handling.

Some LCT(5) and (6) vessels supplied to the British were lengthened by about 12 m (39 ft 5 in). At about this same time in 1943, the Americans designed their first large craft from scratch, designated the **Landing Craft, Tank Mk 7** or **LCT(7)** for a time but then, as a blend of LCT and LST, known as an **LSM (Landing Ship, Medium)**.

Though larger than an LCT(3), it had finer lines and a ship-type bow with vertically hinged doors to be capable of ocean passages at 12 kts. As a result, its capacity was a reduced three heavy or five medium tanks and its draught increased. The LSM had enclosed accommodation for over 50 troops.

Final version

The LSM was not suitable for use by the British, who used the basic idea for their final **Landing Craft, Tank Mk 8** or **LCT Mk 8**. This was limited to eight medium tanks, production of which could be undertaken only as supply problems relaxed near the war's end.

SPECIFICATION	
LCT(7) or LSM	
Displacement: 513 tons light and 900 tons full load	**Performance:** maximum speed 13 kts; range 6485 km (4,030 miles) at 11 kts
Dimensions: length 62.03 m (203 ft 6 in); beam 10.36 m (34 ft); draught 1.07/2.13 m (3 ft 6 in/7 ft)	**Armament:** two 40-mm AA and four or six 20-mm AA guns
Propulsion: two diesels delivering 2088 kW (2,800 shp) to two shafts	**Capacity:** three heavy or five medium tanks, and 48 troops
	Complement: 60 men

Landing Craft, Infantry Large and Small LCI(L) and (S)

First described as a **Giant Raiding Craft**, the **Landing Craft, Infantry (Large)** or **LCI(L)** was designed to carry 210 troops on sea crossings of up to 48-hour duration. The type was first mooted in 1942 for raiding the coast of occupied Europe and, as the troops needed to get ashore rapidly, a gangway

(or 'brow') was included on either bow. Once lowered, these had to put the troops down in water shallow enough to wade ashore. This demanded such a shallow beaching draught forward as to necessitate steel, rather than wood construction, so the LCI(L) was American-built to British requirements.

Bow ramp

From **LCI(L)-351** onwards, a centreline bow ramp operating

through bow doors was adopted (though not universally), more protective for the troops but more vulnerable mechanically. As it did not carry vehicular cargo, the LCI(L) was comparatively finely built, with a ship-type bow. The propulsion system was a product of war

An American LCI(L). Fast by landing craft standards, these craft stemmed from a 1942 requirement for a raiding type able to land 200 infantrymen. Built in the US to British requirements, the shallow beaching draught forward necessitated the use of steel rather than wood construction.

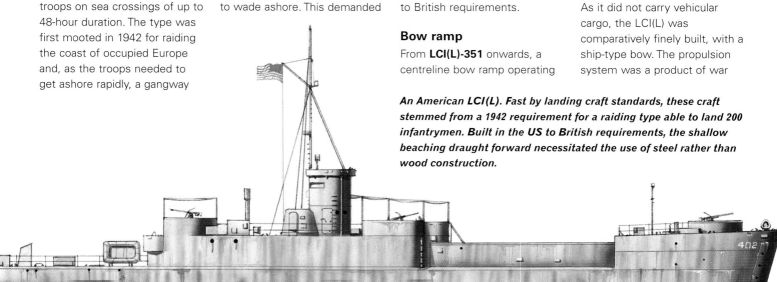

ingenuity, with eight General Motor diesel truck engines driving the twin shafts through rubber friction rollers. Numbers up to **LCI(L)-1139** were allocated, but few over 900 were completed as designed. Over 300 further hulls were completed for special roles, 160 armed as inshore fire support craft. Though known as **Landing Craft, Infantry (Gun)** or **LCI(G)**, i.e. gunboat, many had 5-in (127-mm) rocket-launchers or mortars. Complementing the LCI(L) in its raiding role was the

Landing Craft, Infantry (Small) or **LCI(S)**, though neither type was ever used as intended. Since only half the number of troops was carried, the originally planned wood construction was adopted, the design being the responsibility of Fairmile, which mass-produced them after the manner in which they built so many coastal forces craft. The double-diagonally laid plywood of much of the craft's external surfaces was overhung with 6.4-mm (0.25-in) HT steel plate for protection, but troops below

still incurred many casualties on approach to landings.

Brow arrangement

No less than four brows were arranged forward, together with

a (typically British) stowage for 12 bicycles. Propulsion was by a pair of the well-tried Hall-Scott petrol engines, and the craft were capable of 15 kts when these were turbocharged.

SPECIFICATION	
LCI(L)	**Performance:** maximum speed 14 kts; range 14822 km (9,210 miles) at 12 kts
Displacement: 194–209 tons light; 385–387 tons full load	
Dimensions: length 48.31 m (158 ft 6 in); beam 7.21 m (23 ft 8 in); draught 0.81/1.52 m (2 ft 8 in/ 5 ft)	**Armament:** four or five 20-mm AA guns
	Capacity: 188–209 troops or 75 tons of cargo
Propulsion: two diesels delivering 1730 kW (2,320 shp) to two shafts	**Complement:** 24–29 men

Landing Craft, Mechanized Mks 1 to 7 LCM(1–7)

Motor Landing Craft (MLC) had been the subject of experiments by the British as far back as 1926, but the progenitor of the species was *MLC10*, completed in 1929. This 12.8-m (42-ft) craft could beach with a 12-ton tank. Waterjet propulsion contributed to its low draught, although the low efficiency of units at this time resulted in a speed of barely 5 kts.

Early in 1940, Thornycroft completed the first 36-ton **Landing Craft, Mechanized Mk 1** or **LCM(1)**, at 14.78 m (48 ft 6 in) slightly longer than the prototype and able to carry a

single 16-ton tank or 100 troops. Screw propulsion increased the overall speed by 50 per cent.

Dunkirk

Described by its designer as a 'powered pontoon with bulwarks', this small craft could be hoisted under heavy davits even when loaded. Trials were not even complete when the Dunkirk evacuation stimulated an order for two dozen more. Eventually some 600 LCM(1)s were constructed, up to 1944.

Meanwhile, the US Marine Corps had its own specification for a similar type of craft. This

The US LCM(2) was based on the design of shallow-draught up-river tugs. This LCM(2) is being used by men of the 30th Infantry Division during the Rhine crossings of March 1945.

was based on the hull of an up-river, shallow-draught tug and became known as the **LCM(2)**. It was similar to the British craft in layout and performance. About 150 were built before an improved 15.24-m (50-ft) version increased its capacity from a single 16-ton tank to one of 30 tons. An immediate success, the **LCM(3)** ran to 8,631 craft, built from 1942 to 1945. Two distinct types, the **'Bureau'** and the **'Higgins'**, were built by the Americans to the same specification.

The **LCM(4)** and **LCM(6)** were essentially the same craft, an LCM(3) with an extra 1.83-m (6-ft) section added amidships for extra capacity. Some 2,700 were built.

The **LCM(5)** was stillborn, but the British-built **LCM(7)**, which first appeared late in 1944, was

really a further-enlarged LCM(3) aimed primarily at operations in the Far East. Its length was over 18.29 m (60 ft), but the extra size also added the capability for more versatile tactical employment, so the type was also in a wide variety of (chiefly unofficial) gunboat guises for fire-support purposes. This would continue the tradition of using landing craft for unorthodox missions such as deploying flak and rockets.

Thornycroft completed the first LCM in 1940, describing it as a 'powered pontoon with bulwarks'. Able to carry a 16-ton light tank, it could be hoisted under davits even when loaded.

SPECIFICATION	
LCM(3)	**Performance:** average speed about 8.5 kts; range 1,577 km (980 miles) at 6 kts
Displacement: 23.2 tons light and 52 tons full load	
Dimensions: length 15.24 m (50 ft); beam 4.29 m (14 ft 1 in); draught 0.91/1.22 m (3 ft/4 ft)	**Armament:** one twin 0.5-in (12.7-mm) machine-gun
	Capacity: one medium tank, or 26.8 tons of cargo or 60 troops
Propulsion: two diesels delivering 164/336 kW (220/450 shp) to two shafts	**Complement:** 4 men

Landing Craft, Flak and Landing Craft, Support
LCF and LCS

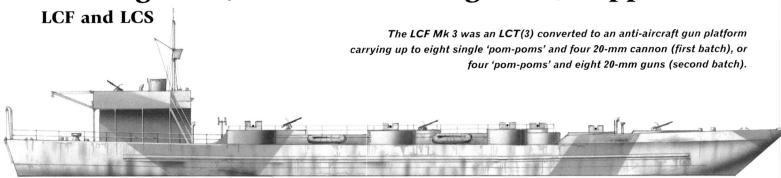

The LCF Mk 3 was an LCT(3) converted to an anti-aircraft gun platform carrying up to eight single 'pom-poms' and four 20-mm cannon (first batch), or four 'pom-poms' and eight 20-mm guns (second batch).

Not all landing craft were used for the carriage of men or machinery: a large number were converted to auxiliary, if unorthodox, warships. Some, the **Landing Craft, Flak** or **LCF** type, were produced to give AA protection where sufficient regular navy back-up was likely to be lacking, while the **Landing Craft, Support** or **LCS** was able to go right inshore to render direct support to personnel actually on the beach, particularly in the awkward gap between the main 'softening-up' barrage lifting or rolling forward and the assault troops actually touching down and getting off

the beach. Two prototype LCFs were produced from LCT(2) hulls in late 1941. The first was a 'Rolls-Royce' with two twin 102-mm (4-in) HA mountings. Besides the work involved, these mountings were already in great demand for a wide range of escort ships, the LCT structure was inherently flimsy and the low-sited director in combination with ship motion made for poor accuracy.

Armament
More realistically, the LCT(2) took eight single 2-pdr 'pom-poms' and four 20-mm guns. Such mountings were more

SPECIFICATION	
LCF(3)	
Displacement: 420 tons light and 515 tons full load	**Performance:** maximum speed 9.5 kts; range 2,688 km (1,670 miles) at 8.5 kts
Dimensions: length 58.1 m (190 ft 9 in); beam 9.4 m (31 ft); draught 1.1/2.1 m (3 ft 7 in/7 ft)	**Armament:** eight single 2-pdr 'pom-poms' and four single 20-mm AA guns
Propulsion: two diesels delivering 746 kW (1,000 shp) to two shafts	**Complement:** 68 men

The LCS was designed for the close support of troops on the beach. This is an LCS(L)2 fitted with the turret of the obsolete Valentine tank, two 20-mm cannon and a 4-in smoke mortar.

A Landing Craft, Flak displays an impressive selection of automatic weapons: visible are 2-pdr 'pom-pom' single mounts, and much smaller 20-mm cannon.

easily come by and could not only hose out a reassuringly large volume of fire against aircraft, but could also work devastatingly against any enemy personnel foolish enough to break cover ashore. Thus the final LCF forms were based on the **LCF(2)**, with the **LCF(3)** and **LCF(4)** being built on LCT(3) and LCT(4) hulls respectively, with the bow ramp permanently secured and a false deck added over the cargo well.

A further refinement was the LCS which carried a medium-calibre weapon for tackling enemy armoured vehicles, or mortars to engage enemy infantry who, all too frequently, were dug-in behind the rise that backed the beach, safe from close range low-trajectory fire.

LCS(S) craft were actually converted from the fast wooden-hulled LCI(S) which were equipped with British armoured tank turrets.

Landing Craft, Assault LCA

'Like floating bootboxes pretending to be motorboats, mere square shells for carrying troops' is a description of a **Landing Craft, Assault (LCA)** by one who spent the war in landing craft.

The LCA was one of the smallest of the practical, mass-produced craft arising from a

specification written by the British Landing Craft Committee in 1938, calling for a craft that, with a loaded weight of under 10 tons, should be capable of being slung under a liner's davits. It should be able to carry an army platoon fully equipped and land the men in less than 50 cm (20 in) of water. Two

prototypes were built, one of aluminium alloy and one of wood with protective plating. Originally called **Assault Landing Craft**, these gave experience for the final design, whose wooden construction let them be built by a wide variety of concerns. Troops along both sides sat covered from the

worst of the elements, but a centreline row had to tolerate both wetness and the inevitable sea sickness.

In any sea, the LCA could make little way and passage times could be protracted when a friendly tow was not available. The low, protected steering position was sited forward and

SPECIFICATION	
LCA	**Performance:** maximum speed
Displacement: 10 tons light and 13	7 kts; range 95–150 km
tons full load	(59–93 miles) depending on sea
Dimensions: length 12.6 m (41 ft	conditions
6 in); beam 3 m (10 ft); draught	**Armament:** two or three
0.5/0.7 m (1 ft 9 in/2 ft 3 in)	machine-guns
Propulsion: two petrol engines	**Capacity:** 35 troops with 363 kg
delivering 97 kW (130 shp) to two	(800 lb) of equipment
shafts	**Complement:** 4 men

on the starboard side, immediately abaft two-element armoured doors, which kept out the water from the leaky bow ramp, while protecting the troops within from end-on fire during the approach to the beach.

An interesting variant was the **LCA(HR)**, the suffix standing, for Hedgerow, which was fitted with four rows of six mortars that were designed to lay their bombs in lanes across the beach in order to explode any buried mines.

The craft were little modified for the function and life could be quite exciting for their crews. Equivalent American designs were the 11.05-m (36-ft 3-in) **LCV** and **LCVP** (**Landing Craft, Vehicle** and **Landing Craft, Vehicle/Personnel**).

Landing Craft, Gun and Landing Craft, Tank (Rocket) LCG and LCT(R)

The LCT(R) Mk 3 could carry over a thousand rockets, which were released in 24 salvoes. Anyone in the target area (measuring some 685 by 145 m/750 by 160 yards) would be confronted with some 17 tons of explosive bursting around them.

Converted from the LCT(3) or LCT(4), the Landing Craft, Gun (Large) or LCG(L) was designed to provide close-in fire support to an amphibious landing, and was armed with two single 4.7-in (119-mm) guns.

Support firepower during landings was expected to be in short supply so, profiting from the successful LCF conversions, 23 LCT(3) craft were fitted with two single 4.7-in (119-mm) guns and recategorized **Landing Craft, Gun (Large)** or **LCG(L)**. They had mountings from ex-destroyers, sited on a new upper deck with deep bulwarks, and the after weapon had only limited arcs on the beam. Range-finding was rudimentary, but the craft had to operate at distance from the beach, firstly to gain some falling trajectory for their guns and secondly to stay out of range of enemy weapons (particularly mortars).

They served well in Europe, so 10 LCT(4) craft were also converted. Extra beam made for a steadier platform, and light armour was added. Only one was completed in time for the war in the Far East.

The **Landing Craft, Gun (Medium)** or **LCG(M)** was designed to go right in and carried two army 25- or 17-pdr guns in single armoured turrets. Considered proof against medium-calibre return fire, they were meant to engage targets on the run in, and then to flood down to reduce freeboard as far as possible and, by sitting on the bottom, shoot accurately. Their hulls were one-offs, with a ship bow and a low initial freeboard. Their metacentric heights meant they manoeuvred poorly.

A modification to LCTs was the **Landing Craft, Tank (Rocket)** or **LCT(R)**. Both LCT(2) and LCT(3) craft were used, the forward end given over for the launch of 792 or 1,064 5-in (127-mm) rockets. These were launched in 24 salvoes to come down at 9.1-m (10-yard) intervals, laying 17 tons of explosive over an area of 685 x 145 m (750 x 160 yards). A set of reloads was carried and, this fired, the craft acted as a ferry.

SPECIFICATION	
LCG(L) Mk 3	**Performance:** maximum speed
Displacement: 495 tons full load	10 kts; range 2688 km (1,670
Dimensions: length 58.5 m (192 ft);	miles) at 8.5 kts
beam 9.4 m (31 ft); draught 1.1/	**Armament:** two single 4.7-in
1.8 m (3 ft 6 in/6 ft)	(119-mm) and one or two twin
Propulsion: two diesels delivering	20-mm AA guns
746 kW (1,000 shp) to two shafts	**Complement:** 47 men

'Wolf' and 'Möwe' classes
Torpedo boat-destroyers

Initially classified as destroyers, the Typ 23 torpedo boats served in the North Sea and English Channel. Armed mainly for surface action, these were the first flotilla craft built for the Weimar navy.

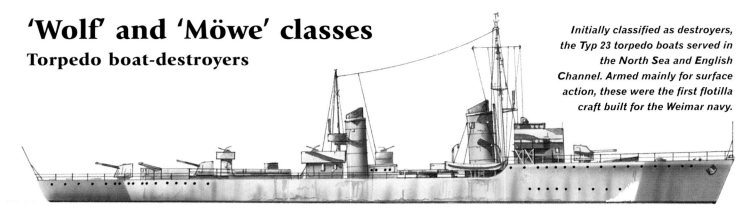

The blockade of the German coast by submarine and mine entailed the covering of warships while coastal traffic needed protection without tying down major fleet units.

The six **'Möwe'-class** (or **Typ 23**) ships were the first flotilla craft built by the 'new' German navy; torpedo boats, they carried two triple mountings. Though not designed for fleet duties, the lack of an alternative accounted for their high speed. Three boilers were required,

necessitating two widely spread funnels. They carried three 105-mm (4.13-in) guns which, with the ambitious torpedo fit, brought up the topweight allowance to the extent that mines could not also be carried.

Improved armament

While the 'Möwe' class was still building, a second group of six, the enlarged **'Wolf'-class** (**Typ 24**) ships, were ordered.

The ships were involved in near-coastal waters, gradually

acquiring more light automatic weapons, some at the expense of a set of torpedo tubes. Later development went for larger torpedo boats and smaller

S-boats. Neither was an ideal escort, leaving the way clear for the 'F'-class *Geleitboote*. All 12 of the Type 23 and 24 vessels became war casualties.

SPECIFICATION	
'Wolf' class (as completed)	shafts
Displacement: 933 tons standard; 1,320 tons full load	**Speed:** 33 kts
Dimensions: length 92.6 m (303 ft 10 in); beam 8.65 m (28 ft 4 in); draught 2.83 m (9 ft 3 in)	**Endurance:** 5750 km (3,575 miles) at 17 kts
Propulsion: two sets of geared steam turbines delivering 17150 kW (23,000 shp) to two	**Armament:** three 105-mm (4.13-in) or 127-mm (5-in) and four 20-mm AA guns, and two triple 533-mm (21-in) torpedo tube mountings
	Complement: 129 men

'F' class Escort

The **'F'-class** ships, a group of 10 *Geleitboote* (escort vessels), were completed in 1935–36 and, though officially escorts, had the peacetime roles of training in the Baltic and general offshore duties. Their wartime role was the escort of larger warships through offshore barriers, for which they were given a high speed and almost destroyer-like proportions, with main parameters that had no equivalent in the Royal Navy. Handsome ships, they looked rather more weatherly than larger German destroyers with plenty of freeboard forward and the angular bridge structure continued to the ship's sides by screens. Though the freeboard aft was low, the after 105-mm (4.13-in) gun was set on a deckhouse at the same height as that on the forecastle. They carried a good outfit of boats for their peacetime duties, which were handled by booms not davits. Spending much time at low speeds, they had anti-rolling

tanks fitted with transfer pumps.

Design changes

The ships' qualities must have left something to be desired for even while still new ships, **F1** to **F4** and **F6** were lengthened and given raked bows. **F2** and **F4** were disarmed for use as auxiliaries but **F1**, **F3** and **F6** had the forecastle deck continued right aft to give a continuous high freeboard and much more accommodation. These were also named **Jagd**, **Hai** and **Königin Luise** respectively, the last name suggesting an unlisted minelaying capacity, though the ships acted as command vessels for minesweeper squadrons. Due to their humble and non-involved status, the tide of war dealt kindly with them, only four of the ships being sunk.

An interesting series of 24 enlarged *Geleitboote* (*G1* to *G24*) was planned to follow on from both German and Dutch

Geleitboote F2 *as it appeared in 1938. The advanced propulsion machinery gave much trouble, and in spite of their destroyer-like lines, the* **Geleitboote** *were poor sea boats. In consequence, most were lengthened forward and revised with a raked stern.*

yards, but just *G1* was laid down, only to be destroyed on the stocks in an air attack in 1943. Like the 'F'-class units, these would have had modest

speed and no torpedo tubes in combination with an enhanced surface armament, a capacity of 50 mines and, remarkably, provision for a helicopter.

SPECIFICATION	
'F' class (as built)	10,440 kW (14,000 shp) to two shafts
Displacement: 712 tons standard; 833 tons full load	**Speed:** 28 kts
Dimensions: length 76 m (249 ft 4 in); beam 8.8 m (28 ft 10 in); draught 2.59 m (8 ft 6 in)	**Endurance:** 2780 km (1,725 miles) at 20 kts
Propulsion: two sets of geared steam turbines delivering	**Armament:** two 105-mm (4.13-in), two twin 37-mm AA and four 20-mm AA guns
	Complement: 121 men

'Spica' class Torpedo boat

Resembling reduced versions of the contemporary 'Freccia'-class fleet destroyers, the 'Spica' class was designed for the torpedo-boat role, but in fact became anti-submarine escorts.

Like its German counterpart, the Italian navy favoured diminutive destroyer-type escorts, usually described as 'torpedo boats'. The type had lapsed for a decade before being resumed with the 32-strong **'Spica' class**, laid down between 1934 and 1937. The design was influenced by the 'Maestrale'-class destroyers. The main armament consisted of 100-mm (3.9-in) guns of a new pattern with a 16,000-m (17,500-yard) range. As these came only in single mountings, three were carried in the usual layout of one forward and two superimposed aft. Previous torpedo boats had been fitted with 533-mm (21-in) torpedo tubes, but the 'Spica'-class units reverted to the 450-mm (17.7-in) weapons of far inferior hitting power and range. The 'Spica'-class units could lay mines, but were also fitted for high-speed minesweeping.

New group

A group of 42 improved 'Spicas' was planned, but only 16, known as the **'Ariete' class**, were laid down, most of them completed by the Germans after the Italian capitulation of 1943.

The **Airone** and **Ariel** were sunk in October 1940 after attacking a British cruiser force covering an early Malta convoy. A year later another pair, the **Aldebaran** and **Altair**, were lost in a minefield laid by the British submarine HMS *Rorqual* in the Gulf of Athens.

SPECIFICATION	
'Spica' class	shafts
Displacement: 795 tons standard; 1,020 tons full load	**Speed:** 34 kts
Dimensions: length 82 m (269 ft); beam 8.2 m (26 ft 11); draught 2.82 m (9 ft 3 in)	**Armament:** three 100-mm (3.9-in), four twin and two single 20-mm AA, and two single 13.2-mm (0.52-in) AA guns, four single or two twin 450-mm (17.7-in) torpedo tubes, and up to 20 mines
Propulsion: two sets of geared steam turbines delivering 14170 kW (19,000 shp) to two	**Complement:** 116

'Gabbiano' class Corvette

The vessels of the diesel-powered 'Gabbiano' class were unusual in being fitted with an electric motor for silent stalking of submarines, for which they were equipped with anything up to 10 depth-charge throwers.

In 1942, with British submarines harrying the supply route to North Africa, the Italians began a programme of **'Gabbiano'-class** corvettes. This was a ship type new to the Italian fleet, like the British 'Flowers' in much the same way that the 'Spicas' equated to the 'Hunts'.

Having a good industrial base for small diesel and petrol engines, the Italians favoured the former for the 'Gabbianos'. Twin-shaft propulsion was adopted to take advantage of established marques of engine, at the same time achieving redundancy and improving manoeuvrability. Propellers with a relatively small diameter reduced draught, an important factor in the shallow and increasingly mine-ridden Mediterranean. The price of this was a complex construction and extremely noisy running, as the diesels were effectively secured to the hull framing and the necessarily high-speed propellers were a source of cavitation. This was recognized as an inevitable drawback in the interests of volume production and, very interestingly for the date, each shaft could be turned by a low-power electric motor for stalking submarines. This permitted not only silent manoeuvring but also improved performance from the ships' own indifferent sonar. The 60-ship class (of which only 42 were completed after launching in 1942–43) defeated the usual Italian lettered pendant system, the ships taking numbers. Few were completed in time to be used by the Italians, but many were used by the Germans. War losses amounted to 20.

SPECIFICATION	
'Gabbiano' class	3,205 kW (4,300 shp) and 112 kW (150 shp) to two shafts
Displacement: 670 tons standard; 740 tons full load	**Speed:** 18 kts
Dimensions: length 64.35 m (211 ft); beam 8.71 m (28 ft 7 in); draught 2.53 m (8 ft 4 in)	**Armament:** one 100-mm (3.9-in) and seven 20-mm AA guns, and (on some) two 450-mm (17.7-in) torpedo tubes
Propulsion: two diesels and two electric motors delivering	**Complement:** 108 men

Kaibokan 'Type A' and 'Type B' Escorts

Kaibokan is a generic title for the main body of Japanese escorts. The term means 'coast defence ship' rather than 'escort'.

Simple draft plans

Draft plans were limited by the London Treaty of 1930, and had to be of a simple type that allowed unlimited construction. Displacement had to be between 600 and 2,000 tons and no guns of a calibre greater than 155 mm (6 in) were to be carried, nor more than four exceeding 76 mm (3 in). No torpedo tubes were allowed, or a speed greater than 20 kts.

Prototype vessels

Not until the 1937 programme were four prototypes of the **'Type A' ('Shimushu') class** firmly ordered, and these were to a reduced specification. Their functions were listed as fishery protection, minesweeping and (lastly) convoy escort. Of robust but complex construction, their short forecastle and continuous superstructure set the style for the whole series.

A single, low-angle 120-mm (4.72-in) gun was sited on the forecastle, with two others superimposed aft. All had good arcs. The ships were built between 1838 and 1941, three of the four were war losses, and during the war the need for

The Kaibokan 'Modified Type B' vessel Shisaka *leaves Osaka in December 1944. Simpler, but faster and more heavily armed than its predecessors, it was handed to China after the war for service as the* Hui An, *which was deleted only in 1986.*

greater armament was reflected in the increase in the depth charge complement from the original 12 to 24 in 1942 and 60 in 1943. The AA armament had also been boosted to 15 25-mm weapons by 1943.

Just months before hostilities developed, an inadequate order was placed for 30 vessels as 14 1,004-ton ships of the **'Modified Type A' ('Etorofu') class** built in 1942–44, of which nine were lost, and 16 ships of the improved and enlarged **'Type B' ('Mikura') class**. The former had a similar gun armament as the 'Type A' ships

Seen on the Inland Sea in about July 1940, the Shimushu *was the first of a class of four general-purpose escorts built between 1938 and 1941, and served as prototype to all Japanese escort programmes in World War II. Unlike many of its successors,* Shimushu *survived the war, and was handed to the USSR in 1947.*

but carried more depth charges and, like the 'Type A' ships, were upgraded in anti-submarine and anti-aircraft armament during their careers. The latter were of a simpler construction than the 'Modified Type A' ships, which reduced the building time. The ships carried three 120-mm DP guns in one twin and one single mounting, and in their detail design reflected their optimization for the anti-submarine role rather than the general-purpose task in the

increase of their depth-charge capacity from 36 to 120. Eight were completed in 1942–44, and the increasing level of air attack led to an increase of the AA armament from the baseline four 25-mm weapons to a total of 18 such guns. Five of the class were lost.

There followed 33 ships of the **'Modified Type B' ('Ukuru') class**. Built in 1944–45, these were simplified to permit a halving of the building time, and strengthened the anti-aircraft armament. Nine were lost.

SPECIFICATION	
Kaibokan 'Type A' ('Shimushu') class (as completed)	delivering 3130 kW (4,200 shp) to two shafts
Displacement: 860 tons standard; 1,020 tons full load	**Performance:** speed 19.5 kts; endurance 14825 km (9,210 miles) at 16 kts
Dimensions: length 77.72 m (255 ft); beam 9.1 m (29 ft 10 in); draught 3.05 m (10 ft)	**Armament:** three 120-mm (4.72-in) and two twin 25-mm AA guns, and12 depth charges
Propulsion: two geared diesels	

General-purpose escorts, the Kaibokan 'Type A' vessels were at first fairly lightly armed. By 1944, the depth-charge fit had increased from 12 to 60, and the AA defences included 15 or more 25-mm AA weapons.

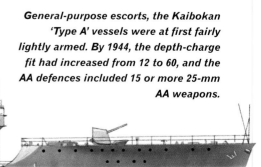

Kaibokan 'Type C' and 'Type D' Escorts

The *Kaibokan* **'Type C'** programme ran virtually parallel with that for the 'Modified Type B' ships, and reflected the belated Japanese realization that sufficient priority for resources and steel had to be made available for escorts in the hope of countering the alarming loss rate in merchant shipping. Whereas the earlier *Kaibokan* units had been named, those of the 'Type C' and later **'Type D'** families were merely numbered, and therefore lacked class names. A two-gun ship of smaller size, the 'Type C' dispensed with every possible complication and was designed for welded construction (reintroduced after major failures in the 1930s) so that smaller yards could handle the task. The forecastle had a straight-line sheer and no camber, flare being not curved but of a composite angle whose discontinuity followed the line of the main deck. Propulsion was a problem inasmuch as the earlier type of diesel could not be produced in sufficient quantities, so alternatives with less than half the power were installed, though this still resulted in an acceptable speed of slightly more than 16 kts. Orders reached 132, but only 53 of the vessels were completed in 1943–45, and 30 of these were lost.

Endless-chain lift

The 'Type C' ships retained the earlier ships' novel arrangement whereby depth charges were

The 'Type D' Kaibokan No. 8 is seen outside Nagasaki in 1944. A steam turbine-powered version of the 'Type C', the 'Type D' was faster but of reduced range. Initially oil-fired, many were converted to coal burning after the sea routes to the oilfields of the East Indies were cut.

SPECIFICATION	
Kaibokan 'Type C' (as completed)	two shafts
Displacement: 745 tons standard; and 810 tons full load	**Performance:** speed 16.5 kts; endurance 12045 km (7,485 miles) at 14 kts
Dimensions: length 67.5 m (221 ft 5 in); beam 8.4 m (27 ft 7 in); draught 2.9 m (9 ft 4 in)	**Armament:** two 120-mm (4.72-in) and two triple 25-mm AA guns, and 120 depth charges
Propulsion: two geared diesels delivering 1417 kW (1,900 shp) to	**Complement:** 136 men

brought up from below by a powered, endless-chain lift and either rolled down an inclined plane over the transom or fed on rollers to 12 throwers, set conveniently at deck level with their firing tubes located below deck. Ingenious, it was a triumph of quantity over quality, for better sonar and training would have placed fewer charges more effectively.

Even the diesels for the 'Type C' vessels ran into production problems, resulting in the design of the 925-ton 'Type D' escort with geared steam turbine propulsion delivering

1,865 kW (2,500 shp) for a slightly increased speed of 17.5 kts. The 'Type D' was a single-shaft ship whose two boilers exhausted via a distinctive, spindly stack, set farther forward than in previous practice. The steam plant had poorer economy than the diesel, so the 'Type D' vessels were slightly enlarged to accommodate extra bunkers, but despite this their endurance was inferior to that of the 'Type C' vessels.

The building time was four to six months, but no sooner were the ships being commissioned than the increasing shortage of

heavy oil for bunkers demanded that they be converted to coal firing, which must have caused acute fuel transfer problems. The effort was largely academic, however, as US submarines finally cut the convoy route to the Dutch East Indies.

With the *Kaibokan* programme now largely superfluous, building ceased to allow a concentration on craft that were designed to contribute to the final struggle for the home islands.

Orders for the 'Type D' vessels amounted to 143, of which just 63 were completed and 27 lost in combat.

The 1943 War Emergency programme required a large number of vessels to be built in a short time. The 'Type C' and 'Type D' Kaibokan were reduced 'Type B' designs, built in four months. Based on prefabricated hulls, the difference between 'Type C' and 'Type D' was in the propulsion.

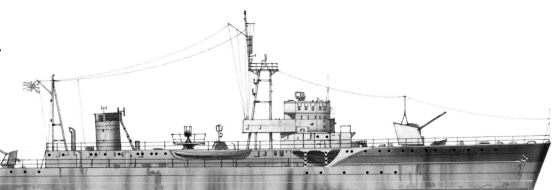

'Flower' class Corvette

The units of the **'Flower' class** (145 built in the UK and 113 in Canada for launch in 1940–42) were regarded by the British as the archetypal escort ship. Though they made their reputation in the early days of the Battle of the Atlantic, they were not suited to the job, the type being developed as a coastal escort fitted for minesweeping.

Ocean work

It was the rapid escalation of the North Atlantic convoy war and a general shortage of escorts that forced these little vessels into ocean work. They were superb seaboats but, being so short, were very lively and wet in the deep ocean, exhausting the best of crews. These limitations convinced the

HMS Lotus is seen before its 1942 transfer to France as the Commandante d'Estienne d'Orves. Lotus is fitted with minesweeping gear, which was to be a secondary task after the designed role as a coastal escort. Only the severe shortage of ocean escorts necessitated service in the North Atlantic.

Admiralty that the larger frigate was the answer.

Early units of the 'Flowers' had a short forecastle with the single mast stepped forward of a mercantile-style bridge structure, but most were later modified to the layout of the **'Modified Flower' class** launched during 1942–44. These had the forecastle extended aft to the funnel, increasing accommodation and reducing

wetness in the waist.

The machinery was simple to ease mass production and operation by rapidly trained personnel.

All the ships had an old-pattern 4-in (102-mm) gun on a 'bandstand' forward, but the

original AA outfit of machine-guns gave way to a 2-pdr 'pom-pom' and as many 20-mm Oerlikons as could be acquired.

They served under a variety of Allied flags, including that of the US. The total wartime losses of the two classes were 31.

SPECIFICATION	
'Flower' class (original specification)	**Speed:** 16 kts
Displacement: 940 tons standard; 1,160 tons deep load	**Endurance:** 6400 km (3,975 miles) at 12 kts
Dimensions: length 62.5 m (205 ft 1 in); beam 10.1 m (33 ft 1 in); draught 3.5 m (11 ft 6 in)	**Armament:** one 4-in (102-mm) and one 2-pdr or quadruple 0.5-in (12.7-mm) AA gun, and depth charges
Propulsion: one triple-expansion steam engine delivering 2,051 kW (2,750 ihp) to one shaft	**Complement:** maximum 85 men

HMS Myosotis at sea displays the battered appearance that constant Atlantic exposure made inevitable. Based upon a commercial whaler hull, the 'Flower' class filled the gap in British escort capacity early in the war, until replaced by new frigates.

'Isles' and 'Castle' classes ASW trawler and corvette

The UK's large fishing fleet in 1939 provided the Royal Navy with a ready source of ships and trained crews for the escort of convoys at a time when escorts were in short supply.

Trawler construction

From its experience in 1914-18 the Admiralty had already formulated plans for trawler

construction at yards that were familiar with them. The 27 ships of the 'Hills', 'Military' and 'Fish' classes were all produced by one yard and had the distinctive lines of the distant-water trawler. Half a dozen 'Lakes' from Smith's Dock were still almost pure whale-catchers. With minor modifications the type went into production first

SPECIFICATION	
'Isles' class (as designed)	steam engine delivering 634 kW (850 ihp) to one shaft
Displacement: 545 tons standard	**Speed:** 12 kts
Dimensions: length 44.2 m (145 ft); beam 8.4 m (27 ft 6 in); draught 3.2 m (10 ft 6 in)	**Armament:** one 12-pdr and three 20-mm AA guns, and depth charges
Propulsion: one triple-expansion	**Complement:** 40 men

HMS Shillay is seen in February 1945. Although the trawler hull gave the type good seakeeping and endurance, it could never be said to have had a sparkling performance. They were easily built, however, and were found in quantity: a total of 168 in four related classes.

as the **'Tree'**, **'Shakespeare'** and **'Dance' classes**, and then as the **'Isles' class**, which became the best-known group. These four groups comprised 218 trawlers. The 'Isles' class numbered 168 units built between 1940 and 1945.

End of the line?

The last of the 'Flowers' were launched in early 1942 and, considering that the true frigate had already been conceived, it may well be assumed that the small escort had reached the end of its development.

But there were several smaller yards which could not physically cope with the larger frigates. Thus a large corvette, of length about midway between the 'Flower' and 'River', was designed by Smith's Dock. This **'Castle' class** embodied all the lessons learned with their forebears, while contriving to look remarkably like them. The hull was, again, of sweet line, although designed for series production with a large proportion of welded seams. This showed itself as minor cranks in the sheerstrake, the

bow and stern sections being of constant sheer angle rather than the earlier continuous curve. Some 44 units were launched in 1943–44.

Spacious bridge

The 'Castles' boasted the same large and spacious bridge as frigates, together with a substantial lattice mast to elevate the considerable mass of the early radars, made possible with the larger hull. Their great advance was the Squid anti-submarine mortar sited at 01 level, forward of the

bridge, with a new-pattern 4-in (102-mm) gun on a bandstand ahead of it. The Squid's advantage was that it could lay a pattern of three heavy bombs around a submerged target up to 500 m (545 yards) ahead.

As the ships retained the single well-tried steam reciprocating engine, the performance of the 'Castle' class did not match that of the frigates and they found their main employment in escort groups of the type being formed in larger numbers toward the end of the war.

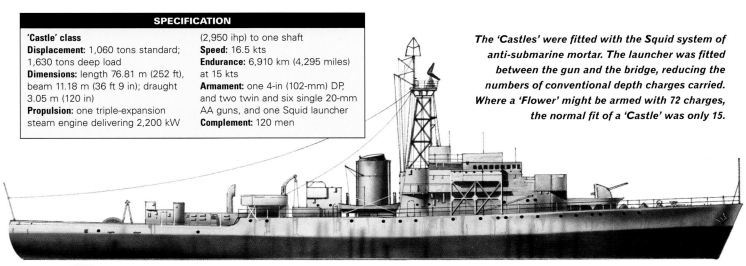

The 'Castles' were fitted with the Squid system of anti-submarine mortar. The launcher was fitted between the gun and the bridge, reducing the numbers of conventional depth charges carried. Where a 'Flower' might be armed with 72 charges, the normal fit of a 'Castle' was only 15.

'Black Swan' class Sloop

The small but powerful ships of the **'Black Swan' class** (13 built) had little in common with the remainder of the Royal Navy's sloops. Earlier units were certainly fitted with minesweeping gear, though under what circumstances such expensive and useful ships were expected to go looking for mines is not clear; at the same time, the space and topweight margin consumed by this gear detracted from the design's anti-submarine capacity. Only with the **'Modified Black Swan' class** (24 built) was this equipment landed, enabling the ships to become capable and dedicated submarine hunters.

The origins of the 'Black Swans' went back to HMS *Enchantress*, launched in 1934. Capable of minesweeping, the

ship had a gun armament comparable to a fleet destroyer. The third of the class, HMS *Bittern*, differed in being completed in 1938 with three of the new high angle 4-in (102-mm) mountings and a prototype fin stabilizer system. This arrangement was so promising that the three follow-on 'Egret'-class units were completed with four such mountings, which was definitely overambitious.

The 'Black Swans', similar in appearance, were slightly larger with a useful quadruple 2-pdr in the 'Y' position, from which it was later removed to improve quarterdeck layout, and as the close-range armament elsewhere was strengthened by the greater availability of 20-mm and 40-mm guns.

Superstructure

The first impression of the appearance of the 'Black Swans' was the mass of superstructure, probably reflecting the desire to produce an easy roll to improve them as AA gun platforms. They did not fare well against aircraft, four of the five lost succumbing to bombing attack. The reason was probably that, unlike the similarly armed 'Hunt'-class ships, they were slow and less nimble. They were, therefore,

little used in the Mediterranean, making their name in ocean warfare, with later units being able to ship over 100 depth charges and a Hedgehog split to flank 'B' mounting. Most of the ships, logically, were sent to the Far East in 1945. The best-known were **HMS *Starling*** of the great U-boat 'killer' Captain Frederic John Walker, and **HMS *Amethyst*** of the 1948 'Yangtse Incident' escape from the communist Chinese.

'Hunt' class Destroyer escort

Aware of its shortage of escorts even in 1938, the Admiralty designed a Fast Escort Vessel (FEV) to give convoys AA and anti-submarine coverage without tying down the fleet destroyers. Perceived needs included speed, to prosecute sonar contacts and rejoin smartly, but not endurance. This was seen to be the province of the true escort vessels, such as the few 'Black Swans'. To improve them as gun platforms the **'Hunt'-class** ships were fitted with active stabilizers as standard, but their power demands and their poor control systems made them so unpopular that later ships replaced them with extra bunker space, which improved their very poor endurance.

Armament

Though their category was simplified to 'destroyer' before they entered service, the 'Hunts' equated to the 'torpedo boats' of the German and Italian fleets, except that most carried no torpedo tubes. This was because the specification for six 4-in (102-mm) AA guns and two/four torpedo tubes was too much on the displacement. Combined with an error in the design calculations, this meant that the first of the class, **HMS Atherstone**, was deficient in stability. The builders therefore sacrificed their tubes and exchanged one twin 4-in

The 'Hunt Type 1'-class destroyer HMS Southdown *lies at its mooring in an English east coast port. These small but relatively powerfully armed vessels did not have the range to operate in the Atlantic, but their comparatively heavy armament made them effective in the Mediterranean and North Sea.*

mounting for a quadruple 2-pdr. Further weight-saving measures created the **'Hunt Type 1' class**, of which 18 were completed.

Hulls at an early stage of construction were split longitudinally and an extra 76 cm (2 ft 6 in) of beam incorporated. These could accommodate the third 4-in mounting originally specified, and became the 30 **'Hunt Type 2'-class** ships that,

The 'Hunt Type 2' class had three rather than two 4-in (102-mm) twin mounts. This is the first Type 2 unit, HMS Avon Vale, *subsequently transferred to Greece.*

because of their fuller hull, were slower. A third variant, the 20 **'Hunt Type 3'-class** units, was produced with only two gun mountings, but with the addition of a twin torpedo tube mounting. The two **'Hunt Type 4'-class** units were completed in 1943–43 to a larger design with three twin 4-in guns.

Experience showed the guns to be the most useful armament, and the 'Hunt'-class ships operated prominently in the Mediterranean as well as for the defence of the British east and south coasts. In all, 21 of the ships were lost but, significantly, only three were to air attack.

The 'Hunt Type 3' differed from the 'Hunt Type 2' mainly in the addition of twin torpedo tubes in place of 'X' turret, providing a more balanced weapon fit. The Type 3s were virtually the last of the 71 'Hunts' built. Some 28 ships went on to serve other navies after World War II.

SPECIFICATION	
'Hunt Type 3' class	endurance 4,819 km (2,900 miles) at 20 kts
Displacement: 1,050 tons standard; 1,590 tons full load	**Armament:** two twin 4-in (102-mm) DP, one quadruple 2-pdr AA, one twin and up to four single 20-mm AA guns, two 21-in (533-mm) tubes, and 70 depth charges
Dimensions: length 85.34 m (280 ft); beam 9.6 m (31 ft 6 in); draught 3.73 m (12 ft 3 in)	
Propulsion: two geared steam turbines delivering 14,170 kW (19,000 shp) to two shafts	**Electronics:** single Type 290/272 and 285 radars, and one hull sonar
Performance: speed 27 kts;	**Complement:** 168 men

'River' class Frigate

Designed as escorts with a range of 12,970 km (8,060 miles), the 'Rivers' were at first fitted with minesweeping gear. Once this was removed, oil storage rose from 440 tons to 646 tons, improving endurance.

With the limitations of the 'Flower'-class corvettes readily apparent, the Admiralty rapidly produced a design for a larger 'twinscrew corvette' that became known as the **'River' class**: the term 'frigate' was not reintroduced until 1942. Overall the 'Rivers' were 28.3 m (93 ft) longer than the later 'Flowers' and this made a great difference in seakeeping, bunker capacity, installed power and armament. Between 1942 and 1944 some 57 were launched in the UK, 70 in Canada and 12 in Australia.

The hull had the raised forecastle extended well aft, with a low quarterdeck for the depth-charge gear and minesweeping equipment. They were the first ships to be fitted as standard with the Hedgehog anti-submarine spigot mortar which, with new sonar gear, made for a more rapid and accurate attack. The Hedgehog was sited well forward and was thus exposed, but later units had the weapon split into two 12-bomb throwers which were

sited one deck higher, winged out abaft the forward 4-in (102-mm) gun. Longer endurance demanded a larger depth-charge capacity, and up to 200 could be carried, compared with a maximum of 70 on the 'Flowers'.

Though not developed from a mercantile hull, the 'Rivers' were built to mercantile standards, which speeded construction. They featured a flat transom, which not only obviated much of the complex curvature of traditionally shaped sterns but also improved the hull in hydrodynamic terms.

Foreign production

It is noteworthy that over half the 'Rivers' were Canadian-built (with more ships coming from Australia), and the contribution of the Canadian yards and the Royal Canadian Navy to victory in the Atlantic is probably overlooked. Most Canadian-built units had a twin 4-in mount forward and a single 12-pdr aft. They also had the full outfit of

SPECIFICATION	
'River' class (1943–44 standard) **Displacement:** 1,445 tons standard; 2,180 tons full load **Dimensions:** length 91.84 m (301 ft 4 in); beam 11.18 m (36 ft 8 in); draught 3.89 m (12 ft 9 in) **Propulsion:** two triple-expansion steam engines delivering 4,100 kW (5,500 ihp) to two shafts **Performance:** speed 20 kts;	endurance 12970 km (8,060 miles) at 12 kts **Armament:** two 4-in (102-mm) guns, two 2-pdr and two 20-mm AA guns (later up to 16 20-mm AA guns), one Hedgehog mortar, and 200 depth charges **Electronics:** single Type 271, 286 and 242 radars, and one hull sonar **Complement:** 140 men

14 20-mm weapons that British-built ships rarely achieved. The machinery was simply that of the 'Flower' doubled. Only four ships were built with steam turbines, as a result of shortages of components. The 'Rivers' were highly successful, but most of the survivors (eight were lost in the war) had been scrapped by the mid-1950s.

'River' variants

Further 'River'-class units, to a slightly modified design, were

built by the Americans as the **PF type** with a full-load displacement of 1,450 tons, overall length of 92.66 m (304 ft), triple-expansion engines delivering 4,100 kW (5,500 ihp) to two shafts for a speed of 20 kts, and primary armament of three 3-in (76-mm) guns as well as one Hedgehog, two depth-charge throwers and two depth-charge rails. Of these ships, 21 served in the Royal Navy as the **'Colony' class**, of which none was lost.

A typically battered Atlantic escort, HMS Spey steams up the line of a convoy during February 1944, when this particular 'River'-class frigate sank the Type VIIC U-boats U-406 on 18 February and U-386 on 19 February.

DE type Destroyer escort

The Americans saw little need of defensive ships such as escorts before World War II and, in the war's early days, had only their unsuitable flush-deck destroyers. It was the Royal Navy, seeking to meet the submarine threat, that produced a specification for an Atlantic escort, followed by orders for 300, placed in the US between November 1941 and January 1942. Termed destroyer escorts

(DE type), they also met the sudden need at home, and the organization was put in hand to build over 1,000 of them, though the earliest still arrived too late to prevent the backyard holocaust known to the U-boat men as the 'Happy Time'.

Well-armed design

The DEs were built like US fleet destroyers, having a flush deck with a prominent sheer line. An

This is one of the earliest of more than 565 DEs built for the US Navy. The six classes delivered were variations on a theme, with differing propulsion arrangements.

emphasis was placed on gun armament, with superimposed 3-in (76-mm) guns forward, a single gun aft and many guntubs with a mixture of weaponry, mostly single 20-mm guns. A Hedgehog projector was sited forward and, by RN standards, the after deck was cramped, though double-depth, sided stowage racks let the 78 units of the British **'Captain' class** stow over 200 depth charges.

Speed of build

Although 'only' 565 DEs were eventually completed, their

construction rate was phenomenal, no less than 425 being commissioned from April 1943 to April 1944 alone. The ships fell into several classes, depending on their propulsion: diesel in 85 **'Edsall'-class** units, diesel-electric in 97 **'Evarts'-** and 76 **'Bostwick'-class** units, and turbo-electric in 152 **'Buckley'-**, 74 **'John C. Butler'-** and 81 **'Rudderow'-class** units. Most of those incorporating diesels were low-powered, as the bulk of existing diesel output was earmarked for landing craft.

Apart from the choice of main armament, most DEs carried similar weaponry. Depth charges were handled by eight DC throwers and two DC racks.

SPECIFICATION	
'Buckley' class	to two shafts
Displacement: 1,400 tons standard; 1,825 tons full load	**Speed:** 24 kts
Dimensions: length 93.27 m (306 ft); beam 11.28 m (37 ft); draught 3.43 m (11 ft 3 in)	**Armament:** three 3-in (76-mm) DP, six 40-mm AA, and two twin and four single 20-mm AA guns, three 21-in (533-mm) torpedo tubes, one Hedgehog projector, and depth charges
Propulsion: geared steam turbines and two propulsion motors delivering 8,948 kW (12,000 shp)	**Complement:** 220 men

PC and PCE types Patrol craft

Given the length of the US's Atlantic and Pacific coasts, together with further major trans-Caribbean routes (to the

Panama Canal and the Venezuelan oil terminals), the US Navy faced a major problem in protecting coastal shipping in

World War II. The vulnerability of the shipping on the eastern seaboard was exposed by the German U-boat campaign in the

first part of 1942, but the problem had been anticipated to the extent that three 53.26-m (174-ft 9-in) **PC type** patrol craft prototypes had been completed before the US entry into the war. These were slim-gutted craft, restricted by their size to inshore work. To expand the escort fleet rapidly and with the PC design to hand, a massive construction programme was instituted and over 350 craft were built.

Not until mid-1943 was the **PCE type** introduced. Only 3 m (10 ft) longer, it was also a full 3 m beamier. These followed British frigate practice in their freeboard and long forecastle. Early units had no funnel, their diesels exhausting through the shell, but later examples had a thin stovepipe and the last a diminutive stack with a curved cap. Some 78 units were built. The armament included a 3-in gun and a full Hedgehog forward, two/three 40-mm and up to five 20-mm AA guns, and depth charges aft. Fifteen, known as the **'Kil' class**, served with the Royal Navy, primarily off Gibraltar and Sierra Leone. **HMS *Kilmarnock*** participated in the only U-boat 'kill' credited to the class – *U-731* off Tangier in May 1944.

Unlike the smaller PC classes, the PCE vessels were adapted from a minesweeper design as an interim coastal escort until the construction of more PCs.

SPECIFICATION

PCE class
Displacement: 795 tons standard; 850 tons full load
Dimensions: length 56.24 m (184 ft 6 in); beam 10.08 m (33 ft 1 in); draught 2.74 m (9 ft)
Propulsion: two diesel engines delivering 1,417 kW (1,900 shp) to

two shafts
Speed: 16 kts
Armament: one 3-in (76-mm) DP, two or three 40-mm AA, and four 20-mm AA guns, one Hedgehog projector, and depth charges
Complement: 100 men

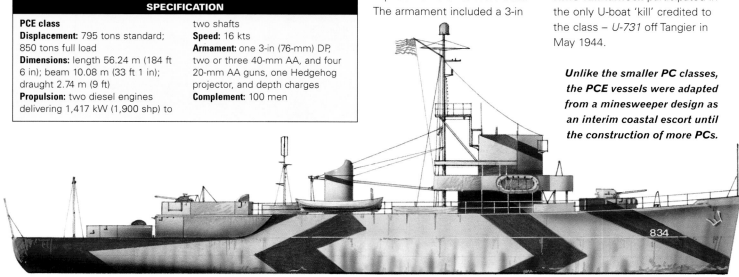

'Elan' class Sloop

At the start of World War II the French navy was poorly served for escorts, those available being intended mainly for colonial service. For effective anti-submarine work during the war, therefore, the Free French relied on frigates, corvettes and DEs transferred from the Royal Navy and the US Navy.

New approach

The 13-strong **'Elan' class** had been completed in 1939–40 as sloop-type vessels with minesweeping capability. Their 78.3 x 8.7 m (256 ft 11 in x 28 ft 6 in) hull dimensions, compared to the 62.5 x 10.1 m (205 x 33 ft) of the British 'Flowers' that served under the same flag, mark a different approach, with speed emphasized.

Despite the fine lines, their low-power twin-shaft diesel machinery drove the 'Elan'-class ships at only 20 kts, but their endurance figures emphasize the economy of diesel. The first group looked very odd, with a distinctively low foredeck. What was in the designer's mind is hard to say, but acute wetness must have been anticipated, as the bridge was perched atop a solid house. No armament was mounted forward and the impact of green seas on the front of the house can only be imagined. A rounded sheerstrake extended the length of the hull, possibly to accommodate stresses in the hull when labouring in heavy seas. Two 100-mm (3.9-in) guns could be carried, though only one was usually fitted on the after house.

Where ships are concerned, it is often said that 'if it looks right, it is right'. The converse apparently holds good, for a follow-on series of nine **'Chamois'-class** ships, whose entry into service was disrupted by the war, repeated the design but incorporated a raised forecastle and looked more workmanlike. Their careers were typically complex. For instance, **L'Impetueuse** was scuttled by the French at Toulon, salvaged by the Italians and then, at their capitulation, taken by the Germans who, finally, scuttled the ship again at Marseilles. Another three units were war losses.

The twin 100-mm (3.9-in) guns originally fitted were replaced in British and later Free French service by British 4-in (102-mm) AA weapons. The minesweeping capability was never used.

SPECIFICATION

'Elan' class (as built)
Displacement: 630 tons standard; 740 tons full load
Dimensions: length 78.3 m (256 ft 11 in); beam 8.7 m (28 ft 6 in); draught 3.28 m (10 ft 9 in)
Propulsion: two diesels delivering 2,982 kW (4,000 shp) to two

shafts
Speed: 20 kts
Endurance: 16,675 km (10,360 miles) at 14 kts
Armament: two 100-mm (3.9-in) guns, and two twin and four single 13.2-mm (0.52-in) machine-guns
Complement: 106 men

The Cold War

The 1960s witnessed a marked development in Soviet maritime activities, involving new construction and an increasingly bold fleet policy. Previously, in accordance with Soviet military doctrine, naval strategy was based on the defence of the homeland. The sight of Soviet warships on the high seas was rare, except for occasional transfers of units between the Baltic and Northern Fleets.

All that began to change after 1961, when the Soviet Union conducted their first significant naval exercise outside home waters. Over the next few years the 'blue water' exercises grew larger, the warships more powerful and sophisticated. This was the true beginning of the Cold War – a naval supremacy race with the US Navy – and the running was dictated by the ballistic missile nuclear submarine, with its ability to wreak destruction from its hiding place under the Arctic ice. The need to track down and kill fast, missile-armed submarines dictated the course of naval construction for decades.

Left: The USS Dwight D. Eisenhower (CVN-69) transits through the Suez Canal, 1989. The development of the US Navy's supercarrier was driven by the advent of the heavier jet combat aircraft, which required longer flight decks.

'Colossus' class Light fleet carrier

Above: HMS Pioneer is seen as completed in 1945 as a maintenance carrier. The carrier was unable to operate aircraft in a combat role, being able to take them aboard only by crane. With its sister ship HMS Perseus, Pioneer continued as a maintenance vessel into the 1950s.

The **'Colossus' class** of light fleet carrier was a World War II design that resembled in many ways a scaled-down 'Illustrious'-class fleet carrier but with a single hangar, no armour and only light self-defence AA guns. The machinery fit was essentially a modified version of that fitted to contemporary cruisers, but with the boilers and engine rooms set one after the other to reduce the effects of a bomb or torpedo hit below decks. Ten units were built and most served with the Royal Navy in the post-war years. **HMS Colossus**, built in 1944, participated in combat operations during the Pacific War, and was loaned to the

French navy as the **Arromanches** in 1946. The vessel was eventually sold to France, while **HMS Pioneer** and **HMS Perseus** were completed as aircraft maintenance ships, continuing in these roles until scrapped in 1954 and 1958 respectively.

Foreign service

Of the remainder, **HMS Venerable** was sold to the Netherlands as the *Karel Doorman* in 1948 *(qv)*, while **HMS Warrior** was lent to the Royal Canadian Navy and then recommissioned into the Royal Navy before being sold to Argentina in 1958 as the *Independencia (qv)*. **HMS**

Seen at Sasebo in company with the American 'Essex'-class carrier USS Oriskany, the 'Colossus'-class carrier HMS Ocean is preparing to depart for Korea in the spring of 1952. Ocean was one of five 'Colossus'-class carriers to serve in that conflict, although Warrior spent time as an aircraft transport

SPECIFICATION	
'Colossus' class	**Aircraft:** 48
Displacement: 13,190 tons standard and 18,040 tons full load	**Armour:** early units 24 2-pdr and 38 to 60 20-mm guns; later units 17 40-mm guns; maintenance ships 16 2-pdr and two 20-mm (later 40-mm)
Dimensions: length 211.84 m (695 ft); beam 24.38 m (80 ft); draught 7.16 m (23 ft 6 in); flight deck width 24.38 m (80 ft)	**Electronics:** Type 281 air search rada; later also fitted with Type 277 height-finding and Type 293 surface search radars
Propulsion: two-shaft geared steam turbines delivering 29,828 kW (40,000 shp)	**Complement:** 1,300
Speed: 25 kts	

Vengeance was also lent, in this instance to the Royal Australian Navy between 1952 and 1955, before being placed in

reserve and then sold to Brazil in 1957 as the *Minas Gerais*. The other four, namely **HMS Glory**, **HMS Ocean**, **HMS Theseus** and **HMS Triumph**, served combat tours off Korea during the war there, with air groups comprising Seafire F.Mk 47s, Sea Fury FB.Mk 11s and Fireflies. The *Ocean* gained an earlier distinction (in December 1945) as the first

HMS Ocean in company with the cruiser HMS Belfast off Korea. Ocean has a considerable claim to fame: providing the flight deck for the world's first jet carrier landing, when the third prototype de Havilland Vampire landed on 3 December 1945.

carrier to receive landings by a jet aircraft, in this case a Vampire. The *Glory*, *Ocean* and *Theseus* were all scrapped in

1961–62, while the *Triumph* was converted over a seven-year period to become a heavy repair ship. *Triumph* took part in the

Beira patrol in the 1960s and was placed in reserve in 1975. Eventually, in 1981–82, it was scrapped, just before the

Falklands War, where the heavy focus on sea-air power meant that its services were most needed.

HMS *Centaur*
Light fleet carrier

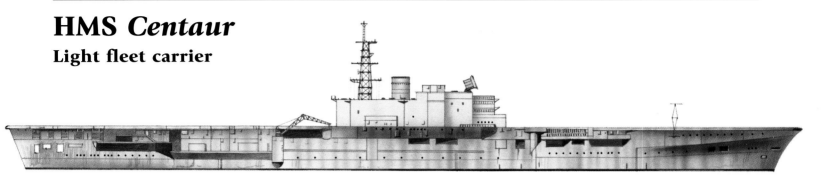

The history of **HMS *Centaur*** (**R06**) lay with the 'Hermes' class of eight carriers that began life in 1943 as ships similar to the 'Colossus' class but with improved capabilities. At the end of World War II, four of those ships already laid down were retained on the stocks for the post-war fleet. Three of the ships were completed to a modified design incorporating as many wartime lessons as possible. These were the *Centaur*, *Albion* and *Bulwark*, which were launched in

1947–48 for completion over the next six years. The *Centaur* was completed to a less capable state than the other two, as it had only a 5° line painted along its landing area to simulate an angled flight deck. The air group was projected as 16 Sea Hawks, 16 Fireflies and four Avenger AEW.Mk 1 aircraft.

In the late 1950s, the *Centaur* received a pair of steam catapults, but it became clear that the ship and its sisters were too small to operate the new generation of aircraft

*HMS **Hermes**, as it appeared in the mid-1960s, was the culmination of the 'Centaur' class, taking some five years longer to complete than the other three vessels in the 'Centaur' class. Hermes was a much more capable vessel, incorporating many of the advances in carrier design which appeared in the 1950s.*

coming into Fleet Air Arm service. *Centaur* served mainly in the Mediterranean and the Far East, including support duties for the Army off the coast of Aden in 1960–64. In January 1964, *Centaur* transported 45 Royal Marine Commando and RAF Belvedere helicopters to quell the rebellion in Tanganyika.

By 1966, *Centaur* had become a depot ship and was stricken in 1971. The vessel's final air group comprised 21 fixed-wing aircraft, including Sea Vixen all-weather fighters, Scimitar strike fighters and Gannet AEW aircraft. Eight Whirlwind helicopters were also embarked for ASW and SAR duties.

SPECIFICATION	
HMS *Centaur* **Displacement:** 22,000 tons standard and 27,000 tons full load **Dimensions:** length 224.64 m (737 ft); beam 27.43 m (90 ft); draught 8.23 m (27 ft); flight deck width 30.48 m (100 ft) **Propulsion:** two-shaft geared steam turbines delivering 58165 kW (78,000 shp) **Speed:** 29.5 kts **Armament:** originally 32 40-mm AA guns (two sextuple, eight twin and	four single mountings), then 20 40-mm AA guns (eight twin and four single mountings) **Aircraft:** originally 42 then 29 (see text) **Electronics:** one Type 982 air search radar, one Type 960 air search radar, one Type 983 height-finding radar, one Type 277Q fighter-direction radar, one Type 974 navigation radar and one Type 275 fire-control radar **Complement:** 1,390

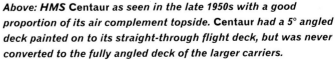

*Above: HMS **Centaur** as seen in the late 1950s with a good proportion of its air complement topside. **Centaur** had a 5° angled deck painted on to its straight-through flight deck, but was never converted to the fully angled deck of the larger carriers.*

*Left: A **Sea Vixen FAW.Mk 1** is launched from one of the newly fitted steam catapults aboard HMS **Centaur**. Along with **Victorious**, the vessel was used for service trials of the aircraft in November 1958, and its final aircraft complement was to include **Sea Vixens** alongside **Scimitars** and **Gannet AEW.Mk 3s**.*

HMS *Albion* and *Bulwark* Light fleet/Commando carriers

Although sisters of HMS *Centaur*, **HMS *Albion* (R07)** and **HMS *Bulwark* (R08)** were completed with an interim 5.75° angled flight deck and two hydraulic catapults. The new flight deck required the removal of three of the twin 40-mm Bofors mountings from the port side in order to accommodate the overhang. Thus built, the two ships served as part of the British carrier force employed in the 1956 Suez Canal landings. The *Albion* served as a fighter carrier with Sea Hawk and Sea Venom jets plus Skyraider AEW aircraft and Sycamore utility/SAR helicopters, while the *Bulwark* carried Sea Hawks and Avenger ASW/bomber aircraft.

Commando role

However, following the success of the carriers HMS *Ocean* and HMS *Theseus* in the helicopter assault role during this operation, and because of the difficulties for this class in operating the new jet generation, it was decided to convert the *Bulwark* to a Commando carrier. This was undertaken between January 1959 and January 1960, and resulted in removal of the catapults, arrester gear and most of the AA guns. Facilities for carrying a 733-man Royal Marine Commando were fitted, as well as the equipment necessary for an air group of up to 16 Whirlwind helicopters and davits for four LCVPs. Although the refit was for the Commando role, the *Bulwark* also retained an ASW capability.

During 1961—the *Albion* was similarly converted, but for 900 Commandos and 16 Wessex

After service in the Far East in the waters off Borneo, Albion was detached to provide Commando facilities in the withdrawal from Aden. Along with Bulwark, Albion was in reserve at the start of the 1970s, but was scrapped in 1972. Needless to say, either vessel could have proved valuable in the Falklands War of 1982.

helicopters. This capability was retrofitted to the *Bulwark* during 1963. The *Albion*'s Commando career was spent mainly in the Far East, and the vessel was present during the 1966 Indonesian confrontation and the subsequent Aden withdrawal. Immediately following this, *Albion* was placed in reserve and was finally stricken from the fleet in 1972 and broken up. In the meantime, the *Bulwark* served in the Mediterranean and the Far East as a Commando carrier, and was also on duty during both the Indonesian and the Aden crises.

Interim ASW

Placed in reserve in 1976, *Bulwark* was refitted in 1977 to act as an interim ASW carrier, and recommissioned in 1979 to release HMS *Hermes* from the amphibious warfare role. With the advent of HMS *Invincible* in 1980, *Bulwark* was relegated to the reserve and paid off in 1981 for disposal. The 1982 Falklands War saw the possibility of the carrier recommissioning again for active service, but following a survey the ship was found to be in such a bad state that the idea was quickly dropped and *Bulwark* was eventually sold for scrap and broken up in 1984.

SPECIFICATION	
HMS *Albion* and HMS *Bulwark* (Commando carriers) **Displacement:** 22,300 tons standard and 27,705 tons full load **Dimensions:** length 224.9 m (737 ft 11 in); beam 27.4 m (90 ft); draught 8.5 m (28 ft); flight deck width 37.6 m (123 ft 6 in) **Propulsion:** two-shaft geared steam turbines delivering 58,165 kW (78,000 shp) **Armament:** (*Albion*) four single	40-mm AA or (*Bulwark*) three twin, and two single 40-mm AA guns **Aircraft:** 20 helicopters **Electronics:** one Type 965 (*Albion*) or Type 982 air search radar (*Bulwark*), one Type 293 air search radar (both), one Type 983 height-finding radar (*Albion*), one Type 974 navigation radar (both) and one Type 275 fire-control radar (both) **Complement:** 325

Two Wessex Mk 5 helicopters make an approach to the Commando carrier HMS Albion after its 1965 refit. Albion spent much of its commando career in the Far East, and within months of this photograph the ship was involved with the Indonesian confrontation.

'Essex' class SCB-27A/C and SCB-125 reconstructions

Fleet carriers

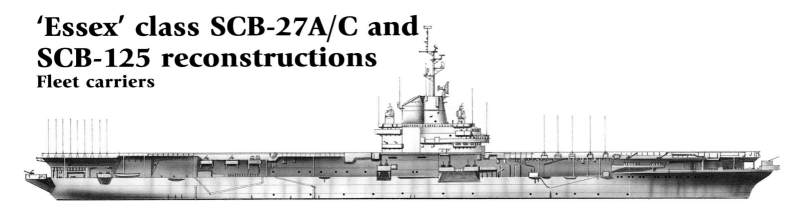

Laid down in 1944 but not completed until 1950, the USS **Oriskany** *was the first of the SCB-27A conversions with the modifications to enable the 'Essex' class to operate the upcoming generation of jet aircraft. These aircraft were much heavier than their World War II forebears, so the flight deck had to be strengthened.*

At the end of World War II in 1945, the US Navy had a carrier force that was in effect obsolescent, as it could not operate the coming generation of jet aircraft. A follow-on carrier design was completed in 1946 but was not built, which forced the US Navy to adopt the policy of reconstructing the carriers of the **'Essex' class** that had been laid up in reserve. The first programme, known as **SCB-27A**, was used as the basis to complete the hull of the incomplete **USS** *Oriskany*. As built, the ship lacked the flight deck guns of its predecessors, but the most powerful hydraulic catapults were fitted and the flight deck itself was strengthened. The island superstructure was rebuilt to improve radar coverage, and a considerable internal rearrangement was made to

enhance habitability and survivability. Eight other vessels, the *Essex* (**CV-9**), *Yorktown* (**CV-10**), *Hornet* (**CV-12**), *Randolph* (**CV-15**), *Wasp* (**CV-18**), *Bennington* (**CV-20**), *Kearsarge* (**CV-33**) and *Lake Champlain* (**CV-39**), were then refitted to this standard. Later all but the *Lake Champlain* were given angled flight decks and enclosed bows.

Over the years, most of the gun armament was removed and the radar systems changed. As rebuilt, the ships each carried

Sikorsky HSS-1 Seabat helicopters aboard the SCB-27A conversion USS **Lake Champlain** *during the late 1950s. The modification entailed tidying up the island and removal of the 5-in (127-mm) flight deck gun mounts.*

1,135,620 litres (300,000 US gal) of AVGAS and 725 tons of aircraft ordnance (including 125 tons of nuclear weapons). As more modern carriers entered service, the SCB-27As were switched to ASW operations with S-2 Trackers and helicopters. Many of these ships (CV-9, 10, 12, 15, 18, 20 and 33) underwent the FRAM

(Fleet Rehabilitation And Modernization) ASW upgrade during the 1960s, in a programme that included the fitting of an SQS-23 bow sonar and a partially automated ASW-orientated Command Information Center. Several of these ASW carriers served tours off Vietnam as screening units to attack units. The air group

SPECIFICATION	
'Essex SCB-27A' class	**Speed:** 30 kts
Displacement: 28,404 tons standard; 40,600 tons full load	**Armament:** eight 5-in (127-mm) and 14 twin 3-in (76.2-mm) guns
Dimensions: length 273.8 m (898 ft 2 in); beam 30.9 m (101 ft 4 in); draught 9.1 m (29 ft 8 in); flight deck width (angled) 59.7 m (196 ft)	**Aircraft:** 45-80 (see text)
	Electronics: SPS-6 (later SPS-12 then SPS-29) air search, SPS-8 (later SPS-30) height-finding and SPS-10 surface search radars, and (FRAM) SQS-23 bow sonar
Propulsion: geared steam turbines delivering 111,855 kW (150,000 shp) to four shafts	**Complement:** 2,900

SPECIFICATION	
'Essex SCB-27C' class	**Speed:** 29 kts
Displacement: 30,580 tons standard; 43,060 tons full load	**Armament:** four 5-in (127-mm) DP guns
Dimensions: length 272.6 m (894 ft 6 in); beam 31.4 m (103 ft); draught 9.2 m (30 ft 4 in); flight deck width 58.5 m (192 ft)	**Aircraft:** 70-80
	Electronics: one SPS-8 (later SPS-37A and SPS-30) height-finding radar, one SPS-12 surface search radar and one ESM system
Propulsion: geared steam turbines delivering 111,855 kW (150,000 shp) to four shafts	**Complement:** 3,545

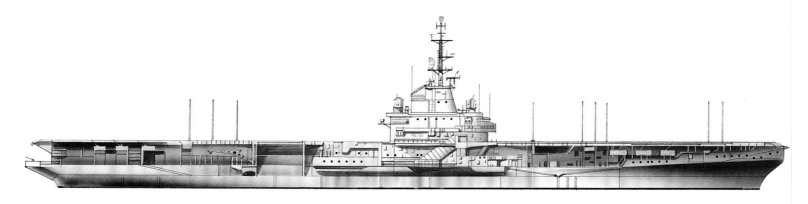

The USS Shangri-La in the late 1950s following its SCB-27C conversion. This was a comprehensive rebuild, with the fitting of an enclosed hurricane bow, steam catapults and a fully angled, sponsoned flight deck. In all, 15 'Essex'-class carriers were modernized to some extent.

normally comprised 30 fixed-wing aircraft and 16-18 Sea King ASW helicopters. The *Essex, Kearsarge, Oriskany* and *Lake Champlain* also saw service off Korea during that war in the conventional attack role.

SCB-27A refit

Once the SCB-27A refit programme was under way, it became apparent that the advances in carrierborne aircraft technology demanded more alterations, and thus the **SCB-27C** programme was born. Three ships, namely the

Intrepid (**CV-11**), *Ticonderoga* (**CV-14**) and *Hancock* (**CV-19**), were so converted in 1951–54 with two steam catapults, revised aircraft lift arrangements and enhanced arrester gear. A further three units to be converted, the **Lexington** (**CV-16**), **Bon Homme Richard** (**CV-31**) and **Shangri-La** (**CV-38**), were then chosen to be refitted to the follow-on **SCB-125** standard, which involved the reconfiguration of the flight deck to an angled landing area and the reshaping of the island superstructure. All three units

were out of dock by late 1955, by which time all the SCB-27Cs, except the *Lake Champlain* of the SCB-27As and the *Oriskany*, were undergoing or had undergone similar conversions. Of the SCB-27Cs, the *Intrepid* was converted to an ASW carrier and underwent the FRAM modernization in the mid-1960s, while the *Ticonderoga* went the same way after serving off Vietnam in the early part of the war as a strike carrier. The *Hancock, Oriskany, Shangri-La* and *Bon Homme Richard* undertook combat tours

off Vietnam, flying a variety of fighter and strike aircraft.

Surviving carriers

By the mid-1980s only five of the carriers were extant, the *Lexington* as the sole active ship (the Atlantic Fleet's training carrier in the Gulf of Mexico), and the other four laid up as part of the Pacific Fleet reserve: the *Bon Homme Richard* and *Oriskany* as an attack aircraft carrier and aircraft carrier respectively, and the *Hornet* and *Bennington* as ASW support carriers. All have now gone.

The USS Intrepid is seen as an ASW carrier in the Atlantic in 1971. The carrier saw action in World War II, suffering many kamikaze attacks. After modernization, Intrepid made three Vietnam tours before decommissioning in 1974. The ship is now preserved as a museum in New York.

'Hancock' and 'Intrepid' classes
Attack carriers/ASW carriers

*The USS **Intrepid** served as an ASW carrier during its later years. The last active ship in the class was USS **Lexington**, which remained operational as a training carrier, in the Gulf of Mexico, into the 1990s.*

Originally units of the 24-strong 'Essex' class, the five ships of these two subclasses were extensively modernized in the 1950s with an enclosed bow, an armoured and angled flight deck, improved aircraft elevators, increased aircraft fuel and new steam catapults. By the mid-1980s, the classes were down to a total of three ships, namely the **Lexington** (**CVT-16**), **Bon Homme Richard** (**CVA-31**) and **Oriskany** (**CV-34**), which had been commissioned in February 1943, November 1944 and September 1950 respectively: the **Intrepid** (**CVS-11**) and **Shangri-La** (**CVS-38**)

had been retired. The subclasses had only one unit, the *Lexington*, in active service with the Atlantic Fleet as the US Navy's deck landing training carrier.

As such, the ship had no aircraft support facilities and the port deck-edge elevator locked as part of the flight deck. The other two ships were in Pacific Fleet reserve and were deleted in the late 1980s, although in 1981 the *Oriskany*, which had suffered a serious hangar fire in October 1966, was the object of a reactivation plan along the lines of the 'New Jersey'-class battleships. But because of

severe limitations in the types of aircraft it could carry (such as the obsolete F-8 Crusader and A-4 Skyhawk), its ordnance load and its fuel stowage, this was vetoed by the US Congress. The *Lexington* ran on to 1999, when it was replaced in the training

role by the USS *Forrestal* after that ship was phased out of front-line service. The aviation ordnance load is believed to have been in the order of 750 tons, and that of aviation fuel about 1,135,620 litres (300,000 US gal).

SPECIFICATION	
'Hancock' and 'Intrepid' classes **Displacement:** (first two) 29,660 tons standard, 41,900 tons full load; (third) 28,200 tons standard, 40,600 tons full load **Dimensions:** length (first) 270.9 m (889 ft) and (other two) 274 m (899 ft); beam (first two) 31.4 m (103 ft) and (third) 32.5 m (106 ft 6 in); draught 9.5 m (31 ft); flight deck width (first) 58.5 m (192 ft), (second) 52.4 m (172 ft) and (third) 59.5 m (195 ft) **Propulsion:** geared steam turbines delivering 111,855 kW (150,000 shp) to four shafts	**Performance:** speed 29.1 kts; range 27800 km (17,275 miles) at 15 kts **Armament:** two or (CV-34) four 5-in (127-mm) DP guns **Aircraft:** 60-70 (none in *Lexington*) **Electronics:** one SPS-10 surface search and navigation radar, one SPS-30 or (CVT-16) SPS-12 air search radar, one SPS-43A or (CV-34) SPS-37 air search radar, one SPN-10 and one SPN-43 aircraft landing aids, several Mk 25/35 fire-control radars (none in CVT-16), one URN-20 TACAN system **Complement:** 2,090 plus 1,185 air group or (CVT-16) 1,440

USS *United States* Attack carrier

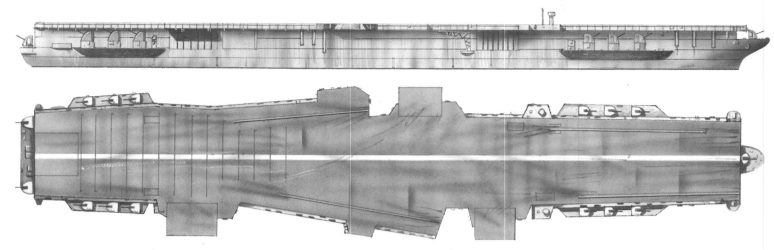

Although cancelled only nine days after its keel had been laid down in April 1949, the **USS United States** (**CVA-58**) is included here because it was the predecessor of the 'Forrestal' class and its successors, and because its advanced design had a profound effect on future development. *United States* was designed to operate a new generation of US Navy heavy strategic bombers (in the 25/45-ton class) and their attendant escort fighters. Because of the size of the bombers, the flight deck had to be large enough both to park them and to fly them on and off. In the end, an armoured and completely flush-deck configuration was chosen with

four catapults: two at the bows, and one each to port and starboard in complementing amidships positions and angled outwards to clear the aircraft forward. *United States* would have been the first large US carrier since the *Langley* that would not have had a navigational bridge on the deck. Four deck-edge lifts were also to be fitted (one to port, two to starboard and one at the stern). The aviation fuel capacity was to be a massive 1,892,700 litres (500,000 US gal), and the ordance load 2,000 tons. Four **'United States'-class** vessels were to have been built, the later ones nuclear-powered. No major electronics were carried, as the escorting warships were

*The startling lines of the **USS** United States design were a result of the fact that early atomic bombs were heavy pieces of equipment, requiring large aircraft, which in turn required large amounts of fuel. To that end, the United States was dedicated solely to the operation of these aircraft and their escorting fighters.*

SPECIFICATION	
USS United States	**Speed:** 33 kts
Displacement: 66,850 tons standard and 83,249 tons full load	**Armament:** eight single 5-in (127-mm) DP, eight twin 3-in (76-mm) AA and 20 single 20-mm AA guns
Dimensions: length 331.6 m (1,088 ft); 38.1 m (125 ft); draught 10.5 m (34 ft 6 in); flight deck width 57.9 m (190 ft)	**Aircraft:** 18 bombers and 54 F2H Banshee fighters
Propulsion: four-shaft geared steam turbines delivering 208,796 kW (280,000 shp)	**Electronics:** one SPS-6 air search radar and one SPS-8 height-finding radar
	Complement: 4,127

expected to take care of this work. The cancellation of the ship was due mainly to its projected role, for the US Air Force objected vigorously to

the US Navy duplicating its strategic mission. The funds released were ploughed back to the US Air Force to increase its bomber fleet.

'Forrestal' class Attack carrier

The four ships of the **'Forrestal' class** were initially conceived as smaller versions of the strategic carrier design, the USS *United States*, with four aircraft catapults and a flush flight deck with no island. However, following a redesign they were completed as the first carriers designed and built for jet aircraft operations, with a conventional island and an angled flight deck to allow the four catapults to be retained. The ships were the

USS *Forrestal*, USS *Saratoga*, USS *Ranger* and **USS *Independence***, and were commissioned in October 1955, April 1956, August 1957 and April 1959 respectively; their aviation ordnance load was 1,650 tons; 2.84 million litres (750,000 US gal) of AVGAS aviation fuel and 2.99 million litres (789,000 US gal) of JP5 aviation fuel were carried for the air wing embarked. The initial total of 90 aircraft carried by

First of the true 'supercarriers', the 'Forrestals' were able to carry over 80 aircraft. The lead ship is seen in the 1980s, with F-14 Tomcats from VF-11 and VF-31 ready for launch on the bow catapults.

Design of the 'Forrestal' class (this is the lead ship) was dictated by the need to operate the new A3D Skywarrior bomber. As a result, these ships were much bigger than the 'Midways', with hangar decks that were 7.2-m (25-ft) high.

SPECIFICATION	
'Forrestal' class	**Aircraft:** 84, comprising two F-14 and two F/A-18 squadrons, one of A-6/KA-6 and E-2, plus EA-6B, S-3 and SH-3 support aircraft
Ships in class (launched): *Forrestal* (1954), *Saratoga* ((1955), *Ranger* (1956) and *Independence* (1958)	
Displacement: (first two) 59,060 tons standard, 75,900 tons full load; (second two) 60,000 tons standard, 79,300 tons full load	**Armament:** three octuple Mk 29 Sea Sparrow SAM launchers, three 20-mm Phalanx CIWS
Dimensions: length (first) 331 m (1,086 ft), (second) 324 m (1,063 ft), (third) 326.4 m (1,071 ft) and (fourth) 326.1 m (1,070 ft); beam 39.5 m (129 ft 6 in); draught 11.3 m (37 ft); flight deck width 76.8 m (252 ft)	**Electronics:** one LN-66 navigation radar, one SPS-10 surface search radar, one SPS-48C 3D radar, one SPS-58 low-level air search (except *Ranger*), two SPN-42 and one SPN-43A aircraft landing aids, two Mk 91 fire-control radars (three in first two), one URN-20 TACAN system, one SLQ-29 ESM suite and three Mk 36 SRBOC chaff launchers
Machinery: four-shaft geared steam turbines delivering 193,880 kW (260,000 shp) in *Forrestal* and 208795 kW (280,000 shp) in others	
Speed: 33 kts (*Forrestal*) or 34 kts	**Complement:** 2,790 plus 2,150 air group

each vessel comprised two fighter squadrons with F2Hs or F9Fs, two light attack squadrons with ADs and A4Ds and supporting reconnaissance, AEW and SAR assets. *Forrestal* and *Ranger* were equipped for Regulus I missile operations in the 1950s. All four vessels saw action off Vietnam and were redesignated as CVs in the 1970s. After serving on the Cuba blockade in 1962, *Independence* was the first

Atlantic Fleet carrier to deploy to Vietnam in June 1965, and supported the A-6 Intruder for its combat debut. *Forrestal* completed just one cruise to the war zone, suffering a fire in August 1967. During the Grenada landings of November 1983, *Independence* provided the air cover and strike support to the US Marine Corps and US Army Ranger assaults while maintaining ASW cover against possible incursions by the two

Cuban 'Foxtrot' conventional attack submarines. In 1985–86 *Saratoga* was involved in skirmishes with Libya.

SLEP refits

Three of the 'Forrestal' ships underwent the SLEP refit in the 1980s (in the order *Saratoga*, *Forrestal*, and *Independence*) to extend their service lives into the 1990s. To rectify deficiencies encountered in combat operations, the SLEP refits improved the habitability, added Kevlar armour to enclose the vital machinery and electronics spaces, improved the NTDS fitted, added TFCC facility and replaced the catapults. The radar outfit was also upgraded and the air defence armament strengthened with the addition of the Phalanx CIWS for anti-missile work complementing the

Sea Sparrow. As built, the 'Forrestals' had been armed with eight 5-in (127-mm) guns on the sponsons either side of the fore and aft deck. These were removed through the 1960s and 1970s, to be replaced by the Mk 25 (and later Mk 29) Sea Sparrow SAM launchers.

In its later years, Forrestal became the US Navy's training carrier as **AVT-59**. The remaining three first-line 'Forrestals' were involved in Operations Desert Shield and Desert Storm. *Saratoga* retired in 1994. Prior to decommissioning, *Independence* replaced *Midway* as the carrier permanently forward deployed at Yokosuka, Japan. The 'Forrestal' class was replaced by new 'Nimitz'-class carriers, *Independence* being the last to retire, in September 1998.

USS **Saratoga**, *the first of the 'Forrestals' to undergo a SLEP, is seen during the 1980s when serving with the Atlantic Fleet. These were the first carriers designed with the hangar and flight decks as an integral part of the hull, with gun positions on outboard sponsons. The class was retired as 'Nimitz'-class ships became available.*

USS **Ranger** *dwarfs the guided missile frigate* **Jacob von Heemskerck** *while refuelling the Dutch ship in the Persian Gulf. The carrier moved into the region in January 1991 to participate in Desert Shield and Desert Storm.*

Minas Gerais 'Colossus'-class carrier

The sister of the Argentinian *25 de Mayo*, the ex-*Vengeance* started life in the Royal Navy in 1945. Three years later the carrier was fitted out for an experimental cruise to the Arctic, and was then lent to the Royal Australian Navy in 1953. She was returned to the Royal Navy in 1955 and purchased by Brazil in December 1956 as the **NAEL *Minas Gerais***. The ship was then transferred to the Netherlands, for a comprehensive refit between 1957 and 1960 with new weapons, a 13365-kg (29,465-lb) capacity steam catapult, an 8.5° angled flight deck, a mirror sight deck landing system, a new island superstructure, new US radars and two centreline aircraft elevators. The hangar was 135.6 m (445 ft) long by 15.8 m (52 ft) wide and 5.3 m (17 ft 6 in) high. In 1976–81, the carrier underwent another refit to allow operations through to the 1990s. A datalink system was installed so that the carrier could co-operate with the 'Niteroi' class of frigates in service with the Brazilian navy,

Above: **Minas Gerais** *operated with a combined Força Aérea Brasileira and navy air group, which until their retirement in 1996 included FAB P-16 Tracker ASW aircraft.*

The **Minas Gerais** *completed its final cruise in February 2001, shortly after having conducted operations with the newly acquired A-4KU Skyhawk (known locally as AF-1) aircraft, which now serve aboard the new 'Clémenceau'-class carrier* **São Paulo.**

SPECIFICATION	
Minas Gerais	**Armament:** two quadruple 40-mm
Displacement: 15,890 tons standard;	AA, and one twin 40-mm AA
19,890 tons full load	**Aircraft:** see text
Dimensions: length 211.8 m (695 ft);	**Electronics:** one SPS-40B air search
beam 24.4 m (80 ft); draught 7.5 m	radar, one SPS-4 surface search
(24 ft 6 in); flight deck width 37 m	radar, one SPS-8B fighter-direction
(121 ft)	radar, one SPS-8A air control radar,
Machinery: two-shaft geared steam	one Raytheon 1402 navigation
turbines delivering 29,830 kW	radar and two SPG-34 fire-control
(40,000 shp)	radars
Speed: 25.3 kts	**Complement:** 1,300 with air group

and the obsolete American SPS-12 radar was replaced with a modern SPS-40B two dimensional air search system. The role of the *Minas Gerais* throughout its service with the Brazilian navy was anti-submarine warfare with an air group (since the late 1970s) of

eight S-2 (P-16) Trackers of the Brazilian air force (the Brazilian navy was not allowed to operate fixed-wing aicraft) plus four navy SH-3/ASH-3 Sea King ASW helicopters, two UH-12/ UH-13 Esquilo and two Bell 206B utility helicopters. The *Minas Gerais* was retired in 2001.

'Clémenceau' class Aircraft carrier

The **Clémenceau** was the first carrier designed as such to be completed in France. Built in the late 1950s and commissioned in November 1961, it incorporated all the advances made in carrier design during the early 1950s, namely a fully angled flight deck, mirror landing sight and a fully comprehensive set of air search, tracking and air control radars.

The flight deck was 165.5 m (543 ft) in length and 29.5 m (96 ft 9 in) in width, and was

The second unit of the 'Clémenceau' class, **Foch** *was laid down in 1957, launched in 1960 and commissioned in 1963. The vessel is seen here after its commissioning into Brazilian navy service as the* **São Paulo.**

angled at 8° to the ship's centreline. Two aircraft lifts, each rated at 2,036 kg (44,895 lb)

were provided, one abaft the island on the deck edge and the other offset to starboard and

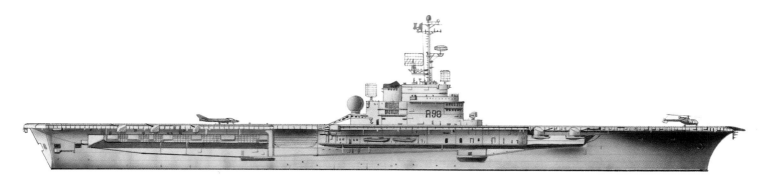

just forward of the island. Two steam catapults were fitted, one on the port side of the bow and the other on the angled flight deck. The hangar had a usable area of 152 m (499 ft) by 24 m (78 ft 9 in) by 7 m (23 ft). The fuel capacity of the *Clémenceau* was 1200 m³ of JP5 aircraft fuel and 400 m³ of AVGAS while its sistership, the **Foch** (commissioned in July 1963), carried 1800 m³ and 109 m³ respectively. During the period September 1977 to November 1978, the *Clémenceau* underwent a major refit, the *Foch* following in 1980–81. During these refits, both ships were converted to operate the Super Etendard strike fighter, for which they carried AN52 15-kt

tactical nuclear gravity bombs in their magazines. They also received SENIT 2 automated tactical information processing systems as part of their C³ suites. Following the refits, the two carriers' air groups comprised 16 Super Etendard, three Etendard IVP reconnaissance aircraft, 10 Crusader interceptors and seven Alizé ASW aircraft, plus two Super Frelon ASW and two Alouette III utility helicopters. The carriers could also act, if required, as helicopter carriers with an air group of 30–40 helicopters, depending upon the types embarked. During the Lebanon crisis of 1983, France used one of the carriers in support of its peace-keeping

After modification, the two 'Clémenceau'-class carriers served on until the 1990s with the French navy. Clémenceau was paid off in March 1998, with Foch following in November 2000. Clémenceau occasionally acted as a helicopter carrier for amphibious operations. During Operation Salamandre, the French deployment to the Gulf in 1990, Clémenceau ferried 30 Gazelles and 12 Pumas to Saudi Arabia.

force, Super Etendards being used to attack several gun positions that had engaged French troops. The *Foch* and *Clémenceau* were refitted again in 1985–88, receiving Crotale missile launchers in place of two 100-mm guns and storing ASMP nuclear missiles in the magazines. In 1992–93, a removable 1.5° mini-ski jump was fitted on the forward catapult of *Foch* for the deck landing trials of the Rafale M in 1993–94 and in 1995–97 *Foch* was further modified to operate the Rafale M as well as two sextuple Sadral launchers for Mistral SAMs.

Refitted by DCN, Foch was commissioned into the Brazilian navy as the **NAE *São Paulo***. The carrier has an airgroup built

around some of the A-4 Skyhawks acquired from Kuwait in 1998 and replaced the *Minas Gerais*. The *São Paulo* has had all gun and missile armament removed except for a few machine-guns; there are at present no defensive systems to protect the ship. However, with the end of the *25 de Mayo*, the *São Paulo* gives Brazil the only operational aircraft carrier in South America. The national prestige value of a major warship remains as potent in that continent as it was at the beginning of the 20th century when Brazil, Chile and Argentina bought dreadnought battleships from European yards in a similar display of conspicuous expenditure, regardless of practical defence strategy.

Left: The São Paulo arrived in Brazil in February 2001, immediately replacing the Minas Gerais.

Left: Seen entering Nice in the early 1980s with Super Etendard, Etendard IVP, Alizé, Lynx and Super Frelon aircraft embarked, Foch, provided air support to the French forces in Lebanon in 1983.

SPECIFICATION
São Paulo
Displacement: 27,032 tons standard, 32,780 tons full load
Dimensions: length 265 m (869 ft 5 in); beam 51.2 m (168 ft); draught 8.6 m (28 ft 3 in)
Machinery: two-shaft geared steam turbines delivering 93,960 kW (126,000 shp)
Speed: 32 kts
Armament: fitted for 12.7-mm (0.5-in) machine-guns
Aircraft: 15 AF-1 Skyhawk, four to six ASH-3 Sea King, three

UH-12/UH-13 Esquilo, two UH-14 Super Puma; Bell 206B can be deployed for training duties
Electronics: one DRBV 23B air search radar, one DRBV 15 air/surface search radar, two DRBI 10 height-finding radars, one Decca 1226 navigation radar, one NRBA 51 aircraft landing aid, one NRBP 2B TACAN system, SICONTA Mk 1 tactical data system (to be fitted), two AMBL 2A Sagaie 10-barrel chaff/flare launchers
Complement: 1,202 (358 aircrew)

HMAS *Melbourne* and HMAS *Sydney* Light fleet carriers

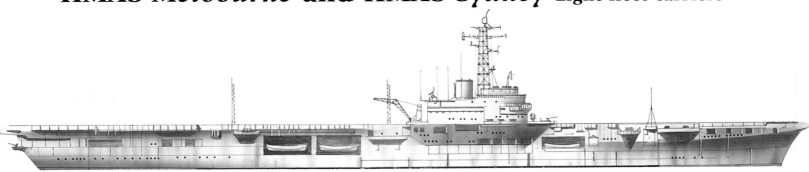

Formerly name ship of the British built 'Majestic'-class light fleet carriers, HMAS Melbourne was bought by Australia in 1949. By 1965 the vessel was notable for the tall lattice mast added to carry the newly fitted LW series main search radar.

Work on all six of the Royal Navy's **'Majestic'-class** carriers was stopped after the end of World War II. However, because of interest expressed by the Royal Australian and Canadian navies in acquiring carriers, two units were subsequently completed as **HMS Terrible** (bought by Australia as **HMAS Sydney**) and **HMS Magnificent** (loaned to Canada under that name), while work on a third, **HMS Majestic**, was started in 1948 to a greatly modified configuration with 25 40-mm AA guns, a 5.5° angle landing deck, new arrester gear, a mirror landing sight system and a steam catapult. The opportunity

to fit a greatly enhanced radar suite was also taken, with no fewer than three Type 277Q height-finding sets, a Type 293 surface search set and a Type 978 navigation set.

Recommissioning as **HMAS Melbourne** in October 1955, the carrier embarked an air group of eight Sea Venoms, 12 Gannet ASW aircraft and two Sycamore SAR helicopters. In 1963–67, the *Melbourne* served as the RAN flagship, and her air group was reduced to four Sea Venoms, six Gannets and ten Wessex HAS.Mk 31B helicopters. In late 1967, the ship was taken in hand for strengthening of the decks,

lifts, catapult and arrester gear, the fitting of new radar and communications equipment and the reduction of the AA armament numbers. This was to allow for the carriage and operation of A-4G Skyhawks and S-2E Tracker ASW aircraft. The

new radars were a mixture of Dutch and American types, together with the old Type 293 and Type 978 sets. The air group now consisted of four Skyhawks, six Trackers and 10 Wessex helicopters, though from 1972 onwards it was again

HMAS Melbourne is seen entering Pearl Harbor in June 1958. The air group at this time comprised 27 aircraft, including Sea Venoms and ASW Gannets. The ship was flagship of the Royal Australian Navy, and remained so until its withdrawal from service in 1982.

SPECIFICATION	
HMS Melbourne **Displacement:** 16,000 tons standard and 20,320 tons full load **Dimensions:** length 213.82 m (701 ft); beam 24.38 m (80 ft); draught 7.62 m (25 ft); flight deck width 32 m (105 ft) **Propulsion:** two-shaft geared steam turbines delivering 31,319 kW (42,000 shp) **Speed:** 23 kts	**Armament:** four twin and four single 40-mm AA guns **Aircraft:** 27 (see text) **Electronics:** one LW-02 air search radar, one Type 293Q surface search radar, one Type 978 navigation radar, one SPN-35 landing aid radar, one TACAN system and one ECM system **Complement:** 1,425 (as flagship)

changed to eight Skyhawks, six Trackers and 10 Sea King HAS.Mk 50 ASW helicopters plus two or three Wessex helicopters in the SAR/planeguard role. After a final refit in 1976, the *Melbourne* was scheduled to serve on until 1985, but as a result of financial constraints she was paid off into reserve during June 1982, and in 1984 was sold for scrap. Although a replacement was

scheduled (including at one stage the Royal Navy's *Invincible*), this was a forlorn hope since all navy fixed-wing aircraft were sold or transferred to the Royal Australian Air Force.

HMAS *Sydney*

HMAS *Sydney* was commissioned into the Australian navy on 16 December 1948, initially carrying a mixed complement of Sea Fury, Firefly

and Sea Otter aircraft. Her complement of 37 aircraft was larger than that of *Melbourne*, despite her being slightly smaller. *Sydney* became the first RAN carrier to serve in combat in October 1951, when she relieved HMS *Glory* during the Korean War. During the conflict, the ship performed seven operational patrols and her air wing completed 2,366 sorties. In May 1958 the

ship was paid off into the reserve, but was then recommissioned as a troop ship in March 1962. Between 1965 and 1972, the vessel undertook operations in Vietnam deploying four Wessex helicopters for ASW protection duties on 22 voyages to the theatre. *Sydney* was decommissioned in November 1973 and was eventually sold for scrap in 1975.

Independencia 'Colossus'-class light fleet carrier

ARA *Independencia* was launched in May 1944 as the British 'Colossus'-class carrier **HMS *Warrior***. *Warrior* was launched on 20 May 1944. The ship was was lent to the Royal Canadian Navy on completion in 1945 for a period of two years until the Canadian carrier HMCS *Magnificent* was ready for service. On return from the Canadian service, *Warrior* was used by the Royal Navy for deck landing trials and in 1948–49 was fitted with a flexible landing

deck to allow jet fighters with skid-type landing gear to make soft landings. In 1952–53 the ship was fitted with a new enlarged bridge and a lattice foremast, while in 1955 it was revised together with a 5° angled right deck and stronger arrester gear.

Operation Grapple

Following more deck landing trials work with this new configuration, *Warrior* was tasked in 1957 to act as the HQ

ship for Operation Grapple (the British H-bomb test programme) at Christmas Island in the Pacific Ocean. On its return, the ship was offered for sale to Argentina. After subsequent negotiations, a deal was signed in the summer of 1958. The vessel was formally handed over to the Argentine navy on 11 November 1958, and the Argentine ensign was raised for

the first time during a ceremony at Portsmouth. The ship sailed under its new name of *Independencia* in December of that year for Argentina, as that nation's first aircraft carrier. As transferred it carried only 12 40-mm AA guns, a number reduced to eight shortly afterwards. However, by May 1962 *Independencia* was spotted with a new battery of

Originally the British 'Colossus'-class carrier HMS Warrior, the Argentine carrier Independencia had a varied career, serving in Korea as well as being lent to the Canadian navy before being acquired in 1958. Among the aircraft types operated were F4U Corsair fighter/attack aircraft and S-2A Tracker ASW aircraft.

SPECIFICATION	
Independencia	turbines delivering 29,828 kW
Displacement: 14,000 tons standard	(40,000 shp)
and 19,540 tons full load	**Speed:** 24 kts
Dimensions: length 211.84 m	**Armament:** one quadruple and nine
(695 ft); beam 24.38 m (80 ft);	twin 40-mm AA guns (removed in
draught 7.16 m (23 ft); flight deck	1970)
width 22.86 m (75 ft)	**Aircraft:** 24 (see text)
Propulsion: two-shaft geared steam	**Complement:** 1,575

one quadruple and nine twin 40-mm guns. In 1963, the carrier was also carrying F4U-5 Corsairs (which formed its most important equipment) and the TF-9J Cougar trainer. Fennec armed trainers were also a common sight aboard the *Independencia*. However, the ship never embarked the F9F Panther on an operational basis, although in theory it could deploy combat jets. By the end of the ship's career in the late 1960s the embarked air group was made up of six S-2A Trackers (introduced to the carrier in 1962) and 14 Fennecs. In 1970, following the acquisition of ARA *25 de Mayo*, the *Independencia* was placed in reserve. Decommissioned, the vessel was finally sold for scrap in March 1971.

Arromanches
'Colossus'-class light fleet carrier

Laid down in June 1942 and launched in September 1943 at the Newcastle yard of Vickers Armstrong Limited as the British 'Colossus'-class carrier **HMS Colossus**, this ship was loaned to the French navy in August 1946 (after 12 months of service in the Far East) for a five-year period. Named **FNS Arromanches** after the beach used by the Allies for landing equipment and supplies after D-Day, the ship made two combat deployments to French Indo-China, flying SBD Dauntless and Seafire Mk XV aircraft on the first, and 24 F6F Hellcats and SB2C Helldivers on the second. *Arromanches* was finally purchased outright in 1951 when the loan expired, and was sent on two more Indo-China deployments before the French defeats of 1954. Transferred to the Mediterranean, the *Arromanches* took part in the 1956 Anglo-French Suez landings, with F4U Corsairs and TBM Avengers attacking targets around Port Said. The carrier also took part in French military operations in Algeria. In 1957–58, the ship underwent a complete rebuild, receiving a 4° angled flight deck and a mirror landing aid. The AA armament then comprised 43 40-mm guns instead of the original armament of 24 2-pdr and 19 40-mm guns. By the early 1960s, all of the 40-mm guns had been removed and the *Arromanches* had been relegated to the training carrier role flying both Alizé ASW aircraft and the Zéphyr jet trainer, to produce personnel for the air groups of the new carriers *Foch* and *Clémenceau*. In 1962, the *Arromanches* also took on the assault role when HSS-1 helicopters from Flotille 33F were embarked. After a further refit in 1968 to carry an

Originally the name ship of the Royal Navy's 'Colossus' class, the **Arromanches** *entered French service in 1946. At the same time as its sisters were in action off Korea, the vessel was involved in the French colonial struggle in Indo-China, making four deployments in eight years.*

air group of 24 helicopters, the carrier was redesignated as a helicopter carrier with ASW, transport, training and intervention missions tasked to it as required. Decommissioned in 1974 after 30 continuous years of British and French service, the *Arromanches* was broken up at Toulon in 1978.

Arromanches *is seen here in the Far East in 1953. On the deck is part of its complement of F6F Hellcat fighters and* **SB2C** *dive-bombers. After Dien Bien Phu and French withdrawal from the east, the ship took part in the Suez landings, operating off Port Said.*

SPECIFICATION	
Arromanches	(40,000 shp)
Displacement: 14,000 tons standard and 19,600 tons full load	**Speed:** 25 kts
	Armament: see text
Dimensions: length 211.84 m (695 ft); beam 24.38 m (80 ft); draught 7.16 m (23 ft); flight deck width 36 m (118 ft)	**Aircraft:** 24 (see text)
	Electronics: one DRBV 22A air search radar, plus various French, American and British radars and aircraft landing aids
Propulsion: two-shaft geared steam turbines delivering 29,828 kW	**Complement:** 1,400

Vikrant 'Majestic'-class carrier

Formerly the British 'Majestic'-class light fleet carrier **HMS Hercules** since May 1946, the **INL Vikrant** (as it was renamed, meaning 'valour') was bought by India in January 1957. Completed with one hangar, two electrically-operated aircraft lifts, an angled flight deck and steam catapult, the carrier was commissioned in 1961.

Vikrant's aircraft deployed to Tamil Nadu for combat in 1962. She was refitting at the time of the 1965 Indo-Pakistan War, although its air units did participate from shore bases.

During the 1971 Indo-Pakistan War, the *Vikrant* operated a mixed air group of 16 Sea Hawk fighter-bombers and four Alizé ASW aircraft off East Pakistan (now called Bangladesh), the Sea Hawks attacking coastal ports, airfields and small craft to prevent the movement of Pakistani men and supplies

during Indian army operations to 'liberate' that country.

Major upgrade

Replacement of the Alizé by the Sea King Mk 42 for ASW duties began in 1971, but the last Alizé launch was not until 1987. In January 1979 the *Vikrant* began a Service Life Extension Programme (SLEP) to enable operations with Sea Harrier FRS.Mk 51 aircraft. Included in the refit was the construction of a 9.75° ski-jump ramp and the provision of new Dutch radars and a new operations control system. The first Sea Harrier ski-jump launch was in March 1990. The new air group consisted of six to eight Sea Harriers, six to eight Alizés, six Sea King Mk 42 ASW/anti-ship missile and Chetak (Alouette III) utility helicopters.

After a long career, *Vikrant* was decommissioned in 1997.

SPECIFICATION	
Vikrant	**Armament:** nine single 40-mm AA
Displacement: 15,700 tons standard; 19,500 tons full load	**Electronics:** one LW-05 air search radar; one ZW-06 surface search radar; one LW-10 tactical search radar; one LW-11 tactical search radar; one Type 963 carrier controlled approach radar
Dimensions: length 213.4 m (700 ft); beam 24.4 m (80 ft); draught 7.3 m (24 ft); flight deck width 39 m (128 ft)	
Propulsion: two-shaft geared steam turbines delivering 29,830 kW (40,000 shp)	**Complement:** 1,075 (including air group) in peace, 1,345 (including air group) in war
Speed: 24.5 kts	

Used extensively in the 1971 Indo-Pakistan War, INS Vikrant was the major Indian Navy unit responsible for the blockade of East Pakistan. The air group of Alizé ASW aircraft and Sea Hawk fighter-bombers sank a number of Pakistani naval and merchant craft.

Dédalo 'Independence'-class carrier

The **Dédalo** was an ex-US 'Independence'-class carrier – the **USS Cabot**, built during World War II – and ended her days in the US Navy as an aviation transport. The vessel was reactivated and modernized as a carrier at the Philadelphia Naval Shipyard before being

The elderly Spanish carrier **Dédalo** *was converted from an ex-US World War II 'Independence'-class carrier. Formerly the flagship of the Spanish fleet, the vessel was replaced by the* **Principe de Asturias**.

transferred to Spain on a five-year loan from 30 August 1967, after Madrid had rejected an 'Essex'-class carrier and a conversion of the Italian cruiser *Trieste*. In 1973 the *Dédalo* was purchased outright and became the Spanish navy's fleet

flagship. The vessel's flight deck was 166 m (545 ft 6 in) long and 32.9 m (108 ft) wide, and the hangar accommodated 18 Sea King helicopters with another six on the flight deck. The *Dédalo*'s normal air wing comprised four air groups,

having at least one with eight AV-8S Matador V/STOL fighters, one with four SH-3D/G Sea King ASW helicopters, one with four AB 212ASW anti-submarine and electronic warfare helicopters, and one of four helicopters. A maximum of seven four-aircraft

groups could be handled aboard. The *Dédalo* was decommissioned in August 1989, having sailed over 804,650 km (500,000 miles) and seeing 50,000 landings during its time in the Spanish navy.

As USS Cabot, Dédalo *had survived a Japanese kamikaze attack during the Battle of Leyte Gulf. Contributing greatly to Spanish carrier aviation doctrine, the vessel survived for 20 years in Spanish fleet service.*

SPECIFICATION	
Dédalo	**Armament:** one quadruple 40-mm
Displacement: 13,000 tons standard; 16,.416 tons full load	AA, and nine twin 40-mm AA
Dimensions: length 189.9 m (623 ft); beam 21.8 m (71 ft 6 in); draught 7.9 m (25 ft)	**Electronics:** one SPS-8 3D radar; one SPS-6 and one SPS-40 air search radar; one SPS-10 surface search/tactical radar; two Mk 29 and two Mk 28 fire-control systems; two navigation radars; one URN-22 TACAN system; one WLR-1 ECM system
Propulsion : four-shaft geared steam turbines delivering 74,570 kW (100,000 shp)	
Speed: 24 kts	
Aircraft: see text	**Complement:** 1,112 minus air group

HMS *Victorious* 'Illustrious'-class carrier

After serving in World War II, **HMS *Victorious*** was completely rebuilt, from the hangar deck up, between 1950 and 1957 at Portsmouth Dockyard. During this modernization the hull was widened, deepened and lengthened while the machinery and boilers were completely renewed. Two steam catapults, new arrester gear and an 8.75° angled flight deck with mirror landing sights (as well as new aircraft lifts and radars) were fitted. A maximum of 35 fixed-

wing aircraft were scheduled as the air group, but in the event the *Victorious* never had more than 28 aboard plus eight helicopters. Initial equipment after recommissioning in 1958 comprised Scimitars, Sea Venoms, Skyraiders and Whirlwinds, with Sea Vixens replacing the Sea Venoms in 1960. The carrier was again refitted in 1962 and 1968, but before the latter was finished a minor fire broke out, which was taken by the government of the day as an excuse for scrapping it

HMS Victorious *was the only wartime fleet carrier to be thoroughly modernized in the 1950s. Seen here just before the start of its protracted refit, the vessel was to emerge after eight years completely rebuilt from the hangar deck up, and able to operate jets of up to 18145 kg (40,000 lb) including the Buccaneer.*

SPECIFICATION	
HMS *Victorious*	**Speed:** 31 kts
Displacement: 30,500 tons standard and 35,500 tons full load	**Aircraft:** 35 (see text)
Dimensions: length 238 m (781 ft); beam 31.5 m (103 ft 6 in); draught 9.4 m (31 ft); flight deck width 47.8 m (157 ft)	**Armament:** six twin 3-in (76-mm) Mk 33 AA and one sextuple 40-mm AA gun
Propulsion: three-shaft geared steam turbines delivering 82,027 kW (110,000 shp)	**Electronics:** one Type 984 3D radar; one Type 293Q height-finding radar; one Type 974 surface search radar; one CCA aircraft landing aid
	Complement: 2,400

in the following year as part of the 1966 carrier rundown programme.

The final air group composition carried by the ship was eight Buccaneer S.Mk 1s, eight Sea Vixens, two Gannet AEW.Mk 3s and five Wessex helicopters. With these aircraft, the vessel conducted air operations during the 1964 Indonesian Confrontation. As one of the fleet's and NATO's strike carrier units, the ship and its Buccaneers were fitted to carry the naval version of the 5/20-kT variable-yield Red Beard tactical nuclear gravity bomb.

Three of the Royal Navy's four angled deck carriers of the time are seen in this 1960s photograph, only HMS Eagle being absent. Victorious, here seen astern of Hermes and Ark Royal, was a very different vessel from the carrier that attacked the Bismarck.

HMCS *Bonaventure* 'Majestic'-class carrier

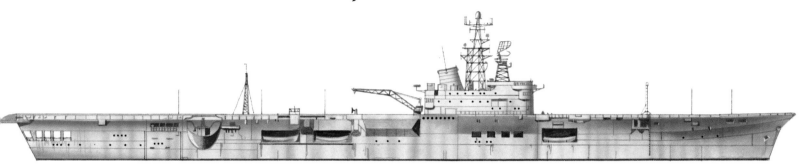

The British 'Majestic'-class aircraft carrier **HMS Powerful** was laid down in November 1943 and launched in an incomplete state in February 1945. In 1952 the hulk was purchased by the Royal Canadian Navy as **HMCS Bonaventure** and redesigned before its completion to accommodate an 8° angled flight deck, a steam catapult, modern arrester gear and a stabilized mirror landing sight. *Bonaventure* was also fitted with four twin 3-in (76-mm) AA guns on four sponsons projecting from the hull sides. The island was rebuilt and a tall lattice mast with US radars erected in place of the original tripod model. Entering Canadian fleet service in 1957, the *Bonaventure* had an air group consisting initially of 16 F2H-3 Banshee jet fighters and eight

The uncompleted 'Majestic'-class carrier HMS Powerful was sold to Canada and completed as HMCS Bonaventure. Originally equipped with F2H Banshees, the carrier had become an ASW-dedicated vessel by 1961. By 1968 Bonaventure appeared as shown, with new Dutch radars and with improved sea-keeping.

Canadian-built CS2F Tracker ASW aircraft. In 1961, it was changed to an all-ASW force with eight Trackers and 13 HO4S-3 Whirlwind helicopters. The latter were replaced by CHSS-2 Sea Kings when they became available. The *Bonaventure*'s last major refit in 1966–67 saw the fitting of new Dutch radar and the Fresnel landing aid, the removal of the two forward gun sponsons to enhance the ship's sea-keeping qualities, and improvements in the accommodation, aircraft handling and anti-fallout protection facilities. The *Bonaventure* was finally paid off in 1970 for disposal because of the costs of keeping the vessel in service. The carrier was subsequently sold and broken up for scrap.

The introduction of Bonaventure allowed a new generation of carrierborne aircraft to be operated, including the Tracker, used for ASW missions.

SPECIFICATION	
HMCS *Bonaventure*	**Speed:** 24.5 kts
Displacement: 16,000 tons standard and 20,000 tons full load	**Armament:** four (later two) twin 3-in (76-mm) Mk 33 AA guns
Dimensions: length 219.5 m (720 ft); beam 24.38 m (80 ft); draught 7.62 m (25 ft); flight deck width 32 m (105 ft)	**Aircraft:** 21–24 (see text)
	Electronics: (before 1967-68 refit) one SPS-12 air search radar; one SPS-8 height-finding radar and one SPS-10 surface search radar
Propulsion: two-shaft geared steam turbines delivering 29,828 kW (40,000 shp)	**Complement:** 1,370

HMS *Ark Royal* Fleet carrier

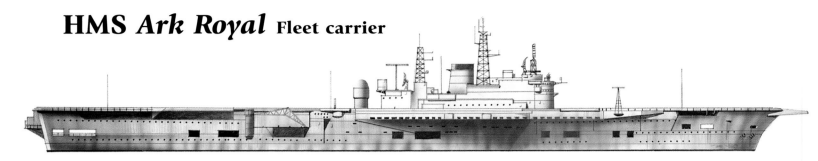

The profile of HMS Ark Royal in 1978 presents a number of features very different to the vessel of the 1950s. The dome abaft the island covers the CCA (Carrier Controlled Approach) radar, an automatic landing aid, and the extra masts and antennae indicate the sophistication of the electronic fit.

SPECIFICATION	
HMS *Ark Royal*	**Aircraft:** 39 (see text)
Displacement: 43,060 tons standard and 50,786 tons full load	**Armament:** fitted for four quadruple GWS.22 Seacat SAM launchers
Dimensions: length 275.6 m (845 ft); beam 34.4 m (112 ft 11 in); draught 11 m (36 ft); flight deck width 50.1 m (164 ft 6 in)	**Electronics:** two Type 965M air search radars, two Type 982 air search radars, two Type 983 height-finding radars, one Type 993 surface search radar, one SPN-35 aircraft landing aid, one Type 974 navigation radar and one ESM system
Propulsion: four-shaft geared steam turbines delivering 113,346 kW (152,000 shp)	
Speed: 31.5 kts	**Complement:** 2,637

Near sister of HMS *Eagle*, **HMS Ark Royal** (**R09**) was completed in 1955 to a more modern configuration with a pair of steam catapults, a 5.5° angled flight deck, a mirror landing sight and a port-side deck-edge lift serving the upper hangar only. The ship's initial air group capacity was 50 aircraft, comprising Sea Hawks, Sea Venoms, Gannet ASW aircraft and Skyraider AEW types plus several utility helicopters. Later in the 1950s, the Wyvern was added to the air group. In 1956 the ship's starboard 4.5-in (114-mm) turrets were removed, and in 1959 the deck-edge lift went.

Returning to sea in 1960, the air wing of the 'Ark' added

Right: Bearer of an honourable name dating back to the time of the Spanish Armada, the Ark Royal ended its career in the 1970s operating Phantoms and Buccaneer fighters. In spite of mechanical problems, it was one of the most powerful vessels in the world at that time.

In October 1957, joint operations with the USS Saratoga enabled Ark Royal to play host to F3H Demons of VF-61. The Seahawk is preparing for launch after the Demons, from one of a pair of BS4 steam catapults, and in the background two Skyraider AEW.Mk 1 aircraft are ranged ready for a free take-off.

Scimitars, Sea Vixens and Gannet AEW aircraft. In 1964, the forward pairs of the aft 5-in guns were removed, while the remaining turrets and the last 40-mm Bofors went during the 1967–70 refit. This was to allow for the operation of Phantom fighters. An 8.5° flight deck was fitted, with new catapults (including a new waist one) and arrester gear. The island was also reconfigured, and the addition of new radars was complemented by the improvement of the older types.

The air group capacity dropped from 48 to 39, a figure that stood for the remainder of the ship's active career. Typically this was 12 Phantom FG.Mk 1s, 14 Buccaneer S.Mk 2s, four Gannet AEW.Mk 3s, six Sea King HAS.Mk 1 (later HAS.Mk 2) ASW helicopters, two Wessex Mk 1 SAR helicopters and Gannet carrier onboard delivery (COD) aircraft. The Buccaneers doubled as tanker aircraft with buddy inflight-refuelling pods and as long-range photo-reconnaissance aircraft with a bomb bay-mounted camera pack, at least one Buccaneer being configured in the latter role at all times.

Retirement

Although suffering throughout its life from mechanical problems, the *Ark Royal* was eventually taken out of service in 1978 as the last of the Royal Navy's conventional carriers. After much public debate as to its future, the vessel was finally towed away from Devonport in 1980 for scrapping.

Like its sister ship, the *Ark Royal* had been fitted in the 1960s to carry the Red Beard and later Green Parrot tactical nuclear bombs.

As completed in 1955, HMS Ark Royal had a heavy gun armament comprising 16 4.5-in (114-mm) and a number of 40-mm Bofors AA guns. The air group of 50 aircraft was to include Sea Hawks, Gannets, Skyraiders and helicopters.

HMS *Eagle* Fleet carrier

Originally to be named **HMS Audacious**, one of a class of four 'Improved Implacable'-class fleet carriers, this hull was fairly advanced at the end of World War II and was therefore chosen to be completed more or less as designed. In January 1946, the name was changed to **Eagle** (**R06**) but the completion of a surviving sistership, HMS *Ark Royal*, was held up to allow for improvements. Completed in 1951, the *Eagle* had, in comparison with the original design, a reduced armament of eight twin 4.5-in (114-mm) DP guns, and eight sextuple, two twin and nine single 40-mm Bofors AA guns, more advanced search radars and a grand total of 12 American Mk 37 radar gun directors. An air group of Firebrands, Fireflies and Attackers was initially embarked, later joined by Sea Hornets and

Seen leaving Wellington, New Zealand, in the late 1960s, Eagle could always be distinguished from Ark Royal by the massive Type 984 radar atop the bridge, and the absence of catapult bridles (extensions).

October 1956, and HMS Eagle, flagship of Vice Admiral Manley Power, leads HMS Bulwark and HMS Albion on exercise off Malta. Within weeks, they were to be involved in the Suez landing.

Skyraider AEW.Mk 1s. A total of 60 fixed-wing aircraft could be carried, although in 1954 the number was 59 Sea Hawks, Avengers, Skyraider and a Dragonfly SAR helicopter.

From mid-1954 to early 1955, the ship underwent a refit that resulted in the building of a 5.5° angled flight deck, the fitting of a mirror landing sight and the removal of three single and one sextuple Bofors mounts. In 1956, the ship served as part of the Anglo-French carrier force during the Suez landings, operating a mixed air group of Sea Hawks, Skyraiders, Wyverns and Sea Venoms on strike missions. From mid-1969 to mid-1964, the *Eagle* was taken in hand for a complete rebuild in which all the forward 4.5-in mounts and all the 40-mm guns were removed, an 8.5° flight deck was fitted, the radar outfit was modernized, and six quadruple Seacat close-range SAM launchers were fitted. The air group number was reduced to 35 fixed-wing and 10 rotary-wing aircraft, this complement

being made up of Sea Vixens, Scimitars, Gannets and Wessex helicopters.

Eagle in action

In 1964, the ship sailed for the Far East and the Indonesian confrontation, which was followed in 1966 by Rhodesia and the Beira patrol to prevent oil reaching the rebel country through Mozambique. In 1967, the carrier moved on to Aden to cover the British withdrawal. It was during a refit between these operations that the *Eagle* was fitted to carry Buccaneers and had a waist catapult added.

SPECIFICATION	
HMS Eagle	**Aircraft:** 36-60 (see text)
Displacement: 44,100 tons standard and 45,100 tons full load	**Armament:** four twin 4.5-in (114-mm) DP guns, and six quadruple GWS.22 Seacat SAM launchers
Dimensions: length 247.4 m (811 ft 8½ in); beam 34.4 m (112 ft 11½ in); draught 11 m (36 ft); flight deck width 52.1 m (171 ft)	**Electronics:** one Type 984 3D radar, one Type 965 air search radar, one Type 963 CCA landing aid, one Type 974 navigation radar and one ESM system
Propulsion: four-shaft geared steam turbines delivering 113,346 kW (152,000 shp)	
Speed: 31.5 kts	**Complement:** 2,750

After a Far Eastern deployment in 1969, *Eagle* was chosen to perform Phantom trials for the Royal Navy, and in the following year embarked its first ASW helicopter squadron. The ship's

career was cut short in the early 1970s by the political decision that it would be too costly to convert *Eagle* to full-time Phantom operations (in fact, only minimal changes were required). *Eagle* paid off in January 1972 and effectively became the floating spares platform for the *Ark Royal*, finally being towed away for scrap in 1978. By the time the carrier was paid off, her air group had again been reduced, this time to 30 fixed- and six rotary-wing aircraft, these being Buccaneers, Sea Vixens, Gannet AEW.Mk 3s and Wessex helicopters.

Two Buccaneers overfly HMS Eagle on deployment in the late 1960s after the addition of a waist catapult. At this late stage of a 20-year career, the carrier's displacement had risen from 45,720 tons in 1951 to a maximum of 54,100 tons.

HMS *Hermes* Aircraft carrier and Commando carrier

The original post-war **HMS Hermes** was the sixth vessel of the 'Centaur' class, but in October 1945 she was cancelled and the name given to the *Elephant* of the same class. As very little work had been done on this hull, the vessel was able to benefit from a complete redesign and was thus commissioned in November 1959 with a 6.5° angled flight deck, a deck-edge aircraft lift as one of the two lifts fitted, and a 3D radar system.

In 1964–6, the new HMS *Hermes* was refitted with two quadruple Seacat SAM systems in place of her original AA armament of five twin 40-mm Bofors mountings, and access to the seaward side of the island was constructed. In 1971, in a further refit, the Type 984 3D radar was replaced by a Type 965 'bedstead' system.

Commando carrier

A comprehensive deck landing light system was fitted after the ship had been paid off for conversion to a commando assault carrier, as she could operate only a 28-aircraft group of Sea Vixen, Buccaneer and Gannet fixed-wing aircraft, but

not the modern Phantoms.

During this conversion, the *Hermes* also lost her arrester wires and catapult, and was converted to carry a complete Marine Commando unit with its associated squadron of Wessex assault helicopters. By 1977, the *Hermes* was again in refit to become an ASW carrier, though she retained the Commando-carrying ability and carried nine Sea King ASW and four Wessex HU.Mk 5 utility helicopters.

In 1980, the *Hermes* began her third major conversion to change her role yet again, this involving a strengthening of the flight deck and the provision of a 7.5° ski-jump ramp overhanging the bow to allow the operation of five Sea Harriers in place of the Wessex helicopters. In 1982, because of her more extensive communications fit and greater aircraft-carrying ability, the *Hermes* was made the flagship of the task force sent to recover the Falklands.

Falklands air wing

During this operation, *Hermes* initially operated an air group of 12 Sea Harriers, nine Sea King HAS.Mk 5s and nine Sea King HC.Mk 4s. However, as the

Below: **HMS** Hermes *with her goalkeeper, a* **Type 22** *frigate, steaming in heavy weather. The Type 22 provided the necessary close-in anti-aircraft and anti-missile defence with the Sea Wolf SAM system that the carrier lacked;* **Hermes** *was equipped with two Seacat launchers.*

Above: After losing its fixed-wing capability in the early 1970s, Hermes' *role was then altered to that of ASW carrier with a secondary* Commando *support role. In this incarnation, fixed-wing aircraft returned to the deck, now equipped with a 7.5° ski-jump ramp.*

The original 6.5° angled flight deck fitted to Hermes was the largest angle that could be contrived in an aircraft carrier of its size. The subsequent ski-jump ramp added during the ship's 1980 refit was accompanied by a strengthened flight deck to allow operations with the V/STOL Sea Harrier FRS.Mk 1.

campaign progressed, this was modified to 15 Sea Harriers, six Harrier GR.Mk 3s, five ASW Sea Kings and two Lynx helicopters (equipped for Exocet decoy operations).

Following her success in the Falklands and after a series of deployments in 1983, *Hermes* underwent a four-month refit, beginning in January 1984. After this, *Hermes* was used in a training ship capacity in harbour because she was considered

too labour-intensive and had not been converted to use the Royal Navy's Dieso fuel type.

Nuclear weapons

Like the 'Invincibles', the Cold War-era *Hermes* carried nuclear depth bombs for her helicopters, and tactical gravity bombs for the Sea Harriers. Based on comparisons with the American carriers, the number of nuclear weapons carried in these ships was probably

around 15, of which approximately 10 would be for ASW purposes. In 1986, *Hermes* was purchased by

India to become ***Viraat***, entering service with that nation's navy in May the following year.

SPECIFICATION	
HMS *Hermes*	nine Sea King ASW helicopters; maximum see text
Displacement: 23,900 tons standard; 28,700 tons full load	**Electronics:** one Type 965 air-search radar, one Type 993 surface-search radar, one Type 1006 navigation radar, two GWS 22 Seacat guidance systems, one TACAN system, one Type 184 sonar, several passive and active ECM systems, two Corvus chaff launchers
Dimensions: length 226.9 m (744 ft 4 in); beam 27.4 m (90 ft); draught 8.7 m (28 ft 6 in); flight deck width 48.8 m (160 ft)	
Machinery: two-shaft geared steam turbine delivering 56,675 kW (76,000 shp)	
Speed: 28 kts	
Armament: two quadruple Seacat SAM launchers (approximately 40 missiles carried)	**Complement:** 1,350 including air group (plus provision for a complete 750-man Marine Commando unit for which four LCVPs were carried)
Aircraft: normally five (later increased to six) Sea Harriers and	

USS *Enterprise* Nuclear-powered aircraft carrier

US studies for a nuclear-powered aircraft carrier date from 1949, when the 'Forrestal' class of carrier was under construction. A nuclear powerplant was earmarked for this class, but was shelved in favour of conventional engines. The attractions of nuclear powerplants were the promises of longer endurance, enormous range, less time in dock, and cleaner operations.

While the **USS *Enterprise*** (**CVAN-65**) was being developed, an argument was raging in defence circles over the future role of aircraft carriers

An F8U-1 Crusader, flown by Commander George C. Talley, made the first ever deck landing on the Enterprise's flight deck. The high approach speed of the Crusader made landings on the earlier 'Essex'-class carriers a significant problem.

in the US Navy. The Kennedy administration was sceptical, and US Defense Secretary McNamara was suspicious of the cost-effectiveness of a ship with a $451,000,000 price tag.

As a result, five further vessels in this class were cancelled.

Construction

The keel was laid down for the *Enterprise* in February 1958.

She was completed in November 1961, when she was commissioned. She entered service as the world's second nuclear-powered warship, being eclipsed by the cruiser USS

The Enterprise's *original boxlike island superstructure was designed to accommodate the SPS-32/33 radar system.*

SPECIFICATION	
USS *Enterprise* (CVAN-65)	(from 1967)
Displacement: 75,700 tons; 89,600 tons full load	**Aircraft:** Up to 85 aircraft; December 1973 air wing included two squadrons each of F-14A and A-7E, one squadron each of A-6A/B, RA-5C, E-2B and EA-6B and one SH-3D detachment
Dimensions: length 342.3 m (1,122 ft 9 in); beam 40.5 m (133 ft); draught 11.9 m (39 ft); flight deck width 76.8 m (252 ft)	
Machinery: four shaft, nuclear, Westinghouse A2W reactors, four geared turbines generating 208.88 MW (280,000 shp)	**Electronics:** SPS-32/33 fixed phased array radar system, including air-search radar, surface-search radar, navigation radar and fire control radar
Speed: 20 kts cruising speed; 35 kts top speed.	
Armament: three Mk 25 Sea Sparrow octuple launchers	**Complement:** 3,325 plus 1,891 air wing

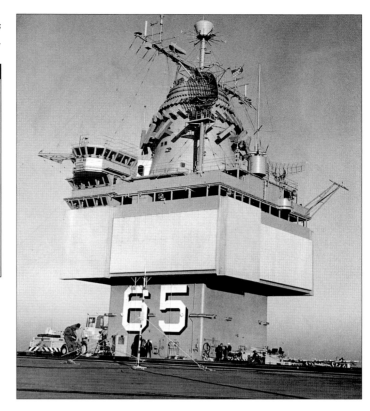

Long Beach, which was launched on 14 July 1959. *Enterprise* would later join the *Long Beach* in the *Enterprise* battlegroup, and two years later the carrier was helping to enforce the Cuban blockade.

In 1964, *Enterprise* began her involvement in the Vietnam War, which would eventually see her completing eight deployments, including helping in the evacuation of Saigon in 1975. In February 1969, she was badly damaged when a rocket explosion tore through the ship, killing 27 sailors and injuring 344. However, fully repaired, she was to become the first aircraft carrier to deploy F-14

Tomcat fighters in 1974.

Enterprise was the world's first 'supercarrier', and was fitted with a nuclear powerplant to give her an impressive top speed of 35 kts. Although the nuclear powerplant was big, it dispensed with the ship's exhaust equipment and fuel oil storage areas, affording valuable extra space, some of which was taken up by enlarged aviation fuel storage areas.

The nuclear powerplant had eight A2W reactors, which drove four geared steam turbines. Power output was rated at 208.88 MW (280,000 shp). Two months after launch, on 2 December 1960,

her reactors went critical. Over the next 11 months, all eight reactors would come on stream, feeding 32 heat exchangers. This gave the *Enterprise* a range of 400,000 nm (740,740 km; 460,230 miles) between refuellings, while operating at a speed of 20 kts. This allowed her to undertake a round-the-world voyage in 1964, with the USS *Long Beach* and USS *Bainbridge*, to demonstrate the capabilities of nuclear-powered marine propulsion. *Enterprise's* impressive performance gave ammunition to the advocates of marine nuclear propulsion, who noted that her performance would increase further as more advanced cores were installed in the reactors over time.

However, the self-sufficiency offered by a nuclear powerplant belied the reality that the ship's vast air wing of over 80 aircraft, and huge crew of over 5,500, required regular replenishment of munitions and food – even

Returning from deployment in Vietnam, Enterprise has an air wing that includes RA-5C Vigilantes, which were active on reconnaissance flights over Vietnam.

though these replenishments were still less frequent than those required for conventionally powered carriers.

The design of the *Enterprise* flight deck drew heavily on lessons learnt from the 'Forrestal' class, and bore a heavy resemblance to the latter. Three deck lifts were arranged on the starboard side of the hull, with a single lift on the port side. The below-deck hangarage of the carrier was also impressive, and a total of 96 aircraft could be carried by the vessel, although the air wing usually comprised 86 aircraft.

Enterprise also featured an unusual island superstructure, notable for its boxlike appearance, and a dome-shaped top. The island featured several sensors and radar, including the SPS-32/33 flat-panelled phased array radar system, which gave the island its slab appearance. The only other ship to be fitted with this system was the nuclear-powered cruiser USS *Long Beach*. However, the system was difficult to maintain and gave a disappointing performance, and was finally removed from *Enterprise* during a major refit in 1980.

'Midway' class

Because of their smaller size, the two 'Midways' had to operate with reduced air groups, which contained no ASW aircraft or helicopters and used the F-4 Phantom II as their main interceptor.

Originally to have numbered six units, the **'Midway' class** suffered the cancellation of three units but entered the post-war years as the only American carriers capable of operating the new generation of heavy attack aircraft without modification.

This meant they were could operate the post-war generation of heavy nuclear-armed attack aircraft. However, it was soon found that a refit was needed in the middle to late 1950s to accommodate all recent carrier innovations.

SPECIFICATION

Midway and Coral Sea
Displacement: *Midway* 51,000 tons standard, 64,000 tons full load; *Coral Sea* 52,500 tons standard, 63,800 tons full load
Dimensions: length 298.4 m (979 ft); beam 36.9 m (121 ft); draught 10.8 m (35 ft 4 in); flight deck width 72.5 m (238 ft)
Machinery: four shaft geared steam turbines delivering 158,090 kW (212,000 shp)
Speed: 30.6 kts
Aircraft: see text
Armament: two octuple Sea Sparrow SAM launchers (no reloads) in *Midway* only, three 20-mm Phalanx CIWS in both
Electronics: (*Midway*) LN-66 navigation radar, SPS-65V air/

surface search radar, SPS-43C air search radar, SPS-49 air search radar, SPS-48C 3D radar, one SPN-035A, two SPN-42 and one SPN-44 aircraft landing aids, two Mk 115 fire-control radars, URN-29 TACAN system, SLQ-29 ESM suite, four Mk 36 SRBOC chaff launchers
Electronics: (*Coral Sea*) one LN-66 navigation radar, one SPS-10 surface search and navigation radar, one SPS-43C air search radar, one SPS-30 air search radar, one SPN-43A aircraft landing aid, one URN-20 TACAN system, one SLQ-29 ESM suite, four Mk 36 SRBOC chaff launchers
Complement: *Midway* 2,615 plus 1,800 air group; *Coral Sea* 2,710 plus 1,800 air group

Above: A stern view of **Midway**, *considered to be the more capable of the two 'Midway'-class vessels that remained in service into the 1980s.*

Left: A US carrier battle group in the Indian Ocean centred on **USS Midway**, *also showing USS* **Bainbridge**, *a missile cruiser and the oiler* **Navasota**.

Modifications

All three eventually underwent modernization programmes which, because they occurred over a long time span, differed considerably in detail. The **USS Midway** (commissioned in September 1945) and **USS Franklin D. Roosevelt** (commissioned in October 1945) were rebuilt under the SCB-110 programme with two steam catapults, the angled flight deck of the SCB-27Cs and a 'hurricane bow', whilst the

last unit, the **USS Coral Sea** (commissioned in October 1947), received the SCB-110A modification, a more extensive refit that included the fitting of a third steam catapult in the waist position.

By the mid-1960s, it was thought necessary for the three vessels to undergo yet another rebuild, and the *Midway* was taken in hand in the latter part of the decade for an SCB-101.66 refit to allow for accommodation of the latest

Above: VF-211 F8U-1 Crusaders overfly Midway in the late 1950s. Arranged on the carrier's deck are A3D Skywarriors, a single AD Skyraider, FJ-4 Furys and a HUP Retriever plane guard helicopter on the forward deck landing spot.

Right: Most thoroughly modernized of the class, USS Midway would have remained a deployable carrier until the turn of the century but was retired in April 1992. In its active life of over 55 years, it may be true to say that Midway experienced a more dramatic enhancement of its capability than any ship in history.

generation of carrier aircraft. However, the final cost proved so great that the *Franklin D. Roosevelt* ended with only an austere version of SCB-101.66 in 1968, whilst the *Coral Sea*, having had the SCB-110A improvement, was deemed sufficiently modern to remain in service unaltered.

First retirement

As the vessel in the worst material condition, the *Franklin D. Roosevelt* was stricken in 1977 and broken up. After being struck off, the vessel's name was assigned to a new 'Nimitz'-

class carrier. All three served off Vietnam during the war there. Under the SCB-110/110A refits, provision was made for 1,376 tons of ordnance, 134,760 litres (35,600 US gal) of AVGAS and 2,271,240 litres (600,000 US gal) of JP5 aircraft fuel.

During the 1980s, only the *Midway* and *Coral Sea* remained in service, the former attached to the Pacific Fleet and homeported in Yokosuka, Japan, the latter serving as a front-line carrier on the strength of the Atlantic Fleet with reduced air groups from carriers that were in refit.

Reduced air wing

Because of their smaller size the 'Midway' class carried the F-4N/S Phantom II in place of the F-14A Tomcat, and did not embark the S-3A Viking. Both carriers were fitted with three deck-edge aircraft elevators, but while the *Midway* had only two steam catapults the *Coral Sea* had three. In their later years, a

total of 1,210 tons of aviation ordnance and 4.49 million litres (1.186 million US gal) of JP5 aircraft fuel was carried for the air wing on each ship. The *Midway* was the more capable on account of its refit in 1966, but both ships were phased out by the late 1980s, the *Coral Sea* in 1990 and the *Midway* two years later.

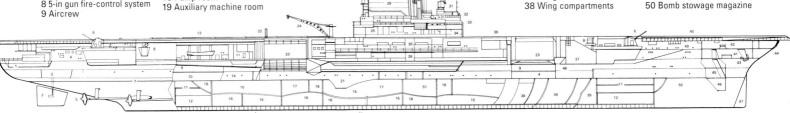

USS *Coral Sea*, 1960s

1 CPO area
2 Balanced rudder
3 Steering compartment
4 Aviation spares/repair shops
5 Screw
6 5-in (127-m) dual-purpose gun
7 Waterline
8 5-in gun fire-control system
9 Aircrew
10 Stores
11 Ammunition
12 Aviation spirit
13 Mk 7 arrester wire system
14 Crew area
15 Engine room
16 Boiler room
17 Ship's service turbo generator
18 Pump room
19 Auxiliary machine room
20 Double bottom
21 Former position of armour belt
22 Frensel deck landing mirror
23 53-ton deck edge lift
24 Aircraft crane
25 Bridge
26 Gallery platform
27 Mast
28 Funnel
29 SPS-43 radar
30 SPS-30 radar
31 Air defence position
32 Navigation bridge
33 Flag bridge
34 Control centre
35 Ventilators
36 Flying deck
37 Hangar
38 Wing compartments
39 Fuel tanks
40 Type C11 catapult
41 Hawser pipe
42 Capstan
43 Anchor
44 Mooring ring
45 Hawser reel
46 Chain locker
47 Forefoot
48 Officer's quarters
49 Walkway
50 Bomb stowage magazine

'Agosta' class Patrol submarine

SPECIFICATION	
'Agosta A90' class	with 533-mm (21-in) liners for 23 550-mm (21.7-in) or 533-mm (21-in) anti-submarine and anti-ship torpedoes, or 46 influence ground mines; provision for SM.39 Exocet or UGM-84 Sub-Harpoon underwater-launched anti-ship missiles on French and Pakistani units, respectively
Displacement: 1,480 tons surfaced; 1,760 tons dived	
Dimensions: length 67.6 m (221 ft 9 in); beam 6.8 m (22 ft 4 in); draught 5.4 m (17 ft 9 in)	
Propulsion: two SEMT-Pielstick diesels delivering 2,685 kW (3,600 shp) and one electric motor delivering 2,200 kW (2,950 shp) to one shaft	
	Electronics: one DRUA 23 surface search radar, one DUUA 2A sonar, one DUUA 1D sonar, one DUUX 2A sonar, one DSUV 2H sonar, one ARUR ESM system, one ARUD ESM system, and one torpedo fire-control/action information system
Speed: 12.5 kts surfaced and 20.5 kts dived	
Diving depth: 300 m (985 ft) operational and 500 m (1,640 ft) maximum	
Torpedo tubes: four 550-mm (21.7-in)	**Complement:** 54

Now decommissioned, the 'Agosta'-class submarines provided the French navy with a very useful capability for anti-ship operations in shallower waters. The last active French vessel in the class, Ouessant, was decommissioned in 2001.

Designed by the French Directorate of Naval Construction as quiet but high-performance submarines for operations in the Mediterranean, the boats of the **'Agosta A90' class** are each armed with four bow torpedo tubes equipped with a pneumatically rammed

rapid-reload system that can launch weapons with the minimum of noise signature. The tubes were of a new design that allows the submarine to fire its weapons at all speeds and at any depth down to its maximum operational limit. The four boats in service with the French navy

as its last conventionally powered submarines up to their decommissioning early in the 21st century were the **Agosta**, **Bévéziers**, **La Praya** and **Ouessant**. All were authorized in the 1970–75 naval programme as the follow-on class to the 'Daphné'-class coastal submarines. *La Praya* was refitted with a removable swimmer delivery vehicle container aft of the sail to replace similar facilities that had been available aboard the *Narval*, lead boat of an obsolete class of six ocean-going submarines deleted during the 1980s.

The Spanish navy received four locally built 'Agosta'-class boats during the early 1980s, namely the **Galerna**, **Siroco**, **Mistral** and **Tramontana**, which

used French electronics as well as French armament in the form of the L5, F17 and E18 torpedoes.

In mid-1978 Pakistan purchased two units (built originally for South Africa but embargoed before delivery) as the **Hashmat** and **Hurmat**, and in 1994 Pakistan ordered three more boats of the improved 'Agosta A90B' class with a number of improved features.

During the 1980s, the French boats were revised with the capability to fire the SM.39 underwater-launched variant of the Exocet anti-ship missile, whereas Pakistan looked to the other side of the Atlantic and sought to procure the UGM-84 submarine-launched version of the US Harpoon anti-ship missile.

The Agosta was the lead ship of the last class of conventionally powered submarines built for the French navy. Later in their careers, all were retrofitted to fire the SM.39 Exocet underwater-launched anti-ship missile.

'Daphné' class Patrol submarine

In 1952 plans were requested from STCAN for a second-class ocean-going submarine to complement the larger 'Narval' class. Designated the **'Daphné' class**, the boats were designed with reduced speed to achieve a greater diving depth and heavier armament than was possible

with the 'Aréthuse' design of conventionally powered hunter-killer submarines. To reduce the crew's workload, the main armament was contained in 12 externally mounted torpedo tubes (eight forward and four aft), which eliminated the need for a torpedo room and reloads.

Further crew reductions were made possible by adopting a modular replacement system for onboard maintenance. The design was based on the double-hull construction technique with the accommodation spaces split evenly fore and aft of the sail, below which was the operations

and attack centre. A total of 11 units was built for the French navy. The **Daphné**, **Diane**, **Doris**, **Eurydicé**, **Flore**, **Galatée**, **Minerve**, **Junon**, **Vénus**, **Psyché** and **Sirène** entered service between 1964 and 1970. Of these two were lost with all hands (the *Minerve* in 1968 and

Once they had reached the ends of their lives and also become obsolete, the 'Daphné'-class submarines were not replaced, as the French navy had decided to concentrate on building only nuclear attack submarines for the future. However, the class remains in service with Pakistan (four boats), Portugal (two), South Africa (two) and Spain (four).

SPECIFICATION	
'Daphné' class	operational and 575 m (1,885 ft) maximum
Displacement: 869 tons surfaced; 1,043 tons dived	**Torpedo tubes:** 12 550-mm (21.7-in) tubes (eight bow and four stern) for 12 anti-ship and anti-submarine torpedoes, or influence ground mines
Dimensions: length 57.8 m (189 ft 8 in); 6.8 m (22 ft 4 in); draught 4.6 m (15 ft 1 in)	
Propulsion: two SEMT-Pielstick diesel generator sets and two electric motors delivering 1,940 kW (2,600 shp) to two shafts	**Electronics:** one Calypso II surface search radar, one DUUX 2 sonar, one DSUV 2 sonar, DUUA 1 and 2 sonars, and one torpedo fire-control/action information system
Speed: 13.5 kts surfaced; 16 kts dived	
Diving depth: 300 m (985 ft)	**Complement:** 54

the *Eurydicé* in 1970) while operating in the western Mediterranean. The remaining boats all underwent an electronics and weapons modernization from 1970 onwards, but have now all been retired. Another 10 were built for export, Portugal receiving the **Albacore**, **Barracuda**, **Cachalote** and **Delfim**, of which *Cachalote* was sold to Pakistan in 1975 as the **Ghazi**. The *Albacore* and

Delfim remained in service in 2003. Pakistan also has the **Hangor**, **Shushuk** and **Mangro**, armed with Sub-Harpoon. Ordered in 1967, South Africa took delivery of the **Maria Van Riebeeck**, **Emily Hobhouse** and **Johanna Van der Merwe**, of which two remained in service in 2003, renamed as the **Umkhonto** and **Assegaai**. These received a weapons system upgrade (including sonar) and

features to improve habitability in 1988–90. A further four, the **Delfín**, **Tonina**, **Marsopa** and **Narval** were built under licence in Spain and were later updated similar to that which was applied to the French boats between

1971–81. In 1971 the Pakistani submarine *Hangor* sank the Indian navy's frigate *Khukri* during the Indo-Pakistan war of that year: this was the first submarine attack since the end of World War II.

'Type 206' and 'Type 209' classes Patrol/ocean-going submarines

In 1962 IKL began studies for a development of its 'Type 205' design. This new **'Type 206'** class, built of high-tensile non-magnetic steel, was to be used for coastal operations and had to conform with treaty limitations on the maximum tonnage allowed to West Germany. New safety devices for the crew were fitted, and the armament fit allowed for the carriage of wire-guided torpedoes. After final design approval had been given, construction planning took place in 1966–68, and the first orders (for an eventual total of 18 units)

*The basic design of the 'Type 206' class is so versatile that customers can opt for different lengths and displacements and an assortment of electronic and armament fits. This is the German navy's **U-24**.*

were placed in the following year. By 1975 all the boats, **U-13** to **U-30** were in service. Since then the class has been given extra armament in the form of two external GRP containers to carry

24 ground mines in addition to their normal torpedo armament. From 1988 onwards, 12 of the class were modernized with new electronics and torpedoes to form the **'Type 206A' class**. In

2003, 12 examples remained in German service.

In the mid-1960s, IKL also designed for the export market a new boat that became the **'Type 209' class** in 1967. Designed

The Peruvian navy took delivery of a total of six 'Type 209/1200' boats in three batches between 1975-83. The Angamos (formerly Casma), SS 31, can carry a total of 14 American NT-37C dual anti-ship and anti-submarine torpedoes as its main armament in preference to the German weapons normally sold with the vessels.

specifically for the ocean-going role, the 'Type 209' can, because of its relatively short length, operate successfully in coastal waters. The 'Type 209' and its variants have proved so popular that 50 have been built or ordered by 12 export customers.

Principal variants

The six main variants of the 'Type 209' are the original **54.3-m 'Type 209/1100'** (178 ft 1 in long, 960 tons surfaced and 1,105 tons dived); **56-m 'Type 209/1200'** (183 ft 9 in long, 980 tons surfaced and 1,185 tons dived); **59.5-m 'Type 209/1300'** 195 ft 2 in long, 1,000 tons surfaced and 1,285 tons dived); **62-m 'Type 209/1400'** (203 ft 5 in long, 1,454 tons surfaced and 1,586 tons dived); **64.4-m 'Type 209/1500'** (211 ft 4 in long, 1,660 tons surfaced and 1,850 tons dived); and the smaller coastal **45-m 'Type 640'** (147 ft 7 in long, 420 tons surfaced and 600 tons dived).

The countries that have bought these vessels are Greece (four 'Type 209/1100' and four 'Type 209/1200'), Argentina (two 'Type 209/1200'), Peru (six 'Type 209/1200'), Colombia (two 'Type 209/1200'), South Korea (nine 'Type 209/1200'), Turkey (six 'Type 209/1200' and eight 'Type 209/1400', most of which have been built locally with German help), Venezuela (two 'Type 209/1300'), Chile (two 'Type 209/1400'), Ecuador (two 'Type 209/1300'), Indonesia (two 'Type 209/1300' plus a further four projected but unlikely to be realized), Brazil (five 'Type 209/1400'), India (four 'Type 209/1500' plus two more projected), South Africa (three 'Type 209/1400') and Israel (three 'Type 640'). Each chose its own equipment fit and crew number according to economic requirements.

During the 1982 Falklands War, the Argentine navy's 'Type 209/1200'-class submarine **San Luis** made three unsuccessful torpedo attacks on vessels of the British task force, but the knowledge of the boat's presence tied up considerable British ship and aircraft resources in efforts to find the submarine.

SPECIFICATION	
'Type 209/1200' class	operational and 500 m (1,640 ft) maximum
Displacement: 1,185 tons surfaced and 1,290 tons dived	
Dimensions: length 56 m (183 ft 9 in); beam 6.2 m (20 ft 4 in); draught 5.5 m (18 ft ½ in)	**Torpedo tubes:** eight 533-mm (210-in) tubes (all bow) for 14 (typically) AEG SST Mod 4 or AEG SUT anti-ship and anti-submarine torpedoes
Propulsion: four MTU-Siemens diesel generators delivering 3730 kW (5,000 shp) and one Siemens electric motor delivering 2685 kW (3,600 shp) to one shaft	**Electronics:** one Calypso surface search radar, one CSU 3 sonar, one DUUX 2C or PRS 3 sonar, one ESM system, and one Sepa Mk 3 or Sinbad M8/24 torpedo fire-control and action information system
Speed: 11 kts surfaced and 21.5 kts dived	
Diving depth: 300 m (985 ft)	**Complement:** 31–35

Above: The multiplicity of sensor and snorting masts rising from the sails of the 'Type 209' is notable. This is Tupi, a 'Type 209 Type 1400' of the Brazilian navy.

The smallest of the 'Type 209' series variants is the 'Type 640'. Israel ordered three from Vickers of the UK, all being commissioned in 1977.

'Ming' class (Type 035) Patrol submarine

Forming the main strength of the Chinese navy's conventionally powered submarine arm, with up to 23 units completed into the early 2000s, the **'Ming' class** or **Type 035 ('ES5' class** for export) diesel-electric submarine is a development of the Soviet 'Romeo'-class submarine designed in the 1950s. The type is now obsolete by Western standards, but retains a vestigial capability for the patrol and coastal defence roles, and was a relatively inexpensive replacement for China's ageing force of Type 033 ('Romeo'-class)

submarines. Some 13 of the boats are allocated to the North Sea Fleet, based at Lushun, Qingdao and Xiapingdao, while the others are allocated to the South Sea Fleet.

After building the Type 033 boats in the 1960s and then undertaking improvements to the class, the Chinese decided in 1967 to develop an improved submarine, although still based on the Soviet original. The task was allocated to the 701 Shipbuilding Institute at Wuhan, and the Wuhan Shipyard was selected to build the boats of the new class. The aim was a

boat offering higher submerged speed and longer range than the 'Romeo' and Type 033 submarines, and the first of the class was laid down in October 1969, launched in July 1971 and commissioned in April 1974.

The first two or three boats, the last completed in 1979, were **'ES5C/D'-class** three-shaft prototypes that were scrapped in the late 1980s. The full production standard then appeared in the **'ES5E' class**, which introduced a number of changes and was produced at the rate of some two boats per year from 1988 to 1995, when the North Sea fleet had 12 such boats in service.

Production resumed

It was planned at this stage to follow the Type 035 with the Type 039 ('Song' class) as the Chinese navy's new diesel-electric submarine, but delays in the programme for the newer boat meant that construction of the Type 035 was resumed in 1997, these later units being

allocated to the South Sea Fleet. These late-production boats were completed to the **Type 035G** standard, which may have been offered for export as the **'ES5F' class**. This standard introduced a number of enhancements suggested by operational experience with the older boats, and introduced the French DUUX 5 passive ranging and intercept sonar, an improved fire-control system, an upgraded command system providing the data required for more effective handling and torpedo launching, and black anechoic tiling on the outside of their hulls to reduced underwater noise and therefore detectability.

One of the Type 035G boats is believed to have a hull 2 m (6 ft 7 in) longer than the other members of the class, but the significance of this change has not been revealed.

It is worth noting that while some sources claim two-shaft propulsion for the 'Ming' class, others state that a single-shaft arrangement is used.

SPECIFICATION	
'Ming' class	**Diving depth:** 300 m (985 ft) operational
Displacement: 1,584 tons surfaced; 2,113 tons dived	**Torpedo tubes:** eight 533-mm (21-in) tubes (six bow and two stern) for 18 Yu-4 (SAET-60) passive-homing and Yu-1 (Type 53-51) torpedoes, or for 32 mines
Dimensions: length 76 m (249 ft 4 in); beam 7.6 m (25 ft); draught 5.1 m (16 ft 9 in)	
Propulsion: two Shaanxi 6E 390 ZC1 diesels delivering 3,880 kW (5,205 hp) and two electric motors powering two shafts	**Electronics:** one 'Snoop Tray' surface search and navigation radar, one 'Pike Jaw' active/passive hull sonar, and one DUUX 5 passive ranging and intercept sonar
Performance: speed 15 kts surfaced and 18 kts dived; endurance 14825 km (9,210 miles) at 8 kts snorting	**Complement:** 57

'Tumleren' class (Type 207) Attack submarine

In 1959 the Norwegian defence ministry ordered from Rheinstahl–Nordseewerke of Emden a class of 15 **Type 207** coastal submarines based on the

West German navy's Type 205 class, but with a stronger hull for deeper-diving capability and, partially reflecting US funding for 50 per cent of the cost, revised

equipment, including the Mk 37 wire-guided torpedo. These 'Kobben'-class boats entered service in 1964–67. Norway also borrowed a German boat for

The cylindrical fairing above the bow of the 'Tumleren'-class coastal attack submarine carries the passive search and attack sonar.

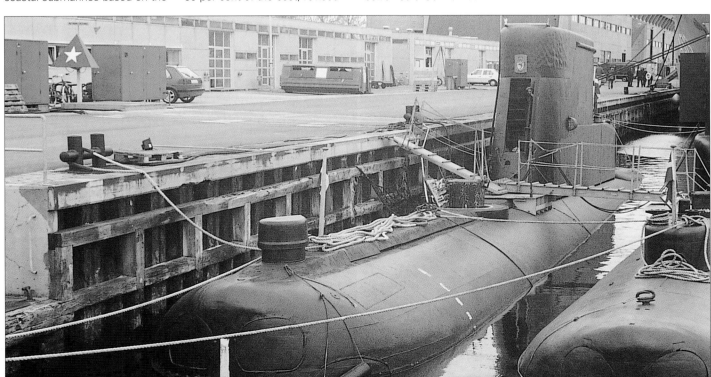

training, and had one of her own submarines modified for officer training with its hull lengthened by 1 m (3 ft 3 in) and a second periscope added.

Six boats were upgraded in 1989–1991 with more modern electronics and new fire-control equipment. Over the same period, three of the class were recommissioned into Danish service as replacements for the four 'Delfinen'-class boats. Bought under a 1986 contract, the boats were the *Utvaer*, *Uthaug* and *Stadt*. The last was badly damaged when it ran aground in 1987, however, and was scrapped and replaced in the Danish contract by the *Stadt*.

In Danish service the three boats became the **Tumleren**, **Saelen** and **Springeren** of the 'Tumleren' class. Before being recommissioned into the Danish navy in October 1989, October 1990 and October 1991 respectively, the boats were upgraded at the same Norwegian yard, the Urivale

Shipyard in Bergen. The process was centred on the structural lengthening of the hull by 1.6 m (5 ft 3 in), increasing the displacement from the Norwegian figures of 370 tons standard and 530 tons full load.

During December 1990, while under unmanned tow in the Kattegat, the *Saelen* sank, but was recovered and had her refurbishment and upgrade completed with spares taken from the ex-Norwegian *Kaura*. The latter was handed over to Denmark in October 1991 and cannibalized, allowing the *Saelen* to re-enter Danish service in August 1993.

As part of their reconditioning before they entered Danish service, the three boats also received a complete overhaul of their propulsion systems, and in electronic terms were upgraded with new and more capable fire-control, ESM, navigation and communications equipment. Further improvement came in 1992–93, when the new Atlas

The **Tumleren** *is caught by the camera as it surfaces. The three boats of the 'Tumleren' class will probably remain in service until replaced by new construction, possibly with the design being considered by Denmark, Norway and Sweden in the Viking programme.*

PSU NU passive search and attack sonar was installed in place of the original equipment. Another modification, which at first sight might seem strange in a Danish submarine, was the 1990 installation in the *Saelen* of an air conditioning and battery cooling system, but this reflected the commitment of the Danish navy to provide one submarine

for NATO operations in the Mediterranean.

In Danish service, the boats are optimized for the attack rather than patrol task, and in this role their primary target-acquisition sensors are the sonar and the Pilkington Optronics CK 34 search periscope. Targets are then engaged with the Swedish FFV Tp 513 anti-ship torpedo.

SPECIFICATION

'Tumleren' class
Displacement: 459 tons surfaced; 524 tons dived
Dimensions: length 47.4 m (155 ft 6 in); beam 4.6 m (15 ft 1 in); draught 4.3 m (14 ft 1 in)
Propulsion: two MTU 12V493 AZ80 diesels delivering 900 kW (1.210 hp) and one electric motor delivering 1,270 kW (1,705 hp) to one shaft
Performance: speed 12 kts surfaced and 18 kts dived; endurance 9,250

km (5,750 miles) at 8 kts snorting
Diving depth: 200 m (655 ft) operational
Torpedo tubes: eight 533-mm (21-in) tubes (all bow) for eight Tp 613 wire-guided passive-homing torpedoes
Electronics: one Furuno 805 surface search radar, one PSU NU passive search and attack sonar, one Tactic fire-control system, and one Sea Lion ESM system
Complement: 24

This is capable of delivering its 240-kg (529-lb) HE warhead to a maximum range of 25 km (15.5 miles) at a speed of 30 kts, though use over shorter distances allows the torpedo to exploit its 45-kt maximum speed. The Tp 513 is wire guided, and its own seeker is of the passive acoustic-homing type.

A distinctive feature of the 'Tumleren'-class submarine is the sail, which has an angled-back front and side fairings for the rearward extension.

'Narhvalen' class Attack submarine

Needing a coastal attack submarine to supplement and complement its indigenously designed 'Delfinen' class, of which four examples (the last funded by the US) had been commissioned in 1958–64, Denmark secured from the West German submarine design house IKL a licence to manufacture an improved version of the Type 205 submarine already in service with the West German navy. Modified to an extent to ensure that it satisfied Denmark's particular requirements, the design was used by the Royal Dockyard in Copenhagen for the construction of the two **'Narhvalen'-class** boats. Named **Narhvalen** and **Nordkaperen**, these were laid down in 1965–66, launched in 1968–69, and were commissioned in

February and December 1970 respectively.

Propulsion systems

In their early form, the boats were powered by two diesels and one electric motor, each half of the diesel-electric propulsion arrangement delivering some 11,125 kW (1,510 hp) for surfaced and submerged speeds of 12 and 17 kts respectively. They had active and passive sonar, and a complement of 22. With Denmark's 1986 purchase of three 'Kobben'-class coastal submarines that had become surplus to the requirements of the Norwegian navy, the decision was made to upgrade the two 'Narhvalen'-class boats to a comparable standard. Work on the Narhvalen began in late 1993 and was completed in February 1995; the same

Now decommissioned, the 'Narhvalen'-class submarines gave the Danish Navy long and useful service, latterly to a virtual 'Tumleren'-class standard.

programme was implemented on the Nordkaperen between the middle of 1995 and the middle of 1998. The work included a propulsion system overhaul, new periscopes, an optronic mast from the French company Sagem, an upgraded ESM system from the British

company Racal, general improvements to the radar, and a modern sonar system from the German company Atlas.

The two boats were relegated to a secondary role after the 2000 arrival of the Kronborg (ex-Swedish Näcken), and were finally decommissioned in 2002.

SPECIFICATION	
'Narhvalen' class	**Diving depth:** 200 m (655 ft) operational
Displacement: 420 tons surfaced; 450 tons dived	**Torpedo tubes:** eight 533-mm (21-in) tubes (all bow) for eight Tp 613
Dimensions: length 44 m (144 ft); beam 4.55 m (14 ft 9 in); draught 3.98 m (13 ft 9 in)	wire-guided passive-homing torpedoes
Propulsion: two MTU 12V493 TY7 diesels delivering 1,680 kW (2,250 hp) and one electric motor delivering 895 kW (1,200 hp)	**Electronics:** one Furuno 805 surface search radar, one PSU NU passive search and attack sonar, one Tactic fire-control system, and one Sea Lion ESM system
Performance: speed 12 kts surfaced and 17 kts dived	**Complement:** 24

'Enrico Toti' class Patrol submarine

The 'Enrico Toti' class was designed specifically for the shallow water areas found around the Italian coastline. Armed with four bow torpedo tubes for the wire-guided A184 heavyweight torpedo, the four vessels had a submerged dash speed of 20 kts, but could sustain 15 kts for one hour.

As the first indigenously built Italian submarine design since World War II, the **'Enrico Toti' class** had a chequered start: the plans had to be recast several times from their origins during the mid-1950s in an American-sponsored NATO project for a small anti-submarine boat. Stricken or decommissioned between 1991 and 1993, the four units were the *Attilio Bagnolini*, *Enrico Toti*, *Enrico Dandolo* and *Lazzaro Mocenigo*, which entered

service in 1968–69 for use in the notoriously difficult ASW conditions encountered in the central and eastern regions of the Mediterranean. For these operations, the boats' relatively small size and minimum sonar cross section stood them in good stead. The main armament was originally four Kanguru anti-submarine and four anti-ship torpedoes, but then revised to six examples of the 533-mm (21-in) Whitehead Motofides A184 wire-guided dual-role anti-

submarine and anti-ship weapon with active/passive acoustic homing that features enhanced ECCM to counter decoys launched or towed by a target. With a launch weight of 1300 kg (2,866 lb), a large HE warhead

and a range of some 20 km (12.4 miles), the electrically powered A184 would have been used by the 'Enrico Totis' at natural 'chokepoints' to attack much larger opponents such as Soviet SSNs or SSGNs.

*Third of the 'Enrico Toti'-class boats was the **Enrico Dandolo**, which shows off the characteristic IPD 64 active sonar system housing on the bow in this view. The crew for the relatively small boats of this class was four officers and 22 other ranks.*

SPECIFICATION	
'Enrico Toti' class	**Diving depth:** 180 m (591 ft)
Displacement: 535 tons surfaced; 591 tons dived	operational and 300 m (984 ft) maximum
Dimensions: length 46.2 m (151 ft 8 in); beam 4.7 m (15 ft 5 in); draught 4 m (13 ft 1 in)	**Torpedo tubes:** four 533-mm (21-in) tubes (all bow) for six A184 torpedoes, or 12 ground influence mines
Propulsion: two diesels and one electric motor delivering 1,641 kW (2,200 shp) to one shaft	**Electronics:** one 3RM 20/SMG surface search radar, one IPD 64 sonar, one MD 64 sonar, torpedo fire-control and action information
Performance: speed 14 kts surfaced and 15 kts dived; range 5,550 km (3,450 miles) at 5 kts surfaced	system, and ESM system **Complement:** 26

'Sauro' class Patrol submarine

During the early 1970s, it became clear to the Italian navy that a new submarine type was required for defence against amphibious landings and for ASW and anti-shipping tasks in the local area.

The result was the Italcantieri design for the **'Sauro' class**, whose first two units were the **Nazario Sauro** and **Carlo Fecia**

Fincantieri as the **Salvatore Pelosi**, **Giuliano Prini**, **Primo Longobardo** and **Gianfranco Gazzana Priaroggia**.

The first pair have displacements of 1,476 tons surfaced and 1,662 tons dived with a length of 64.4 m (211 ft 3 in), and the second pair have displacements of 1,653 tons surfaced and 1,862 tons dived

Above: The boats of the 'Sauro' class are welded from HY-80, a US-developed high-tensile steel, and thus possess a usefully greater diving depth than the earlier 'Totis'. Nazario Sauro decommissioned in 2001.

Left: Salvatore Pelosi is one of the sub-class of four 'Improved Sauros'. A Harpoon or Exocet capability may be added to the last two of these vessels. The current armament options are limited to the 12 Whitehead A184 torpedoes normally carried for the boats' six 533-mm (21-in) bow tubes. Alternatively, mines can be stowed.

di Cossato, which entered service in 1980 and 1979 respectively, following major problems with their batteries. A further two units, the **Leonardo da Vinci** and the **Guglielmo Marconi**, were then for commissioning in 1981 and 1982. The class has a single pressure hull with external ballast tanks at the bow and stern, and a buoyancy tank in the sail. The pressure hull is made from the US-developed HY-80 steel, which provides a deeper diving depth than was possible with the preceding 'Enrico Toti'-class boats. The main armament is the A184 wire-guided dual-role torpedo.

The *Sauro* and *Marconi* were deleted in 2001 and 2002 respectively. In March 1983 and July 1988, two additional pairs of boats were ordered to the **'Improved Sauro' class** design, and these were delivered in 1988–89 and 1994–95 by

Above: Leonardo da Vinci was modernized in 1993 to receive new batteries of greater capacity, and improved habitability. Fecia di Cossato was similarly upgraded in 1990.

with a length of 66.4 m (217 ft 10 in). Uprated machinery provides surfaced and dived speeds of 11 and 19 kts respectively.

SPECIFICATION	
'Sauro' class	and 465 km (290 miles) at 4 kts
Displacement: 1,456 tons surfaced;	dived
1,631 tons dived	**Diving depth:** 250 m (820 ft)
Dimensions: length 63.9 m (209 ft	operational and 410 m (1,345 ft)
8 in); beam 6.8 m (22 ft 4 in);	maximum
draught 5.7 m (18 ft 8 in)	**Torpedo tubes:** six 533-mm (21-in)
Propulsion: three diesel engines	tubes (all bow) for 12 A184
delivering 2,395 kW (3,210 shp)	torpedoes or 24 ground mines
and one electric motor delivering	**Electronics:** BPS 704 surface search
2,720 kW (3,650 shp) to one shaft	radar, IPD 70 and Thomson
Performance: speed 12 kts surfaced	sonars, fire-control and action
and 20 kts dived; range 20,385 km	information system, and ESM
(12,665 miles) at 11 kts surfaced	**Complement:** 45

'Zwaardvis' & 'Walrus' classes
Patrol submarines

Ordered in the late 1970s, the two 'Walrus'-class submarines are much improved versions of the 'Zwaardvis' design with more modern electronics, greater automation and therefore a smaller crew.

Based on the US Navy's teardrop-hulled 'Barbel' class of conventional submarine, the Dutch **Zwaardvis** and **Tijgerhaai** of the **'Zwaardvis' class** were ordered in the mid-1960s. Because of the requirement to use indigenous Dutch equipment wherever possible, the design was modified to include the placement of all noise-producing machinery on a false deck with spring suspension for silent running. The two submarines entered service with the Dutch navy in 1972 and were decommissioned in 1994–95. A buyer is still sought for the boats.

At the same time, the need arose for the design of a new class to replace the boats of the elderly 'Dolfijn' and 'Potvis' classes. The new design evolved as the **'Walrus' class**, which was based on the hull form of the 'Zwaardvis' with similar dimensions and silhouette but with more automation allowing

a significant reduction in the number of crew needed, more modern electronics, X-layout control surfaces and fabrication in the French MAREI high-tensile steel, allowing a 50 per cent increase in the maximum diving depth.

The first unit, the **Walrus**, was laid down in 1979 in

Rotterdam (where all the boats were built) for commissioning in 1986 and the **Zeeleeuw** a year

later for service entry in 1987. A further two, the **Dolfijn** and **Bruinvis**, were laid down in 1986 and 1988 for commissioning in 1993 and 1994.

Above: Although fitted for the Sub-Harpoon SSM, the 'Walrus' class does not carry these weapons. The lead ship of the class is illustrated.

Left: For their time the 'Zwaardvis' class of conventionally powered submarines were capable boats well suited to the demands of the Dutch navy for littoral defence. Both vessels underwent an upgrade in 1988–90.

In 1987–88 Taiwan received two **'Improved Zwaardvis'** or **'Hai Lung'-class** units **Hai Lung** and **Hai Hu**. The Tawainese navy intends these to carry Hsiung Feng II SSMs.

SPECIFICATION

'Walrus' class
Displacement: 2,390 tons surfaced; 2,740 tons dived
Dimensions: length 67.7 m (222 ft 1 in); beam 8.4 m (27 ft 7 in); draught 6.6 m (21 ft 8 in)
Propulsion: three diesel engines delivering 4,700 kW (6,300 shp) and one electric motor delivering 5,150 kW (6,910 shp) to one shaft
Performance: speed 13 kts surfaced and 20 kts dived; range 18,500 km (11,495 miles) at 9 kts snorting
Diving depth: 450 m (1,476 ft) operational and 620 m (2,034 ft) maximum
Torpedo tubes: four 533-mm (21-in)

tubes (all bow) for 20 Mk 48 dual-role wire-guided torpedoes, or 40 influence ground mines, or Sub-Harpoon underwater-launched anti-ship missiles
Electronics: one ZW-07 surface search radar, one TSM 2272 Eledone Octopus active/passive bow sonar, one Type 2026 towed-array passive sonar, one DUUX 5 passive ranging and intercept sonar, GTHW torpedo/missile fire-control system, Gipsy data system, SEWACO VIII action information system, and ARGOS 700 ESM
Complement: 52

SPECIFICATION

'Zwaardvis' class
Displacement: 2,350 tons surfaced; 2,640 tons dived
Dimensions: length 66 m (216 ft 6 in); beam 8.4 m (27 ft 7 in); draught 7.1 m (23 ft 4 in)
Propulsion: three diesel engines delivering 3,130 kW (4,200 shp) and one electric motor delivering 3,725 kW (4,995 shp) to one shaft
Performance: speed 13 kts surfaced and 20 kts dived
Diving depth: 300 m (984 ft) operational and 500 m

(1,640 ft) maximum
Torpedo tubes: six 533-mm (21-in) tubes (all bow) for 20 Mk 37C anti-submarine and Mk 48 dual-role wire-guided torpedoes, or 40 influence ground mines
Electronics: one Type 1001 surface search radar, one low-frequency sonar, one medium-frequency sonar, one WM-8 torpedo fire-control/action information system, and one ESM system
Complement: 67

'Sjöormen' class Patrol submarine

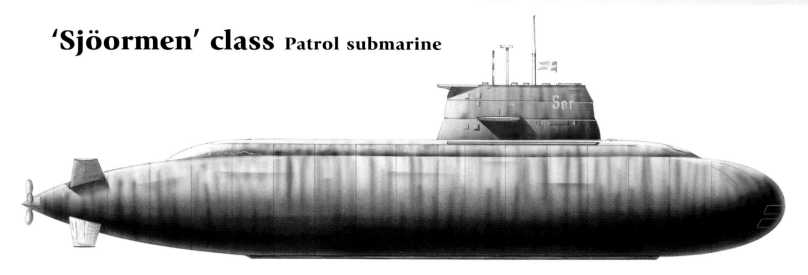

The first of the modern type of submarines for the Swedish navy was the **'Sjöormen' class** designed in the early 1960s by Kockums, Malmö and built by that company (three units) and Karlskronavarvet (two units). The class comprised the **Sjöormen**, **Sjölejonet**, **Sjöhunden**, **Sjöbjörnen** and **Sjöhästen**. With an 'albacore' type hull for speed and a twin-deck arrangement, the class was extensively used in the relatively shallow Baltic, where its excellent manoeuvrability and silent-running capabilities greatly aided the Swedish navy's ASW operations. The control surface and hydroplane arrangements were the same as those fitted to the latter Swedish submarine classes, and these, together with the hull design, allowed the optimum manoeuvrability characteristics to be used throughout the speed range, though they were more

The Sjölejonet of the 'Sjöormen' (sea serpent) class runs on the surface in the submarine's major operating area of the Baltic. In such a region, speed and manoeuvrability is of greater importance than diving depth, since much of the sea is relatively shallow.

The five vessels of the 'Sjöormen' class were designated the Type A12 by their builders. Fitted with X-configuration stern planes for increased manoeuvrability, they carried four 533-mm (21-in) and two 400-mm (15.75-in) calibre torpedo tubes for anti-ship and ASW torpedoes respectively. Four vessels transferred to Singapore.

SPECIFICATION	
'Sjöormen' class **Displacement:** 1,125 tons surfaced and 1,400 tons dived **Dimensions:** length 51 m (167 ft 4 in); beam 6.1 m (20 ft); draught 5.8 m (19 ft) **Propulsion:** four diesels delivering 1,566 kW (2,100 shp) with one electric motor driving one shaft **Speed:** 15 kts surfaced and 20 kts dived **Diving depth:** 150 m (492 ft) operational and 250 m (820 ft) maximum	**Torpedo tubes:** four 533-mm (21-in) bow and two 400-mm (15.75-in) bow **Basic load:** 10 Type 61 533-mm (21-in) anti-ship wire-guided torpedoes or 16 influence ground mines, plus four Type 431 anti-submarine wire-guided torpedoes **Electronics:** one Terma surface search radar, one low-frequency sonar, one torpedo fire-control/action information system, and one ESM system **Complement:** 18

The **Sjöbjörnen** *shows the sail-mounted hydroplanes that increased the vessel's underwater manoeuvring capabilities. The class could, at medium speeds submerged, out-turn most of the Western and Warsaw Pact ASW vessels it was likely to encounter in the Baltic.*

noticeable at the lower end. For example, a 360° turn could be achieved in five minutes within a 230-m (755-ft) diameter circle at a speed of 7 kts underwater; if the speed was increased to 15 kts, the same turn would take only two and a half minutes, which meant the class could easily out-turn most of the Warsaw Pact ASW escorts encountered in the Baltic, as well as most of the NATO escorts.

Sjöbjörnen was modified and upgraded for tropical conditions 1996–97 and re-launched as **Challenger** on 26 September

1997, as one of four submarines of the **'Challenger' class** on order for the Republic of Singapore Navy. The other vessels comprise **Centurion** (ex-Sjöormen), **Conqueror** (ex-Sjölejonet) and **Chieftain** (ex-Sjöhunden) and together will form 171 Squadron. The weapons options for the reconditioned boats comprises a combination of FFV Type 613 anti-ship torpedoes (10 carried) and FFV Type 431 ASW torpedoes (four).

'Näcken' class Patrol submarine

Since World War II, Sweden has placed considerable emphasis on the possession of a small but capable force of conventional submarines as a key element in the preservation of its long coastline against the incursions of other nations' surface and

Sweden's 'Näcken'-class submarines were extremely capable boats by the standards of their day, their wire-guided torpedoes providing high capability against surface ships as well as submarines. The lead unit is illustrated.

The 'Näckens' were typical diesel-electric 'submersibles', with limited submerged endurance, until the addition of air-independent propulsion in the lead boat. Neptun and Najad are seen at Karlskrona.

underwater forces for the purposes of reconnaissance and/or aggression. The Swedish navy's first post-war submarines were the six boats of the 'Hajen' class, built during the 1950s on the basis of the German Type XXI class design: the design data were derived from the *U-3503*, which its crew scuttled off Göteborg on 8 May 1945 and which the Swedes salvaged.

From 1956, the Swedes followed with six examples of the indigenously designed 'Draken' class, and in 1961 the Swedish government approved plans for five more advanced submarines of the Type A12 or 'Sjöormen' class. This latter introduced a teardrop-shaped hull with two decks and X-configured stern planes.

'Sjöormen' successor

The Swedish navy considers the effective life of its conventional submarines to be something in the order of 10 years, and in the early 1970s raised the matter of a class to succeed the 'Sjöormen' class from a time later in the same decade. The Swedish government gave its approval to the request in 1972, and the Swedish defence ministry was therefore able to contract in March 1973 with Kockums of Malmö (two boats) and Karlskronavarvet naval dockyard (one boat) for the three **Type A14** or **'Näcken'-class** diesel-electric submarines. The boats were all laid down in 1976 and launched between April 1978 and August 1979 for commissioning between April 1980 and June 1981 as the **Näcken**, **Neptun** and **Najad**. The Baltic, which is the primary operational theatre for Sweden's submarine arm, is shallow, so the diving depth of the 'Näcken'-class boats was fixed at some

The submarines of the 'Näcken' class were characterized by their good fire-control system, the data being derived from the single Kollmorgen periscope.

150 m (500 ft). The boats were based on the same type of teardrop-shaped two-deck hull as the 'Sjoormen' class, and were completed with Kollmorgen periscopes from the US as well as the Data Saab NEDPS combined ship control and action information system.

In 1987–88 the *Näcken* was lengthened by 8 m (26 ft 3 in) to allow the installation of a neutrally buoyant section containing two liquid-oxygen tanks, two United Stirling Type V4-275 closed-cycle engines and the relevant control system, this air-independent propulsion arrangement boosting the submerged endurance to 14 days and in effect making

the boat a true submarine rather than just an advanced submersible.

Danish service

From the early 1990s, the boats were upgraded to a partial 'Västergötland' class standard in their electronics, but were discarded later in the same decade. The sole surviving boat is the **Kronborg** of the Danish navy, which was the *Näcken*

SPECIFICATION	
'Näcken' class (upgraded)	**Diving depth:** 150 m (492 ft) operational
Displacement: 1,015 tons surfaced; 1,085 tons dived	**Torpedo tubes:** four 533-mm (21-in) and two 400-mm (15.75-in) tubes (all bow) with eight and four torpedoes respectively; up to 48 mines can be carried in an external girdle
Dimensions: length 57.5 m (188 ft 8 in); beam 5.7 m (18 ft 8); draught 5.5 m (18 ft)	
Propulsion: one MTU 16V 652 MB80 diesel delivering 1,290 kW (1,730 shp), two Stirling engines and one Jeumont Schneider electric motor delivering 1,340 kW (1,800 shp) to one shaft	**Electronics:** Terma navigation radar, IPS-17 (Sesub 900C) fire-control system, AR700-S5 ESM, and Thomson-Sintra passive sonar with bow and flank arrays
Performance: speed 10 kts surfaced and 20 kts dived	**Complement:** 27

until transferred in August 2001, after a refit by Kockums, under a lease to buy or return (in 2005).

The boat is armed with wire-guided torpedoes, the 533-mm (21-in) Type 613 passive anti-ship weapons attaining 45 kts over a range of 20 km (12.4 miles), and the 400-mm (15.75-in) Type 431 active/passive anti-submarine weapons having a speed of 25 kts over the same range.

'Romeo' class
Diesel-electric submarine

The Soviets built the first **'Romeo' class** (**Project 633**) submarines in 1958 at Gorky, as an improvement on their 'Whiskey' design. Their construction coincided with the successful introduction of nuclear propulsion into Soviet submarines. As a consequence, only 20 of these diesel electric powered boats were actually completed out of the 560 boats originally planned.

Chinese production

However, the design was passed to the Chinese as part of the development of their weapons production industry, and the class was built in China from 1962, the first being completed at the Wuzhang shipyard under the local designation **Type 033**.

Three further shipyards, located at Guangzhou (Canton), Jiangnan (Shanghai) and Huludao, then joined the programme to give a maximum yearly production rate of nine units during the early 1970s.

A total of 84 'Romeos' was constructed by the Chinese. However, it is now thought that only 31 remain in service with the People's Liberation Army Navy, with a further nine vessels in reserve. A total of four were exported to Egypt during 1982–84, and these have since been fitted with Sub Harpoon missiles. North Korea is believed to operate 22 'Romeo'-class boats, some of which were locally built with Chinese

The Chinese adopted the Soviet 'Romeo' class as their main submarine production type and exported the type to North Korea. Today numbers of PLAN 'Romeo' ships are decreasing, and construction ceased in 1987 in favour of the 'Ming' class.

SPECIFICATION

Type 033 'Romeo' class
Displacement: 1,475 tons surfaced and 1,830 tons dived
Dimensions: length 76.6 m (251 ft 3 in); beam 6.7 m (22 ft); draught 5.2 m (17 ft 1 in)
Propulsion: two diesels delivering 2.94 MW (4,000 shp) with two electric motors driving two shafts
Speed: 15.2 kts surfaced and 13 kts dived
Range: 14,484 km (9,000) miles at 9 kts surfaced
Torpedo tubes: eight 533-mm (21-in), six located in the bows and two at the stern
Basic load: 14 533-mm (21-in) anti-ship or anti-submarine torpedoes (including Yu-4 and Yu-1 weapons) or 28 mines
Electronics: one 'Snoop Plate' or 'Snoop Tray' surface search radar, one Thomson Sintra interception sonar (some vessels), one high-frequency Herkules or Tamir 5 active/passive search and attack hull-mounted sonar
Complement: 54 (10 officers)

With only a few 'Romeo' class units left in service, the Soviet navy transferred surplus vessels to Algeria, Bulgaria, Egypt and Syria. Algeria's boats were on loan and were used to train naval personnel in submarine operations. The Algerian navy have since replaced the boats with the 'Kilo'-class.

assistance from 1976. Bulgaria operates a single Soviet-built vessel named **Slava**.

Of the original Soviet boats, all had been decommissioned by 1987. Two boats were loaned to Algeria in 1982–83 for a five-year period as training boats, before

Algeria's acquisition of the more modern 'Kilo'-class submarines. In physical appearance both the Chinese and Soviet 'Romeos' are essentially identical, except that the Soviet boats tend to have extra sonar installations around the bow.

'Foxtrot' class
Diesel-electric submarine

Built in the periods 1958–68 (45 units) and 1971–74 (17 units) at Sudomekh for the Soviet Union, the **'Foxtrot' class** (**Project 641**) has proved to be the most successful of the post-war Soviet conventional submarine designs, a total of 62 entering service with the Soviet navy. Two were subsequently struck off as a result of damage sustained in accidents, one of them apparently caused by a collision with the Italian liner *Angelino Lauro* in the Bay of

Naples on 10 January 1970, after which the unit was seen later at a Soviet naval anchorage off Morocco with 8 m (26 ft 2 in) of its bow missing. All four Soviet navy fleet areas operated 'Foxtrot'-class diesel-electric submarines , and the Mediterranean and Indian Ocean squadrons regularly had units attached to them as part of their subsurface forces.

The first foreign recipient of the type was India, which took eight brand new boats between

A total of up to 79 'Foxtrot'-class units were built from 1958 onwards in several subgroups. Surprisingly, even after this period of time the basic design is still being built for the export market, with new-build ships transferred to India, Libya and Cuba (three boats received between 1979 and 1984), albeit with downgraded electronic systems.

1968 and 1975, although it now deploys only two of the vessels. India was followed by Libya, with six units received between 1976 and 1983, of which two remain operational. Poland intended to operate two vessels, **Wilk** and **Dzik**, until 2003, while a single boat remains in the Russian navy. Export versions differed from the standard Soviet units by having export-grade electronic and weapon fits, although the eight Indian navy units (received 1968–75) were of a very similar standard to the Soviet vessels. Like all Soviet conventional and

nuclear submarine classes, the 'Foxtrots' were fitted to carry the standard Soviet 15-kT yield anti-ship torpedo as part of its weapons load, but liners for 400-mm (16-in) ASW torpedoes were not apparently fitted. The Soviet 'Foxtrots' were built in three distinct subclasses that differed only in the propulsion plant. The last group is thought to have served as prototypes for the follow-on 'Tango' design. The submerged non-snorkelling endurance of the class is estimated to have been around 5 to 7 days when operating at very low speeds (2–3 kts).

Of the 62 'Foxtrot' boats that entered service with the Soviet navy, a single boat remains in service with the Russian navy. This, the last of the class, is used for basic ASW training. Another four units were transferred to the Ukraine in 1997.

SPECIFICATION	
'Foxtrot' class	at 2 kts dived
Displacement: 1,952 tons surfaced and 2,475 tons dived	**Torpedo tubes:** 10 533-mm (21-in) located as six at the bows and four at the stern
Dimensions: length 91.3 m (299 ft 5 in); beam 7.5 m (24 ft 6 in); draught 6 m (19 ft 7 in)	**Basic load:** 22 533-mm (21-in) anti-ship and anti-submarine torpedoes or 32 mines
Propulsion: three Type 37-D diesels delivering 4.4 MW (6,000 shp) with three electric motors driving three shafts	**Electronics:** one 'Snoop Tray' or 'Snoop Plate' surface-search radar, one 'Pike Jaw' high-frequency passive/active search and attack hull sonar, one 'Stop Light' ESM system
Speed: 16 kts surfaced and 15 kts dived	**Complement:** 75 (12 officers)
Range: 32186 km (20,000) miles at 8 kts surfaced; 612 km (380 miles)	

'Tango' class
Diesel-electric submarine

Built as the Soviet navy's interim long-range successor to the 'Foxtrot' class in the Black Sea and Northern Fleet areas, the first unit of the **'Tango' class** (**Project 641B**) was completed at Gorky in 1972. A total of 18 were constructed in two slightly different versions, the later type being several metres longer than the first, perhaps due to the installation of ASW missile equipment.

The bow sonar installations appear similar to those fitted to the latter classes of contemporary Soviet nuclear attack submarines, while the

Production of the 'Tango' class was completed in 1982. The design succeeded the 'Foxtrot' and offered increased battery storage capacity and more advanced electronics systems. The hull was also more streamlined than that of the 'Foxtrot', making it more suitable for submerged operations.

SPECIFICATION

'Tango' class
Displacement: 3,100 tons surfaced and 3,800 tons dived
Dimensions: length 91 m (298 ft 6 in); beam 9.1 m (29 ft 9 in); draught 7.2 m (23 ft 6 in)
Propulsion: three diesels delivering 4.6 MW (6,256 shp) with three electric motors driving three shafts
Speed: 13 kts surfaced and 16 kts dived
Diving depth: 250 m (820 ft) operational and 300 m (984 ft) maximum

Torpedo tubes: six 533-mm (21-in) located in the bow
Basic load: 24 533-mm (21-in) anti-submarine and anti-ship torpedoes, or equivalent load of mines
Electronics: one 'Snoop Tray' surface-search radar, one medium-frequency active/passive search and attack hull-mounted sonar, one high-frequency active attack hull-mounted sonar, one 'Brick Group' or 'Squid Group' ESM system
Complement: 62 (12 officers)

The casing and fin of the long-range 'Tango'-class submarines are fitted with a continuous acoustic coating, and at least one vessel was completed with a towed sonar tube in the stern and a reel mounted in the casing forward of the fin.

propulsion plant was the same as that tested on the last subgroup of the 'Foxtrot' design. The battery capacity was much higher than in any preceding Soviet conventional submarine class as a result of the increased pressure hull volume. This allowed an underwater endurance in excess of a week before snorkelling was required. Coupled with the new armament and sensor fit, this made the 'Tangos' ideal for use in 'ambush' operations against Western nuclear submarines at natural 'chokepoints'.

Construction of this class has now stopped. However, four 'Tango'-class boats remain in service. These are operated by the Russian navy's Northern Fleet at Polyarny and were inherited from the Soviet navy. The current condition of these vessels is unknown.

The 'Tango' class prototype with its characteristic raised forecasing was first identified at the July 1973 Sevastopol Naval Review in the Black Sea. Directly ahead of the 'Tango' is a 'Whiskey Twin Cylinder' boat.

'Oberon' class Patrol submarine

The 'Oberon'-class boats were considered to be among the quietest conventional submarines ever built, and continued to serve with the Royal Navy into the 1990s as training boats.

Left: HMS Olympus is seen against the icy background of a Norwegian fjord. The 'Oberon'-class boats were optimized for operations in shallow waters such as these fjords.

Above: Australia's fleet included six 'Oberon' boats. Canadian and Australian units were modernized to a standard higher than that of the Royal Navy's boats.

Built in the late 1950s to the mid-1960s as the follow-on design to the 'Porpoise' class, the **'Oberon'-class** submarine was outwardly identical to its predecessor. Internally there were a number of differences. These included soundproofing of all the equipment for silent running and the use of a higher-grade steel for the hull to allow a greater maximum diving depth. A total of 13 units was commissioned into the Royal Navy between 1960 and 1967 as **HMS Oberon**, **HMS Odin**, **HMS Orpheus**, **HMS Olympus**, **HMS Osiris**, **HMS Onslaught**, **HMS Otter**, **HMS Oracle**, **HMS Ocelot**, **HMS Otus**, **HMS**

Opossum, **HMS Opportune** and **HMS Onyx**. The *Oberon* was later modified with a deeper casing to house equipment for the initial training of personnel for the nuclear submarine fleet, and several other units were modified for the same role. The *Opossum* later operated with a new GRP bow sonar dome and was used as a trials vessel for an integrated combat operations centre that was under development for use in future submarine classes. The *Orpheus* was also fitted with a special five-man lock-out diving chamber in its forecasing for covert operations, and for training by the Special Boat Squadron and

Unlike the US Navy, which abandoned diesel-electric submarines, the Royal Navy valued conventional vessels such as the 'Oberon' class for the hunter-killer role in the Greenland–Iceland–UK gap and for clandestine spying operations.

SAS Regiment. The *Onyx* served in the South Atlantic during the Falklands War on periscope beach reconnaissance operations and for landing special forces, and while performing these duties rammed a rock, which caused a live torpedo to become stuck in one of the bow tubes. This weapon had to be removed

in dry dock after *Onyx* had returned to Portsmouth. The two shortened 21-in (533-mm) stern tubes, designed for Mk 20S anti-escort torpedoes, were later converted to carry additional stores.

The 'Oberon' design was also sold to other navies. Chile bought the **O'Brien** and **Hyatt**;

Brazil the **Humaita**, **Tonelero** and **Riachuelo**; Canada the **Ojibwa**, **Onondaga** and **Okanagan**; and Australia the **Oxley**, **Otway**, **Onslow**, **Orion**, **Otama** and **Ovens**. The type is obsolescent, and all of the boats have been retired. The *O'Brien* was ther last of the class to be taken out of service in 2004.

'Guppy' class Patrol submarine

At the end of World War II Nazi Germany was poised to introduce a new fleet of U-boats. The Type XXI class were potentially revolutionary. Standard U-boats were essentially submersibles rather than true underwater weapons platforms; they spent as much time as possible on the surface, as their submerged speed was very slow, slower even than many of the lumbering merchant ships they were trying to sink. The Type XXIs were faster underwater than on the surface.

Indeed, they could out-run many of the warships hunting them. Built too late, and often to

shockingly bad production standards, they had no effect on the war. However, the Allies were

impressed by their potential; several navies commissioned captured Type XXIs into service

Snorkel-equipped 'Guppy'-class submarines were typical of the fast US underwater fleet that was built up as part of the race with the USSR for control of the seas. Each such boat was capable of a two-month patrol, covering 22,240 km (13,820 miles) without refuelling. At the top and bottom are the USS Pickerel and USS Cubera respectively.

and elements of their design were incorporated in many post-war submarine classes.

The US Navy developed Project 'GUPPY' (Greater Underwater Propulsive Power) as a conversion programme in which current submarines were provided with greater battery capacity (at the cost of four reload torpedoes, some fresh water tanks, and magazine space) and streamlined topside with their superstructures remodelled and guns removed. Though snorkels were not fitted to the **'Guppy I'-class** prototypes, **USS Odax** and **USS Pomodon**, all subsequent conversions had them. On trials, the *Pomodon* made 18.2 kts submerged. The streamlining made a great difference, the

snorkel-equipped **'Guppy II' class** needing only about 44 per cent of the power of the standard fleet boat, submerged, at 10 kts. Twelve 'Guppy II' conversions were approved in 1947, and in 1951 there was approval of 12 **'Guppy IA'-class** conversions (including two for the Netherlands) as well as 16 austere **'Fleet Snorkel'** conversions with the hull unchanged but the original superstructure replaced by a 'Guppy' fin with a snorkel fitted. By this time the boats' ASW training role had been eclipsed by a conventional attack submarine function.

Snorkel-equipped fleet boats could be distinguished by their raked bows, whereas those of the 'Guppy' boats were rounded;

underwater they could not make much more than the 10 kts of a fleet boat, though they could snorkel at 6.5 kts (compared to 7.5 and 9.5 kts for a 'Guppy IA' and 'Guppy II' respectively).

Some 16 more fleet submarines became **'Guppy IIA'-class** conversions under a 1952 programme. These had improved sonar performance with one main engine removed to permit the relocation of auxiliary machinery farther away from the sonar transducers. Two of the 'Guppy IIA' boats were used as underwater targets, but

A Lockheed P-3 Orion patrol aircraft exercises with a 'Guppy' in the Gulf of Mexico in May 1967. The submarine is the USS Chopper, a 'Guppy IA', originally launched in 1945 as a 'Balao'-class boat.

were easily convertible back to the 'Guppy IIA' standard. Under the FRAM (Fleet Rehabilitation And Modernization) programme, nine 'Guppy IIs' were rebuilt to the **'Guppy III'-class** standard with a 3.05-m (10-ft) lengthening for a plotting room and longer conning tower, together with new fire-control systems for the Astor (Mk 45) nuclear ASW torpedo. They also received a new plastic fin similar to that of the nuclear submarines. In the 1960s US yards converted several fleet boats (including some already transferred abroad) to the late 'Fleet Snorkel' layout with the plastic fin.

'Guppy' conversions were transferred to several friendly nations: Argentina, Brazil, Peru and Venezuela in South America, Greece, Italy, Spain and Turkey in Europe, and Taiwan in Asia.

A US submarine squadron visits Portsmouth in June 1962. The front row comprises the 'Guppy IIs' USS Dogfish, USS Halfbeak, USS Tirante and the 'Tench C1' USS Torsk. The second row comprises USS Sablefish ('Balao' class), USS Trutta ('Guppy IIA'), USS Sennett ('Balao') and USS Irex ('Tench').

SPECIFICATION

'Guppy IIA' class

Displacement: 1,848 tons surfaced; 2,440 dived

Dimensions: length 93.6 m (307 ft); beam 8.2 m (27 ft); draught 5.2 m (17 ft)

Propulsion: Fairbanks-Morse diesel engines delivering 2557 kW (3,430 shp) and two electric motors delivering 3,579 kW (4,800 shp) to two shafts

Speed: 16 kts surfaced; 18 kts dived

Armament: 10 21-in (533-mm) tubes (six bow, four stern) for 24 torpedoes

Electronics: BQR-2, BQS-3 and SQR-3 sonars; one Type 1006 surface search radar, one Type 187 sonar, one Type 2007 sonar, one Type 186 sonar, one torpedo fire-control/action information system, and one ESM system

Complement: 85

'Colbert' class Cruiser

A development of the pre-war 'De Grasse' design with a shortened transom stern providing better stability, greater beam, a knuckle in the hull forward, and a new system of armour protection, the **Colbert** (**C 611**) was laid down at the Arsenal de Brest in December 1953, launched on 24 March 1956 and commissioned on 5 May 1959.

The ship represented a major addition to the surface strength of the French navy, and a feature then comparatively new on French ships was the incorporation of a helicopter platform on the ship's wider stern. The ship's primary and secondary armament in its major task of fleet air defence was 16 127-mm (5-in) guns in eight twin mountings and 20 57-mm guns in 10 twin mountings, and like *De Grasse*, the ship was fitted out as a flagship and command vessel with the additional capability for the carriage of 2,400 troops under emergency conditions. Other changes were the alteration of the machinery arrangement to include two compartments (each with two boilers and one set of geared turbines) separated by an 18-m (59-ft) watertight bulkhead, and the relocation of the funnel to a position farther aft (with a lattice mast just forward of it) to clear the bridge structure.

Major upgrade

From April 1970 until October 1972, the *Colbert* underwent a major refit to equip it with the Masurca area-defence SAM system for fleet defence duties. The original upgrade plan involved the removal of all the 127- and 57-mm guns in favour of the Masurca system and six 100-mm (3.94-in) single gun mountings installed as a superfiring pair forward and two on each beam, but financial restraints meant the original refit plan had to be modified to include the retention of six 57-mm beam mountings in place of the four 100-mm beam mountings.

The bridge structure was rebuilt, bedplates were added forward of the bridge structure for the later addition of Exocet anti-ship missiles, air-conditioning was installed throughout, and the complement was cut to 560. The radar fit was upgraded, as required for effective use of the Masurca SAM system, and to cope with the increased power requirements of these and other systems, the electrical generator system was uprated to give a 5000-kW (6,705-shp) output. A modernized electronics suite was also installed, and a SENIT-1 action information system was fitted in the operations room to enable the *Colbert* to act as a flagship for the French Mediterranean fleet, a role in which it served from the end of her 1970 refit.

From August 1981 to November 1982, the *Colbert* underwent a second major refit to extend its operational life into

SPECIFICATION

'Colbert' class
Displacement: 8,500 tons standard and 11,300 tons full load
Dimensions: length 180 m (590 ft 6 in); beam 20.2 m (66 ft 4 in); draught 7.9 m (25 ft 11 in)
Propulsion: geared steam turbines delivering 64,130 kW (86,000 shp) to two shafts
Speed: 31.5 kts
Armament: four MM 38 Exocet SSM launchers with four missiles, one twin Masurca SAM launcher with 48 missiles, two 100-mm (3.94-in) DP guns and six twin 57-mm AA guns

Aircraft: none embarked, though a helicopter platform was provided
Electronics: one DRBV 23C air search radar, one DRBI 10D height finder radar, one DRBV 50 tactical radar, one Decca RM 416 navigation radar, one DRBV 20 air search radar, two DRBR 51 SAM fire-control radars, one DRBR 32C gun fire-control radar, two DRBC 31 100-mm fire-control radars, one URN-20 TACAN, one SENIT-1 action information system, one passive ECM suite, and two Syllex chaff launchers
Complement: 562

Serving as the flagship of the French Mediterranean Fleet between 1981 and 1982, the **Colbert** *underwent a refit to extend its operational life past the year 1995. This refit included an upgrade of the Masurca SAM system to meet the threat of Soviet bombers and anti-ship missiles.*

the 1990s. During this second refit, a satellite communications system was fitted and improvements made to extend the range of the Masurca system beyond 60 km (37 miles) by replacing the original Mk 2 Mod 2 beam-riding missiles with Mk 2 Mod 3 semi-active radar homing missiles; the altitude engagement limits of the missile were 30–22,500 m (100–73,820 ft). The *Colbert* was finally decommissioned from service in May 1991.

'Vittorio Veneto' class
Helicopter cruiser

Originally to have been a third unit of the 'Andrea Doria' class, the **Vittorio Veneto** (**C 550**) was conceived in basically the same role as a helicopter cruiser, with the ship's after end devoted to a major ASW capability and its forward end to area defence against air attack through the use of guided missiles, some of which could be replaced on a one-for-one basis by RUR-5 ASROC rockets carrying homing torpedoes as their payload.

The ship was altered in basic design after it was realized that the two earlier ships were too small. The *Vittorio Veneto* thus emerged as half as large again as an 'Andrea Doria', with a raised 40 x 18.5 m (131 ft 2 in x 60 ft 8 in) flight deck aft and a hangar, two decks deep and measuring 27.5 x 15.3 m (90 ft

Originally to have been a third 'Andrea Doria'-class hybrid cruiser/helicopter carrier, the Vittorio Veneto was radically altered in design when it became apparent to the Italian navy that the earlier ships were much too small for their assigned tasks.

2 in x 50 ft 2 in), below this. The hangar could accommodate up to nine AB.204A or AB.212ASW or six SH-3D Sea King ASW helicopters, although the two 18 x 5.3 m (59 ft 1 in x 17 ft 5 in) aircraft lifts preclude the Sea Kings from being struck down into the hangar.

The extra space forward allowed the fitting of an American Mk 20 SAM/ASW launcher system in place of the Mk 10 used on the 'Andrea Doria' class. As first installed, the launcher had three rotary drums loaded with 40 SAMs and 20 ASROC ASW missiles so that the operations centre could choose the missile type to be fired according to the nature of the threat detected. During its 1981–83 refit, the *Vittorio Veneto* was modified to fire the Standard SM-1ER SAM, and was also fitted with four Teseo launchers fitted for Otomat SSMs, and two Dardo close-in weapon system mountings with three 40-mm Breda twin-gun mountings. The *Vittorio Veneto* was launched on 5 February 1967, and was the flagship of the Italian navy until the late 1980s. The ship will be decommissioned in 2006 with the arrival of the new aircraft carrier *Andrea Doria*.

*The **Vittorio Veneto** was the Italian navy's flagship until replaced in this role by the **Giuseppe Garibaldi**. The ship operates up to nine AB.212ASW or six SH-3D Sea King helicopters from its flight deck, and has missiles forward of the superstructure.*

SPECIFICATION	
'Vittorio Veneto' class	(12.75-in) ASW torpedo tube mountings for Mk 46 and A244 torpedoes
Displacement: 7,500 tons standard and 9,500 tons full load	**Aircraft:** six to nine AB.212ASW or six SH-3D Sea King ASW and ASV helicopters
Dimensions: length 179.6 m (589 ft 3 in); beam 19.4 m (63 ft 7 in); draught 6 m (19 ft 8 in)	**Electronics:** one SPS-52C 3D radar, one SPS-40 air search radar, one SPS-70 surface search radar, two SPG-55C SAM fire-control radars, four RTN10X 76.2-mm gun fire-control radars and two Dardo CIWS fire-control radars, three RM7 navigation radars, one Abbey Hill passive ESM suite, two SCLAR flare/chaff launchers, and one SQS-23 sonar.
Propulsion: geared steam turbines delivering 54,435 kW (73,000 shp) to two shafts	
Speed: 30.5 kts	
Armament: one Mk 10 Mod 9 twin-arm launcher with a normal load of 40 Standard SM-1ER and 20 ASROC missiles, four Teseo Mk 2 SSM launchers with four Otomat missiles, eight OTO Melara 76.2-mm (3-in) DP guns, three twin Breda 40-mm CIWS mountings, and two triple Mk 32 324-mm	**Complement:** 565

'De Ruyter' class Cruiser/helicopter cruiser

The 'De Ruyter' class was laid down on 5 September 1939, part of a building programme inspired by the Japanese threat to the Netherlands' colonial possessions in the Pacific. These were conventional cruisers to accompany *Scharnhorst* style battlecruisers planned for construction the following year. In the event, Germany attacked and occupied the Netherlands in May 1940. At that time there was already a cruiser named *De Ruyter* in service, but this was sunk in action with the Japanese in early 1942. The new **De Ruyter** was launched in December 1944 to clear the slipway. A sister ship, laid down in May 1939 was not launched until 1950. Cruisers for colonial protection·had little relevance in the immediate post-war era. However, the two cruisers were completed and commissioned at the end of 1953 and served for 20 years in the Royal Netherlands Navy.

Gun obsolescence

Developments in surface-to-surface missiles made 6-in (152-mm) gun cruisers obsolete during the 1960s. However, there was interest from South America, where large World War II relics retained a potent symbolism if not great combat power. Argentina was to discover the difference when the *Belgrano* sortied during its invasion of the Falkland Islands.

Peru expressed interest in the Dutch cruisers and *De Ruyter* was commissioned into its navy in March 1973 as the **Almirante Grau**. The vessel returned to the Netherlands in 1985–88 (during which it was known as the **Proyecto 01**) for comprehensive modernization, including the fitting of Otomat Teseo Mk 2 SSMs. Carrying a 210-kg (463-lb) warhead, these active radar-homing sea-skimming missiles have a range of some 160 km (99.4 miles). It was subsequently planned to fit Exocet missiles from the old 'Daring' class instead of the Otomats, but this has never taken place. Newly added defensive capabilities for *Almirante Grau* were provided by Aspide semi-active radar homing SAMs launched from an octuple Selenia Elsag Albatros launcher.

The second vessel, **De Zeven Provincien** was acquired by Peru in August 1976 and converted into a helicopter carrier. Renamed **Aguirre**, the vessel served until 1992 when it was placed in reserve. In 1977 *Aguirre* was converted into a helicopter cruiser, with its original Terrier SAM system and aft turrets removed and replaced by a 20.4 x 16.5 m (67 x 54 ft)

The two cruisers of the 'De Ruyter' class carried two twin 152-mm gun mountings forward of the bridge in the 'A' and 'B' positions and two similar mountings on the afterdeck in the 'X' and 'Y' positions. The latter were removed from Aguirre *when that vessel was converted into a helicopter cruiser.*

hangar and flight deck built between the midships and the stern, and with a second landing spot on the hangar roof. In its new configuration, the vessel could operate three SH-3D Sea King helicopters carrying AM 39 Exocet missiles. Although brought back into service in 1994, the vessel was finally decommissioned in 1999. *Almirante Grau* remained in service with the Peruvian navy in 2002.

SPECIFICATION

De Ruyter class
Displacement: 12,165 tons full load
Dimensions: length 190.3 m (624 ft 6 in), beam 17.3 m (56 ft 8½ in), draught 6.7 m (22 ft)
Propulsion: two turbines delivering 63,410 kW (85,000 shp) to two shafts
Speed: 32 kts
Armament: eight Otomat Teseo Mk 2 SSMs (*Grau*), one Albatros octuple launcher for Aspide SAMs (*Grau*), eight Bofors 152-mm (6-in) guns (four in *Aguirre*), six Bofors 57-mm

(2.24-in) guns (removed from *Grau*), six Bofors 40-mm guns (four in *Aguirre*), two depth charge racks; two CSEE Dagaie and one Sagaie chaff launchers (*Grau*, after refit)
Electronics: Signaal Sewaco SATCOM, Signaal LW08 air search radar, Signaal DA08 surface search/target indication radar, Signaal WM25 (152-mm) and Signaal STIR fire-control radars
Complement: 953 (including 49 officers)

'Leahy' and 'Bainbridge' classes Guided missile cruisers

The 'Leahy'-class cruiser USS Harry E. Yarnell (CG 17). The primary mission of these ships was anti-air warfare, for which they carried two twin launchers for a total of 80 Standard SM-2ER SAMs. These missiles could engage targets out to over 140 km (87.5 miles) at altitudes of up to 24,390 m (80,000 ft).

The **'Leahy' class** was the first US warship design with the SAM as primary armament. The SAM launchers were two twin Mk 10 Terrier launchers fore and aft, the former being protected in heavy seas by the knuckling of the hull (a feature previously unseen in US ships).

ASW equipment

The ASW outfit was limited, as the ships' primary mission was anti-air warfare defence. The nine ships comprised the **USS**

Leahy (**CG 16**), USS *Harry E. Yarnell* (**CG 17**), USS *Worden* (**CG 18**), USS *Dale* (**CG 19**), USS *Richmond K. Turner* (**CG 20**), USS *Gridley* (**CG 21**), USS *England* (**CG 22**), USS *Halsey* (**CG 23**) and USS *Reeves* (**CG 24**), commissioned between 1962 and 1964, and in their careers these all underwent modernization. An NTDS (Naval Tactical Data System) was fitted, the missile fire-control systems were upgraded for the Standard SM-

SPECIFICATION

'Leahy' class
Displacement: 5,670 tons standard and 8,203 tons full load
Dimensions: length 162.5 m (533 ft); beam 16.7 m (54 ft 9 in); draught 7.9 m (24 ft 8 in)
Propulsion: geared steam turbines delivering 63,385 kW (85,000 shp) to two shafts
Speed: 32.7 kts
Aircraft: none embarked, though a helicopter platform was provided
Armament: two quadruple Harpoon SSM launchers with eight missiles, two twin Standard SM-2ER SAM launchers with 80 missiles, one octuple ASROC ASW launcher with

eight missiles, two 20-mm Phalanx CIWS mountings, and two 324-mm (12.75-in) Mk 32 ASW torpedo tube mountings with six Mk 46 torpedoes
Electronics: one SPS-48E 3D air search radar, one SPS-49 air search radar, one SPS-1OF surface search radar, four SPG-55C Standard fire-control radars, one URN-25 TACAN, one SLQ-32(V)3 ESM suite, four Mk 36 SRBOC chaff/flare launchers, one SLQ-25 Nixie towed torpedo decoy and one SQS-23B active search/attack sonar
Complement: 423 (26 officers)

The nuclear-powered USS Bainbridge turning to port. Bainbridge was like the 'Leahy'-class cruisers, but had larger dimensions and tonnage to accommodate the two General Electric D2G pressurized-water cooled reactors that gave it a speed in excess of 30 kts.

SPECIFICATION

'Bainbridge' class
Displacement: 7,804 tons standard and 8,592 tons full load
Dimensions: length 172.3 m (565 ft); beam 17.6 m (57 ft 9 in); draught 9.5 m (31 ft 2 in)
Propulsion: General Electric D2G pressurized-water cooled reactors powering geared steam turbines delivering 52,199 kW (70,000 shp) to two shafts
Speed: over 30 kts
Aircraft: none embarked
Armament: two quadruple Harpoon SSM launchers with eight missiles, two twin Standard SM-2ER SAM launchers with 80 missiles, one octuple ASROC ASW launcher with

eight missiles, two 20-mm Phalanx CIWS mountings, two 324-mm (12.75 in) Mk 32 ASW torpedo tube mountings with six Mk 46 torpedoes
Electronics: one SPS-48C 3D air search radar, one SPS-49 air search radar, one SPS-67 surface search radar, four SPG-55C Standard fire-control radars, one URN-25 TACAN, one SLQ-32(V)3 ESM suite, four Mk 36 SRB0C chaff/flare launchers, one Mk 6 Fanfare towed torpedo decoy and one SQQ-23 sonar
Complement: 558 (42 officers)

The USS England's forward twin Mk 10 missile launcher displays a pair of Mach-2.5 Standard SAMs. A Mk 16 octuple ASROC ASW missile launcher was located between the forward missile launcher and the bridge on the main deck level.

1ER (later SM-2ER) missile, two quadruple Harpoon launchers were fitted, and the 3-in mountings were replaced by two 20-mm Phalanx CIWS mountings.

At the same time as the 'Leahy'-class cruisers were built, a single nuclear-powered variant was constructed in the form of the **USS Bainbridge (CGN 25)**. It was essentially similar, with larger dimensions and tonnage to accommodate the nuclear powerplant. The entire fleet of 'Leahy'-class cruisers and USS *Bainbridge* were retired from US Navy service by the mid 1990s.

'Belknap' and 'Truxtun' classes Guided missile cruisers

The **'Belknap' class** suffered a long and tortuous development history even by US standards, being redesigned on a number of occasions as the costs gradually increased. The design eventually stabilized as a single-ended missile ship with hangar facilities for the DASH (Drone Anti-Submarine Helicopter) and a single 5-in (127-mm) DP gun at the other end. The nine ships were the **USS Belknap (CG 26)**, **USS Josephus Daniels (CG 27)**, **USS Wainwright (CG 28)**, **USS Jouett (CG 29)**, **USS Horne (CG 30)**, **USS Sterett (CG 31)**. **USS William H. Standley (CG 32)**, **USS Fox (CG 33)** and **USS Biddle (CG 34)**.

Trials ships

After completion between 1964 and 1967, the class was used as trials ships for a number of new systems: for example, the *Wainwright* was the test ship for the first NTDS data system integrated into a fire-control system and for the Standard SM-2ER missile, while the *Fox* evaluated the Tomahawk cruise missile box-launcher

The sole nuclear-powered version of the 'Belknap' class was USS Truxtun (CGN 35). It normally operated in the US Pacific Fleet as the partner to USS Bainbridge escorting a nuclear-powered carrier. Although adapted from the 'Belknap' class, Bainbridge's gun/missile launcher arrangement was reversed from that of the non-nuclear ships.

arrangement. On 22 November 1975 the *Belknap* suffered very severe fire damage following a collision with the carrier USS *John F. Kennedy* in the Mediterranean, and had to be towed back to the US for rebuilding. Before that time, several of the *Belknap*'s sister ships had accumulated great combat experience in the Vietnam War, both as combat air

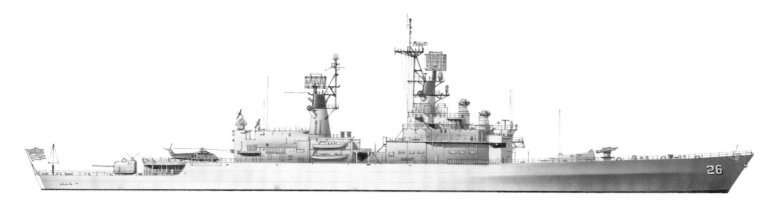

patrol fighter-guidance controllers and as air-defence ships. The 1972 North Vietnamese invasion of South Vietnam, and the subsequent US bombing, mining and naval bombardment of North Vietnam coastal areas, resulted in two air attacks on the US fleet that involved 'Belknap'-class ships. The first, on 19 April 1972, saw the *Sterret* fighting off a combined air and surface attack on a gunfire support group, its Terrier missiles destroying a 'Styx' SSM (the first occasion on which a SAM was used to destroy an anti-ship cruise missile in combat) and two MiGs (one at 9-km/5.6-mile range and the other at 27.5-km/ 17-mile range).

Later, on 19 July, the *Biddle* engaged an incoming raid of five MiGs attempting a night attack on Task Force 77 off the North Vietnamese coast, its Terriers shooting down two MiGs at about 32 km (20 miles) and driving the rest off. As had

Above: USS Belknap (CG 26) had to be rebuilt following a devastating fire that followed a collision with the aircraft carrier USS John F. Kennedy off Sicily in 1975. During the Vietnam War, USS Biddle and USS Sterett of the 'Belknap' class shot down four MiGs and a single 'Styx' SSM in two separate incidents off the North Vietnamese coast.

occurred with the 'Leahy' class, a larger and nuclear-powered version of the 'Belknap'-class ships was constructed, the **USS Truxtun (CGN 35)**, basically similar in weapon and electronic fits. The deployment pattern of

the class was similar to that of the 'Leahy' class, with the nuclear-powered vessel in the Pacific Fleet as the partner to the USS *Bainbridge*. All vessels had been decommissioned by the mid 1990s.

Above: 'Belknap' vessels, with the exception of the name ship of the class, were equipped with a hangar for operating a single SH-2F Seasprite LAMPS I helicopter. USS Belknap served as 6th Fleet Flagship.

SPECIFICATION
'Truxtun' class

Displacement: 8,200 tons standard and 9,127 tons full load
Dimensions: length 171.9 m (564 ft); beam 17.7 m (58 ft); draught 9.4 m (31 ft)
Propulsion: two General Electric D2G pressurised-water cooled reactors powering geared steam turbines delivering 52199 kW (70,000 shp) to two shafts
Speed: 30 kts
Aircraft: one SH-2F Seasprite LAMPS I helicopter
Armament: two quadruple Harpoon SSM launchers with eight missiles, one twin Standard SM-2ER SAM/ASROC ASW launcher with 40 Standard and 20 ASROC missiles, one 5-in (127-mm) DP gun, two

20-mm Phalanx CIWS mountings, and two twin 324-mm (12.75-in) Mk 32 ASW torpedo tube mountings with four Mk 46 torpedoes
Electronics: one SPS-48E 3D air search radar, one SPS-49 air search radar, one SPS-67 surface search radar, one LN-66 navigation radar, two SPG-55C Standard fire-control radars, one Mk 68 gun fire-control system, one URN-205 TACAN, one NTDS combat data system, one SLQ-32(V)3 ESM suite, four Mk 36 SRBOC chaff/flare launchers, one SLQ-25 Nixie towed torpedo decoy and one SQS-26 bow-mounted active search/attack sonar
Complement: 561 (39 officers)

SPECIFICATION
'Belknap' class

Displacement: 6,570 tons standard and between 8,065 and 8,575 tons full load (depending on ship)
Dimensions: length 166.7 m (547 ft); beam 16.7 m (54 ft 8 in); draught 8.8 m (28 ft 8 in)
Propulsion: geared steam turbines delivering 63385 kW (85,000 shp) to two shafts
Speed: 32.5 kts
Aircraft: one SH-2F Seasprite LAMPS I helicopter
Armament: two quadruple Harpoon SSM launchers with eight missiles, one twin Standard SM-2ER SAM/ASROC ASW launcher with 40 Standard and 20 ASROC missiles, one 5-in (127-mm) DP gun, two 20-mm Phalanx CIWS

mountings, and two triple 324-mm (12.75-in) Mk 32 ASW torpedo tube mountings with six Mk 46 torpedoes
Electronics: one SPS-48C/E 3D air search radar, one SPS-40F (CG 31-34) or SPS-49(V)3/5 (CG 26-30) air search radar, one SPS-67 surface search radar, one LN-66 navigation radar, two SPG-55D Standard fire control radars, one SPG-53F gun fire-control radar, one URN-25 TACAN, one NTDS combat data system, one SLQ-32(V)23 ESM suite, four Mk 36 SRBOC chaff/flare launchers, one SLQ-25 Nixie towed torpedo decoy and one SQS-26BX or SQS-53C (CG 26) sonar
Complement: 479 (26 officers)

USS *Long Beach* Nuclear-powered cruiser

The first US surface warship to have nuclear power, the **USS Long Beach** (**CGN 9**) was to have been built as a frigate-sized vessel. However, the ship's design concept grew rapidly, the vessel eventually assuming the dimensions of a heavy cruiser.

It was the largest surface combatant, with the exception of the US Navy aircraft carriers, built after World War II. It was also the only ship of cruiser dimensions to be built for the US Navy after the war.

The *Long Beach*'s reactors were of a similar design to those of the USS *Enterprise* (CVAN 65). It first sailed under nuclear power on 6 July 1961. From August 1965 to February 1966, it underwent its first refuelling, having travelled over 191,716 km (167,000 miles).

It was built with two twin long-range Talos SAM systems (with 52 missiles), two Terrier medium-range SAM systems (with 120 missiles), and what was then the revolutionary SPS-32/33 fixed-array air-search radar system with an early version of the naval tactical data system (NTDS).

MiGs over Vietnam

Although homeported at San Diego, *Long Beach* saw extensive service during the Vietnam War. It used its Talos missiles to attack MiGs on seven occasions during 1967–68 while they flew deep within North Vietnamese territory, shooting down two aircraft (in May and June 1968) at ranges of more than 120 km (75 miles). As a result of experiences in the Vietnam War, *Long Beach* had a conventional SPS-12 air search radar fitted in 1968 to supplement the fixed arrays, while an integral identification friend or foe (IFF) and digital Talos fire-control system were added in 1970.

By 1979, the Talos system was becoming obsolete, and the launchers and radars were removed. Meanwhile, two

quadruple Harpoon SSM launchers were added. The next year, the inadequate fixed-array systems were removed and replaced by SPS-48 and SPS-49 radars, the original planar array panels being replaced on the superstructure by armour plate. Two 20-mm Phalanx CIWS mountings were added, and the sonar was modified to improve its passive capabilities. In 1981 the Standard SM-2ER missile replaced the SM-1ER model that had been used since the late 1970s. During the next major refit in 1984–85, *Long Beach* received a Tactical Flag Command Center and additional Kevlar armour.

Tomahawk

After several years of US Navy reliance on the aircraft-carrier for

USS Long Beach *(CGN 9) was fitted with the Talos air defence missile system with 185-km (114-mile) range RIM-8J SAMs. These missiles could carry either a 130-kg (286-lb) conventional warhead or a 2.5-kT W-30 nuclear warhead. The conventional variant proved successful during the Vietnam War.*

SPECIFICATION	
USS *Long Beach* **Displacement:** 15,540 tons standard and 17,525 tons full load **Dimensions:** length 219.8 m (721 ft 2½ in); beam 22.3 m (73 ft 2½ in); draught 9.5 m (31 ft 2½ in) **Propulsion:** two Westinghouse C1W pressurised-water cooled reactors powering geared steam turbines delivering 59,655 kW (80,000 shp) to two shafts **Speed:** 36 kts **Aircraft:** none embarked, although a helicopter platform was provided **Armament:** (after 1981 refit) two quadruple Harpoon SSM launchers with eight missiles, two Mk 10 twin Standard SM-2ER SAM launchers with 120 missiles, one Mk 16 octuple ASROC ASW launcher with	20 missiles, two 5-in (127-mm) DP guns, two 20-mm Phalanx CIWS mountings, and two triple 324-mm (12.75-in) Mk 22 ASW torpedo tube mountings with six Mk 46 torpedoes **Electronics:** (after 1981 refit) one SPS-48C 3D radar, one SPS-10 surface search radar, one SPS-49B air-search radar, four SPG-55A Standard fire-control radars, two SPG-49 gun and two SPW-2 fire-control radars, one NTDS, one ESM suite, Mk 36 Super-Rapid Bloom Offboard Countermeasures (SRBOC) chaff launchers, and one pair SQQ-23B search and attack sonar **Complement:** 1,160 plus flag accommodation of 68

The slab-sided superstructure of the USS Long Beach *housed the ship's SPS-32/33 air search radar, although these were deactivated in 1980. The superstructure's appearance went largely unchanged, despite the addition of an SPS-48C air search radar and the SPS-49 long-range air search radar.*

its primary land attack capability, ships began to be reconfigured for the role with the advent of the ship-launched cruise missile. Between January and October 1985, the *Long Beach* was installed with the Tomahawk cruise missile anti-ship/land-attack system. In 1986, *Long Beach* was part of the first battleship battlegroup to deploy to the western Pacific area since

the Korean War, sailing in a task group with the USS *Wabash*, USS *Merril*, USS *Gray*, USS *Thach* and the battleship

USS *New Jersey*. *Long Beach* was destined to undergo a major refit in the 1990s, but this was shelved, and the ship was

deactivated on 2 July 1994 at Norfolk Naval Station. It was finally scrapped at Bremerton on 1 May 1995.

'California' class Guided missile cruiser

The **'California' class** was originally to have comprised five nuclear-powered guided-missile frigate versions of the conventionally powered guided-missile destroyer design from the ill-fated fiscal year 1966, but this was cut back to to only two vessels, the **USS *California*** (**CGN 36**) and the **USS *South Carolina*** (**CGN 37**). The money

saved went towards the follow-on 'Virginia' class.

The 'California'-class ships were intended to be the first nuclear-propelled surface combatants destined for serial production, and the basic design for the class was a nuclear-powered version of an original design first proposed in the early 1960s.

An aft side view of the USS California *displays the ship's antenna array before its major upgrade, including the SPS-48 (on the top of the forward support tower) and SPS-40 (rear support tower) air search radars and the SPS-10 surface search radar (mast-mounted on the forward support tower).*

Multi-role platforms

The purpose of the nuclear-powered guided-missile cruisers was to operate offensively against air, surface and sub-

surface threats, either independently or while escorting convoys or aircraft-carrier battlegroups. The nuclear powerplant allowed the ship to

SPECIFICATION

'California' class (as modified)
Displacement: 9,561 tons standard and 11,100 tons full load (CGN 36) or 10,473 tons full load (CGN 37)
Dimensions: length 181.7 m (596 ft); beam 18.6 m (61 ft); draught 9.6 m (31 ft 6 in)
Propulsion: two General Electric D2G pressurised water-cooled reactors powering geared steam turbines delivering 44,740 kW (60,000 shp) to two shafts
Speed: 39 kts
Aircraft: none embarked, though a helicopter platform was provided
Armament: two quadruple Harpoon SSM launchers with eight missiles, two single Mk 13 launchers with 80 Standard SM-2MR missiles, one Mk 16 octuple Anti-Submarine ROCket (ASROC) launcher with 24 missiles, two Mk 45 5-in (127-mm) DP guns, two Mk 15 20-mm Phalanx CIWS mountings, four 0.5-in (12.7-mm) machine-guns, and two Mk 32 twin 324-mm (12.75-in) ASW torpedo tubes with 16 Mk 46 Mod 5 torpedoes
Electronics: one AN/SPS-48 3D radar, one AN/SPS-49 air search radar, one LN 66 navigation radar, one AN/SPS-10 surface search radar, four AN/SPG-51D Standard fire-control radars, one AN/SPQ-9A fire-control radar, one AN/SPG-60 5-in gun fire-control radar, one URN-25 TACAN, one AN/SLQ-32 ECM suite, one NTDS, one AN/SQS-26CX sonar, four Mk 36 SRBOC chaff/flare launchers, and one SATCOM system
Complement: 563

*This bow view of the USS **South Carolina** shows the anchor located well forward to clear the **SQS-26CX** sonar dome fitted in the underwater chin position.*

deploy rapidly over extended distances and periods.

The USS *California* was commissioned in 1974 while the USS *South Carolina* was commissioned in 1975. They were the first warships to have the improved D2G reactor system installed with three times the core life of the original plants installed on the USS *Bainbridge* (CGN 25) and USS *Truxtun* (CGN 35) 'one-off' guided-missile cruisers.

A helicopter landing pad was provided, but no hangar or maintenance facilities were fitted. Two torpedo tubes for the Mk 48 heavyweight ASW

The two 'California'-class vessels (nearest to camera) and the four 'Virginia'-class CGNs in company. The differences between the two classes are readily apparent, with the latter carrying twin-rail launchers for the Standard SAM.

torpedo were fitted in the transom, but these were discarded, together with the original heavy Mk 42 5-in (127-mm) guns, the latter being replaced by a pair of Mk 45 lightweight 5-in mountings. The ship's weapons systems were reinforced with rapid data

processing and command and control equipment that acted as a force multiplier. Both 'California'-class ships served as a pair with the Atlantic Fleet as aircraft-carrier escorts. The 'California' class was able to project force over 130 km (81 miles) with its eight Harpoon missiles.

Missile armament

After upgrading, the main SAM battery comprised two single-rail Mk 13 launchers with SPG-51D digital fire-control radars; the missile was the semi-active radar-homing Standard SM-2MR (replacing the SM-1MR following the conversion of the necessary launcher and fire control systems). The principal ASW armament was provided

by a reloadable eight-round Mk 16 ASROC launcher with 24 Mk 46 Mod 5 Neartip/Mk 50 weapons.

In 1993, the USS *California* underwent a major upgrade. Kevlar armour protection was added to major sections of the ship's superstructure. Moreover, the original SPS-40 air search target-tracking radar was replaced by the AN/SPS-49 system. Between 1992 and 1993, the ship underwent a refuelling of its reactors, along with the sister ship, the USS *South Carolina*.

In 1998, the USS *South Carolina* entered Norfolk Naval Shipyard, Virginia to begin the process of formal decommissioning, and was followed by USS *California*.

'Virginia' class Nuclear-powered missile cruiser

Above: The USS Arkansas *was the last of the 'Virginia'-class cruisers in commission. Extremely capable air defence ships, the nuclear-powered vessels were too expensive for the US Navy to refuel and maintain.*

Right: *The Mk 26 missile launcher carried by the 'Virginia'-class cruisers was the fastest and most versatile system in use by the US Navy until the introduction of vertical launch systems.*

Initially planned as nuclear counterparts of the 'Spruance'-class destroyers, the **USS Virginia (CGN 38), Texas (CGN 39), Mississippi (CGN 40)** and **Arkansas (CGN 41)** eventually evolved into an improved derivative of the 'California' class.

Like most of the US Navy's guided-missile frigates (DLG or DLGN), the ships of the **'Virginia' class** were re-designated as nuclear-powered guided-missile cruisers (CGN) during 1975. The four new cruisers commissioned between 1976 and 1980, and were

---

SPECIFICATION

'Virginia' class (modernised)
Type: Nuclear-powered cruiser
Displacement: 8,623 tons standard and 10,420 tons full load
Dimensions: length 177.3 m (581 ft 8 in); beam 19.2 m (63 ft); draught 9.5 m (31 ft 2½ in)
Propulsion: two General Electric D2G pressurized-water cooled reactors powering geared steam turbines delivering 52,200 kW (70,000 shp) to two shafts
Speed: 40 kt
Aircraft: one Kaman SH-2D Seasprite multi-role helicopter (a second could be carried)
Armament: two quadruple Harpoon SSM launchers with eight missiles, two quadruple Tomahawk SSM launchers with eight missiles; two twin Standard

SM2-ER/ASROC ASW launchers with 50 Standard; 20 ASROC and two test missiles; two 127-mm (5-in) DP guns, two 20-mm Phalanx CIWS mountings, and two triple 324-mm (12¾-in) Mk 32 ASW torpedo launchers with 14 Mk 46 torpedoes
Electronics: one SPS-51D surface search radar, one SPS-40B air-search radar, one SPS-48A or SPS-48C radar, two SPG-51D Standard fire control radars, one SPQ-9A fire control system, one SPG-60D gun fire control system, one URN-20 TACAN, one SLQ-32(V)3 ESM suite, four Mk 36 Super RBOC chaff launchers, one NTDS suite, one SATCOMM system, and one SQS-53A sonar
Complement: 519

---

expected to have a service life of four decades. A fifth unit was projected but not funded by the US Congress.

Some 3.35 m (11 ft) shorter than the 'Californias', they were fitted with two multi-purpose Mk 26 launcher systems. These could fire long-range Standard SM-1 SAMs, ASROC ASW missiles and, if required, Harpoon SSMs. The Virginias were completed with a

helicopter hangar beneath the fantail flight deck, housing a single Kaman SH-2 Seasprite. The telescoping hatch cover tended to leak badly in heavy weather. The normal role of the 'Virginia' class ships was to act as fast area-defence SAM escorts to nuclear-powered aircraft carriers. Deployed in pairs, one pair was assigned to the Atlantic Fleet, the other to the Pacific.

Seeing six nuclear-powered cruisers steaming together was an unusual sight. Normally operating in pairs to provide cover to carrier battle groups, the four 'Virginias' and two 'Californias' came together for Exercise READEX 1 in the Caribbean in 1981.

away helicopter capability. The advanced SQR-19 tactical towed sonar array was not fitted due to the ships' inherently noisy reactor machinery systems.

Had funds been available, the AEGIS system would have been fitted, and an improved 'Virginia' class would have been built in the 1990s. However, refuelling overhauls were cancelled due to the expense of maintaining nuclear components, and the four ships were laid off. *Texas* decommissioned in 1993, *Virginia* in 1994, and *Mississippi* and *Arkansas* in 1997. The ships had served only half the time that their builders had anticipated.

Updated

During the 1980s, all four ships were modernized. They received Phalanx CIWS mountings, the SAM systems were adapted to fire the long-range Standard SM-2ER missiles, Kevlar armour was applied to vulnerable command and machinery spaces, and eight Tomahawk cruise missiles in launcher boxes added, as well as two quadruple Harpoon launchers.

The box launchers were mounted at the stern, taking

'Iowa' class Modernized battleship

Although constructed for service during World War II, the four battleships of the 'Iowa' class saw much action after the war. The **USS *Iowa* (BB 61)**, ***New Jersey* (BB 62)**, ***Missouri* (BB 63)** and ***Wisconsin* (BB 64)** were the largest examples of their type ever built, apart from the Japanese *Yamato* and *Musashi*. Straight after the war, the *Missouri* served as a training ship, while the others were mothballed. All were soon in action again, however, as the Korean War (1950–3) created a need for naval gunfire support. Afterwards, they were transferred to the reserve, and in 1958 were again mothballed.

Vietnam

On 6 April 1967 the *New Jersey* began her second reactivation for active service in Vietnam. During her deployment to South Vietnam and the North Vietnamese panhandle region, she spent 120 days on the gun line, firing 5,688 406-mm (16-in) rounds and 14,891 127-mm (5-in) rounds at targets. In 1969 she fell foul of economy cuts, when she decommissioned for her third period of mothballing,

By the 1970s the four battleships were considered as little more than relics from a bygone age, but in 1980 the need to augment the US

*In 1983, a modernized **New Jersey** opens fire on militia positions threatening **US** Navy aircraft flying missions in Lebanon.*

surface combat fleet and match new Soviet warship classes resulted in the US Congress authorizing funds to reactivate and modernize the battleship force. After much debate, the *New Jersey* was recommissioned on 27 December 1982, beginning her first operational deployment with the Pacific Fleet in March 1983, where she served off Nicaragua. By the end of that year, she had made a high-speed run to the Mediterranean and was off Lebanon, supporting the US Marine Corps units ashore. She used her main armament to bombard Syrian AA positions that had fired on US Navy aircraft.

Upgrades

The initial modernization programme included the upgrading of the electronics, conversion of the propulsion plant to burn Navy distillate fuel and the fitting of a Combat Engagement Center. Armament upgrades – at the expense of four twin 127-mm (5-in) mountings – included the addition of Harpoon anti-ship missiles, Tomahawk cruise missiles and Phalanx CIWS.

Eventually all four ships were returned to fleet service, *Iowa* following in 1984, *Missouri* in 1986 and *Wisconsin* in 1988. They were intended to operate with battle groups with or without organic air cover, providing US amphibious units with much-needed heavy fire

The USS **New Jersey** *opens fire with a full broadside during her deployment to Vietnam in 1968. She was the only battleship activated for the conflict in Asia.*

SPECIFICATION	
'Iowa' class **Type:** Battleship **Displacement:** 45,000 tons standard and 57,450 tons full load (BB 61 and 63); 59,000 tons full load (BB 62); 57,216 tons full load (BB 64) **Dimensions:** length 270.4 m (887 ft 2½ in); beam 33 m (108 ft 2½ in); draught 11.6 m (38 ft) **Propulsion:** geared steam turbines delivering 158,090 kW (212,000 shp) to four shafts **Speed:** 32.5 kt , (BB 63 was limited to 27.5 kt) **Aircraft:** up to four Kaman SH-2 Seasprite multi-role helicopters on the fantail landing pad **Armament:** eight quadruple Tomahawk	SSM launchers with 32 missiles, four quadruple Harpoon SSM launchers with 16 missiles, three triple 406-mm (16-in) guns, six twin 127-mm (5-in) DP guns, and four 20-mm (0.8-in) Phalanx CIWS mountings **Electronics:** one SPS-10F surface-search radar, one SPS-49 air-search radar, one LN66 navigation radar, two Mk 38 gun fire-control systems, four Mk 37 gun fire-control systems, one Mk 40 gun director, one Mk 51 gun director, one SLQ-32 ESM suite, eight Mk 36 Super RBOC chaff launchers, one NAVSAT system, and one SATCOMM system **Complement:** 1,571

support. In 1991, *Missouri* and *Wisconsin* served off Kuwait, providing gunfire support to Marines ashore and firing Tomahawk missiles against targets inside Iraq.

The four battleships had been activated primarily to fill a temporary gap in US Navy capabilities, and were never expected to serve for a long time. *Iowa* decommissioned for the last time in October 1990, followed by *New Jersey* and *Wisconsin* in 1991, and *Missouri* in 1992. *New Jersey* and *Wisconsin* have been preserved as museum ships, while the *Iowa* and *Missouri* remain mothballed until such time as the US Navy has enough fire support capacity to be confident that the old battleships will not be needed again.

'Tiger' class Cruiser/helicopter cruiser

The three **'Tiger'-class** ships were the last cruisers operated by the Royal Navy. The units of this class were laid down during World War II as the final three units of the 'Swiftsure' class: 11,000-ton light cruisers armed with nine Mk XXIII 6-in (152-mm) rapid-fire guns. These water-cooled weapons were automatic and capable of firing 20 rounds per minute. The vessels would have overwhelmed any comparable German or Japanese cruiser they encountered. Work was suspended once the new hulls had cleared the slipways in 1944–45, and was not resumed for 10 years after a much-criticised Admiralty decision of 1951 to have the ships completed to a more advanced design with two 6-in Mk 26 dual-purpose twin mountings (one forward and one aft) and three 3-in (76.2-mm) AA twin mountings in the 'B' position and abreast the after funnel.

Belated completion

HMS *Tiger* was finally commissioned in 1959, **HMS Blake** and **HMS Lion** following in 1960 and 1961 respectively. The *Lion* served for just four years before being paid off, and spent the period 1964–72 on the reserve list before it was broken up in 1975. There was little place for a World War II cruiser – even one with

Above: This view of HMS Lion reveals the ship's forward section with two 6-in (152-mm) DP guns in the 'A' position and two 3-in (76.2-mm) AA guns in the 'B' position. Lion was the first of the class to be deactivated and was used as a parts hulk from 1972.

automatic 6-in guns – in the post-war era, when the primary threat had become Soviet submarines.

The *Tiger's* claim to fame was that the vessel was used for the 'Tiger talks' between Harold Wilson and Ian Smith on the eve of Rhodesia's ill-fated bid for unilateral independence. The vessel arrived at Gibraltar for the talks during a Mediterranean patrol without the crew having being informed of the situation.

It was decided to convert the two other ships to ASW

HMS Tiger is seen leaving Valletta harbour in Malta. It is claimed the 'Tiger' class had the fastest primary guns of any surface combatants.

SPECIFICATION

'Tiger' class
Displacement: 9,500 tons standard and 12,080 tons full load
Dimensions: length 169.32 m (555 ft 6 in); beam 19.51 m (64 ft); draught 5.48 m (18 ft)
Propulsion: Parsons geared steam turbines delivering 59,680 kW (80,000 shp) to four shafts
Speed: 31.5 kts
Armament: two 6-in (152-mm) Mk 26

DP guns in one twin mounting, two 3-in (76.2-mm) Mk 6 DP guns in one twin mounting, two GWS22 Seacat SAM launchers
Aircraft: 4 Sea King ASW helicopters
Electronics: one Type 965 air surveillance radar, one Type 992Q surface/low-level air search radar, one Type 278 height-finding radar, and two Type 903 gunnery radars
Complement: 885

helicopter carrier standard. *Blake* was modified at Portsmouth in a conversion effort that lasted from 1965–69. *Tiger* was similarly altered at Devonport during 1968–72. The conversion involved the removal of the aft 6-in turret and the installation of a flight deck and hangar. Much of their armour was removed and Sea Cat SAM

launchers were installed in place of the 3-in guns abreast the funnel. Four Sea King or Wessex ASW helicopters were shipped.

These large cruisers were a luxury the Royal Navy could not afford in an era of repeated defence cuts. In their original configuration they required a crew of over 700, but the helicopter carriers demanded nearly 900 personnel. The ships did not last long: *Tiger* was paid off after only six years, placed on the disposal list in 1980 and broken up in 1986, and *Blake* paid off in December 1979 (making it the last cruiser to serve with the Royal Navy), and was broken up in 1982.

HMS **Blake**, *the Royal Navy's last active cruiser is seen in its final **ASW** helicopter cruiser configuration during September 1970.*

'Sverdlov' class Light cruiser/command ship

Dzerzhinski *is seen in SAM trials form with a twin-arm launcher aft.*

Destined to be a 24-ship class in the post-World War II plan for the development of the Soviet navy as a blue-water force, the **'Sverdlov'** (or **Project 68bis**) **class** of cruisers finally comprised 20 hulls laid down, of which only 17 were launched, and of these three were not completed but instead laid up in the Neva river at Leningrad (now St Petersburg) for a number of years before being scrapped.

The remaining 14 ships were completed during the period 1951–55 in two slightly different forms. This notwithstanding, all of the ships were completed to what was in effect an improved **'Chapayev' class** (**Project 68K**) standard. This earlier class was

The 'Sverdlov'-class cruiser **Dzerzhinski.** *Following the addition of the Volkhov SAM system, this vessel was redesignated as a **Project 68E** cruiser.*

A light cruiser of the 'Chapayev' (Project 68K) class, the type that paved the way for the 'Sverdlov'-class cruisers. First laid down in 1939, only five of this planned class of 17 were completed following World War II.

The Royal Navy's 'County'-class destroyer HMS Norfolk surveys one of the Baltic Fleet's 'Sverdlov'-class light cruisers anchored off the Shetland Islands in July 1981.

designed and laid down before World War II and commissioned in 1950–51.

Export vessel

Only one of the 'Sverdlov'-class cruisers, the **Ordzhonikidze**, was transferred, in this instance to Indonesia during 1962 as the **Irian** (and scrapped in 1972 in Taiwan following a chronic spares problem). In the late 1950s, the **Dzerzhinski** was converted into an experimental SAM cruiser with a launcher for the Volkhov (SA-N-2 'Guideline') surface-to-air missile system in place of the 152-mm (6-in) gun turret in the 'X' position. This conversion proved unsuccessful, and by the late 1970s the vessel had been placed in reserve with the Black Sea Fleet. The **Admiral Nakhimov** was also converted around the same time as the trials ship for the P-1

Shchuka (SS-N-1 'Scrubber') anti-ship missile system, but was subsequently scrapped in 1961 without ever having left Soviet waters. Of the remaining ships, two (the **Admiral Senyavin** and **Zhdanov**) were converted to the KU (*Korabl' Upravleuiye*, or command ship – designated **Project 68U**) role in 1971–72: the former served as the flagship of the Pacific Fleet for special deployments, and the latter operated with the Black Sea Fleet for the same purposes.

Fire-support role

The nine remaining ships were the **Admiral Lazarev**, **Admiral Ushakov**, **Aleksandr Nevski**, **Aleksandr Suvorov**, **Dmitri Pozharski**, **Mikhail Kutuzov**, **Molotovsk**, **Murmansk**, and **Sverdlov**. These were conventional cruisers (Soviet designation KR, for *Kreyser*) and were deployed as three with the Pacific Fleet (one soon being placed in reserve), and two each with the Black Sea, Baltic and Northern Fleets. Three of these units, the *Admiral Ushakov*

(Black Sea), the *Aleksandr Suvorov* (Pacific) and the *Molotovsk* (Baltic), underwent refits in 1977–79, which

included the extension of the bridge superstructure aft, the fitting of eight twin 30-mm AA guns with four 'Drum Tilt' fire-control radars, and the removal of the 'Egg Cup' 100-mm (3.94-in) gun fire-control radars from the main turrets. By the 1980s, the primary use for these vessels lay with their main and secondary armaments for the support of Soviet and Warsaw Pact army and Naval Infantry units in amphibious assaults and ground attacks on NATO and other Western targets. This capability was unmatched in all NATO navies other than the American, which used the reactivated 'Iowa'-class battleships with an even heavier armament. All the ships in the class had been deleted by 1992.

SPECIFICATION

'Sverdlov' class
Displacement: 12,900 tons standard and 17,200 tons full load
Dimensions: length 210 m (689 ft); beam 22 m (72 ft 2½ in); draught 7.2 m (23 ft 7 in)
Propulsion: geared steam turbines delivering 82,025 kW (110,000 shp) to two shafts
Speed: 32.5 kts
Armament: one twin Volkhov (SA-N-2 'Guideline') SAM launcher with eight missiles (in *Dzerzhinski*) or one Osa-M (SA-N-4 'Gecko') SAM twin launcher and 18 missiles (in *Admiral Senyavin* and *Zhdanov*), four triple 152-mm (6-in) guns (three triple mountings in *Dzerzhinski* and *Zhdanov*; two in *Admiral Senyavin*), six twin 100-mm (3.94-in) DP guns, 16 twin 37-mm AA guns (14 twin mountings in 1977–79 modifications, and eight twin mountings in the *Dzerzhinski*, *Admiral Senyavin* and *Zhdanov*), four twin 30-mm AA (in *Zhdanov* only; the *Admiral Senyavin* and 1977–79 modifications had eight twin mountings), and up to 200 mines (none in *Admiral Senyavin* and *Zhdanov*)
Aircraft: one Kamov Ka-25PS 'Hormone-C' utility helicopter (in

Admiral Senyavin only)
Electronics: *(Dzerzhinski)* one 'Big Net' air search radar, one 'Low Sieve' air search radar, one 'Slim Net' air search radar, one 'Fan Song-E' SA-N-2 fire-control radar, two 'Sun Visor' 152-mm fire-control radars, one 'Top Bow' gun fire-control radar, and one 'Neptune' navigation radar
Electronics: *(Admiral Senyavin and Zhdanov)* one 'Top Trough' air search radar, one 'Pop Group' SA-N-4 fire-control radar, one 'Sun Visor' 152-mm fire-control radar, two 'Top Bow' 152-mm fire-control radars, four 'Drum Tilt' 30-mm fire-control radars (only two in *Zhdanov*), and six 'Egg Cup' gun fire-control radars
Electronics: (others) one 'Big Net' or 'Top Trough' air search radar, one 'High Sieve' or 'Low Sieve' air search radar, one 'Knife Rest' air search radar (in some ships only), one 'Slim Net' air search radar, one 'Don-2' or 'Neptune' navigation radar, two 'Sun Visor' gun fire-control radars, two 'Top Bow' 152-mm fire-control radars, eight 'Egg Cup' gun fire-control radars, and one 'Watch Dog' ECM system
Complement: 1,010

'Kynda' class Rocket cruiser

Launched between 1961 and 1964, in a programme that was curtailed after only four ships had been built, the **'Grozny' class** cruisers were known as the **'Kynda' class** to NATO. They were the first ships in the Soviet navy to introduce a pyramid superstructure supporting the type's numerous radar and ESM systems. Classed as RKR units by the Soviets, these were dedicated anti-surface ship vessels tasked with countering US Navy carriers. For this role the main armament comprised two trainable four-round launcher banks of P-35 Progress (SS-N-3B 'Shaddock') cruise missiles, one reload for each tube located within magazines in the superstructure behind each launcher unit. The reloading operation was a difficult process, however, and required a relatively calm sea. The ships had no aircraft, being equipped

One of the Soviet Pacific Fleet's two 'Kynda' class rocket cruisers (RKR), which were designed for destroying US Navy aircraft carriers.

only with a helicopter landing pad aft. For targeting, they relied on third-party sources such as naval air force Tupolev Tu-95RTs 'Bear-Ds'.

Propulsion was provided by a set of pressure-fired geared stem turbines. The air-defence armament was limited to a single Volna (SA-N-1 'Goa') twin launcher forward and two twin 76-mm (3-in) DP gun turrets aft, while the ASW armament was a pair of RBU 6000 ASW rocket-launchers and two triple ASW torpedo tube banks. The RBU 6000 fires a 75-kg (165-lb) HE projectile with optional depth or magnetic proximity fusing. The 533-mm (21-in) torpedoes were acoustic-homing types.

SPECIFICATION	
'Kynda' class	(21-in) ASW torpedo tubes
Displacement: 4,400 tons standard and 5,600 tons full load	**Electronics:** two 'Head Net-A' (Grozny and Admiral Golovko), or one 'Head Net-A' and one 'Head Net-C' (Admiral Fokin) or two 'Head Net-C' (Varyag) air-search radars, two 'Plinth Net' surface-search radars (none in Admiral Golovko), two 'Don-2' navigation radars, one 'Owl Screech' 76.2-mm gun fire-control radar, one 'Peel Group' SAM fire-control radar, two 'Scoop Pair' SSM fire-control radars, two 'Bass Tilt' CIWS fire-control radars (Varyag only), 'Bell Clout', 'Bell Slam' and 'Bell Tap' ECM system, one 'Top Hat' ECM system, and one high-frequency hull sonar
Dimensions: length 141.7 m (465 ft); beam 16.0 m (52 ft 6 in); draught 5.3 m (17 ft 5 in)	
Propulsion: geared steam turbines delivering 74,570 kW (100,000 shp) to two shafts	
Speed: 35 kts	
Aircraft: none	
Armament: two quadruple P-35 Progress (SS-N-3B 'Shaddock') SSM with 16 missiles, one twin Volna (SA-N-1 'Goa') SAM with 16 missiles, two twin 76-mm (3-in) DP guns, four 30-mm ADG6-30 CIWS mountings (in Varyag only), two 12-barrel RBU 6000 ASW launchers, and two triple 533-mm	
	Complement: 375

The lead ship of the class, the **Grozny**, served with the Northern, Black Sea and Baltic fleets. Decommissioned in 1991, it was scrapped in 1993. **Admiral Fokin** (formerly the **Vladivostok**) served with the Pacific Fleet and was scrapped

in 1994. The **Admiral Golovko** transferred from the Northern Fleet to the Black Sea in 1968, serving as the flagship from 1995. It was decommissioned in 1997 and will be scrapped. **Varyag** served in the Pacific until she was scrapped in 1994.

'Kresta I' and 'Kresta II' classes Rocket/ASW cruisers

Built at the Zhdanov Shipyard in Leningrad, the first **'Kresta I' class** BPK (later changed by the Soviets to RKR) was completed in 1967. Four ships were built (**Admiral Zosulva, Vladivostok,**

Vitse-Admiral Drozd and **Sevastopol**, commissioned 1967–9), and it is likely that they were an interim design between the anti-ship **'Kynda'** and the ASW **'Kresta II' classes**.

The 'Kresta I' class ships were larger than the former class with a different hull form, half the P-35 Progress (SS-N-3B 'Shaddock') SSM battery (but with no reloads) and increased

anti-air warfare capabilities. The ships were also the first Soviet surface combatants to have a helicopter hanger, for a single Kamov Ka-25K 'Hormone-B' missile-targeting helicopter. Two

A Soviet 'Kresta II' class BPK, armed with Rastrub (SS-N-14 'Silex') ASW missiles in two quadruple launcher boxes either side of the bridge. The class also has a useful anti-ship capability in its 'Silexes' and Shtorm (SA-N-3 'Goblet') SAM missiles. The latter can be fitted with a 10 kt nuclear warhead in place of its HE warhead.

were modified, the *Vitse-Admiral Drozd* also having two 'Bass Tilt' fire-control radars and four 30-mm CIWS fitted. The Volna (SA-N-1 'Goa') SAM systems carried in this class had a secondary anti-ship capability, with an alternate 10-kiloton yield nuclear warhead in place of the usual 60-kg (132-lb) HE type.

All four 'Kresta Is' were stricken in the early 1990s, and by 1995 all had been sold for scrap.

'Kresta II'

Following the last 'Kresta I' on the slipway came the first of 10 'Kresta II' BPK hulls (the **Kronshtadt, Admiral Isakov,**

Admiral Nakhimov, Admiral Makarov, Marshal Voroshilov, Admiral Oktyabrisky, Admiral Isachenkov, Vasily Chapayev and **Admiral Yumashev**), all commissioned between 1970 and 1978. These were similar in design, but being primarily ASW ships they had significantly different SAM, ASW and electronic outfits.

The 'Shaddock' launchers were replaced by two quadruple Rastrub (SS-N-14 'Silex') ASW missile-launcher boxes (although the first missiles were not actually carried for several years) while the Volna system was replaced by the Shtorm (SA-N-3 'Goblet') system. For operation

in heavy weather, fin stabilizers were fitted. The same hangar arrangement was adopted, but with a Kamov Ka-25BSh 'Hormone-A' ASW helicopter.

The 'Krestas' served with the Northern, Baltic and Pacific

Fleets. All of them were withdrawn from service and subsequently decommissioned between 1990 and 1994, and most have since been sold abroad (primarily to India) for scrap.

SPECIFICATION
'Kresta I' class

'Kresta I' class
Displacement: 6,000 standard and 7,600 tons full load
Dimensions: length 155.5 m (510 ft 3 in); beam 17.0 m (55 ft 8 in); draught 6.0 m (19 ft 7 in)
Propulsion: geared steam turbines delivering 100,000 shp (74570 kW) to two shafts
Speed: 34 kts
Aircraft: one Kamov Ka-25K 'Hormone-B' missile-guidance helicopter
Armament: two twin P-35 Progress (SS-N-3B 'Shaddock') SSM launchers with four missiles, two Volna (SA-N-1 'Goa') SAM launchers with 32 missiles, two twin 57-mm DP guns, four 30-mm ADG6-30 CIWS mountings (in Vitse-Admiral Drozd only), two 12-barrel RBU 6000 ASW rocket-launchers, two six-barrel RBU 1000 ASW rocket-launchers, and two quintuple 533-mm (21-in) ASW torpedo tube mountings
Electronics: one 'Big Net' air-search radar one 'Head Net' 3D radar, two 'Peel Group' SAM fire-control radars, two 'Muff Cobb' 57-mm fire-control radars, 'Bass Tilt' CIWS fire-control radars (in Vitse-Admiral Drozd only), two 'Plinth Net' surface-search radar, two 'Don-2' navigation radars, one 'Scoop Pair' SSM-guidance radar, one 'Side Globe' ESM suite, 'Bell Clout', 'Bell Tap' and 'Bell Slam' ECM systems, and one high-frequency hull sonar
Complement: 380

SPECIFICATION
'Kresta II' class

'Kresta II' class
Displacement: 6,000 standard and 7,600 tons full load
Dimensions: length 158.6 m (520 ft); beam 17.0 m (55 ft 8 in); draught 6.0 m (19 ft 7 in)
Propulsion: geared steam turbines delivering 100,000 shp (74,570 kW) to two shafts
Speed: 34 knots
Aircraft: one Kamov Ka-25BSh 'Hormone-A' ASW helicopter
Armament: two quadruple Rastrub (SS-N-14 'Silex') ASW with 8 missiles, two twin Shtorm (SA-N-3 'Goblet') SAM with 48 missiles, two twin 57-mm DP guns, four 30-mm ADG6-30 CIWS, two 12-barrel RBU 6000 and six-barrel RBU 1000 ASW rocket-launchers, and two quintuple 533-mm (21-in) ASW torpedo tube mountings
Electronics: one 'Head Net-C' 3D radar, one 'Top Sail' 3D radar, two 'Head Light' SAM fire-control radars, two 'Muff Cob' 57-mm fire-control radars, two 'Bass Tilt' CIWS fire-control radars, two 'Don Kay' navigation radars, two 'Don-2' navigation radars, one 'Side Globe' ESM suite, 'Bell Clout', 'Bell Tap' and 'Bell Slam' ECM system, and one medium-frequency bow sonar
Complement: 400

The 'Berkut' class (known to NATO as the 'Kresta I') was classed as an RKR (Raketnyy Kreyser, or Missile Cruiser). Like the 'Kyndas', it carried launchers for the long-range Progress (SS-N-3B 'Shaddock') anti-ship cruise missile on either side of the bridge. The 'Krestas' were the first Soviet warships equipped with hangars, which housed the Kamov Ka-25K used for over the horizon targetting.

'Moskva' class ASW cruiser

The **PKR** **Moskva** *was a hybrid helicopter-carrier and missile cruiser designed originally to counter western ballistic missile submarines in seas close to the Soviet homeland. An air group of 14 Kamov Ka-25BSh 'Hormone A' helicopters was normally carried, which worked in four aircraft flights to form medium range ASW screens.*

Classified by the Soviets as PKRs (Protivolodochnyy Kreyser, or anti-submarine cruiser), the two 'Moskva' class ships were in fact hybrid helicopter carriers and missile cruisers, and were developed to counter the Western strategic missile submarines in the regional seas adjacent to the Soviet Union. However, by the time the first two vessels, the **Moskva** and the **Leningrad**, had been completed at the Nikolayev South Shipyard in 1967 and 1968, it was found that they were incapable of coping with both the numbers of submarines and their capabilities, so the programme was terminated. The 'Moskva' class ships were deployed primarily to the Mediterranean as part of the Soviet 5th Eskadara. They also occasionally deployed to the North Atlantic, North Sea, Baltic and Indian Ocean as part of deployed task forces or on transit.

Minesweeping

In appearance the two ships were missile cruisers forward. Extensive anti-air warfare and ASW systems were located step-wise on the forward superstructure. This ended abruptly in a large combined turbine exhaust stack and main radar mast assembly. A 15-m (49.2-ft) long hangar suitable for two helicopters side by side

was located within this structure between the stack uptakes.

The after end of the ship was taken up by an 86 x 34 m (282.2 x 111.5 ft) flight deck with five helicopter take-off and landing spots. Two 16.5 x 4.5 m (54.1 x 14.8 ft) aircraft lifts served the flight deck from the 65 x 24 m (213.25 x 78.75 ft) hangar deck below. The hangar could accommodate a maximum of 18 Kamov Ka-25BSh 'Hormone-A' ASW helicopters, although 14 is a more usual load. The Leningrad was seen with two modified Mil Mi-8T 'Hip-C' helicopters stowed on her flight deck for minesweeping duties when she assisted in the clearing of the southern end of the Suez Canal zone following the Yom Kippur War of 1973.

Nuclear depth bomb

The ASW armament included two 6000-m (6,500-yard) range 250-mm (9.84-in) calibre automatically reloaded rocket-launchers and a twin Metel (SUW-N-1) unguided ballistic missile-launcher firing the 30-km (18.6-mile) range 82-R FRAS-1 (Free Rocket Anti-Submarine) rocket fitted with a 15-kiloton nuclear depth bomb as the warhead.

The 'Hormone-A' helicopters provided an ASW screen at medium ranges (55–74 km/ 34–46 miles from the ship)

'Moskva' class ships were equipped with full command and control facilities to coordinate both hunter-killer task groups and maritime patrol aircraft, including their own ASW helicopters, to 'sanitize' areas of ocean.

SPECIFICATION

'Moskva' class
Displacement: 11,200 tons standard and 19,200 tons full load
Dimensions: length 189.0 m (620 ft 1 in); beam 25.9 m (85 ft 4 in); draught 8.5 m (25 ft 3 in)
Propulsion: geared steam turbines delivering 100,000 shp (74,670 kW) to two shafts
Speed: 31 kts
Aircraft: 14–18 nuclear-capable and torpedo-armed Kamov Ka-25BSh 'Hormone-A' anti-submarine helicopters
Armament: eight twin Shtorm (SA-N-3 'Goblet') SAM launchers with 48 missiles, two twin 57-mm DP guns, one twin Metel (SUW-N-1)

ASW launcher with 20 82-R (FRAS-1) rockets, and two 12-barrel RBU 6000 ASW rocket-launchers
Electronics: one 'Top Sail' 3D radar, one 'Head Light' 3D radar, two 'Head Light' SAM fire-control radars, two 'Muff Cob' 57-mm fire-control radars, three 'Don-2' navigation radars, one 'Side Globe' ESM suite, two 'Bell Clout' ECM systems, two 'Bell Slam' ECM systems, two 'Bell Tap' ECM systems, two twin-barrel flare/chaff launchers, one low-frequency bow sonar, and one medium-frequency variable-depth sonar
Complement: 850

using dipping sonar, sonobuoys, 450-mm (17.7-in) ASW torpedoes, and conventional and nuclear depth bombs. The 'Moskvas' were fitted to serve

as command ships. Both *Leningrad* and *Moskva* were stricken in the 1990s, and were sold for scrap in 1995 and 1997 respectively.

'Wielingen' class
Guided-missile frigate

Distinguished by their low superstructure and relatively massive funnel, the 'Wielingens' were the first warships designed and built in Belgium after World War II. The gun armament includes a 100-mm (3.9-in) DP weapon, but the planned Goalkeeper 30-mm CIWS mounting was cancelled.

The **'Wielingen' class** is the first post-war warship type designed and built wholly in Belgium. The programme was approved in June 1971, the final studies being completed in July 1973. The first two ships were laid down in 1974, the remaining two in 1975. All units were commissioned in 1978.

Based at Zeebrugge, the three surviving ships (the **Westhinder** having been decommissioned) are the largest surface warships in the Belgian navy and form its only seagoing escort ship element. They are fitted with Vosper fin stabilizers and a hull sonar. The armament and sensor fits, from

SPECIFICATION

'Wielingen' class
Displacement: 1,880 tons standard; 2,430 tons full load
Dimensions: length 106.4 m (349 ft 1 in); beam 12.3 m (39 ft 9 in); draught 5.6 m (18 ft 5 in)
Propulsion: CODOG with one Rolls-Royce Olympus TM3B gas turbine delivering 20,880 kW (28,000 shp) and two Cockerill 240 CO diesels delivering 4474 kW (6,000 shp) to two shafts
Performance: speed 26 kts; range 8350 km (5,190 miles) at 18 kts
Armament: two twin launchers for four MM.38 Exocet anti-ship missiles, one Mk 29 octuple launcher for eight RIM-7P Sea

Sparrow SAMs, one 100-mm (3.9-in) Creusot-Loire Mod 68 DP gun, one 375-mm (14.76-in) Creusot-Loire sextuple launcher for Bofors ASW rockets, and two 533-mm (21-in) launchers for 10 ECAN L5 ASW torpedoes
Electronics: one DA05 air and surface search radar, one WM25 fire-control radar, one Vigy 105 optronic director, one Scout navigation radar, one SEWACO IV tactical data system, one Argos AR 900 ESM system, two Mk 36 SRBOC chaff launchers, one SLQ-25 Nixie ASW decoy system, one SQS-510 hull search/attack sonar
Complement: 159 (13 officers)

various NATO countries, were chosen to make the class as well-armed as possible for so compact a size. The combined diesel or gas turbine (CODOG) machinery outfit comprises one gas turbine and two diesels to drive two shafts fitted with controllable-pitch propellers. The three extant ships are the **Wielingen**, **Westdiep** and **Wandelaar**, and these will remain in operational service until the second decade of the 21st century.

Wielingen has no helicopter facilities, but is well armed for a small ship. First of four vessels, the Wielingen and its sisters (one now decommissioned) provide Belgium's only ocean-going escort capability.

'Niteroi' class Guided-missile frigate

Ordered in September 1970 from Vosper Thornycroft in ASW and general-purpose versions, the **'Niteroi'-class** ships were

based on the company's Mk 10 frigate design and were constructed in the UK and Brazil. The four ASW ships were

the **Niteroi**, **Defensora**, **Independência** and **União** fitted with the Branik missile launcher system derived specifically for

Brazil from the Australian Ikara ASW missile system for the delivery of Mk 46 torpedoes. The two general-purpose units were the **Constituição** and **Liberal,** similar to the ASW variant but with a second 4.5-in (114-mm) Vickers Mk 8 DP gun mounting aft instead of the Branik system and two pairs of container-launchers for MM.38 Exocet anti-ship missiles located between the bridge and funnel.

Fitted with a combined diesel or gas turbine (CODOG) propulsion plant, the design is considered to offer exceptional economy in terms of manpower compared with previous warships of this size. A CAAIS action information system is fitted to allow coordinated surface ship ASW and surface strike operations with other vessels of the Brazilian navy, including the aircraft carrier *São Paulo.* A major programme is updating the weapons and sensors to create more capable air-defence frigates.

Training vessel
In June 1981 a single ship to a modified 'Niteroi'-class design was ordered as the **Brasil**, for commissioning in 1985 as a training ship for the naval and merchant marine academies. Fitted only with a light anti-aircraft armament as well as classrooms, the vessel has a hangar and landing platform aft for two Super Lynx Mk 21 helicopters.

As built, the 'Niteroi'-class general-purpose frigate **Liberal** *was not fitted with the Branik launcher system aft to fire the Australian Ikara rocket carrying a Mk 46 torpedo payload. Instead, this vessel carried an additional 4.5-in (114-mm) gun aft (removed in 2001 after a refit) and Exocet missile launchers amidships.*

SPECIFICATION

'Niteroi' class (modernized)
Displacement: 3,200 tons standard; 3,707 tons full load
Dimensions: length 129.2 m (423 ft 11 in); beam 13.5 m (44 ft 4 in); draught 5.5 m (18 ft 1 in)
Propulsion: CODOG arrangement with two Rolls-Royce Olympus TM3B gas turbines delivering 37,935 kW (50,880 shp) and four MTU 16V 956 TB91 diesels delivering 11,752 kW (15,760 shp) to two shafts
Performance: speed 30 kts; range 9815 km (6,100 miles) at 17 kts
Armament: two twin container-launchers for four MM.40 Exocet anti-ship missiles, a Branik launcher for 10 missiles carrying Mk 46 torpedo payload (ASW ships, but being removed), one Albatros launcher for Aspide SAMs replacing two triple launchers for Seacat SAMs (60 Seacat missiles), one or two 4.5-in (114-mm) Mk 8 DP guns,

two 40-mm Bofors DP guns in Trinity single CIWS mountings, one Bofors 375-mm (14.76-in) trainable twin launcher with 54 ASW rockets, two triple 324-mm (12.76-in) STWS-1 tube mountings for six Mk 46 lightweight anti-submarine torpedoes, and one rail for five depth charges (on GP ships)
Electronics: RAN 20 S (3L) air/surface search radar replacing AWS 3, TM 1226 surface search radar replacing ZW06, Scanter navigation radar, two RTN 30X fire-control radars replacing RTN 1OX, one EOS 450 optronic director, one CAAIS 400 action information system, one SDR-2/7 or Cutlass B-1B ESM system replacing RDL-2/3, one Cygnus or Elebra SLQ-1 jammer, one EDO 61OE Mod 1 hull-mounted active sonar, and (Niteroi and Defensora) one EDO 700E variable-depth sonar
Aircraft: one Super Lynx Mk 21
Complement: 217

'Jiangnan' and 'Jianghu' classes Guided-missile frigates

In the late 1950s China assembled four 'Riga'-class frigates from Soviet-supplied components, which were known as the 'Chengdu' class. In 1965 the Chinese laid down the first of an enlarged and modified indigenous variant at the Jiangnan yard in Shanghai, resulting in the designation **'Jiangnan' class.** Four further units were completed at the Tung Lang yard in Guangzhou (Canton) in 1967–69.

At least one of the 'Jiangnans' took part in the combat operations against South Vietnamese naval vessels in the January 1974 occupation of the Paracel Islands. The 'Jiangnans', now deleted, had a diesel rather than geared steam turbine propulsion arrangement, and were not refitted with the SY-1 (CSS-N-1 'Scrubbrush') Chinese copy of the Soviet P-15 series (SS-N-2 'Styx') anti-shipping missile.

Following the Cultural Revolution, the first new frigate design to emerge was the 'Jiangdong' class, of which two examples were constructed at the Hudong yard in Shanghai between 1970 and 1978. The long building and commissioning times were caused by the fact that the ships were due to carry the first naval SAM system designed and made in China. The class also introduced into service the first Chinese 100-mm (3.9-in) twin gun mounting.

SPECIFICATION

'Jianghu I' class
Displacement: 1,425 tons standard; 1,702 tons full load
Dimensions: length 103.2 m (338 ft 7 in); beam 10.8 m (35 ft 5 in); draught 3.1 m (9 ft 11 in)
Propulsion: two Type 12E 390V diesels delivering 10,740 kW (14,405 shp) to two shafts
Performance: speed 26 kts; range 7400 km (4,600 miles) at 15 kts
Armament: two twin container-launchers for HY-2 (CSS-N-2 'Safflower') anti-ship missiles, two single or two twin 100-mm (3.9-in) guns, six or four twin 37-mm AA guns, two or four RBU-1200 five-barrel launchers for anti-submarine

rockets, two BMB-2 depth charge projectors, in some vessels two depth charge racks, and between 40 and 60 mines
Electronics: one Type 517 air search radar, one Type 354 'Eye Shield' or 'Rice Screen'/'Rice Shield' air/surface search radar, one Type 352 'Square Tie' surface search and fire-control radar, one 'Sun Visor'/'Wasp Head' or 'Rice Lamp' fire-control radar, one 'Fin Curve' or Don-2 navigation radar, 'Jug Pair' or 'Watch Dog' ESM system, 'Wok Don' weapons director, two Mk 33 RBOC chaff launchers, and one Type 5 hull-mounted sonar
Complement: 200

SPECIFICATION

'Jianghu III' class
as 'Jianghu I' class except:
Displacement: 1,924 full load
Armament: four twin container-launchers for eight YJ-1 (CSS-N-4 'Sardine') anti-ship missiles, two twin 100-mm (3.9-in) guns, four twin 37-mm AA guns (may be replaced by PL-8H gun/missile CIWS in some vessels), two RBU-1200 five-barrel launchers for anti-submarine rockets, two BMB-2 depth charge projectors, two depth

charge racks, and between 40 and 60 mines according to type
Electronics: one Type 517 air search radar, one Type 354 'Eye Shield' air/surface search radar, one 'Square Tie' surface search and fire-control radar, one 'Sun Visor-B'/ 'Wasp Head' and one 'Rice Lamp' fire-control radar, one 'Fin Curve' navigation radar, Newton ESM system, Type 981 ECM system, two 26-barrel chaff launchers, and one Type 5 hull-mounted sonar

The People's Republic of China has built the 'Jianghu' frigate in four versions (including five subvariants of the 'Jianghu I' with funnel and bridge changes). Egypt bought two 'Jianghu I' units with revised gun armament; these are very active in the Red Sea.

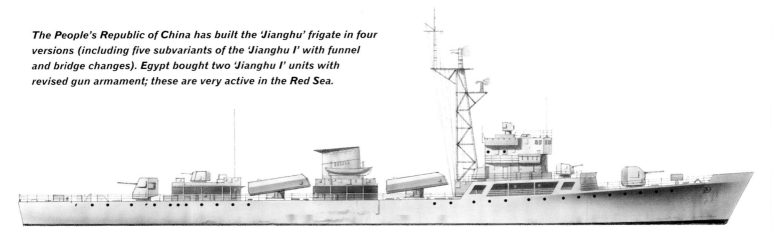

Anti-ship variant

While the 'Jiangdongs' were being built, a half-sister variant for the anti-ship rather than anti-air role was planned. The first units of what became known as the **'Jianghu I' (Type 053) class** were laid down in 1973–74 at

Hudong, launched in 1975 and commissioned in 1976. The Jiangnan and Huangpu yards also joined the programme, and at least 31 units were completed, including two and one transferred to Egypt and Bangladesh respectively.

Developments have included one **'Jianghu II'-class** conversion with only two HY-2 (CSS-N-2 'Safflower') anti-ship missiles and a number of Western weapons and sensors, and six new-build **'Jianghu III/IV' (Type 053HT)** units

(including three for Thailand) with more advanced sensors and weapons, the latter including eight YJ-1 or C-802 (CSS-N-4 'Sardine' or CSS-N-8 'Saccade') anti-ship missiles in III and IV design configuration respectively.

'Madina' class
Guided-missile frigate

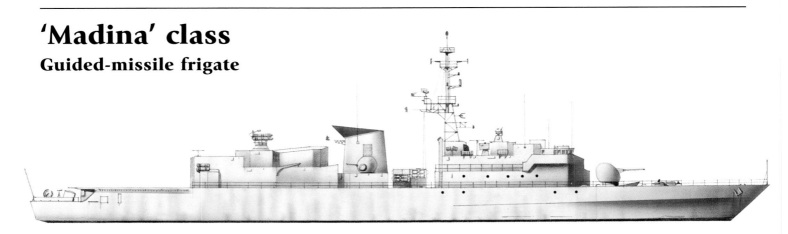

Ordered from France in October 1980 as a part of the 'Sawari I' weapons supply contract, the first of of four frigates of the **'Madina' (F 2000S) class** was laid down in the Lorient shipyard in 1981 and launched in 1983 for commissioning in 1985 as the **Madina**. The other three vessels are the **Hofouf**, **Abha** and **Taif**, laid down at the CNIM shipyard at Seyne-sur-Mer in 1982–83 for delivery during 1985–86.

The class is a very complex design and uses much untried state-of-the-art electronics technology, and at first it was seen as too sophisticated for so young a navy as that of Saudi Arabia. The weapon systems are predominantly French, though the anti-ship missiles are the Franco-Italian Otomat

Mk 2 rather than the more usual member of the Exocet family, which indicates a long-range anti-ship role, especially as the SA 365F Dauphin 2 embarked helicopter can provide mid-course guidance.

Inevitably, the presence of the class in an area of particularly sensitive strategic importance to both major power blocs was of considerable interest to all the Arabian Gulf oil states, and the 'Madinas' would have been matched only by Iraq's Italian-built 'Lupo' frigates had their delivery not been embargoed.

Class upgrade

Between 1997 and 2000, the 'Madinas' underwent an upgrade by DCN Toulon. Improvements included the

addition of a Thomson-CSF TAVITAC combat data system, a helicopter handling system and the hull-mounted active search/attack sonar with integrated Sorel VDS. Based at Jiddah, the class spend only a few weeks at sea each year.

A 'Madina' frigate of the Saudi Arabian navy. The purchase of this sophisticated class from France is typical of the tendency of oil-rich Arab nations to buy weapons with more capacity than is necessary for local defence duties.

SPECIFICATION	
'Madina' class	two twin Breda 40-mm AA guns, four single 533-mm (21-in) tubes for ECAN F17P anti-submarine torpedoes
Displacement: 2,000 tons standard; 2,870 tons full load	
Dimensions: length 115 m (377 ft 4 in); beam 12.5 m (41 ft); draught 4.9 m (16 ft 1 in)	**Electronics:** DRBV 15 air/surface search radar, Castor II fire-control radar, DRBC 32 SAM fire-control radar, two TM 1226 navigation radars, TAVITAC action information system, DR 4000 ESM system, two Dagaie chaff/flare launchers, Diodon TSM 2630 hull-mounted sonar, Sorel variable-depth sonar
Propulsion: four SEMT-Pielstick diesels delivering 28,630 kW (38,400 shp) to two shafts	
Performance: speed 30 kts; range 14825 km (9,210 miles) at 18 kts	
Armament: two quadruple container-launchers for Otomat Mk 2 anti-ship missiles, one octuple launcher for 26 Crotale Naval SAMs, one 100-mm (3.9-in) DP and	**Aircraft:** one SA 365F Dauphin 2 helicopter
	Complement: 179

'Esmeraldas' class Guided-missile corvette (FSG)

Although strictly rated as missile corvettes rather than small light frigates, the units of the **'Esmeraldas' class** must, thanks to their multi-purpose capabilities, be ranked with the latter. Ordered in 1978 from the Italian firm CNR del Tirreno, the design is based on the **'Wadi M'ragh'** (now **'Assad') class** for Libya but with more powerful diesel engines, the addition of a helicopter landing platform amidships and a SAM launcher aft of the bridge.

All six units of the class, the **Esmeraldas (CM11)**, **Manabi (CM12)**, **Los Rios (CM13)**, **El Oro (CM14)**, **Los Galapagos**

Above: The 'Esmeraldas' class are the principal surface combatants of the Ecuadorian navy.

Below: Although more correctly classed as missile corvettes, the Ecuadorian navy's 'Esmeraldas'-class vessels have more firepower per ship than a number of light frigate classes. They are armed with six MM.40 Exocets, a quadruple Albatros SAM launcher, guns and torpedoes.

SPECIFICATION	
'Esmeraldas' class	one twin 40-mm AA guns, and two
Displacement: 620 tons standard;	triple 324-mm (12.75-in) ILAS-3
685 tons full load	tubes for six Whitehead A244/S
Dimensions: length 62.3 m (204 ft	anti-submarine torpedoes
5 in); beam 9.3 m (30 ft 6 in);	**Aircraft:** provision for one light
draught 2.5 m (8 ft 2 in)	helicopter on a landing pad
Propulsion: four MTU diesels	**Electronics:** one RAN 10S
delivering 18,195 kW (24,400 shp)	air/surface search, one Orion 10X
to four shafts	fire-control, one Orion 20X fire-
Speed: 37 kts	control and one 3RM20 navigation
Armament: six container-launchers	radars, one IPN20 data information
for MM.40 Exocet anti-ship	system, one Gamma ESM system,
missiles, one Albatros launcher for	and one Diodon hull-mounted
four Aspide SAMs, one 76-mm	sonar
(3-in) OTO Melara Compact and	**Complement:** 51

(CM15) and **Loja (CM16)**, have been in service with the Ecuadorian navy since the first half of the 1980s as the country's primary anti-ship surface strike force.

The helicopter platform is used to operate one of the navy's Bell Model 206B light helicopters in the surface-search and air-sea-rescue roles.

The vessels' anti-ship missile system is the 65-km (40-mile) range MM.40 version of the

Exocet, with two banks (each of three single container-launchers, firing outward) located between the landing platform and the bridge. The SAM system is the lightweight four-round launcher version of the Italian Albatros weapon system, which uses the Aspide multi-role missile. Only self-defence ASW torpedo tubes are fitted, together with a hull-mounted sonar set, for the conduct of anti-submarine warfare operations.

'Chikugo' class Frigate (FF)

Designed with structural features to reduce noise and vibration, the **'Chikugo'-class** frigates were used primarily for coastal ASW missions around the Japanese home islands. To facilitate their use in this role, they were retrofitted with the SQS-35(J) variable-depth sonar from an open well offset to starboard at the stern. They were also the smallest warships in the world to carry the octuple

launcher for the ASROC ASW rocket-launcher system, though no reloads were carried: the amidships launcher was trained to the bearing and then elevated to fire a two-round salvo of the solid-fuel RUR-5A rockets, with their Mk 46 parachute-retarded homing torpedo payloads, out to a maximum range of 9.2 km (5.7 miles). The Japanese vessels did not carry the alternative payload of a 1-kiloton

SPECIFICATION	
'Chikugo' class	DP gun, twin 40-mm AA gun, one
Displacement: (DE215 and DE220)	ASROC octuple ASW launcher with
1,480 tons standard, (DE216-DE219	eight rockets, and two 324-mm
and DE221) 1,470 tons standard	(12.75-in) Type 68 triple ASW tubes
and (DE222-DE225) 1,500 tons	with Mk 46 torpedoes
standard; 1,700–1,800 tons full load	**Electronics:** one OPS 14 air search
Dimensions: length 93.1 m (305 ft	radar, one OPS 28 surface search
5 in); beam 10.8 m (35 ft 5 in);	radar, one GCFS 1B fire-control
draught 3.5 m (11 ft 6 in)	radar, one OPS 19 navigation radar,
Propulsion: four diesels delivering	one NORL 5 ESM system, one
11,930 kW (16,000 shp) to two	OQS 3 hull sonar, and one SQS-
shafts	35(J) variable-depth sonar
Speed: 25 kts	**Aircraft:** none
Armament: twin 3-in (76-mm) Mk 33	**Complement:** 165

The Tokachi *(DE218) pays a courtesy visit to Hawaii. As in all but the most recent Japanese designs, the 'Chikugo' class had significant ASW capability but little surface-to-surface or surface-to-air equipment.*

Mk 17 nuclear depth charge that was carried by some US ships. The propulsion plant comprised four Mitsubishi-Burmeister & Wain UEV30/40 diesels in DE215, 217–219, 221, 223 and 225, or four Mitsui 28VBC-38 diesels in the remainder. A Mk 51 fire-control director with no radar controlled the twin 40-mm mount aft. The hull-mounted OQS-3 sonar was a licence-built version of the US SQS-23 set, a variant of which is used on the 'Spruance'-class ASW destroyers. The 11 vessels were the *Chikugo* (**DE215**), *Ayase* (**DE216**), *Mikumo* (**DE217**), *Tokachi* (**DE218**), *Iwase* (**DE219**), *Chitose* (**DE220**), *Niyoda* (**DE221**), *Teshio* (**DE222**), *Yoshino* (**DE223**), *Kumano* (**DE2224**) and *Noshiro* (**DE2225**).

'Yubari' class
Guided-missile frigate (FFG)

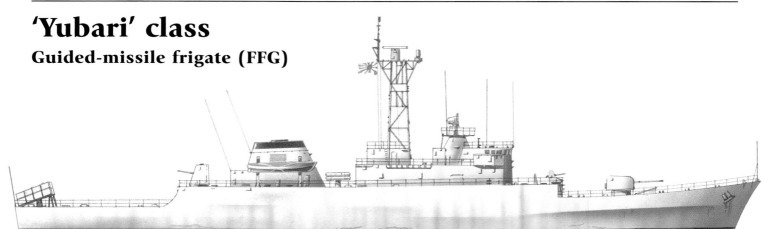

Smaller than the preceding 'Chikugo' class, the 'Yubari' class is highly automated with a crew of under 100. Designed to operate under land-based air cover, the design has little AAW capability. There is capability for the retrofit of the Phalanx 20-mm close-in weapon system if required.

The **'Yubari'-class** frigate is basically an improved and enlarged variant of the 'Ishikari' design authorized in 1977–78. The greater length and beam have improved the seaworthiness and reduced the internal space constrictions of the earlier design. The original number of units to be built was three, but this was reduced by one when the Japanese government deleted funds from the naval budget in the early 1980s. A new three-vessel 'Improved Yubari' class was to have been constructed in the 1983–87 five-year plan, but what

SPECIFICATION
'Yubari' class

Displacement: 1,470 tons standard; 1,690 tons full load
Dimensions: length 91 m (298 ft 7 in); beam 10.8 m (35 ft 5 in); draught 3.6 m (11 ft 10 in)
Propulsion: CODOG with one Kawasaki/Rolls-Royce Olympus TM3B gas turbine delivering 21170 kW (28,390 shp) and one Mitsubishi 6DRV diesel delivering 3,470 kW (4,650 shp) to two shafts
Speed: 25 kts
Armament: two quadruple launchers for eight Harpoon anti-ship missiles, one 76-mm (3-in) OTO Melara Compact gun, provision for one 20-mm Phalanx CIWS, one 14.76-in (375-mm) Bofors quadruple ASW rocket launcher, and two triple 12.75-in (324-mm) Type 68 ASW tubes with Mk 46 lightweight anti-submarine torpedoes
Electronics: one OPS 28 surface search radar, one OPS 19 navigation radar, one GFCS 1 gun fire-control radar, one NOLQ 6 ESM system, one OLT 3 ECM jammer, two Mk 36 SRBOC chaff launchers, and one OQS 1 hull sonar
Aircraft: none
Complement: 98

Developed from the 'Ishikari' interim design, the Yubari *and* Yubetsu *were enlarged in both length and beam, the better to handle the armament mounted. Two quadruple Harpoon launchers give the class considerable anti-ship capability.*

emerged was the six-strong 'Abukuma' class.

Although not heavily armed and having no helicopter facilities in comparison with contemporary Western designs, the 'Yubaris' are ideal for use in the waters around Japan, where they operate under shore-based air cover. Most of the weapons, machinery and sensors have been built under licence from foreign manufacturers. The propulsion plant is a CODOG arrangement with a licence-built British gas turbine and a Japanese diesel. Extensive automation of the machinery reduced the crew requirement to below 100, which is extremely good for a warship of this size.

The vessels that comprise the class are the **Yubari** (**DE227**) and **Yubetsu** (**DE228**).

'Tromp' class Guided-missile frigate

Although designated by the Dutch navy as frigates, the **'Tromp'-class** vessels *Tromp* and *De Ruyter* were more akin to guided-missile destroyers. They were equipped with an admiral's cabin and supporting command and control facilities to serve as the flagships of the two Dutch navy ASW hunter-killer groups assigned to EASTLANT control during wartime. Fitted with fin stabilizers, they were excellent seaboats and weapons platforms in most weathers. The propulsion was of the COGOG type with pairs of Rolls-Royce Olympus and Tyne gas turbines that were downrated to improve gas generator life and ease of maintenance. A full NBC citadel defence was built into the hull to operate under high-intensity warfare.

SAM defence

The ships provided area SAM defence against aircraft and missiles to the hunter-killer group or convoy they escorted, while offering secondary ASW and anti-surface vessel roles. A single-rail Mk 13 Standard SM-1MR SAM launcher was the main armament, backed up by an octuple NATO Sea Sparrow SAM launcher with a large reload magazine. The appearance of the vessels was characterized by the plastic radome fitted over the forward SPS-01 3D radar.

The *Tromp* was decommissioned in 1999 with the *De Ruyter* following in 2001.

SPECIFICATION
'Tromp' class **Displacement:** 3,665 tons standard; 4,308 tons full load **Dimensions:** length 138.4 m (454 ft 1 in); beam 14.8 m (48 ft 7 in); draught 4.6 m (15 ft 1 in) **Propulsion:** COGOG with two Rolls-Royce Olympus TM313 gas turbines delivering 37285 kW (50,000 shp) and two Rolls-Royce Tyne RM1C gas turbines delivering 6,115 kW (8,200 shp) to two shafts **Speed:** 28 kts **Armament:** two quadruple launchers for eight Harpoon anti-ship missiles, one Mk 13 Standard single-rail launcher for 40 SM-1MR SAMs, one Mk 29 octuple launcher for 60 NATO Sea Sparrow SAMs, one twin 120-mm (4.72-in) Bofors DP gun, one 30-mm Goalkeeper CIWS mounting, two 20-mm Oerlikon AA guns, and two 324-mm (12.75 in) Mk 32 triple tubes for Mk 46 anti-submarine torpedoes **Electronics:** one SPS-01 3D radar, two ZW-05 surface search radars, one Decca 1226 navigation radar, one WM-25 fire-control radar, two SPG-51C SAM fire-control radars, one SEWACO I data information system, one Sphinx ESM system, two Corvus chaff launchers, one Type 162 hull sonar, and one CWE610 hull sonar **Aircraft:** one SH-14B/C Lynx ASW helicopter **Complement:** 306

Replacing two cruisers in service with the Royal Netherlands navy, **HNLMS** Tromp *and* De Ruyter *were among the largest and most capable of frigates afloat. Weapons fitted included Harpoon, Standard and Sea Sparrow missiles.*

'Kortenaer' and 'Jacob van Heemskerck' classes FFGs

The **'Kortenaer'**- or **'Standard'**-**class** frigate design was authorized in the late 1960s as the replacement for the 12 ASW destroyers of the 'Holland' and 'Friesland' classes. The propulsion plant and machinery layout was taken from the 'Tromp' design. A single pair of fin stabilizers is fitted, and as far as possible internal systems have been automated to reduce crew numbers. Eight ships were ordered in 1974, and a further four in 1976. In 1982, however, two newly completed units were purchased by Greece as the **Elli** and **Limnos**. These were replaced in the Dutch order by two vessels built to an air-defence variant design known as the **'Jacob van Heemskerck' class**. The two ships are the **Jacob van Heemskerck** and **Witte de With**, and were planned to alternate as the flagship of the Dutch navy's third ASW hunter-killer group.

The helicopter facilities of these two ships have been replaced by a Mk 13 Standard SAM missile launcher. The two vessels entered service in 1986.

The 10 vessels of the ASW class were the **Kortenaer**, **Callenburgh**, **Van Kinsbergen**,

The **Banckert** *was the fourth 'Kortenaer'-class frigate to enter service with the Royal Netherlands navy. The 'Kortenaers' have a well-balanced armament fit, the primary ASW weapons being two Lynx helicopters. The vessel now serves as* **Aegeon** *with the Greek navy.*

Banckert, **Piet Hein**, **Abraham Crijnssen**, **Philips van Almonde**, **Bloys van Treslong**, **Jacob van Brakel** and **Pieter Florisz**. The *Treslong* is still in Dutch service, the *Crijnssen* and *Heyn* became the UAE's **Abu**

Dhabi and **Al Emirat** in 1997–98, and the others went to Greece in 1993–2001 (without the 30-mm Goalkeeper CIWS mounting) as the **Aegeon**, **Adrias**, **Navarinon**, **Kountouriotis** and **Bouboulina**.

SPECIFICATION

'Kortenaer' class
Displacement: 3,050 tons standard; 3,630 tons full load
Dimensions: length 130.5 m (428 ft 2 in); beam 14.6 m (47 ft 11 in); draught 4.3 m (14 ft 1 in)
Propulsion: COGOG with two Rolls-Royce Olympus TM3B gas turbines delivering 37,935 kW (50,880 shp) and two Rolls-Royce Tyne RM1C gas turbines delivering 7,380 kW (9,900 shp) to two shafts
Performance: speed 30 kts; range 5,405 miles (8,700 km) at 16 kts
Armament: two quadruple container-launchers for Harpoon anti-ship

missiles, one Mk 29 octuple launcher for 24 Sea Sparrow SAMs, one 76-mm (3-in) DP gun, one 30-mm Goalkeeper CIWS, and two twin 324-mm (12.75-in) tubes with Mk 46 ASW torpedoes
Electronics: one LW-08 air search radar, one ZW-06 navigation radar, one WM-25 and one STIR fire-control radars, one SEWACO II data information system, one Ramses ESM system, two decoy launchers, and one SQS-509 bow sonar
Aircraft: two SH-14B Lynx helicopters
Complement: 176–200

SPECIFICATION

'Jacob van Heemskerck' class
as 'Kortenaer' class except:
Displacement: 3,000 tons standard; 3,750 tons full load
Armament: as 'Kortenaer' class without 76-mm (3-in) DP gun but with one Mk 13 single-rail launcher with 40 Standard SM-1MR SAMs
Electronics: one LW-08 air search radar, one SMART 3D radar, one

Scout surface search radar, two STIR and one STIR 180 fire-control radars, one SEWACO VI data information system, one Ramses ESM/ECM system, two Mk 36 SRBOC six-tube chaff/IR flare launchers, and one SQS-509 hull-mounted search/attack sonar
Aircraft: none
Complement: 176 plus 20 flag staff

'Oslo' class FFG

Displacement of the 'Oslo' class was increased by 200 tons between 1995-96, when the hulls were strengthened for **VDS** *operations in heavy seas.* **Oslo***, the lead-ship of the class, sank under tow south of* **Bergen** *in 1994 after an engine failure caused the vessel to run aground in heavy weather.*

The 'Oslo'-class frigates are a modification of the 'Dealey' class of destroyer escort built in the US during the 1950s. Freeboard was increased in order to improve handling in the more challenging sea conditions off Norway. This is **Bergen.**

SPECIFICATION

'Oslo' class

Displacement: 1,650 tons standard; 1,950 tons full load
Dimensions: length 96.6 m (316 ft 11 in); beam 11.2 m (36 ft 9 in); draught 4.4 m (14 ft 5 in)
Propulsion: geared steam turbines delivering 14,915 kW (20,000 shp) to one shaft
Performance: speed 25 kts; range 8,350 km (5,190 miles) at 15 kts
Armament: four container-launchers for Penguin Mk 1 anti-ship missiles, one Mk 29 octuple launcher with 24 RIM-7M Sea Sparrow SAMs, one twin 3-in (76-mm) Mk 33 DP gun, one 40-mm Bofors AA gun, one sextuple Terne III ASW rocket launcher, and two triple 324-mm (12.75-in) Mk 32 tubes for Stingray ASW torpedoes.
Electronics: AWS-9 air search radar, TM 1226 surface search radar, Decca navigation radar, 9LV 218 Mk 2 and Mk 95 fire-control radars, MSI-3100 action information system, Argo AR 700 ESM system, two chaff launchers, TSM 2633 combined hull sonar and VDS, and Terne III active attack sonar
Aircraft: none
Complement: 125

Based on the US 'Dealey'-class destroyer escorts, the **'Oslo'-class** frigates have a higher freeboard forward (to suit the sea conditions off Norway). They were built under the 1960 five-year naval plan, with half the cost borne by the US. The class was modernized in the late 1970s, and fitted with Penguin Mk 1 SSMs, a NATO Sea Sparrow SAM launcher and Mk 32 ASW self-defence torpedo tubes. Five 'Fridtjof Nansen' class have been ordered as replacements to enter service from 2005.

Norway's largest surface combatants, the 'Oslos' provide the only major ASW force in the region. They carry a forward-mounted sextuple launcher for the 120-kg (265-lb) Terne III anti-submarine rocket: once fired, the launcher is automatically trained to the vertical and reloaded within 40 seconds. For self-defence the ships have the American 11-km (6.8-mile) range Mk 46 acoustic-homing torpedo, fired from the Mk 32 torpedo tubes and capable of 45 kts.

The five ships built were the **Oslo**, which sank in 1994, **Bergen**, **Trondheim**, **Stavanger** (laid up in 1999) and **Narvik**.

'Grisha' class Light frigate (FFL)

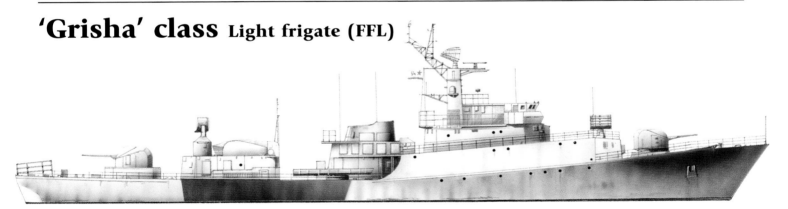

The 'Grisha II' was used solely by the maritime element of the KGB but has been retired. Exports amount to two 'Grisha IIIs' to Lithuania, and one 'Grisha V', one 'Grisha II' and two 'Grisha IIs' to Ukraine. The official name of the class is Project 1124 'Albatros'. The single 'Grisha IV' was a testbed for the SA-N-9 SAM system.

Built as a *malyy protivolodochnyy korabl'* (MPK, or small anti-submarine ship) between 1968 and 1974, the **'Grisha I' class** included only 16 units. These gave more specialized ASW capability than the earlier 'Mirka' and 'Petya' classes. They were followed during 1974 and 1976 by eight **'Grisha II'-class** *pogranichnyy storozhevoy korabl'* (PSKR, or border patrol ship) units for the Maritime Border Directorate of the KGB. These differed from the 'Grisha Is' in having a second twin 57-mm AA mount substituted for the Osa-M (SA-N-4 'Gecko') SAM launcher forward and in having no 'Pop Group' fire-control radar. In 1973–85 the **'Grisha III' class** was the Soviet

SPECIFICATION

'Grisha' classes

Displacement: 950 tons standard; 1,200 tons full load
Dimensions: length 71.2 m (233 ft 7 in); beam 9.8 m (32 ft 2 in); draught 3.7 m (12 ft 2 in)
Propulsion: CODAG with one gas turbine delivering 11,185 kW (15,000 shp) and two diesels delivering 11,30 kW (16,000 shp) to two shafts
Performance: speed 30 kts; range 4,600 km (2,860 miles) at 14 kts
Armament: one twin launcher for 20 Osa-M (SA-N-4 'Gecko') SAMs, one twin 57-mm DP or ('Grisha V') one 76-mm (3-in) DP gun, one 30-mm CIWS mount ('Grisha III and V'), two or ('Grisha V') one 12-barrel RBU 6000 250-mm (9.8-in) launchers for 120 ASW rockets, two twin 533-mm (21-in) tubes for anti-submarine torpedoes, two rails for 12 depth charges, and between 20 and 30 mines according to type
Electronics: one 'Strut Curve' or ('Grisha V') 'Strut Pair' or 'Half Plate Bravo' air search radar, one 'Pop Group' SAM fire-control radar, one 'Muff Cob' or ('Grisha III and V') 'Bass Tilt' gun fire-control radar, two 'Watch Dog' ECM systems, one 'High Pole-B' IFF, one 'Bull Nose' high/medium-frequency hull-mounted sonar, and one 'Elk Tail' high-frequency VDS
Aircraft: none
Complement: 60–70

navy's production model. A 'Bass Tilt' gun fire-control radar (atop a small deckhouse to port on the aft superstructure) replaced the 'Muff Cob' system on earlier versions, while the space previously occupied by this radar was taken by a single early 1980s, one 'Grisha III' was

modified as the sole **'Grisha IV' class** unit for trials of the Klinok (SA-N-9 'Gauntlet') SAM system. The final variant was the **'Grisha V' class** development of the 'Grisha III', the after 57-mm twin mount replaced by a 76-mm (3-in) single mount.

A 'Grisha I' unit in heavy weather shows that there is no bow sonar dome. There is a hull set and a VDS housed in the deckhouse aft beneath the hump-shaped superstructure. In the early 2000s, there were only 23 'Grishas' left in Russian service.

'Riga' class Frigate (FF)

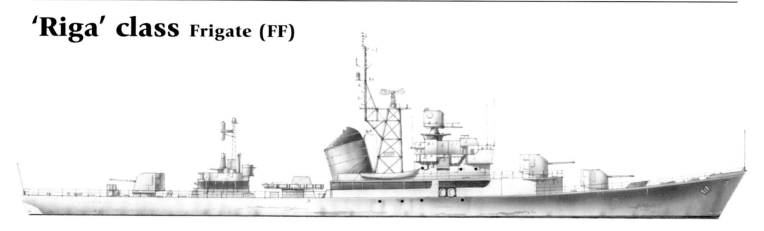

Built at the Kaliningrad, Nikolayev and Komsomolsk shipyards in the USSR, the 64 (including eight export) units of the **'Riga' class** were the successors to the six 'Kola'-class escorts. Designated *storozhevoy korabl'* (SKR, or patrol ship) by the Soviets, the type was an excellent coast-defence design and followed the Soviet practice in the 1950s of

flush-decked hulls with a sharply raised forecastle. The 'Rigas' became one of the largest Soviet ship classes, and were exported in some numbers. In all, 17 were transferred: two to Bulgaria, five to East Germany (of which one was retained in service as a self-propelled barracks ship), two to Finland (one modified as a minelayer) and eight to Indonesia. China

Now retired, the 'Riga' class remained in service with the Soviet navy in relatively large numbers into the 1980s for second-line duties and as training vessels.

built four further units in its shipyards from Soviet components, and these too have been retired. The last Soviet vessels were taken out of service by the early 1990s.

Modifications

A few of the operational vessels were modified in the 1970s, a twin 25-mm AA gun being added each side of the funnel and a dipping sonar fitted

abreast of the bridge. Before this, however, all units were fitted with two hand-loaded 16-barrel RBU 2500 ASW rocket-launchers forward to replace the original ASW armament of a single MBU 600 'Hedgehog' and four BMB-2 depth-charge throwers. One of the active units was also fitted with a taller stack cap and several 'Bell' ECM systems, possibly for trials.

One of the most popular pastimes practised by the Soviets in warm climates was relaxation on deck away from their spartan living conditions, as the majority of the crew of this 'Riga'-class frigate are doing.

SPECIFICATION

'Riga' class
Displacement: 1,260 tons standard; 1,510 tons full load
Dimensions: length 91.5 m (300 ft 2 in); beam 10.1 m (33 ft 2 in); draught 3.2 m (10 ft 6 in)
Propulsion: geared steam turbines delivering 14900 kW (19,985 shp) to two shafts
Performance: speed 28 kts; range 3700 km (2,300 miles) at 13 kts
Armament: three 100-mm (3.9-in) DP, two twin 37-mm AA and (some units) two twin 25-mm AA guns, two 16-barrel RBU 2500 250-mm

(9.8-in) launchers with 160 ASW rockets, two racks for 24 depth charges, one twin or triple 533-mm (21-in) tube mounting for anti-ship torpedoes, and 28 mines
Electronics: one 'Slim Net' air search radar, one 'Sun Visor-B' and one 'Wasp Head' fire-control radars, one 'Don-2' or 'Neptune' navigation radar, one 'High Pole-B' IFF, two 'Square Head' IFF, two 'Watch Dog' ECM systems, and one high-frequency hull sonar
Aircraft: none
Complement: 175

'Petya' classes Light frigates (FFLs)

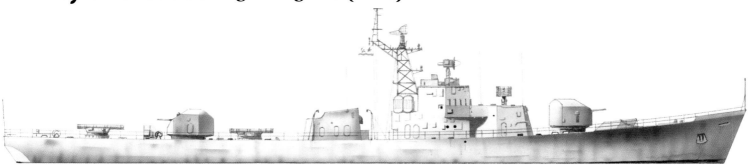

The 18 units of the **'Petya I' class** were constructed at the Kaliningrad and Komsomolsk shipyards between 1961 and 1964. From the latter year until 1969, both yards switched to building 27 units of the **'Petya II' class**, which differed from their predecessors in having an extra quintuple 406-mm (16-in) ASW torpedo tube mounting in place of the two aft ASW rocket launchers. The two forward-mounted RBU 2500 rocket launchers were also exchanged for the RBU 6000 system with automatic loading facilities. Both variants also had mine rails.

Conversion

From 1973 onwards, eight 'Petya I' vessels were modified to give the **'Petya I (Mod)' class**. The conversion involved

the addition of a medium-frequency variable-depth sonar system in a new raised stern deckhouse, which necessitated the removal of the mine rails. A further three were then converted as trials vessels and given the same sub-group designation: one was fitted with a larger VDS system with no deckhouse at the stern; the second had a deckhouse installed abaft the stack (following the removal of the torpedo tubes) and fitted with a complex reel/winch installation for what may have been either a towed non-acoustic ASW sensor or a towed surface-ship sonar array; the third vessel had a small boxlike structure built at the stern for a towed sensor deployed from a hole in the stern. In 1978 a single unit of

The 'Petya II' has heavier ASW armament than the 'Petya I' in the form of RBU 6000 rocket launchers and additional torpedo tubes.

SPECIFICATION
'Petya' classes **Displacement:** 950 tons standard; 1,150 tons or ('Petya II') 1,180 tons full load **Dimensions:** length 81.8 m (268 ft 4 in) or ('Petya II') 82.5 m (270 ft 8 in); beam 9.1 m (29 ft 10 in); draught 2.9 m (9 ft 6 in) **Propulsion:** CODAG with one diesel delivering 4,000 kW (5,365 shp) and two gas turbines delivering 22,370 kW (30,000 shp) to three shafts **Performance:** speed 32 kts; range 5,590 miles (9000 km) at 10 kts **Armament:** two ('Petya I (Mod)' towed-array trials ship one) twin 76-mm (3-in) DP guns, four 16-barrel RBU 2500 250-mm (9.84-in) ASW launchers with 320 rockets or ('Petya II' and 'Petya II (Mod)' only) two 12-barrel RBU 6000 250-mm ASW launchers with 120 rockets or ('Petya I (Mod)' only) two 16-barrel RBU 2500 launchers with 160 rockets, two ('Petya I (Mod)' only one) racks for 24 or 12 depth charges, one ('Petya II (Mod)' two; and 'Petya I (Mod)' towed-array trials ship none) 533-mm (21-in) quintuple tube mounting for five or 10 ASW torpedoes and between 20 and 30 mines (none in 'Petya I (Mod)') according to type **Electronics:** one 'Slim Net' or 'Strut Curve' air search radar, one 'Hawk Screech' gun fire-control radar, one 'Don-2' navigation radar, one 'High Pole-B' and ('Petya I' only) two 'Square Head' IFF, two 'Watch Dog' ECM systems, one hull-mounted sonar, one dipping sonar, and (in some) one variable-depth sonar **Aircraft:** none **Complement:** 98

the 'Petya II' type was also converted into a **'Petya II (Mod)'-class** trials vessel. The conversion was along the lines of the 'Petya I (Mod)' but with a slimmer VDS deckhouse, which allowed retention of the minelaying capability.

In 1984 the Soviet navy had a total of seven 'Petya I', 11 'Petya I (Mod)', including three trials vessels, 23 'Petya II' and one 'Petya II (Mod)' (for trials) in service with all four fleets. A further four 'Petya IIs' of the

This unmodified member of the 'Petya I' class of light frigates is easily identified by the presence of the RBU 2500 ASW rocket launchers in front of the bridge and the lack of any stern superstructure for a variable-depth sonar system.

Soviet navy were transferred to Vietnam (three ships) and Ethiopia (one ship), and another 16 were built specifically for export with a triple 533-mm (21-in) torpedo tube mounting and RBU 2500 ASW rocket-launchers for the navies of India (12 **'Arnala'-class** ships), Vietnam (two ships) and Syria (two ships).

In the final stages of their Soviet careers, now ended, the 'Petyas' were rated as *stororzhevoy korabl'* (SKR, or patrol ship). In 2003, the only survivors were to be found in India (one ship on the verge of deletion), Syria (two, of which one may no longer be operational) and Vietnam (a single 'Petya II').

'Mirka' classes FFLs

Black Sea Fleet 'Mirka I' and 'Mirka II' units regularly deployed to the Mediterranean squadron to provide ASW protection to higher-value surface units and the Soviet navy's many deep water anchorages in the region.

Built between 1964 and 1965 at the Kaliningrad shipyard, the nine vessels of the **'Mirka I' class** were followed on the stocks during 1965 and 1966 by nine units of the **'Mirka II' class**. They were constructed as a specialized variation of the early 'Petya' design and were initially rated by the Soviets as *malyy protivolodochnyy korabl'* (MPK, or small anti-submarine ship). As with some other ASW-oriented ship classes, this was changed in 1978 to *stororzhevoy korabl'* (SKR, or patrol ship).

Retired vessels

The vessels of the two 'Mirka' classes, now all retired, served only with the Soviet Baltic and Black Sea Fleets. The propulsion plant was similar in concept to the combined diesel and gas turbine plant of the 'Petyas', the

combination of the two types of engine offering long endurance at modest speed for routine patrolling or escort, and high speed (and acceleration) to close as rapidly as possible on the location of suspected targets in preparation for attacks on submerged submarines.

Dual-purpose guns

Both classes carried a mixed armament based on four 76-mm (3-in) dual-purpose guns in a pair of two-gun mountings over the forecastle and abaft the mast. The difference between the models lay in their anti-submarine armaments. In the 'Mirka I' class this comprised four 250-mm (9.84-in) 12-barrel launchers for anti-submarine rockets (two abreast of each other ahead of the bridge and two abreast of each other near

the stern, flanking the forward unit of the two large centreline exhaust arrangements for the gas turbines) and one quintuple mounting for anti-submarine torpedoes on the centreline abaft the lattice mast with its mass of antennae. In the 'Mirka II' class, the two after rocket

launchers were omitted in favour of a second quintuple mounting on the centreline in the area between the mast and the superstructure rear: both mountings carried 533-mm (21-in) electrically powered anti-submarine torpedoes. The later 'Mirka II' units had a 'Strut Curve' air search radar in place of the earlier 'Slim Net' set.

Dipping sonar

Almost all the units of both classes were later fitted with a dipping sonar, either instead of the internal depth charge rack in

SPECIFICATION	
'Mirka' classes	240 or 120 rockets, and one
Displacement: 950 tons standard;	('Mirka I') or two ('Mirka II')
1,150 tons full load	533-mm (21-in) quintuple tube
Dimensions: 82.4 m (270 ft 4 in);	mountings for five or 10 anti-
beam 9.1 m (29 ft 10 in); draught	submarine torpedoes
3 m (9 ft 10 in)	**Electronics:** one 'Slim Net' or (some
Propulsion: CODAG with two diesels	'Mirka II' only) 'Strut Curve' air
delivering 4,470 kW (5,995 shp) and	search radar, one 'Hawk Screech'
two gas turbines delivering 23100	gun fire-control radar, one 'Don-2'
kW (30,980 shp) to two shafts	navigation radar, two 'High Pole-B'
Performance: speed 35 kts; range	IFF, two 'Square Head' IFF, two
4600 km (2,860 miles) at 20 kts	'Watch Dog' ECM systems, one
Armament: two twin 76-mm (3-in)	hull-mounted sonar and one
DP guns, four ('Mirka I') or two	dipping sonar
('Mirka II') 250-mm (9.84-in) RBU	**Aircraft:** none
6000 12-barrel ASW launchers with	**Complement:** 98

All the nine 'Mirka II'-class frigates built were subsequently fitted with a new type of dipping sonar in place of the internal depth charge rack on the port side of the stern to improve their ASW capabilities in the Mediterranean and Baltic.

the port side of the stern or abreast the bridge. This was intended to improve the submarine-detection capabilities in regions such as the Baltic, where oceanographic conditions for anti-submarine warfare are notoriously difficult.

The 'Mirka' light frigates remained in declining service into the early 1990s before the last units were finally deleted.

'Koni' class Frigate/guided-missile frigate

Although constructed in the USSR at the Zelenodolsk Shipyard on the Black Sea, the **'Koni' class** of *storozhevoy korabl'* (SKR, or patrol ship) was intended only for export, a mere one unit, the **Timofey Ul'yantsev**, being retained by the Soviets as a crew training ship for the personnel of the countries which bought vessels of this class. There are two distinct subclasses, the **'Koni Type II' class** differing from the **'Koni Type I' class** in having the space between the funnel and the aft superstructure occupied by an extra deckhouse for the air-conditioning units required for

service in hot climates.

The countries that took delivery of 'Koni'-class units were East Germany ('Type I' **Rostock** and **Berlin**), Yugoslavia ('Type I' **Split**, now named **Beograd**; and **Podgorica**, now cannibalized), Algeria ('Type II'

The East German navy had two 'Koni Type I'-class frigates, the ***Rostock (141)*** *and the* ***Berlin (142)***. *They differed slightly from other 'Koni'-class units in having no chaff launchers, and carried East German-built TSR333 navigation radars in place of the more usual 'Don-2' sets.*

Murat Reis, **Ras Kellich** and **Rais Korfou**) and Cuba ('Type II' **Mariel** plus an unnamed vessel). The Yugoslavs themselves modified their ships to carry two single aft-firing launchers for P-20 (SS-N-2c 'Styx') anti-ship missiles on each side of the rear superstructure, which houses the Osa-M (SA-N-4 'Gecko') SAM unit, and in the mid-1980s also built in their Tito

Yard in Kraljevica the two **'Kotor'-class** ships **Kotor** and **Novi Sad**: these have various structural differences from the Soviet original, different diesel engines and the SS-N-2c missiles in forward-facing launchers abreast the forward end of the bridge superstructure. A similar ship was sold to Indonesia as a training vessel.

The 'Koni Type I'-class frigate was built in the USSR primarily for export. The 'Koni Type II' class differs in having additional superstructure, which houses air-conditioning systems for use in tropical climates.

SPECIFICATION	
'Koni' class	30-mm AA guns, two 250-mm
Displacement: 1,440 tons standard;	(9.84-in) RBU 6000 12-barrel ASW
1,900 tons full load	launchers with 120 rockets, two
Dimensions: length 96.4 m (316 ft	racks for 24 depth charges, and
3 in); beam 12.6 m (41 ft 4 in);	between 20 and 30 mines
draught 3.5 m (11 ft 6 in)	according to type
Propulsion: CODAG with two	**Electronics:** one 'Strut Curve' air
diesels delivering 11,400 kW	search radar, one 'Pop Group' SAM
(15,290 shp) and one gas turbine	fire-control radar, one 'Hawk
delivering 13,420 kW (18,000 shp)	Screech' gun fire-control radar, one
to three shafts	'Drum Tilt' 30-mm gun fire-control
Performance: speed 27 kts; range	radar, one 'High Pole-B' IFF, two
2,500 km (1,555 miles) at 14 kts	'Watch Dog' ECM systems, and
Armament: one twin launcher for 20	one hull-mounted sonar
Osa-M (SA-N-4 'Gecko') SAMs, two	**Aircraft:** none
twin 76-mm (3-in) DP and two twin	**Complement:** 120

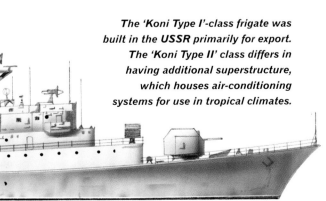

'Krivak' classes Guided-missile frigates (FFG)

Right: 'Krivak'-class frigates were optimized for the anti-submarine role, in time of war operating against marauding NATO submarines in Soviet coastal waters and protecting Soviet SSBNs. Note the twin 76-mm (3-in) guns in the aft turrets of this 'Krivak I' ship.

In 1970 the first gas turbine-powered **'Krivak I'-class** or **Project 1135** frigate of *bol'shoy protivolodochnyy korabl'* (BPK, or large anti-submarine ship) entered service with the Soviet navy. Built at the Zhdanov Shipyard in Leningrad, the Kaliningrad Shipyard and the Kamish-Burun Shipyard in Kerch between 1970 and 1980, 21 units of this variant were constructed. In 1975 the **'Krivak II' class**, of which 11 were built at Kaliningrad between that year and 1981, was first seen. This differed from the previous class

in having single 100-mm (3.9-in) guns substituted for the twin 76-mm (3-in) turrets of the earlier version, and a larger variable-depth sonar housing at the stern. Both classes were re-rated to *storozhevoy korabl'*

(SKR, or patrol ship) status in the late 1970s, possibly in view of what some Western observers considered to be the type's deficiencies in terms of size and limited endurance for ASW operations in open waters.

New and improved

The first unit of the **'Krivak III' class**, designed to remedy some of the probable defects, appeared in mid-1984. This has a hangar and flight platform for one Ka-27 helicopter in place of

Above: Three 'Krivak'-class frigates refuel from a 'Dubna'-class replenishment oiler. Two 'Krivak I'-class ships have been upgraded with two launchers for eight Uran (SS-N-25 'Switchblade') anti-ship

Right: The 'Krivak I'-class frigate Storozhevoy is seen in the North Atlantic, the overhead view revealing the layout of the ship's weapons and sensors. The largest item is the quadruple Rastrub (SS-N-14) ASW missile launcher.

SPECIFICATION

'Krivak I' and 'Krivak II' classes

Displacement: 3,100 tons standard; 3,650 tons full load

Dimensions: length 123.5 m (405 ft 2 in); beam 14.3 m (46 ft 11 in); draught 7.3 m (23 ft 11 in)

Propulsion: COGAG with two M8K gas turbines delivering 41,400 kW (55,525 shp) and two M-62 gas turbines delivering 10,150 kW (13,615 shp) to two shafts

Performance: speed 32 kts; range 7,400 km (4,600 miles) at 14 kts

Armament: one quadruple Rastrub launcher for RPK-3 Metel (SS-N-14 'Silex') ASW missiles, two twin launchers for 40 Osa-M (SA-N-4 'Gecko') SAMs, two twin 76-mm (3-in) DP or ('Krivak I') two 100-mm (3.9-in) DP guns, two RPK-8 Zapad

(RBU 6000) 12-barrel ASW launchers with 120 rockets, two quadruple 533-mm (21-in) tube mountings for ASW torpedoes, and 20 to 40 mines according to type

Electronics: one 'Head Net-C' 3D radar, two 'Pop Group' SAM fire-control radars, two 'Eye Bowl' SS-N-14 fire-control radars, one 'Owl Screech' ('Krivak I') or 'Kite Screech' ('Krivak II') gun fire-control radar, one 'Don Kay' or 'Palm Frond' surface search radar, two 'Bell Shroud' and two 'Bell Squat' ECM systems, four 16-barrel PK-16 chaff launchers, one 'High Pole-B' or 'Salt Pot' IFF, one 'Bull Nose' hull-mounted sonar, and one 'Mare Tail' VDS

Aircraft: none

Complement: 194

Right: The long rake of the bow of the 'Krivak' class with the anchor well forward betrays the presence of a large bow sonar dome for a 'Bull Nose' (Titan-2) medium-frequency active sonar. For under-layer searching, a low-frequency VDS is fitted aft. Russia had 15 'Krivak' frigates remaining in active service in 2003.

the after gun turrets and Osa-M (SA-N-4 'Gecko') SAM launcher, and one 100-mm gun turret in place of the forward quadruple Rastrub (SS-N-14 'Silex') launcher for ASW missiles.

The variable-depth sonar remains under the flight deck at the stern, and single 30-mm AK-630 CIWS are located on each

side of the hangar. The other ASW armament of the 'Krivak I/II' classes and the forward Osa-M launcher are also retained. The 'Krivak III' was built at Kamish-Burun and became the standard ASW frigate of the Soviet (now Russian) navy. A number of ships were exported.

Below: The 'Krivak I'-class frigate is distinguishable from the 'Krivak II' by its two twin 76-mm (3-in) DP gun turrets aft and a smaller housing at the stern for the VDS towed body. Other operators of the 'Krivak'-class frigate are India and Ukraine.

'Nanuchka' classes Guided-missile corvettes (FSG)

Classed by the Soviets as a *malyy raketnyy korabl'* (MRK, or small rocket ship), the 17 **'Nanuchka I'-class** or **Project 1234 Ovod** units were built between 1969 and 1974 at Petrovsky, Leningrad, with a variant, the **'Nanuchka II' class**, following at that yard and at a Pacific coast shipyard from 1977.

In 1978 came the **'Nanuchka III'**, a development with one 76-mm (3-in) DP gun and one 30-mm CIWS mounting.

The 'Nanuchkas' are considered by Western observers to be coastal missile corvettes, although the fact that they are sometimes seen far from home waters (in such areas as the North Sea, the Mediterranean and the Pacific) tends to put them in the light frigate category, especially when the firepower of the class is considered. The anti-ship missile carried is the Malakhit (SS-N-9 'Siren'), which can carry either a 500-kg (1,102-lb) HE or 250-kT nuclear warhead over a range of 110 km (68 miles). The SS-N-9 uses a dual active radar and passive IR terminal homing system, with third-party targeting and mid-course corrections to guide it in over-the-horizon engagements.

Export vessels

In 1977 an export version of the 'Nanuchka II' class was delivered to India with twin SS-N-2c 'Styx' SSM launchers in place of triple 'Siren' launcher systems. India received three units, two being deleted in 1999 and 2000. Algeria and Libya received three and four ships respectively, Libya losing one in 1986 to US air attack.

SPECIFICATION
'Nanuchka' classes

'Nanuchka' classes
Displacement: 560 tons standard; 660 tons full load
Dimensions: length 59.3 m (194 ft 7 in); beam 11.8 m (38 ft 9 in); draught 2.6 m (8 ft 6 in)
Propulsion: six M-504 diesels delivering 19,470 kW (26,115 shp) to three shafts
Performance: speed 33 kts; range 4,000 km (2,485 miles) at 12 kts
Armament: two triple launchers for Malakhit (SS-N-9 'Siren') anti-ship missiles, one twin launcher for 20 Osa-M (SA-N-4 'Gecko') SAMs, one

twin 57-mm AA gun or ('Nanuchka III' only) one 76-mm (3-in) DP gun and one 30-mm AK-630 CIWS mounting
Electronics: ('Nanuchka III') one 'Peel Pair' or 'Plank Shave' search radar, one 'Pop Group' and one 'Bass Tilt' SAM and gun fire-control radars, one Nayada navigation radar; 'High Pole', 'Square Head', 'Spar Stump' and 'Salt Pot-A/B' IFFs, 'Foot Ball' and 'Half Hat-A/B' ESM, and four chaff PK 10 launchers
Aircraft: none
Complement: 42

Above: A 'Nanuchka I'-class small missile ship under way. The 'Nanuchka II' class for export differs mainly in carrying SS-N-2c 'Styx' missiles, while the last Soviet operational variant, the 'Nanuchka III', has a different gun armament, with a single 76-mm gun and CIWS.

Below: The 'Nanuchka I' class of small missile ship carries the SS-N-9 anti-ship missile as its main armament. For maximum range, a third-party OTH targeting source is required. The single 'Nanuchka IV' is a trials vessel for the Yakhont (SS-N-26) missile, carried in two sextuple launchers. Twelve 'Nanuchka IIIs' remained in Russian service in 2003.

Modified Type 12 'Rothesay' class Anti-air frigate

The **Modified Type 12-** or **'Rothesay'-class** frigates were repeats of the 'Whitby'-class design, somewhat improved in their internal features, and were ordered under the 1954–55 programme to the extent of a planned 12 units.

Though the 'Whitby'-class ships had been designed with a vertical funnel, the 'Rothesay' ships were completed with the slightly raked funnel that had been retrofitted in HMS *Torquay* of the 'Whitby' class, but in other respects there were but few external differences between the two classes.

The 12 torpedo tubes (two twin and eight single) were later removed as being superfluous to modern requirements, and only the early ships carried the two 40-mm Bofors AA guns in the high-capability STAAG Mk 2 radar-controlled automatic twin mount. In the STAAG Mk 2's place was put a large deckhouse so that the GWS.20 missile system, with the Seacat short-range SAM, could be shipped, but for some years all of the ships were fitted instead with a single 40-mm Bofors gun in a manually operated mount.

New Zealand ships

Two ships were completed for the Royal New Zealand Navy as **Otago** and **Taranaki**, but the

Above: Deleted in 1982, HMNZS Otago was the first of the Royal New Zealand Navy's two 'Rothesay'-class frigates.

Right: HMS Berwick was completed by Harland & Wolff in June 1961, and was finally expended as a target in 1986.

last three hulls under British contract were cancelled and completed to the 'Leander'-class design, leaving the British class as **Rothesay**, **Londonderry**, **Brighton**, **Falmouth**, **Yarmouth**, **Rhyl**, **Lowestoft**, **Berwick** and **Plymouth**, which were completed in 1960–61.

The clear superiority of the 'Leander' class led to a major upgrade for the 'Rothesays'. The most significant of the enhancements was the incorporation of a Wasp light helicopter carrying Mk 44 and later Mk 46 anti-submarine lightweight homing torpedoes. The fire-control arrangements were updated, with the MRS3 system replacing the Mk 6M system. The ships' appearance was slightly changed by a new plated foremast and the raising of the funnel. In other respects the layout remained the same with an armament that now comprised two 4.5-in (114-mm) guns in a single mount, one

Above: The lines and general layout mark the 'Rothesay' class as a virtual repeat of the 'Whitby'-class frigate and the immediate ancestor of the immensely successful 'Leander'-class frigate.

SPECIFICATION	
'Rothesay' class (as built)	(533-mm) torpedo tubes, and two
Displacement: 2,150 tons standard;	Limbo Mk 10 ASW mortars
2,560 tons full load	**Electronics:** single Type 975 surface
Dimensions: length 112.7 m (370 ft);	search, Type 293 air/surface search
beam 12.5 m (41 ft); draught 3.9 m	and target indicating, Type 974
(17 ft)	navigation, Type 262 (later Type 903)
Propulsion: two geared steam	aircraft-control, Type 994 air/surface
turbines delivering 22370 kW	search and Type 978 navigation
(30,000 shp) to two shafts	radars, and single Type 170 attack,
Performance: speed 29 kts;	Type 174/177 medium-range search,
endurance 8370 km (5,200 miles)	and Type 162 bottom search sonars
Armament: one twin 4.5-in (114-in)	**Aircraft:** none, but see text
DP gun, one twin 40-mm Bofors AA	**Complement:** 200–235
gun, two twin and eight single 21-in	

GWS.20 quadruple launcher for Seacat SAMs, two 20-mm cannon, and a single Limbo Mk 10.

Trials

In 1978 the *Falmouth* was used in trials of the quarterdeck winch gear for towed-array sonar, and in 1975–79 the *Londonderry* was reconstructed as a trials ship for the Admiralty Surface Weapons Establishment.

This involved the removal of the 4.5-in guns, altering the propulsion system to waterjets for quietness, and stepping a large, plated mizzen mast to carry the new Type 1030 STIR radar. In the autumn of 1980 the ship also received the 30-mm RARDEN cannon for trials.

The cuts in the 1981 Defence Review marked the end of the class, although some lasted longer as a result of the Falklands War. The *Lowestoft* was fitted with the first Type 2031(I) towed-array sonar in 1981–82.

Seen in updated form with a Westland Wasp light anti-submarine helicopter onboard, **HMS** *Falmouth was completed by Swan Hunter in July 1961 as the fourth of the nine 'Rothesay'-class frigates for Royal Navy service. Prominent on the quarter-deck is the three-barrel Limbo Mk 10 anti-submarine mortar.*

Improved Type 12 'Leander' class General-purpose frigate

The **Isaac Sweers** *was completed in 1968 as the fifth of the six Dutch 'Van Speijk'-class frigates modelled on the 'Leander' class, and became the Indonesian* **Karel Satsuitubun.**

A total of 26 general-purpose **'Leander'-class** frigates was built for the Royal Navy in three sub-groups: eight **'Leander Batch 1'**, eight **'Leander Batch 2'** and 10 broad-beam **'Leander Batch 3'** ships. After entering service from 1963, the class underwent numerous refit and modernization programmes that created what were in effect six separate subclasses. The five Batch 3 ships **Andromeda**, **Hermione**, **Jupiter**, **Scylla** and **Charybdis** underwent the most radical conversion, involving the addition of a GWS.25 Sea Wolf automatic point-defence missile system plus numerous new

sensor systems to give the most capable of the subclasses.

Economic cutbacks

The conversion of the remaining five Batch 3 units was shelved for economic reasons. One of the five, the **Bacchante**, was sold to New Zealand in 1991,

becoming **Wellington** and joining the existing 'broad-beam' **Canterbury** and the standard version **Waikato**. The remaining four Batch 3 units were **Achilles**, **Diomede**, **Apollo** and **Ariadne**, which retained their twin 4.5-in (114-mm) guns and Seacat SAM armament. The

eight Batch 2 units were due to form a single Exocet-armed class, but this was changed to three different types. The first comprised **Cleopatra**, **Sirius**, **Phoebe** and **Minerva** and became the **'Leander Batch 2 Towed Array Exocet Group'**, as the ships had the Type

SPECIFICATION

'Ahmad Yani' class
Displacement: 2,255 tons standard;
2,835 tons full load
Dimensions: length 113.4 m (372 ft);
beam 12.5 m (41 ft); draught 4.2 m
(13 ft 10 in)
Propulsion: two geared steam
turbines delivering 22,370 kW
(30,000 shp) to two shafts
Performance: speed 28.5 kts;
endurance 8,300 km (5,160 miles)
at 12 kts
Armament: two quadruple Harpoon
anti-ship missile launchers, two
quadruple launchers for 32 Seacat
SAMs being replaced by two twin

Simbad launchers for Mistral
SAMs, one 76-mm (3-in) DP gun,
and two triple 324-mm (12.75-in)
Mk 32 tubes for Mk 46 anti-
submarine torpedoes
Electronics: single LW-03 air search,
DA-05 surface search, TM 1229C
navigation and M-45 fire-control
radars, SEWACO V data information
system, passive ESM system, two
Corvus chaff launchers, and single
CWE-610 hull and SQR-18A towed-
array sonars
Aircraft: one Wasp or NBO-105
helicopter
Complement: 180

SPECIFICATION

**'Leander' class (RN Sea Wolf
conversion)**
Displacement: 2,500 tons, later
2,790 tons standard; 2,962 tons,
later 3,300 tons full load
Dimensions: length 113.4 m (372 ft);
beam 13.1 m (43 ft); draught 4.5 m
(14 ft 10 in)
Propulsion: two geared steam
turbines delivering 22,370 kW
(30,000 shp) to two shafts
Performance: speed 27 kts;
endurance 7,400 km (4,600 miles)
at 15 kts
Armament: four MM.38 Exocet anti-
ship missile launchers, one sextuple

GWS.25 launcher with 30 Sea Wolf
SAMs, two 20-mm AA guns, and
two triple 324-mm (12.75-in) STWS-
1 tubes for Mk 46 and Stingray
ASW torpedoes
Electronics: single Type 967/978
air/surface search, Type 910 SAM-
control and Type 1006 navigation
radars, one CAAIS combat data
system, one UAA-1 ESM system,
two Corvus chaff launchers, one
Type 2016 hull sonar and one Type
2008 underwater telephone
Aircraft: one Lynx HAS.Mk 2 ASW
helicopter
Complement: 260

2031(I) general-purpose
surveillance and tactical towed-
array sonar on the starboard
side of the stern. Three of the
remaining Batch 2 vessels were
Danae, **Argonaut** and
Penelope, which constituted the
original Exocet conversion group
with the 4.5-in Mk 6 twin gun
mount replaced by four MM.38
Exocet launchers and a third
GWS.22 Seacat SAM launcher.
The last Batch 2 ship, **Juno**, had
its Exocet conversion halted in
favour of modification as a
navigation training ship.

The eight Batch 1 vessels
were converted to ASW ships
by the fitting of a GWS.40 Ikara
ASW missile installation in place
of the gun mount. To
compensate for the loss in AA
capability, a second GWS.22
Seacat launcher was added aft
atop the hangar. One vessel,
Dido, was sold to New Zealand
in 1991, becoming **Southland**,
while the other seven remained
in Royal Navy service as **Aurora**,

Right: Completed in 1971, HMAS
Torrens was one of two 'Swan'-
class frigates built in Australia
to a modified 'Leander' design.

Euryalus, **Galatea**, **Arethusa**,
Naiad, **Ajax** and **Leander**. All
the ships remaining in British
service were deleted in the late
1980s and early 1990s.

Overseas exports

In addition to the vessels for the
Royal Navy, a number of other
nations have either purchased
British-built 'Leanders' or
constructed their own under
licence. The former vessels are
the Chilean navy's **Condell** and
Almirante Lynch, while the
latter included the Royal
Australian Navy's **Swan** and
Torrens, the Indian navy's
Nilgiri, **Himgiri**, **Udaygiri**,
Dunagiri, **Taragiri** and
Vindhyagiri, and the Dutch

navy's **Van Speijk**, **Van Galen**,
Tjerk Hiddes, **Van Nes**, **Isaac
Sweers** and **Evertsen**, which
became the Indonesian navy's
Ahmad Yani, **Slamet Riyadi**,
Yos Sudarso, **Oswald Siahaan**,
Abdul Halim Perdanakusuma
and **Karel Satsuitubun** in the
later 1980s. In all cases the
countries obtained ships with
better armament and sensor fits
than the Royal Navy vessels,
apart from the final Sea Wolf
conversions.

The Dutch doubled the
surface-to-surface missile
armament to eight by using
Harpoon, and the Indians fit the
last two of their vessels to carry
accompanying Sea King ASW
helicopters.

Above: HMS Andromeda was
the first of the 'Leanders' to be
fitted with Sea Wolf and Exocet
missiles, re-commissioning in
1980. After refitting, Andromeda
and the other four 'Leander
Batch 3' ships were the most
powerful of the 'Leander'-class.
The planned conversion of the
other five Batch 3s fell victim to
cuts in the defence budget.

As they left British service, a
number of the ships were sold,
the Chilean navy receiving the
Achilles and *Ariadne* as the
Ministro Zeneno and **General
Baquedano**, and the Ecuadorian
navy receiving the *Penelope* and
Danae as the **Presidente Eloy
Alfar** and **Moran Valverde**.

Type 21 'Amazon' class Guided-missile frigate

Above: HMS Amazon leads Antelope through calm sea. Royal Navy Type 21s carried four Exocet missile launchers.

Left: The ill-fated HMS Antelope. Type 21 frigates handle well, but lack the capacity to handle the most up-to-date weapon systems.

The **Type 21** or **'Amazon'-class** general-purpose frigate was a private shipbuilder's design to replace the Type 41 (or 'Leopard'-class) and Type 61 (or 'Salisbury'-class) frigates. Private and official ship designers were not brought together on the project, resulting in a class that handled well but lacked sufficient growth potential to take the new generation of sensor and weapon fits. Thus the vessels

did not receive new equipment when refitted.

Falklands War

During the 1982 Falklands War, **Avenger**, **Ardent**, **Arrow**, **Antelope** and **Alacrity** served in the combat zone, while **Active** and **Ambuscade** assisted in supporting operations and the occasional shore bombardment. Only the lead ship, **Amazon**, missed the war, as it was in the Far East. On 21 May 1982, the

HMS Ambuscade. These vessels suffered severe cracking in the upper deck.

SPECIFICATION
'Amazon' class (as built)

Displacement: 2,750 tons standard; 3,250 tons full load
Dimensions: length 117.04 m (384 ft); beam 12.73 m (41 ft 9 in); draught 5.94 m (19 ft 6 in)
Propulsion: COGOG with two Rolls-Royce Olympus TM3B gas turbines delivering 41,755 kW (56,000 shp) and two Rolls-Royce Tyne RM1A gas turbines delivering 6,340 kW (8,500 shp) to two shafts
Performance: speed 32 kts; range 7,400 km (4,600 miles) at 17 kts
Armament: four container-launchers for four MM.38 Exocet anti-ship missiles (not in *Amazon* and *Antelope*), one GWS 24 quadruple launcher for 20 Seacat short-range

SAMs, one 4.5-in (114-mm) DP gun, two or four 20-mm AA guns, and two triple 324-mm (12.75-in) STWS Mk 1 tubes with Mk 46 and Stingray anti-submarine torpedoes
Electronics: one Type 992Q air/surface search radar, one Type 978 navigation radar, two RTN10X fire-control radars, one CAAIS combat data system, one UAA-1 ESM system (in some vessels), two Corvus chaff launchers, one Type 162M hull sonar, and one Type 184M hull sonar
Aircraft: one Lynx HAS.Mk 2 or HAS.Mk 3 ASW helicopter
Complement: 175 normal and 192 maximum

Ardent sank after air attacks, and two days later the *Antelope* was destroyed when an unexploded bomb detonated while being defused.

After the war, the remaining class members were found to have severe hull cracking;

indeed *Arrow* required an emergency refit. All the ships were strengthened with steel inserts welded to the hull

structure, but the future of the class remained clouded, and in 1993–94 the six ships were sold to Pakistan as the **Tariq**, **Babur**,

Khaibar, **Badr**, **Shajahan** and **Tippu Sultan** of the **'Tariq' class** and have been fittted with new missiles.

The 'Oliver Hazard Perry'-class frigate USS Rueben James *(rear) alongside Pakistan's* Shahjahan *and* Tippu Sultan. *The 'Tariq' class replace the obsolete Seacat SAM system with either the Chinese LY 60N (a copy of Aspide) or Harpoon missiles carried in place of the Exocet added to the Royal Navy ships.*

Type 22 'Broadsword' class Guided-missile frigate

Originally to have been a class of 26 to follow the 'Leanders', the **Type 22** or **'Broadsword'-class** design was conceived as an ASW type for service in the Greenland–Iceland–UK gap against modern high-performance nuclear submarines. As has happened to most modern British naval

programmes, however, the 'chop' fell during defence cuts and the procurement schedule was changed somewhat. The original four **'Broadsword Batch 1'** vessels were **Broadsword**, **Battleaxe**, **Brilliant** and **Brazen**. Although rated as frigates, these are in fact larger than the contemporary Type 42

destroyers, and were designated frigates for purely political reasons. The hull, which has greater freeboard than that of the destroyers, is an

Batch 3 variants of the 'Broadsword' class are highly capable ships, although the frigate description may seem odd for a vessel with a full-load displacement of 4,800 tons and a length of 148.1 m (485 ft 10 in) with significant anti-air, surface and submarine capabilities.

improved Type 12 design for capability in rough weather without a significant reduction in speed. The *Brilliant* and *Broadsword* distinguished

The four Batch 1 vessels were transferred to Brazil during 1995–97. HMS Battleaxe is illustrated before its transfer to Brazil as the Rademaker. Original plans to place a single 57-mm gun on the bow of the Brazilian ships was shelved in favour of a 40-mm weapon on each beam.

Sheffield and **Coventry**. These also differ among themselves, as the *Brave* has a Rolls-Royce COGAG arrangement with two Spey SM1A (later SM1C) and two Tyne RM1C gas turbines. The *Brave* was also the first Type 22 unit to have an enlarged platform to take a Sea King or Merlin ASW helicopter.

Following the ships' success in the 1982 Falklands War, a **'Broadsword Batch 3'** variant was ordered: the four units were **Cornwall**, **Cumberland**, **Campbeltown** and **Chatham**. These have the same basic hull as the Batch 2s but with eight Harpoon missiles, a single 4.5-in (114-mm) DP gun and one 30-mm Goalkeeper CIWS. All ships still in British service now have Type 2050 rather than Type 2016 sonar.

themselves in the Falklands, the former being the first to fire the Seawolf in anger.

Unfortunately, because of design shortcomings, the Type 22s could not be fitted with the definitive Type 2031(Z) towed-array sonar at the stern, so a lengthened **'Broadsword Batch 2'** of six ships was authorized as **Boxer**, **Beaver**, **Brave**, **London**,

Brazilian service

The Batch 1 ships have been sold to Brazil as the **Bosisio, Greenhalgh, Dodsworth** and **Rademaker** (with an aditional 40-mm gun added on each beam and MM.40 Exocets) and the *London, Boxer, Beaver, Brave* and *Coventry* were deleted in 1999–2001.

SPECIFICATION

'Broadsword Batch 1' class
Displacement: 3,500 tons standard; 4,400 tons full load
Dimensions: length 131.06 m (430 ft); beam 14.78 m (48 ft 6 in); draught 6.05 m (19 ft 10 in)
Propulsion: COGOG with two Rolls-Royce Olympus TM3B gas turbines delivering 40,710 kW (54,600 shp) and two Rolls-Royce Tyne RM1A gas turbines delivering 7,230 kW (9,700 shp) to two shafts
Performance: speed 29 kts; range 8335 km (5,180 miles) at 18 kts
Armament: four container-launchers for four MM.38 Exocet anti-ship missiles, two GWS 25 sextuple launchers for 60 Seawolf SAMs, two 40- or 30-mm AA guns, two

20-mm AA guns, and (*Brilliant* and *Brazen*) two triple 324-mm (12.75-in) STWS Mk 1 tubes for Mk 46 and Stingray ASW torpedoes
Electronics: one Type 967/968 air/surface search radar, two Type 910 Seawolf fire-control radars, one Type 1006 navigation radar, one CAAIS combat data system, one UAA-1 ESM system, two Corvus chaff launchers, two Mk 36 SRBOC chaff launchers, one Type 2016 hull sonar, and one Type 2008 underwater telephone
Aircraft: one or two Lynx HAS.Mk 2/3 or HMA.Mk 8 ASW/anti-ship helicopters
Complement: 223 normal and 248 maximum

The Batch 2 vessel HMS Boxer was retired from Royal Navy service in 1999. The 'Broadswords' were designed primarily for the ASW and are also capable of acting as OTC (Officer in Tactical Command). A single Lynx is normally embarked and additional EW equipment is added for deployments.

'Garcia' and 'Brooke' classes Frigate and Guided-missile frigate

SPECIFICATION

'Garcia' class
Displacement: 2,620 tons standard; 3,560 tons full load
Dimensions: length 126.3 m (414 ft 6 in); beam 13.5 m (44 ft 4 in); draught 4.4 m (14 ft 6 in)
Propulsion: geared steam turbines delivering 26,100 kW (35,000 shp) to one shaft
Performance: speed 27.5 kts; endurance 7,400 km (4,600 miles) at 20 kts
Armament: two 5-in (127-mm) Mk 30 DP guns, one octuple Mk 16 ASROC launcher with eight (first five ships) or 16 (other ships)

RUR-5A rockets, two triple 12.75-in (324-mm) Mk 32 tubes for Mk 46 ASW torpedoes (12 reloads)
Electronics: one SPS-40 air search radar, one SPS-10 surface search radar, one SPG-35 fire-control radar, one LN66 navigation radar, one WLR-1 ECM system, one WLR-3 ECM system, one ULQ-6 ECM system, one SQS-26 bow sonar, and (*Garcia* and *McDonnell* only) one BQR-15 towed sonar
Aircraft: one SH-2F Seasprite LAMPS I helicopter (not in *Garcia* and *McDonnell*)
Complement: 239–247

The USS **Brooke** *was the name ship of its class, essentially a derivative of the 'Garcia' class of ocean escort with the after 5-in (127-mm) gun replaced by a single-rail SAM launcher. The ship became the Pakistani* **Khaibar** *for a time after 1988.*

Designed in the late 1950s as successors to World War II destroyers in the oceanic escort role, the **'Garcia'-class** ASW and **'Brooke'-class** AAW ships were ordered by the US Navy to the extent of 10 and six units respectively. Further production of the latter ended during fiscal year 1963 because of the ships'

high cost and limited capability. Although they were relatively modern, the US Navy evinced little real interest in the process of steady modernization for the ASW ships *Garcia*, **Bradley**, **Edward McDonnell**, **Brumby**, **Davidson**, **Voge**, **Sample**, **Koelsch**, **Albert David** and **O'Callahan** (laid down at four yards between 1962 and 1964 for completion between 1964 and 1967) with new guns, Harpoon anti-ship missiles and modern ESM equipment. Over the years the ships of the class, initially classified in USN service as destroyer escorts, were frequently used for the testing of several prototype items of systems, including the SQR-15 linear towed-array sonar, which was installed in the *Garcia* and

Evident in the after part of the 'Brooke'-class USS **Ramsey** *is the hangar for the LAMPS I light multi-role (SH-2F Seasprite) helicopter and, between the hangar and the superstructure, the Mk 22 single-arm launcher for medium-range SAMs.*

Left: The USS O'Callahan *was the last unit of the 'Garcia' class of oceanic escorts optimized for the anti-submarine role. The 16 'Garcia'- and 'Brooke'-class ships were complemented by a 17th unit, the experimental USS* Glover *with pump-jet propulsion.*

Edward McDonnell in place of the otherwise standard LAMPS I ASW helicopter. An automated ASW tactical data system (TDS) was carried by the *Voge* and *Koelsch*, while on the ships from the *Voge* onward a reload magazine for the ASROC anti-submarine system was built into the superstructure, boosting the number of RUR-5A rocket-launched weapons from eight to 16.

SAM ships

The SAM ships **Brooke**, **Ramsey**, **Schofield**, **Talbot**, **Richard L. Page** and **Julius F. Furer** (built and completed by two yards in the period 1962–1967) were identical to the 'Garcias' except for the incorporation of a single-rail Mk 22 launcher, originally for 16 Tartar and later for the same number of Standard SM-1MR missiles, in place of the aft 5-in (127-mm) gun mount. From the *Talbot* onward, an ASROC reload magazine was also incorporated into the forward part of the superstructure. The *Talbot* was used as the test ship for the weapons and sensor fit for the 'Oliver Hazard Perry' class, but was then returned to normal appearance. The only major modernization of the ships was the fitting of the SLQ-32(V)2 ESM suite to replace older systems.

The ships were retired from US service in the late 1980s, four 'Garcias' being leased to Brazil as the **Pernambuco**, **Paraíba, Paraná** and **Pará**. Four of each class were leased to Pakistan as the **Saif, Harbah, Siqqat, Aslat, Khaibar, Hunam, Tabuk** and **Badr**, but were later returned when the US refused to renew the leases.

'Knox' class Frigate

The USS Knox *(FF-1052) was the first ship of its class. Evolved from the preceding 'Garcia' and 'Brooke' classes, the 'Knox'-class vessels were later fitted with Harpoon anti-ship missiles and the 20-mm Phalanx close-in weapon system (CIWS) for last-ditch defence against sea-skimming anti-ship missiles.*

The 'Knox' class is similar to the 'Garcia' and 'Brooke' classes but with slightly larger dimensions as a result of the use of non-pressure fired boilers. The type was designed in the early 1960s, and the first of these ocean escort vessels (now generally regarded as frigates) entered US Navy service in 1969, while the last units of the 46-strong class were delivered in 1974. They are specialized ASW ships and were heavily criticised for their single-shaft propulsion and gun armament of just one 5-in (127-mm) weapon.

Spanish derivative

A five-ship class based on the design but with a Mk 22 missile launcher for 13 Standard SM-1MR and three Harpoon missiles was constructed in Spain for the Spanish navy. Built with US aid, the ships are the **Baleares, Andalucia, Cataluña, Asturias** and **Extremadura**, which also carried two Mk 25 ASW torpedo tubes (now no longer used) as well as the two twin Mk 32 systems, for which a total of 22 Mk 44/46 and 19 Mk 37 ASW torpedoes was stored in each ship's magazines.

From 1980 onwards the American 'Knox' ships were taken in hand to receive raised bulwarks and spray strakes forward to improve their seakeeping in heavy weather. Like the 'Garcia' class, numerous 'Knox' ships have been used over the years to test individual prototype weapon and sensor systems. The first 32 ships were equipped with an octuple launcher for the Sea Sparrow SAM, but this was replaced by a 20-mm Phalanx CIWS of the type eventually fitted to all 46 ships. The port pair of the four twin cells of the ASROC launcher were retrofitted to fire the Harpoon anti-ship missile, while all of the vessels were fitted to carry the SQR-18A TACTASS towed-array sonar, which in 34 of the ships replaced the SQS-35A VDS system carried in a stern well. For helicopter operations an SRN-15 TACAN is carried and the SLQ-32(V)1 ESM system was upgraded to the SLQ-32(V)2 configuration. To reduce underwater radiated noise, the Prairie/Masker bubble system is used on the hull and propeller. The ASW TDS first evaluated in the 'Garcia' class was fitted as the ships were refitted. By 1986 eight units had been reassigned to the Naval Reserve Force as replacements for old World War II destroyers as these were retired.

American class

The class comprised the **Knox**, **Roark**, **Gray**, **Hepburn**, **Connole**, **Rathburne**, **Meyerkord**, **W. S. Sims**, **Lang**, **Patterson**, **Whipple**, **Reasoner**, **Lockwood**, **Stein**, **Marvin Shields**, **Francis Hammond**, **Vreeland**, **Bagley**, **Downes**, **Badger**, **Blakely**, **Robert E.**

Right: Seen in US Navy service, the USS Cook was completed by Avondale in December 1971 as one of the 'Knox' class of ASW frigates. In August 1995 it was recommissioned as the Taiwanese navy's Hae Yang.

Below: The USS Pharris is seen during an exercise off the South American coast. The 46 'Knox'-class vessels were built as dedicated oceanic ASW escorts, and later in their lives were revised to improve their seakeeping qualities.

Peary, **Harold E. Holt**, **Trippe**, **Fanning**, **Ouellet**, **Joseph Hewes**, **Bowen**, **Paul**, **Aylwin**, **Elmer Montgomery**, **Cook**, **McCandless**, **Donald B. Beary**, **Brewton**, **Kirk**, **Barbey**, **Jesse L. Brown**, **Ainsworth**, **Miller**, **Thomas C. Hart**, **Capodanno**, **Pharris**, **Truett**, **Valdez** and **Moinester**.

The ships were decommissioned from US service in the early 1990s, and many of the vessels were transferred to the navies of friendly nations. At the beginning of the 21st century, considerable numbers of the 'Knox'-class ships were still in extensive service with Egypt (two of four **'Damyat'-class**

ships), Greece (one of three **'Epirus'-class** ships), Mexico (four **'Allende'-class** ships), Taiwan (eight out of nine **'Chin**

Yang'-class ships), Thailand (two **'Phutta Yofta Chulalok'-class** ships) and Turkey (six out of nine **'Tepe'-class** ships).

SPECIFICATION
'Knox' class

Displacement: 3,011 tons standard; 3,877 tons (first 26 ships) or 4,250 tons (last 20 ships) full load
Dimensions: length 133.5 m (438 ft); beam 14.3 m (47 ft); draught 4.6 m (15 ft)
Propulsion: geared steam turbines delivering 26,100 kW (35,000 shp) to one shaft
Performance: speed 27 kts; endurance 8335 km (5,180 miles) at 20 kts
Armament: one 5-in (127-mm) Mk 42 DP gun, one 20-mm Mk 15 Phalanx CIWS replacing one octuple launcher for eight RIM-7 Sea Sparrow SAMs, one octuple

Mk 16 ASROC launcher for 12 RUR-5A anti-submarine rockets and four Harpoon anti-ship missiles, and two twin 12.75-in (324-mm) Mk 32 launchers for 22 Mk 46 ASW torpedoes
Electronics: one SPS-40B air search radar, one SPS-10 surface search radar, one SPG-53 fire-control radar, one LN66 navigation radar, one ASW tactical data system, one SRN-15 TACAN, one SQS-26 bow sonar, and one SQS-35 variable-depth sonar (34 ships); all later had one SQR-18A towed-array sonar
Aircraft: one SH-2F Seasprite LAMPS I helicopter
Complement: 283

'Ulsan' & 'Bangabandhu' classes Guided-missile frigates

In the mid-1970s, the South Koreans came to the decision that the development of their shipbuilding industry and the continuing threat of aggressive action by the north Koreans in and around South Korean waters made it sensible to procure a new class of small frigates built in South Korean yards with imported weapons and electronics.

This was the genesis of the **'Ulsan' class** of nine frigates built by Hyundai at Ulsan, Korean SEC, Korea Tacoma, and Daewoo. The ships are the **Ulsan**, **Seoul, Chung Nam**, **Masan**, **Kyong Buk**, **Chon Nam**, **Che Ju**, **Busan** and **Chung Ju**, which were laid down in 1979–1990, launched in 1980–1992, and commissioned in 1981–93. The design was based on a steel hull with an aluminium alloy superstructure,

and the ships were completed to three standards. The first four ships are basically similar and carry the light armament of eight 30-mm Oerlikon cannon, for use against aircraft and fast attack craft, in four Emerson Electric twin turrets. The fifth ship, the *Kyong Buk*, was completed to a standard that differed only in its light armament of six 40-mm Bofors guns in three Otobreda twin turrets, and the last four ships were completed with a built-up after gun platform but the same light armament as the *Kyong Buk*, and also with different surface search, target indication and navigation radars.

Some problems were encountered with the integration of the weapons, and in the last five ships a Ferranti combat data system has been fitted.

The 'Ulsan'-class light frigate marked the emergence of South Korea as a country able to design and build warships, albeit with major imported influence in their all-important weapons, electronics and engines.

In 1998 Bangladesh ordered the **Bangabandhu**, built by Daewoo. She has a full-load displacement of 2,370 tons,

SEMT-Pielstick diesels, Dutch radars, other European electronics, and lighter armament.

SPECIFICATION

'Ulsan' class
Displacement: 1,496 tons light; 2,180 tons or, from *Chon Nam*, 2,300 tons full load
Dimensions: length 102 m (334 ft 8 in); beam 11.5 m (37 ft 9 in); draught 3.5 m (11 ft 6 in)
Propulsion: CODOG with two LM 2500 gas turbines delivering 39995 kW (53,640 shp) and two MTU 16V538 TB82 diesels delivering 4430 kW (5,940 shp) to two shafts
Performance: speed 34 kts; endurance 7400 km (4,600 miles) at 15 kts
Armament: two 76.2-mm (3-in) Otobreda Compact DP guns, four

twin 30-mm EMERLEC-30 AA guns, four twin launchers for eight Harpoon anti-ship missiles, two triple 324-mm (12.75-in) tubes for Mk 46 anti-submarine torpedoes, and 12 depth charges
Electronics: one DA-05 air search radar, one ZW-06 surface search radar, one SPS-10C navigation radar, one WM-28 or ST 1802 fire-control radar, one Lirod or Radamec System 2000 optronic director, one WSA 423 or Litton combat data system, one ULQ-11K ESM systee SLQ-25 Nixie towed torpedo decoy
Aircraft: none
Crew: 150

'Pará' ('Garcia') class Frigate

As changing operational requirements coincided with the completion of the 'Oliver Hazard Perry' class of ocean escort

frigates in the mid-1980s, the US Navy decided that it could discard most of its older frigates. Among the classes that

were selected for this process was the 'Garcia' class, which was still comparatively new but had for some time been

treated with operational suspicion because of its single-shaft propulsion, which was deemed a hindrance to agility

*At one time known as the **USS** Albert **D**avid, she became the* Pará *upon entering Brazilian service. This vessel was launched on 19 December 1968.*

Navigating the tropical waters off the northern coast of South America, the Brazilian navy's Paraíba, *formerly the ex-**USS** **D**avidson, is seen here on manoeuvres.*

and a factor rendering the ship liable to total disablement through a single hit.

In 1989 the Brazilian navy leased four of the ships. These were the USS *Albert David, Davidson, Sample and Bradley*, which had been constructed by Lockheed Shipbuilding & Construction, Avondale Shipyards, Lockheed, and Bethlehem Steel respectively, for commissioning in 1968, 1965, 1968 and 1965.

The ships all arrived in Brazil in December of that year, and in 1994 the lease on the ships was extended. In Brazilian service these frigates are classified as destroyers, and constitute the **'Pará' class,** comprising the **Pará**, **Paraíba**, **Paraná** and **Pernambuco**. The ships operate

as the 1st Destroyer Squadron from the base at Niteroi close to Rio de Janeiro, and have proved somewhat difficult to maintain at an adequate state of operational readiness.

Hangar

The ships have been little altered since their arrival from the US, but it is worth noting that while the hangar was originally sized for the Sikorsky SH-3 Sea King anti-submarine helicopter, it is now used for the somewhat smaller Westland Lynx helicopter, which has a similar anti-submarine tasking with a secondary anti-ship role. In their original US service, the *Albert David* and *Sample* had had their helicopter flight decks adapted for the accommodation

and use of the SQR-15 towed-array sonar, but this equipment was removed from the ships before their transfer to Brazil.

The ships are not notably fast, but speedy enough for the anti-submarine role that is their primary task. Here the primary long-range weapon is the

embarked helicopter, as noted above, while a shorter-range capability is provided by the Mk 112 octuple launcher for ASROC weapons. This is located abaft the forward 5-in (127-mm) gun, and the *Pará* and *Paraná* have an automatic reload system.

SPECIFICATION

'Pará' class
Displacement: 2,620 tons standard; 3.560 tons full load
Dimensions: length 126.3 m (414 ft 6 in); beam 13.5 m (44 ft 3 in); draught 4.4 m (24 ft)
Propulsion: one Westinghouse or General Electric steam turbine delivering 26,095 kW (35,000 shp) to one shaft
Performance: speed 27.5 kts; endurance 7400 km (4,600 miles) at 20 kts
Armament: two 5-in (127-mm) DP

guns, one octuple launcher for ASROC anti-submarine rockets, and two triple 324-mm (12.75-in) tubes for Mk 46 anti-submarine torpedoes
Electronics: one SPS-40B air search radar, one SPS-10C surface search radar, one LN66 navigation radar, one Mk 35 fire-control radar, one WLR-6/ULQ-6 EW system, two Mk 33 RBOC chaff launchers, and one T Mk 6 Fanfare torpedo decoy system
Aircraft: none
Crew: 286

*She used to be called the **USS** **B**radley, but today this frigate is a proud member of Brazil's navy. The* **Pernambuco** *was commissioned into service with the force on 25 September 1989.*

The Brazilian frigate **Paraná**, *the ex-**USS** **S**ample, was acquired from the US Navy in the late 1980s. She was recommissioned on 24 August 1989.*

'Type FS 1500' class Guided-missile frigate

In 1980 Colombia contracted with a West German company, Howaldtswerke of Kiel, for the design and construction of four frigates. The design was known to its originator as the **'Type FS 1500' class**, and to the Colombian navy as the **'Almirante Padilla' class**. The ships are the **Almirante Padilla**, **Caldas**, **Antioquia** and **Independiente**, and these were laid down in 1981, launched in 1982–83, and commissioned in 1983–84. In 1999, the ships were reclassified from frigate to light frigate standard.

With eight MM.40 Exocet missiles, the ships pack a heavyweight anti-ship punch. It has been reported that the short-range defensive capability against aircraft has been bolstered by the retrofit of one or more launchers for Mistral SAMs, and the anti-submarine

Colombia's four 'Almirante Padilla'-class light frigates offer a considerable capability by the standards prevailing on the western side of South America and in the Caribbean.

capability has been enhanced by the replacement of the original MBB (later Eurocopter) BO 105CB helicopter by a larger and more capable Bell Model 412 helicopter. This required the lengthening of the flight deck by some 2 m (6 ft 7 in) at its rear edge to a point close above the Breda twin mounting for two 40-mm Bofors guns that provide capability against aircraft and fast attack craft.

It is also reported that there have been changes to the ships' superstructure, and possibly an upgrade of the ships' systems.

In 1982 Malaysia ordered two similar ships as the **'Kasturi' class** units **Kasturi** and **Lekir**. These too were built by Howaldtswerke in 1983, and were both commissioned in August 1984. Despite the fact that they are larger than the service's frigate *Rahmat*, now used in the training role, the ships are classified by the Malaysian navy as corvettes.

The specification for the 'Kasturi' class includes a full-load displacement of 1,850 tons, an overall length of 97.3 m

(319 ft 2 in), and the same propulsion arrangement as the 'Almirante Padilla' class for a speed of 28 kts. The armament is different, with the long-range anti-ship capability provided by two twin launchers for four MM.40 Exocet missiles.

The gun armament comprises one 100-mm (3.94-in) Creusot-Loire Compact Mk 2 DP gun, one 57-mm (2.24-in) Bofors DP gun, and four 30-mm cannon in two Emerson Electric twin turrets. Anti-submarine capability was vested in a Westland Wasp HAS.Mk 1 light

helicopter (no longer operational) without a hangar, and a 375-mm (14.76-in) Bofors twin-tube mortar.

The electronics are mainly Dutch, French and German. The radars are the DA-08 air/surface search and WM-22 fire-control units, the latter backed by two LIOD optronic directors, the combat data system is the Sewaco-MA system, EW capability rests with a DR 3000 ESM system and two Dagaie chaff/flare launchers, and the sonar is the DSQS-21C hull-mounted unit.

SPECIFICATION	
'Almirante Padilla' class	launchers for eight MM.40 Exocet anti-ship missiles, and two 324-mm (12.75-in) tubes for A244S anti-submarine torpedoes
Displacement: 1,500 tons standard; 2,100 tons full load	
Dimensions: length 99.1 m (325 ft 2 in); beam 11.3 m (37 ft 2 in); draught 3.7 m (12 ft 2 in)	**Electronics:** one Sea Tiger air/surface search radar, one Furuno navigation radar, one Castor IIB fire-control radar, two Canopus optronic directors, one TAVITAC combat data system, one EW system, one Dagaie chaff/flare launcher, and one ASO 4-2 hull sonar
Propulsion: four MTU 20V1163 TB92 diesels delivering 17,440 kW (23,390 shp) to two shafts	
Performance: speed 27 kts; endurance 9,250 km (5,750 miles) at 18 kts	
Armament: one 76.2-mm (3-in) Otobreda Compact DP gun, one twin 40-mm DP guns, two twin 30-mm AA cannon, twin quadruple	**Aircraft:** one BO 105CB or Bell 412 helicopter
	Crew: 94

'St Laurent' and 'Restigouche' classes DDE/DDH

In 1949 Canada announced the construction of seven new anti-submarine escorts, the units of the **'St Laurent' class**, which were the first dedicated ASW ships designed and built (by four yards) in Canada. They were some of the most sophisticated destroyers of their time. The first ship in the class, **HMCS St Laurent**, was commissioned in 1955. New features included a dedicated command operations room, air conditioning, and a pre-wetting system to counter NBC contamination.

In the late 1950s, the ships were rmodified to permit helicopter operations through the provision of a platform, hangar and maintenance facilities for the CHSS-2 Sea King. The original single funnel was reconfigured into a twin funnel, and the aft 3-in (76-mm) Mk 33 twin gun mount and aft Limbo Mk 10 ASW mortar were replaced by the midships

helicopter pad and hangar. A variable-depth sonar, fin stabilizers and Beartrap helicopter recovery system were also added, and the displacement rose to more than 3,000 tons. The first of the ships to be adapted was **HMCS Assiniboine**, which was recommissioned in June 1963. To signify helicopter capability, the ships' designation was changed from DDE to DDH.

DELEX programme

The next milestone for the class came in the 1970s, when the Destroyer Life Extension Program upgraded various onboard systems to keep the ships viable as surface combatants into the 1980s. The name ship was the only unit not to receive this DELEX upgrade, and paid off in 1974.

HMCS Fraser had a lattice mast fitted between the twin funnels to support a TACAN

HMCS **Terra Nova** *was built by Victoria Machinery and commissioned in June 1959. The vessel was one of four within the 'Restigouche' class to receive* **ASROC** *aft, a* **VDS** *and a lattice foremast.*

antenna. *Fraser* was also used as a test-bed for the Nixie torpedo decoy system, and the Experimental Towed-Array Sonar System. After decades of service, all of the ships (the others being **Saguenay**, **Skeena**, **Ottawa** and **Margaree**) had been paid off by 1994.

Seven similar DDEs of the **'Restigouche' class** were ordered in 1952 and commissioned in 1958–59. Distinguishing them from the 'St Laurents', the forward main battery was changed to two 3-in

Mk 6 guns in a single mount. In the late 1960s **Gatineau**, **Restigouche**, **Kootenay** and **Terra Nova** were given a tall lattice mast, an ASROC launcher and VDS. And in the 1980s, they received the DELEX upgrade.

For the 1991 Gulf War, Canada upgraded *Restigouche* and *Terra Nova* with Harpoon missiles, a Vulcan Phalanx CIWS, two twin-mount 40-mm Bofors guns, and Blowpipe shoulder-launched SAMs. The *Terra Nova* was the last active ship, and was finally paid off in 1997.

SPECIFICATION

'St Laurent' class
Displacement: 2,800 tons full load (DDE) or 3,050 tons full load (DDH)
Dimensions: length 113.1 m (371 ft); beam 12.8 m (42 ft); draft 4.2 m (13 ft 2 in)
Propulsion: geared steam turbines delivering 22,370 kW (30,000 shp) to two shafts
Speed: 28 kts
Armament: two twin 3-in (76-mm) Mk 33 guns (aft mount removed in DDH refit), two Mk 10 Limbo ASW mortars (one removed in DDH

refit), two 40-mm Bofors guns (removed in DDH refit), and two triple 324-mm (12.75-in) Mk 32 tubes for Mk 44 or Mk 46 ASW torpedoes (added in DDH refit)
Electronics: one SPS-12 air search radar, one SPS-10 surface search radar, one navigation radar, SPG-48 fire-control radar on gun mounts; SQS-501, SQS-502, SQS-503, SQS-504 and VDS sonars
Aircraft: one CHSS-2/CH-124 (DDH)
Complement: 290

HMCS Fraser, *seen in heavy weather, reveals the subtle differences of the 'St Laurent' class. This was the sole vessel in the class with a* **TACAN** *aerial.*

'Surcouf' class Destroyer escort/air defence/ASW ship

The destroyers of the **'Surcouf'** or **T47 class**, which were larger than other European destroyers of the time, were authorized in 1949–52 and, as an *escorteur d'escadre* type, were designed to give AAW protection to the new carriers and other fleet units. A 127-mm (5-in) calibre was adopted, backed by a heavy

secondary battery of 57-mm twin AA mountings.

Completed in 1955–57, the 12 ships were the **Surcouf**, **Kersaint**, **Cassard**, **Bouvet**, **Dupetit-Thouars**, **Chevalier Paul**, **Maillé-Brézé**, **Vauquelin**, **D'Estrées**, **Du Chayla**, **Casabianca** and **Guépràtte**. In the plans little provision, other

than depth charges, was made for ASW operations, and finally four triple tubes were mounted along the deck edge on each beam: the forward pair fired L3 anti-submarine torpedoes, of which 12 were carried, and the after pair either L3 ASW or K2 anti-ship torpedoes. Hull sonars of French design were used,

and the increased air threat led to the employment of new-generation French radars, supported by single main- and secondary-armament directors. As the new fleet escorts with carriers, a high speed was not needed. Early in the 1960s the *Surcouf*, *Cassard* and *Chevalier Paul* had their forward 57-mm

mounting removed to allow the bridge to be extended, making the ships suitable for command purposes.

In 1962–65 the *Dupetit-Thouars*, *Kersaint*, *Bouvet* and *Du Chayla* were revised with the single-rail Mk 13 launcher for US Tartar (and from the 1970s, Standard SM-1MR) SAMs in place of the after pair of 127-mm mountings, and two associated SPG-51 tracker/illuminator radars mounted on a raised deckhouse between the after pair of 57-mm mountings. A sextuple 375-mm (14.76-in) Bofors ASW rocket launcher also replaced the forward 127-mm mounting, and the anti-ship torpedo tubes were removed. The masts and funnels were made taller, and the antenna for the SPS-39A 3D radar replaced that of the DRBV 11 at the head of the mainmast.

From 1968 onwards, these

277-crew conversions (the **'Du Chayla' class**) were updated with more capable electronics, and all four ships had been deleted by 1991.

Malafon conversions

After the concept had been validated by the experimental installation of a bow sonar and VDS on *D'Estrées* early in the 1960s, five ships were converted to ASW standard by the replacement of their whole armament and sensor outfit. A single launcher and magazine for 13 Malafon ASW missiles were fitted aft, single 100-mm (3.9-in) guns (controlled by a DRBC 32A director) were fitted forward and aft, and a sextuple Bofors rocket launcher was installed in the 'B' position. Only the two forward sets of tubes were retained, and the antenna for a DRBV 22A air search radar replaced the original model at

The D'Estrées was one of the 'Surcouf'-class destroyers adapted later in its career as a specialized anti-submarine destroyer with the Malafon missile system. Additional ASW armament incuded one sextuple Bofors mortar and two sets of triple tubes for L3 torpedoes. The ASW conversions were known as the 'D'Estrées' class.

the head of the single tripod foremast with that for a DRBV 50 air/surface radar beneath it. The sensors were completed by DUBV 23 and DUBV 43 sonars, the new bow sonar involving the reshaping of the clipper bow for an overall length of 132.5 m

(434 ft 6 in), and the crew was reduced to 260 in more habitable accommodation.

These served into the mid-1980s before being replaced by the ASW destroyers of the 'Georges Leygues' class. The last was deleted in 1985.

SPECIFICATION	
'Surcouf' class (as built)	DP, three twin 57-mm AA and
Displacement: 2,750 tons standard; 3,740 tons full load	three 40-mm guns, and four triple 550-mm (21.65-in) tubes for anti-ship and ASW torpedoes (see text)
Dimensions: length 128.6 m (422 ft); beam 12.7 m (42 ft); draft 5.4 m (18 ft)	**Electronics:** one DRBV 20A air surveillance radar, one DRBV 11 air/surface search radar, one DRBC 11 127-mm fire-control radar, one DRBC 30 57-mm fire-control radar, one DUBV 1 sonar, and one DUBA 1 sonar
Propulsion: geared steam turbines delivering 46,975 kW (63,000 shp) to two shafts	
Performance: speed 34 kts; endurance 9250 km (5,750 miles) at 18 kts	**Aircraft:** none
Armament: three twin 127-mm (5-in)	**Complement:** 347

'Suffren' class Guided-missile destroyer

Originally classed as light cruisers, the **Suffren** and **Duquesne** were later reclassified as destroyers of the **'Suffren' class**. In fact the ships were guided-missile destroyers to a design specifically created to provide an area anti-air warfare and ASW protection

capability within the screens of lighter warships protecting the French navy's two 'Clemenceau'-class aircraft carriers. As first drafted, the plan demanded the initial construction of three ships, with more to follow as and when the country's financial resources

permitted, but ultimately only two ships were ever laid down and completed. The *Suffren* was built by the Arsenal de Brest, being laid down in November 1962, launched in May 1965 and commissioned in July 1967, while the *Duquesne* was built by the Arsenal de Lorient, being

laid down in November 1964, launched in February 1966 and commissioned in April 1970.

Distinguishable craft

Completed almost exclusively with French weapons and sensors, the two ships were the first French naval vessels to be

SPECIFICATION

'Suffren' class
Displacement: 5,090 tons standard; 6,090 tons full load
Dimensions: length 157.6 m (517 ft); beam 15.54 m (51 ft); draught 7.25 m (23 ft 9 in)
Propulsion: geared steam turbines delivering 54,065 kW (72,500 shp) to two shafts
Performance: speed 34 kts; endurance 9,450 km (5,870 miles) at 18 kts
Armament: four launchers for four MM.38 Exocet anti-ship missiles, one twin launcher for 48 Masurca SAMs, two 100-mm (3.9-in) DP guns, four 20-mm AA guns, one launcher for 13 Malafon ASW

missiles (non-operational after 1997), and four 533-mm (21-in) launchers for 10 L5 ASW torpedoes
Electronics: one DRBI 23 air search and target designation radar, one DRBV 50 surface search radar, two DRBR 51 SAM-control radars, one DRBC 32A fire-control radar, one DRBN 32 navigation radar, one SENIT 1 tactical data system, one ESM suite, two Dagaie chaff/decoy launchers, one DUBV 23 hull sonar, and one DUBV 43 variable-depth sonar
Aircraft: none
Complement: 355

Above: Classed initially as light cruisers and later as frégate lance-missiles (FLMs), the 'Suffren'-class ships were the first French warships designed primarily for missile armament from the outset.

designed round a primary armament of surface-to-air missiles, and with three pairs of gyro-controlled non-retractable stabilizers the ships proved themselves very stable missile platforms. They were readily distinguishable in French service by the isolated tall central 'mack' (combined mast and stack) and, forward of this, the distinctive radome for the DRBI 23 3D surveillance and tracking radar (unique to the two vessels of this class). Data from the full range of each ship's sensors were fed to the SENIT 1 tactical data system for co-ordination as part of the process of creating a complete picture of the tactical situation around the ship to the maximum range of the sensors.

Air defence upgrade

During the mid-1970s both the vessels were modified to install new weapons and to improve the area-defence SAM system to fire only the Masurca Mk 2 Model 3 medium-range missile

with semi-active radar guidance in place of the earlier variant's beam-riding guidance.

Both ships were transferred to the Mediterranean in 1975, then serving with the Toulon-based Mediterranean Fleet as escorts to the carriers.

For the area-defence anti-submarine role the weapon carried was the Malafon, a 1500-kg (3,307-lb) command-guided glider platform with a maximum range of 13 km (8.1 miles). This was launched with the aid of twin solid-propellant booster rockets, and carried as its payload the 533-mm (21-in) L4 ASW torpedo with active/passive acoustic homing, a weight of 540 kg (1,190 lb), a speed of 30 kts and a range of around 5.5 km (3.4 miles) to deliver a 104-kg (229-lb) warhead. The vessels used the 1000-kg (2,205-lb) L5 torpedo with active/passive acoustic homing for self-defence. The *Suffren* was deleted in 2001.

Above: The Suffren at its home port of Toulon, the major base of the French navy in the Mediterranean. The vessels escorted the French carriers, protecting them from air and submarine attack. The surviving Duquesne is due to remain in service until 2007.

Below: The Suffren was the lead ship of a two-ship class, the vessels being characterized by the distinctive radome over the antenna for the DRBI 23 3D radar system, which provides target data for the stern-mounted twin-rail Masurca area defence SAM launcher. The Malafon ASW missile launcher was carried amidships.

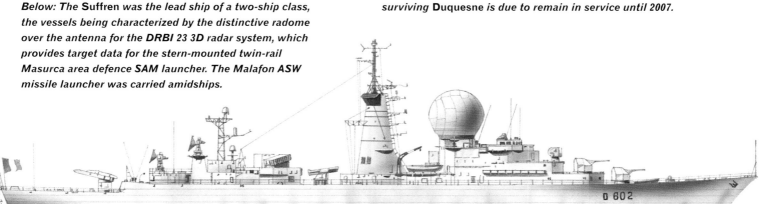

'Tourville' class Guided-missile destroyer

In 1973 the French navy commissioned the 'C 65' class destroyer *Aconit* as the prototype for a series of escorts optimized for the anti-submarine role in the North Atlantic. The ship was 127 m (417 ft) long and had single-shaft propulsion for a speed of 27 kts. Even as the ship was being built, however, it was clear that it was too small and limited in capabilities, so the following **'F 67'** or **'Tourville'-class** destroyers enlarged dimensions, leading to a 1,350-ton increase in standard displacement, a doubling of power delivered to two shafts, hangarage for two Westland Lynx helicopters, and an enhanced anti-ship capability through the addition of Exocet missiles.

Completed in 1974–77 at the Lorient naval dockyard, the three ships were commissioned as the **Tourville**, **Duguay-Trouin** and **de Grasse**. The first two ships were completed with three 100-mm (3.9-in) guns, but the *de Grasse* was completed with only the two forward guns, as it had been decided that the ships would have a Crotale SAM installation (with 26 missiles) above the hangar.

The ships were to have been completed with the same electronic fit as the *Aconit*, but a more modern and capable suite was adopted during the ships' construction, including the

DRBV 26 air surveillance radar, the DRBV 50 (later DRBV 51B) target designation radar, and a lightweight version of the DRBC 32 fire-control radar. The *Aconit*'s SENIT 3 tactical data system was retained.

The ships have two sets of non-retracting stabilizers, and helicopter capability is enhanced by the provision of a downhaul system on the flight platform and a SPHEX traverse system serving the double hangar. Habitability was improved over that of earlier ships, and the capability of the electronics (especially the sonar) has been upgraded, although the Malafon system was removed in the 1990s. The *Tourville* and *de Grasse* are still in service.

Above: Like its sister ship de Grasse, *the destroyer* Tourville *is based at Brest in north-west France as part of the French navy's forces allocated to operations in the North Atlantic.*

*Above: The 'Tourville-class' destroyers (*de Grasse *being seen here) were designed for the oceanic anti-submarine role with the Malafon rocket-launched torpedo system and two embarked helicopters.*

SPECIFICATION	
'Tourville' (F 67) class (as built) **Displacement:** 4,580 tons standard; 5,950 tons full load **Dimensions:** length 152.5 m (500 ft 4 in); beam 15.3 m (50 ft 2 in); draught 6.5 m (21 ft 4 in) **Propulsion:** geared steam turbines delivering 40,560 kW (54,400 shp) to two shafts **Performance:** speed 31 kts; endurance 9,250 km (5,750 miles) at 18 kts **Armament:** two triple launchers for MM.38 Exocet SSMs, two 100-mm	(3.9-in) DP guns, one Crotale launcher for 26 R.440 short-range SAMs), and one launcher for 13 Malafon torpedo-carrying rockets **Electronics:** one DRBV 26 air search radar, one DRBV 51B air/surface search radar, two navigation radars, one DRBC 32D fire-control radar, one SENIT 3 tactical data system, one DUBV 23 hull sonar, and one DUBV 43 variable-depth sonar **Aircraft:** two Lynx helicopters **Complement:** 282

'Hamburg' class Guided missile destroyer

In the mid-1950s West Germany was authorized to start the process of creating armed forces, prohibited after the 1945 defeat, to participate in the country's defence under the auspices of the Western European Union and later NATO. The new West German navy started to train personnel in 1956, and in 1958 received its first major warships in the form of six World War II-vintage 'Fletcher'-class destroyers,

transferred from the US Navy on five-year leases under the terms of the US's Mutual Defense Assistance Program. The ships were modernized before transfer and adapted to facilitate their operation within the context of West German operational practices. The ships were finally phased out of West German service in 1968–82.

The next type of destroyer intended for service with the West German navy was a class

designed and built in West Germany but featuring weapons and sensors from several European sources.

Otherwise known as **Type 101** units, these **'Hamburg'-class** destroyers were originally to have numbered 12, and were ordered in August 1957. It then emerged that the ships could not be built to the 2,500-ton limit imposed on West German ships, but although the Western European Union raised the limit

to 6,000 tons, the West Germans opted for a class of four ships each with a standard displacement in the order of 3,350 tons.

Built in Germany

The ships were built by Stülcken of Hamburg, being laid down in 1959–61 and commissioned in 1964–68 as the **Hamburg**, **Schleswig-Holstein**, **Bayern** and **Hessen**. The ships were conceptually akin to the definitive destroyers of World War II, and featured West German propulsion equipment, including four Wahodag boilers, fired by a maximum of 600 tons of oil, supplying steam to four sets of Wahodag-geared steam turbines driving two shafts.

In their original form, the ships were wholly conventional gun-armed destroyers with the primary armament of four 100-mm (3.9-in) L/55 guns in paired superfiring turrets fore and aft. In the period 1974–77 all four of the ships were updated: the boilers were modified to burn light oil, the lattice main mast was removed, and 'X' turret was replaced by two pairs of launchers for MM.38 Exocet anti-ship missiles.

Further change came in the following year, when the ships received an enclosed bridge for better operability in adverse conditions. Later modifications included the modification of the superstructure and the funnel caps, the replacement of the five fixed tubes (three bow and two stern) for 533-mm (21-in) heavyweight anti-submarine torpedoes by two pairs of short tubes for 324-mm (12.8-in) lightweight anti-submarine torpedoes, the replacement of the original 40-mm AA guns in four twin mountings by more modern weapons, and the

Right: During Exercise 'Northern Wedding' in 1986, the 'Hamburg'-class destroyer **Hessen** *refuels from the 'Cimarron'-class fleet oiler USS* **Platte** *in the Norwegian Sea.*

steady upgrade of the electronics.

The four ships were decommissioned in 1990–94 and replaced by 'Brandenburg'-class frigates.

Below: The **Bayern** *was the third of the 'Hamburg'-class ships. It was completed in July 1965 and taken out of service in December 1993 before being sold for scrap.*

SPECIFICATION	
'Hamburg' class (1982)	100-mm (3.9-in) guns, four twin
Displacement: 3,340 tons standard;	40-mm AA guns, five 533-mm
4,330 tons full load	(21-in) torpedo tubes, and two
Dimensions: length 133.7 m (438 ft	375-mm (14.76-in) launchers for
9 in); beam 13.4 m (44 ft); draught	anti-submarine rockets
5.2 m (17 ft)	**Electronics:** one LW-04 air
Propulsion: geared steam turbines	surveillance radar, one DA-08
delivering 53,685 kW (72,000 shp)	surface search radar, one Kelvin
to two shafts	Hughes 14/9 navigation radar, four
Performance: speed 36 kts;	WM-45 fire-control radars (100-mm
endurance 11,000 km (6,835 miles)	and 40-mm guns), and one ELAC
at 13 kts	1BV hull-mounted sonar
Armament: two twin launchers	**Aircraft:** none
for MM.38 Exocet SSMs, three	**Complement:** 284

'Lütjens' class Guided-missile destroyer

Reformed after Germany's 1945 defeat in the mid-1950s, the West German navy was initially confined to a limited capability by the obsolescence of the ships it initially operated and the limited skills of its personnel. During the late 1950s and early 1960s, however, the capabilities of the Soviet navy increased dramatically and it became

reasonable to expect the West German navy to shoulder an increasing proportion of the naval burden associated with the NATO alliance's defence of Western Europe.

Limited capability

The West Germany navy's obsolescent American-supplied 'Fletcher'-class and German-built

'Hamburg'-class destroyers, supplemented by 'Köln'-class frigates also built in West Germany, were limited in operational capability, so in May 1964 West Germany and the US signed an agreement for the purchase of **'Modified Charles F. Adams'-class** guided missile destroyers, to be known in West German service as **Type 103A**

or **'Lütjens' class**-units.

After the abandonment of the initial plan for six units of the class to be built in West German yards, during April 1965 the US Navy ordered just three ships from the Bath Iron Works of the US on behalf of the West German navy, and the vessels were laid down in 1966–67, launched in 1967–69, and

SPECIFICATION

'Lütjens' (Type 103B) class
Displacement: 3,370 tons standard; 4,500 tons full load
Dimensions: length 133.2 m (437 ft); beam 14.3 m (47 ft); draught 6.1 m (20 ft)
Propulsion: geared steam turbines delivering 52,190 kW (70,000 shp) to two shafts
Performance: speed 32 kts; endurance 8,350 km (5,190 miles) at 20 kts
Armament: one launcher for 40 Standard medium-range SAMs and Harpoon SSMs, two launchers for 42 RAM short-range SAMs, two 5-in (127-mm) DP guns, one octuple launcher for eight

ASROC rocket-delivered anti-submarine torpedoes, and two triple 12.8-in (324-mm) tubes for Mk 46 lightweight anti-submarine torpedoes
Electronics: one SPS-52 3D search radar, one SPS-40 air search radar, one SPS-67 surface search radar, two SPG-51 fire-control radars, one SPQ-9 and one SPG-60 fire-control radars, one SATIR 1 action information system, FL-1800S-II ESM system, Mk 36 SRBOC decoy launcher, and DSQS-21B hull sonar
Aircraft: none
Complement: 337

By the standards of the late 1960s and early 1970s, the 'Lütjens'-class destroyer offered a excellent blend of performance and capability in the anti-air and anti-submarine roles.

commissioned in 1969–70 as the **Lütjens**, **Mölders** and **Rommel**, who were respectively sea, air and land leaders of World War II lacking in any Nazi taint and therefore politically acceptable to both West Germany and NATO.

The 'Charles F. Adams'-class destroyer had been designed as a fleet escort optimized for the anti-air and anti-submarine roles with the Tartar short/medium-range SAM and RUR-5 ASROC rocket-delivered torpedo respectively: the single-arm SAM launcher was located over the after part of the ship and supported by two fire-control radars for the simultaneous engagement of two aerial targets, while the octuple ASROC launcher was located amidships between the forward and after superstructure blocks.

Revised standard

The West German ships were based on the standard of the US Navy's later 'Charles F. Adams'-class ships modified by the adoption of two combined masts and stacks (or 'macks') with side exhausts for the

The Lütjens *was completed as the lead ship of the Type 103 class, in its time the most capable major surface combatant class in West German naval service.*

propulsion arrangement's wastes in place of the US ship's separate masts and stacks.

At the end of the 1970s, the ships were taken in hand by two Kiel-based organizations, the naval dockyard and Howaldtswerke, for a major upgrade to **Type 103B** standard. The upgrades to the *Lütjens*, *Mölders* and *Rommel* were completed in 1986, 1984 and 1985 respectively, and included modification of the Mk 13 launcher for the Standard medium-range SAM and

Harpoon anti-ship missile, modernization of the fire-control system with digital rather than analogue computers, and heightening of the superstructure abaft the bridge with a platform for the SPG-60 and SPQ-9 fire-control radars.

From 1993 the ships received a short-range AA capability through the addition of two launchers for RAM missiles. The *Rommel* was taken out of service in 1998, and the other two were scheduled for retirement at the end of 2003.

'Holland' and 'Friesland' classes Destroyers

In 1948 the Dutch navy ordered 12 anti-submarine destroyers, of which six were to be completed in 1952 and the other six in 1953–54. The destruction caused by World War II made this an impossible schedule, so the first four were completed in 1954–55 to the **'Holland' class** standard with stored propulsion equipment delivering 33,550 kW (45,000 shp) for a speed of 32 kts.

The ships were the **Holland**, **Zeeland**, **Noord Brabant** and **Gelderland**, the first sold to Peru in 1978 as the **Garcia y Garcia** that was deleted in

Below: The 'Friesland'-class destroyers carried four 120-mm (4.72-in) DP guns in two fully automatic and radar-controlled turrets fore and aft, and forward of the bridge were two 40-mm AA guns and the two quadruple launchers for 375-mm (14.76-in) anti-submarine rockets.

1986, and the others scrapped in 1973–79.

The other eight ships, completed in 1956–58, were the **'Friesland'-class** units **Friesland**, **Groningen**, **Limburg**, **Overijssel**, **Drenthe**, **Utrecht**, **Rotterdam** and

*The **Overijssel** was the fourth of the eight 'Friesland'-class destroyers, and was built for the Dutch navy by Wilton-Fijenoord, where the ship was commissioned in October 1957.*

Amsterdam. These had the higher-rated propulsion arrangement originally envisaged as well as six rather than just one 40-mm AA gun. The lead ship was broken up in

1979, and the others became the Peruvian **Galvez**, **Capitan Quinones**, **Colonel Bolognesi**, **Guise**, **Castilla**, **Diez Canseco** and **Villar**, which were finally deleted in 1985–91.

SPECIFICATION	
'Friesland' class	Bofors AA guns, two quadruple
Displacement: 2,497 tons standard; 3,070 tons full load	375-mm (14.76-in) anti-submarine rocket launchers, and two depth charge racks
Dimensions: length 116 m (380 ft 7 in); beam 11.7 m (38 ft 5 in); draught 5.2 m (17 ft 1 in)	**Electronics:** one LW-02 long-range surveillance radar, one DA-01 medium-range air/surface search radar, one ZW-01 radar, one
Propulsion: two geared steam turbines delivering 44,735 kW (60,000 shp) to two shafts	WM-45 fire-control radar, Type 170B hull sonar, and Type 162 hull sonar
Performance: speed 36 kts; endurance 7,400 km (4,600 miles) at 18 kts	**Aircraft:** none
Armament: two twin 120-mm (4.72-in) DP guns, six 40-mm	**Complement:** 284

'Halland' and 'Ostergotland' classes DDG/DD

In 1948 the Swedish navy was authorized to order two **'Halland'-class** destroyers, which were completed in 1955–56 as the **Halland** and **Småland** with a standard displacement of 2,630 tons, length of 121 m (397 ft), speed of 35 kts on 43,245 kW (58,000 shp), and armament of two twin 120-mm (4.72-in) automatic guns, one twin

57-mm AA gun, six 40-mm AA guns, one quintuple and one triple launchers for 533-mm (21-in) torpedoes, and two quadruple launchers for 375-mm (14.76-in) anti-submarine rockets. Two more ships, the *Lappland* and *Varmland*, were cancelled in 1958.

In 1967 the ships become the first non-Soviet units to be equipped with anti-ship missiles

SPECIFICATION	
'Ostergotland' class	(4.72-in) DP guns, seven 40-mm
Displacement: 2,150 tons standard; 2,600 tons full load	Bofors AA guns reduced to four with Seacat system, one sextuple launcher for 533-mm (21-in)
Dimensions: length 112 m (367 ft 6 in); beam 11.2 m (36 ft 10 in); draught 3.7 m (12 ft 2 in)	torpedoes, one Squid Mk 3 anti-submarine mortar, and 60 mines
Propulsion: two geared steam turbines delivering 3,5045 kW (47,000 shp) to two shafts	**Electronics:** one Saturn search radar, one WM-44 Seacat and one WM-45 gun fire-control radars, and
Performance: speed 35 kts; endurance 5,500 km (3,420 miles) at 20 kts	hull-mounted search and attack sonars
Armament: two twin 120-mm	**Aircraft:** none
	Complement: 244

in the form of Rb 315 weapons, which were later replaced by Rb 08 missiles. Steadily upgraded, the ships were retired in 1982 and 1985 respectively.

The destroyers of the **'Ostergotland' class**, completed in 1958–59, were the **Ostergotland**, **Sodermanland**, **Gåstrikland** and **Hålsingland**. The ships' main and light AA armament were similar to those of the 'Halland'-class ships, but the anti-submarine armament was different, and from 1963 three of the 40-mm guns were replaced by a quadruple launcher for Rb 07 (Seacat) short-range SAMs. All four ships were deleted in 1982–83.

The **Smaland** *was the second of the 'Halland'-class destroyers, and is seen here in its later form with an anti-ship missile launcher abaft the after funnel.*

'Skoriy' class Destroyer

Work on the **Project 30B** or **'Skoriy'-class** destroyer began in October 1945, using the basic arrangement, machinery and armament of the earlier Project 30 or 'Ognevoy'-class destroyer in order to speed design and construction. The design was approved in January 1947, and fixed the parameters of the first Soviet type with a longitudinally framed and all-welded hull. By comparison with the 'Ognevoy' class, the 'Skoriy' class had a strengthened hull, the changes adding just under 50 per cent to the hull's weight. To speed completion, the vessels were built in 101 prefabricated modular sections, and one was completed within a year.

Flawed design

Although the design had higher freeboard than the earlier 'Strashniy' and 'Ognevoy' classes, it still allowed the ships to take water in heavier weather, reducing speed and making many of the guns inoperable. The turning circle was deemed too great, and bilge keels were later fitted.

From the early 1950s, the seven 37-mm guns were replaced by four twin mountings, the initial fit of heavy machine-guns was replaced by two or six 25-mm weapons, and the Tamir-5H sonar was replaced by a Pegas-2 set.

SPECIFICATION	
'Skoriy' class	(5.1-in) guns, one twin 85-mm
Displacement: 2,316 tons standard;	(3.35-in) AA gun, seven 37-mm AA
3,066 tons full load	guns, two quintuple launchers for
Dimensions: length 120.5 m (395 ft	533-mm (21-in) torpedoes, and 52
4 in); beam 12 m (39 ft 4 in);	depth charges or 60 mines
draught 3.9 m (12 ft 10 in)	**Electronics:** one Gyus-1B air search
Propulsion: two geared steam	radar, one Ryf-1 surface search and
turbines delivering 44,735 kW	fire-control radar, one Redan-2
(60,000 shp) to two shafts	radar, one Vympel-2 fire-control
Performance: speed 35.5 kts;	radar, and one Tamir-5H hull-
endurance 6,500 km (4,040 miles)	mounted sonar
at 15.7 kts	**Aircraft:** none
Armament: two twin 130-mm	**Complement:** 286

Upgrade

While the first 14 ships had a standard displacement of 2,316 tons, the last 56 were 35 tons heavier as a result of their improved radar and the strengthening of their hulls to prevent sagging as a result of

The Project 30 destroyers reflected the initial Soviet thinking about destroyer operations in World War II, and were fairly simple ships in weapons and sensors.

water taken over the bow.

In 1957 a modernization requirement was issued, and nine ships were later upgraded to the **Project 31** standard for improved capability in the anti-submarine, anti-aircraft,

anti-FAC, patrol and intelligence-gathering roles: the 130-mm (5.1-in) gun director and one set of torpedo tubes were landed, the light armament became five 57-mm AA guns, and two RBU 2500 anti-submarine rocket

launchers were mounted forward of the bridge.

Foreign export
Six **Project 30-BA** ships were transferred in pairs to Egypt in 1956, 1962 and 1968, and seven

Project 30-BK ships to Indonesia (four in 1959, one in 1962, and two in 1964). These ships had improved habitability features and revised armament and radar. None of the ships remains in service.

'Kotlin' and 'Kildin' classes Destroyer/guided-missile destroyer

The **Project 56** destroyer (NATO designation **'Kotlin' class**) was a scaled-down Project 41 or 'Tallinn'-class destroyer, created from June 1951 with the full-load displacement trimmed from 3,770 to 3,150 tons, speed increased from 36 to 39 kts, cruising range reduced, lighter torpedo tubes shipped, and unstabilized quadruple 45-mm AA mounts in place of stabilized twin mounts. Some 110 units were planned, but only 27 were completed in 1955–58, another four being completed in 1958 as **Project 56M** ('Kildin' class) missile ships.

There were differences in the armament scheme from Project

41, with a new Sfera-56 director, the 45-mm mounts disposed in a rhomboidal pattern to allow a concentration of the fire along the centreline, and no anti-submarine rocket launchers.

The accommodation of the Project 41's armament and powerplant in a smaller hull meant some volume had to be raised above the main deck, so an aluminium/magnesium alloy was used in the superstructure to reduce topweight. The Project 56 ships may have been the first Soviet vessels with fin stabilizers.

Trials of **Spokoynyy**, the first ship, revealed problems that were overcome by the use of

SPECIFICATION	
'Kotlin' class	(4.72-in) DP guns, four quadruple
Displacement: 2,662 tons standard; 3,230 tons full load	45-mm AA guns, two quintuple launchers for 533-mm (21-in)
Dimensions: length 126.1 m (413 ft 9 in); beam 12.7 m (41 ft 8 in); draught 4.19 m (13 ft 9 in)	torpedoes, and 48 depth charges or 50 mines
Propulsion: two geared steam turbines delivering 53,685 kW (72,000 shp) to two shafts	**Electronics:** one Fut-N air search radar, one Ryf surface search and fire-control radar, and one Pegas-2 hull-mounted sonar
Performance: speed 38 kts	**Aircraft:** none
Armament: two twin 120-mm	**Complement:** 284

four- rather than three-blade propellers, and the replacement of the two rudders abaft the propellers by a single centreline unit.

One incomplete ship, **Bedovyy**, was completed for evaluation of the new SS-N-1

anti-ship missile, for which the Project 57 or 'Krupny' class destroyer was already being developed. The *Bedovyy* then became operational, and three others units were completed to this Project 56M standard with six missiles. The ships had a new secondary armament of four quadruple 57-mm guns, two replacing the forward 130-mm mount and two aft, and two beam-mounted twin torpedo launchers. Three were modified in 1973–75 with SS-N-2 missiles, and all were deleted in the late 1980s.

Modifications
Twelve ships were modified in 1958 to the **Project 56PLO** improved ASW standard with one torpedo tube launcher and depth charge capability removed, better sonar fitted, and two RBU 2500 and two RBU 600 rocket launchers added forward and aft. Nine other ships were upgraded to the **Project 56K** ('SAM Kotlin' class) standard with the SA-N-1 system (one launcher and 16 SAMs) in 1959–71, in place of the armament over the after part of the hull. One was transferred to Poland in 1970. All of the ships were decommissioned between 1986 and 1990.

Above: In its definitive form the Project 56M ('Kildin' class) destroyer had an aft-mounted launcher for six SS-N-1 anti-ship missiles.

Left: The Project 56K ('SAM Kotlin' class) conversions had the after part of each ship revised with a twin-arm launcher for up to 16 SA-N-1 (navalized SA-3) surface-to-air missiles.

'Kashin' and 'Kashin (Mod)' classes DDG

The first major warship class with gas turbine propulsion, the 20-ship **'Kashin' class** was produced from 1963 to 1973. The last unit of **Project 61** was the **Sderzhanny**, completed to a **Project 61M** design (known as the **'Kashin (Mod)' class** by NATO). The hull was lengthened and four P-15M Termit SSMs installed, later replaced by eight Uran SSMs, AK-630 CIWS

mountings and a variable-depth sonar. Five other ships were thus modified in 1973–80.

Explosion

In 1981 the **Provorny** re-entered service with the Black Sea Fleet after conversion to the trials ship for the Uragan SAM system. All but two of the ships had been stricken by the end of the 20th century.

The 'Kashin' class were completed between 1964 and 1973, the 20 ships were operated in two forms as the 'Kashin' class without anti-ship missiles and the 'Kashin (Mod)' class with such weapons.

SPECIFICATION

'Kashin' class
Displacement: 4,010 tons standard; 4,750 tons full load
Dimensions: length 144 m (472 ft 5 in); beam 15.8 m (51 ft 10 in); draught 4.7 m (15 ft 5 in)
Propulsion: COGAG with four DE 59 gas turbines delivering 53,700 kW (72,025 shp) to two shafts
Performance: speed 32 kts; range 7,400 km (4,600 miles) at 18 kts
Armament: two twin launchers for 32 Volna (SA-N-1 'Goa') SAMs except Provorny, one single launcher for 23 Uragan (SA-N-7 'Gadfly') SAMs, two twin 76-mm (3-in) AK-726 DP guns, two 250-mm (9.84-in) RPK-8 Zapad (RBU 6000) 12-tube ASW rocket launchers, one quintuple 533-mm (21-in) ASW torpedo tube mounting (except Provorny), and 20-40 mines depending on type

Electronics: (Provorny) one 'Head Net-C' 3D radar, one 'Top Steer' 3D radar, two 'Don Kay' navigation radars, eight 'Front Dome' SA-N-7 fire-control radars, two 'Watch Dog' ECM systems, one 'High Pole-B' IFF system, two 'Owl Screech' gun fire-control radars and one high-frequency hull sonar
Electronics: (rest) eight ships one 'Big Net' air search and one 'Head Net-C' 3D radars, or four ships two 'Head Net-A' air search radars, or Soobrazitelny two 'Head Net-C' 3D radars; two 'Peel Group' SAM fire-control radars, two 'Don Kay' or 'Don 2' navigation radars, two 'Owl Screech' gun fire-control radars, two 'Watch Dog' ECM systems, two 'High Pole-B' IFF systems, and one high-frequency hull sonar
Aircraft: helicopter platform only
Complement: 280

SPECIFICATION

'Kashin (Mod)' class
Displacement: 4,975 tons full load
Dimensions: length 146.2 m (479 ft 8 in); beam 15.8 m (51 ft 10 in); draught 4.7 m (15 ft 5 in)
Propulsion: as 'Kashin 'class
Performance: speed 31 kts
Armament: four P-15M Termit (SS-N-2c 'Styx') SSMs later replaced by eight Uran (SS-N-25 'Switchblade') SSMs, two twin launchers for 32 Volna (SA-N-1 'Goa') SAMs, four 30-mm AK-630 CIWS mountings, two 250-mm (9.84-in) RPK-8 Zapad 12-tube ASW rocket launchers, and one quintuple 533-mm (21-in) ASW torpedo tube mounting

Electronics: one 'Big Net' air search radar, one 'Head Net-C' 3D radar (except Ognevoy two 'Head Net-A' air search radars), two 'Don Kay' navigation radars, two 'Owl Screech' gun fire-control radars, two 'Bass Tilt' CIWS fire-control radars, two 'Peel Group' SAM fire-control radars, two 'Bell Shroud' and two 'Bell Squat' ECM systems, four 16-barrel chaff and IR decoy launchers, one medium-frequency hull sonar, and one low-frequency variable-depth sonar
Aircraft: helicopter platform only
Complement: 300

Ships of the 'Kashin' class played anti-air and anti-submarine roles. The former capability was provided by a pair of two-arm missile launchers, the latter by two 12-tube launchers for rockets and a PTA-53-61 quintuple 533-mm (21-in) torpedo tube mounting.

'Daring' class Destroyer

The eight destroyers of the **'Daring' class** were the first built in the UK after World War II, although their design was prepared in the closing stages of that conflict. The vessels reflected the experience of six years of war, although they marked a departure in that they were larger and more capable than most British destroyers

other than the 'Battle'-class units. Although destroyers of a similar size were created in other countries, the Admiralty decided in 1953 that these were in effect small light cruisers rather than large destroyers.

Construction

Completed between February 1952 and March 1954, the ships

fell into two groups. **Dainty**, **Daring**, **Defender** (ex-**Dogstar**) and **Delight** (ex-**Disdain**, ex-**Ypres**) had a 220-volt DC electrical system, whereas **Decoy** (ex-**Dragon**), **Diamond**, **Diana** (ex-**Druid**) and **Duchess** had the 440-volt AC system that became the navy's standard.

From 1963, the ships in the class were modernized. The

after 21-in (533-mm) quintuple torpedo tube mounting had been removed in 1958–59, and the other was now removed, as were the radar-controlled STAAG mountings (each with two 40-mm Bofors AA guns) in the bridge wings. The Mk 6M director was replaced by an MRS3 director, and the four ships with the DC electrical system received a pair of more reliable Mk 5 mountings for two 40-mm Bofors guns, while the four ships with the AC electrical system received Mk 7 mountings for single 40-mm Bofors guns.

Updated destroyer

In 1963 the *Decoy* was updated with a quadruple launcher for Seacat short-range surface-to-air missiles abaft the second funnel. This system used the radar-controlled MRS8 (Medium-Range System Mk 8) fire-control system, a development of the CRBF (Close-Range Blind Fire) system with the predictor units replaced by a computer. The trials were successful, but the Admiralty did not standardize the system for the 'Daring'-class

and the first installation was then removed from the *Decoy*.

The *Diana* and *Daring* were revised with a streamlined after funnel casing for a short period after their completions. The change improved the ships' appearances but also limited the firing arcs of the after twin Bofors mounting and the ships were returned to the standard after a few years.

The ships served at a time when ships' capabilities were being enhanced rapidly by emergent technologies, and the 'Darings' lacked the deck area and volume for the introduction of new weapons and sensors.

Replacement

The *Duchess* was transferred to the Royal Australian Navy in

1964 to replace HMAS *Voyager* (name ship of a four-strong class based on the 'Daring' class), and was stricken in 1979. In 1970 the *Decoy* and *Diana* were sold to Peru, becoming the **Ferré** and **Palacios**. The latter was stricken in 1993, but the former survives, with upgraded radar,

six 4.5-in guns, two twin 40-mm Bofors guns in radar-controlled Breda mountings and provision for up to eight MM.38 Exocet anti-ship missiles.

The *Diamond* became a harbour training ship in 1970–81, and the other British ships were stricken in the early 1970s.

SPECIFICATION	
'Daring' class **Displacement:** 2,830 tons standard; 3,580 tons deep load **Dimensions:** length 118.8 m (390 ft); beam 13.1 m (43 ft); draught 4.1 m (13 ft 7 in) **Propulsion:** two double-reduction steam turbines delivering 40,620 kW (54,000 shp) to two shafts **Performance:** speed 34.75 kts; range 5,550 km (3,450 miles) at 20 kts **Armament:** three twin Mk III 4.5-in	(114-mm) guns, two to six 40-mm Bofors AA guns, and one Squid three-barrel anti-submarine mortar **Electronics:** one Type 293 air search and target-indication radar, one navigation radar, one Type 903 4.5-in gun fire-control radar, one or two Type 262 40-mm gun fire-control radars, one Type 174/177 hull-mounted medium-range search sonar, and one Type 170 hull-mounted Squid attack sonar **Aircraft:** none **Complement:** 297–330

'County' class Guided-missile destroyer (DDG)

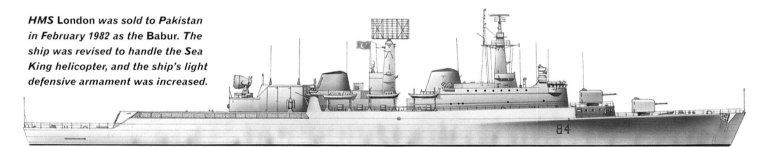

HMS **London** *was sold to Pakistan in February 1982 as the* **Babur.** *The ship was revised to handle the Sea King helicopter, and the ship's light defensive armament was increased.*

The title 'destroyer' was applied to the **'County'-class** ships to obtain Treasury approval, but

they were little short of guided-missile cruisers. Built around the beam-riding Seaslug, the UK's

first-generation area-defence SAM system, the 'County' class was ordered in batches. Completed in 1962–63, the four **Batch 1** ships were **Devonshire**, **Hampshire**, **London** and **Kent**: The first was sunk as a target in 1984, the third was sold to Pakistan in 1982 as the **Babur** (after the Seaslug system had been removed) and has now been deleted, and the other two were deleted in 1979–80. Completed in 1966–70, the **Batch 2** ships were **Fife**, **Glamorgan**, **Antrim** and **Norfolk**, with Exocet SSMs in place of one of their two 4.5-in (114-mm) gun mountings and the Seaslug Mk 2 SAM with limited SSM capability.

With extensive command and control facilities, the *Glamorgan* and *Antrim* served in the

Falklands War, the former surviving a hit from an MM.38 Exocet and the latter a hit from a bomb that failed to explode.

Chilean service

Due to the 1981 British defence cuts, however, the *Norfolk* had been sold to Chile as the **Capitán Prat**, while the *Fife* was undergoing a refit. Later disposals saw the departure of the *Antrim*, *Glamorgan* and *Fife* to Chile as the **Almirante Cochrane**, **Almirante Latorre** and **Almirante Blanco Encalada** in 1984, 1986 and 1987. The *Latorre* was deleted in 1998, and the other three vessels now have two octuple launchers for the Israeli Barak 1 SAM in place of the Seaslug system, in addition to the quadruple Exocet launcher.

SPECIFICATION	
'County Batch 2' class **Displacement:** 6,200 tons standard; 6,800 tons full load **Dimensions:** length 158.7 m (520 ft 6 in); beam 16.5 m (54 ft); draught 6.3 m (20 ft 6 in) **Propulsion:** COSAG with two geared steam turbines delivering 22,370 kW (30,000 shp) and four G6 gas turbines delivering 22,370 kW (30,000 shp) to two shafts **Performance:** speed 32.5 kts; range 6,435 km (4,000 miles) at 28 kts **Armament:** one GWS.50 launcher for four MM.38 Exocet anti-ship missiles (no reloads), one twin launcher for 30 Seaslug Mk 2 SAMs, one twin Mk 6 4.5-in (114-mm) DP gun, two GWS.22 quadruple launchers for 32 Seacat SAMs, two 20-mm AA guns, and two 12.75-in (324-mm) STWS.1 triple tubes for 12 Mk 46 anti-	submarine torpedoes in *Fife* and *Glamorgan* only **Electronics:** one Type 965M air search radar, one Type 992Q air search and target-designation radar, one Type 901 Seaslug fire-control radar, one Type 278M height-finder radar, two Type 904 Seacat fire-control radars, one MRS3 gun fire-control system, one Type 1006 navigation and helicopter-control radar, one ADAWS 1 action information system, one ESM suite, two Corvus chaff launchers, one Type 184 hull-mounted sonar, one Type 170B hull-mounted attack sonar, one Type 182 torpedo decoy system and one Type 185 underwater telephone **Aircraft:** one Lynx HAS.Mk 2 or 3 helicopter **Complement:** 471

Type 82 Guided-missile destroyer (DDG)

The British Admiralty decided that the new aircraft carriers planned for the 1970s would require specialized escorts to protect them from aircraft and submarine threats. Thus a class of four guided-missile destroyer leaders was planned to follow the ships of the 'County' class. The ships were given the designation **Type 82** in the general-purpose frigate series. With the cancellation of CVA-01 in 1966, the type was trimmed to a single ship to serve as the trials ship for new weapons.

Advanced concepts

The Type 82 destroyer incorporated advanced thinking and also a later generation of equipment. For instance, the GWS.30 SAM system was based on vertical stowage and a zero-length twin-arm launcher firing a semi-active homing missile with a much greater capacity to handle multiple targets. The funnel arrangement shifted from one to two and finally three funnels, the after uptakes being divided into two separate funnels to provide fuller access to the Olympus gas turbines.

Bristol fashion

HMS Bristol was the first Royal Navy ship designed around the notion of upkeep by replacement. Although nearly 1,000 tons larger than the 'Counties', the ship needed 70 men less in its crew. It was also the first British warship to go to sea with the Anglo-Australian Ikara ASW missile system, mounted in a 'zareba' forward of the bridge. One 4.5-in (114-mm) Vickers Mk 8 gun replaced

HMS Bristol was a 'single-ended' ship with the magazine and launcher for the Sea Dart long/medium-range SAM abaft the superstructure, though the capability for the simultaneous engagement of two targets was provided by two fire-control radars.

the previous two Mk 6 twin mountings.

Work had been proceeding on a joint Anglo-Dutch project to produce a CDS (Comprehensive Display System) radar, mounted above the bridge for air warning, surveillance and aircraft direction. However, the rising cost led to a British withdrawal from the scheme. At the same time, the Dutch were worried about the cost and volume of the Sea Dart missile system. The CDS was dropped, and the *Bristol* was completed with the less capable Type 965 (AKE-2).

Versatile warship

The *Bristol* emerged as a very versatile ship. The only failing was the lack of a helicopter hangar, which had been omitted because the ship was to have operated with carriers. After completion, the *Bristol* was used for trials of weapons and systems.

The core of the vessel's weapon systems was the ADAWS-2 (Action Data Automation Weapon System Mk 2) to co-ordinate data from the radar, sonar, INS and other sources, and process them by means of digital computers.

In 1991 the *Bristol* became a harbour training ship.

A Westland Wessex helicopter flies past HMS Bristol, a multi-role destroyer whose tactical deficiency was its lack of an embarked helicopter. This stemmed from its origins as a carrier escort.

SPECIFICATION	
Type 82 **Displacement:** 6,700 tons standard; 7,700 tons full load **Dimensions:** length 154.53 m (507 ft); beam 16.76 m (55 ft); draught 6.8 m (22 ft 6 in) **Propulsion:** COSAG with two geared steam turbines delivering 22,370 kW (30,000 shp) and two Rolls-Royce Olympus TM1A gas turbines delivering 32805 kW (44,000 shp) to two shafts **Performance:** speed 30 kts; range 5,750 miles (9255 km) at 18 kts **Armament:** one GWS.30 twin launcher with 40 Sea Dart SAMs one 4.5-in (114-mm) DP gun; two twin 30-mm AA guns four 20-mm AA guns one GWS.40 ASW system with 32 Ikara weapons and one triple Mk 10 Limbo ASW	mortar (later removed) **Electronics:** one Type 965 (AKE-2) air search radar, one Type 992Q air search and target designation radar, two Type 909 Sea Dart fire-control radars, one Type 1006 navigation and helicopter-control radar, two Ikara fire-control radars, one ADAWS-2 action information system, one Abbey Hill ESM suite two Corvus chaff launchers, two SCOTT satellite communications systems, one Type 184 medium-frequency hull sonar, one Type 162 classification sonar, one Type 182 torpedo decoy system, one Type 185 underwater telephone, and one Type 170 Limbo attack sonar **Aircraft:** helicopter landing platform only **Complement:** 407

'Decatur' class Guided-missile destroyer

The 18 'Forrest Sherman'-class ships were completed in the 1950s as gun destroyers for the oceanic escort role. The ships were the first in US Navy service with greater firepower aft than forward, and as completed had a primary anti-submarine armament of two Mk 10/11 Hedgehog mortars.

In 1959 it was decided to convert the class to offer greater air-defence and anti-submarine

The USS John Paul Jones was completed as DD-932, but became DDG-32 after its conversion to a 'Decatur'-class missile ship. The lattice masts and radar antennae are evident.

capability, including the Tartar SAM system. High costs limited the programme to four ships, the **'Decatur' class**, including the *Decatur*, *John Paul Jones*, *Parsons* and *Somers*.

SPECIFICATION

'Decatur' class
Displacement: 4,150 tons full load
Dimensions: length 127.6 m (418 ft 5 in); beam 13.7 m (45 ft); draught 6.1 m (20 ft)
Propulsion: two geared steam turbines delivering 52190 kW (70,000 shp) to two shafts
Performance: speed 32.5 kts
Armament: 5-in (127-mm) Mk 42 DP gun, Mk 13 Mod 1 single-arm launcher for 40 RIM-24 Tartar

SAMs, Mk 16 ASROC launcher for RUR-5A ASW weapons, two Mk 32 triple tubes for 12.75-in (324-mm) ASW torpedoes
Electronics: one SPS-48 3D radar SPS-29E or -40 air search radar one SPS-10B surface search radar one SPG-51C missile-control radar various fire-control systems; and one SQS-23 hull-mounted sonar
Complement: 333-344

Conversions

The conversions began in 1965–66 and were completed in 1967–68. The Tartar system was capable of launching eight RIM-24 missiles per minute, but the engagement capability was limited by the provision of only one SPG 51C target-designation radar (all other US air-defence destroyers had two). This led to their early retirement to reserve status in 1982–83, and then to deletion only a short time later.

'Kidd' class Guided-missile destroyer (DDG)

In 1978, the government of Iran ordered four examples of an improved 'Spruance'-class destroyer to form what would be the world's most capable guided-missile destroyers with additional armour protection and superior air-defence and anti-submarine capabilities. Provision for such capabilities had been incorporated into the basic

design of the 'Spruance' class, but these four ships were the only units ordered to the DXG missile standard rather than the DX standard optimized for the anti-submarine role.

Cancelled order

The ships were at an early stage of their construction when the overthrow of the Shah of Iran

SPECIFICATION

'Kidd' class
Displacement: 6,950 tons standard; 9,574 tons full load
Dimensions: length 171.7 m (563 ft 4 in); beam 16.8 m (55 ft); draught 9.1 m (30 ft)
Propulsion: four General Electric LM2500 gas turbines delivering 64120 kW (86,000 shp) to two shafts
Performance: speed 33 kts
Armament: two 5-in (127-mm) Mk 45 DP guns, two Mk 26 twin-arm launchers for 52 Standard SM-2MR SAMs and 16 ASROC ASW missiles, two quadruple Mk 141

launchers for eight Harpoon anti-ship missiles, two 20-mm Mk 15 Phalanx CIWS mountings, and two triple Mk 32 tubes for 12.75-in (324-mm) Mk 46 or Mk 50 ASW torpedoes
Electronics: single SPS-48E and SPS-49(V)5 air search radars, SPS-55 air/surface search radar, SPS-64 navigation radar, two SPG-51D SAM-control radars, single SPG-60 and SPQ-9A fire-control radars; weapons control systems, ACDS combat data system, ESM/ECM systems, and SQS-53A bow-mounted sonar
Aircraft: two medium helicopters
Complement: 363

The USS Kidd was completed as the lead ship of its class in July 1981. Notable in this view of the ship's forward end is the clean deck carrying a single 5-in (127-mm) 54-calibre DP gun in a Mk 45 mounting, and the forward Mk 26 twin-arm missile launcher.

and the establishment of the Khomeni regime in 1979 led to the cancellation of the order. The US Navy took over the order for $1.353 billion, and these ships of the **'Kidd' class** were completed between June 1981 and March 1982. Named the *Kidd*, *Callaghan*, *Scott* and *Chandler*, they were allocated in pairs to the Atlantic and Pacific Fleets. Their capabilities made them precursors of the later 'Ticonderoga'-class cruisers

but without the AEGIS radar and missile-control system.

The 'Kidd'-class ships have a large central superstructure surmounted by two large four-legged lattice masts to carry antennae, and are double-ended ships with two 5-in (127-mm) guns and two Mk 26 twin-arm launchers for Standard SM-2MR surface-to-air missiles.

High operating costs led to their retirement from US service in 1998–99.

'Gearing' and 'Sumner' class FRAM Destroyers

The US Navy appreciated by 1958 that its destroyers of World War II vintage were starting to wear out, and therefore launched the FRAM (Fleet Rehabilitation And Modernization) programme to prolong their lives and so delay the huge cost of replacing them. At the time, the US Navy had a requirement for more than 200 destroyers, and the demands of the Vietnam War delayed the building of successors, trimmed the numbers of the 'Spruance' class that was the sole replacement type being built, and required that the 'Gearing'-class ships be kept in service (albeit reserve service) into the 1980s, more than a decade after their scheduled deletions.

Upgrade programmes

The more costly of the two programmes, the **FRAM I** upgrade was implemented on 75 'Gearing'-class destroyers. To give them eight more years of useful life, the **'Gearing (FRAM I)'-class** ships had their shipboard components rehabilitated; one 5-in (127-mm) mount and all smaller-calibre guns removed; ASROC rocket-launched torpedo, DASH drone helicopter, triple ASW torpedo tubes and the SQS-23 long-range hull sonar added. Some 16 'Gearing'-class ships (six radar pickets, four ex-radar

The USS Norris was a 'Gearing'-class fleet destroyer converted to DDE standard in 1949, and then modified to FRAM II standard. The ship was retired from US Navy service in the early 1970s and in 1974 became the Turkish Kocatepe, which was stricken in 1993.

pickets and six ex-DDE adaptations) were converted to the less capable **'Gearing (FRAM II)'-class** standard.

The ships retained little effective anti-aircraft capability, so an attempt was made to enhance defence against air attack, nine ships intended for service off South Vietnam receiving the Sea Chaparral short-range SAM system. All the ships had been retired by 1984.

The FRAM II programme was intended to provide a five-year life extension and was applied to the 16 'Gearings' already mentioned and to 32 'Sumner'-class ships, thereby creating the **'Sumner (FRAM II)' class**. All three 5-in gun mounts were kept; a new bridge, radar and ECM were installed; the SQS-4 sonar was improved and moved forward and supplemented by a variable-depth sonar using the

same signal generator; Mk 32 tubes for lightweight ASW torpedoes and a DASH drone helicopter were added; and two tubes for Mk 37 torpedoes were incorporated between the funnels. Six destroyer escorts kept the Mk 15 Hedgehog forward, with DASH aft and a pair of long torpedo tubes amidships; they also received the new SQS-23 sonar. The six ships retained as radar pickets received only minor ASW refits: they kept their fixed Hedgehogs and received SQS-4 improvements, variable-depth sonar, a new bridge, a larger CIC and new radars. The ultimate failure of DASH left the ships without a long-range ASW weapon.

As they left US service, many of the FRAM ships were passed to allies, mainly in Asia, South America and southern Europe.

SPECIFICATION	
'Gearing (FRAM I)' class **Displacement:** 2,405 tons standard; 3,495 tons full load **Dimensions:** length 119 m (390 ft 5 in); beam 12.5 m (40 ft 11 in); draught 4.4 m (14 ft 4 in) **Propulsion:** geared steam turbines delivering 44,736 kW (60,000 shp) to two shafts **Performance:** speed 32 kts; endurance 7,400 km (4,600 miles) at 20 kts **Armament:** two twin Mk 38 5-in	(127-mm) DP guns, one Mk 112 octuple launcher with 17 RUR-5A ASROC anti-submarine missiles, and two triple 12.75-in (324-mm) Mk 32 tubes for lightweight ASW torpedoes **Electronics:** one SPS-29 surface search radar, one SPS-37 or SPS-40 air search radar, and one SQS-23 hull-mounted sonar **Aircraft:** one DASH anti-submarine drone helicopter **Complement:** 310

The USS William M. Wood was a fleet destroyer of the 'Gearing' class, adapted as a radar picket (DDR) in 1953. It received the FRAM I update, allowing it to remain in US Navy service up to December 1976, when it was stricken.

'Charles F. Adams' class Guided-missile destroyer

Guided-missile destroyers of the **'Charles F. Adams' class** are currently serving with the navies of Germany and Greece, the former operating the 'Lütjens'- or 'Modified Charles F. Adams'-class ships *Lütjens* and *Mölders*, and the latter four ex-US Navy ships as the **Kimon**, **Nearchos**, **Formion** and **Themistocles** of the **'Kimon' class**. Until their deletions in 1999–2001, the Royal Australian Navy had **Perth**, **Hobart** and **Brisbane**, and until their deletions or transfers in the 1989–1992 period, the US Navy operated 23 of these ships.

Minor variations

The three new-build variants differed from each other, the Australian ships having two single-rail Ikara ASW missile launchers amidships with 32 missiles in place of the ASROC launcher, the German vessels having 'mack' (combined funnel and radar mast) layout. All 23 US Navy ships were to have received extensive refits, but cost factors limited it to six ships, the **Conyngham**, **Tattnall**, **Goldsborough**, **Benjamin Stoddart**, **Richard E. Byrd** and **Waddell**.

Designed with a medium-range armament of SAMs and

At the beginning of the 21st century, the Greek navy retained four 'Kimon'-class ('Charles F. Adams') destroyers in service. These vessels, including Formion (D 220), are armed with six Harpoon AShMs stowed in the magazines in addition to the 34 Standard SM-1MR air defence missiles. The Mk 13 launcher can load, direct and fire six missiles per minute.

ASROC anti-submarine weapons, the 'Charles F. Adams' class was built to a revised 'Forrest Sherman'/'Hull' design to accommodate either a single- or twin-arm Tartar launcher. After completion some units were fitted with a four-round ASROC reload magazine on the starboard side alongside the forward funnel. The modernized vessels had a three-computer NTDS action data system, an integrated combat system, and the Standard SM-2MR (RIM-66C) missile. The ships not modernized were the **Charles F. Adams**, **John King**, **Lawrence**, **Claude V. Ricketts**, **Barney**, **Henry B. Wilson**, **Lynde McCormick**, **Towers**, **Sampson**, **Sellers**, **Robison**, **Hoel**, **Buchanan**, **Berkeley**, **Joseph Strauss**, **Semmes** and **Cochrane**.

SPECIFICATION

'Charles F. Adams' class (US Navy)
Displacement: 3,370 tons standard; 4,526 tons full load
Dimensions: length 133.2 m (437 ft); beam 14.3 m (47 ft); draught 6.1 m (20 ft)
Propulsion: geared steam turbines delivering 52,200 kW (70,000 shp) to two shafts
Performance: speed 31.5 kts
Armament: one Mk 11 twin-arm launcher (36 RIM-24 Tartar or RIM-66C Standard SAMs and six RGM-84 Harpoon SSMs) or one Mk 13 single-arm launcher (36 RIM-24 Tartar or RIM-66C Standard SAMs and four RGM-84 Harpoon SSMs), three or (after 1966) two 5-in (127-mm) Mk 42 DP guns, one Mk 16 octuple launcher for eight or

(some ships) 12 RUR-5A ASROC ASW missiles, and two triple 12.75-in (324-mm) Mk 32 tubes for six Mk 46 lightweight ASW torpedoes
Electronics: one SPS-39A 3D radar, one SPS-40B or SPS-37 air search radar, one SPS-10F surface search radar, two SPG-51C Tartar fire-control radars, one SPG-53A gun fire-control radar, one URN-20 or URN-25 TACAN, one WLR-6 ECM system, one ULQ-6B ECM system, two Mk 36 SRBOC chaff launchers, one SQS-23A bow sonar (some ships), one SQQ-23 PAIR hull sonar (some ships), and one Fanfare torpedo decoy system
Complement: 354

One of the best of the earlier guided-missile ship designs, the 'Charles F. Adams'-class vessels were initially armed with the Mk 11 twin-arm launcher for the Tartar SAM. The USS John King was a unit of this subvariant of the class.

The last 10 'Charles F. Adams'-class destroyers, including the USS Semmes seen here, carried the Mk 13 single-arm missile launcher, which was more reliable than the Mk 11 twin-arm launcher of earlier ships. This variant attracted the Australian and West German navies.

Soviet destroyers

Perhaps nowhere was the rise of Soviet power more evident than in the expansion of the Soviet navy. What was basically a coastal force in 1945 matured into a potent blue-water fleet, and the destroyer forces underwent a similar transformation. The extremely capable later generation of Soviet fighting ships posed a severe problem to NATO planners.

In the West there is a wide range of warships grouped together as 'destroyers'. The Soviet fleet operated a similarly wide band of ships and, though Western references tended to apply the same terminology to them, the Soviets grouped them differently in a scheme broadly based on function.

The Soviet term 'destroyer' initially meant a flotilla-type vessel of classical layout such as the 'Skory' and 'Kotlin' classes, built to the ideas of World War II and only superficially modernized. Beginning in 1980, however, the 'Sovremenny' class began to commission ships with over twice the displacement and a heavy bias toward anti-surface ship operations. Taken in conjunction with the functions of the older vessels, this would seem to point to the Soviet idea of a destroyer as having been

essentially a ship for fighting other ships.

There were, of course, anomalies. For instance, the 'Kotlin SAM' conversions changed their function but not, apparently, their categorization. The 'Kildins', which once carried the monstrous SS-N-1 'Scrubber' SSM on their 'Kotlin'-type hulls, were mostly rearmed with the smaller SS-N-2c 'Styx'. They reverted from their earlier Soviet label of 'large missile ship' to 'large anti-submarine ship' in the mid-1970s.

The third category of Soviet 'destroyer' was the 'large anti-submarine ship', a bracket that extended upward to embrace the 'Kara' and 'Kresta II' classes, known as 'cruisers' in the West. Anomalies existed here also, the oldest of the type, the 'Kanins', having limited ASW capacity. Perversely, the 'Kashin' class had a strong AAW

bias. Both these and the older 'Kanins' had only rocket-launchers and torpedo tubes for AS work, neither type boasting variable-depth sonar (VDS) or organic helicopter. Their classification may, therefore, have represented their dedication to an ASW group rather than having referred to any individual potential.

Only in 1980, in fact, did a destroyer-sized 'large AS ship' class with any real potential in this direction enter service. This was the 'Udaloy' which, together with the 'Sovremenny' and 'Kashin' classes, represented the state of the art in ASW, ASUW and AAW as applied to Soviet destroyer-sized ships.

An aerial view of the BPK Udaloy. The main armament is two quadruple launchers for the SS-N-14 'Silex' ASW missile and two Ka-27 'Helix' ASW helicopters, backed up by an extensive array of electronics and an anti-aircraft defence of 100-mm (3.9-in) guns, AK-630 'Gatling' guns and vertical-launch SA-N-9 'Gauntlet' SAMs.

Although not carrying anti-ship torpedoes, the major weapon system of the 'Sovremenny' class is the supersonic sea-skimming SS-N-22 'Sunburn' anti-ship cruise missile. This is backed up by two twin fully-automatic 130-mm (5.12-in) gun turrets capable of very high rates of fire.

Soviet initiative

Only latterly did the Soviet fleet reach the point where it began to initiate problems for the West, rather than to respond to developments. This new threshold was marked by the entry into service of the

THE NORTHERN PATROL: ASW OPERATIONS IN THE NORTH ATLANTIC

Photographed by an RAF Nimrod maritime patrol aircraft, this 'Kotlin'-class destroyer was having a close look at an Esso oil rig off the Orkney islands as part of the Soviet navy's intelligence-gathering role. In severe northern conditions, hull-mounted sonars and helicopters are, for perhaps half the time, either inoperable or degraded in performance, and it was noticeable that the Soviets concentrated on producing alternative means of locating and attacking submerged targets. They fitted VDS and towed passive arrays from an early date and accumulated much experience in their use. By virtue of temperature and density effects, sound energy travelling through water is ducted and distorted, tending to be concentrated in the so-called 'convergence zones', spaced regularly (about 60 km/37 miles) at intervals from the source. A quiet ship, streaming a passive array at depth, can easily locate a target at this range and, as modern submarines carry stand-off anti-ship missiles, they also needed an AS weapon to hit the target first at this considerable range.

so-called 'battlecruiser' *Kirov*. A powerful ship, the *Kirov* was perceived to play a role similar to the US 'Iowa'-class battleships in forming the core of a Surface Action Group (SAG). Soviet doctrine emphasized the importance of surface ship support for submarine operations. Geography demanded that their submarines needed to transit certain 'choke points' which would, inevitably, be hotly contested with the West. There was an obvious role for a surface group that could not only frustrate Western formations in their efforts but also survive in a very high threat environment while, if possible, extending further Soviet ASW on the spot. It was, therefore, to be expected that the Soviets would produce ships complementary to the 'Kirov' class – the 'Slava' cruiser and the 'Sovremenny' class.

Surface warfare

The *Sovremenny* was the first Soviet destroyer designed with an ASUW bias since the post-war period. The class was assigned to the Northern and Pacific Fleets to control the vital GIUK and Okhotsk Sea gaps; in the former case particularly, the weather proved as tough a problem as opposing fleets.

A new range of sensors and weapons was installed, and a high level of training was required for their use. It was likely, therefore, that the 'Sovremenny'-class ships were drafted with career men rather than conscripts.

The 'Sovremennys' are robust, high freeboard ships, configured to operation in unpleasant weather. ASW gear is minimal. No VDS is fitted and the hull-mounted sonar is of only intermittent use in northern waters.

ASW complement

The 'Udaloy'-class ASW destroyer makes an interesting contrast. Of comparable size to the 'Sovremenny', its concepts are widely different. The 'Udaloys' also have the solid look of a ship designed for use in hostile climatic environments and their Cold War role was important, not only in the prevention of Western SSNs' efforts to interdict Soviet submarines but possibly also in the prosecution of Western SSBNs themselves. Two 'Helix' AS helicopters are carried, their bulk demanding an all-aft location for flightpad and hangar. The pad itself gains useful freeboard from being sited above the stowage for the

towed VDS. Compared with that of the 'Sovremenny' class, the more steeply raked bow of the 'Udaloy' betrays larger, lower-frequency sonar.

In the principal 'Udaloy I' subclass, this weapon is the SS-N-14 'Silex', set in quadruple launchers beneath each bridge wing. Although this weapon normally carries a conventional homing torpedo out to the first convergence zone, this could be inaccurate if targeted only on the data from a passive sonar. If the helicopters were inoperable for the purposes of pinpointing the target, a saturation approach using a nuclear warhead may have been attractive to the Soviets during the Cold War.

Dedicated to ASW, the 'Udaloys' would probably need the support of another vessel

with area-defence SAMs, as the class is armed only with point-defence missiles. However, the Soviets lacked a modern AAW destroyer, the latest being the 'Kashin' class of 'double-enders', the earliest of these having been commissioned in 1962.

A feature of Soviet ships was their heavy armament. Even before the Falklands War underlined the need of close-in weapons systems, they commonly fitted several 30-mm Gatling-type guns. All carried long torpedo tubes that could be used against either surface or submarine targets. Most could lay mines. The Soviets recognized that ships need to defend themselves in order to carry out their tasks and that vessels unable to do this are liabilities.

A 'Kynda'-class missile cruiser and a 'Kanin'-class SAM-equipped destroyer (foreground) practise underway replenishment with a 'Boris Chilkin'-class tanker off Hawaii.

'Jeanne d'Arc' class Helicopter carrier

Commissioned in 1964, the Jeanne d'Arc is equipped to act as an amphibious command ship to transport a battalion of marines, or to operate up to eight Super Frelon and Lynx helicopters. By April 1997, Jeanne d'Arc had conducted 33 training cruises and was docked for extensive repairs to its propulsion machinery. This was the vessel's third major refit, following upgrades in 1989 and 1990.

The single vessel of the **'Jeanne d'Arc' class** was laid down at Brest Naval Dockyard in 1960, launched in 1961 and commissioned in 1964. Although used in peacetime as a training ship for 158 officer cadets, *Jeanne d'Arc* (**R 97**) can be rapidly converted for wartime use as an amphibious assault, anti-submarine warfare or troop transport vessel. The helicopter platform is 62 m (203 ft 5 in) wide and is connected to the hangar deck by a 12218-kg (26,935-lb) capacity elevator located at the after end of the flight deck. The deck is capable of flying-on two Super Frelon heavy-lift helicopters and can accommodate a further four parked. The hangar, with some internal modifications, can accommodate a further eight helicopters. At the aft end extensive machine, inspection and maintenance workshops are sited with weapon handling rooms and magazines for the armaments carried by the helicopters. In the commando carrier or troop transport role the ship has facilities for a 700-man infantry battalion with light equipment in its fully air-conditioned interior.

A modular type action information and operations room is fitted, together with a separate helicopter control bridge and a combined command and control centre for amphibious warfare operations. A SENIT-2 combat data system was to be installed, but was cancelled as a cost-saving measure. On each side of the funnel two LCVPs are normally carried.

In the future, *Jeanne d'Arc* may lose its two 100-mm (3.9-in) guns from the quarterdeck. The vessel's service life may be extended to 2010, in order that it can be replaced by a dedicated training ship, rather than a 'Mistral'-class LND as is planned for 2006.

SPECIFICATION	
Jeanne d'Arc	war inventory includes up to eight
Commissioned: 1 July 1964	Super Frelon and Lynx; four LCVPs
Displacement: 10,000 tons standard	**Armament:** two single 100-mm
and 13,270 tons full load	(3.9-in) DP guns, two triple MM 38
Dimensions: length 182 m (597 ft	Exocet surface-to-surface missile
1 in); beam 24 m (78 ft 8½ in);	launcher-containers, four 12.7-mm
draught 7.5 m (24 ft 7 in)	(0.5-in) machine-guns
Propulsion: two geared steam	**Electronics:** one DRBV 22D air
turbines delivering 29828 kW	search radar, one DRBV 51
(40,000 shp) to two shafts	air/surface search radar, one DRBN
Speed: 26.5 kts	34A navigation radar, three DRBC
Complement: 455 (33 officers) plus	32A fire-control radars, one SRN-6
13 instructors and 158 cadets	TACAN, one SQS-503 sonar, DUBV
Troops: 700 (commando carrier)	24C active hull sonar, two Syllex
Cargo: three Dauphin helicopters,	ECM rocket launchers

The French navy's helicopter carrier, Jeanne d'Arc. Used as a training ship in peacetime, the vessel can be rapidly converted in wartime to a commando ship or ASW helicopter carrier.

'Ropucha' class Tank landing ship

Designated *bol'shoy desantnyy korabl'* (BDK) or large landing ship by the Soviets, the **'Ropucha I'** class was in series production at the Polish Polnocny shipyard, Gdansk, in 1974–78 and 1980–88 for the Soviet navy. The class is designed for roll-on/roll-off operations with both bow and stern doors. The 630-m² (6,780-sq ft) vehicle deck stretches throughout the conventional LST-type hull. Two spaces for 122-mm (4.8-in) BM-21 multiple rocket-launchers are provided forward. Some units had four quadruple Strela-2 (SA-N-5 'Grail') SAM launchers fitted to supplement the two twin

SPECIFICATION	
'Ropucha I' class (Project 775)	quadruple Strela-2 SAM launchers
Displacement: 4,400 tons full load	**Electronics:** one 'Don-2' navigation
Dimensions: length 112.5 m (369 ft);	radar, one 'Strut Curve' air search
beam 15 m (49 ft 2½ in); draught	radar, one 'Muff Cob' fire-control
3.7 m (12 ft 1½ in)	radar, one 'High Pole' or 'Salt Pot'
Propulsion: two diesels delivering	IFF system
14,340 kW (19,230 shp) to two	**Complement:** 95 (7 officers)
shafts	**Troops and cargo:** 230 troops, or 10
Armament: two twin 57-mm	MBTs and 190 troops, or 24 AFVs
(2.24-in) guns, 92 mines, and four	and 170 troops

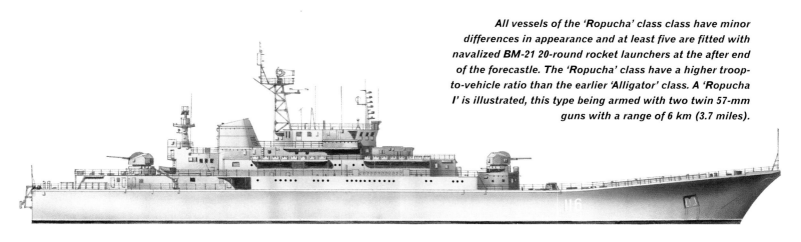

All vessels of the 'Ropucha' class class have minor differences in appearance and at least five are fitted with navalized BM-21 20-round rocket launchers at the after end of the forecastle. The 'Ropucha' class have a higher troop-to-vehicle ratio than the earlier 'Alligator' class. A 'Ropucha I' is illustrated, this type being armed with two twin 57-mm guns with a range of 6 km (3.7 miles).

57-mm (2.24-in) guns carried. The multi-level superstructure was specially built to accommodate the 230 men of two Soviet Naval Infantry companies for extended periods. This, together with the capacity for carrying 24 AFVs or 450 tons of cargo, allowed the Soviet navy to employ these ships on distant ocean operations.

Between 1990 and 1992, a further three vessels were built to an improved **'Ropucha II'** design, with a single 76-mm (3-in) gun forward and two 30-mm AK 630 guns aft. There are currently some 16 of both types in service with the Russian navy, whilst another was transferred to South Yemen in 1979 and another to Ukraine in 1996.

'Alligator' class Tank landing ship

The 'Alligator' class is now operated in only small numbers by the Russian navy, with one Type IV ship with the Pacific Fleet, one vessel with the Baltic Fleet and two with the Black Sea Fleet. The Soviet navy, who knew the type as the 'Tapir' class, operated four Type Is, two Type IIs, six Type IIs and two Type IVs.

Designated *bol'shoy desantnyy korabl'* (BDK) or large landing ship by the Soviets, the **'Alligator' class** was built at Kaliningrad and commissioned between 1966 and 1976. During this time, the roll-on/roll-off bow and stem door design evolved to form four distinct sub-classes. The first two series are primarily for the transport role whilst the remaining two are primarily for the over-the-beach assault role.

The latter two classes have a navalized split 40-round BM-21 122-mm (4.8-in) rocket launcher pedestal mount fitted for shore bombardment purposes. The deck crane equipment also varies within the variants: **Type I** has one 15-ton capacity and two 5-ton capacity cranes, whilst **Types II**, III and IV have only one 15-ton capacity crane. The **Type III** also has a raised superstructure and a forward deckhouse for the rocket launcher; the **Type IV** is similar to the Type III but with two additional twin 25-mm AA gun mountings on the centreline abaft the bridge superstructure.

The ships were designed to carry the equipment required by a Naval Infantry battalion landing team, although the ships can also accommodate a Naval Infantry company for long periods. As well as a 91.4-m (300-ft) tank deck stretching across the hull, there are two smaller deck areas and a hold. The vehicle parking area includes the upper deck, and both the Strela-1 (SA-9 'Gaskin')

SAM mounted on the BRDM-2 and the tracked ZSU-23-4 AA gun system have been observed on this deck, operating in pairs to supplement the ship's normal AA armament.

Most of the class were subsequently fitted with two quadruple Strela-2 (SA-N-5 'Grail') SAM close-range launcher systems. The class regularly operated off the coastline of West Africa, in the Mediterranean and the Indian Ocean, usually with Naval Infantry units embarked.

Approximately half the class are now scrapped or laid up, and a single vessel was sold to Ukraine in 1995.

SPECIFICATION	
'Alligator' class (Project 1171)	(2.24-in) gun, two twin 25-mm
Displacement: 3,400 tons standard and 4,700 tons full load	AA guns (Type IV), one 40-round BM-21 122-mm (4.8-in) rocket
Dimensions: length 113 m (370 ft 8 in); beam 15.5 m (50 ft 10 in); draught 4.5 m (14 ft 8½ in)	launcher (Types III and IV), two quadruple Strela-2 SAM launchers
Propulsion: two diesels delivering 6,711 kW (9,000 shp) to two shafts	**Electronics:** two 'Don Kay' or one 'Don-2' and one 'Spin Trough' navigation radars, one 'Muff Cob'
Speed: 18 kts	fire-control radar in some, one
Cargo: typically 20 tanks and various trucks or 40 AFVs	'High Pole-B' IFF system
Armament: one twin 57-mm	**Complement:** 100
	Troops: 120 normal, 300 maximum

'Sir Lancelot' and 'Sir Bedivere' classes Landing Ships Logistic

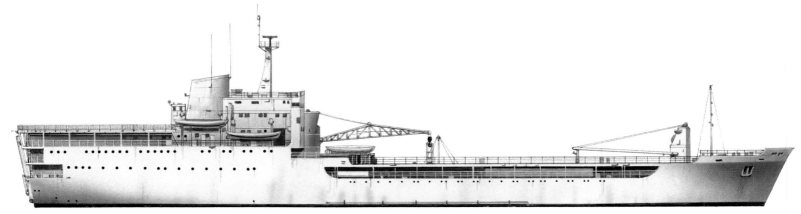

The **Sir Lancelot** was ordered in 1963 as the prototype vessel of the **'Sir Lancelot' class**, designed to furnish the British Army with ships capable of landing troops, vehicles and tanks. The remaining five ships in the class, comprising **Sir Bedivere**, **Sir Geraint**, **Sir Galahad**, **Sir Percivale** and **Sir Tristram** were built to a slightly modified design known as the **'Sir Bedivere' class**. In 1970, the ships of the 'Sir Lancelot' and 'Sir Bedivere' classes were handed over to the Royal Fleet Auxiliary.

Falklands

The six ships sailed with the Royal Navy Task Force during the Falklands War of 1982. *Sir Galahad* and *Sir Tristram* were attacked by Argentine aircraft on 8 June. *Sir Galahad* was so

badly damaged that it was taken out into the Atlantic and sunk. *Sir Tristram* was salvagable and spent the rest of the Falklands campaign as an accomodation vessel in Port Stanley. After the conflict, she was towed back to the UK for extensive repairs.

Tyne Ship repairers were tasked with restoring *Sir Tristram*. She received major modifications. She was lengthened by 7 m (29 ft) to accomodate an enlarged flight deck, to enable the vessel to operate Chinook helicopters. The aluminium bridge was replaced by a steel construction. The ship was also fitted with a new systems suite, including a SATCOM system and helicopter control radar. The refit was completed in October 1985.

The remaining vessels in the 'Sir Lancelot'/'Sir Bedivere'

The 'Sir Lancelot' and 'Sir Bedivere' class of LSL were essentially similar. Manned by the RFA from 1970, the LSLs were heavily committed during the Falklands War. One, the Sir Galahad, was sunk as a war grave on 8 June 1982 after sustaining damage during an air attack at Bluff Cove while another, the Sir Tristram, suffered such severe damage that it had to be rebuilt.

classes were subsequently modified to the same standard. The remaining four of the class were deployed during Operation Desert Storm in 1991. They were outfitted with additional 20-mm (0.79-in) guns, missile decoy systems and navigation equipment.

The 'Sir Lancelot'/'Sir Bedivere' classes were designed for amphibious operations. Ramps are fitted to the bow and stern for roll-

on/roll-off operations. Interior ramps conect the ship's two cargo decks. The cargo decks can carry 16 main battle tanks, 34 mixed vehicles, 30 tons of ammunition and 120 tons of petrol, oil and lubricants. Two 4.5-ton cranes and a single 20-ton crane assist loading and unloading. In addition, two Mexeflote self-propelled floating platforms can be carried on the hull for use as pontoons to ferry troops and vehicles ashore.

The Royal Fleet Auxilliary Sir Bedivere comes under air attack in 'Bomb Alley' (San Carlos Water) from an Argentine Dagger during the Falkands War in May 1982.

As well as having a helicopter deck astern, the vessels also have a helicopter deck fitted on the foredeck. However, both classes lack either hangarage or maintenance facilities for helicopters. Nine helicopters can be stored on the vehicle deck while a further 11 can be stored on the tank and armoured vehicle deck.

Four vessels of the 'Sir Lancelot' and 'Sir Bedivere' class are still in service – Sir Bedivere, Sir Tristram, Sir Geraint and Sir Percivale – together with the new Sir Galahad, which was commissioned in 1987 as a replacement for the original of that name. All of these ships are scheduled to be replaced by the four 'Bay'-class LSLs (Landing Ships Logistic) in 2004–2005.

SPECIFICATION	
'Sir Lancelot' and 'Sir Bedivere' classes	4-ton trucks plus 90 tons of general cargo; 120 tons of petrol, oil and lubricants and 30 tons of ammunition (*Sir Lancelot* the same except only 16 MBTs and 25 4-ton trucks); all vessels can carry two Mexeflote floating platforms
Ships in class (commissioned): *Sir Lancelot* 1964, *Sir Galahad* (original vessel) 1966, *Sir Bedivere* 1967, *Sir Tristram* 1967, *Sir Geraint* 1967 and *Sir Percival* 1968	
Displacement: *Sir Lancelot* 5,550 tons and rest 5,674 tons full load	**Aircraft:** three Wessex HU.Mk 5 or two Sea King HC.Mk 4 or three Gazelle or Lynx helicopters
Dimensions: length 125.1 m (412 ft 1 in); beam 19.6 m (59 ft 9½ in); draught 4.3 m (13 ft)	**Armament:** two Mk 9 40-mm AA guns, two Oerlikon 20-mm AA guns, plus several 0.3-in (7.62-mm) GPMGs and Blowpipe man-portable SAM launchers
Propulsion: two diesels delivering 7,010 kW (9,400 bhp) to two shafts; *Sir Lancelot* 7,099 kW (9,520 bhp)	**Electronics:** one Type 1006 navigation radar
Speed: 17 kts	
Troops: 340 normal, 534 maximum	**Complement:** 69 (18 officers and 51 men)
Cargo: maximum 18 MBTs and 32	

HMS Fearless *(right) and the Falklands veteran* **LSL** Sir Tristram *(left) undergo alongside refuelling at speed from one of the RFA's 'Leaf'-class support ships.*

'Fearless' class Amphibious Transport Dock

The two British **'Fearless'-class** LPDs, **HMS** *Fearless* and **HMS** *Intrepid*, were formerly under the command of Flag Officer Third Flotilla (FOF3), which was concerned with the larger warships of the Royal Navy and the naval air elements. The infamous 1981 Defence Review forecast the disposal of *Intrepid*

HMS Fearless *signals* **HMS** Antrim *prior to the San Carlos landings. The run of the Falkland Sound was made at night, with the first troops landing at San Carlos at 04.00 hours on 21 May 1982.*

A Wessex HU.Mk 5 commando assault helicopter departs HMS Fearless. Note the single LCU in the well deck, one of four that could be accommodated. Each LCU could carry one or two MBTs or up to 250 troops.

(**L 11**) in 1982 and of *Fearless* (**L 10**) in 1984, but sanity finally prevailed within the Ministry of Defence in February 1982, and it was decided that both ships would continue in service, their worth later being proved during the Falkland Islands war, since without them there could not have been an assault landing to recapture the islands.

Assault capacity

The 'Fearless'-class ships were tasked to provide amphibious assault lift capabilities using an onboard naval assault group/brigade headquarters unit with a fully equipped assault operations room from which the force commanders could mount and control all the air, sea and land force assets required for the operation. The ships also carried an amphibious detachment that consisted of an assault squadron subdivided into a landing craft (LC) squadron with four LCUs (ex-LCM9s) and four LCVPs, an amphibious beach unit (ABU) with its own Land Rover and a Centurion

Beach Armoured Recovery Vehicle (BARV) to attend to stranded vehicles and landing craft, and a vehicle deck party (VDP) for marshalling vehicles for embarkation on the landing craft. The LCU could carry either one Chieftain or two Centurion MBTs, or four 4-ton trucks or eight Land Rovers and trailers, or 100 tons of cargo, or 250 troops as its payload. The LCVP carried either 35 troops or two

Land Rovers. A 50.29 x 22.86 m (165 x 75 ft) flight deck was built over the well deck and was capable of operating most NATO helicopter types or, if required, Sea Harrier V/STOL fighter aircraft. Three vehicle decks were provided, in the form of one for tracked vehicles such as tanks or self-propelled guns, one for wheeled trucks, and a halfdeck that was reserved for Land Rover vehicles and trailers.

The overload troop capacity was sufficient for a light infantry battalion or Royal Marine Commando with an attached artillery battery.

Further light vehicle stowage space could be obtained by using the helicopter flight deck. The vessels could also act as training ships, in which 150 midshipmen and naval cadets could be embarked for nine-week courses.

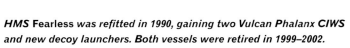

HMS Fearless was refitted in 1990, gaining two Vulcan Phalanx CIWS and new decoy launchers. Both vessels were retired in 1999–2002.

SPECIFICATION

HMS *Fearless* (L 10) and *Intrepid* (L 11)
Commissioned: L 10 25 November 1965 and L 11 11 March 1967
Displacement: 12,210 tons full load
Dimensions: length 158.5 m (520 ft); beam 24.4 m (80 ft); draught 6.2 m (20 ft 6 in)
Propulsion: two geared steam turbines delivering 22,000 shp to two shafts
Speed: 21 kts
Cargo: maximum 20 MBTs, one BARV, 45 4-ton trucks with 50 tons of stores, or up to 2,100 tons of stores; four LCUs and four LCVPs; five Wessex HU.Mk 5 or four Sea King HC.Mk 4 plus three Gazelle or Lynx helicopters
Armament: two GWS 20 quadruple Sea Cat SAM launchers, two twin

Oerlikon 30-mm DP guns (L 11), two Oerlikon 20-mm AA guns, variable numbers of 0.3-in (7.62-mm) GPMGs and Blowpipe man-portable SAM launchers; L 10 later received two 20-mm Mk 15 Vulcan Phalanx guns
Electronics: one Type 978 navigation radar, one Type 994 air and surface search radar, one SCOT satellite communications system, one ESM system with Knebworth/Corvus chaff launchers, one CAAIS operations room command and control system
Complement: 617 (37 officers, 500 ratings and 80 Royal Marines)
Troops: 330 normal, 500 overload and 670 maximum

'Blue Ridge' class Amphibious Command Ships (LCC)

The two integrated air, land and sea amphibious assault command ships of the **'Blue Ridge' class** are the first and only ships constructed by any nation solely for that role. A third ship of the class (designed at the outset for both amphibious and fleet command) was also programmed but was cancelled. In the late 1970s, as a result of the retirement of the elderly 'Cleveland'-class flagship cruisers, the two 'Blue Ridge' vessels also took on fleet flagship duties. The **USS Blue Ridge** became the flagship of the West Pacific 7th fleet and **USS Mount Whitney** the flagship of the Atlantic 2nd fleet.

The basic hull design and propulsion machinery is like that of the 'Iwo Jima'-class LPHs, with the larger hangar area devoted to accommodation, offices and operations rooms required by the maximum possible 200 officers and 500 enlisted men of the embarked flag group. The ships have comprehensive satellite communications, command, control and intelligence analysis facilities fitted: the Amphibious Command Information System (ACIS); the Naval Intelligence Processing System (NIPS); the Naval Tactical Data System (NTDS) with its AN/UYK-20 and AN/UYK-7 digital computers to give an overall picture of the tactical underwater, surface and air warfare situations; Link 11 and Link 14 automatic data transmission systems to allow the exchange of tactical information with NTDS-equipped ships and Airborne Tactical Data System (ATDS) equipped aircraft; extensive photographic laboratories and document publication facilities; and the satellite communications system with OE82 antenna, SSR-1 receiver and WSC-3 transceiver. The vessels each carry three LCPs, two LCVPs and one 10-m (32.8-ft) personnel launch in Welvin davits situated in prominent sponsons projecting from the ships' sides. A helicopter landing area is located at the stern, but there are no hangar or maintenance facilities aboard. A small vehicle garage and elevator are provided. When necessary, the ships operate a single SH-3H Sea King utility helicopter as the ship's flight. A Mk 23 Target Acquisition System (TAS) and RAM missiles are due to be added.

USS Blue Ridge (LCC-19) before the addition of Phalanx CIWS. Fitted with a vast array of command, control and communications systems, the vessel is well suited for its additional role of fleet flagship.

The nerve centre of an amphibious assault, the command ship USS Blue Ridge. The vessel serves as the US 7th Fleet flagship and is home ported at Yokosuka. Mount Whitney is based at Norfolk, Virginia.

SPECIFICATION	
Blue Ridge (LCC-19) and Mount Whitney (LCC-20) **Commissioned:** LCC-19 14 November 1970 and LCC-20 16 January 1971 **Displacement:** 19,290 tons full load **Dimensions:** length 189 m (620 ft); beam 25 m (82 ft); draught 8.8 m (29 ft) **Propulsion:** one geared steam turbine delivering 16,405.4 kW (22,000 shp) to one shaft **Speed:** 23 kts maximum and 20 kts sustained **Armament:** two twin Mk 33 3-in (76-mm) AA (removed 1996-97), two 8-tube Mk 25 Sea Sparrow BPDMS launchers replaced by two 20-mm Mk 16 Phalanx CIWS	**Electronics:** one SPS-48 3D search radar, one SPS-10 surface search radar, one SPS-40 air search radar, two Mk 115 missile fire-control systems, one target designation system, two Mk 56 gun fire-control systems, two Mk 35 fire-control radars, one Mk 36 Super RBOC launcher system and associated ESM equipment, one URN-20 TACAN **Complement:** LCC-19 799 (41 officers plus 758 enlisted men) and LCC-20 516 (41 officers plus 475 enlisted men) **Flag group:** LCC-19 250 (50 officers plus 200 enlisted men) and LCC-20 420 (160 officers, 260 enlisted men

'Iwo Jima' class Amphibious Assault Ships Helicopter (LPH)

Since 1955, when the escort carrier *Thetis Bay* was converted to a helicopter assault ship, the United States Navy has maintained a vertical airlift capability for the US Marine Corps. The ships of the **'Iwo Jima' class** were built to an improved World War II escort carrier design with accommodation for a US Marine infantry battalion landing team fore and aft of the centrally located box hangar. These vessels were the first to be designed specifically to carry and operate helicopters, and as such no catapult or arrester gear was fitted. The flight deck was able to operate or recover seven

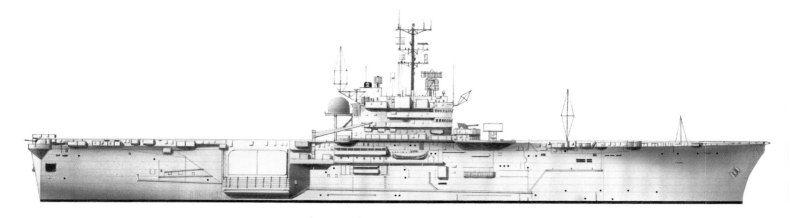

CH-46 Sea Knight or four CH-53 Sea Stallions simultaneously. The hangar deck, with a 6.1-m (20-ft) height clearance, could accommodate 19 CH-46s or 11 CH-53s. The normal air group was a mixture of 24 CH-46, CH-53, AH-1 and UH-1 helicopters. On **LPH-2**, **LPH-3**, **LPH-11** and **LPH-12** two foldable 22,727-kg (50,100-lb) capacity deck-edge lifts were carried, whilst on **LPH-7**, **LPH-9** and **LPH-10** the lifts were reduced to 20,000-kg (44,090-lb) capacity. They did not

carry landing craft (with the exception of LPH-12, which had two LCVPs on davits), so the ships were limited in the size of equipment they could carry for the embarked US Marines. Two small elevators carried palletized cargo from the cargo holds to the flight deck, and a parking area for light vehicles and towed artillery pieces also provided.

During 1972–74, LPH-9 operated as an interim sea control ship carrying AV-8A Harriers and SH-3 Sea King

The 'Iwo Jima'-class LPHs were the world's first ship class designed and constructed specifically to operate helicopters. Each LPH could carry a Marine battalion landing team with all its equipment, a reinforced helicopter squadron and supporting personnel.

ASW helicopters. When converted back to an LPH, it retained the Air Surface Classification and Analysis Centre (ASCAC) that was fitted for the experimental role. Other LPHs also operated as minesweeping headquarters boats, embarking US Navy RH-53 helicopter minesweeping units. These cleared North Vietnamese ports in 1973 and the Suez Canal in 1974. All helicopter operations were controlled from a dedicated

command and control centre located in the flight deck island. All except LPH-10 carried the same satellite communications equipment as the LCCs, and they had the same 300-bed hospital unit as the LHAs. Four ships served with the Atlantic fleets and three with the Pacific fleets. LPH-12 was later permanently converted for the mine warfare role as **MCS-12**. The remaining five vessels in the class were decommissioned between 1993 and 1997.

USS Inchon, the sole surviving 'Iwo Jima'-class ship, now serves in the mine warfare role and embarks eight MH-53E Sea Dragons, having undergone conversion to become a Mine Countermeasures Command, Control and Support Ship (MCS) by 1996.

SPECIFICATION

'Iwo Jima' class
Iwo Jima (LPH-2), *Okinawa* (LPH-3), *Guadalcanal* (LPH-7), *Guam* (LPH-9), *Tripoli* (LPH-10), *New Orleans* (LPH-11) and *Inchon* (LPH-12)
Commissioned: LPH-2 26 August 1961, LPH-3 14 April 1962, LPH-7 20 July 1963, LPH-9 16 January 1965, LPH-10 6 August 1966, LPH-11 16 November 1968 and LPH-12 20 June 1970
Displacement: 18,300 tons full load
Dimensions: length 183.7 m (602 ft 3½ in); beam 25.6 m (84 ft); draught 7.9 m (26 ft)
Propulsion: one geared steam turbine delivering 16,405.4 kW (22,000 shp) to one shaft
Speed: 23 kts maximum and 20 kts sustained
Cargo: total 399.6-m² (4,300-sq ft) vehicle parking area; LPH-12 two

LCVPs; maximum 19 CH-46 helicopters in hangar plus seven on deck; 24,605 litres (6,500 US gal) MOGAS vehicle fuel; 1,533,090 litres (405,000 US gal) JP5 aviation fuel; 1059.8 m³ (37,425 cu ft) palletized stores
Armament: two twin Mk 33 3-in (76-mm) AA guns, two 8-tube Mk 25 Sea Sparrow BPDMS launchers, two 20-mm Mk 16 Phalanx CIWS
Electronics: one SPS-10 surface search radar, one SPS-40 air search radar, one SPN-10 or SPN-43 aircraft landing aid radar system, one Mk 36 Super RBOC launcher system with associated ESM equipment, one URN-20 TACAN
Complement: 652 (47 officers plus 605 enlisted men)
Troops: 2,090 (190 officers and 1,900 enlisted men)

'Raleigh' and 'Austin' classes Amphibious Transport Docks (LPD)

The LPD is a development of the dock landing ship (LSD) with an increased troop and vehicle capacity at the expense of a

reduction in the dock well size. The LPD combines the troop-carrying of the APA with part of the cargo-carrying AKA, and the

vehicle and landing craft capabilities of the LSD designs in one hull. Of the three-ship **'Raleigh' class**, one was

converted to the Command Middle East Force flagship. This ship, **USS La Salle**, serves as flagship in the Mediterranean.

An SH-60B from HSL-41 'Seahawks' shadows USS Denver during operations in the Pacific. Six 'Austin'-class vessels can now operate the Pioneer UAV.

Similar to but larger than the 'Fearless' class, USS Shreveport, can, like several of its sisters, act as an amphibious squadron flagship. Two additional Mk 38 25-mm guns can be carried for self-defence.

The 'Raleigh'-class ships have a stern docking well 51.2 m (168 ft) long and 15.2 m (50 ft) wide that can accommodate one LCU and three LCM6s, or four LCM8s, or 20 AAV7 amphibious vehicles. In addition, two LCM6s or four LCPLs are carried on the helicopter deck and lifted overboard by crane. The helicopter deck covers the landing craft well, but there are no onboard hangar or maintenance facilities. Up to six CH-46 helicopters can be operated for short times from the deck.

An overhead monorail stores transfer system is used to load the landing craft in the well deck from the forward cargo holds. Ramps connect the vehicle decks, docking well and flight deck, which can also be used to park additional vehicles if required. Side ports in the hull provide a roll-on/roll-off

capability when docks are available.

The later **'Austin'-class** ships are enlarged versions of the 'Raleigh' class. The docking well is the same size, but a 12-m (39.4-ft) extension has been inserted just forward of the well to increase the vehicle- and cargo-carrying capacities. A fixed flight deck is located above the well with two landing spots. All except **LPD-4** are fitted with a variable hangar – 17.7–19.5 m (58–64 ft) long, 5.8–7.3 m (19–24 ft) wide – which can be extended to about 24.4 m (80 ft) long if required. Up to six CH-46s can be operated, although the hangar can accommodate only one utility helicopter. The AAV7 capacity is increased to 28 with alternative loads of one LCU and three LCM6s or nine LCM6s or four LCM8s. **LPD-7** to **LPD-13** are fitted with amphibious squadron flagship

SPECIFICATION	
'Raleigh' and 'Austin' classes *Raleigh* (LPD-1), *Vancouver* (LPD-2), *Austin* (LPD-4), *Ogden* (LPD-5), *Duluth* (LPD-6), *Cleveland* (LPD-7), *Dubuque* (LPD-8), *Denver* (LPD-9), *Juneau* (LPD-10), *Shreveport* (LPD-12), *Nashville* (LPD-13), *Trenton* (LPD-14) and *Ponce* (LPD-15) **Commissioned:** 1962 to 1971 **Displacement:** LPD-1/2 13,900 tons full load; LPD-4/6 15,900 tons full load; LPD-7/10 16,550 tons full load; LPD-11/13 16,900 tons full load; LPD-14/15 17,000 tons full load **Dimensions:** (LPD-1/2) length 159.1 m (521 ft 10 in); beam 30.5 m (100 ft); draught 6.7 m (22 ft); (LPD-4 to LPD-15) length 173.8 m (570 ft); beam 30.5 m (100 ft); draught 7 m (23 ft) **Propulsion:** two geared steam turbines delivering 17,896.8 kW (24,000 shp) to two shafts **Speed:** 21 kts maximum **Flag group:** LPD-7 to LPD-13 90 **Troops:** LPD-1 to LPD-6 930; LPD-7 to LPD-13 840; LPD-14 and LPD-15 930	**Cargo:** LPD-4 to LPD-15 (LPD-1/2 figures are reduced slightly) total 1034.1-m² (11,130-sq ft) vehicle parking area; one LCU and three LCM6s; or nine LCM6s or four LCM8s or 28 AAV7s; 616 m³ (21,750 cu ft) of palletized stores or 472 m³ (16,670 cu ft) of ammunition; 5900 litres (22,335 US gal) of MOGAS vehicle fuel; 368,425 litres (97,328 US gal) of AVGAS aviation fuel; 17,035 litres (4,500 US gal) of AV-LUB oil; 850,095 litres (224,572 US gal) of JP5 aviation fuel **Armament:** LPD-1/2 three twin Mk 33 3-in (76-mm) AA guns, LPD-4/15 two twin Mk 33 guns (now removed); two 20-mm Mk 16 Phalanx CIWS (all vessels) **Electronics:** one SPS-10 surface search radar, one SPS-40 air search radar, one URN-20 TACAN, one Mk 36 Super RBOC system **Complement:** LPD-1 413 (24 officers plus 389 enlisted men); LPD-2 410 (23 officers plus 387 enlisted men); LPD-4 to LPD-15 410–447 (24–25 officers plus 386-442 enlisted men)

duties with an additional superstructure deck. Both classes have satellite communications systems of the

type fitted to the LCCs. Five 'Austin'-class ships serve with the Atlantic fleets, whilst six 'Raleigh'-class ships serve in the Pacific fleets. *Coronado* (**LPD-11**) was converted to become a command ship in 1980, as a temporary replacement for *La Salle*, and is now based at San Diego; it has served as a Joint Force Command Ship since 1997. **LPD-1** and **LPD-2** decommissioned in 1991-92.

The 'Austin'-class LPD USS Dubuque. From 1986 onwards this class, together with the 'Iwo Jima'-class LPHs, underwent a service life extension programme.

'Newport' class Landing ships tanks (LST)

Above: The 'Newport'-class LST USS Fairfax County is seen in company with the 'Iwo Jima'-class LPH USS Inchon. A ramp just ahead of the forward superstructure on the 'Newport' connects the lower tank deck with the main deck. A vehicle passage through the superstructure provides access to the parking area amidships.

Left: A 'Newport'-class LST unloads a cargo of medium trucks. The hull form required to achieve 20 kts does not permit bow doors, hence the use of the 34.14-m (112-ft) ramp over the bow.

Below: USS Newport standing just offshore and in the process of lowering its bow ramp for vehicle disembarkation during a landing exercise. Note the size of the twin supporting derrick arms.

The **'Newport' class** is the ultimate design in post-World War II LST design. The vessels use a pointed bow, allowing them to sustain 20 kts, the speed required by American amphibious ships. The 34-ton aluminium bow ramp is 34.14 m (112 ft) long and can carry loads of up to 75 tons. It is handled over the bow by two supporting derrick arms. The stern ramp has direct access to the tank deck to allow the unloading of AAV7s directly into the water. The stern ramps can also be mated to a landing craft or a pier for unloading purposes.

Lower deck

Vehicles are driven onto the lower deck via a 75-ton capacity ramp or through a passage in the superstructure that leads to the helicopter deck aft. This has no hangar or helicopter maintenance facilities. Four pontoon causeway sections can be carried on the hull sides, and handled by two derrick cranes located aft of the two funnel

intakes. The vehicle decks can also be used for 500 tons of general cargo if required. Cargo space for ammunition, diesel fuel, MOGAS vehicle fuel and AVGAS aviation fuel supplies are also available.

At peak deployment, nine ships served with the US Atlantic fleets, nine with the Pacific fleets, and two with the Naval Reserve Force. Throughout the 1990s, transfers were made to Australia (two vessels), Brazil (one), Chile (one), Malaysia (one), Morocco (one), Spain (two leased) and Taiwan (two).

USS **Frederick,** *the last 'Newport'-class ship in US Navy service, is seen shortly after its final berth shift. Finally decommissioned in October 2002, the 'Fast Freddy' had played an active role in both the Vietnam War and the 1991* **Gulf War.**

SPECIFICATION	
'Newport' class	cargo; three LCVPs and one LCPL;
Commissioned: 1969–72	72.3 m² (2,550 cu ft) ammunition;
Displacement: 8,342–8,450 tons full load	508,900 litres (134,438 US gal) of AVGAS, 27,230 litres (7,194 US gal)
Dimensions: length 159.2 m (522 ft 4 in); beam 21.2 m (69 ft 6 in); draught 5.3 m (17 ft 6 in)	of MOGAS; 96,150 litres (25,400 US gal) of diesel fuel
Propulsion: six diesels delivering 12,304 kW (16,500 shp) to two shafts	**Armament:** two twin Mk 33 3-in (76-mm) AA guns (replaced by one 20-mm Mk 15 Phalanx CIWS)
Speed: 20 kts sustained	**Electronics:** one SPS-10 surface search radar, one LN/66 navigation radar, one Mk 36 SRBOC launcher
Cargo: total 1765-m² (19,000-sq ft) vehicle parking area for 25 AAV7s and 17 2½-ton trucks, or 21 M48/M60 MBTs and 17 2½-ton trucks, or 500 tons of general	**Complement:** 225 (14 officers plus 211 enlisted men)
	Troops: 431 (20 officers plus 211 enlisted men)

'Cabildo', 'Thomaston' and 'Anchorage' classes LSD

The LSD (Landing Ships Dock) is a World War II design for carrying landing craft and heavy vehicles such as tanks. There are no **'Cabildo' class** LSDs still in service with the US Navy, but one remains in service with Taiwan as *Chung Cheng* (and was fitted with a Sea Chaparral SAM system in 1992). Single vessels of the class were also operated by Greece and Spain. The 9,375-ton full load 'Cabildo' class can carry three LCUs or 18 LCM6s or 32 LVTP-5/7 amphibious carriers in its well dock, which is 103 m (338 ft) long and 13.3 m (43 ft 8½ in) wide. The class can also carry 1,347 tons of cargo, and 100 2½-ton trucks or 27 M48 MBTs or 11 helicopters as well. Troop accommodation is limited to 137 overnight or 500 for short day runs. The crew numbers 18 officers and 283 enlisted men.

The 'Anchorage'-class LSD USS **Mount Vernon** *and the 'Oliver Hazard Perry'-class guided missile frigate USS* **Sides** *steam together off the coast of Japan.* **Mount Vernon** *was the first West Coast ship to operate the* **LCAC** *air cushion assault craft.*

Above: The 'Anchorage'-class **LSD USS** *Portland is viewed from the* **LHA USS** *Saipan in the Atlantic Ocean during Operation Enduring Freedom in 2003.*

Left: Lead ship of its class, **USS** *Anchorage is seen off the Australian coast during a routine deployment to the Western Pacific. These ships can accommodate three* **LCUs** *or* **LCACs** *or up to 48* **AAV7** *amphibians.*

Maximum speed is 15.4 kts and the original armament was a variable number of 40-mm AA guns. A helicopter platform is fitted over the well deck although no hangar or maintenance facilities are carried.

The **'Thomaston' class** was the first post-war LSD design, and stemmed from Korean War experiences. The docking well is 119.2 m (391 ft) long and 14.6 m (48 ft) wide, and can accommodate three LCUs or 19 LCM6s or nine LCM8s or 48 AAV7s. A vehicle-parking area forward of the dock can accommodate a further 30 AAV7s if required. The ship carries two LCVPs and two LCPLs in davits, but no palletized cargo is carried. The 'Thomaston'-class ships were replaced by the new 'Whidbey Island' class.

The **'Anchorage' class** is similar to the 'Thomaston' class, but the ships have a tripod mast to distinguish them. A removable helicopter landing platform is fitted over the major

The 'Thomaston'-class **LHD USS** *Hermitage. This class was very similar to the later and marginally larger 'Anchorage'-class* **LSD.** *Two 'Thomaston'-class vessels,* **Ceará** *and* **Rio de Janeiro,** *continued to be operated by the Brazilian navy in 2003.*

part of the docking well; the size of which was increased to 131.1 m (430 ft) long by 15.2 m (50 ft) wide to accommodate three LCUs or 21 LCM6s or eight LCM8s or 50 AAV7s. The vessels also carry one or two LCM6s stowed on deck and one LCPL and one LCVP on davits. Troop capacity is also increased.

Three 'Anchorage'-class vessels (**USS Anchorage, USS Portland** and **USS Mount Vernon**) remained in service with the US Navy in 2003, two with the Pacific Fleet and one with the Atlantic Fleet. One further vessel was sold to Taiwan in 2000 and serves as **Shiu Hai**. A second such vessel may be acquired by Taiwan in the future.

SPECIFICATION

'Thomaston' and 'Anchorage' classes
Names: *Thomaston* (LSD-28), *Plymouth Rock* (LSD-29), *Fort Snelling* (LSD-30), *Point Defiance* (LSD-31), *Spiegel Grove* (LSD-32), *Alamo* (LSD-33), *Hermitage* (LSD-34) and *Monticello* (LSD-35); *Anchorage* (LSD-36), *Portland* (LSD-37), *Pensacola* (LSD-38), *Mount Vernon* (LSD-39), *Fort Fisher* (LSD-40)
Commissioned: 1954 to 1972
Displacement: LSD-28/31 and LSD-35 11,270 tons full load; LSD-32/34 12,150 tons full load; LSD-36/40 13,700 tons full load
Dimensions: (LSD-28 to LSD-35) length 155.5 m (510 ft), beam 25.6 m (84 ft); draught 5.8 m (19 ft); (LSD-36 to LSD-40) length 168.6 m (553 ft 4 in); beam 25.6 m (84 ft); draught 6 m (20 ft)
Propulsion: two geared steam turbines delivering 17,896.8 kW (24,000 shp) to two shafts

Speed: 22.5 kts maximum and 20 kts sustained
Cargo: LSD-28/35 total 975-m² (10,500-sq ft) vehicle parking area, LSD-36/40 1115-m² (12,000-sq ft) vehicle parking area; three LCUs or 19 LCM6s or LCM8s or 48 AAV7s; 85 m³ (3,000 cu ft) ammunition; 4,540 litres (1,200 US gal) of AVGAS or MOGAS; 147,650 litres (39,000 US gal) of diesel fuel
Armament: three twin Mk 33 3-in (76-mm) AA guns (replaced by two 20-mm Mk 16 Phalanx CIWS and two 25-mm Mk 38 Bushmaster)
Electronics: one SPS-10 surface search radar, one SPS-6 (or SPS-40 in LSD-36/40) air search radar, one Mk 36 SRBOC system with associated ESM equipment
Complement: LSD-28/35 331–341; and LSD-36/40 341–345
Troops: LSD-28/35 340, and LSD-36/40 376

'Charleston' class Amphibious cargo ship

SPECIFICATION

'Charleston' class LKA
Ships in class: Charleston (LKA-113), Durham (LKA-114), Mobile (LKA-115), St Louis (LKA-116) and El Paso (LKA-117)
Commissioned: LKA-113 19 December 1968, LKA-114 24 May 1969, LKA-115 29 September 1969, LKA-116 22 November 1969 and LKA-117 17 January 1970
Displacement: 18,600 tons full load
Dimensions: length 175.4 m (575 ft 6 in); beam 18.9 m (62 ft); draught 7.7 m (25 ft 6 in)

Propulsion: one steam turbine delivering 14,354.7 kW (19,250 shp) to one shaft
Speed: 20 kts sustained
Armament: three twin Mk 33 3-in (76-mm) AA guns; two 20-mm Mk 16 Phalanx CIWS
Electronics: One LN/66 navigation radar, one SPS-10 surface search radar, one Mk 36 Super RBOC chaff/flare launcher system
Complement: 325 (24 officers)
Troops: 226 (15 officers)

Originally designated Attack Cargo Ship (AKA), USS Durham was redesignated as an Amphibious Cargo Ship (LKA) in 1969. The five-vessel 'Charleston' class was the first class in the US Navy fitted with fully automated main propulsion plants.

The **'Charleston'-class** amphibious cargo ship (LKA) was designed to carry all the heavy equipment and supplies for an amphibious assault landing, and was the first vessel to be designed specifically and built for this role. All previous ships of either the LKA or assault transport (LPA) types were either converted from or built to merchant ship designs. The class was fitted with a helicopter landing pad aft, but no hangar or maintenance facilities were carried. Troop accommodation was limited to 226, but four LCM8s, four LCM6s, two LCVPs and two LCPs were normally carried as deck cargo. The landing craft and super heavy equipment were offloaded by two 78.4-ton capacity heavy-lift cranes. There were also two 40-ton capacity booms and eight 15-ton capacity booms aboard. Cargo holds for palletized stores and ammunition were provided together with extensive vehicle parking areas.

By the early 1980s, only one of the five 'Charleston' class LKAs was still assigned as a fully active unit. The vessel was assigned to the Atlantic fleet whilst the others were assigned in pairs to the Naval Reserve Force Units of the Atlantic and Pacific fleets. Although these four ships briefly returned to the active fleet in the 1980s, all vessels in the class were decommissioned by 1994.

Above: USS St Louis (LKA-116) pictured in 1976. Control of the various cranes and booms was conducted from either the bridge or a central machinery console.

Right: An aerial view of Da Nang harbour in July 1971 shows USS Durham (rear) in company with the LST USS Fresno (LST-1182) and commercial transport ships during the withdrawal from Vietnam.

'Grayback' class Transport submarine

Although latterly classed as an attack submarine (SS), the **USS Grayback** was originally built, together with USS Growler, as a cruise-missile submarine fitted to carry four SSM-N-8 (subsequently RGM-6) Regulus I strategic missiles in two hangars located forward. The Grayback operated in this role until decommissioned on 25 May 1964. The planned conversion of Growler was cancelled due to a lack of funds. The vessel was then converted as a **'Grayback' class** transport

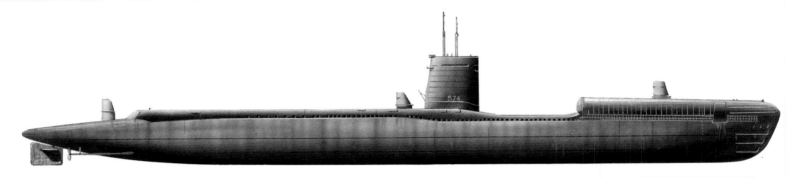

Above: USS Grayback was one of the US Navy's last five conventionally powered submarines in service. From the late 1960s, the vessel acted as a transport submarine for the United States' military covert action Special Forces Units, and saw action during the Vietnam War.

submarine and listed as APSS. In August 1968, this designation was changed to LPSS and then to SS in 1975 for administrative reasons, to guarantee funding support from the US Congress.

Transport role

The conversion to the transport role was carried out at the Mare Island Naval Shipyard, San Francisco Bay from November 1967 to May 1969, and involved lengthening the hull from 98.25 m (322 ft 4 in) to 101.8 m (334 ft) and fitting mess and sleeping accommodation for the 67 troops to be carried. The work also involved the modification of the missile hangars to carry six swimmer

Above: The USS Grayback is seen in its previous incarnation as an attack submarine. The bulbous hangars formerly housed four Regulus I cruise missiles, which were launched from just ahead of the conning tower.

Below: Transport submarines allow Special Forces troops to approach close to enemy coasts without detection and reduce the amount of time such troops spend in the water.

delivery vehicles (SDV) and to be used to launch and recover both the SDVs and scuba-equipped divers underwater. The fin height was also increased and a Sperry BQG-4 Passive Underwater Fire Control System (PUFFS) sonar was fitted.

The submarine was intended to carry commando or other covert forces on missions against targets that required approach from the sea. Units that might have been carried were the US Army's Green Berets, the US Navy's Sea, Air and Land (SEAL) teams and Naval Underwater Demolition Teams (UDT). The last would have been used to clear the approaches to

beaches and to reconnoitre likely landing zones for amphibious assault units.

Attack capability

During the early 1980s, the *Grayback* was on active service with the US Pacific Fleet, and was based at Subic Bay in the Philippines. The vessel retained its full submarine attack capability and carried the thermal-powered anti-ship Mk 14 torpedo with a range of 8200/4100 m (8,975/ 4,480 yards) together with the electric-powered ASW Mk 37 torpedo with a range of 8000 m (8,750 yards). The more modern Mk 48 was not carried because of the lack of support facilities at

Subic Bay. The torpedo fire control system was the Mk 106 Model 12.

In 1982, five US Navy divers were killed in *Grayback*'s starboard chamber when a vacuum was rapidly drawn. Following the investigation,

substantial upgrading of design, procedures, and training took place in all US Navy Deep Submergence Systems.

Grayback was finally decommissioned on 16 June 1984 and was sunk as a target near Subic Bay on 13 April 1986.

SPECIFICATION	
USS *Grayback* (SS-574)	**Speed:** 20 kts surfaced and 16.7 kts dived
Commissioned: 9 May 1969 (as LPSS)	**Cargo:** six SDVs
Displacement: 2,670 tons surfaced and 3,650 tons dived	**Torpedo tubes:** six 21-in (533-mm) Mk 52 bow and two 21-in stern
Dimensions: length 101.8 m (334 ft); beam 8.3 m (27 ft 2½ in); draught 5.8 m (19 ft)	**Sonar:** one BQS-4, one BQG-4 (PUFFS)
Propulsion: three diesels delivering 3,579.4 kW (4,800 shp) and two electric motors delivering 4101.4 kW (5,500 shp) to two shafts	**Complement:** 96 (10 officers)
	Troops: 67 (7 officers)

'Atsumi' and 'Miura' class Landing Ships Tank (LST)

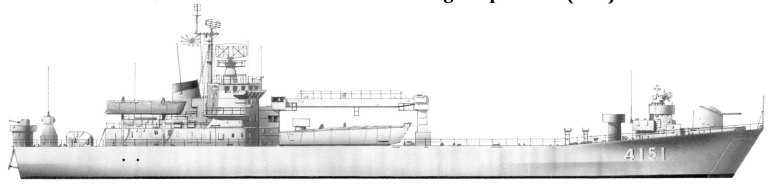

Although composed of several large and many smaller islands, Japan has traditionally maintained relatively few amphibious assault ships, the reason being that such vessels tend to suggest an offensive rather than defensive naval role. Hence there has been a distinct reluctance on the part of Japanese politicians to have a large number of such units available.

Prior to the introduction of the more capable 'Oosumi'-class, the JMSDF operated two main classes of amphibious warfare vessels, the **'Atsumi'** and the **'Miura' class**. Both these LSTs were of conventional bow ramp 'assault-over-the-beach' design. The 'Miura'-class ships were larger in tonnage and dimensions and could carry more cargo. The 'Atsumi' class,

In spite of its many islands Japan does not maintain a significant amphibious warfare capability. For a long period the largest vessels were the 'Miura' class, although these have now been overtaken by the 8,900-ton 'Oosumi' class LPD/LSTs. The 'Miuri'-class vessels (illustrated) could accommodate and land up to 190 troops at a time, together with up to 10 MBTs. Miura was finally decommissioned in 2000, followed by Ojika (2001) and Satsuma (2002).

of which one example (**Nemuro, LST 4103**) remains in service, was built by Sasebo Heavy Industries and commissioned between 1972 and 1977. The 'Miura' class was built by the Ishikawajima Harima shipyard of Tokyo and commissioned between 1975 and 1977.

The 'Atsumi' class can carry 130 troops and 20 vehicles, together with two LCVPs in davits and a third on deck, amidships. The 'Miura' class could carry 190 troops and 1,800 tons of cargo or 10 Type 74 MBTs plus two LCVPs in davits and two LCM6s on deck. The LCMs were handled by a

travelling gantry with folding rails that extended over the ship's side to lower the craft into the water. Any ground

forces embarked would have come from the Japanese Ground Self-Defence Force (JGSDF).

SPECIFICATION	
'Atsumi' and 'Miura' classes	**Propulsion:** two diesels delivering 3,281.1 kW (4,400 shp) to two shafts
Names: *Atsumi*, *Motobu* and *Nemuro*; *Miura*, *Ojika* and *Satsuma*	**Speed:** 14 kts
Commissioned: 'Atsumi' class 1972–7; 'Miura' class 1975–7	**Cargo:** 'Atsumi' 20 vehicles and three LCVPs; 'Miura' 1,800 tons of stores or vehicles, or 10 MBTs, plus two LCVPs and two LCM6s
Displacement: 'Atsumi' 2,400 tons; 'Miura' 3,200 tons full load	**Armament:** 'Atsumi' two twin 40-mm AA guns; 'Miura' one twin 76-mm (3-in) Mk 33 AA gun, one twin 40-mm AA gun
Dimensions: 'Atsumi' class length 89 m (291 ft 11 in); beam 13 m (42 ft 7 in); draught 2.6 m (8 ft 6 in); and 'Miura' class length 98 m (321 ft 5 in); beam 14 m (45 ft 11 in); draught 3 m (9 ft 9½ in)	**Complement:** 'Atsumi' 100, 'Miura' 118
	Troops: 'Atsumi' 130, 'Miura' 190

The Modern Era

For many years after the end of World War II, the warships of the major powers were designed to fight a major war between the Communist countries and the West, and the Falklands war of 1982 proved that the amphibious task force was still one of the most effective means of projecting power over long distances.

With the sudden and unexpected end of the Cold War in the early 1990s, naval force projection assumed new dimensions. Rapid reaction became the key phrase, and this meant the fullest possible integration of naval task forces with other supporting forces – notably air – for the primary purpose of imposing stability on flashpoints around the world. The aircraft carrier remains at the core of the rapid reaction doctrine, with its mix of aircraft for all purposes, from early warning to long-range strike and short-range V/STOL operations.

However, a key element in rapid reaction is surprise, and here a new factor comes into play. The warships being designed today for future deployment will be stealthy, the products of technology that has already proved its worth in the conflicts of recent years.

The USS Philippine Sea *launches a Tomahawk cruise missile against Al Qaeda targets in Afghanistan, November 2001. The US Navy has increasingly been used in support of ground operations in the 'War on Terror'.*

25 de Mayo 'Colossus'-class carrier

The **ARA** *25 de Mayo* was a 'Colossus'-class carrier purchased from the UK by the Dutch and commissioned into the Royal Netherlands navy on 28 May 1948. In April 1968 the ship suffered a serious boiler room fire, and was later judged to be uneconomical to repair. In the following October, Argentina bought the vessel, which was refitted in the Netherlands. The vessel sailed for Argentina on 1 September 1969.

The vessel was fitted with a modified Ferranti CAAIS data-processing system and Plessey Super CAAIS console displays. This allowed the ship to control its carrier-based aircraft and to communicate via datalinks with the two Type 42 destroyers of the Argentinian navy and their ASAWS 4 action information systems.

The deck of the 25 de Mayo *in the mid-1980s supported A-4Q Skyhawk and Super Etendard aircraft. The steam from the catapult indicates that an aircraft has just left the flight deck.*

In 1980–81, the ship was again refitted to increase the strength of the flight deck and add extra deck space to allow two extra aircraft to be parked in readiness for the Super Etendards that Argentina was acquiring.

Falklands War

None of these strike aircraft had qualified to land on the carrier by the time of the Falklands War, and the carrier's air group consisted of eight A-4Q Skyhawks, six S-2E Trackers and four SH-3D Sea Kings. The *25 de Mayo* played

a major part in the initial landings on the Falklands and was ready to strike against the British task force on 2 May 1982 when poor flying conditions intervened. The sinking of the *Belgrano* then forced the Argentine carrier to retire to the relative safety of Argentina's coastal waters, where it landed its air group for land-based operations.

After the war, the remaining Super Etendards were delivered. These were rapidly

deck-qualified and the new make-up of the air group was 20 fixed-wing and four rotary-wing aircraft: eight Super Etendards, six A-4Q Skyhawks, six S-2E Trackers and four Agusta-built AS-61D Sea Kings. The vessel was officially retired in 1997.

The main target for the British SSN force during the Falklands conflict was 25 de Mayo, *the flagship of the original task force that invaded the islands.*

SPECIFICATION

25 de Mayo
Displacement: 15,892 tons standard
Dimensions: length 211.3 m (693 ft 3 in); beam 24.4 m (80 ft); draught 7.6 m (25 ft); flight deck width 42.4 m (138 ft 5 in)
Propulsion: two-shaft geared steam turbines delivering 29,830 kW (40,000 shp)
Speed: 24.25 kts

Armament: nine single 40-mm AA
Electronics: one LW-01 and one LW-02 air search radar, one SGR-109 height-finder radar, one DA-02 target indicator radar, one ZW-01 navigation/surface search radar, one URN-20 TACAN system, and one CAAIS action information system
Complement: 1,000 plus 500 air group

'Charles de Gaulle' class Nuclear-powered carrier

In September 1980, the French government approved the construction of two nuclear-powered aircraft carriers to replace its two conventionally powered 'Clemenceau'-class carriers dating back to the 1950s. However, the French CVN programme has been bedevilled by political opposition and technical problems, both with the vessel and the aircraft. The first ship of the class, **FS Charles de Gaulle** was laid down in April 1989 and launched in May 1994, but commissioned only in May 2001. Budget cuts delayed work as did a number of errors in its construction. Thus, even in 2003 the *Charles de Gaulle* is non-operational and still lacks a proper air group. The navalized Rafale remains delayed, leaving the carrier to operate an air group comprising 20 Super Etendards. As

completed, the *Charles de Gaulle* was unable to operate E-2C Hawkeye aircraft because critical dimensions were wrongly measured. In 1999–2000, the angled flight deck was lengthened accordingly, and additional radiation shielding was also added. Prospects for a second (perhaps conventionally-

Charles de Gaulle has a pair of 75-m (246-ft) US Type C13F catapults, which can launch 23-tonne aircraft. Enhanced weight capability allows the flight deck to allow AEW aircraft operations.

The island of the Charles de Gaulle is located well forward in order to provide protection from the weather for the two 36-ton capacity aircraft lifts.

SPECIFICATION

Charles de Gaulle
Displacement: 40,600 tons full load
Dimensions: length 261.42 m (857 ft 8 in); beam 64.4 m (211 ft 4 in); draught 8.5 m (27 ft 10 in)
Machinery: two Type K15 reactors delivering 300 MW (402,145 shp) and two turbines delivering 56,845.2 kW (76,000 shp) to two shafts
Speed: 28 kts (limited to 25 kts)
Aircraft: up to 40 aircraft, including 24 Super Etendard, two E-2C Hawkeye, 10 Rafale M, and two SA 365F Dauphin (plane-guard) or AS 322 Cougar (CSAR)
Armament: four Sylver octuple VLS

launchers for Aster 15 anti-missile missiles, two Sadral PDMS sextuple launchers for Mistral SAMs, eight Giat 20-mm guns
Countermeasures: four Sagaie 10-barrel decoy launchers, LAD offboard decoys, SLAT torpedo decoys (to be fitted)
Electronics: DRBJ 11B air search radar, DRBV 26D Jupiter air search radar, DRBV 15D air/surface search radar, two DRBN 34A navigation radars, Arabel 3D fire-control radar
Complement: 1,150 plus 550 aircrew and 50 flag staff; can accommodate 800 marines

powered) ship of the 'Charles de Gaulle' class remain poor; the navy has pressed for one, but political and popular support for such an expensive investment may never be forthcoming.

The *Charles de Gaulle* is equipped with a hangar for

20–25 aircraft (around half the air group) and carries the same reactor units as the 'Le Triomphant'-class SSBN: this permits five years of continuous steaming at 25 kts before refuelling. Seakeeping behaviour is improved through the fitting of four pairs of fin stabilizers.

Viraat 'Hermes'-class carrier

HMS *Hermes* was commissioned into the Royal Navy in November 1959, having been built at Barrow-in-Furness between 1944 and 1953. Four years after playing a crucial role in the liberation of the Falklands, *Hermes* was sold to India. Refitted, the ship was commissioned into the Indian Navy as the **INS *Viraat*** in May

1987. Refitted again from July 1999 to December 2000, *Viraat* returned to the fleet in June 2001 and is planned to remain in service until 2010, by which time a 32,000-ton CTOL carrier (which has been approved for construction) is scheduled to enter service.

Modifications since its Falklands days include the

substitution of Russian AK-230 six-barrel 30-mm guns for the old Sea Cat SAM system (these may in turn be replaced by Kashtan CIWS); new fire control, search and navigation radars; new deck-landing aids; improved NBC protection; conversion of boilers to use distillate fuel; and after 2001, the IAI/Rafael Barak SAM. Like

Hermes, *Viraat* is fitted to carry up to 750 troops and four LCVPs are carried for amphibious landings, and in addition up to 80 lightweight torpedoes can be carried in the magazine. However, *Viraat* may be retired early now that India has finally completed a deal with Russia to buy the 'Kiev'-class carrier *Admiral Gorshkov*

Flagship of the Indian fleet, **V**iraat *has been modified several times since it was commissioned into Indian service in 1986. These include new safety features and defences, including the Israeli Barak close-in missile defence system with anti-missile capability.*

and with it, a number of MiG-29K fighters – a $700 million refit and through-deck conversion for the *Gorshkov* is supposed to be completed by 2008. The Sea Harriers carried by the *Viraat* are scheduled for modernization too but this may be shelved with the advent of the MiG-29Ks.

Viraat *is fitted with a 12° ski jump and a reinforced flight deck with armour over the magazines and machinery spaces. Capacity is provided for 30 Harriers.*

SPECIFICATION	
Viraat	**Armament:** two octuple VLS launchers for Barak missiles, four Oerlikon 20-mm guns, two 40-mm Bofors guns, and four AK-230 30-mm guns
Displacement: 28,700 tons full load	
Dimensions: length 208.8 m (685 ft); beam 27.4 m (90 ft); draught 8.7 m (28 ft 6 in)	
Machinery: four boilers generating 56,673 kW (76,000 shp) to two shafts	**Countermeasures:** two Corvus chaff launchers
Speed: 28 kts	**Electronics:** Bharat RAWL-02 Mk II air search radar, Bharat RAWS air/surface search radar, Bharat Rashmi navigation radar, Graseby Type 184M hull-mounted active search/attack sonar
Range: 6,500 miles (10,460 km) at 14 kts	
Aircraft: (normal) 12-18 Sea Harrier FRS.Mk 51/60, up to seven Sea King Mk 42 or Ka-28 'Helix-A'; three Ka-31 on order	**Complement:** 1,350 including 143 officers with the air group

Giuseppe Garibaldi ASW carrier

Designed as a gas turbine-powered helicopter carrier, the **ITS** *Giuseppe Garibaldi* incorporates features suiting it for the carriage and operation of V/STOL fighters. The flight deck is 173.8 m (570 ft 2 in) long and 21 m (68 ft 11 in) wide, and is fitted with a 6.5° ski-jump ramp. The hangar is 110 m (360 ft 11 in) long, 15 m (49 ft 3 in) wide and 6 m (19 ft 8 in) high, and is built to accommodate 12 SH-3D or EH 101 ASW helicopters, or 10 AV-8B aircraft and one SH-3D, although the available height permits the embarkation of CH-47C helicopters if required. A maximum air wing comprising 18 helicopters (six on deck) or 16 AV-8Bs can be embarked. Two aircraft lifts are fitted (one forward and one abaft the island), and there are six marked flight deck spaces for helicopter operations.

Flagship of the Italian navy, the **Giuseppe Garibaldi** *and its air group are one of the more powerful naval forces in the Mediterranean. As well as regular air group operations, the ship can act as an assault carrier, and has operated army CH-47Cs, AB 205s and A 129s.*

ASW role

The *Garibaldi* was designed to provide ASW support for naval task forces and merchant convoys, and as such is fitted with full flagship facilities plus command, control and communication systems for naval and air force operations. In emergencies, it can carry up to 600 troops for short periods.

The extensive weaponry fitted also allows it to operate as an independent surface unit. The carrier carries a bow-mounted active search sonar. To permit helicopter operations in heavy weather, the vessel has been fitted out with two pairs of fin stabilizers, and the aircraft maintenance facilities are sufficient not only to service the

ship's own air group but also the light ASW helicopters of any escorting warships.

Commissioned in September 1985, the *Garibaldi* operated solely as an assault carrier with SH-3s and AB 212s embarked. After the Italian navy was given political clearance to operate

fixed-winged types, AV-8Bs were acquired, although these have been routinely embarked only since December 1994. Under modernization, the Teseo Mk 2 SSM launchers are to be removed and replaced with SATCOM domes, and Aster 15 missiles will replace Aspide.

SPECIFICATION

Giuseppe Garibaldi
Displacement: 10,100 tons standard; 13,139 full load
Dimensions: length 179 m (587 ft 3 in); beam 30.4 m (99 ft 9 in); draught 6.7 m (22 ft)
Machinery: two-shaft gas turbine (four Fiat/GE LM2 500) delivering 59,655 kW (80,000 shp)
Speed: 30 kts
Aircraft: 12–18 helicopters or 16 AV-8B Harrier II or combination
Armament: eight OTO Melara Teseo Mk 2 SSM launchers, two octuple Albatros launchers for Aspide SAMs (48 missiles), three twin 40-mm Breda guns, two triple 324-mm (12.75-in) B-515 torpedo tubes for

Mk 46 ASW torpedoes
Countermeasures: various passive ESM systems, two SCLAR chaff launchers and one DE 1160 sonar
Electronics: one SPS-52C long-range 3D air search radar, one SPS-768 D-band air search radar, one SPN-728 I-band air search radar, one SPS-774 air/surface search radar, one SPS-702 surface search/target indication radar, three SPG-74 gun fire-control radars, three SPG-75 SAM fire-control radars, one SPN-749(V)2 navigation radar, one SRN-15A TACAN system, one IPN-20 combat data system
Complement: 550 normal, 825 maximum including air group

Garibaldi is well defended for a Western carrier, with eight Teseo Mk 2 anti-ship missile launchers and two octuple Albatros launchers for 48 Aspide SAMs.

'Kuznetsov' class Heavy aviation cruiser

The 'Kiev' class cannot be considered true aircraft carriers. From the 1960s onwards, the expanding Soviet Navy began to see its lack of such a vessel to be a handicap, especially to a navy looking to spread its influence around the world.

Several abortive projects were started, including the 1973 design for a nuclear-powered aircraft carrier of 85,000 tons capable of accommodating 60 to 70 aircraft. In the early 1980s, two less ambitious projects began to make progress, the

Vastly more capable than the preceding vessels of the 'Kiev' class, the Kuznetsov is also vastly more expensive. The cash-strapped Russian navy can ill afford such a vessel, and no more are to be built in the foreseeable future.

The huge expanse of the Kuznetsov's flight deck is as large as that of a US Navy supercarrier, though it operates with a much smaller air wing.

Project 1143.5 (which was to become the **Kuznetsov**) and the 75,000-ton **Project 1143.7** which, had it been built, would have been the **Ulyanovsk**. This nuclear-powered ship with twin catapults was proposed to carry the upgraded Su-27KM and Yak-44 AEW/ASW fixed-wing aircraft within its complement of 60–70 aircraft.

Propulsion

Initially, Western analysts anticipated that the ships would have a combined nuclear and steam (CONAS) propulsion plant similar to the *Kirov* battle cruiser and the *SSV-33* support/ command ship. However the class was in fact conventionally propelled with oil-fired boilers.

Although superficially similar to American carriers, the 60,000-ton Soviet aircraft carrier was intended to be subordinate to missile submarines operating in their 'bastions' in the Arctic. It is capable of engaging surface, subsurface and airborne targets. The lack of catapults precludes launching aircraft with heavy strike loads, and the air superiority orientation of the air wing is apparent.

The flight deck area is 14,700 m² (158,235 sq ft) and aircraft take-off is assisted by a bow ski-jump angled at 12° in lieu of steam catapults. The flight deck is equipped with

arrester wires. Two starboard lifts carry the aircraft from the hangar to the flight deck. The ship was designed to operate Su-27K, MiG-29K, Yak-41 (and later the more capable Yak-43) supersonic STOVL fighters, but the only fixed wing aircraft regularly taken to sea have been the Su-27K (Su-33) and Su-25UTG, the latter used as an unarmed trainer.

The first unit was originally named **Riga**. The name was changed to **Leonid Brezhnev** and then to **Tbilisi** before settling in October 1990 on **Admiral Flota Sovetskogo Soyuza Kuznetsov**, normally shortened to **Admiral Kuznetsov**.

Abortive construction

Construction of a sister ship (**Project 1143.6**), initially named **Riga** and later **Varyag**, started in December 1985, and the ship was launched in November 1988. Late in 1991 the Russian Defence Ministry stopped financing the carrier, and gave the hulk to Ukraine. In 1998, the sale of the *Varyag* was announced – to a Macau-based entertainment company. The unfinished hull was towed to the Far East and converted into an entertainment complex and casino – though Russian media reports claim the company is a front for the Chinese navy.

SPECIFICATION
'Kuznetsov' class
Type: Heavy Aviation Cruiser (Aircraft Carrier)
Displacement: 46,600 tons standard; 59,400 tons full load
Dimensions: length 304.5 m (999 ft); beam 67 m (219 ft 10 in); hangar deck length 183 m (600 ft); draught 11 m (36 ft 1 in)
Propulsion: 8 boilers powering four turbines delivering 149 MW (200,000 shp) to four shafts
Speed: 29 kts
Aircraft: Designed to carry the cancelled Yak-41 STOVL fighter and MiG-29K; typical complement of twelve Sukhoi Su-27K/33 plus 24 Kamov Ka-27/31 Helix for utility, ASW, AEW and missile targetting; in future will carry Su-27KUB combat trainer
Armament: Twelve-cell VLS for P-700 Granit (SS-N-19 'Shipwreck') SSMs, 24 eight-round Kinshal (SA-N-9 'Gauntlet') vertical SAM launchers with 192 missiles, eight combined gun/missile close air defence systems with eight twin 30-mm Gatling guns and Klinok (SA-N-11 'Grison') missiles, two RPK-5 (UDAV-1) ASW rocket systems with 60 rockets
Electronics: One 'Top Plate' (MR-710 Fregat-MA) 3D air/surface search radar, two 'Strut Pair' (MR-320M Topaz) 2D search radars, three 'Palm Frond' navigation radars, four 'Cross Sword' (MR-360 Podkat) SA-N-9 fire control radars, eight 'Hot Flash' (3P37) SA-N-11 fire control radars, one 'Fly Trap B' aircraft control system, one Zvezda-2 sonar suite including an 'Ox Yoke' (MGK-345 Bronza) hull mounted system, one Sozbezie-BR ESM/ECM suite, two PK-2 and ten PK-10 chaff and decoy launchers
Complement: 2,626 including 626 air personnel and 40 flag staff

Like its predecessors, the **Kuznetsov** *is primarily an* **ASW** *platform, and as such is armed mainly with helicopters. However, the* **Su-27K** *'Flanker' interceptor gives it a considerable counter-air capability.*

'Kiev' class Aviation cruiser

An aviation capability was developed by the Soviet Navy in response to the US navy's Polaris missile submarines. The two 'Moskva'-class helicopter carriers were completed in the late 1960s, but were fairly limited and notoriously unreliable. Work on an

improved helicopter carrier began in 1967. The **Project 1143** vessels, known in the USSR as the 'Krechyet' class, were much larger than the 'Moskva'-class.

Into service

The new carriers were built at the Chernomorsky yard at

The 'Kievs' were hybrid carrier/cruisers, carrying a very heavy missile armament capable of engaging submarine, surface ship and airborne targets.

First seen in the Mediterranean in 1976, the 44,000 ton 'Kiev'-class V/STOL carriers of the Soviet Navy were impressive vessels.

Nikolayev on the Black Sea. The 42,000-ton **Kiev** was the first of the class. It passed through the Bosphorous on 18 July 1976, to international protests about possible infractions of the Montreaux Convention. Three more ships were later built in this class; **Minsk**, **Novorossiysk** and **Baku** (later renamed **Admiral Gorshkov**). Because of improvements which included a phased array radar, extensive electronic warfare installations, and an enlarged command and control suite, the *Baku* was sometimes considered a separate class. A fifth unit was approved in 1979, but not built.

Aviation cruisers

Classified as PKRs (*Provtivolodochny Kreyser*, or aviation cruiser), they were much closer to conventional aircraft carriers than the 'Moskva' class. They had a large island superstructure to starboard, with an angled flight deck to port. However, unlike American carriers, the bow of the ships carried a very heavy armament fit, including the long-range, nuclear-capable P-500 Bazalt anti-ship missile, known to NATO as the SS-N-12 'Sandbox'.

The air wing consisted of up to 22 Yakovlev Yak-38 'Forger' VTOL fighters and 16 Kamov Ka-25 'Hormone' or Ka-27 'Helix' helicopters.

Ten of the helicopters were ASW machines, with two utility/SAR machines and four missile-guidance aircraft. None of the vessels are in service today – *Kiev*, *Minsk* and *Novorossiysk* were decommissioned in 1993 and were later sold for scrap. The *Admiral Gorshkov*, inactive since 1991, is to due to be transferred to the Indian navy, following the addition of a redesigned 'Kuznetsov'-style flight deck incorporating a 'ski-jump' built into a newly raised bow.

SPECIFICATION

'Kiev' class
Type: Anti-submarine/aviation cruiser
Displacement: 36,000 tons (38,000 tons *Gorshkov*) standard; 43,500 tons (45,500 tons *Gorshkov*) full load
Dimensions: length 274 m (899 ft); beam 32.7 m (107 ft 4 in); flight deck 53 m (173 ft 10 in); max draught 12 m (39 ft 4 in)
Propulsion: eight turbo-pressurized boilers powering four steam turbines delivering 149 MW (200,000 shp) to four shafts
Speed: 32 kts
Aircraft: 12 Yakovlev Yak-38 'Forger' VTOL fighters; up to 17 Kamov Ka-25 'Hormone' or Ka-27 'Helix' ASW helicopters
Armament: Two Shtorm (SA-N-3 'Goblet') twin SAM launchers with 72 missiles, two Osa-M (SA-N-4 'Gecko') twin SAM launchers with 40 missiles, four Kinshal (SA-N-9 'Gauntlet') eight-cell vertical launchers with 96 missiles (*Novorossisk* only) or 192 missiles (*Gorshkov* only), eight P-500 Bazalt (SS-N-12 'Sandbox') anti-ship missile tubes for 16 missiles, four 76-mm (3-inch) guns in two twin DP mounts (two single 100-mm/3.9-inch in *Gorshkov*), eight AK 630 six-barrel 30-mm CIWS, two RBU 6000 ASW rocket launchers, ten 533-mm (21-in) torpedo tubes
Electronics: 'Plate Steer' air search radar, 'Sky Watch 4' phased array radar (on *Gorshkov*), two 'Strut Pair' surface search radars, three 'Palm Frond' navigation radars, one 'Trap Door', one 'Kite Screech', four 'Bass Tilt' and four 'Cross Sword' fire control radars, one 'Fly Trap' and one 'Cake Stand' aircraft control and landing system, 'Horse Jaw', 'Horse Tail' and variable depth sonars, two twin chaff launchers plus full ECM/ESM and IFF suite
Complement: 1,600

Lacking catapults and arrester gear, the 'Kiev'-class carriers were much less capable aviation platforms than the US Navy's supercarriers.

Principe de Asturias Light aircraft carrier

In 1977, to replace the *Dédalo* (ex-'Independence'-class light aircraft carrier USS *Cabot*) from 1986, the Spanish navy placed a contract for a vessel with gas turbine propulsion. The design of the new Spanish ship, prepared by Gibbs and Cox of New York, was based on the Enal design variant of the US Navy's abortive Sea Control Ship. Originally to have been named the **SPS Almirante Carrero Blanco** but then renamed as the **Principe de Asturias** before being launched, the new ship is analogous in many respects to the three British light aircraft carriers of the 'Invincible' class.

Slow completion

The *Principe de Asturias* was laid down on 8 October 1979, launched on 22 May 1982, and commissioned on 30 May 1988. The long period between the launch and the commissioning

was attributable to the need for changes to the command and control system, and also to the addition of a flag bridge to facilitate the ship's use in the command role.

The *Principe de Asturias* has a flight deck measuring 175.3 x 29 m (575 ft 2 in x 95 ft 2 in), and this is fitted with a 12° 'ski-jump' ramp blended into the bow. Two aircraft lifts are fitted, one at the extreme stern, and these are used to move aircraft (both fixed- and rotary-wing) from the hangar, which has an area of 2300 m² (24,760 sq ft).

For the *Principe de Asturias*' air wing, Spain ordered the EAV-8B (VA.2) Harrier II V/STOL multi-role warplane (from early 1996, radar-equipped Harrier II Plus were delivered) and the SH-60B Seahawk ASW helicopter. The standard aircraft complement is 24, although this can be increased to 37 with the

*The **Principe de Asturias** has a straight flight deck and a substantial 'ski jump' rise at the bow for the launch of heavily laden Harrier II aircraft.*

SPECIFICATION

Principe de Asturias
Displacement: 16,700 tons full load
Dimensions: length 195.9 m (642 ft 9 in); beam 24.3 m (79 ft 9 in); draught 9.4 m (30 ft 10 in)
Machinery: two General Electric LM 2500 gas turbines delivering 34,300 kW (46,000 shp) to one shaft
Speed: 26 kts
Aircraft: see text

Armament: four 12-barrel Meroka 20-mm CIWS
Electronics: one SPS-55 surface search radar, one SPS-52 3D radar, four Meroka fire-control radars, one SPN-3SA air control radar, one URN-22 TACAN system, one SLQ-25 Nixie towed decoy and four Mk 36 SRBOC chaff launchers
Complement: 555 plus a flag staff and air group of 208

---

aid of flight-deck parking. The standard aircraft mix is six to 12 AV-8Bs, two SH-60Bs, two to four AB 212ASW helicopters,

and six to 10 SH-3H Sea King helicopters, including three fitted with Searchwater radar to operate in the AEW role.

The fully digital Tritan command and control system is fitted with the Link 11 and Link 14 data transmission/reception terminals of the Naval Tactical Display System, and there is also the standard complex of air- and surface surveillance radars, aircraft and gun control radars, and countermeasures both electronic and physical. The ship also carries two LCVPs, and two pairs of stabilizers are fitted for stability in heavier seas.

*The hangar of the **Principe de Asturias** opens at its after end onto one of the two aircraft lifts. On ship's two sides and the stern are the four Meroka defensive guns.*

Chakri Naruebet Light aircraft carrier

The **HTMS *Chakri Naruebet*** ('The Great of the Chakri Dynasty') is the most powerful warship of the Royal Thai navy, which otherwise comprises a dozen frigates and a similar number of corvettes and fast attack craft plus amphibious forces. The ship is the first aircraft carrier to be operated by a country in Southeast Asia. Built in Spain, the vessel was launched on 20 January 1996. The ship spent the first months of 1997 working up with the Spanish fleet. (*Chakri Naruebet* is similar to the Spanish *Principe de Asturias*.)

Arriving in Thailand in August 1997, the vessel serves with the Third Naval Area Command. The planned primary anti-aircraft armament (a Mk 41 LCHR 8-cell VLS launcher for Sea Sparrow

The **Chakri Naruebet** *was ordered to give the Thai navy the means to support the country's amphibious forces, but the country's financial problems then prevented the addition of the defensive weapons vital to survival in contested waters.*

missiles and four Vulcan Phalanx CIWS mountings) has not been installed, leaving the vessel protected by Mistral infrared homing missiles with a range of 4000 m (4,375 yards). The

Chakri Naruebet makes few operational sorties, and when she does put to sea it is usually to carry members of the Thai Royal family. Is she the most expensive royal yacht afloat?

A side view of the **Chakri Naruebet** *reveals the considerable similarity between this major element of the Royal Thai navy and the* **Principe de Asturias** *of the Spanish navy, which was built by the same yard.*

SPECIFICATION	
Chakri Naruebet	SAM launchers
Displacement: 10,000 tons standard; 11,485 tons full load	**Aircraft:** up to six AV-8S Matador fixed-wing aircraft and six S-70B
Dimensions: length 182.6 m (599 ft 1 in); beam 21.9 m (73 ft 10 in); draught 6.21 m (20 ft 4in)	Seahawk; alternatively Sea King, S-76 or Chinook helicopters
Propulsion: two gas turbines and two diesels delivering 32,985 and 8785 kW (44,240 and 11,780 shp) respectively to two shafts	**Electronics:** SPS-32C air-search and SPS-64 surface-search radars, MX1105 navigation radar, hull-mounted sonar, four SRBOC decoy launchers, and SLQ-32 towed decoy
Speed: 26 kts	**Complement:** 455 plus 146 aircrew and 175 marines
Armament: two 0.5-in (12.7-mm) machine guns and two Mistral	

'Invincible' class Light aircraft carrier

The demise of the British fixed-wing aircraft carrier, with the cancellation of the CVA-01 fleet carrier programme in 1966, led in 1967 to a Staff Requirement for a 12,500-ton command cruiser equipped with six Sea King ASW helicopters. A redesign of this basic concept to give more deck space showed that a nine-helicopter air group was much more effective. A

new specification resulted in a design that became known as the 19,500-ton 'through deck cruiser' (TDC), a term used for what was essentially a light carrier design because of the political difficulties of resurrecting a carrier at the time. Despite this, the designers showed initiative in allowing sufficient space and facilities to be incorporated from

the outset for a naval version of the RAF's Harrier V/STOL warplane. The designers were duly awarded for such foresight in May 1975 when it was announced officially that the TDC would carry the Sea Harrier. The first of the **'Invincible' class**, **HMS *Invincible***, which had been laid down in July 1973 at the Vickers shipyard at Barrow-in-Furness,

was not delayed during building. In May 1976 the second ship, **HMS *Illustrious***, was ordered, and in December 1978 the third, **HMS *Indomitable***, was contracted. However, in response to public disquiet, the Admiralty, in placatory mood, renamed the ship **HMS *Ark Royal***. The ships were commissioned in July 1980, July 1982 and November 1985.

Gas turbines

The ships of the class are the largest gas turbine-powered warships in the world, with virtually every piece of below-deck equipment, including engine modules, suitable for maintenance by exchange. During building, both the *Invincible* and the *Illustrious* were fitted with 7° 'ski-jump' ramps, while the *Ark Royal* has a 15° ramp.

In 1982 it was announced that the *Invincible* was to be sold to Australia as a helicopter carrier to replace HMAS *Melbourne*, leaving only two carriers in British service. However, the deal was cancelled after the Falklands campaign, as it was realized by the government that three carriers ought to be available to ensure two in service at any one time. During Operation Corporate, the *Invincible* started with an air group of eight Sea Harriers and nine Sea King ASW helicopters. However, as a result of losses and replacements, this was modified to a group of 11 Sea Harriers, eight ASW Sea Kings and two Lynx helicopters configured to decoy Exocet missiles. A significant problem was that it was necessary to accomodate most of the extra aircraft on the deck, as there was insufficient room for them in the hangar.

The *Illustrious* was hurried through to completion in time to relieve the *Invincible* after the war, and went south with 10 Sea Harriers, nine ASW Sea Kings and two Sea King AEW conversions.

The vessels were also fitted with two 20-mm Phalanx CIWS mountings for anti-missile defence and two single 20-mm AA guns to improve on the previous non-existent close-in air defences. The normal air group consisted of five Sea Harriers and 10 Sea Kings (eight ASW and two AEW).

TDCs in service

Since the 1980s, the Royal Navy has run two ships while the third undergoes a refit. The *Invincible* was brought to the standard of the *Ark Royal*, and then *Illustrious* followed. The *Ark Royal itself* started a two-year refit in 1999.

In recent years six RAF GR.Mk 7 Harriers have been regularly embarked for ground-attack missions under Joint Force Harrier. *Illustrious* has had her Sea Dart missile launcher removed to allow space for a flight extension. The *Invincible* was on station off the Adriatic in 1994 when Sea Harrier F/A.Mk 2s were first operationally deployed.

SPECIFICATION	
'Invincible' class	**Aircraft:** see text
Displacement: 16,000 tons standard and 19,500 tons full load	**Electronics:** one Type 1022 air search radar, one Type 992R air search radar, two Type 909 Sea Dart guidance radars, two Type 1006 navigation/helicopter direction radars, one Type 184 or Type 2016 bow sonar, one Type 762 echo sounder, one Type 2008 underwater telephone, one ADAWS 5 action information data processing system, one UAA-1 Abbey Hill ESM suite, two Corvus chaff launchers
Dimensions: length 206.6 m (677 ft); beam 27.5 m (90 ft); draught 7.3 m (24 ft)	
Propulsion: four Rolls-Royce Olympus TN1313 gas turbines delivering 83,520 kW (112,000 shp) to four shafts	
Speed: 28 kts	
Armament: one twin Sea Dart SAM launcher with 22 missiles, two 20-mm Phalanx (replaced by Goalkeeper on *Illustrious*) CIWS, and two single 20-mm AA	**Complement:** 1,000 plus 320 air group (provision for emergency Marine Commando)

Above: The primary long-range air defence weapon installed on the carriers of the 'Invincible' class was the Sea Dart surface-to-air missile fired from a twin-arm launcher beside the forward edge of the flight deck.

Left: The 'Invincible'- class carriers carry fixed- and rotary-wing aircraft, the former comprising various Harrier and Sea Harrier V/STOL multi-role warplane marks in blends suiting the task in question.

'Improved Forrestal' class

America, Constellation, John F. Kennedy & Kitty Hawk

USS America (CVA 66), commissioned in January 1965, first entered service with the Atlantic Fleet and made three combat deployments to Southeast Asia during 1968–73. In 1975 the vessel was modified to handle F-14 and S-3 aircraft, and in 1980 became the first carrier to receive the Phalanx CIWS. America was involved in action against Libya in 1986 and Iraq in 1991.

Built to an **'Improved Forrestal'-class** design, these four carriers in reality constitute three sub-classes that are easily distinguished from their predecessors by the fact that their island superstructures are set farther aft. In addition, two of their four aircraft elevators are forward of the island, the 'Forrestals' having only one in this location. A lattice radar mast is also carried abaft of the island.

USS *America*

The **USS *America*** (which was (commissioned in January 1965) was very similar to the first two ships (**USS *Kitty Hawk*** and **USS *Constellation***, commissioned in June 1961 and January 1962), and was built in preference to an austere-version nuclear-powered carrier. It was, however, the only US carrier of post-war construction to be fitted with a sonar system. The last unit, the **USS *John F. Kennedy***, was built to a revised design incorporating an underwater protection system developed originally for the nuclear carrier programme, and was commissioned in September 1968. All four were

Above: **Kitty Hawk** *refuels the 'Sumner'-class destroyers* **McKean** *and* **Harry E. Hubbard** *in 1962, a year after entering service with the US Pacific Fleet.*

Below: USS **Kitty Hawk** *is pictured in Apra Harbor, Guam, in April 2000 during a two-month deployment to the western Pacific. Since 1998 the vessel has operated as the Japan-based US carrier.*

USS **Constellation** *(foreground)
and* **Kitty Hawk** *conduct joint
carrier operations in the western
Pacific Ocean in August 1999.*
Constellation *was retired in
favour of USS* **Ronald Reagan** *in
2003, whilst* **Kitty Hawk** *will be
replaced by CVN 77 in 2008.*

built with steam catapults and
carried some 2,150 tons of
aviation ordnance plus about
7.38 million litres (1.95 million
US gal) of aviation fuel for their
air groups. These are again
similar in size and composition
to those of the 'Nimitz' class.
The tactical reconnaissance
element in each of the air wings
is usually provided by a handful
of Grumman F-14 Tomcats
equipped with a digital TARPS
(tactical airborne reconnaissance
system) pod. Replacement of
the Tomcat in all its roles by the
Boeing F/A-18E/F Super Hornet
multi-role fighter and strike
aircraft is under way, although
this aircraft has initially deployed
on units of the 'Nimitz' class.

The ships were all fitted with
full Anti-Submarine Classification
and Analysis Center (ASCAC),
Navigational Tactical Direction
System (NTDS) and Tactical Flag
Command Center (TFCC)

facilities, *America* being the first
carrier to be fitted with the
NTDS. The ships all had the OE-
82 satellite communications
system, and were the first
carriers able simultaneously to
launch and recover aircraft
easily; on previous carriers this
was difficult.

Three of the ships passed
through a SLEP (service life
extension programme), but
America was retired in the early
1990s without SLEPing.
Constellation was retired in
2003 and *Kitty Hawk* is due to
remain with the Pacific Fleet
until 2008. *John F. Kennedy* is
scheduled to remain on Atlantic
Fleet strength until 2018.

SPECIFICATION

USS *John F. Kennedy*
Displacement: 81,430 tons full load
Dimensions: length 320.6 m
(1,052 ft); beam 39.60 m (130 ft);
draught 11.40 m (37 ft 5 in);
flightdeck width 76.80 m (252 ft)
Machinery: four-shaft geared steam
turbines delivering 209 MW
(280,000 shp)
Speed: 32 kt
Aircraft: air wing depends on
mission; includes up to 20 F-14
Tomcat, 36 F/A-18 Hornet, four
EA-6B Prowler, four E-2C
Hawkeye, six S-3B Viking, two
ES-3A Shadow (until 1999), four
SH-60F Ocean Hawk and two HH-
60H Rescue Hawk
Armament: three octuple Mk 29 Sea
Sparrow SAM launchers (no
reloads), three 20-mm Vulcan
Phalanx close-in weapons systems
(CIWSs); two Phalanx mountings

scheduled to be replaced by Sea
RAM (Rolling Airframe Missile)
CIWS
Electronics: one SPN-64(V)9
navigation radar, one SPS-49(V)5 air
search radar, one SPS-48E 3D
radar, one Mk 23 TAS (Target
Acquisition System), one SPS-67
surface search radar, six Mk 95 fire
control radars, three Mk 91 MFCS
(Missile Fire Control System)
directors; one SPN-41, one
SPN-43A and two SPN-46 CCA
(Carrier-Controlled Approach)
radars, one URN-25 TACAN
system, one SLQ-36 Nixie towed
torpedo decoy, SLQ-32(V)4/SLY-2
ESM/ECM suite, SSTDS (Surface
Ship Torpedo Defence System),
four SRBOC Mk 36 chaff/flare
launchers
Complement: 2,930 (155 officers)
plus 2,480 air group (320 officers)

USS *Enterprise* (Post-refit) Nuclear-powered carrier

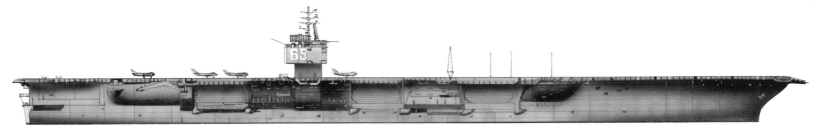

The use of nuclear power as the propulsion plant allows **USS
Enterprise** *to carry sufficient aircraft fuel and ordnance for 12 days
of sustained air operations before having to undergo replenishment.*

The world's first nuclear-
powered aircraft-carrier, the
Enterprise was laid down in
1958 and commissioned in
November 1961, as what was
then the largest warship ever
built. Since exceeded in size by
the 'Nimitz'-class ships, the
Enterprise was built to a

modified 'Forrestal'-class
design, with its larger
dimensions dictated by the
powerplant of eight A2W
pressurized water enriched-
uranium fuelled nuclear
reactors. The high cost of its
construction prevented five
other vessels in the naval

building programme from being
built.

Major refit
From January 1979 to March
1982, *Enterprise* underwent an
extensive refit, which included
the rebuilding of its island
superstructure and the fitting of
new radar systems and a mast
to replace the characteristic
ECM dome and billboard radar
antenna that had been used

since it was built. *Enterprise* is
equipped with four steam
catapults, four deck-edge aircraft
elevators and carries 2,520 tons
of aviation ordnance plus
10.3 million litres (2.72 million
US gal) of aircraft fuel. Like that
of other US carriers, the
Enterprise's ordnance has
included 10-kT B61, 20-kT B57,
60-kT B43, 100-kT B61, 200-kT
B43, 330-kT B61, 400-kT B43,
600-kT B43 and 900-kT B61

tactical nuclear gravity bombs, 100-kT Walleye air-to-surface missiles and 10-kT B57 depth bombs, while 1.4-MT B43 and 1.2-MT B28 strategic bombs could be carried as and when required. The air group is similar in size and configuration to that carried by the 'Nimitz'-class carriers, and the *Enterprise* is fitted with the same ASCAC, NTDS and Tactical Flag Command Center (TFCC) facilities. In addition to its OE-82 satellite system, it also carries two British SCOT satellite communications antenna units for use with British fleet units and NATO. These two systems were fitted in 1976.

Enterprise is currently deployed with the Atlantic Fleet and was SLEPed between 1991 and 1994. It is estimated that it will be eventually paid off in about 2014.

*Right: Air traffic controllers on board **USS** Enterprise assist in guiding strike aircraft in and out of Iraq during **Operation Desert Fox** in December 1998.*

SPECIFICATION	
USS *Enterprise*	three 20-mm Vulcan Phalanx CIWS
Displacement: 75,700 tons	(may be replaced by Sea RAM)
standard, 93,970 tons full load	**Electronics:** SPN-64(V)9 navigation
Dimensions: length 342.30 m	radar, SPS-49(V)5 air search radar,
(1,123 ft); beam 40.50 m (133 ft);	SPS-48E 3D radar, Mk 23 TAS,
draught 10.90 m (39 ft); flightdeck	SPS-67 surface search radar, six
width 76.80 m (252 ft)	Mk 95 fire control radars, three Mk
Machinery: four-shaft geared steam	91 MFCS directors; one SPN-41,
turbines (eight A2W nuclear	one SPN-43A and two SPN-46
reactors) delivering 209 MW	CCA radars, URN-25 TACAN
(280,000 shp)	system, SLQ-36 Nixie towed
Speed: 33 kt	torpedo decoy, SLQ-32(V)4/SLY-2
Aircraft: see 'Improved Forrestal'	ESM/ECM suite, SSTDS, four
class	SRBOC Mk 36 chaff/flare launchers
Armament: three octuple Mk 29 Sea	**Complement:** 3,215 (171 officers)
Sparrow launchers (no reloads),	plus 2,480 air group (358 officers)

***USS** Enterprise (top) and **USS** George Washington (second top), the fast combat support ship **USS** Supply (centre) and the ammunition ship **USS** Mount Baker (bottom) steam in formation in the western Mediterranean during turnover operations in 1996.*

'Nimitz' class Nuclear-powered aircraft carrier

The first three **'Nimitz'-class** carriers were designed as replacements for the 'Midway' class. The largest and most powerful warships ever built, they differ from the earlier nuclear-powered USS *Enterprise* in having two reactors rather than eight, with ordnance magazines between and forward of them. This increases the internal space available to allow some 2,570 tons of aviation weapons and 10.6 million litres (2.8 million US gal) of aircraft fuel to be carried – sufficient for 16 days of continuous flight operations. The class is also fitted with the same torpedo protection arrangement as carried by the USS *John F. Kennedy*, and also shares the same general arrangement and electronic fit.

Flight deck

Four deck-edge aircraft elevators are available: two forward and one aft of the island on the starboard side and one aft on the port side. The hangar is 7.80 m (25 ft 7 in) high, and like those of other US carriers can

USS **Eisenhower** *steams in company with the guided missile cruiser* **California** *in the early 1980s. For a quarter of a century, the 'Nimitz'-class carriers have been the world's most powerful warships.*

accommodate, at most, only half of the aircraft embarked at any one time; the remainder is spotted on the flight deck in aircraft parks. The flight deck measures 333 x 77 m (1,093 x 253 ft), the angled section being 237.70 m (780 ft) long. It is fitted with four arrester wires and an arrester net for recovering

aircraft. Four steam catapults are carried, two on the bow launch position and two on the angled flight deck. With four catapults, the carrier can launch one aircraft every 20 seconds.

Air Wing

The standard US Navy air wing at the beginning of the 21st

Century includes 20 F-14D 'Bomcats' (Tomcats with a strike role), 36 F/A-18 Hornets, eight S-3A/B Vikings, four E-2C Hawkeyes, four EA-6B Prowlers, four SH-60F and two HH-60H Seahawks. Air wings can be varied according to the nature of the operation: for example, in 1994, 50 army helicopters

The USS **Carl Vinson** *displays about a third of a standard air wing on deck. Most of the strike aircraft can fight both air-to-air and air-to-ground.*

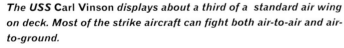

replaced the usual air wing on the Eisenhower during peacekeeping operations off Haiti. There are also facilities for a Grumman C-2A Greyhound carrier on-board delivery aircraft.

A million miles

The core life of the A4W reactors fitted is, under normal usage, expected to provide a cruising distance of 1,287,440–1,609,300 km (800,000–1,000,000 miles) and last for about 13 years before the cores have to be replaced. Although the class is relatively new, it is planned for the 'Nimitz'-class to undergo Service Life Extension Program (SLEP) refits by 2010 in order to extend their service life by 15 years.

As the primary means of American power projection, the ships of the 'Nimitz' class have seen a considerable amount of

use around the hotspots of the world. The USS *Nimitz* (CVN-68), commissioned in May 1975, was the base for the abortive Iranian hostage rescue mission in 1980. In 1981 her fighters were in action against Libya. Transferring from the Atlantic to the Pacific in 1987, *Nimitz* often deployed to the Persian Gulf and Asian waters over the next decade. In 1998 the carrier returned to Norfolk for a two-year refuelling refit.

Eisenhower

Commissioned in October 1977, USS *Dwight D. Eisenhower* (CVN-69) serves with the Atlantic Fleet. The carrier has made eight Mediterranean deployments, and was the first US carrier to respond to the Iraqi invasion of Kuwait. In 1994, 'Ike' supported peacekeeping operations off Haiti, and in

succeeding deployments supported US policy in the Persian Gulf.

Assigned to the Pacific fleet in 1982, the USS Carl Vinson (CVN-70) has conducted

numerous deployments in the Pacific and Indian Oceans, as well as the Arabian Sea. Most recently, the Vinson has played a major part in the war in Afghanistan.

SPECIFICATION	
'Nimitz' class	two triple 32-cm (12.6-in) torpedo tubes
Displacement: 81,600 tons standard, 91,487 tons full load	**Electronics:** (first three) one SPS48E 3D air-search, one
Hull dimensions: length 317 m (1,040 ft); beam 40.80 m (134 ft); draught 11.30 m (37 ft);	SPS-49(V)5 air-search; one SPS-67V surface-search; one SPS-67(V)9 navigation; five aircraft landing aids
Flightdeck dimensions: length 332.90 m (1,092 ft); width 76.80 m (252 ft)	(SPN-41, SPN-43B, SPN-44 and two SPN-46); one URN-20 TACAN system; six Mk 95 fire-control
Machinery: two A4W/A1 G nuclear reactors powering four geared steam turbines delivering 20,8795 kW (280,000 shp) to four shafts	radars; one SLQ-32(V)4 ESM suite; four Mk 36 Super RBOC chaff launchers; SSTDS torpedo defensive system; SLQ-36 Nixie
Speed: over 35 kt	sonar defence system; ACDS
Aircraft: capacity for up to 90, but current USN air wings usually comprise 78–80 aircraft	combat data system; JMCIS combat data system; four UHF and one SHF SATCOM systems
Armament: three octuple Sea Sparrow SAM launchers (no reloads); four 20-mm Phalanx close-in weapon systems (CIWS);	**Complement:** 3,300 plus 3,000 air group

Improved 'Nimitz' class   Nuclear-powered aircraft carrier

In 1981 the first of at least six **Improved 'Nimitz'-class** carriers was ordered after much discussion both within the Congress and the Pentagon.

New armour

These vessels were completed with Kevlar armour over their vital areas and have improved hull protection arrangements.

The Kevlar armour has been retrofitted to the earlier carriers, as have many of the advanced systems built into the more recent ships.

US Navy personnel man the status board in the control centre of the 'Nimitz' class USS **Theodore Roosevelt** *(CVN-71).*

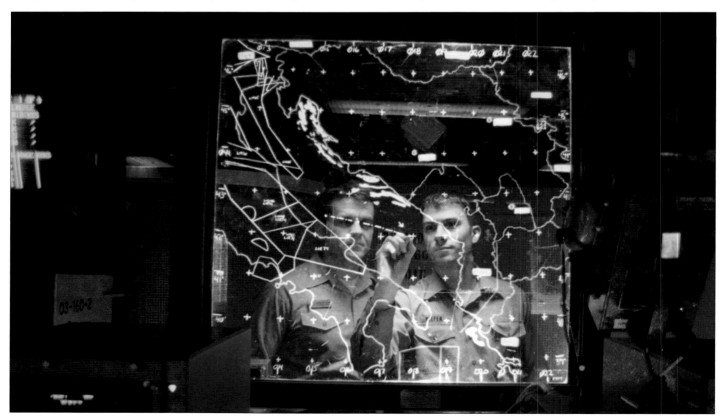

The massive flight deck of the
USS Harry S. Truman is as large
as three football fields, and
provides the base for an air wing
stronger than most of the
world's smaller air forces. The
aircraft carrier is a powerful
element of US foreign policy.
Bill Clinton once said that the
first thing any President asked
when being presented with a
new crisis anywhere in the
world was, 'Where are the
nearest carriers?'

Enlarged

Broader in the beam by about
two metres, the newer carriers
have a full-load displacement in
excess of 102,000 tons (and
may exceed 106,000 tons in
some circumstances). The ship's
complement of 3,184 personnel
(203 officers) does not include
the air wing of 2,800 aircrew
(with 366 officers); and 70 flag
staff (with 25 officers).

The combat data systems
fitted to the improved carriers
are based around the Naval
Tactical and Advanced Combat
Direction System (ACDS), with
Links 4A, 11, 14, and 16
communication and data links.
Weapons control is managed by
three Mk 91 Mod 1 MFCS
directors for the Sea sparrow
missile. USS *Nimitz* is being
fitted with the SSDS Mk2 Mod
0 ship self-defense system,
developed by Raytheon. The
SSDS will provide automated
self-defence against anti-ship
cruise missiles (ASCMs) by
integrating and co-ordinating the
ship's weapon and electronic
warfare systems.

Electronic war

The Raytheon AN/SLQ-32(V)
electronic warfare system
detects hostile radar emissions
by two sets of antennae and the
system analyzes the pulse
repetition rate, the scan mode,
the scan period, and the
frequency. The system identifies

the threat and direction,
provides a warning signal and
interfaces to the ship's
countermeasures systems.

The first improved 'Nimitz'
was the USS *Theodore*
Roosevelt (CVN-71), which
commissioned in October 1986.
Roosevelt saw extensive action
in the Gulf War. USS *Abraham*
Lincoln (CVN-72) was
commissioned in November
1989 and her first major
operation was the evacuation
of American forces from the
Philippines after the eruption of
Mount Pinatubo. USS *George*
Washington (CVN-73) was
commissioned in July 1992,
followed by USS *John C.*
Stennis (CVN-74) in December

1995 and USS *Harry S. Truman*
(CVN-75) in 1998. USS *Ronald*
Reagan (CVN-76) was christened
by Mrs Nancy Reagan in 2001.

The 10th and last of the class,
CVN-77, will enter service in
2008. This will be a transitional

design, incorporating new
technology that will significantly
reduce the crew requirement.
It will test systems intended
for a new class of carriers
(CVNX) due in the following
decade.

An F-14B Tomcat launches from the flight deck of the aircraft
carrier USS George Washington (CVN 73) on June 26, 2004.
The Tomcat was assigned to Carrier Air Wing Seven for a
deployment in support of Operation Iraqi Freedom.

CVNX Aircraft carrier

The **CVNX** programme is the core of the US Navy's determination to procure a new generation of large aircraft carriers that will enable it to maintain its capability for long-range power projection right through the 21st century. The long-term goal is the placing in service of up to 10 new aircraft carriers, built at the rate of about one every five years and based on a design derived from the current 'Nimitz' class but with considerable 'upgradability' built into the design so that new technologies can be incorporated as they become available. Within this concept is a desire to ensure a reduction in ownership cost while keeping the Navy's core capabilities for the delivery of high-volume firepower and at the same time enhancing survivability, sustainability and mobility.

Newport News

To be built by Northrop Grumman Newport News, in line with a decision of July 2003, the **CVNX 1** (now redesignated the **CVN 21**) will follow the last of the current series of 'Nimitz'-class carriers, and is to be ordered in the 2007 fiscal year to attain operational capability in 2014, replacing the USS *Enterprise*, commissioned in 1961.

The CVN 21 will feature a new nuclear propulsion plant developed via three generations of submarine reactor

The CVNX is based on the hull of the 'Nimitz'-class carrier, but will be built in a new steel for lighter weight and greater strength. This artist's impression conveys one of several options for the layout of the new ships.

technology. The use of a new powerplant arrangement indicates the need for reductions in acquisition, manning, maintenance and life cycle costs, and this powerplant will provide the CVN 21 with all the electrical power that will be required for the operation of 21st century shipboard technology. A new system for generating and distributing electrical power will also be a vital element of the design, and will enhance combat capability in aspects such as survivability, availability and flexibility.

Enhanced survival

For survivability, a redundant grid electrical system will enhance damage control features, and electrical auxiliary systems will reduce maintenance and allow the more efficient use of electrical power. This should mean the CVN 21 requires shorter shipyard maintenance visits. The advanced electrical features of this new powerplant will allow the CVN 21 to make maximum use of advanced technologies as they become available. It is also intended that the CVN 21 will

trim operating costs and crewing requirements.

Interim standard

The transitional CVN 21 is to be followed by the **CVNX 2** (presumably to be redesignated as the **CVN 22**), which will mark the culmination of the evolution of the aircraft carrier in the programme inaugurated with the CVN 76. The most important features of CVNX 2 will be an electromagnetic aircraft launching system for reduced crewing and maintenance needs, as well as lower wind-over-deck requirements for the launch and recovery of aircraft, and extended airframe life as peak loads will be reduced. Based on technology similar to that used by 'maglev' trains, the system will liberate catapults from reliance on ship-generated steam, while increasing the available energy and markedly reducing weight and volume.

The CVNX 2 will have systems reconfigurable to enhance operational flexibility, an advanced protective system to boost survivability in combat

and, wherever possible, adaptations of commercial systems for tasks such as ship operations, habitability, mooring, and manoeuvring. An advanced information management system will automate weapons' inventory control, movement and deployment from the magazines to the aircraft. Long-term objectives for the CVNX 2 are further major reductions in total operating costs and crew requirements.

Power projection

Thus the US Navy is firmly committed to the aircraft carrier in the 21st century on the basis of the use and retrofit of advanced technological applications, the service's object being the operation of a sea-based tactical air platform retaining the full operational capabilities of the 'Nimitz' class in conjunction with an architecture optimized for the introduction of changes.

The CVNX will be 'stealthier' than current carriers, but perhaps unsurprisingly will not be a completely stealth design.

ex-*Admiral Gorshkov* & 'Vikrant' class Aircraft carriers

In accordance with its doctrine of a blue-water navy, India has operated aircraft carriers since 1961, when its navy commissioned the ex-British light aircraft carrier **Hercules** as the 19,500-ton **Vikrant**. It was long appreciated that the ship was too small to operate later-generation naval warplanes, and too elderly to be worth major

modification, so pending the advent of more advanced carriers in 1986 India bought another British carrier, the larger 28,700-ton **Hermes**, to be refitted before entry to service in the following year as the **Viraat**. In her refitted form the ship can embark 12 Sea Harrier FRS.Mk 51 STOVL and seven rotary-wing aircraft.

Then in 1999 India accepted the gift of the ex-Soviet carrier **Baku**, already renamed as the **Admiral Gorshkov**, of the **'Modified Kiev'** or **Type 1143.3 class**, which had first been commissioned in January 1987 and was then laid up in 1994. The arrangement was that India received the ship essentially free of charge, as she was in

poor condition and costing the Russians too much even for simple maintenance, on condition that the Indian government paid for the ship's reconditioning and upgrade in a Russian yard. It was only in the later stages of 2003 that the final arrangements were agreed for the three/four-year refurbishment of the ship, which had been gutted of her weapons and most of her operational equipment by the Russians when they laid up the vessel.

The refurbishment and update, which will amount to some 70 per cent of the ship, will include a squadron of MiG-29K warplanes, six Kortik/Kashtan SAM/gun systems for anti-aircraft and anti-missile defence, and a 14° ski-jump at the forward end of the flight deck. The flight deck is of the angled type with a length of 198 m (649 ft 7 in) and three arrester wires, and the two lifts can move 30 tons and 20 tons between the flight deck and the hangar, which measures 130 x 22.5 m (426 ft 6 in x 73 ft 10 in).

In the longer term, the Indian navy is to operate two new carriers built in India. The plan was first announced in 1989 with the first ships, to be built by the Kochi Shipyard, scheduled to enter service in 1997 as successor to the original *Vikrant*, which was decommissioned in January 1997. The task of creating the concept of a 28,000-ton design was entrusted to the Direction des Constructions Navales in France, the object being the creation of a ship capable of exceeding 30 kts and carrying either STOVL or CTOL warplanes. In 1991 the Indian navy was instructed to forget large aircraft carriers and instead base its thinking on smaller ships akin to the Italian 'Garibaldi' class in size and capability, but then in June 1999 the Indian government authorized the funding for a single 'Air Defence Ship' with a full-load displacement of 32,000 tons, speed of 32 kts, overall length iof 250 m (820 ft 3 in), angled flight deck with a ski-jump take-off aid on the non-angled section, ability to operate 36 aircraft (16 fixed-wing of the MiG-29 type and 20 rotary-wing), and armament of SAM launchers and CIWS mountings.

The whole future of aircraft carriers in India, be they Russian or otherwise, is still speculative.

SPECIFICATION	
'Modified Kiev' class	search radar, two 'Strut Pair'
Displacement: 45,400 tons full load	surface search radars, one
Dimensions: length 283 m (928 ft 5 in); beam 51 m (167 ft 4 in); draught 10 m (32 ft 10 in)	navigation radar, one aircraft control radar, one Lesorub 11434 combat data system, one Bharat
Propulsion: four GTZA 674 steam turbines delivering 149,200 kW (200,105 shp) to four shafts	EW system, two PK2 chaff launchers, one MG 355 'Horse Jaw' active hull hull sonar, and two
Performance: speed 28 kts; endurance 25500 km (15,845 miles) at 18 kts	towed torpedo decoys
Armament: six Kortik/Kashtan SAM/gun mountings	**Aircraft:** up to 30 fixed- and rotary-wing (see text)
Electronics: one 'Plate Steer' air	**Crew:** 1,200 plus an air group of undetermined size

'Andrea Doria' class Aircraft carrier

In 2000 the Italian ministry of naval defence contracted with Fincantieri for the construction of the **Andrea Doria**, a NUM (*Nuova Unita Maggiore*, or new major vessel) of the light aircraft carrier type. The ship will be delivered in 2007.

The vessel will be capable of the command and amphibious operations roles, with provision for 145 command staff and 380 marines (rising to 470 for short-endurance operations), plus 24 MBTs, or 60 smaller AFVs or 100 wheeled vehicles, or a mix of these. Vehicles enter and leave the ship via two ro/ro ramps (one stern and one starboard side), and one 7- and two 15-ton cranes are provided for the loading and unloading of logistic and ordnance items.

Aster-15

The ship will be very flexible in tactical terms, able to perform the aircraft carrier role as well as deliver men and/or wheeled and tracked vehicles for military and humanitarian tasks.

The vessel will have a flight deck for both fixed- and rotary-wing aircraft, and a hangar/garage of 2500 m² (26,910 sq

ft). The ship will also have an amphibious capacity through rapid transport via helicopter. Other features will be a hospital with three operating rooms, X-ray and CT equipment, dentist's surgery, and a laboratory.

The carrier will be armed with the Aster-15 SAM fired from vertical-launch systems and operated in conjunction with the EMPAR multi-function phased-array radar, offering surveillance, tracking and weapons control. The vessel will be armed with two Otobreda 76.2-mm (3-in) Super Rapid guns and three 25-mm anti-aircraft guns, and include advanced radar and EW systems.

Melding two naval power projection concepts (assault ship and aircraft carrier) into one ship, the **Andrea Doria** *will be one of the most versatile ships on the high seas.*

SPECIFICATION	
'Andrea Doria' class	and three 25-mm cannon
Displacement: 26,500 tons full load	**Electronics:** RAN-40S or S-1850M
Dimensions: length 234.4 m (769 ft); beam 39 m (128 ft); draught 7.5 m (24 ft 7 in)	long-range air search radar, EMPAR air search and missile guidance radar, SPS-791 surface search
Propulsion: COGAG with four LM 2500 gas turbines delivering 87.980 kW (118,000 shp) to two shafts	radar, SPN-753G(N) navigation radar, Vampir optronic director, SPN-41 aircraft control radar, 'Horizon'-based combat data
Performance: speed 30 kts; endurance 13.000 km (8,080 miles) at 16 kts	system, EW system, two SCLAR-H chaff/decoy launchers, and one SNA-2000 mine avoidance sonar
Armament: four Sylver 8-cell vertical-launch systems for Aster-15 medium-range SAMs, two 76.2-mm (3-in) Super Rapid DP guns,	**Aircraft:** eight AV-8B or F-35 fixed-wing aircraft and 12 EH.101 helicopters
	Crew: 456 plus 211 air group

Chinese SSBNs Types 092 'Han' and 094

The Chinese navy's SSBN programme began in the 1970s but has yet to produce a functioning weapons platform. The sole Chinese SSBN, the **Changzheng 6**, is a modified 'Han'-class (NATO designation) SSN, laid down in 1978 and launched in 1981. Commissioned in 1987, the NATO designation is **'Xia' class**; to the Chinese it is the **Type 092**. Construction of both boat and intended missile system was a catalogue of disasters. The 'Xia' class is slow, noisy and its reactor unreliable. The JL-1 missile failed on its first live firings in 1985, and it took three years to achieve a successful test launch. The JL-1 (CSS-N-3) has a single 250-kT

warhead and its comparatively short range of 2,150 km (1,336 miles) would force the vessel to patrol perilously close to enemy shores. In fact, the 'Xia' class has never left Chinese coastal waters and seldom put to sea before a refit that lasted from 1995 to 2000. It emerged from dockyard hands with a new coat of black paint – replacing the previous steel blue – a bow-mounted sonar, re-designed missile casing that would allow for longer missiles and (presumably) new firing systems for a different missile, the JL-1A SLBM, which has a reported range of 2,800 km (1,740 miles).

It was reported that a second unit was constructed but lost

with all hands in an accident in 1985, but Chinese secrecy remains at Cold War levels. A solitary SSBN has little strategic value but whatever plans there might have been to extend the 'Xia' class have come to nought. Even if all systems are functioning, the boat's performance is poor. The sole 'Xia'-class boat would not

survive long in wartime against western ASW platforms. A new class of SSBN, the **Type 094**, reportedly with 16 JL-2 (CSS-N-5 'Sabbot') SLBMs (8,000-km/ 4,971-mile range) is under construction with an estimated launch date of 2006. This new vessel may well be based on the hull of the new Type 093 SSN with an additional missile 'plug'.

SPECIFICATION	
'Xia' class (Type 092)	**Diving depth:** 300 m (984 ft)
Displacement: 6,500 tons dived	**Armament:** 12 JL-1A (CSS-N-3)
Dimensions: length 120 m (393 ft 6 in); beam 10 m (33 ft); draught 8 m (26 ft 2 in)	SLBMs, six 533-mm (21-in) bow tubes for Yu-3 torpedoes
Machinery: one pressurized watercooled reactor delivering 90 MW (120,643 shp) to one shaft	**Electronics:** 'Snoop Tray' surface search radar; 'Trout Cheek' hull-mounted active/passive search, Type 921A ESM
Speed: 22 kts dived	**Complement:** 140

'Le Triomphant' class New generation SSBN/SNLE

Ordered in March 1986 to replace the 'Redoutable' class, the **'Le Triomphant' class** are known to the French as SNLE-NGs (*Sous-marins Nucléares Lanceurs d'Engines-Nouvelle Génération*) or 'new generation' SSBNs. **Le Triomphant** was laid down at Cherbourg in 1989, launched in 1994 and entered service in 1997. Six boats were planned, but this was reduced to four after the end of the Cold War, and the M5 SLBM, which was proving very expensive to develop, has been abandoned. The 'Triomphant' class will be armed with the cheaper M51 missile although the two vessels currently in service carry the M45.

A first submerged M45 launch was conducted by *Le Triomphant* in February 1995. Operated by

Le Triomphant undertook its first cruise in summer 1995, while Le Téméraire began trials in April 1998. The next vessel, Le Vigilant, began trials in December 2003, and the fourth and final boat (and the first to carry the definitive M51 SLBM), Le Terrible, is scheduled to enter service in 2010.

two crews ('amber' and 'blue') *Le Triomphant* is France's primary nuclear deterrent – only one of the 'L'Inflexible' M4 class is still operational. The 'Triomphant' class submarines are significantly quieter than their predecessors: the primary objective of the design team was to reduce noise levels to

the point that even the best acoustic sensors would have problems detecting and tracking the vessels.

The second of the class, *Le Téméraire* was laid down in 1993, launched in 1998 and commissioned in December 1999. *Le Vigilant*, laid down in 1997, entered service in 2004. *Le Terrible* was laid down in October 2000 and is planned to join the fleet in 2010. The M45 SLBM has a maximum range of 5,300 km (3,293 miles) and each missile has six MIRVs, each carrying a 150-kT nuclear

warhead. The 'Triomphant' class can launch SM39 Exocet anti-ship missiles from their torpedo tubes to attack surface targets, in addition to dual purpose L5

active/passive homing torpedoes. Between 2010-15 the class of four boats, beginning with *Le Terrible*, is to be equipped with the M51.

Le Téméraire *was the second of the 'Le Triomphant'-class SSBNs, launched in August 1997 and commissioned in 1999. This boat and the name ship currently carry the M45 SLBM.*

SPECIFICATION	
'Le Triomphant' class	**Speed:** 25 kts dived
Displacement: 12,640 tons surfaced; 14,335 tons dived	**Diving Depth:** 500 m (1,640 ft)
Dimensions: length 138 m (453 ft); beam 12.5 m (41 ft); draught 12.5 m (41 ft)	**Armament:** 16 M45 SLBMs each with six 150-kT MIRVs, four 533-mm (21-in) tubes for 18 L5 torpedoes/SM39 Exocet missiles
Machinery: one pressurized water-cooled reactor delivering 150 MW (201,072 shp), two diesels delivering 700 kW (939 shp), one pump jet propulsor, one shaft	**Electronics:** Dassault search radar, Thomson-Sintra DMUX multi-function passive bow and flank arrays, towed array passive sonar
	Complement: 111

'Le Redoutable' and 'L'Inflexible' classes SSBNs/SNLEs

The first French SSBN (or more correctly *Sous-marin Nucléare Lanceurs d'Engine* or SNLE) **Le Redoutable** was authorized in March 1963, laid down in November 1964 and commissioned in 1971 after being employed for 2½ years on trials as the prototype for the French naval deterrent known as the *Force de Dissuasion* in official circles. This vessel and her **'Le Redoutable' class** sister ship **Le Terrible** were

initially equipped with the 2400-km (1,490-mile) range two-stage solid-propellant inertially-guided M1 SLBM that had a single 500-kT nuclear warhead and a CEP of 930 m (3,050 ft). In 1974 the third unit, **Le Foudroyant**, was commissioned with the improved 3100-km (1,925-mile) range M2 SLBM with a more powerful second-stage motor but carrying the same warhead and having a similar CEP. The two previous

SPECIFICATION	
'L'Inflexible' class	**Armament:** 16 launch tubes for 16 M4 SLBMs (16 M45 SLBMs fitted in *l'Inflexible* in 2001), and four 533-mm (21-in) bow tubes for total of 18 L5 dual-purpose and F17 anti-ship torpedoes and SM39 Exocet anti-ship missiles
Displacement: 8,080 tons surfaced and 8,920 tons dived	
Dimensions: length 128.7 m (422 ft 3 in); beam 10.6 m (34 ft 9 in); draught 10 m (32 ft 10 in)	
Propulsion: one pressurized water-cooled reactor powering two steam turbines driving one shaft	**Electronics:** one surface search radar, one passive ESM system, one DLT D3 torpedo and Exocet fire-control system, one DSUX 21 sonar, and one DUUX 5 underwater telephone
Speed: 20 kts surfaced and 25 kts dived	
Diving depth: 350 m (1,150 ft) operational and 465 m (1,525 ft) maximum	**Complement:** 135

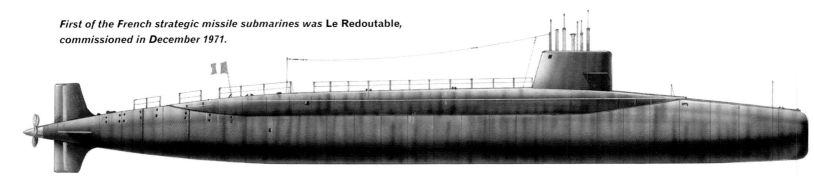

First of the French strategic missile submarines was **Le Redoutable,** *commissioned in December 1971.*

vessels were then retrofitted with the M2 system during their normal overhauls. The fourth boat, **L'Indomptable**, was commissioned into service in 1977 with the vastly improved M20 missile that had the same range and accuracy as the M2 but carried a new 1.2-MT yield hardened warhead with what is believed to be chaff-dispensing penetration aids to confuse defending radar systems. The last vessel, **Le Tonnant**, was also completed with the M20 while the three units equipped with the M2 were subsequently brought up to the same standard. From 1985 the last four units built underwent another modification to carry the M4 SLBM that entered service aboard **L'Inflexible**.

All five boats were also converted to carry the SM39 Exocet anti-ship missile and sonars of the **'L'Inflexible' class**. After the paying off of *Le Redoutable* in December 1991, the remaining submarines of the class were classified as the **'L'Inflexible' class SNLE M4**. The

better streamlining of the M4 conversion gave the boats a silhouette similar to that of *L'Inflexible*. The last such boat remaining in service was *L'Indomptable*, which received M4 missiles in 1989 and was decommissioned in late 2004. The similarly upgraded *Le Tonnant* was paid off into the reserve in 1999.

'L'Inflexible' class

Ordered in September 1978, the sole boat of the 'L'Inflexible' class, *L'Inflexible* is an intermediate design between the 'Le Redoutable' class and the 'Le Triomphant' class. *L'Inflexible* retains most of the external characteristics of the earlier class, but the internal fittings and sensors differ by taking advantage of the advances made in the propulsion system, electronics and weapons since the 'Le Redoutable'-class boats were constructed. The rationale behind this intermediate boat lay in the fact that France required three SSBNs to be continuously available, of which two were to be on patrol. In order to achieve

Le Foudroyant *and its sister ships were designed and built in France without any help from the US, unlike the British Polaris boats, which required considerable design assistance.*

SPECIFICATION	
'Le Redoutable' class	**Diving depth:** 250 m (820 ft) operational and 330 m (1,085 ft) maximum
Displacement: 8,045 tons surfaced and 8,940 tons dived	
Dimensions: as 'L'Inflexible' class	
Propulsion: one pressurized water-cooled reactor powering two steam turbines driving one shaft	**Armament:** 16 launch tubes for 16 M20 SLBMs, and four 550-mm (21.7-in) bow tubes for 18 L5 dual-purpose and F17 anti-ship torpedoes
Speed: 18 kts surfaced and 25 kts dived	

this, the French navy had to have six submarines in service, a number one more than the 'Le Redoutable' class total.

Laid down in March 1980, *L'Inflexible* achieved operational status in April 1985 and is due to remain in service until at least 2008. Like all French missile submarines, *L'Inflexible* has two crews, *Bleu* (blue) and *Ambre* (amber), to crew the vessel in rotation in order to maximize the time spent on patrol between reactor-refuelling refits. French

SSBNs normally undertake patrols of two months' duration, with three months as the absolute maximum. All the French SSBNs are based at Île Longue near Brest and have special protection when transiting to and from the port.

In April 2001 *L'Inflexible* conducted a successful test launch of the M45 SLBM, containing components of the new generation M51 missile with which it is planned to equip the 'Le Triomphant' -class SSBNs.

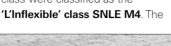

France tries to maintain a minimum of two SNLEs on patrol at any one time, and submarines such as the **Le Terrible** *('Le Redoutable' class) were screened on departure and return by navy surface units, submarines and ASW aircraft in order to maintain security.*

'Golf' class SSBN

The **'Golf' class** is NATO's designation for the Soviet **Project 629**, a 22-strong class of conventionally powered submarines armed with nuclear missiles. Authorized in 1955, a year ahead of the 'Hotel'-class nuclear boats, the 'Golfs' carried the same SLBMs, the R-13 or SS-N-4. The first boat was launched at Severodvinsk in 1960 and another 14 followed there while seven were built at Komsomolsk-na-Amur for the Pacific Fleet. The boats were commissioned between 1959 and 1962 and served for upwards of twenty years. **K-36** and **K-91** were transferred to the Pacific Fleet; six spent their last years with the Baltic Fleet; and **K-113** was converted to a minelayer, then stricken in 1974. The other vessels were decommissioned in 1980–91.

K-129 was lost with all hands 66 km (600 miles) northwest of Hawaii on 11 April 1968 in circumstances that remain classified. The Soviets were unable to locate K-129, but the US did. By then, these were not the most modern boats in the Soviet fleet, but K-129 was carrying nuclear missiles and associated command equipment plus sonar and radar and communications systems that would amount to a major intelligence windfall. The recovery, codenamed 'Project Jennifer', was undertaken using a specially built 63,000-ton ship financed by Howard Hughes, the *Glomar Explorer*. The CIA and US Navy brought up the submarine in September 1974. The operation was conducted in great secrecy and many details remain unclear. Officially the whole boat was never raised because the crane snapped, leaving the US with a 11.6-m (38-ft) section of the hull and the mortal remains of eight Soviet submariners, who were later reburied at sea. Tactical nuclear warheads from two torpedoes were recovered, but the SLBMs fell back to the ocean floor. Exactly what coding equipment ended up in US hands was never confirmed.

'Golf' exports

Three 'Golf'-class submarines were supplied to China without nuclear missiles. One sank in an accident. Soviet specialists were withdrawn from China in 1960 as Sino-Soviet relations broke down, but China launched an SSBN almost identical to the 'Golf' in 1966. This remains in service and was used to test launch China's first SLBM, the JL-1 (CSS-N-3) in 1982. Refitted in 1995 for the JL-2 (CSS-N-5) missile, it has been used in trials for China's first submarine launched missile with global reach – the missiles have a range of 12,070 km (7,500 miles) – since 1999.

Of the 22 'Golf I' boats with SS-N-4 missiles, 14 were refitted with SS-N-5 weapons (as 'Golf IIs') and a further boat was built to Project 629B standard as a testbed for new liquid-fuel and solid-propellant missile systems. A 'Golf II' is pictured.

SPECIFICATION	
'Golf' class (Project 629) **Displacement:** 2,794 tons surfaced and 3,553 tons dived **Dimensions:** length 98.4 m (32 ft 4 in); beam 8.2 m (26 ft 11 in), draft 7.85 m (25 ft 9 in) **Propulsion:** three diesels delivering 4,474 kW (6,000 shp) with electric motors driving three shafts **Speed:** 15 kts surfaced; 12.5 kts submerged **Diving depth:** 260 m (853 ft)	operational; 300 m (984 ft) maximum **Armament:** ('Golf I') D-2 missile system with three R-13 (SS-N-4) missiles, or ('Golf II') D-4 missile system with three R-21 (SS-N-5 'Sark') missiles **Electronics:** one 'Snoop Tray' or 'Snoop Plate' surface search radar, one Herkules sonar, one Feniks sonar **Complement:** about 80

'Golf'-class boats carried their three missiles within upright launch tubes located directly behind the conning tower. Launches were conducted on the surface.

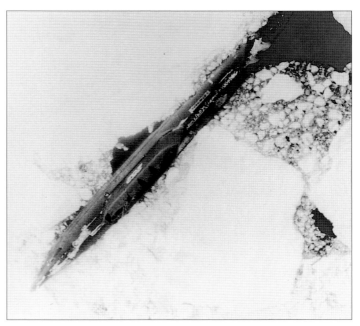

The combat control system of the 'Golf' class allowed the flight path of the submarine's missiles to be automatically corrected as the boat's position changed, reducing launch time.

'Hotel' class SSBN

Assigned the NATO reporting name **'Hotel' class**, the Soviet Union's first SSBN was designated **Project 658**. The first of the class was laid down on 17 October 1958 and eight boats were completed, all at Severodvinsk from 1960 to 1962. All were decommissioned between 1988 and 1991. As built, they carried three R-13 nuclear missiles (Western designation SS-N-4) nearly 12 m (40 ft) long and positioned upright in the sail, which required a bulge in the submarine's keel underneath the rear part of the sail. By later standards, the missile had a very short range, just 650 km (404 miles), so the submarines would have had to cross the Atlantic from their base in the Barents Sea in order to threaten America. The submarines had to surface to fire, and it took 12 minutes to launch all three missiles. From 1965 to 1970 they were refitted with the R-21 system (SS-N-5 'Sark'); this had a range of 1400 km (870 miles).

K-55 and **K-178** had their SLBMs removed and served in the Pacific fleet until decommissioned. The others served with the Northern Fleet. **K-145** was given a major refit in 1969–70 just six years after it was commissioned. The hull was lengthened by 13 m (43 ft) and the sail enlarged to carry R-29 SLBMs (NATO designation SS-N–8 'Sawfly'). **K-40** was converted to a communications boat in 1977 (the Soviets lacked global coverage in HF stations and relied on command boats to relay orders).

K-19 became the most infamous Soviet nuclear

submarine in history, known to submariners as 'Hiroshima' after successive reactor breakdowns irradiated two complete crews. The first disaster took place on 4 July 1961, when a leak in the reactors was detected. Several crew members entered the contaminated compartments to attempt repairs – knowing this would doom them to certain death. Repairs proved impossible, the crew was taken off and K-19 was towed into port. Eight men died of radiation burns soon after and cancer rates among their comrades are horrendous. The reactor was replaced during 1962–64 but K-19 caught fire while on patrol off

The 'Hotel' class was the first Soviet nuclear-powered ballistic missile submarine. The armament of SS-N-4 missiles was replaced by SS-N-5s on the 'Hotel II'.

Newfoundland on 4 February 1972. More than 30 ships were involved in the rescue, but fighting the fire cost the lives of 28 of its crew. A movie version of this grisly saga was released in 2002 (*K-19*

Widowmaker). The ill-fated submarine was finally decommissioned in 1991. The single **'Hotel III'** vessel refitted in 1969–70 for test of the new R-29 (SS-N-8 'Sawfly') SLBM carried six missile launchers.

SPECIFICATION	
'Hotel' class (Project 658)	maximum
Displacement: ('Hotel II') 5500 tons dived	**Armament:** ('Hotel I') D-2 missile system with three R-13 (SS-N-4) missiles, or ('Hotel II') D-4 missile system with three R-21 (SS-N-5 'Sark') missiles
Dimensions: length 114 m (374 ft); beam 9.2 m (30 ft 2 in); draft 7.31 m (24 ft)	
Propulsion: diesel electric	
Speed: 18 kts surfaced; 26 kts dived	**Electronics:** one 'Snoop Tray' surface search radar, one Herkules sonar, one Feniks sonar
Diving depth: 240 m (787 ft) operational; 300 m (984 ft)	**Complement:** 104

'Yankee' class SSBN

The **'Yankee' class (Project 667A Navaga)** was the first modern Soviet SSBN to be built. The design was apparently based on the plans of the US 'Benjamin Franklin' and 'Lafayette' classes,

which were covertly obtained by Soviet military intelligence (GRU) in the early 1960s. A total of 34 units were built between 1967 and 1974 at the shipyards in Severodvinsk and Komsomolsk,

the peak year being 1970, when 10 vessels were completed. The 'Yankees' were distinguishable from the later 'Deltas' by having a smaller rise to the 'turtle-back' missile compartment abaft the

sail. In 1976, one unit was converted to a **'Yankee II' class (Project 667AM)** configuration in which the original 16 missile tubes were replaced by 12 larger units for the solid-propellant R-31

(SS-N-17 'Snipe') SLBM. The 'Yankee II' also differed from the similar 12-round 'Delta Is' by having a sloping forward edge to the 'turtle-back' casing of the missile tubes.

To comply with the SALT agreement, a number of 'Yankee I' SSBNs were deactivated as SLBM carriers. By mid-1984, 10 had been so treated, a number being converted to SSNs by the complete removal of the ballistic missile section of the hull. These are now inactive.

SLCM conversion

Another was converted for the highly accurate RK-55 Granat (SS-N-21 'Sampson') cruise missile with a single 200-kT yield warhead and a range of 3,000 km (1,865 miles). This **'Yankee Notch'** vessel now operates with the Northern Fleet. The 35 Granat SLCMs are launched from torpedo tubes.

During the early 1980s, three or four of 14 **'Yankee I'** boats, plus the sole 'Yankee II' in the Northern Fleet, were on station at any one time off the eastern seaboard of the US, with a further unit either on transit to or from a patrol area. Overlaps did occur, and these occasionally raised the number of boats on patrol. Of the nine 'Yankee Is' in the Pacific Fleet, two were on permanent patrol off the western US seaboard with another on transit to or from the patrol zones. The forward-deployed 'Yankees' were assigned the wartime role of destroying time-sensitive area targets such as SAC bomber alert bases and carriers/SSBNs in port, and of disrupting the American higher command echelons as much as possible to ease the task of follow-up ICBM strikes. Subsequently, NATO sources

The 'Yankee I'-class boat **K-219** *suffered a launch tube decompression resulting in a fire in October 1986. The vessel was conducting a combat patrol east of Bermuda. The vessel surfaced but could not be towed and later sank.*

indicated that several of the 'Yankees' in each theatre had been switched to operate against theatre nuclear targets, with the submarines operating in sanctuary areas closer to the Soviet homeland. These vessels replaced the older 'Hotel' and 'Golf II' submarines in this role. Two 'Yankee' vessels operate in the research and development role, one undertaking sonar trials and the other taking part in underwater operations in support of the 'Paltus'-class auxiliary submarines.

A single boat was refitted in 1982 to test the Meteorit-M (SS-N-24 'Scorpion') supersonic cruise missile as the **'Yankee Sidecar'**.

The 'Yankee I' class, with its armament of SS-N-6 missiles, formed the major part of the Soviet SSBN fleet in the early 1970s. 'Snipe'). The boat carried 12 of these weapons, each of which was equipped with a 500-kT warhead.

With an increased displacement, the single 'Yankee II' was equipped with the Soviet's first solid-propellant SLBM, the the R-31 (SS-N-17 'Snipe'). The boat carried 12 of these weapons, each equipped with a 500-kT warhead.

SPECIFICATION
'Yankee' class (Project 667A)

Displacement: 7,700 tons surfaced and 9,300 dived
Dimensions: length 132 m (433 ft); beam 11.6 m (38 ft 1 in); draught 8 m (26 ft 4 in)
Propulsion: two pressurized watercooled reactors powering four steam turbines driving two shafts
Speed: 13 kts surfaced and 27 kts dived
Diving depth: 400 m (1,315 ft) operational and 600 m (1,970 ft) maximum
Armament: ('Yankee I') 16 launch tubes for R-27 (SS-N-6 'Serb')

SLBMs, or ('Yankee II') 12 launch tubes for R-31 (SS-N-17 'Snipe') SLBMs, and (both classes) four 533-mm (21-in) and two 400-mm (15.7-in) torpedo tubes
Electronics: one 'Snoop Tray' surface search radar, one low-frequency bow sonar, one medium-frequency torpedo fire-control sonar, VHF/SHF/UHF communications systems, one VLF towed communications buoy, one ELF floating antenna, one 'Brick Group' ESM suite, and one 'Park Lamp' direction-finding antenna
Complement: 120

'Delta I' and 'Delta II' class SSBNs

The first 'Delta I'-class ballistic missile submarine was paid off in 1992, and a decade later all but a single vessel had been scrapped or laid up at operational bases in the North and the Pacific.

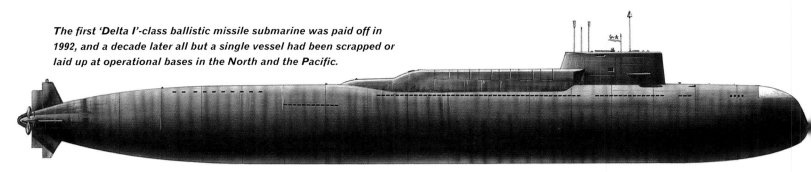

The **'Delta I'** SSBN or **Project 667B Murena** was a larger vessel than the previous 'Yankee' class. Built initially at Severodvinsk and then at Komsomolsk in the Soviet Far East, the 'Delta I' was the world's largest undersea craft when the first unit entered Northern Fleet service in 1972. The 18th and last of the class was completed at Komsomolsk and commissioned in 1977. Designated a ballistic missile submarine (*podvodnaya lodka raketnaya laylataya,* or PLRK) by the Soviet Union, the class carried two parallel rows of six D-9 missile launch tubes for the R-29 (SS-N-8 'Sawfly') missile aft of the sail, which was set forward with diving planes on each side.

'Sawfly' missiles

Unlike its predecessor, the 'Delta I' with its long-range SLBMs was capable of mounting sustained patrols within the marginal ice seas of the Soviet arctic littoral, including the Barents and Norwegain seas. As a result, they did not need to pass Western SOSUS sonar barriers before their targets were within range. Cold War tactics saw the 'Delta I' ships deployed in friendly waters, protected by Soviet naval 'bastions'.

The R-29 missiles themselves

Only four 'Delta II'-class vessels were built at Severodvinsk between 1973 and 1975. Their lengthened hulls were capable of carrying a load of 16 R-29D missiles.

incorporated accurate Topol-B navigation and Cyclone-B satellite navigation. The 'Sawfly' missiles could be launched in a single salvo whilst the submerged vessel was moving at a speed of 5 kts.

'Delta I' SSBNs served with the 41st Division of Strategic Submarines with the Northern Fleet from 1973 (based at Yagyelnaya Bay) and with the 25th Division, Pacific Fleet, beginning patrols in 1976. Pacific Fleet vessels were originally based at Kamchatka, but were transferred to Pavlovsk in the early 1990s. Nine survivors were operational in 1991, and their decommissioning under START-1 began in 1994. In 2002,

SPECIFICATION

'Delta I' and 'Delta II' class
Displacement: 7,800 tons surfaced and 10,000 tons dived for 'Delta I', and 9,350 tons surfaced and 10,500 tons dived for 'Delta II'
Dimensions: length 139 m (456 ft) for 'Delta I' and 155 m (508 ft 6 in) for 'Delta II'; beam 12 m (39 ft 5 in); draught 9 m (29 ft 6 in)
Propulsion: two pressurized water-cooled reactors powering two steam turbines driving two shafts and each developing 38.7 MW (52,000 shp) for 'Delta I' and 41 MW (55,000 shp) for 'Delta II'
Speed: 12 kts surfaced and 25 kts submerged ('Delta I'); 12 kts surfaced and 24 kts submerged ('Delta II')
Diving depth: ('Delta I' and 'Delta II') 390 m (1,279 ft 6 in) operational and 450 m (1,476 ft 4½ in) maximum

Armament: D-9 launch tubes for 12 R-29 (SS-N-8 'Sawfly') SLBMs and four 533-mm torpedo tubes ('Delta I') or D-9D launch tubes for 16 R-29D SLBMs, four 533-mm and two 400-mm torpedo tubes ('Delta II')
Electronics: ('Delta I' and 'Delta II') one 'Snoop Tray' I-band surface search radar, one 'Shark Teeth' low-/medium-frequency hull-mounted sonar, one 'Mouse Roar' high-frequency hull-mounted sonar, one medium-frequency torpedo fire-control sonar, HF/SHF/UHF comms systems, one VLF towed comms buoy, one ELF floating antenna, one 'Brick Group' ESM suite, one 'Park Lamp' direction finding antenna, and one 'Pert Spring' satellite navigation system
Complement: 120 ('Delta I') or 130 ('Delta II')

a single 'Delta I', **K 447**, remained in Russian service.

Interim class

Between 1972 and 1975 at Severodvinsk, an interim batch of four **'Delta II'** (**Project 667BD Murena-M**) class units was constructed. These were essentially similar to the earlier design but were lengthened by 16 m (52 ft 6 in) to make possible the incorporation of a further four missile tubes. The 'Delta II' carried improved R-29D missiles and introduced several features to decrease noise levels, including a new hydroacoustic coating. The first vessel entered service with the Northern Fleet in September 1975. In accordance with START-1, decommissioning of the 'Delta II' began in 1996.

The range of its D-29 'Sawfly' missiles allowed the 'Delta I' to maintain constant patrol in remote areas or remain on combat alert whilst moored at their bases.

'Typhoon' class SSBN

The 'Typhoon' does not need to submerge or even go to sea in order to launch its payload of up to 200 nuclear warheads: during the Cold War, targets in the continental US could be attacked while the vessel was moored at its Northern Fleet home base.

The **'Typhoon'-class** (**Project 941 Akula**) boats are the largest undersea vessels ever built, and are based on a catamaran-type design that comprises two separate pressure hulls joined by a single outer covering to give increased protection against ASW weapons.

The class was built specifically for operations with the Soviet Northern Fleet in the Arctic ice pack. The reinforced sail, advanced stern fin with horizontal hydroplane fitted aft of the screws and retractable bow hydroplanes allow the submarine to break easily through spots of thin ice within the Arctic ice shelf.

'Sturgeon' SLBM

The first unit was laid down in 1977 at Severodvinsk and commissioned in 1980, becoming operational in 1981. To arm the 'Typhoon', design of a fifth-generation SLBM, the

SPECIFICATION
'Typhoon' class

'Typhoon' class
Displacement: 23,200–24,500 tons surfaced; 33,800–48,000 tons dived
Dimensions: length 170–172 m (558-564 ft); beam 23–23.3 m (75–76 ft); draught 11–11.5 m (36–38 ft)
Propulsion: two OK-650 190-MW (254,750 shp) pressurized water-cooled reactors and two 37.3 MW (50,000 shp) steam turbines driving two shafts
Speed: 12–16 kts surfaced and 25–27 kts dived
Diving depth: 500 m (1,640 ft)
Armament: D-19 launch tubes for 20 R-39 (SS-N-20 'Sturgeon') SLBMs, two 650-mm and four 533-mm torpedo tubes for RPK-7 Vodopei (SS-N-16 'Stallion') and RPK-2 Viyoga (SS-N-15 'Starfish') or VA-111 Shkval respectively
Electronics: surface-search radar, ESM system, low-frequency bow sonar, medium-frequency torpedo fire-control sonar, VHF/SHF/UHF communications systems. one VLF towed communications buoy, and one ELF floating antenna
Complement: 150–175 (50–55 officers)

Soviet doctrine envisaged the 'Typhoon' as a 'doomsday weapon', capable of emerging from the polar ice and launching a devastating second strike after an initial nuclear exchange. The high maintenance and manpower costs of these vessels is likely to result in their retirement in the medium term, although Russia is keen to maintain them as short term force multipliers.

R-39 Taifun (SS-N-20 'Sturgeon'), began in 1973. Six vessels were constructed between 1981 and 1989, and served as part of the 1st Flotilla of Atomic Submarines, within the Western Theatre of the Northern Fleet, and based at Nyerpicha. Construction of a seveth vessel was not completed.

The R-39 allowed the submarine to fire the weapon from within the Arctic circle and still hit a target anywhere within the continental US. The 'Typhoons', were originally to be retrofitted with the improved R-39M (SS-N-28) missile.

Two vessels were decommissioned in 1997, and in 2002 only two remained in service, although it has been reported that three of the class will remain active in order to test the R-39M or the new Bulava SLBM, contravening the Co-operative Threat Reduction Program. However, the status of the R-39M, intended to arm the fourth-generation Borei-class SSBN, is uncertain.

SPECIFICATION

R-39 (SS-N-20 'Sturgeon')
Type: SLBM
Dimensions: total length 16 m (52 ft 6 in); length without warhead 8.4 m (27 ft 7 in); diameter 2.4 m (7 ft 11 in)
Payload: 2550 kg (5,622 lb)
Performance: range 8,300 km (5,158 miles); CEP 500 m (1,640 ft)
Warhead: up to 10 MIRVs of 200 kT each
Propulsion: three-stage solid-propellant rocket
Guidance: stellar-inertial

'Delta III/IV' class
Ballistic missile submarine

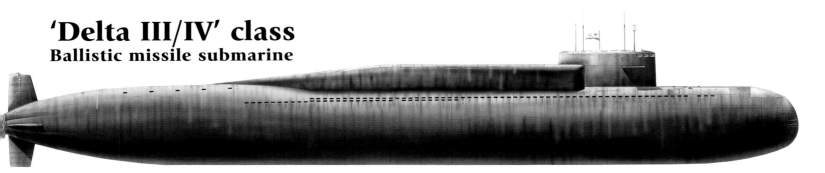

Although the Soviets were pioneers in firing missiles from submarines, their early systems were short-ranged. The 34 units of the 'Yankee' class, built between 1967 and 1974, were apparently based on stolen American plans for the 'Benjamin Franklin' class. These provided the foundation for the follow-on **'Delta'** class, an enlarged development of the 'Yankee' design. The first Deltas entered service in 1972, the original **'Delta I'** design being succeeded by the interim **'Delta II'** with 16 missiles rather than the original 12.

'Delta III'

These were followed from 1976 by the **Type 667 BDR 'Kalmar' class**, better known to NATO as the **'Delta III'**. These had a larger and longer 'turtle-back' abaft the sail. This housed R-29R missiles (NATO designation SS-N-18), the first Soviet sea-based multiple-warhead

system. Fourteen submarines were built at Severodvinsk.

The 'Delta III' submarines that served in the Northern fleet formed a division and were based at Sayda and at Olyenya port. In the early 90s the ballistic missile submarines were transferred to Yagyelnaya. Pacific Fleet 'Delta IIIs' were based on Kamchatka.

Development of the **Type 667 BDRM 'Delfin'** or **'Dolphin' class**, known to NATO as the **'Delta IV'**, began on 10 September 1975. The first boat, *K-51*, was commissioned into the Northern fleet in December 1985. Between 1985 and 1990, seven 'Delta IVs' were constructed. The 'Delta IVs' were constructed in parallel to the 'Typhoon' class, in case the larger boats proved unsuccessful. The 'Dolphin' is a further modification of the 'Delta III', with an increased diameter pressure hull and a

At more than 16,000 tons submerged displacement, the 'Kalmar' class, known to NATO as the Delta III, were the largest submarines in the world when they entered service in 1976.

longer bow section. Displacement has increased by 1,200 tons and it is 12 m (39 ft) longer.

'Delta IV'

The 'Delta IV' is a strategic platform, designed to strike military and industrial installations and naval bases. The submarine carries the RSM-54 Makeyev missile (NATO designation: SS-N-23

'Skiff'). The RSM-54 is a three-stage liquid-propellant ballistic missile with a range of 8300 km (5,158 miles). The warhead consists of four to ten multiple independently targeted re-entry vehicles (MIRVs), each rated at 100 kT. The missile uses stellar inertial guidance for a CEP of 500 m (1,640 ft).

The submarine can also launch the Novator (SS-N-15

Since 'Delta'-class boats remain a mainstay of Russia's nuclear deterrent force, they are kept in better condition than other nuclear submarines.

SPECIFICATION

Type 667 'Delfin' or 'Delta IV' class

Type: Nuclear-powered ballistic missile submarine

Displacement: 13,500 tons surfaced, 18,200 tons submerged

Dimensions: length 166 m (544 ft 7 in); beam 12.3 m (39 ft 6 in); draught 8.8 m (29 ft)

Machinery: two pressurized water-cooled reactors powering two steam turbines delivering 44700 kW (60,000 shp) to two seven-bladed fixed-pitch shrouded propellers; 3 x 3200-kW (4,294-hp) turbo generators; two 800-kW (1074-hp) diesel generators; one 750-kW (1007-hp) auxiliary motor powering screw rudders bow and stern

Speed: c.14 kt surface; 24 kt dived

Patrol endurance: 90 days

Diving depth: 300 m (985 ft) operational and 400 m (1312 ft) max

Weapons tubes: 16 missile and 4 x 533-mm (21-in) torpedo in bow

Weapons load: 16 x Makeyev RSM-54 Shtil (SS-N-23 'Skiff') nuclear ballistic missiles; 18 tube-launched weapons including RPK-7 Vodopei (SS-N-16 'Stallion') ASW missiles, and Type 65K, SET-65, SAET-60M 533-mm torpedoes

Electronics: one Snoop Tray I-band Surface Search radar; Skat-BDRM ('Shark Gill') LF active/passive sonar; 'Shark Hide' passive LF flank sonar; Pelamida passive VLF thin-line towed array sonar; 'Mouse Roar' active HF attack sonar; ESM/ECM; D/F radar warning; 'Brick Spit' optronic mast; Satellite/Inertial/ Radiometric navigation; satcom plus two floating aerials for VLF/ELF radio

Complement: 135

Although the Russian navy is a shadow of its former self, it still maintains sufficent force to keep a minimum missile deterrent at sea at all times.

submarines, while the Russians had destroyed another five ballistic missile subs on their own using US equipment.

As of June 2003, the Russian Navy claimed that it operated five 'Typhoon'-class submarines, six 'Delta IV'-class submarines, and 13 'Delta III'-class submarines, which between them carry 2,272 nuclear warheads on 440 ballistic missiles. With the chronic funding shortages affecting the Soviet navy, it is likely that many of these boats are of suspect seaworthiness.

However, the Russian navy reportedly believes that 12 nuclear ballistic missile submarines is the minimum necessary force structure for national security, and this force goal is likely to be maintained up until 2010 at least.

'Starfish') anti-ship missile or Mk 40 anti-ship torpedo. 'Starfish' is armed with a 200 KT nuclear warhead and has a range of 45 km (28 miles).

The operational lifetime of these submarines was estimated to be 20–25 years,

but in the 1990s everything changed. When the START-1 treaty was signed in 1991, five 'Delta IIIs' served in the Northern and nine in the Pacific Fleet.

Russia is scheduled to dismantle one 'Yankee'-class,

five 'Typhoon'-class and 25 assorted 'Delta'-class ballistic missile submarines by the year 2003.

By September 1999, US specialists had helped Russia to disassemble one 'Yankee'-class and six 'Delta'-class

'R' class
Ballistic missile submarines

The missile compartment of the 'R'-class SSBN was based on a US Navy design, but the rest of the boat and equipment was British.

SPECIFICATION	
'Resolution' class **Displacement:** 7,500 tons surfaced and 8,400 tons dived **Dimensions:** length 129.5 m (425 ft); beam 10.1 m (33 ft); draught 9.1 m (30 ft) **Propulsion:** one pressurized watercooled reactor powering two steam turbines driving one shaft **Speed:** 20 kt surfaced and 25 kt dived **Diving depth:** 350 m (1,150 ft) operational and 465 m (1,525 ft) maximum	**Armament:** 16 launch tubes for 16 Polaris A3TK submarine-launched ballistic missiles, and six 533-mm (21-in) bow tubes for approximately 16 tube-launched weapons **Electronics:** one Type 1003 surface search radar, one type 2001 bow sonar, one Type 2007 sonar, one Type 2023 retractable towed-array sonar, one ESM suite, and an extensive communications outfit **Complement:** 135

Britain's initial nuclear-deterrent was carried by the RAF's V-bombers, but developments in radar and surface-to-air weaponry in the late 1950s and early 1960s made it clear that manned bombers were becoming increasingly vulnerable. In January 1963, the Defence Committee decided that the nation's deterrent should be carried in submarines.

In February 1963, the

government announced that it was to order four **'Resolution'-class** nuclear-powered, Polaris missile-equipped 7,000-ton submarines, with an option on a fifth. The SSBNs would take over the nuclear deterrent role from the Royal Air Force's V-Bomber force from 1968 onwards.

The first two pairs of boats were ordered in May 1963 from Vickers Shipbuilding Ltd, Barrow-in-Furness, and

Cammell Laird & Co. Ltd, Birkenhead; the option on a fifth unit was cancelled in February 1965.

Missile boats

Although designed in the United Kingdom, the new missile boats incorporated a number of design features used on the contemporary 'Lafayettes' design. The lead ship, **HMS Resolution** (S22) was launched in September 1966 and commissioned in October of the following year. **HMS Repulse** (*S23*), followed in September 1968, with **HMS Renown** (*S24*), and **HMS Revenge** (*S27*), commissioning in November 1968 and December 1969.

Early in 1968, the *Resolution* sailed to Florida for missile launch trials, making the UK's first successful Polaris launch on 15 February. Four months later, HMS *Resolution*, armed with Polaris A3P missiles, deployed on the first of more than 230

consecutive Polaris patrols by the Royal Navy. As with French and American SSBNs, two crews (Port and Starboard) were used to maximize the time spent at sea, each patrol lasting around three months. When not aboard, the submarine crews took leave and underwent refresher training at the 10th Submarine Squadron base at Faslane on the Clyde.

All four boats underwent conversion in the 1980s, being fitted to carry the improved Polaris A-TK missile, which was

*Right: HMS **Renown** heads for her home port at Faslane. The SSBN base became a focus for anti-nuclear protesters.*

*Below: In 1983 HMS **Revenge** became the second British SSBN to go on patrol with Chevaline. The new warheads were designed to penetrate Soviet ABM defences in place around Moscow.*

fitted with the British-developed Chevaline MRV warhead.

Obsolete

In spite of these extremely costly improvements to the Polaris system, it had been clear as early as 1980 that the rapidly ageing **'R-class'** boats, together with potential improvements in Soviet anti-missile capability, meant that capability had to be

upgraded still further. In July of that year, the British Government announced that it would acquire American-built Trident C-4 missiles, a decision modified in 1982 when it was announced that the Trident II system with the even larger D-5 missiles would be purchased.

As the 'V'-class boats entered service through the 1990s, their 'R' predecessors were retired.

'Vanguard' class SSBN

The 'Vanguard' class is fitted with state-of-the art periscopes for both search and attack. TV cameras and infra-red technology aid reconnaissance.

Unlike its Polaris missile-armed predecessor, the 'Resolution' class, the British **'Vanguard'-class** nuclear powered ballistic missile submarine (SSBN) is a completely new design. It has, however, utilized several of the successful design features from previous SSBNs.

The 'Vanguard' class is the largest submarine type ever constructed in the UK, and the third largest type of vessel in Royal Navy service. However, it is cloaked in tight secrecy. Despite the ending of the Cold War and the downgrading of its strategic mission, details on 'Vanguard' weapon systems and patrols are still highly classified. All four of the boats, **HMS Vanguard**, **HMS Victorious**, **HMS Vigilant** and

HMS Vengeance, were built by Vickers Submarine Engineering Limited (now BAE Systems Marine) at its dockyard in Barrow-in-Furness, Cumbria. Such was their size that a special production facility, the Devonshire Dock Hall, had to be constructed. The boat's large hull was prompted by the Trident D5 Submarine-Launched Ballistic Missile (SLBM), of which it can deploy 16. However, the vessels patrol with a smaller complement of crew than that of the previous 'Resolution' class (132 as oppposed to 149).

This 'Vanguard'-class submarine is pictured being escorted out of port by a tug and a French naval Alouette III, after paying a courtesy visit to a French port.

Transition

The first major transition from Polaris to Trident occurred in 1996, when HMS *Victorious* was deployed on patrol with a complement of Trident SLBMs. Trident has since become the sole component of the UK's nuclear deterrent, following the decommissioning of the WE177 tactical nuclear gravity/depth bomb in 1998, as part of the UK Strategic Defence Review. Furthermore, the 'Vanguard'-class boats had their 'readiness to fire' changed from a matter of minutes to 'a matter of days' according to the UK Secretary of State for Defence.

The 'Vanguard'-class missile suite contains 16 tubes and is based on the 24-tube design, which the US Navy deploys on its 'Ohio'-class Trident boats. The Trident missile system was built by Lockheed Martin, and is technically leased from the US. The Trident D5 is a MIRV (Multiple Independently-targeted Re-entry Vehicle) system, and it

is capable of deploying 12 warheads per missile.

Missile maintenance for the Trident missile system occurs in the US. However, the UK Atomic Weapons Establishment at Aldermaston undertakes all of the design, construction, installation and maintenance of the warheads.

Deployment

Each 'Vanguard'-class submarine can carry a maximum of 192 nuclear warheads, although the Royal Navy originally insisted that each boat would carry no more than 96, deployed across eight missiles. Since the Strategic Defence Review, this has been further reduced to 48 warheads per boat, spread across four missiles. Although the Ministry of Defence refuses to comment on how many missiles are deployed when a boat is on patrol, it has indicated that the complement of Trident missiles now only carries one warhead per missile, which is probably in the sub-strategic

SPECIFICATION	
'Vanguard' class **Displacement:** 15,900 tonnes dived **Dimensions:** length 149.9 m (492 ft); beam 12.8 m (42 ft); draught 12 m (32 ft). **Machinery:** (nuclear) one Rolls-Royce Pressurised Water Reactor; (conventional) two GEC turbines developing 20.5 MW (27,500 shp) **Speed:** 25 kts dived **Torpedo tubes:** four 21-in (533-mm) tubes **Missiles:** 16 Lockheed Trident 2	(D5) 3-stage 12000-km (6,500 nm) range solid-fuel nuclear-armed missiles. Each D5 can carry 12 MIRV of 100–120-kT, sub-strategic warheads introduced in 1996 **Electronics:** Type 1007 I-band nav radar, Type 2054 composite multi-frequency sonar suite including Type 2046 towed array, Type 2043 hull-mounted active/passive search and Type 2082 passive intercept and ranging **Complement:** 132 (14 officers)

Above: At least one 'Vanguard'-class boat is permanently at sea, providing the UK's nuclear deterrent. The submarines now perform a sub-strategic role.

kiloton range. A single 'Vanguard'-class boat is on deterrence patrol at any one time, and a reserve boat is also available.

New systems

As well as having a new strategic weapons system, the Vanguard also features several other new systems. These include a Rolls-Royce nuclear Pressurized Water Reactor propulsion system, and new tactical weapons fit, including Tigerfish and Spearfish torpedoes for short and medium defence. Tigerfish has a range of 13–29 km (8–18 miles) depending on the homing configuration, while Spearfish can hit targets up to 65 km (40 miles) away. The submarine also features a greatly improved Electronic Counter Measures (ECM) suite, and state-of-the-art attack and search periscopes. These are fitted with a TV camera and thermal imager as well as the traditional optical channel.

'Lafayette' class SSBN

Underrated and underplayed, the 'Lafayette' was, for many years, backbone of the USN strategic missile submarine fleet and was a highly successful design.

The **Lafayette' class** followed a successful series of US strategic submarines, which had begun with the 'George Washington' class, America's first strategic nuclear submarine. The 'Ethan Allen' class submarines followed the 'George Washington' class, the vessels being constructed between 1961 and 1963. However, unlike the 'George Washington' submarines, the 'Ethan Allen' class had the advantage of being designed as SSBNs from the start.

Nevertheless, both classes faced a distinct tactical disadvantage in having to operate close to Soviet shores. This so-called 'Moscow criteria' meant that the US Navy's ballistic missile submarines had to operate close to the USSR in

An officer on the sail scans the horizon for hostile vessels and anti-submarine aircraft while his 'Lafayette'-class vessel carries out deterrence patrol.

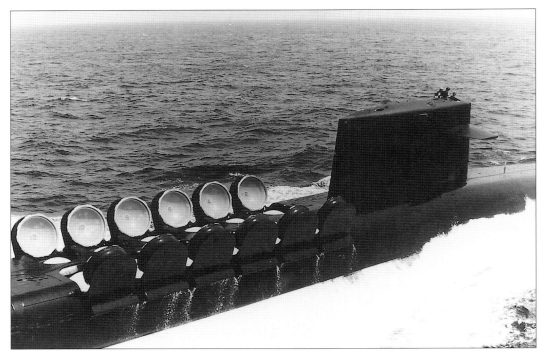

The 'Lafayette'-class submarines represented a formidable nuclear deterrent. This submarine displays 12 of its missile tubes. The 'Lafayette' class were the largest Western submarines completed during the 1960s.

order to destroy targets in Moscow, due to the range of their Polaris missiles. For example, Polaris A3, the model with the longest range, could still only hit targets at a maximum range of 4,600 km (2,858 miles).

Construction

Construction of the **USS Lafayette** began in 1963, before the first 'Ethan Allen'-class vessel had been completed. Between 1963 and 1967, a total of 31 'Lafayette'-class boats

were constructed. All of the vessels were fitted with Polaris missiles, originally the Polaris A2 with a range of 2,800 km (1,740 miles). However, in 1968, the **USS James Monroe** became the first submarine to receive the longer-range Polaris A3. Another four boats were planned, although they were never constructed. Between 1970 and 1978, all of the vessels were converted to deploy the Poseidon SLBM system. Later on, between 1978 and 1983, 12 of these boats

were converted to deploy the Trident C4 system. The first of these Trident vessels, the **USS Francis Scott Key**, began its maiden patrol on 20 October 1979.

Although the Lafayette-class began its life deploying the Polaris missile, it was converted to take the Poseidon, for which the class had originally been designed. The Lafayette-class earned its place in Cold War history as the first SLBM to be fitted with Multiple Independently-targetted Re-entry Vehicles (MIRVs). Each MIRV contained a single 50-kT warhead. However, Poseidon proved to be a troubled system,

being unreliable and prone to mechanical failure. Nevertheless, it set the standard and the ensuing Trident series still equips the US Navy SSBN fleet today.

Technically speaking, the 'Lafayette' class was divided into three separate classes, each group having only minor differences. The original 'Lafayette' class consisted of nine vessels; the modified **'James Madison' class** comprised 10 boats; and the **'Benjamin Franklin' class** was the largest, with 12 submarines. One vessel in the 'James Madison' class, the **USS Daniel Boone**, was the first ever fleet SSBN to visit Hawaii.

Modernization

The 'Lafayette' class and its Poseidon missile system would eventually succumb to modernization as the US Navy's 'Ohio' class came on stream deploying the Trident missile. The 'Lafayette' class would be an important platform for the Trident, with the USS *Daniel Boone* being the first boat to be converted to carry the Trident.

This submarine is pictured preparing to dive. One of the strengths of nuclear-powered boats is the length of time for which they can remain submerged on patrol.

SPECIFICATION	
'Lafayette' class	**Missiles:** first eight vessels fitted
Displacement: 7250 tons standard	with Polaris A2 missiles, next 23
surfaced; 8250 tons dived	with Polaris A3 missiles, five
Dimensions: length 129.5 m	vessels rearmed with Polaris A3
(424 ft 11 in); beam 10.1 m	during 1968–70, vessels of class
(33 ft); draught 9.6 m (31 ft 6 in)	subsequently converted to carry
Machinery: one pressurized-water	Poseidon C3 in 16 tubes, from
cooled Westinghouse S5W	1978-82 12 vessels fitted with
reactor; two geared turbines	Trident I/C4 missiles
developing 11,186 kW (15,000	**Electronics:** Mk 113 Mod 9
shp)	torpedo fire control system,
Speed: 20 kts surfaced;	WSC-3 satellite communication
approximately 30 kts dived	transceiver, Mk 2 Mod 4 Ship's
Torpedo tubes: four 21-in (533-mm)	Inertial Navigation System (SINS)
Mk 65 (bow)	**Complement:** 140

'George Washington' class First-generation SSBN

On 28 June 1960, the **USS George Washington**, first of the eventually five-strong **'George Washington' class**, made the world's first successful test launch of a ballistic missile from a submerged submarine. The vessel launched two Polaris missiles, the second two hours after the first, while cruising off Cape Canaveral, Florida. Since the practicality of submerged launches was demonstrated, the SSBN (nuclear-powered ballistic missile submarine) has been a key element in the concept and practice of nuclear deterrence. It is the proud boast of the SSBN fleets of the US Navy and Royal Navy that there were no fully confirmed detections of their boats by any potential enemy in some 40 years of operational patrols. The enormous difficulty in detecting and fixing the position of an SSBN means that the US, British, French and Soviet (now Russian) nuclear forces are constantly ready to retaliate against a nuclear strike on their homelands.

'Skipjack'-class SSN

The *George Washington* was actually laid down by Electric Boat of Groton, Connecticut, as the *Scorpion*, a 'Skipjack'-class SSN, but the boat was cut in half during construction to allow the insertion of an an additional 39.64-m (130-ft) section to carry the vertical tubes required for the stowage and launch of 16 Polaris A1 ballistic missiles. These each carried a 600-kT warhead and had a range of 2200 km (1,367 miles). From the 'Skipjack' class the boats inherited the S5W reactor and six bow torpedo tubes, albeit with a reduced number of torpedo reloads.

Launched in June 1959, the *George Washington* sailed on its first operational patrol on 15 November 1960 as a member of Submarine Squadron 14. In 1966 the **Patrick Henry** (built by Electric Boat and launched in April 1960) was modified during a refit to carry the Polaris A3, an improved version of the Polaris A1 to deliver the 200-kT W58 warhead over the significantly greater range of 4,360 km (2,709 miles) and in the process vastly enlarge the ocean areas in which the submarines could patrol but still be within range of their designated targets, and this missile soon became the core of

the missile armament carried by all of the 'George Washington'-class SSBNs.

In 1977 the **USS Abraham Lincoln** (built by Portsmouth Navy Yard and launched in March 1961) became the first SSBN to complete 50 patrols. But by this time newer SSBNs were entering service and the strategic arms limitation talks led to three of the class being converted to attack submarines. The *George Washington*, *Patrick Henry* and **USS Robert E. Lee** (built by Newport News of Norfolk, Virginia) had their Polaris missiles and associated systems (including the control room) removed in 1982, and at that stage were reclassified as SSNs even though they lacked sufficient torpedo stowage and the large bow sonars that would have made them effective in the attack submarine role. It is worth noting, though, that the 'George Washington'-class boats were quieter than the 'Skipjack' boats,

The USS Robert E. Lee is seen November 1960. The volume of the missile compartment added to the 'Skipjack' design is readily apparent.

though because of their greater size somewhat slower. As it was, the Polaris missile tubes were filled with cement ballast, as it had been decided that the boats were too old to warrant modification to carry the newer Poseidon C3 missile.

Final chapter

The *George Washington* was decommissioned in 1985 and scrapped in 1998. The *Robert E. Lee* was scrapped in 1991 and the *Abraham Lincoln* in 1994, while the **USS Theodore Roosevelt** (built by Mare Island Navy Yard and launched in February 1961) was decommissioned in 1981 and scrapped 1995. The *Patrick Henry* was decommissioned in 1984 and scrapped in 1997. Some consideration had been given to revising the boats to carry other weapons (each Polaris missile tube could carry eight cruise missiles, for instance), but nothing came of the plans.

The USS Theodore Roosevelt was the third of the 'George Washington'-class boats to be ordered but the fourth to be launched. This and the last two boats were based at Guam in the Marianas Islands.

SPECIFICATION	
'George Washington' class	**Speed:** 18 kts surfaced and 25 kts dived
Displacement: 5,959 tons surfaced; 6,709 tons dived	**Diving depth:** 180 m (700 ft)
Dimensions: length 116 m (381 ft 8½ in); beam 10.5 m (33 ft); draught 8.1 m (26 ft 8 in)	**Armament:** 16 Polaris A1 (later Polaris A3) submarine-launched ballistic missiles (SLBMs), and six 21-in (533-mm) torpedo tubes
Propulsion: one S5W pressurized water-cooled reactor powering two geared steam turbines delivering 11,185 kW (15,000 shp) to one shaft	**Electronics:** BQS-4 sonar later replaced by BQR-19 sonar
	Complement: 112

'Benjamin Franklin' class SSBN

The 'Benjamin Franklin'-class boat USS Mariano G. Vallejo, equipped with the Trident I C4 SLBMs each with eight re-entry vehicles.

Although actually two classes, the 12 **'Benjamin Franklin'-class** and 19 'Lafayette'-class submarines were very similar in overall appearance and in many physical and operational aspects. The main difference between the two classes was that the boats of the 'Benjamin Franklin' class

were built with quieter machinery outfits than those of the 'Lafayette' class. An additional four boats were proposed for the FY65 shipbuilding programme so that there would be 35 submarines in these two related classes to complete the planned total of 45 SSBNs (including both earlier classes, the 'Ethan Allen' and 'George Washington' classes each of five boats) required for an SSBN force of five squadrons each of nine boats. The additional boats were cancelled by

Secretary of Defense Robert McNamara.

The 'Lafayette'- and 'Benjamin Franklin'-class boats had a small diesel-electric arrangement for stand-by propulsion in the event of problems with the nuclear propulsion system, snort masts, and an auxiliary propeller. The individual submarines that comprised the 'Benjamin Franklin' class were the **USS Benjamin Franklin**, **USS Simon Bolivar**, **USS Kamehameha**, **USS George Bancroft**, **USS Lewis and Clark**, **USS James K. Polk**, **USS George C. Marshall**, **USS Henry L. Stimson**, **USS George Washington Carver**, **USS Francis Scott Key**, **USS Mariano G. Vallejo** and **USS Will Rogers**.

The boats were built by the Electric Boat Division of the General Dynamics Corporation (six boats), Newport News Shipbuilding (four boats), and Mare Island Navy Yard (two boats), and were laid down

between April 1963 and March 1965 for launch between August 1964 and July 1966, and commissioning between October 1965 and April 1967. The boats served with the Atlantic Fleet (from New London, Connecticut; Charleston, South Carolina; King's Bay, Georgia; and Holy Loch, Scotland) until decommissioned (or in two cases converted to SSN/special operations standard with provision for carrying, launching and recovering SEAL commando teams) between July 1992 and January 1999.

Armament

Completed with provision for the Polaris A3 SLBM, the boats were later converted to carry first the altogether more capable Poseidon C3 missile with up to 14 re-entry vehicles (RVs) carrying W68 warheads and then the longer-range Trident C4 missile with up to eight RVs carrying W76 warheads.

The 'Benjamin Franklin'-class SSBN USS Simon Bolivar underway off Hampton Roads, Virginia, at the beginning of the boat's sea trials in October 1965.

SPECIFICATION	
'Benjamin Franklin' class **Displacement:** 7,250 tons surfaced; 8,250 tons dived **Dimensions:** length 129.6 m (425 ft); beam 10.06 m (33 ft); draught 9.6 m (31 ft 6 in) **Propulsion:** one S5W pressurised water-cooled reactor powering two steam turbines delivering 11,185 kW (15,000 shp) to one shaft **Speed:** 28 kts surfaced; 25 kts dived **Diving depth:** 350 m (1,150 ft) operational and 465 m (1,525 ft) maximum	**Armament:** 16 launch tubes for 16 Poseidon C3 or Trident I C4 SLBMs, and four 21-in (533-mm) tubes (all bow) for 12 Mk 48 ASW/anti-ship torpedoes **Electronics:** one BPS-11A or BPS-15 surface search radar, one ESM system, one BQR-7 sonar, one BQR-15 towed-array sonar, one BQR-19 sonar, one BQR-21 sonar, one BQS-4 sonar, and extensive communications and navigation systems **Complement:** 143

The last 12 units built to the 'Lafayette' SSBN design were officially designated as the 'Benjamin Franklin' class because they were completed with quieter propulsion machinery. Six boats were converted to carry the Trident I C4 instead of the Polaris A3 SLBM.

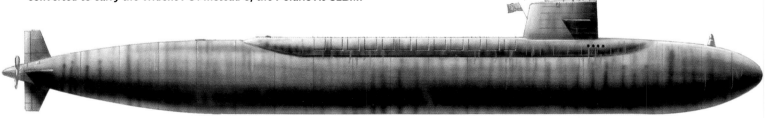

'Ohio' class SSBN

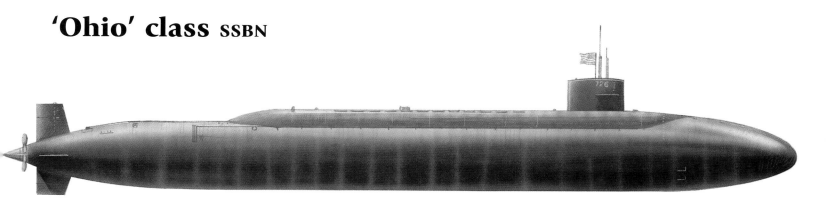

Designed in the early 1970s as successor to the 'Benjamin Franklin' and 'Lafayette' classes in the SSBN role, the lead boat of the **'Ohio' class**, the **USS Ohio**, was contracted to the Electric Boat Division of the General Dynamics Corporation in July 1974. As the result of an unfortunate series of problems both in Washington, DC, and at the shipyard, the lead vessel did not run its first sea trials until June 1981, and was not finally commissioned until November of that year, three years late. Production then improved, and the **USS Louisiana**, the last of these 18 'boomers', was commissioned in September 1997. The Atlantic and Pacific Fleets have 10 and eight boats with the Trident II D5 and Trident I C4 missiles respectively; the latter are being replaced from

1996 with the D5 weapon. The Trident I carries up to eight re-entry vehicles each with one 100-kT W76 warhead delivered over a range of up to some 7780 km (4,835 miles), while the larger Trident II carries up to a maximum of 14 but more typically eight RVs each with one 475-kT W88 warhead delivered to a classified range some hundreds of miles longer than that of the Trident I.

Each submarine carries 24 rather than the earlier standard of 16 SLBMs, is expected to have a 12-month reactor refuelling refit every nine years, and works a patrol period of 70 days followed by 25 days spent alongside a tender or jetty readying for the next patrol. Because of their longer-range Trident missiles, the 'Ohio'-class boats have patrol areas in

The mainstay of the American SSBN fleet, the 'Ohio' class carry the longer-range Trident II D5 SLBM that allows these submarines to operate in patrol zones close to the American coasts, where they can be protected more easily by other submarines, surface vessels and maritime patrol aircraft.

waters either close to the US or in the remoter parts of the world's oceans, making virtually impossible effective ASW measures, the more so as the boats are acoustically extremely quiet. Other than the Ohio and Louisiana, the 'Ohio'

class boats are the **Michigan**, **Florida**, **Georgia**, **Henry M. Jackson**, **Alabama**, **Alaska**, **Nevada**, **Tennessee**, **Pennsylvania**, **West Virginia**, **Kentucky**, **Maryland**, **Nebraska**, **Rhode Island**, **Maine** and **Wyoming**.

Based on the streamlining of a fish, the clean shape and smooth contours of the 'Ohio'-class SSBN produce a boat that is fast. The shape is also designed for highly efficient and quiet cruising while underwater.

SPECIFICATION

'Ohio' class
Displacement: 16,764 tons surfaced; 18,750 tons dived
Dimensions: length 170.69 m (560 ft); beam 12.8 m (42 ft); draught 11.1 m (36 ft 6 in)
Propulsion: one S8G pressurized water-cooled natural-circulation reactor powering two geared steam turbines delivering 44,735 kW (60,000 shp) to one shaft
Speed: 20 kts surfaced; 25 kts dived
Diving depth: 300 m (985 ft) operational and 500 m (1,640 ft) maximum

Armament: 24 launch tubes for 24 Trident I C4 or Trident II D5 SLBMs, and four 21-in (533-mm) tubes (all bow) for Mk 48 anti-ship/ submarines torpedoes
Electronics: one BPS-15 surface search radar, one WLR-8(V) ESM system, one BQQ-6 bow sonar, one BQS-13 active sonar, one BQR-19 navigation sonar, one TB-16 towed-array sonar, and extensive communications and navigation systems
Complement: 155

USS *Ohio*
The ultimate submarine

Submarines are the ultimate deterrent: stealthy, hard to find, and armed with the most destructive weapons man has ever devised. Their existence is a shield that has protected both East and West from the horrors of nuclear war for half a century. Lurking stealthily beneath the surface of the world's oceans, nuclear-powered ballistic missile submarines carry the threat of ultimate destruction, and it is that threat which has made the prospect of nuclear war too frightening to contemplate.

Early theorists felt that the submarine's main target role would be against the battlefleet, but in practice its greatest successes have been against enemy trade, and in denying the enemy control of the sea. However, in a single lifetime its ability to wage strategic war has increased beyond belief.

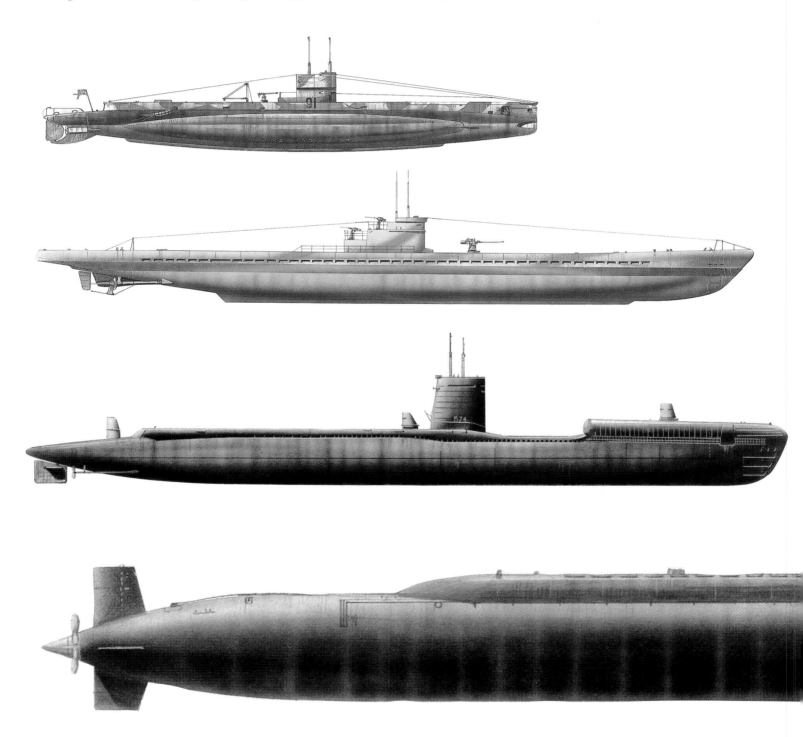

The Trident D-5 is the first submarine-launched intercontinental ballistic missile to be as accurate as its land-based equivalents. Each of its 12 warheads can strike to within 90 m (295 ft 4 in) of a target at ranges in excess of 12000 km (7,456 miles).

E-Class 1914 (opposite, top)

One of the first truly effective submarines fielded by the British Royal Navy, the 'E'-class boats showed just what the new submersible weapon could do when unleashed against economic targets. Under the command of hard-driving young captains like Max Horton and Martin Naismith, they wrought havoc among German trade along the North Sea Coast and in the Baltic, and among Germany's Turkish allies in the Eastern Mediterranean and the Sea of Marmora.

Type IX 1939 (opposite, second down)

In spite of their small numbers, Admiral Karl Doenitz U-Boats were the only weapons in Adolf Hitler's arsenal which had a truly strategic mission. Their purpose was to cut off Britain's vital Atlantic lifeline, and in 1941 and 1942 their wolfpack tactics accounted for millions of tons of Allied shipping. Large ocean-going boats like this Type IX were able to extend the war to as far as the Gulf of Mexico, the Caribbean and the South American coasts. However, Allied countermeasures were eventually to prove more effective, and by 1943 the U-Boat threat had been minimized, if not actually defeated.

Grayback 1958 (opposite, third down)

The advent of nuclear weapons changed the face of warfare. In the 1950s, the US Navy envisaged that supersonic cruise missiles would provide its ships with their primary nuclear capability. Submarines like the USS *Grayback* were completed with hangars for firing two Regelus II missiles, each weighing four tons and with a range of over 1,600 km (1,000 miles). However, boats had to surface to fire, negating the submarine's primary advantage. As long as it is underwater, the submarine is the original stealth machine. Once it surfaces, it becomes a target.

Metres	**5**	**10**	**15**	**20**

Feet	**15**	**30**	**45**	**60**

Ohio 1981 (opposite, bottom)

The advent of Polaris changed the face of the world forever. Now a nuclear-powered submarine could remain on patrol for months at a time, with the ability to attack targets from beyond any possible enemy defences. By launching from underwater, the submarine was as near to invulnerable as any weapon system ever built. A continual process of development saw submarines and missiles getting larger and more destructive; by the time the USS *Ohio* set off on its first patrol in 1981, a single submarine could carry more explosive power than had ever been used in combat history.

Inside the *Ohio*

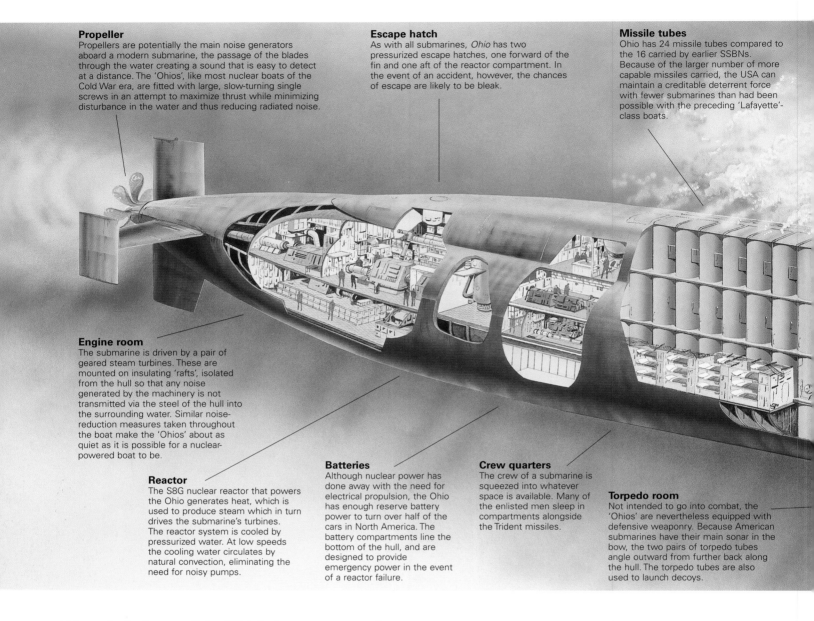

Propeller
Propellers are potentially the main noise generators aboard a modern submarine, the passage of the blades through the water creating a sound that is easy to detect at a distance. The 'Ohios', like most nuclear boats of the Cold War era, are fitted with large, slow-turning single screws in an attempt to maximize thrust while minimizing disturbance in the water and thus reducing radiated noise.

Escape hatch
As with all submarines, *Ohio* has two pressurized escape hatches, one forward of the fin and one aft of the reactor compartment. In the event of an accident, however, the chances of escape are likely to be bleak.

Missile tubes
Ohio has 24 missile tubes compared to the 16 carried by earlier SSBNs. Because of the larger number of more capable missiles carried, the USA can maintain a creditable deterrent force with fewer submarines than had been possible with the preceding 'Lafayette'-class boats.

Engine room
The submarine is driven by a pair of geared steam turbines. These are mounted on insulating 'rafts', isolated from the hull so that any noise generated by the machinery is not transmitted via the steel of the hull into the surrounding water. Similar noise-reduction measures taken throughout the boat make the 'Ohios' about as quiet as it is possible for a nuclear-powered boat to be.

Reactor
The S8G nuclear reactor that powers the Ohio generates heat, which is used to produce steam which in turn drives the submarine's turbines. The reactor system is cooled by pressurized water. At low speeds the cooling water circulates by natural convection, eliminating the need for noisy pumps.

Batteries
Although nuclear power has done away with the need for electrical propulsion, the Ohio has enough reserve battery power to turn over half of the cars in North America. The battery compartments line the bottom of the hull, and are designed to provide emergency power in the event of a reactor failure.

Crew quarters
The crew of a submarine is squeezed into whatever space is available. Many of the enlisted men sleep in compartments alongside the Trident missiles.

Torpedo room
Not intended to go into combat, the 'Ohios' are nevertheless equipped with defensive weaponry. Because American submarines have their main sonar in the bow, the two pairs of torpedo tubes angle outward from further back along the hull. The torpedo tubes are also used to launch decoys.

Although the boats of the 'Ohio'-class are among the largest submarines ever built – only the massive Russian 'Typhoons' are larger – there is no wasted space aboard. The missile compartment, with its 24 launch tubes for the 60-tonne missiles, takes up almost half the available volume. By the time a reactor system and a propulsion system have been fitted, together with a comprehensive sonar suite, an incredible amount of advanced electronics and defensive weaponry, there is not much room for crew and supplies, and they are squeezed in wherever space can be found. Even though the crew is less than half the size of that found on a comparable surface ship, they are still expected to spend 60 days either at work or in a personal space not much bigger than their bunk, with a tiny locker for their personal kit.

The 18 'Ohio'-class Trident missile boats are now the only SSBNs in US Navy service, replacing more than 40 Polaris- and Poseidon-carrying boats.

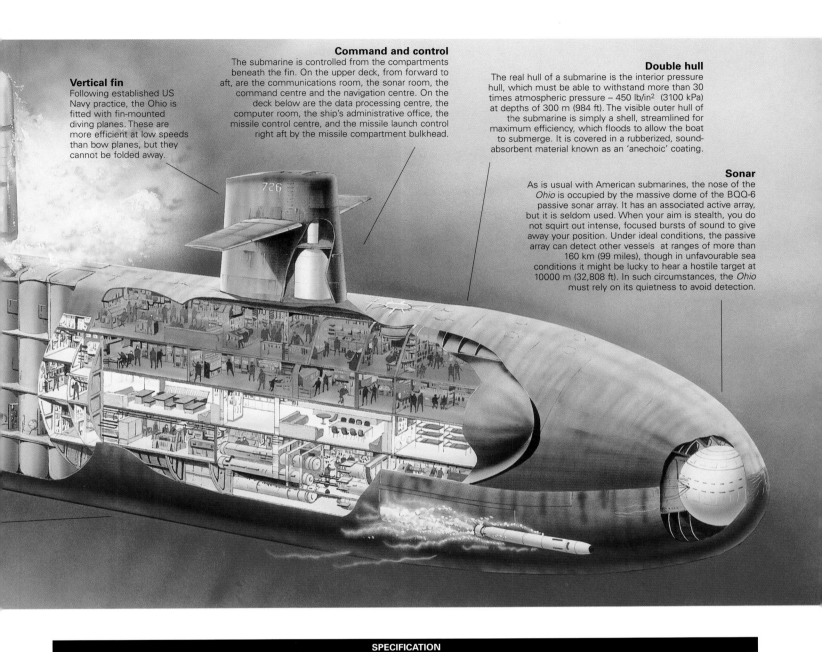

Vertical fin
Following established US Navy practice, the Ohio is fitted with fin-mounted diving planes. These are more efficient at low speeds than bow planes, but they cannot be folded away.

Command and control
The submarine is controlled from the compartments beneath the fin. On the upper deck, from forward to aft, are the communications room, the sonar room, the command centre and the navigation centre. On the deck below are the data processing centre, the computer room, the ship's administrative office, the missile control centre, and the missile launch control right aft by the missile compartment bulkhead.

Double hull
The real hull of a submarine is the interior pressure hull, which must be able to withstand more than 30 times atmospheric pressure – 450 lb/in^2 (3100 kPa) at depths of 300 m (984 ft). The visible outer hull of the submarine is simply a shell, streamlined for maximum efficiency, which floods to allow the boat to submerge. It is covered in a rubberized, sound-absorbent material known as an 'anechoic' coating.

Sonar
As is usual with American submarines, the nose of the Ohio is occupied by the massive dome of the BQQ-6 passive sonar array. It has an associated active array, but it is seldom used. When your aim is stealth, you do not squirt out intense, focused bursts of sound to give away your position. Under ideal conditions, the passive array can detect other vessels at ranges of more than 160 km (99 miles), though in unfavourable sea conditions it might be lucky to hear a hostile target at 10000 m (32,808 ft). In such circumstances, the Ohio must rely on its quietness to avoid detection.

SPECIFICATION

'Ohio'-class SSBN
Builders: General Dynamics Electric Boat Division
Type: nuclear-powered ballistic missile submarine (SSBN)

Dimensions
Length 170.69 m (560 ft); beam 10.06 m (42 ft); draught 11.01 m (36 ft 6 in)

Displacement
16,764 tons surfaced; 18,750 tons submerged

Performance
Speed: 18 kt (33 km/h; 21 mph) surfaced; 20+ kt (37+ km/h; 23 mph) official submerged; actual probably more than 25 kt (46 km/h; 29 mph)
Range: effectively unlimited: primary factor is crew endurance – patrols last up to 90 days, six months supplies carried
Hull: HY-80 steel, outer hull covered in anechoic coating
Operating depth: 'More than 800 feet' admitted to by US Navy; actual depth may be 365.80 m (1,200 ft)

Armament
24 missile tubes for Trident I and II, each missile with up to 12 Mk 4 RVs with 100 kiloton W76 warheads or Mk 5 RVs with variable yield (45–300 kiloton) W88; 4 torpedo tubes to fire Mk 48 or Mk 48 ADCAP torpedoes, MK 57 MOSS torpedo decoy; 8 x launchers for Emerson Mk 2 decoys

Periscopes
One Kollmorgen Type 82, one Kollmorgen Type 152

Electronics
Fire control: CCS Mk 3 combat data system; Mk 98 missile fire control system; Mk 118 digital torpedo fire control system
Radar: BPS-15A surface search/nav
ESM: WLR-8(V)5 intercept; WRL 10 radar warning
Navigation: 2 SINS (Ship's Inertial Navigation System)

Sonar
BQQ-6 bow-mounted passive search with BQS-13 spherical array active search; BQR-15 towed array with BQQ-9 processors BQS-15 high-frequency active/passive BQR-19 high-frequency navigation/under ice

Crew
14/15 officers, 140 enlisted

Units (commissioned)
Ohio (SSBN 726) November 1981; Michigan (SSBN 727) September 1982; Florida (SSBN 728) June 1983; Georgia (SSBN 729) February 1984; Henry M. Jackson (SSBN 730) October 1984; Alabama (SSBN 731) May 1985; Alaska (SSBN 732) January 1986; Nevada (SSBN 733) August 1986; Tennessee (SSBN 734) December 1988; Pennsylvania (SSBN 735) September 1989; West Virginia (SSBN 736) October 1990; Kentucky (SSBN 737) July 1991; Maryland (SSBN 738) June 1992; Nebraska (SSBN 739) July 1993; Rhode Island (SSBN 740) July 1994; Maine (SSBN 741) July 1995; Wyoming (SSBN 742) July 1996; Louisiana (SSBN-743) September 1997

'Han' class
Nuclear anti-ship submarine

China began building its submarine force in the 1950s, basing its boats primarily on Soviet designs. However, with the split between Mao Tse Tung and Khrushchev, developments in the 1960s had to be carried out without outside assistance. China lacked the scientific, engineering or technological resources to match the USSR or Western navies, and development of an indigenous nuclear submarine was protracted.

The first of the **'Type 91'** class attack boats, also known as the **'Han' class**, was laid down in 1967. It was commissioned in 1974, but because of continuing problems with the nuclear reactor **Submarine 401** was probably not truly operational for a decade. Four more boats were commissioned through the 1980s. The last three are several metres longer, and have vertical launch tubes fitted to allow anti-ship missiles to be carried without cutting into the torpedo load.

These boats are rather noisy, even by the standards of the time they were built. Their equipment, based on Soviet designs of the 1950s, was primitive. However, the original Soviet ESM system, as well as the ineffective passive sonar, have been replaced by French equipment, and the last three boats have been given an even more extensive refit.

Anti-ship

The primary function of the Han class appears to be anti-surface-ship: the boats carry a mix of straight-running and homing torpedoes, as well as the C-801 Ying-Ji (Eagle Strike) anti-ship missile. They are too noisy to be effective anti-submarine vessels, but they have the capability to strike at shipping lanes far beyond China's coastal waters.

The next-generation 'Type 93' SSN is intended to replace the 'Hans'. Being built with Russian help, the design is reportedly based on the Soviet Victor III, which would make it the equivalent of one of the US Navy's 'Sturgeon'-class boats of the 1970s and 1980s. But although the first of the class has been under construction at the Huludao ship yard since 1994, the programme has been considerably delayed.

As an interim measure, it is believed that the PLA Navy has been looking into the possibility of leasing or buying an 'Akula' class boat from Russia.

Submarine 404 is a stretched and improved version of the 'Han' class. It serves as part of the North Sea Fleet at Jianggezhuang.

SPECIFICATION	
'Han' class	**Diving depth (estimated):** 200 m
Type: Nuclear-powered attack submarine	(656 ft) normal and 300 m (985 ft) maximum
Displacement: 4,500 tons surfaced and 5,550 tons dived	**Torpedo tubes:** six 533-mm (21-in)
Dimensions: length 98 m (321 ft 6 in); beam 10 m (32 ft 10 in); draught 7.4 m (24 ft 2½ in)	**Basic load:** 18 weapons, usually a mix of homing and straight-running torpedoes, or up to 36 mines
Machinery: one 90-MW pressurized water reactor driving one shaft	**Electronics:** Snoop Tray surface search radar; Trout Cheek medium frequency sonar; DUUX-5 low frequency sonar; Type 921A ESM
Speed: 12 kts surfaced and 25 kts dived	**Complement:** 75

The 'Han' class is a key part of China's expansion plans, which aim to project power out into the Pacific beyond Japan and Taiwan.

'Rubis' class

France's refusal to accept American aid meant that her first nuclear attack boats entered service 20 years after their British equivalents.

In 1964 the French Navy began the design of a 4,000-ton nuclear-powered attack submarine. This was cancelled in 1968, before construction started. A smaller design was then initiated, based on the hull form of the diesel-electric 'Agosta' class and with basically the same fire-control, torpedo-launching and sonar detection systems.

The resulting **'SNA72'** class, built at Cherbourg, is the smallest SSN type in service with any navy, and was made possible by the development of a small 48-megawatt integrated reactor-heat exchanger system driving two turbo-alternators and a main electric motor.

The hull depth was increased compared with the earlier 'Agosta' class, and this has allowed the typical three-deck layout of larger SSNs to be used for the areas forward and immediately aft of the fin. The forward diving planes of the Agostas have been relocated to the fin to improve underwater manoeuvrability.

Service entry

The first boat, the **Rubis**, was laid down at Cherbourg in 1976, and was commissioned in February 1983. It was followed by three further boats, the **Saphir**, the **Casabianca**, and the **Émeraude**, which were commissioned between 1984 and 1987. The French Navy had originally planned for two squadrons of these SSNs, one to be based at Brest to cover the SSBN base, and the other at Toulon. In the event, all of the boats are based at Toulon, together with the two boats of the follow-on **'Améthyste'** class. All, however, operate frequently in the Atlantic.

Although initially a little slower and noisier than contemporary British and American boats, the 'Rubis' class has evolved into a highly effective ASW platform.

Currently the world's smallest front-line SSN, the 'Rubis'-class boats are essentially a heavily-modified version of the conventionally-powered 'Agosta'-class boats.

Originally, the 'Rubis' class were tasked primarily with anti-surface warfare. Endurance, limited primarily by the amount of food which can be carried, is estimated at 45 days.

All of the boats carry versions of the F 17 and L5 torpedoes and, from the middle of the 1980s, have been equipped with the underwater-launched, encapsulated SM.39 Exocet anti-ship missile.

However, in the early 1990s, the 'Rubis'-class submarines were joined by two improved boats, the **Améthyste** and the **Perle**. Built to the same basic design as their predecessors,

---

SPECIFICATION

'Rubis' class
Boats in class: *Rubis* (S601), *Saphir* (S602), *Casabianca* (S603), *Émeraude* (S604), *Améthyste* (S605) and *Perle* (S606)
Type: Nuclear-powered attack submarine
Displacement: 2,385 tons surfaced and 2,670 tons dived
Dimensions: length 72.1 m (236 ft 6½ in); beam 7.6 m (24 ft 11 in); draught 6.4 m (21 ft)
Machinery: one 48-MW pressurized water reactor (PWR) powering two turbo-alternators driving one shaft

Speed: 18 kts surfaced and 25 kts dived
Diving depth: 300 m (985 ft) normal and 500 m (1, 640 ft) max
Torpedo tubes: four 550-mm (21⅝-in), all bow
Basic load: 10 F 17 wire-guided anti-ship and/or L5 mod.3 ASW torpedoes; four SM.39 Exocet missiles; or up to 28 TSM35 10 ground mines
Electronics: one Kelvin-Hughes surface search radar; one DMUX 20 multi-function sonar and one DSUV 62C passive towed array sonar; ARUR 13/DR 3000U ESM system
Complement: 66

but stretched by about two metres, the new boats were designed primarily as anti-submarine platforms. They have a more advanced sonar and electronic fit, and are quieter than the original boats.

Between 1989 and 1995, the early boats underwent the Améthyste modernization programme. Standing for AMElioration Tactique HYdrodynamique Silence Transmission Ecoute, it brings them up to the standard of their successors. A new, even larger class of SSN is currently in development, and is expected to enter service some time after 2010.

'November' class Nuclear-powered anti-shipping submarine

The 14-vessel **Project 627** class of submarine was called the **'November'** class by NATO. They were the first operational Soviet nuclear-powered boats, built from 1958 at Severodvinsk. Contemporary with the American 'Nautilus', 'Seawolf' and 'Skate', they were built primarily for performance rather than stealth.

Armed with nuclear torpedoes, the original task of these boats was to get close enough to American ports to fire their torpedoes into the harbours. However, the role rapidly changed, the primary function of the 'Novembers' for most of their lives being to attack carrier battle groups in the hope of getting a clear shot at the carrier itself.

Noise makers

By modern standards, the 'Novembers' were very noisy, thanks to their hull form, elderly reactor design and the many free flood holes in the casing. Retractable hydroplanes were carried just aft of the bow sonar systems, and two 406-mm (16-in) anti-escort torpedo tubes were fitted aft. The first of the class was the **Leninskiy Komsomol**, also known as **K3**. Becoming operational in July 1958, the *Leninskiy Komsomol* was the first Soviet submarine to reach the North Pole, in July 1962. However, it also suffered two major reactor accidents in the 1960s, accidents that would become typical of the class.

The 'Novembers', along with the related 'Echo'- and 'Hotel'-class missile boats, were a definite radiation hazard to their crews, because of design defects and poor shielding. It is known that several specialist hospitals were set up in the Soviet Union to treat the radiation casualties from these boats, and they acquired the nickname 'widow-makers' amongst Soviet submarine crews.

Four of the submarines were lost to reactor accidents, and there were numerous incidents of machinery breakdown whilst on operational patrol.

Most of the 'Novembers' served with the Northern Fleet, though four of the class were transferred to the Far East in the 1960s. The surviving vessels were decommissioned between 1988 and 1992.

All survivors, except K3, which was preserved as a memorial, remain to this day as radioactive hulks in Russian ports.

SPECIFICATION	
'November' class	(16-in) at stern
Type: Nuclear-powered attack submarine	**Basic load:** maximum of 20 533-mm (21-in) torpedoes; normally a mix of 14 533-mm (21-in) anti-ship or anti-submarine and six 533-mm (21-in) anti-ship 15-kiloton nuclear torpedoes, plus two 406-mm (16-in) anti-ship torpedoes
Displacement: 4,200 tons surfaced and 5,000 tons dived	
Dimensions: length 109.7 m (359 ft 11 in); beam 9.1 m (29 ft 10 in); draught 6.7 m (22 ft)	
Machinery: two liquid metal or pressurized water-cooled reactors powering two steam turbines driving two propellers	**Electronics:** one RLK-101 search radar; one MG-100 Arktika active sonar, one MG-10 Feniks passive sonar, one MG-13 sonar intercept receiver, one Luch mine-detector sonar; VHF/UHF communications and one underwater telephone
Speed: 15 kts surface; 30 kts dived	
Diving depth: 214 m (790 ft) operational and 300 m (980 ft)	
Torpedo tubes: eight 533-mm (21-in) in bow and two 406-mm	**Complement:** 24 officers, 86 men

Above: In April 1970, a 'November'-class boat got into difficulty south west of the British Isles. Crewmen are seen here escaping a fire in the reactor room. They were taken off by a Soviet support ship just before the submarine sank.

The 'November' class lacked the efficient 'teardrop' hull standard on later boats. However, it was quite fast, and nuclear-tipped torpedoes gave it a big punch.

'Echo' class SSGN/SSN

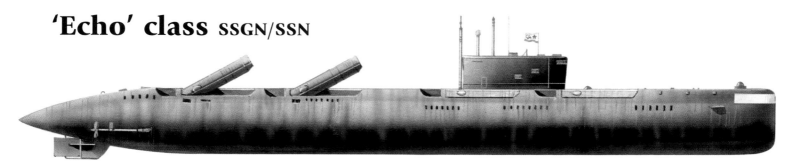

The five **'Echo'-class** SSNs were originally completed at Komsomolsk in the Soviet Far East in 1960–62 as **Project 659** or **'Echo I'-class** SSGNs. Armed with six launchers for the P-5 (SS-N-3c 'Shaddock-B') cruise missile, they had to operate in the strategic rather than ship-attack role, as they lacked the fire-control and guidance radars of the later 'Echo II' class. As the

The forward part of the 'Echo II' sail structure rotated through 180° to expose 'Front Piece' and 'Front Door' missile guidance radar antennae before firing. The holes and hull protuberances made the boats very noisy under water.

SPECIFICATION

'Echo I' class
Displacement: 4,500 tons surfaced; 5,500 tons dived
Dimensions: length 110 m (360 ft 11 in); beam 9.1 m (29 ft 10 in); draught 7.5 m (24 ft 7 in)
Propulsion: one pressurized water-cooled reactor powering two steam turbines delivering 18,640 kW (25,000 shp) to two shafts
Performance: speed 20 kts surfaced and 28 kts dived
Diving depth: 300 m (985 ft) operational and 500 m (1,640 ft) maximum
Torpedo tubes: six 533-mm (21-in)

tubes (bow) and four 406-mm (16-in) tubes (stern) for 20 533-mm torpedoes (16 anti-ship or anti-submarine HE and four anti-ship 15-kT nuclear) and two 406-mm anti-ship torpedoes
Missiles: six P-5 (SS-N-3c 'Shaddock-B') with 1000-kg (2,205-lb) HE or 350-kT nuclear warheads
Electronics: one 'Snoop Tray' surface search radar, one Hercules sonar, one Feniks sonar, one 'Stop Light' ESM system and one underwater telephone
Complement: 75

SPECIFICATION

'Echo II' class
Displacement: 5,000 tons surfaced; 6,000 tons dived
Dimensions: length 115 m (377 ft 4 in); beam 9 m (29 ft 6 in); draught 7.5 m (24 ft 7 in)
Propulsion: one pressurized water-cooled reactor powering two steam turbines delivering 17,900 kW (24,010 shp) to two shafts
Performance: speed 20 kts surfaced and 25 kts dived
Diving depth: as for 'Echo' class
Torpedo tubes: as for 'Echo' class

except only two 406-mm (16-in) stern tubes
Missiles: eight P-6 (SS-N-3a 'Shaddock-A'), four with 1000-kg (2,205-lb) HE and four with 350-kT nuclear warheads or, in 14 converted boats, eight Bazalt (SS-N-12 'Sandbox'), same mix as SS-N-3a
Electronics: 'Snoop Tray' surface search radar, 'Front Door/Front Piece' missile-guidance radars, 'Stop Light' ECM, and Arktika-M, Feniks-M and Herkules sonars
Complement: 90

Soviet SSBN force was built up so the need for these boats diminished, and they were converted to **Project 659T** SSNs between 1969 and 1974. The conversion involved the removal of the 'Shaddock' launchers, the plating over and streamlining of the hull to reduce the underwater noise of the launchers, and modification of the sonar systems to the standard carried by the 'November' class SSNs. All were then deployed with the Pacific Fleet, although **K-45** was badly damaged by fire in 1979 off Okinawa and had to be towed back to its base near Vladivostok for emergency dry-docking. The last two boats were deleted in the early 1990s.

'Echo II' class

The follow-on **Project 675** or **'Echo II' class** was built at Severodvinsk (18 vessels) and Komsomolsk (11 vessels) between 1962 and 1967 as the Soviet Navy's primary anti-carrier missile submarines. They carried

eight P-6 (SS-N-3a 'Shaddock-A') anti-ship cruise missiles mounted in pairs above the pressure hull, and before firing had to surface and elevate the pairs to about 25–30°. The forward section of the sail structure then rotated through 180° to expose the two 'Front' series missile-guidance radars. The paired firing of all eight missiles took some 30 minutes, the submarine then having to remain on the surface until the missile mid-course correction and final target-selection commands had been sent, unless guidance had been passed to a third party such as a Tupolev Tu-95RTs 'Bear-D' fitted with the appropriate system.

From the mid-1970s, 14 of the 'Echo II'-class boats were converted during overhauls to carry the more capable Bazalt (SS-N-12 'Sandbox') anti-ship cruise missile. The conversions could be distinguished by the fitting of bulges to each side of the sail and at the forward end of the missile tubes abreast the bridge.

The 'Echo II' boats were divided evenly between the Pacific and Northern Fleets. The boats were obsolete by the mid-1980s, and were deleted in 1989–94.

Some 29 units of the 'Echo II' SSGN entered service with the Soviet navy with the primary armament of SS-N-12 'Sandbox' or SS-N-3a 'Shaddock-A' missiles. The boats' primary failing was that they had to surface to fire and guide their missiles.

'Charlie' class SSGN

*A 'Charlie I'-class **SSGN** of the sub-class armed with the **SS-N-7** J-band active radar homing anti-ship missile in two banks of four tubes, angled upward on each side of the bow external to the pressure hull.*

SPECIFICATION

'Charlie I' class
Displacement: 4,000 tons surfaced; 4,900 tons dived
Dimensions: length 95 m (311 ft 8 in); beam 10 m (32 ft 10 in); draught 8 m (26 ft 3 in)
Propulsion: one pressurized water-cooled reactor powering two steam turbines delivering 11,185 kW (15,000 shp) to one shaft
Performance: speed 20 kts surfaced and 24 kts dived
Diving depth: 400 m (1,315 ft) operational and 600 m (1,970 ft) maximum
Torpedo tubes: six 533-mm (21-in) tubes (all bow) for a maximum of 12 torpedoes, but normally a mix of four anti-ship or anti-submarine HE torpedoes, two anti-ship 15-kT

nuclear torpedoes, and two Tsakra (SS-N-15 'Starfish') 15-kT anti-submarine missiles, or a total of 24 AMD-1000 ground mines
Missiles: eight P-70 Ametist (SS-N-7 'Starbright') anti-ship missiles (four with 500-kg/1,102-lb HE and four with 200-kT nuclear warheads)
Electronics: one 'Snoop Tray' surface search radar, one 'Shark Teeth' low-frequency bow sonar, one medium-frequency missile and torpedo fire-control sonar, one 'Brick Spit' and one 'Brick Pulp' passive intercept and threat-warning ESM system, one 'Park Lamp' direction-finding antenna, VHF and UHF communications, and one underwater telephone
Complement: 100

The first **Project 670 Skat,** or 'Charlie I'-class SSGN, was launched at the inland shipyard at Gorky in 1967. Over the next five years, a further 10 were completed there, with two banks of four missile tubes angled upward on each side of the bow outside the pressure hull. The tubes had large outer doors and were designed to carry the P-120 Malakhit (SS-N-9 'Siren') medium-range anti-ship missile, but delays in the development of this underwater-launched weapon meant that the boats were completed for the short-range P-70 Ametist (SS-N-7 'Starbright') submerged-launch anti-ship missile, a development of the P-15 Termit (SS-N-2 'Styx') surface-launched missile, for pop-up surprise attack on high-value surface targets such as a carrier.

In 1972–79 six units of the improved **Project 670M Skat-M** or **'Charlie II' class** design were

built at Gorkiy with an 8-m (26-ft 3-in) insertion in the hull forward of the fin for the electronics and the launch systems necessary for targeting and firing the longer-range P-120 Malakhit anti-ship missile.

Mass production

The 'Charlie' classes were conceived for production on a mass-production basis, and it was this that probably prompted the finalization of the design with a single reactor and five-blade main propeller (supplemented by a pair of two-blade propellers for quiet running) instead of the arrangement of two reactors and two propellers that was preferred by the Soviet navy. One consequence of this cost-cutting measure was that the 'Charlie' boats lacked the speed to operate effectively with high-speed surface battle groups.

It was once thought that there

SPECIFICATION

'Charlie II' class
Displacement: 4,300 tons surfaced; 5,100 tons dived
Dimensions: length 103 m (340 ft); beam 10 m (32 ft 10 in); draught 8 m (26 ft 3 in)
Propulsion: one pressurized water-cooled reactor powering two steam turbines delivering 11,185 kW (15,000 shp) to one shaft
Performance: speed probably slightly less than 20 kts surfaced and 24 kts dived
Diving depth: 400 m (1,315 ft) operational and 600 m (1,970 ft) maximum
Torpedo tubes: six 533-mm (21-in) tubes (all bow) for a maximum of 12 torpedoes, but normally a mix

of eight anti-ship or anti-submarine HE torpedoes, two anti-ship 15-kT nuclear torpedoes, and two Tsakra (SS-N-15 'Starfish') 15-kT anti-submarine missiles, or a total of 24 AMD-1000 ground mines
Missiles: eight P-120 Malakhit (SS-N-9 'Siren') anti-ship missiles
Electronics: one 'Snoop Tray' surface search radar, one 'Shark Teeth' low-frequency bow sonar, one medium-frequency missile and torpedo fire-control sonar, one 'Stop Light' ESM system, one 'Park Lamp' direction-finding antenna, VHF and UHF communications, and one underwater telephone
Complement: 98

---

was a 'Charlie III' class to fire a variant of the P-80 Zubr (SS-N-22 'Sunburn') anti-ship missile, but this was not the case. In both the 'Charlie I' and 'Charlie II' classes, the boat had to be reloaded back at port once the missiles had been fired, although the secondary torpedo

armament and sonar systems provided a useful anti-ship and ASW capability. The last boats were retired in 1994. India leased one 'Charlie I' as the **Chakra** between 1988 and 1991, mainly to gain experience in the operation of nuclear-powered submarines.

*A total of 17 'Charlie'-class **SSGN**s were completed in two subclasses between 1967 and about 1981 at the **Gorky** shipyard. Primarily used for surprise 'pop-up' missile attacks on high-value surface targets such as carriers, the 'Charlies' also had a secondary **ASW** capability.*

'Papa' and 'Oscar' class SSGNs

In 1970, the Soviet shipyard at Severodvinsk launched a single **Project 661 Anchar** unit that became known in NATO circles as the **'Papa' class**. This boat was considerably larger and carried two more missile tubes (for the P-120 Mlakhit/SS-N-9 'Siren' anti-ship missile) than the contemporary 'Charlie'-class SSGNs, and it was for many years a puzzle to Western intelligence services.

The answer appeared in 1980 at the same shipyard, however, with the launch of the even larger **Project 949 Granit** or **'Oscar I' class** SSGN. The 'Papa'-class unit had been

conceived from 1958 as the cruise missile-launching predecessor to the titanium-hulled 'Alfa' class high-speed/deep-diving SSN. Its high underwater noise levels contra-indicated series production, so it had then become the prototype for advanced SSGN concepts with a considerably changed powerplant and revised propeller arrangement.

The missile system had been created to test the underwater-launched version of the P-120 for the subsequent 'Charlie II' series of SSGN. The 'Oscar' design introduced more improvements, including two 12-round banks of

underwater-launched P-700 Granit (SS-N-19 'Shipwreck') long-range supersonic anti-ship missile tubes outside the main pressure hull on each side of the fin. In common with other Soviet submarines, the 'Oscars' feature a double hull, comprising an inner pressure hull and an outer hydrodynamic hull. The two 'Oscar I' boats paved the way for 11 of a planned 12 **Project 949A Antei** or **'Oscar II'-class** SSGNs with a hull lengthened by some 10 m (32 ft 10 in) and an enlarged fin. Four serve with the Northern and two with the Pacific Fleets, designated PLARK (*Podvonaya Lodka*

The 'Oscar'-class SSGNs are among the largest submarines in the world, and offer very considerable capabilities at several levels. **Kursk***, the tenth unit of the 'Oscar II' class, was lost with all hands after an internal weapons explosion in August 2000.*

Atomnaya Raketnaya Krylataya, nuclear-powered cruise missile submarine). The two 'Oscar I' boats are laid up, and the remaining four 'Oscar IIs' are awaiting disposal. As with preceding classes, the 'Oscars' were primarily intended to attack US aircraft carrier battle groups.

SPECIFICATION

'Papa' class
Displacement: 5,200 tons surfaced; 7,000 tons dived
Dimensions: length 106.9 m (350 ft 9 in); beam 11.5 m (37 ft 9 in); draught 8 m (26 ft 3 in)
Propulsion: one pressurized water-cooled reactor powering two steam turbines delivering 59,650 kW (80,005 shp) to two shafts
Performance: speed 20 kts surfaced and 42 kts dived
Diving depth: 400 m (1,315 ft) operational and 600 m (1,970 ft) maximum
Torpedo tubes: six 533-mm (21-in), tubes (all bow) for a maximum of 12 torpedoes, but normally a mix of eight anti-ship or anti-submarine HE, two anti-ship 15-kT

nuclear torpedoes and two Tsakra (SS-N-15 'Starfish') 15-kT anti-Stallion' anti-submarine missiles, or a total of 24 AMD-1000 ground mines
Missiles: 10 P-120 Malakhit (SS-N-9 'Siren'), six with 500-kg (1,102-lb HE) and four with 200-kT nuclear warheads
Electronics: one 'Snoop Tray' surface search radar, one Rubin low-frequency bow sonar, one medium-frequency torpedo and missile fire-control sonar, one 'Brick Spit' and one 'Brick Pulp' passive intercept and threat-warning ESM system, VHF/UHF communications, one 'Park Lamp' direction-finding antenna, and one underwater telephone
Complement: 82

SPECIFICATION

'Oscar II' class
Displacement: 13,900 tons surfaced; 18,300 tons dived
Dimensions: length 154 m (505 ft 3 in); beam 18.2 m (59 ft 9 in); draught 9 m (29 ft 6)
Propulsion: two pressurized water-cooled reactors powering two steam turbines delivering 73,070 kW (98,000 shp) to two shafts
Performance: speed 15 kts surfaced and 28 kts dived
Diving depth: 500 m (1,640 ft) operational and 830 m (2,725 ft) maximum
Torpedo tubes: four 533-mm (21-in) and two 650-mm (25.6-in) tubes (all bow) for a maximum of 28 533- and 650-mm weapons including Tsakra (SS-N-15 'Starfish') anti-submarine

missiles with 15-kT nuclear warheads and Vodopad/Veder (SS-N-16 'Stallion') anti-submarine missiles with a 200-kT nuclear warhead or Type 40 anti-submarine torpedo, or 32 ground mines
Missiles: 24 P-700 Granit (SS-N-19 'Shipwreck'), with 750-kg (1,655-lb) HE or 500-kT nuclear warheads
Electronics: one 'Snoop Pair' or 'Snoop Half' surface search radar, one 'Punch Bowl' third-party targeting radar, one 'Shark Gill' active/passive hull-mounted search and attack sonar, one 'Shark Rib' passive flank-array sonar, one 'Mouse Roar' active attack hull sonar, one Pelamida passive towed-array sonar, and one 'Rim Hat' ESM system
Complement: 107

'Victor I', 'Victor II' and 'Victor III' class SSNs
Nuclear attack submarines

The **'Victor I' class** was designated by the Soviets as a PLA (*podvodaya lodka atomnaya*, or nuclear-powered submarine), and together with the contemporary 'Charlie I' SSGN and 'Yankee' SSBN classes formed the second generation of Soviet nuclear submarines. The **Project 671** boats, known to the Soviets as the **'Yersey' class**, were the first Soviet submarines built to the teardrop hull design for high underwater speeds. **K 38**, the first 'Victor,' was completed in 1967 at the Admiralty Shipyard, Leningrad, where the last of 16 units was completed in 1974. The 'Victor Is' were the fastest pressurized-water reactor-powered SSNs afloat, even with the advent of the American 'Los Angeles' class. The enriched uranium-fuelled reactor was of the same type as installed in both the 'Charlie' and 'Yankee' class vessels.

In 1972, the first of the improved **'Victor II' class** was built at the Gorky shipyard, being produced in alternate years to the 'Charlie II' design there. Four were built there, whilst another three were

A Soviet 'Victor I' class SSN in the Malacca Straits during 1974. The personnel seen on the sail structure are sunbathing, a favourite pastime of Soviet sailors in warm climate regions.

constructed at the Admiralty Shipyard in 1975

Initially called the **'Uniform' class** by NATO, the 'Victor II' class is marked by a 6.1-m (20-ft) extension inserted into the hull forward of the sail. This was to make room for the new generation of 65-cm (25-in) heavy torpedoes together with the power equipment to handle them.

Silent Victors

In 1976, the first of the **'Victor III'** units was launched at the Admiralty Shipyard. In 1978, the Komsomolsk yard joined the production team, building two

boats per year after the end of 'Delta I' class production. A total of 26 'Victor III' class boats were built between 1978 and 1992. Given the Soviet designation of

Schuka, the 'Victor IIIs' are unofficially known to the US Navy as the 'Walker' class, since many of the improvements in quieting the boats and in

SPECIFICATION	
'Victor III' class **Displacement:** 5,000 tons surfaced and 7,000 tons dived **Dimensions:** length 107.2 m (351 ft 6 in); beam 10.8 m (35 ft 4 in); draught 7.4 m (24 ft 2 in) **Machinery:** as for 'Victor I' class **Speed:** 18 kts surfaced and 30 kts dived **Diving depth:** as for 'Victor I' class	**Torpedo tubes:** as for 'Victor II' class **Basic load:** as for 'Victor II' class **Missiles:** as for 'Viktor II' plus two Granat (SS-N-21 'Sampson') cruise missiles or two Vodopei (SS-N-16 'Stallion') rocket torpedoes **Electronics:** as for 'Victor II' class plus one Pithon towed sonar **Complement:** 115

SPECIFICATION	
'Victor I' class **Displacement:** 4,100 tons surfaced and 6,085 tons dived **Dimensions:** length 92.5 m (303 ft 5 in); beam 11.7 m (38 ft 5 in); draught 7.3 m (23 ft 11 in) **Machinery:** two VM-4T PW reactors powering one OK-300 steam turbine delivering 22.7 MW 31,000 shp one five-blade propeller. Two two-blade 'creep' props also fitted **Speed:** 12 kts surfaced and 32 kts dived **Diving depth:** 320 m (1,050 ft) operational and 396 m (1,300 ft) maximum **Torpedo tubes:** six 533-mm (21-in), two with 406-mm (16-in) liners, all bow **Basic load:** maximum of 18 533-mm (21-in) torpedoes, but	normally a mixture of eight 533-mm (21-in) anti-ship or anti-submarine, 10 406-mm (16-in) anti-submarine and two 533-mm (21-in) anti-ship 15-kiloton nuclear torpedoes, or a total of 36 AMD-1000 ground mines **Missiles:** two Tsakra (SS-N-15 'Starfish') nuclear anti-submarine 15-kiloton missiles **Electronics:** one MRK-50 Topol surface-search radar, one low-frequency MGK-300 Rubin active/passive bow sonar, one MG-24 Luch mine-detection sonar, one Zhaliv-P passive intercept and threat-warning ESM system, one MG-14 sonar intercept receiver, VHF/UHF communications, and one MG-29 Khost underwater telephone **Complement:** 100

A Soviet 'Victor III' class vessel. The pod on the top of the upper rudder is for a towed sonar array, which was the first such installation on a Soviet submarine. To match the sonar's long range, the class can carry both SS-N-15 and SS-N-16 ASW missiles.

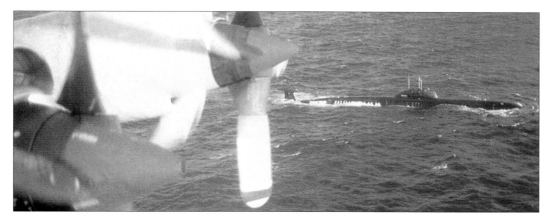

A windfall for Western naval intelligence, this Soviet 'Victor III' class SSN got into difficulties off the North Carolina coast in November 1983. The vessel had to be towed to Cuba for repairs after becoming the most photographed submarine in the Soviet navy.

providing them with more effective sensors were the product of the activities of the Walker spy ring during the 1970s and 1980s.

The 'Victor III's have a 3-m (9 ft 10-in) hull extension forward of the fin and a pod mounted atop the upper rudder, which deployed a brand new towed sonar array. The extension provided the extra volume for the additional electronic equipment required to process the data from the towed array and two new flank arrays.

'Clusterguard' anechoic coatings helped to decrease radiated noise levels as the design was improved, the 'Victor III' class being described officially in US Navy circles as the equivalent to the USS 'Sturgeon' class SSN in quietness. They also have bow hydroplanes that retract into the hull at high underwater speeds or when a boat is on the surface. Like all boats after the 'Hotel' SSBN, 'Echo' SSGN and 'November' SSN classes, the 'Victor' class submarines had two of their 533-mm (21-in)

SPECIFICATION	
'Victor II' class	
Displacement: 4,700 tons surfaced and 7,190 tons dived	**Basic load:** as for 'Victor I' class plus six 650-mm weapons
Dimensions: length 101.8 m (334 ft); beam 10.8 m (35 ft 4 in); draught 7.3 m (23 ft 11 in)	**Missiles:** as for 'Victor I' class **Electronics:** one low-frequency MGK-400 Rubikon active/passive bow sonar; rest as for 'Victor I' class plus one Paravan towed VLF communications buoy and one floating ELF communications antenna for Molniya-671 communication system **Complement:** 110
Machinery: as for 'Victor I' class **Speed:** 12 kts surfaced and 31.7 kts dived **Diving depth:** as for 'Victor I' class **Torpedo tubes:** as for 'Victor I' plus two 650-mm (25.6-in) bow	

tubes fitted with 406-mm (16-in) ASW torpedo liners for self-defence use. Two of these weapons are carried in the place of every 533-mm (21-in)

reload offloaded. Surviving Victor I and II boats had been decommissioned by 1996, together with about a dozen of the first Victor IIIs.

'Akula' class Nuclear-powered attack submarine

The 'Akula' class of nuclear-powered attack submarines was designed to provide the Soviet navy with much enhanced attack submarine capability. Officially designated Shuka-B (pike) by the Russians, it is commonly known in service as the Bars (snow leopard).

The steel-hulled submarines of the **Project 971 Shuka-B** or **'Akula' class** were easier and cheaper to build than the

'Sierras', and are essentially successors to the 'Victor' class. Today, they make up about half of Russia's dwindling fleet of

SPECIFICATION

'Akula' class (Project 971)
Displacement: 7,500 tons surfaced and 9,100 tons submerged
Dimensions: length 111.7 m (366 ft 5½ in); beam 13.5 m (44 ft 3½ in); draught 9.6 m (31 ft 6 in)
Propulsion: one OK-650B pressurised water reactor powering a steam turbine delivering 32,060 kW (43,000 shp) to one shaft
Speed: 20 kts surfaced and 35 kts submerged
Diving depth: 450 m (1,475 ft) maximum
Torpedo tubes: four 650-mm (25.6-in) and four 533-mm (21-in) tubes
Armament: 3M10 (SS-N-21 'Sampson') SLCMs, RPK-6/7 (SS-N-16 'Stallion') rocket-delivered nuclear depth charges/torpedoes,

VA-111 Shkval underwater rockets, 533-mm SET-72, TEST-71M and USET-80 torpedoes, 650-mm Type 65-76 torpedoes, or 42 mines
Electronics: (Russian designations) Chiblis surface search radar, Medvyedista-945 navigation system, Molniya-M satcom; Tsunami, Kiparis, Anis, Sintez and Kora communications, Paravan towed VLF receiver, Vspletsk combat direction system, MGK-503 Skat-3 active/passive sonar, Akula flank-array sonar, Pelamida towed-array sonar, MG-70 mine-detection sonar, Bukhta integrated ESM/ECM system, two MG-74 Korund decoys, MT-70 sonar intercept receiver, and Nikhrom-M IFF
Complement: 62 (25 officers and 26 enlisted)

nuclear-powered attack submarines. The first seven boats (designated in the West as the **'Akula I' class**) were constructed between 1982 and 1990, and are the **Puma**, **Del'fin**, **Kashalot**, **Bars**, **Kit**, **Pantera** and **Narval**. Five more (the **Volk**, **Morzh**, **Leopard**, **Tigr** and **Drakon** built between 1986 and 1995) are classified as the **Project 971U** or **'Improved Akula' class**, while a 13th boat, the **Vepr** of the **Project 971M**

or **'Akula II' class**, was launched in 1995 but is still incomplete at the end of 2002. Three more boats – the **Belgograd**, **Kuguar** and **Nerpa**, launched between 1998 and 2000 as 'Akula II' boats – are also incomplete. At least two more were projected but were not built.

Evolutionary design

The design was approved in the early 1970s but modified in 1978–80 to carry the Granat (SS-N-21 'Sampson') land attack cruise missile. The 'Akula' marks a significant improvement in Soviet submarine design, as it is far quieter than the 'Victor' and earlier SSNs. The use of commercially available Western technology to reduce noise levels played an important role in this, eroding a long-held NATO advantage in the underwater Cold War. Sensors were also much improved, the

use of digital technology enabling them to detect targets at three times the range possible in a 'Victor'.

The 'Akulas' sport a massive tear-drop shaped pod on the after fin: this houses the Skat-3 VLF passive towed array. There is an escape pod built into the fin. The 'Improved Akula' and 'Akula II' boats are fitted with six additional 533-mm (21-in) external torpedo tubes: as these cannot be reloaded from within the pressure hull, it is probable that they are fitted with the Tsakra (SS-N-15 'Starfish') anti-submarine missile. Additionally, the 'Akula II' boats are credited with an increased operational diving depth.

Four 'Akula I' boats were paid off in the late 1990s and are unlikely to return, and the surviving boats are divided between the Northern and Pacific Fleets.

Left: A notable feature of the 'Akula' class design is its highly streamlined shaping, a fact that reduces underwater noise and enhances speed.

Below: The large fairing atop the upper fin of the 'Akula' class submarine carries the sensor array and cable for the Skat-3 'Shark Gill' active/passive towed sonar system.

'Valiant' and 'Churchill' classes
Nuclear-powered attack submarines

Essentially an enlarged 'Dreadnought' design with all-British reactor plant and systems, **HMS Valiant** was ordered in August 1960 as the lead boat of the **'Valiant' class** and completed in July 1966, a year later than planned because of the priority accorded to the British Polaris programme. A sister ship, **HMS Warspite**, was followed by three others built to a modified and quieter-running **'Churchill' class** design as **HMS Churchill**, **HMS Conqueror** and **HMS Courageous**.

All of the submarines were fitted with the Type 2001 long-range active/passive LF sonar mounted in the optimum 'chin' position, although from the late 1970s the five submarines were retrofitted with the Type 2020 set as a replacement during overhauls. They were also retro-fitted with the clip-on Type 2026 towed-array LF sonar. Other sonars identified with the submarines were the Type 2007 long-range passive set and the joint Anglo-Dutch-French Type 2019 PARIS (Passive/Active Range and Intercept Sonar). A Type 197 passive ranging sonar to detect sonar transmissions was also carried. When completed, the submarines each carried a main armament of Mk 8 anti-ship torpedoes dating from before World War II,

Essentially an enlarged version of the 'Dreadnought' class design, HMS Valiant was built at the same time as the Polaris boats with an all-British reactor plant and associated control systems.

the 1950s technology wire-guided Mk 23 ASW torpedo, and World War II Mk 5 ground and Mk 6 moored mines. The armament was later modernized to include, in addition to the Mk 8 anti-ship torpedo, the Mk 24 Tigerfish wire-guided dual-role torpedo, the Sub- Harpoon anti-ship missile, and the new Stonefish and Sea Urchin ground mines. The *Churchill* tested the Sub-Harpoon for the Royal Navy. During the 1982 Falklands War the *Conqueror*, *Courageous* and *Valiant* were deployed to the Maritime Exclusion Zone, the first sinking the Argentine cruiser *General Belgrano* on 2 May 1982. All five submarines were gradually switched to the anti-surface ship role as quieter boats entered

anti-submarine service. The *Valiant*, *Warspite*, *Churchill*, *Conqueror* and *Courageous*

Remaining in service until the mid-1990s, the five 'Valiant'- and 'Churchill'-class vessels were committed to modernization refits as they came in for overhauls during the 1980s.

were decommissioned in 1997, 1993, 1990, 1990 and 1992 respectively.

SPECIFICATION	
'Valiant' and 'Churchill' classes **Displacement:** 4,400 tons surfaced and 4,900 tons submerged **Dimensions:** length 86.9 m (285 ft); beam 10.1 m (33 ft 3 in); draught 8.2 m (27 ft) **Propulsion:** one Rolls-Royce pressurised water-cooled reactor powering two steam turbines driving one shaft **Speed:** 20 kts surfaced and 29 kts dived **Diving depth:** 300 m (985 ft) operational and 500 m (1,640 ft) maximum **Torpedo tubes:** six 21-in (533-mm) bow	**Basic load:** 32 Mk 8 and Mk 24 Tigerfish torpedoes or 64 Mk 5 and Mk 6 mines, later changed to 26 torpedoes and six UGM-84B Sub-Harpoon anti-ship missiles, or Stonefish and Sea Urchin mines **Missiles:** see above **Electronics:** one Type 1006 surface search radar, one Type 2001 sonar, one Type 2026 towed sonar, one Type 2007 sonar, one Type 2019 sonar, one Type 197 sonar, one direction-finding antenna, one ESM system, one DCB torpedo fire-control system, and one underwater telephone **Complement:** 103

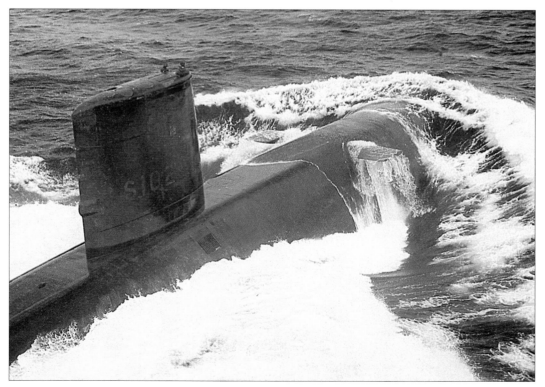

'Swiftsure' class
Nuclear-powered attack submarine

In 1971 the first of the UK's **'Swiftsure' class** of second-generation SSNs was launched at the Vickers shipyard at Barrow-in-Furness. This **HMS Swiftsure** introduced a hull form shorter and fuller than that of the 'Valiant' class in order to provide greater volume and create a stronger pressure hull for operation at greater depths and speeds than the previous

Quieter than their predecessors, the 'Swiftsure'-class submarines proved to be excellent anti-submarine platforms, especially after the original sonar equipment had been upgraded and the Mk 24 Tigerfish heavyweight torpedo added to the armament. Refits have also added upgraded tactical weapons systems, Spearfish torpedoes, improved decoys and Tomahawk missiles. Spartan (below left) can be fitted with a dry deck hangar.

class. The fin is smaller and the retractable diving planes are located below the water line. The *Swiftsure* was followed by five sister ships, **HMS Sovereign**, **HMS Superb**, **HMS Sceptre**, **HMS Spartan** and **HMS Splendid**. The submarines are currently used both in the ASW screening role for task forces, and in the independent anti-ship and ASW roles because of the quieter machinery used. Their sonar fit is basically the same as that of the 'Valiant' class, and all had the Type 2020 fitted as the Type 2001 replacement during normal refits. The armament is reduced by one tube and seven torpedoes, but this reduction is balanced by the fact that it takes only 15 seconds to reload individual tubes. Emergency

power is provided by the same 112-cell electric battery and associated diesel generator and electric motor as fitted in the 'Valiant' and 'Churchill' classes.

In 1976 the *Sovereign* demonstrated the Royal Navy's ability to conduct ASW operations under the ice pack when it undertook a trip to the North Pole, the operational aspects being combined with a successful scientific voyage.

The *Spartan* and *Splendid* were both involved in the Falklands War. At the end of 2002, four of the submarines were still in service with the Royal Navy, the *Swiftsure* having been decommissioned in 1992 after cracks were found in its reactor during a refit. Since 1998 two boats have been armed with Tomahawk cruise missiles.

SPECIFICATION
'Swiftsure' class

Displacement: 4,200 tons surfaced and 4,900 tons submerged
Dimensions: length 82.9 m (272 ft); beam 9.8 m (32 ft 4 in); draught 8.2 m (27 ft)
Propulsion: one pressurized water-cooled reactor powering two steam turbines driving one shaft
Speed: 20 kts surfaced and 30 kts submerged
Diving depth: 400 m (1,315 ft) operational and 600 m (1,970 ft) maximum
Torpedo tubes: five 21-in (533-mm) bow

Basic load: 20 Mk 8 or Mk 24 Tigerfish torpedoes plus five UGM-84B Sub-Harpoon AShMs, or 50 Stonefish and Sea Urchin mines; Tomahawk Block III SLCM since 1998 (*Spartan* and *Splendid* only)
Missiles: see above
Electronics: one Type 1006 surface search radar, one Type 2001 sonar, one Type 2026 towed sonar, one Type 2007 sonar, one Type 2019 sonar, one Type 197 sonar, one ESM system, one DCB torpedo and missile fire-control system, and one underwater telephone
Complement: 97

'Trafalgar' class Nuclear-powered attack submarine

Essentially an improved 'Swiftsure'-class design, the **'Trafalgar' class** constitutes the third generation of British SSNs built at the Vickers shipyard in Barrow-in-Furness. The lead boat, **HMS *Trafalgar***, was launched in 1981 and commissioned into the Royal Navy in March 1983, serving with the 'Swiftsure'-class boats at the Devonport naval base. The class total of seven boats also includes **HMS *Talent*, HMS *Tireless*, HMS *Torbay*, HMS *Trenchant*, HMS *Triumph*** and **HMS *Turbulent***.

Major improvements over the 'Swiftsure' class include features to reduce the underwater radiated noise. These comprise a new reactor system, a pumpjet propulsion system rather than a conventional propeller, and the covering of the pressure hull and outer surfaces with anechoic tiles to give the same type of

protection as afforded by the Soviet 'Clusterguard' coating in reducing noise. The *Trafalgar* was the first boat to be fitted with the Type 2020 sonar, and was used as the development test platform for the system. According to other reports, there has also been a rearrangement of the internal compartments to allow a rationalization and centralization of the operations, sound and ESM/radar rooms. The remaining systems, the armament and the sonars are the same as fitted to the 'Swiftsure'-class boats, although a thermal imaging periscope is now carried as part of the search and attack

*Similar in many respects to the 'Swiftsure' class, HMS **Trafalgar** was the first Royal Navy submarine to be covered with anechoic tiles reducing underwater radiated noise.*

*With the aircraft carrier **HMS** Illustrious in the background, **HMS** **Trafalgar** enters Devonport naval base to tie up at the 2nd Submarine Squadron berth.*

periscope fit, and Type 197 sonar is no longer carried. The fin, like those of the earlier British SSNs, houses an SHF DF antenna, communications antennae, and snort induction, radar and ESM masts. Underwater communications are believed to be conducted via a towed buoy

and/or a floating antenna.

The primary mission of the 'Trafalgar'-class submarines, all of which remain in service with the Royal Navy, is anti-submarine warfare, with anti-surface ship warfare as a secondary role. The boats can launch the Tomahawk Block IIIC cruise missile.

SPECIFICATION	
'Trafalgar' class	**Torpedo tubes:** five 21-in (533-mm) bow
Displacement: 4,800 tons surfaced and 5,300 tons submerged	**Basic load:** 20 Spearfish and Mk 24 Tigerfish torpedoes and five UGM-84B Sub-Harpoon anti-ship missiles, or 50 Stonefish and Sea Urchin mines; Tomahawk SLCM carried from 1999
Dimensions: length 85.4 m (280 ft 3 in); beam 9.8 m (32 ft 4 in); draught 8.2 m (27 ft)	
Propulsion: one Rolls-Royce pressurized water-cooled reactor powering two steam turbines driving one shaft with pumpjet propulsion	**Missiles:** see above
	Electronics: one Type 1007 surface search radar, one Type 2020 sonar, one Type 2026 towed sonar, one Type 2007 sonar, one Type 2019 sonar, one ESM system, and one DCB torpedo and missile fire-control system
Speed: 20 kts surfaced and 29 kts submerged	
Diving depth: 400 m (1,315 ft) operational and 600 m (1,970 ft) maximum	
	Complement: 97

USS *Nautilus*, USS *Seawolf* and 'Skate' class Early SSNs

Seen on initial sea trials, USS Nautilus was the world's first nuclear-powered warship. The S2W reactor delivered 11185 kW (15,000 shp) for a submerged speed of 25 kts. Six bow torpedo tubes were fitted.

The **USS *Nautilus*** was the world's first nuclear-powered submarine. Launched in January 1954, the boat was commissioned only eight months later. In January 1955, *Nautilus* cast off and made the historic signal 'Under way on nuclear power'. Establishing a succession of speed and endurance records, the boat made the first underwater passage to the North Pole in August 1958, travelling 2,945 km (1,830 miles) beneath the ice and establishing the Pole as a new region of strategic importance. Overhauled in 1959, *Nautilus* was assigned to the US 6th Fleet in the Mediterranean, steaming 321,850 km (200,000 miles) during the next six years. *Nautilus* continued to serve alongside subsequent classes of SSN until being decommissioned in 1980.

Launched in 1955 and commissioned two years later, the second nuclear-powered submarine, the **USS *Seawolf*** was generally similar to the *Nautilus* in terms of overall design, but was fitted with a liquid sodium reactor, which did not prove satisfactory, steam leaks occurring shortly after it first went critical in 1956. It was replaced by a pressurized water-cooled reactor during an overhaul of 1958–60. With the 6th Fleet in the early 1960s, *Seawolf* formed part of the first all-nuclear task force, a carrier group built around the CVN USS *Enterprise* and two nuclear-powered cruisers. The boat was transferred to the Atlantic Fleet and then to the Pacific Fleet in 1970. The *Seawolf* was decommissioned in 1987.

'Skate' class

These two 'one-off' designs were followed by the **'Skate' class** of four SSNs (**USS *Skate*, USS *Swordfish*, USS *Sargo* and USS *Seadragon***) launched in 1957–58 and commissioned in 1957–59. These were the first series production SSNs for the US Navy, and utilized certain technologies tested by the *Nautilus* and *Seawolf*. Three of them took part in further exploration missions to the Arctic. The *Skate* sailed for the Pole in March 1959, testing the practicality of operations there during the winter when the ice is at its thickest. The boat travelled nearly 6440 km (4,000 miles) under the ice, surfacing through it 10 times. The *Sargo* made another voyage to these frigid waters 12 months later, carrying new scientific instruments for a sustained exploration of the Arctic basin. *Sargo* covered 17700 km (11,000 miles), 9661 km (6,003 miles) of them below the ice, and

gathered vital information for subsequent operations, including the discovery of very deep water at the western end of the north-west passage. In July 1962, the *Skate* returned to the Pole for a rendezvous with *Seadragon*: the two boats operated in company under the ice and surfaced together at the Pole on 2 August. The 'Skate' class was decommissioned in 1984–89 and all were scrapped in 1995.

Right: A stern view of the USS Sargo, the third of four 'Skate'-class SSNs. The first six US Navy SSNs all retained the long, thin hull and twin propellers of the German Type XII of World War II.

*Below: The **USS** Seawolf was the prototype used for evaluation of the S2G reactor cooled by liquid sodium. The installation was unsuccessful and replaced by an S2Wa pressurized water-cooled reactor (PWR) powering two steam turbines.*

SPECIFICATION	
'Skate' class	turbine delivering 11,185 kW (15,000 shp) to two shafts
Ships in class (launched): *Skate* (1957), *Swordfish* (1957), *Sargo* (1957) and *Seadragon* (1958)	**Speed:** 15.5 kts surfaced; 18 kts dived
Displacement: 2,550 tons surfaced; 2,848 tons dived	**Diving depth:** 244 m (800 ft)
Dimensions: length 102.72 m (337 ft); beam 8.23 m (27 ft); draught 8.53 m (28 ft)	**Torpedo tubes:** six 21-in (533-mm) Mk 59 torpedo tubes (six forward, two aft)
Propulsion: one S5W pressurized water-cooled reactor powering one	**Electronics:** one Mk 88 missile and torpedo fire-control system, one WLR-1 countermeasures system
	Complement: 101

'Skipjack' class SSN

Although built in the late 1950s, the five-strong **'Skipjack' class** of SSNs had a long operational career and, until the advent of the 'Los Angeles' class, were the fastest submarines available to the US Navy. A sixth boat, the **USS Scorpion**, whose original hull was used in the construction of the first American SSBN, the USS *George Washington*, was lost in May 1968 south-west of the Azores while en route from the Mediterranean to Norfolk, Virginia, with all 99 men aboard. The class was notable for being the first to use the S5W reactor design, which was subsequently used in all US nuclear submarine classes up to the 'Glenard P. Lipscomb' class.

The 'Skipjack' class also introduced the classic teardrop hull shape, and as such acted as the model for the British 'Dreadnought' and 'Valiant'/ 'Churchill' classes, the long rearward taper of the hull forcing the designers to dispense with stern torpedo tubes and adopt a single-shaft propulsion arrangement. The diving planes were also relocated to the fin to increase underwater manoeuvrability, a feature which the British did not copy.

All the engine room fittings except the reactor and steam turbines were duplicated to minimize total breakdown possibilities.

In the later parts of their careers, four boats (**USS Skipjack**, **USS Scamp**, **USS Sculpin** and **USS Shark**) served in the Atlantic Fleet and one (**USS Snook**) in the Pacific

*The USS **Shark** is seen at its maximum surfaced speed of 18 kts. With an underwater speed of 30 kts, the 'Skipjack'-class submarines were long considered to be effective front-line boats.*

Fleet. By the mid-1980s, age was catching up with the boats, however, and after the *Snook* had been decommissioned in 1986 following severe damage in a rescue operation, the other boats were decommissioned in 1990–91.

SPECIFICATION	
'Skipjack' class	**Speed:** 18 kts surfaced; 30 kts dived
Ships in class (launched): *Skate* (1958), *Scamp* (1960), *Scorpion* (1959), *Sculpin* (1960), *Shark* (1960) and *Snook* (1960)	**Diving depth:** 300 m (985 ft) operational and 500 m (1,640 ft) maximum
Displacement: 3,075 tons surfaced; 3,515 tons dived	**Torpedo tubes:** six 21-in (533-mm) tubes (all bow) for 24 Mk 48 dual-purpose torpedoes or 48 Mk 57 moored mines
Dimensions: length 76.7 m (251 ft 9 in); beam 9.6 m (31 ft 6 in); draught 8.5 m (27 ft 10 in)	**Electronics:** one surface search radar, one modified BQS-4 sonar suite, one Mk 101 torpedo fire-control system, and one underwater telephone
Propulsion: one Westinghouse S5W pressurized water-cooled reactor powering two steam turbines delivering 11,185 kW (15,000 shp) to one shaft	**Complement:** 114

*Compared with subsequent US nuclear-powered attack submarines, the boats of the 'Skipjack' class were limited in their armament and sonar, having only Mk 48 torpedoes and a modified **BQS**-4 sonar system. No **ASROC ASW** missiles or towed sonar array were carried as the expense of retrofitting them was considered too great.*

USS *Triton*, USS *Halibut* and USS *Tullibee*
Radar picket/SSN, SSGN/SSN and experimental SSN

Laid down in 1958, **USS *Triton*** made the first underwater circumnavigation of the earth on its shakedown cruise in 1960, taking 60 days and 21 hours to do so. (The *Triton*'s sail did break the surface once – to transfer a sick sailor to a surface ship off Uruguay.) The achievement and the speed were both significant,

demonstrating the global reach of nuclear submarines. The *Triton* was conceived as a radar picket, a short-lived concept developed from experience in World War II. With two reactors for an unprecedented speed (achieving over 30 kts on trials), the *Triton* was to operate on the surface, using radar and ESM to detect

enemy air and surface forces well ahead of a US task force. It was even envisaged that the boat could control interceptions by carrierborne fighters. Its role as a command platform complete, *Triton* would then submerge and operate as a conventional submarine. The rapid pace of Soviet submarine construction made ASW the overriding priority, however, and the radar picket concept was abandoned. The *Triton* was reconfigured as an attack submarine in 1962 with four 21-in (533-mm) torpedo tubes. The vessel was the flagship of the Atlantic Fleet's submarine force in 1964–67, but was one of

50 boats to be decommissioned at the end of the 1960s.

Halibut SSGN

The 'one-off' **USS *Halibut*** was the first nuclear-powered submarine designed to launch guided missiles (SSGN) and was launched in 1959. The boat's odd shape was determined by the need to keep the main deck as dry as possible once it had surfaced to fire its five RGM-6 Regulus I cruise missiles. *Halibut* undertook a first test-firing in March 1960, but emerging technology ages quickly and the system was phased out in 1964. The *Halibut* was converted to an attack submarine in 1965–67 and served in the ASW role in the Pacific Fleet until being decommissioned in 1976.

Laid down in 1958, the diminutive **USS *Tullibee*** was commissioned in 1960 for the ASW role, and served as an experimental platform for sonar systems and other ASW equipment and tactics. The boat was the first with turbo-electric nuclear power, and was the world's quietest SSN until the arrival of the 'Glenard P. Lipscomb' class, and the first with bow sonar. As a result of the latter, the four 21-in (533-mm) torpedo tubes were moved back. Extensively overhauled in 1965–68, *Tullibee* served with the 6th Fleet and then returned to the US in 1971 for further evaluation of SSN tactics, and tested PUFFS sonar equipment in a 'shark fin' installation. Highly automated, it operated with a small crew of around 50. The boat alternated between the Mediterranean and the Atlantic for the remainder of its service life before being decommissioned in 1988.

SPECIFICATION	
USS *Halibut* **Displacement:** 3,655 tons surfaced; 5,002 tons dived **Dimensions:** length 106.7 m (350 ft); beam 9 m (29 ft 6 in); draught 6.3 m (20 ft 9 in) **Propulsion:** one S3W pressurized water-cooled reactor power two steam turbines delivering 11185 kW	(15,000 shp) to two shafts **Performance:** speed 15 kts surfaced; 28 kts dived **Armament:** five Regulus I SSMs, and six 21-in (533-mm) Mk 59 torpedo tubes (four bow, two stern) **Diving depth:** 214 m (700 ft) **Complement:** nine officers and 108 enlisted men

The first nuclear submarine designed specifically for the ASW mission, the USS Tullibee had vertical dorsal-like fins fore and aft containing sonar gear.

'Permit' class SSN

The 'Permit' class (USS Permit is seen here) received new sonars and weapon-control systems so that they could operate as first-line units into the 1990s to pave the way for the 'Los Angeles' class.

The first of the SSNs in the US Navy with a deep-diving capability, advanced sonars mounted in the optimum bow position, midships angled torpedo tubes with the SUBROC ASW missile, and a high degree of machinery quieting, the **'Thresher' class** remained an important part of US attack capability until the early 1990s. The lead boat of this class, the **USS Thresher**, was lost with all 129 crew on board during diving trials off the coast of New England on 10 April 1963, midway through the period between 1960 and 1966 in which the 14 boats of

the class were being built by five yards (three each by Portsmouth Navy Yard, New York Shipbuilding, Electric Boat and Ingalls, and two by Mare Island Navy Yard).

The class was then renamed as the **'Permit' class** after the second boat. As a result of the lessons learned from the enquiry following the *Thresher*'s loss, the last three of the class were modified during construction with improved safety features as part of the 'Sub-safe' programme, heavier machinery, the hull lengthened from 84.89 m (278 ft 6 in) to 89.08 m (292 ft 3 in) to

allow the incorporation of the BQQ-5 bow sonar in place of the BQQ-2 system that had been fitted in the earlier boats, and the sail increased in height to 6.1 m (20 ft) from the figures of 4.22 m or 4.57 m (13 ft 10 in or 15 ft) that had been typical of the earlier boats. As such, these three boats were the prototypes for the follow-on 'Sturgeon' class.

Altered design

In addition, the **USS Jack** was built to a different design, with two propellers on one shaft and a

contra-rotating turbine without reduction gear to test a new method of reducing machinery operating noises. This system was unsuccessful, however, and the vessel was refitted with standard machinery. During the boats' normal refit programme, the original Mk 113 torpedo fire-control system and the BQQ-2 sonar suite were replaced by the all-digital Mk 117 FCS and the BQQ-5 sonar suite with clip-on towed sonar array facilities. All the submarines were also later fitted to carry and fire the tube-launched

USS Barb executes a high-speed turn on the surface. Underwater, the submarine would be 'flown' throught the water, using controls similar to those found aboard aircraft, exploiting its maximum manoeuvrability and speed.

SPECIFICATION

'Permit' class
Displacement: 3,750 tons surfaced; 4,311 tons dived, except *Jack* 3,800 tons surfaced; 4,470 tons dived, and *Flasher*, *Greenling* and *Gato* 3,800 tons surfaced; 4,642 tons dived
Dimensions: length 84.89 m (278 ft 6 in) except *Jack* 85.9 m (297 ft 5 in) and *Flasher*, *Greenling* and *Gato* 89.08 m (292 ft 3 in); beam 9.6 m (31 ft 8 in); draught 8.8 m (28 ft 10 in)
Propulsion: one Westinghouse S5W pressurized-water reactor powering two steam turbines delivering 11,185 kW (15,000 shp) to one shaft
Performance: speed 18 kts surfaced and 27 kts dived, except *Jack*, *Flasher*, *Greenling* and *Gato* 18 kts surfaced and 26 kts dived
Diving depth: 400 m (1,315 ft) operational and 600 m (1,970 ft)

maximum
Torpedo tubes: four 21-in (533-mm) Mk 63 amidships with a load initially comprising 17 Mk 48 wire-guided active/passive-homing torpedoes and six UUM-44A SUBROC ASW missiles but later modified to 15 Mk 48 torpedoes, four SUBROC missiles and four UGM-84A/C Harpoon anti-ship missiles; an alternative load was 46 Mk 57 deep water mines, Mk 60 Captor mines or Mk 67 mines
Missiles: initially none, but see above
Electronics: one BPS-11 surface search radar, one BQQ-2 or BQQ-5 sonar suite (the latter with towed array), one Mk 113 or Mk 117 torpedo fire-control system, one WSC-3 satellite communications system, one ESM system, and one underwater telephone
Complement: 122–134

The first US Navy SSN class with a deep-diving capability, advanced sonars, midships torpedo tubes and machinery-quietening systems, the 'Permit' class is epitomized by the USS Plunger off the coast of Hawaii during its first fleet deployment in 1963.

version of the Harpoon anti-ship missile, but no provision was made for the carriage of Tomahawk cruise missiles.

SUBROC was to be replaced by a new stand-off ASW missile in the late 1980s, with the choice of either a nuclear depth bomb or an ASW torpedo as the payload, but this project was cancelled. Eight boats in the 'Permit' Class (**Permit**, **Plunger**, **Barb**, **Pollack**, **Haddo**, **Guardfish**, **Flasher** and **Haddock**) served with the Pacific Fleet and five (**Jack**, **Tinosa**, **Dace**, **Greenling** and **Gato**) served with the Atlantic Fleet. The last of these boats, the *Gato*, was finally withdrawn from US Navy service in 1996.

'Narwhal' class SSN

SPECIFICATION

'Narwhal' class
Displacement: 4,450 tons surfaced; 5,350 tons dived
Dimensions: length 95.9 m (314 ft 8 in); beam 11.6 m (38 ft); draught 7.9 m (25 ft 11 in)
Propulsion: one General Electric S5G pressurized-water reactor powering two steam turbines delivering about 12,675 kW (17,000 shp) to one shaft
Performance: speed 18 kts surfaced and 26 kts dived
Diving depth: 400 m (1,315 ft)

operational and 600 m (1,970 ft) maximum
Torpedo tubes: four 21-in (533-mm) Mk 63 amidships for 17 Mk 48 wire-guided active/passive-homing torpedoes and six SUBROC ASW missiles (later modified to 15 Mk 48 torpedoes, four SUBROC and four Harpoon anti-ship missiles), or 46 Mk 57, Mk 60 or Mk 67 mines; by the late 1980s the load comprised 11 Mk 48 torpedoes, four Harpoon missiles and eight Tomahawk

(TASM) anti-ship cruise missiles
Missiles: initially none, but see above
Electronics: one BPS-11 surface search radar, one BQQ-2 or BQQ-5 sonar suite (the latter with towed array), one Mk 113 or Mk 117 torpedo fire-control system, one WSC-3 satellite communications system, one ESM system, and one underwater telephone
Complement: 120

The **'Narwhal' class** was one of two single-boat classes built as testbeds for major new submarine technology. The **USS Narwhal** was constructed in 1966–67 to evaluate the natural-circulation S5G nuclear reactor plant. This used natural convection rather than several circulator pumps, with their associated electrical and control equipment, for heat transfer operations via the reactor coolant to the steam generators, thus effectively reducing at slow speeds one of the major sources of self-generated radiated machinery noise within ordinary nuclear-

The USS Narwhal was the testbed for the natural-circulation S5G nuclear reactor, which used natural convection rather than circulator pumps for heat transfer to the steam turbines in order to reduce the self-generated noise levels at low speeds. The boat was claimed to be the quietest submarine when introduced.

powered submarines. In all other respects, the boat was similar to the units of the 'Sturgeon' class, and was retrofitted with new electronic equipment and missiles (including Tomahawk cruise and Harpoon anti-ship missiles) in the course of a regular refit. The *Narwhal* operated with the Atlantic Fleet as a operational unit up to 1999.

'Glenard P. Lipscomb' class SSN

In contrast to the USS *Narwhal*, the **USS *Glenard P. Lipscomb*** was laid down in June 1971 and launched in August 1973, again by the Electric Boat Division of the General Dynamics Corporation at Groton in Connecticut, as a considerably larger submarine. The type was the later of the two single-boat SSN types designed and built as testbeds, in this instance for the evaluation under operational conditions of a turbine-electric drive propulsion plant as first pioneered, more than a decade earlier, by the USS *Tullibee*.

This propulsion arrangement eliminated the noisy reduction gear of the steam turbine plant that was otherwise standard in the US Navy's nuclear-powered submarine fleet, and introduced a number of new and quieter machinery systems into the boat. It was confirmed in trials, however, that the inevitable penalty which had to be paid for the system's greater weight and volume (and thus the hull's greater size) was a significant reduction in underwater speed by comparison with that of other US Navy SSN classes of the time.

Ongoing project

The *Glenard P. Lipscomb* was used in an ongoing project designed to allow a realistic at-sea evaluation of noise-reduction techniques as a counter to current and possible anti-submarine measures. Some of the concepts were seen to offer very real

advantages, and some of the quietening techniques that caused no degradation of underwater speed were accordingly worked into the design of the 'Los Angeles' class.

The *Glenard P. Lipscomb* served with the Atlantic Fleet as a fully operational unit until retirement in 1989.

SPECIFICATION	
'Glenard P. Lipscomb' class **Displacement:** 5,800 tons surfaced; 6,840 tons dived **Dimensions:** length 111.3 m (365 ft); beam 9.7 m (31 ft 9 in); draught 9.5 m (31 ft) **Machinery:** one Westinghouse S5Wa pressurized-water reactor powering two steam turbines delivering power to one shaft **Performance:** speed 18 kts surfaced	and 24 kts dived **Diving depth:** 400 m (1,315 ft) operational and 600 m (1,970 ft) maximum **Torpedo tubes:** four 21-in (533-mm) Mk 63 amidships for the same basic load as the *Narwhal* **Missiles:** initially none, but later fitted for Harpoon and Tomahawk **Electronics:** as for *Narwhal* **Complement:** 120

Though quiet at low speeds, the* Glenard P. Lipscomb *had a special propulsion arrangement that demanded the use of an enlarged hull. This meant that underwater speed was adversely affected.

'Sturgeon' class SSN

Essentially an enlarged and improved 'Thresher'/'Permit' design with additional quieting features and electronic systems, the **'Sturgeon' class** of SSNs built between 1965 and 1974 were the largest class of nuclear-powered warships built

anywhere until the advent of the boats of the 'Los Angeles' class. Like the previous class they were intended primarily for ASW, and employed the standard American SSN amidships torpedo battery aft of the fin, with two tubes firing

USS Queenfish (SSN-651) surfaces in the Arctic ice pack at a region of thin ice known as a polynya. Such ASW patrols beneath the ice-cap were vital to search out Soviet nuclear-armed SSBNs.

diagonally outwards from the hull on each side. This allows a larger torpedo handling room than in bow-battery boats, and

facilitates fast access, weapon choice and reloading of the tubes. The last nine of the class were lengthened to accommodate more electronic equipment. What is not widely known, however, is that these were the boats used in one of the most closely guarded and classified naval intelligence programmes of the Cold War. Codenamed 'Holy Stone', the programme was initiated in the late 1960s and involved the use of these submarines in highly specialized intelligence-gathering missions close to the coasts of nations unfriendly towards the

USS Queenfish at its maximum surface speed of 18 kts. During a patrol an SSN rarely surfaces or comes to periscope depth, preferring to remain deep.

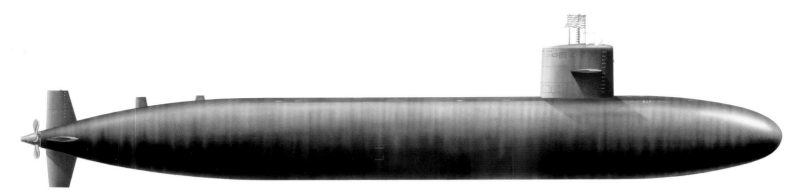

USS Sturgeon (SSN-637). The clean external lines have no unnecessary protuberances that could radiate noise. The 'Sturgeons' were armed with the 10-kT yield SUBROC ASW missiles and any orders to fire this weapon had to be cleared by the President of the United States, as it was considered to be a theatre tactical nuclear weapon.

US. The additional intelligence-gathering equipment was located in special compartments and was operated by National Security Agency personnel specifically carried for the task. During these operations, several collisions with other underwater and surface craft occurred, resulting sometimes in damage to the US boats involved; and on one occasion a 'Holy Stone' submarine was accidentally grounded for several hours during a mission within the territorial waters of the Soviet Far East.

As in the case of the 'Thresher'/'Permit' class, the boats were retrofitted with the Mk 117 FCS and BQQ-5 sonar suite, and both the SubHarpoon and Tomahawk. A total of 22 (including five 'Holy Stone') vessels served in the Atlantic and 15 (including the remaining four 'Holy Stone' vessels) in the Pacific. The **USS Hawkbill**, **USS Pintado** and several others were also converted to carry a DSRV (deep submergence rescue vehicle) aft for launch and recovery underwater during SUBSMASH rescue operations.

US attack submarines, like USS Pogy (SSN-647) were increasingly seen in British waters, as they took mid-patrol rest between voyages at selected ports during their extensive patrol periods.

Of the 22 'Sturgeon'-class SSNs that were operational with the Atlantic Fleet, it is thought that the 'standard' boats were the **USS Sturgeon**, **USS Whale**, **USS Grayling**, **USS Sunfish**, **USS Pargo**, **USS Ray**, **USS Lapon**, **USS Hammerhead,** **USS Sea Devil**, **USS Bergall**, **USS Spadefish**, **USS Seahorse**, **USS Finback**, **USS Flying Fish**, **USS Trepang**, **USS Bluefish** and **USS Billfish**, while the 'Holy Stone' boats were probably the **USS Archerfish**, **USS Silversides**, **USS Batfish**, **USS L. Mendel Rivers** and **USS Richard B. Russell**. The Pacific Fleet's 15 'Sturgeons' were the 'standard' **USS Tautog**, **USS Pogy**, **USS Aspro**, **USS Queenfish**, **USS Puffer**, **USS Sand Lance**, **USS Gurnard**, **USS Guitarro**, **USS Hawkbill**, **USS Pintado** and

USS Drum, and the 'Holy Stone' **USS William H. Bates**, **USS Tunny**, **USS Parche** and **USS Cavalla**. Nuclear power can regenerate onboard air for considerable periods and, with a hull optimized for submerged performance, the 'Sturgeon' did not need to surface for the duration of its patrol. The endurance was really that of the 107-strong crew. At 26 kts, the

submerged speed of a 'Sturgeon' was high because, unlike conventionally-powered boats, it was driven by steam turbines. Steam for these was raised by a boiler heated, via a heat exchanger, from the reactor. The water operated in a closed circuit to minimize loss.

Hull profile

In contrast with the sharply

SPECIFICATION

'Sturgeon' class
Displacement: 4,266 tons surfaced and 4,777 tons dived
Dimensions: length 89 m (292 ft 3 in) except *Archerfish*, *Silversides*, *William H. Bates*, *Batfish*, *Tunny*, *Parche*, *Cavalla*, *L. Mendel Rivers* and *Richard B. Russell* 92.1 m (302 ft 2 in); beam 9.65 m (31 ft 8 in); draught 8.9 m (29 ft 3 in)
Machinery: one Westinghouse S5W pressurized-water reactor powering two steam turbines driving one shaft
Speed: 18 kts surfaced and 26 kts dived
Diving depth: 400 m (1,315 ft) operational and 600 m (1,970 ft) maximum
Armament: four 21-in (533-mm) Mk 63 torpedo tubes amidships; basic

load 17 Mk 48 21-in torpedoes and six SUBROC anti-submarine missiles (later modified to 15 Mk 48 torpedoes, four SUBROC missiles and four Sub-Harpoon anti-ship missiles), or 46 Mk 57, Mk 60 or Mk 67 mines; in the late 1980s a typical load comprised 15 Mk 48 torpedoes, four Sub-Harpoon missiles, and four Tomahawk cruise missiles. SUBROC was phased out in 1990
Electronics: one BPS-15 surface search radar, one BQQ-2 or BQQ-5 sonar suite (the latter with towed array), one Mk 113 or Mk 117 torpedo fire-control system, one ESM suite, one WSC-3 satellite communication system, one underwater telephone
Complement: 121–134

Above: USS Ray (SSN-653) carried a BQR-7 passive bow conformal sonar array (effective at 30-100 nm against a snorkling submarine, and 10-50 nm against a cavitating target), and a BQS-6 active spherical bow array that could operate in bottom-bounce and convergence-zone modes near to the coasts of Cold War rivals for intelligence gathering operations.

Above: USS Silversides (SSN-679), one of the nine 'Holy Stone' special intelligence-gathering submarines in the US Navy that operated near to the coasts of countries 'unfriendly' towards the US.

tapered 'high speed' hulls of earlier classes, the 'Sturgeons' had a long, low freeboard over a parallel midbody that offered more internal volume. The external hull was smooth and featureless, with no unnecessary protuberances that could cavitate and cause noise. The single, large-diameter propeller turned on a centreline shaft abaft the cruciform rudder and after hydroplane assembly. The boats' great speed was used sparingly, for to be fast is to be noisy.

For the greater part of a patrol, a 'Sturgeon' would progress at 'loiter' speeds, not only to reduce the chances of detection but also to decrease the interference to its own sensors caused by water and hull noise. These can be passive, active or dual function. Active sets were not used indiscriminately, being equivalent to a beacon that advertizes a boat's presence and

USS *Sturgeon*					
1 Propeller	**13** Under-ice navigation sonar	**21** Reactor room, lower level	**33** Galley	**46** Ballast tanks	**51** Diesel generating room
2 Navigation light	**14** Aft hatch	**22** Boiler	**34** Mess room	**47** Inner hull easing	**52** Sonar sphere
3 Upper rudder	**15** Auxiliary machinery upper level no. 1	**23** Bulkheads	**35** Leisure room	**48** Fore escape/access hatch	**53** Sail (conning tower)
4 Starboard diving plane	**16** Auxiliary machinery lower level no. 2	**24** Nuclear reactor	**36** Sonar equipment	**49** Machine room	**54** Sail plane
5 Lower rudder	**17** Auxiliary machinery lower level no. 3 (generators etc)	**25** Stores	**37** Crew quarters	**50** Escape capsule	**55** Sail decks
6 Shaft		**26** Air-conditioning plant	**38** Wardroom		**56** Bridge
7 Turbine	**18** Tunnel through reactor area	**27** Radio room	**39** Auxiliary machine room (generators etc)		**57** BPS-15 search radar
8 Steam pipe	**19** Reactor room, upper level	**28** Hatch	**40** Passage		**58** Periscopes
9 Condenser	**20** Reactor deck	**29** Sonar operating room	**41** Laundry		**59** Snorkel
10 Upper engine room		**30** Control room and attack centre	**42** Torpedo room		**60** ECM mast
11 Lower engine room		**31** Access to sail (conning tower)	**43** Torpedo control area		**61** WSC-3 satellite receive
12 Engine control area		**32** Frozen food store	**44** Pump room		**62** Radio aerial
			45 Battery compartment		

so invites a homing weapon.

American designers take the view that the sonars are important enough to occupy prime siting. For this reason, the torpedo tubes of the 'Sturgeon' were not right forward but amidships, releasing the bow position for the enormous AN/BQS-6 sonar, an active set with the many individual transducers built into a 4.5-m (15-ft) diameter sphere. For surveillance purposes, an AN/BQR-7 passive sonar was used.

The 'teeth' of the 'Sturgeon' were the weapons launched from the four amidships tubes. Dependent upon target, these could be full-sized Mk 48 torpedoes with wire guidance, homing and considerable intelligence for use against submarine or surface targets out to a claimed 50 km (31 miles), encapsulated Harpoon missiles for 'pop-up' tactics against surface targets, or nuclear-tipped SUBROC missiles for countering high-value submerged targets at long range or mines.

'Los Angeles' class SSN

Comprising the largest number of nuclear-powered vessels built to one design, the **'Los Angeles' class** couples the speed advantage of the 'Skipjack' class with the sonar and weapons capability of the 'Permit' and 'Sturgeon' classes. The increase in size is mainly the result of doubling the installed power available by the fitting of a new reactor design, the S6G pressurized-water reactor based on the D2G reactor fitted in the nuclear-powered cruisers of the 'Bainbridge' and 'Truxtun' classes. Reactor refuelling takes place every 10 years. The boats originally carried the BQQ-5 passive/active search and attack sonar system. From the **USS San Juan (SSN-751)** onward, the BSY-1 system was fitted. The **USS Augusta** and the **USS Cheyenne** were both fitted with a BQG-5D wide-aperture flank array. All boats have the BQS-15 active close-range high-frequency sonar for ice detection. Other sensors include a MIDAS (Mine and Ice Detection Avoidance System) first fitted in the *San Juan*, and all the boats from this onward were fitted with sound-reducing tiles and hydroplanes relocated from the fin to the forward part of the hull.

Soviet 'Victor'?

Thanks to its electronic systems, the class has proved to be an exceptionally good ASW platform although, on one occasion on the first out-of-area 'Alpha I' deployment, a Soviet 'Victor' was easily able to outrun a trailing 'Los Angeles'-class boat off Iceland just by using its superior underwater speed.

Against more conventional Soviet-designed nuclear-powered boats, the success rate of detection and tracking is high. The advanced BQQ-5 system on one occasion acquired and held contact with two Soviet 'Victor'-class SSNs for an extended time.

The class features a potent weapons array, including the Tomahawk Tactical Land Attack Missile (TLAM) ranging 900–1,700 km (559–1,056 miles). Current versions of the missile are the TLAM-C, which can carry a single 454-kg (1,000-lb) warhead, and the TLAM-D, which carries a submunition payload to 900 km. The standard unitary HE warhead can be replaced by a 318-kg (692-lb) shaped-charge warhead. To overcome the problem of limited weapons stowage, all boats from the **USS Providence (SSN-719)** onward are fitted with a vertical launch system in which the launch tubes for the TLAMs are placed outside the pressure hull behind the sonar array. The Tomahawk is nuclear-capable, but such weapons are not now deployed routinely.

Furthermore, the boats can also carry the 21-in (533-m) Mk 48 active/passive homing torpedo with a wire-guidance

The USS Birmingham (SSN-695) shows off an emergency surfacing drill during its sea trials. Note the large volumes of water pouring from the fin and the early fin-mounted diving planes. A normal surfacing is achieved gradually by selective blowing of ballast tanks. This boat was withdrawn in 1999.

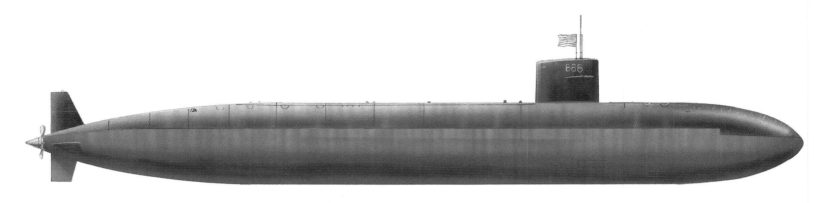

'Los Angeles' class
Displacement: 6,082 tons surfaced; 6,927 tons dived
Dimensions: length 110.34 m (362 ft); beam 10.06 m (33 ft); draught 9.75 m (32 ft)
Propulsion: one S6G pressurized water-cooled reactor powering two steam turbines delivering 26,095 kW (35,000 shp) to one shaft
Speed: 18 kts surfaced; 32 kts dived
Diving depth: 450 m (1,475 ft) operational and 750 m (2,460 ft)

maximum
Torpedo tubes: four 21-in (533-mm) tubes amidships for 26 weapons including Mk 48 torpedoes, Sub-Harpoon and Tomahawk missiles, plus (from SSN-719) 12 external tubes for Tomahawk SLCMs (TLAM-C and TLAM-D now carried)
Electronics: one BPS-15 surface search radar, one BQQ-5 or BSY-1 passive/active search and attack low-frequency sonar, DY-1/BQS-15 sonar array, TB-18 passive towed array and MIDAS
Complement: 133

Above: With a total of 51 boats still in service out of a total of 62 hulls completed, the 'Los Angeles' design is the most numerous nuclear-powered warship class, as well as being the second most expensive SSN type after the new 'Seawolf' class.

Right: Full steam ahead on the USS City of Corpus Christi as it heads towards the Colombian city of Cartagena. The boat's commander is seen on the right and is flanked by a navigator and an observer.

option. This guidance is suitable for ranges up to 50 km (31 miles) or 38 km (23 miles) in the active or passive modes respectively. The torpedo has a 267-kg (588-lb) warhead, and 26 Mk 48 weapons can be carried by a 'Los Angeles'-class boat, though another load is 14 torpedoes and 12 tube-launched TLAMs. These are fired out of

four tubes placed amidships in the vessel. The 'Los Angeles' class has participated in operations in Iraq, Kosovo and Afghanistan. The boats have also continued their under-ice operations, and in mid-2001, the **USS Scranton (SSN-756)** surfaced through the Arctic ice cap. Eleven of the class have been retired.

'Seawolf' class SSN

The boats of the **'Seawolf' class** are the most advanced but also the most expensive hunter-killer submarines in the world. The first completely new American submarine design for some 30 years, the **USS Seawolf** was laid down in 1989 as the lead boat in a class of 12. The cost of the 'Seawolf' class in 1991 was estimated at $33.6 billion (25 per cent of the naval construction budget), making it the most expensive

naval building programme ever. At that time the US Navy planned an additional 17 boats. Then the 'peace dividend' resulting from the collapse of the USSR and the end of the Cold War caused US politicians to question the need for more ultra-quiet boats, the class was capped at three units, and the replacement for the 51 current 'Los Angeles'-class boats will be a much cheaper design.

The 'Seawolf' class was

intended to restore the technological edge which the US Navy had enjoyed over the Soviets from 1945 until the mid-1980s, when espionage and the cynical trading practices of some US allies eroded it. The new boats were designed to operate at greater depths than

existing US submarines and to operate under the polar ice cap. New welding materials have been used to join the hull subsections and the 'Seawolf' class are the first attack submarines to use HY-100 steel rather than the HY-80 used for previous boats. (HY-100 was

The US Navy's 'Seawolf' class is the most expensive submarine design: the research costs for the pressurized water reactor alone are thought to have cost in excess of $1 billion. Retractable bow planes improve surfacing capabilities through thick polar ice.

SPECIFICATION	
'Seawolf' class	**Diving depth:** 487 m (1,600 ft)
Displacement: 8,080 tons surfaced; 9,142 tons dived	**Armament:** eight 26-in (660-mm) torpedo tubes with up to 50 Tomahawk cruise missiles; Mk 48 ADCAP torpedoes or 100 mines
Dimensions: length 107.6 m (353 ft); beam 12.9 m (42 ft 4 in); draught 10.7 m (35 ft)	**Electronics:** one BPS-16 navigation radar, one BQQ-5D sonar suite with bow spherical active/passive array, TB-16 and TB-29 surveillance and tactical towed sonar arrays, and BQS-24 active close-range detection sonar
Propulsion: one S6W pressurized water-cooled reactor powering steam turbines delivering 38,770 kW (52,000 shp) to one pumpjet propulsor	
Speed: 18 kts surfaced; 35 kts dived	**Complement:** 134

used in experimental deep-diving submarines during the 1960s.) The most important advantage of the 'Seawolf' class design is its exceptional quietness even at high tactical speeds. Whereas most submarines need to keep their speed down to as little as 5 kts to avoid detection by passive sonar arrays, the 'Seawolf' class are credited with being able to cruise at 20 kts and still be impossible to locate.

Sound of silence

The US Navy describes the 'Seawolf' as 10 times as quiet as an improved 'Los Angeles' and 70 times as quiet as the original 'Los Angeles' boat: a

'Seawolf' at 25 kts makes less noise than a 'Los Angeles' tied up alongside the pier! However, during their construction and subsequent trials, several problems were experienced on the *Seawolf* after acoustic panels kept falling off the boat.

Equipment

With eight torpedo tubes in a double-decked torpedo room, the 'Seawolf' class are capable of dealing with multiple targets simultaneously. Now that the original targets are rusting at anchor in Murmansk and Vladivostok, it is the 'Seawolf's ability to make a stealthy approach to enemy coasts that makes it so valuable.

The last unit, the **USS *Jimmy Carter***, which was commissioned in December 2001, incorporates a dry deck shelter, for which its hull was lengthened by 30.5 m (100 ft).

The dry deck hangar is an air transportable device that can be fitted piggy-back style to carry swimmer delivery vehicles and combat swimmers. There is a combat swimmer silo too, an internal lock-out chamber that can fit up to eight swimmers and their equipment.

Armament

The class is completed by its second unit, the **USS *Connecticut***, and all three of the boats can carry Tomahawk TLAM cruise missiles. The boats also have eight 26-in (660-mm) torpedo tubes. A complement of 50 torpedoes and missiles can be carried by the boats of the 'Seawolf' class, but an alternative is up to 100 marine mines in place of either the torpedoes or the cruise

missiles. It is thought that in the future the vessels may also be fitted for the carriage, deployment and recovery of Uninhabited Underwater Vehicles (UUVs).

The state of the art electronic system on the boats features a BSY-2 sonar suite with an active or passive sonar array and a wide-aperture passive flank array; TB-16 and TB-29 surveillance and tactical towed arrays are also fitted. The class features a BPS-16 navigation radar and a Raytheon Mk 2 weapons control system. A countermeasures suite includes the WLY-1 advanced torpedo decoy system.

The boats have great manoeuvrability, and additional space was built into the class for improvements in weapons development. Despite their potent weapons load, their ultra-quietness, and their robust electronics fit, the 'Seawolf' class are yet to be deployed in combat.

*The USS **Seawolf**, the first boat in the class, conducts 'Bravo' trials in September 1996. The 'Seawolf' class is arguably the quietest design of submarine constructed.*

'Astute' class Nuclear-powered attack submarine

Ordered by the Ministry of Defence for service with the Royal Navy, the **'Astute'-class** boat is an SSN (nuclear-powered attack submarine). It is of the type designed to replace the service's five 'Swiftsure'-class nuclear-powered attack submarines commissioned in 1974–81, and therefore nearing the end of their operational lives. The Ministry of Defence issued invitations to tender in July 1994 for the construction of an initial three submarines with an option on a further two, and in December 1995 GEC-Marconi (now BAE Systems Marine) was selected as the prime contractor. The initial order was for a first tranche of three submarines, as fixed in the original invitation to tender, but the Ministry of Defence later announced that it was planning a follow-on order for another three submarines. The contract decision for the

second tranche was expected in 2002, but is now likely to be placed in 2004 for the commissioning of the resulting submarines in 2012–14.

The performance specification for the 'Astute'-class submarines is essentially a development of that which characterizes the 'Trafalgar Batch 1'-class boats operated by the 2nd Submarine Squadron from the Royal Navy's base at Devonport. The design requirements included a 50 per cent increase in weapons load and a significant reduction in radiated noise levels. The design matured into what was in effect a development of the fully modernized 'Trafalgar'-class submarine with a longer fin and two Thales (originally Pilkington) Optronics CM010 optronic periscopes, whose masts do not penetrate the hull.

As prime contractor, BAE Systems Marine is building the

The 'Astute'-class SSN is designed to replace the 'Swiftsure'-class submarines, and is notable for its quiet operation, large weapons load and use of a life-long reactor core.

'Astute Batch 1'-class submarines at its facility in Barrow-in-Furness. The first metal was cut late in 1999, and the manufacture of prefabricated components allowed the formal laying down of the first submarine in January 2001. The unit was launched in 2005.

Initial batch of three

The 'Astute Batch 1'-class submarines are to be named HMS **Astute**, **Ambush** and **Artful**, and are scheduled to enter service in 2008, 2009 and 2010 respectively.

The electronic core of the submarines' capabilities is the ACMS (Astute Combat Management System) developed by Alenia Marconi Systems as an improved version of the SMCS (Submarine Command System) in service with all current classes of British submarines. The ACMS receives data from the sonars and other sensors and, employing advanced algorithms and data handling, displays real-time images on the command consoles.

Factory acceptance of the operational software was received in July 2002. Tied into the ACMS is the WHLS (Weapon Handling and Launch

System) created by Strachan and Henshaw.

The 'Astute'-class submarines' major long-range weapon systems, each carrying a high explosive rather than nuclear warhead, are the Raytheon (originally General Dynamics) Tomahawk Block III land-attack cruise missile and the Boeing (originally McDonnell Douglas) Sub-Harpoon anti-ship missile, each launched from the 21-in (533-mm) torpedo tubes. The Tomahawk uses an inertial navigation system with TERCOM (Terrain Contour Mapping) update for accurate long-range navigation, the Block III missile having improvements such as upgraded propulsion, enhanced terminal guidance, and improved navigation through the installation of a GPS receiver. The Sub-Harpoon is a sea-skimming missile with high subsonic cruising speed, a range of more than 80 miles (129 km) and active radar terminal guidance.

Sensor equipment

For the launch of these missiles and also the torpedoes that constitute their primary shorter-range weapons system, the 'Astute'-class submarines have six 21-in (533-mm) torpedo

---

SPECIFICATION	
'Astute' class	
Displacement: 6,500 tons surfaced; 7,200 tons dived	**Armament:** six 21-in (533-mm) tubes (all bow) for 36 Spearfish wire-guided torpedoes, Harpoon anti-ship missiles, Tomahawk land-attack cruise missiles, and mines in proportions dependent on the tactical requirement
Dimensions: length 97 m (318 ft 3 in); beam 10.7 m (35 ft 1 in); draught 10 m (32 ft 10 in)	
Propulsion: one Rolls-Royce PWR 2 nuclear reactor supplying steam to two Alsthom steam turbines delivering not available power to one shaft driving one pump jet propulsor	
	Electronics: one surface search and navigation radar, one ACMS combat data system, one UAP 4 ESM system, and one Type 2076 integrated sonar suite with reelable towed array
Performance: speed 29 kts dived; endurance limited only by consumables	**Crew:** 98 plus 12 spare

tubes, and will be equipped with Spearfish torpedoes with mines as an alternative. There is capacity for a total of 36 torpedoes and missiles. The Spearfish torpedo from BAE Systems is a wire-guided weapon with active/passive homing and a range of 65 km (40.4 miles) at 60 kts while carrying an advanced directed-energy warhead.

The submarines' suite of countermeasures equipment includes the Racal UAP 4 ESM system and decoys, the former using non-penetrating Thales Optronics and McTaggart Scott masts. The Ministry of Defence also has a requirement for a new CESM (Communications-band Electronic Support Measures) system for the 'Astute'-class submarines and also for the 'Trafalgar'-and 'Swiftsure'-class submarines. The system is designed to ensure that all of

the submarines possess a suitably advanced means of intercepting, recognizing, localizing and in general monitoring a wide range of communications signals.

The 'Astute'-class submarines are fitted with I-band navigation radars, but of considerably greater operational importance is the Thales Underwater Systems (formerly Thomson Marconi Sonar) Type 2076 integrated active/passive search and attack sonar suite with bow, intercept, flank and reelable towed arrays. This sonar suite is also being retrofitted on four of the 'Trafalgar'-class submarines. Atlas Hydrographic is providing the DESO 25 high-precision echo sounder, which is able to provide depth measurements down to 10000 m (32,810 ft). The two Thales CM010 optronic masts, with much of the hardware developed by

McTaggart Scott, carry thermal imaging, low-light-level TV and colour CCD (charge-coupled device) TV sensors. Raytheon Systems is providing the submarines' SIFF (Successor Identification, Friend or Foe) transponder system.

Advanced powerplant

The considerable quantities of power needed by these large submarines is provided by the Rolls-Royce PWR 2 nuclear reactor, and propulsion is entrusted to a pair of two Alsthom (originally GEC) turbines driving a single shaft powering a Rolls-Royce pump jet propulsor unit. This last comprises rotor blades turning in a fixed duct to provide 'jet' propulsion. There are also two diesel alternators as well as a single emergency drive motor powering a retractable auxiliary propeller. The digital integrated controls, and the

associated instrumentation system for steering, diving, depth control and overall platform management, are provided by CAE Electronics.

The PWR 2 is a second-generation pressurized water-cooled nuclear reactor developed for the 'Vanguard' class of Trident SLBM submarines. Most current PWRs provide a range equivalent to 20 circumnavigations of the world, but the PWR 2 with Core H offers about twice that capability. In effect, this means that the submarines so fitted will not have to be refuelled during their operational lives. The key sub-elements of the PWR 2 are the reactor pressure vessels from Babcock Energy, the main coolant pumps from GEC and Weir, and the protection and control instrumentation from Siemens Plessey and Thorn Automation.

'Virginia' class Nuclear-powered attack submarine

The US Navy's **'Virginia'-class** nuclear-powered attack submarine, which is also called the **New Attack Submarine**, was conceived as an advanced 'stealthy' type with multi-mission capability for the

completion of deep-ocean service in the anti-submarine role and also for shallow-water service in a whole range of littoral tasks. It may seem odd that this class was designed so soon after that of the 'Seawolf'

class, created as the successor to the 'Los Angeles' class and whose first unit was commissioned in July 1997.

In the oceanic role, the primary weapon of the 'Virginia'-class submarine is the Mk 48 torpedo, of which 26 can be carried.

However, the 'Seawolf' class soon showed itself to be too costly and insufficiently versatile at a time when the USS had

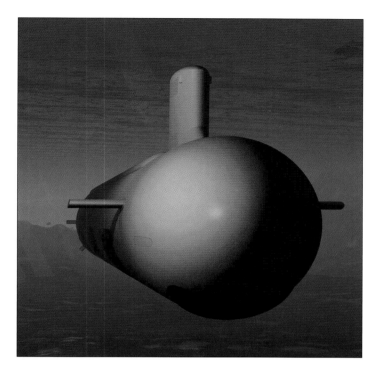

In the littoral role, the 'Virginia'-class boat can be used for the delivery of special forces troopers, of whom 40 (with all their gear) can be embarked in place of the torpedoes.

dissolved into the CIS, removing the grand strategic threat of the Soviet forces and ushering in a new world order demanding cheaper solutions to a range of lower-threat operational tasks. The US Navy therefore wanted a new generation of SSNs smaller than the 'Seawolf' class.

The Electric Boat Division of the General Dynamics Corporation is the lead design authority for the new submarine after it was contracted by the US Department of Defense for the first and third units, namely the **USS** *Virginia* and **USS** *Hawaii*, to be laid down in 1999 and 2001 for commissioning in 2006 and 2008 respectively. Northrop Grumman Newport News are contracted for the

second and fourth units, which are the **USS** *Texas* and **USS** *North Carolina*. They are to be laid down in 2000 and 2002 for commissioning in 2007 and 2009 respectively. The building programme is in fact collaborative, with Electric Boat making the cylindrical central section of the hull, and Newport News the bow and stern sections as well as three modules to be inserted in the central hull; each of the companies makes the reactor plant module for the submarines it completes.

The hull contains structurally integrated enclosures carrying equipment of two standard widths to facilitate the installation, maintenance, repair and upgrade of major systems. The design also includes modular isolated deck structures: the command centre, for example, is fitted as a unit resting on cushioned mounting points. Control is based on computer touch screens, and the steering and diving are controlled by means of a two-axis 'joystick' fitted with four buttons.

The requirement for the 'Virginia' class demanded an acoustic signature no greater than that of the notably quiet 'Seawolf' class, so the 'Virginia' class uses new types of anechoic coatings, isolated deck structures, and a new design of pump jet propulsor.

Command and control

The C³I (Command, Control, Communication and Intelligence) system is the responsibility of a team under the leadership of Lockheed Martin Naval Electronics & Surveillance Systems – Undersea Systems. Based on open system architecture, this integrates the entirety of the submarine's tactical systems (the sensors, countermeasures, navigation and weapons control). Weapons control is the responsibility of a variant of the Raytheon CCS Mk 2 combat system. The launch of weapons is allocated to 12 vertical-launch tubes for Tomahawk submarine-launched cruise missiles and to four 21-in (533-mm) torpedo tubes. The latter are used to fire up to 26 Mk 48 ADCAP Mod 6 wire-guided heavyweight torpedoes and UGM-84 Sub-Harpoon anti-ship missiles. Additionally, Mk 60 CAPTOR mines can also be delivered from the torpedo tubes.

The submarines each carry the Northrop Grumman WLY-1 acoustic countermeasures

system, which provides range and bearing data to the fire-control system, and the Lockheed Martin BLQ-10 mast-mounted ESM system.

For littoral operations, an inbuilt lock-out/lock-in chamber provides a special operations capability. This chamber can also support a mini-submarine such as the Northrop Grumman ASDS (Advanced SEAL Delivery System) for the insertion of special forces teams.

Multi-faceted sonar

The primary sensor for the underwater warfare role is the sonar suite, which includes a version of the BQQ-10 acoustic data processing system and an active/passive bow array, two passive wide-aperture flank array, active high-frequency keel and fin arrays, a TB-16 towed array and a TB-29A thin-line towed array. Surface navigation is enhanced by the provision of a BPS-16 radar. Each of the submarines has a pair of BVS-1 Universal Modular Mast 'photonic' masts, which do not penetrate the hull, rather than traditional optical periscopes. Sensors mounted on the 'photonic' masts include low-light-level TV and thermal imaging cameras as well as a laser rangefinder. The UMM was created by Kollmorgen and Calzoni, an Italian subsidiary.

Developed by Boeing, the LMRS (Long-term Mine Reconnaissance System) comprises two autonomous unmanned underwater vehicles each 6 m (19 ft 8 in) long, one robotic recovery arm at 18 m (59 ft) long, and the relevant support electronics.

The core of the boat's propulsion system is the General Electric S9G pressurized water reactor with a core designed to last as long as the submarine and thereby remove the need for refueling. Steam from the reactor drives a pair of turbines geared to a single shaft powering the pump jet propulsor unit.

SPECIFICATION
'Virginia' class **Displacement:** 7,800 tons dived **Dimensions:** length 114.9 m (377 ft); beam 10.4 m (34 ft); draught 9.3 m (30 ft 6 in) **Propulsion:** one General Electric S9G nuclear reactor supplying steam to two steam turbines delivering 29,825 kW (40,000 shp) to one shaft driving a pump jet propulsor **Performance:** speed 34 kts dived; endurance limited only by consumables **Armament:** four 21-in (533-mm) tubes for 26 Mk 48 ADVCAP Mod 6 wire-guided torpedoes and/or Harpoon anti-ship missiles, or	Mk 67 Mobile and/or Mk 60 CAPTOR mines, and 12 vertical-launch system tubes for 12 Tomahawk land-attack missiles **Electronics:** one BPS-16 navigation radar, one CCSM combat data system, one WLQ-4(V) ESM system, one WLY-1 acoustic countermeasures system, 14 external and one internal countermeasures launchers, and an advanced sonar suite including an active/passive bow array, two passive wide-aperture flank arrays, active keel and fin arrays, and TB-16 and TB-19 towed arrays **Crew:** 134

'Upholder' and 'Victoria' classes Patrol submarines

To meet the requirement for a diesel-electric submarine type to succeed the 'Oberons' in Royal Navy service, Vickers Shipbuilding and Engineering Ltd developed the **Type 2400** or **'Upholder' class**. As in most new submarine classes, the priority was for standardization and automation to reduce manning requirements. The first of the class was ordered in 1983 and completed in June 1990, and another three boats were ordered in 1986 for completion in 1991–93. The original plan was to order 12 such boats, but this scheme was trimmed to 10 and then nine before being curtailed at just four as part of the 'peace dividend' at the end of the Cold War in the early 1990s.

The design also included advanced noise-attenuation features to reduce the radiated noise levels below those of the already quiet 'Oberon' class. There was also a reduction in the short time required to recharge the batteries to ensure a minimum exposure time of any part of the masts above the water. The armament fit includes a new positive discharge and fully automated weapon-handling system to

The 'Upholder' class had only a very short British career, being deemed surplus to requirements in the early 1990s and laid up before being purchased by Canada.

avoid the stability problems at torpedo launch and the limitations that are sometimes made on the platform's speed and manoeuvrability.

HMS **Upholder**, HMS **Unseen**, HMS **Ursula** and HMS **Unicorn** were laid up in 1994, and in 1998 were bought by Canada for service from 2000 as the **'Victoria' class**. These are named HMCS **Chicoutimi**, HMCS **Victoria**, HMCS **Cornerbrook** and HMCS **Windsor** respectively.

SPECIFICATION	
'Victoria' class	**Torpedo tubes:** six 21-in (533-mm) tubes (all bow) for 18 Mk 48 Mod 4 wire-guided active/passive-homing dual-role torpedoes; provision for mines and Sub-Harpoon anti-ship missiles has been removed. Anti-aircraft capability may be added.
Displacement: 2,168 tons surfaced; 2,455 tons dived	
Dimensions: length 70.3 m (230 ft 7 in); beam 7.6 m (25 ft); draught 5.5 m (17 ft 8 in)	
Propulsion: two Paxman Valenta 16SZ diesels delivering 2,700 kW (3,620 shp) and one GEC electric motor delivering 4,025 kW (5,400 shp) to one shaft	**Electronics:** one Type 1007 navigation radar, one Type 2040 passive bow sonar, one Type 2007 passive flank-array sonar, one MUSL passive towed-array sonar, one Librascope fire-control system, one AR 900 ESM system, and two SSE decoy launchers
Performance: speed 12 kts surfaced and 20 kts dived; range 14,805 km (9,200 miles) at 8 kts snorting	
Diving depth: 300 m (985 ft) operational and 500 m (1,640 ft) maximum	**Complement:** up to 53

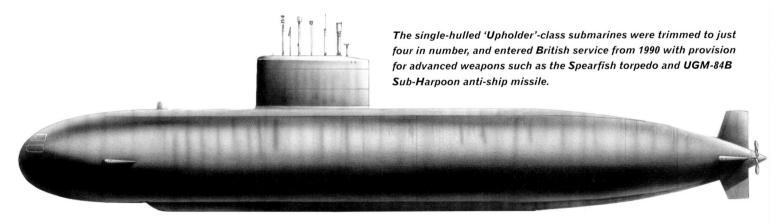

The single-hulled 'Upholder'-class submarines were trimmed to just four in number, and entered British service from 1990 with provision for advanced weapons such as the Spearfish torpedo and UGM-84B Sub-Harpoon anti-ship missile.

'Shishumar' class Patrol submarine

In December 1981, the Indian government reached an agreement with Howaldtswerke-Deutsche Werft, a German organization based in Kiel, for a four-section contract covering four conventional submarines of the Type 1500 variant of the very successful boats of the Type 209 class. The four-part contract covered the construction in Germany of an initial pair of submarines of the **'Shishumar' class**, packages of equipment and components for the building of another two boats by the Mazagon Dock Ltd. of Mumbai (Bombay), the training of specialized design and construction personnel

The Type 1500 is the largest of the sub-classes derived from the basic Type 209 class, and submarines of this very successful and long-lived design are also operated by the navies of Argentina, Brazil, Chile, Colombia, Ecuador, Greece, Indonesia, Peru, South Korea, Turkey and Venezuela.

capabilities in terms of range and speed are 28 km (17.4 miles) at 23 kts and 12 km (7.5 miles) at 35 kts. The fifth and sixth boats were to have been completed with provision for the carriage and firing of anti-ship missiles, but the existing boats lack this facility. They do have, however, provision for the addition of external 'strap-on' carriers.

The *Shishumar* started a mid-life refit in 1999, with the other boats in the 'Shishumar' class following in order of completion. Improvements that may be retrofitted are French Eledone sonar and an Indian action data system.

employed by Mazagon, and the provision of logistical support and consultation services during the manufacture and early service of the boats. In 1984, it was announced that another two boats would be built at Mazagon, giving the Indian navy a total of six 'Shishumar'-class submarines, but this scheme was overtaken in the later part of the decade by changes in the thinking of the Indian navy, and in 1988 it was revealed that the arrangement with Howaldtswerke would end with the completion of the fourth boat.

The decision was reviewed 1992 and 1997, and in 1999 the Indian navy decided to move ahead with its Project 75 for the Indian construction of three submarines of the French 'Scorpène' class design.

The four 'Shishumar' boats are the **Shishumar**, **Shankush**, **Shalki** and **Shankul**. Built in Germany, the first two boats were laid down in May and September 1982 for launching in December and May 1984 and completion in September and November 1986, while the last two boats, built in India, were laid down in June 1984

and September 1989 for launching in September 1989 and March 1992 and completion in February 1992 and May 1994.

The submarines are basically conventional with a single central bulkhead, their most notable operational features being the provision of an IKL-designed escape system. This latter comprises an integrated escape sphere able to accommodate the entire 40-man crew. This sphere can withstand the same pressure as the hull, has its own eight-hour air supply, and is outfitted for short-term survival and communications.

Bow tubes

The eight torpedo tubes are all grouped in the bows, and provision is made for the embarkation of six reload torpedoes. The standard weapon for these tubes is a German torpedo, the AEG SUT, which is a wire-guided weapon

The 'Shishumar'-class boats have given the Indian navy effective operational capability and also invaluable experience in modern submarine thinking.

with active/passive onboard terminal guidance. The weapon carries a 250-kg (551-lb) HE warhead, and its two primary

SPECIFICATION	
'Shishumar' class	**Diving depth:** 260 m (855 ft) operational
Displacement: 1,660 tons surfaced; 1,850 tons dived	**Torpedo tubes:** eight 533-mm (21-in) tubes (all bow) for 14 torpedoes; provision for mines
Dimensions: length 64.4 m (211 ft 2 in); beam 6.5 m (21 ft 4 in); draught 6 m (19 ft 8 in)	**Electronics:** one Calypso surface search radar, one CSU 83 active/passive hull sonar, one
Propulsion: four MTU 12V 493 AZ80 diesels delivering 1,800 kW (2,415 shp) and one Siemens electric motor delivering 3,430 kW (4,600 shp) to one shaft	DUUX 5 passive ranging sonar, Librascope Mk 1 fire-control system, AR 700 or Sea Sentry ESM, and C 303 acoustic decoys
Performance: speed 11 kts surfaced and 22 kts dived; range 14,825 km (9,210 miles) at 8 kts snorting	**Complement:** 40

'Collins' class Patrol submarine

Needing a successor to its obsolescent 'Oberon' class diesel-electric submarines, the Royal Australian Navy decided in the first part of the 1980s to consider the full range of foreign-designed submarines that would meet its operational requirement and also be suitable for construction in an Australian yard. The decision eventually went to a Swedish design, the Type 471 designed by Kockums, and in June 1987 the Australian Submarine Corporation contracted with Kockums for six such submarines, to be built in Adelaide, South Australia, and known in Australian service as the **'Collins'-class**. The contract included an option for another two boats, but this option was not exercised.

Fabrication of the boats' initial assemblies began in June 1989, and the bows and midships sections of the first submarines were produced in Sweden and

shipped to Adelaide to be mated with locally built sections. The boats were laid down between

February 1990 and May 1995, launched between August 1993 and November 2001, and completed between July 1996 and 2003, and are named **HMAS Collins**, **HMAS Farncomb**, **HMAS Waller**, **HMAS Dechaineux**, **HMAS Sheean** and **HMAS Rankin**.

The armament and fire-control/combat system are along American lines, while the sonar is of French and Australian origins. The Boeing/Rockwell combat system proved troublesome during development and initial service, and only after the Raytheon CCS Mk 2 system has been installed will the boats be regarded as fully operational, from about 2007. All but the *Collins*, which was retrofitted, were built with anechoic tiles on their outer surfaces, and the periscopes are British, in the form of the Pilkington (now Thales) Optronics CK43 search and CH93 attack units. The tubes

The RAN's six-strong class of 'Collins' boats are typical of modern submarine design, and may be retrofitted with an air-independent propulsion system (AIPS).

Above: The 'Collins'-class submarines are based at the Royal Australian Navy's Fleet Base West (HMAS Stirling) in Western Australia, with pairs of boats making regular deployments to the east coast.

are all located in the bows, and are designed to fire either the Mk 48 Mod 4 heavyweight torpedo or the UGM-84B Sub-Harpoon underwater-launched anti-ship missile, of which a combined total of 22 can be shipped. An alternative is 44 mines. The Mk 48 Mod 4 is a wire-guided dual-role weapon with active/passive homing, and can carry its 267-kg (590-lb) warhead to a range of 38 km (23.6 miles) at 55 kts or 50 km (31.1 miles) at 40 kts. The tube-launched weapons are discharged by an air turbine pump arrangement.

Great development effort has improved the boats' reliability and quietness. The revision of the boats with a Stirling air-independent propulsion system in a lengthened hull is being considered, and a test rig has been bought from Sweden.

SPECIFICATION	
'Collins' class	**Diving depth:** 300 m (985 ft) operational
Displacement: 3,051 tons surfaced; 3,353 tons dived	**Torpedo tubes:** six 533-mm (21-in) tubes (all bow) for 22 torpedoes or missiles, or 44 mines
Dimensions: length 77.8 m (255 ft 3 in); beam 7.8 m (25 ft 5 in); draught 7 m (23 ft)	**Electronics:** one Type 1007 navigation radar, one Scylla sonar with active/passive bow and passive flank arrays; one Kariwara, Narama or TB 23 passive towed-array sonar; Boeing/Rockwell data system, AR740 ESM, and two SSE decoys
Propulsion: three Hedemora V18B/14 diesels delivering 4,500 kW (6,035 shp) and one Jeumont Schneider electric motor delivering 5,475 kW (7,345 shp) to one shaft	
Performance: speed 10 kts surfaced and 20 kts dived; range 21,325 km (13,250 miles) at 10 kts surfaced	**Complement:** 42

'Dolphin' class Patrol submarine

Left: The three 'Dolphin'-class submarines provide Israel with a capable cruise missile deterrent, interdiction, surveillance and also a swimmer delivery capability.

internal revisions to permit the incorporation of a 'wet and dry' compartment so that underwater swimmers can leave and re-enter the boat. It is also likely that the boats are fitted with the Triten anti-helicopter SAM system.

Weapons fit

Primary anti-ship and anti-submarine armament is the STN Atlas DM2A4 Seehecht wire-guided torpedo carrying a 260-kg (573-lb) warhead to a range of 13,000 m (14,215 yards) in active mode at 35 kts, or to 28,000 m (30,620 yards) in passive mode at 23 kts. Pending the delivery of the complete DM2A4 package from Germany, NT 37E torpedoes are included in the torpedo fit. Tube-laid mines are an alternative to the 16 torpedoes, and other weapons that can be launched are up to five UGM-84C Sub-Harpoon underwater-launched AShMs, or conventionally armed cruise missiles of Israeli design and manufacture. As well as the six 533-mm (21-in) conventional tubes, the boats have four 650-mm (25.6-in) tubes optimized for the launch of swimmer delivery vehicles (SDVs) but with provision for the carriage of liners so that they can also be used as conventional torpedo tubes.

The boats are painted in blue and green for reduced visibility in the shallow water of the East Mediterranean.

SPECIFICATION	
'Dolphin' class **Displacement:** 1,640 tons surfaced; 1,900 tons dived **Dimensions:** length 57.3 m (188 ft); beam 6.8 m (22 ft 4 in); draught 6.2 m (20 ft 4 in) **Propulsion:** three MTU 16V 396 SE 84 diesels delivering 3,165 kW (4,245 shp) and one Siemens electric motor delivering 2,890 kW (3,875 shp) to one shaft **Performance:** speed 11 kts snorting and 20 kts dived; range 14,825 km (9,210 miles) at 8 kts surfaced and	780 km (485 miles) at 8 kts dived **Diving depth:** 350 m (1,150 ft) operational **Torpedo tubes:** six 533-mm (21-in) and four 650-mm (25.6-in) tubes (all bow); for weapons see text **Electronics:** Elta surface search radar, CSU 90 active/passive hull sonar, PRS-3 passive ranging sonar, FAS-3 passive flank-array sonar, ISUS 90-1 torpedo fire-control system, and Tinmex 4CH(V) 2 ESM **Complement:** 30

To replace three elderly Type 206 coastal submarines deleted in 1999–2000, the Israeli navy decided in 1988 to purchase two boats of the the **'Dolphin'** or **Type 800 class** as variants of the German Type 212 class design by IKL. On the basis of promised American FMS (Foreign Military Sales) funding, Israel contracted with the Ingalls Shipbuilding Division of the Litton Corporation as prime contractor for the boats, to be built in Germany by Howaldtswerke of Kiel with participation by Thyssen Nordseewerke of Emden. Funding was made available in July 1989 and the contract became effective in January 1990, but in November it was cancelled because of funding pressures in the period leading up to the 1991 Gulf War. The programme was revived with German funding in April 1991, and then in July 1994 Israel exercised its option for a third boat of the same class.

The first steel for the three boats was cut in April 1992, and the boats were laid down in October 1994, April 1995 and December 1996 for completion in July 1999, November 1999 and July 2000 as the **Dolphin**, **Leviathan** and **Tekuma**.

The three boats are similar to the Type 212 class except for

'Västergötland' class Patrol submarine

In the late 1970s, the Swedish navy began to consider building a class of patrol submarines to replace the 'Draken'-class boats built in the late 1950s and early 1960s, and to supplement the 'Sjöormen' classes built in the second half of the 1960s, which were eventually sold to Singapore as training boats in the second half of the 1990s. The result was the **'Västergötland' class** of diesel patrol submarines.

The design of this class was contracted to Kockums of Malmö during April 1978. The type was conceived with a single hull, X-type after control surfaces combining rudder and hydroplane functions, and a Pilkington Optronics CK 38 optronic search periscope enhanced with night vision capability. Four boats in the class were commissioned in the period 1987–90. They were constructed by Kockums on the basis of its own central section and bow and stern sections by Karlskrona varvet.

Operations in the acoustically tricky shallow waters of the Baltic demanded special consideration

Commissioned in January 1990, Östergötland was the last 'Västergötland' completed, and is being modernized. The first pair may be leased to Denmark.

SPECIFICATION	
'Västergötland' class	operational
Displacement: 1,070 tons surfaced; 1,143 tons dived	**Torpedo tubes:** six 533-mm (21-in) and three 400-mm (15.75-in) tubes
Dimensions: length 48.5 m (159 ft 1 in); beam 6.06 m (19 ft 11 in); draught 5.6 m (18 ft 4 in)	(all bow) for 12 and six torpedoes respectively; 48 mines can be carried in an external girdle
Propulsion: two Hedemora V12A/ 15-Ub diesels delivering 1,640 kW (2,200 shp) and one Jeumont Schneider electric motor delivering 1,350 kW (1,810 shp) to one shaft	**Electronics:** Terma surface search and navigation radar, CSU 83 active/passive hull sonar, passive flank-array sonar, IPS-17 (Sesub 900A) torpedo fire-control system, and Argo AR-700-S5 or Condor
Performance: speed 10 kts surfaced and 20 kts dived	CS 3071 ESM
Diving depth: 300 m (985 ft)	**Complement:** 28

There are four boats in the 'Västergötland' class: Västergötland, Hälsingland, Södermanland and Östergötland.

of quietening features, and the boats are also coated with an anechoic layer to reduce their reflection of active sonar pulses. The torpedo tubes are all located in the bow, and comprise six 533-mm (21-in) tubes over three 400-mm (15.75-in) tubes. All the tubes are used for wire-guided torpedoes, the larger-diameter tubes firing swim-out FFV Type 613 passive-homing anti-ship weapons carrying a 240-kg (529-lb) warhead to a range of 20 km (12.4 miles) at 45 kts, and the smaller-diameter tubes firing

FFV Type 431/451 active/passive-homing anti-submarine weapons carrying a 45-kg (99-lb) shaped-charge warhead to a range of 20 km at 25 kts.

The last two boats are being lengthened by 10 m (32 ft 10 in) to allow the incorporation of a Stirling-cycle AIPS (Air-Independent Propulsion System) providing a submerged endurance of some 14 days.

The first two boats may be passed to Denmark, which already has one 'Näcken' class submarine from Sweden.

'Kilo' class Patrol submarine

The **Project 877** or **Vashavyanka** diesel-electric submarine, better known in the West as the **'Kilo' class**, was designed in the early 1970s for the anti-submarine and anti-ship defence of Soviet naval bases, coastal installations and sea lanes, and also for the patrol and surveillance tasks. First delivered from the shipyard at Komsomolsk in eastern Siberia, but then built in the western USSR at Nizhny Novgorod and the Admiralty Yard in Leningrad (now St Petersburg), the boat is of the medium-endurance type.

Below: Built at Komsomolsk and two other yards, the 'Kilo' diesel-electric submarines were derived from the longer-range 'Tango' class, and despite problems with its batteries in hotter conditions has achieved respectable export sales to countries of North Africa, the Middle East and the Far East.

Above: Poland received a single 'Project 877E' class submarine, the letter suffix indicating export, in June 1986. Based at Gdynia, the submarine is named Orzel.

Between 1986 and 2000, India received 10 'Kilos'. Known as the 'Sindhughosh' class, after the name of the first boat delivered, the submarines are allocated to the 11th Submarine Squadron (four boats at Vishakapatnam) and the 10th Submarine Squadron (six boats based at Mumbai). Five boats are armed with 3M54 Alfa (SS-N-27) active radar homing SLCMs with a supersonic attack phase and a range of 180 km (112 miles).

SPECIFICATION	
'Kilo' (Project 4B) class	**Diving depth:** 240 m (790 ft) operational
Displacement: 2,325 tons surfaced; 3,076 tons dived	**Torpedo tubes:** six 533-mm (21-in) tubes (all bow) for 18 torpedoes or 24 mines, and provision for one short-range SAM launcher
Dimensions: length 73.8 m (242 ft 2 in); beam 9.9 m (32 ft 6 in); draught 6.6 m (21 ft 8 in)	**Electronics:** one 'Snoop Tray' radar, one 'Shark Teeth'/'Shark Fin' active/passive hull sonar, one 'Mouse Roar' active attack hull sonar, MVU-110EM or MVU-119EM torpedo fire-control system, and 'Squid Head' or 'Brick Pulp' ESM
Propulsion: two diesels delivering 2,720 kW (3,650 shp) and one electric motor delivering 4,400 kW (5,900 shp) to one shaft	
Performance: 10 kts surfaced and 17 kts dived; range 11,125 km (6,915 miles) at 8 kts snorting and 740 km (460 miles) at 3 kts dived	**Complement:** 52

The first example of this boat was launched in 1979 for completion in 1982.

Soviet deletions

Some 24 'Kilos' were built for the Soviet navy, and by the first part of the 21st century the Russian navy had deleted 15 of these, leaving it with nine boats with the Northern and Pacific Fleets (three and four respectively), and single boats with the Baltic and Black

Sea Fleets, the latter's boat having been modified with pumpjet propulsion.

In design, the 'Kilo' class is a development of the 'Tango' class with an improved hull form. Even so, the boat can be considered only basic by comparison with contemporary Western submarines. The Soviets procured the submarine in four variants: the Project 877 baseline model, **Project 877K** with improved fire-control, **Project 877M** with provision for wire-guided torpedoes from two tubes, and the slightly longer **Project 4B** with uprated diesels, an electric motor turning more slowly for less noise, and an automated data system to provide fire-control data for two simultaneous interceptions. Boats have been exported to Algeria (two), China (four), India (10), Iran (three), Poland (one) and Romania (one). Some of these boats are **Type 636** submarines with improved propulsion and fire-control systems.

With the retirement of its more maintenance-intensive vessels, the earlier 'Kilo'-class submarines have disappeared from the Russian navy's active submarine list.

'Tupi' class Patrol submarine

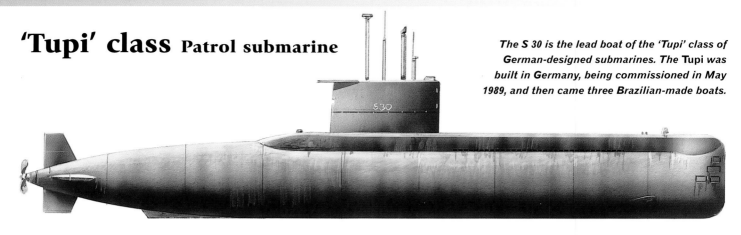

The S 30 is the lead boat of the 'Tupi' class of German-designed submarines. The Tupi was built in Germany, being commissioned in May 1989, and then came three Brazilian-made boats.

In 1984, Brazil contracted with Howaldtswerke-Deutsche Werft for six **'Tupi' class** submarines to the 'Type 1400' subvariant of the 'Type 209' model, the first built in Kiel and the other five in Rio de Janeiro. Financial constraints trimmed the Brazilian-built quantity to three, while the pair of **'Tikuna'-class** boats, to an improved 'Tupi' class standard, are far behind schedule: the *Tikuna*'s commissioning date is delayed from 2000 to 2005 and work on the *Tapuia* has been suspended. Brazil established an uranium-enrichment plant in 1988 with the intention of building an SSN, but this project has not proceeded beyond the design stage. The 'Tikuna'-class boats were described as intermediate between the older SSKs and an SSN.

Brazilian torpedoes

The 'Tupi' class boats operate from Moncangue island's Base Almirante Castro e Silva, across the bay from Rio.

These are well armed small boats, carrying a combination of British Mk 24 Tigerfish torpedoes and an anti-submarine torpedo developed by the IPqM (Instituto de Pesquisas da Marinha, or naval research institute). Eight torpedoes are carried in the tubes and there are eight reloads. The Tigerfish is a wire-guided torpedo capable of

The Tamoio was built in Brazil as the second unit of the 'Tupi' class, and was completed in December 1994 at the end of a construction effort lasting more than eight years.

SPECIFICATION
'Tupi' class
Boats in class: *Tupi, Tamoio, Timbira* and *Tapajo*
Displacement: 1,400 tons surfaced; 1,550 tons dived
Dimensions: length 61.2 m (200 ft 9 in); beam 6.2 m (20 ft 4 in); draught 5.5 m (18 ft)
Propulsion: four MTU 12V 493 AZ80 diesels delivering 1,800 kW (2,414 shp) and one Siemens electric motor delivering 3,425 kW (4,595 shp to one shaft)
Performance: speed 11 kts surfaced/snorting and 21.5 kts dived; range 15,000 km (9,320 miles) at 8 kts surfaced and 740 km (460 miles) at 4 kts dived
Diving depth: 250 m (820 ft)
Armament: eight 533-mm (21-in) tubes with up to 16 Mk 24 Mod 1 or 2 Tigerfish torpedoes or IPqM anti-submarine torpedoes
Electronics: Calypso navigation radar; DR-4000 ESM, CSU 83/1 hull-mounted passive search/attack sonar
Complement: 30

The Brazilian 'Tupi'-class submarines offer generally good capabilities, and it is planned that their torpedo armament should be upgraded in the future with the advanced Bofors 2000 torpedo.

active homing at 35 kts to a range of 13 km (8 miles) or passive homing at 24 kts to 29.6 km (18.4 miles).

The IPqM torpedo has a swim-out launch system and travels up to 18.5 km (11.5 miles) at 45 kts.

The 'Tikuna'-class boats are larger, at 2,425 tons dived, and have a crew of 39. Designed for an endurance of 60 days, they are designed to carry MCF-01/100 acoustic-magnetic mines (produced by IPqM) instead of some torpedoes.

'Type 212A' Patrol submarine

Above: The U 31 under way just off the yard in which its final assembly was undertaken. The 'Type 212A'-class boats are notable for their AIPS and their streamlined exterior lines.

Below: The AIPS, created and manufactured by Siemens and HDW, offer extended underwater endurance. The attack periscopes are by Zeiss.

Since the 1980s, there has been a steadily rising level of interest among the world's navies in the advantages offered by the introduction of an air-independent propulsion system to create true 'submarines' out of what are otherwise conventionally powered 'submersibles'.

Germany trialled such a system in a 'Type-205' boat adapted with an AIPS in 1988–89, and then moved forward to the creation of a highly streamlined boat designed from the outset with an AIPS, in this case using a hybrid fuel cell/battery propulsion arrangement based on Siemens PEM fuel cell technology. In 1992, ARGE 212 (a consortium of Howaldtswerke-Deutsche Werft and Thyssen Nord-seewerke, supported by IKL) completed the initial design of the **'Type 212A' class**, and an initial four boats were

SPECIFICATION	
'Type 212A' class	**Torpedo tubes:** six 21-in (533-mm) tubes (all bow) for 12 DM2A4 wire-guided torpedoes
Displacement: 1,450 tons surfaced; 1,830 tons dived	
Dimensions: length 55.9 m (183 ft 5 in); beam 7 m (23 ft); draught 6 m (19 ft 8 in)	**Electronics:** Type 1007 navigation radar, DBQS-40 passive ranging and intercept sonar, FAS-3 flank and passive towed-array sonar, MOA 3070 or ELAK mine-detection sonar, MSI-90U weapon-control system, FL 1800 ESM, and TAU 2000 torpedo decoy system
Propulsion: one MTU diesel delivering 3,165 kW (4,245 hp) and one electric motor delivering 2,890 kW (3,875 shp) to one shaft	
Performance: speed 12 kts surfaced and 20 kts dived; range 14,805 km (9,200 miles) at 8 kts surfaced	**Complement:** 27

authorized in July 1994. However, it was only in July 1998 that the first metal was cut, as the programme had been slowed to allow the incorporation of changes (including improved habitability and a greater diving depth) to maximize commonality with two boats ordered by Italy.

The four German boats, which may be complemented by a further eight, are the **U 31** to **U 34**. These are based on forward and after sections produced by HDW at Kiel and TNSW at Emden, with the boats completed alternately at the two yards. The first boat was launched in 2002, and the schedule allows thorough testing of this boat before the other three are finalized.

The design is based on a partial double hull in which the larger-diameter forward section is connected to the narrower-diameter after section (carrying the two liquid oxygen tanks and the hydrogen tankage) by a tapered section accommodating the fuel cell plant. The underwater propulsion can provide a maximum speed of 20 kts, declining to 8 kts on just the fuel cells.

The two Italian boats, of which the first is to be called the **Salvatore Todaro**, are being built at Muggiano by Fincantieri, and are scheduled for completion in 2006 to a standard essentially similar to that of the German boats.

Key features of the 'Type 212A' class design are the diving planes on the conning tower, the X-configured control surfaces at the stern, and the propeller with seven scimitar-shaped blades.

'Type 214' Patrol submarine

Ordered by Greece and South Korea, the **'Type 214'-class** submarine is basically a development of the 'Type 209'-class design with a hull further optimized for hydrodynamic efficiency and therefore 'stealthiness', but with the 'Type 212A' class's AIPS (Air-Independent Propulsion System) based on the Siemens PEM (Polymer Electrolyte Membrane) fuel cell technology rather than the Stirling system used in Swedish submarines. Each of the boats boasts two PEM cells, producing 120 kW (161 shp) per module, and this translates into a submerged endurance of 14 days.

In October 1998 the Greek government announced that the Greek navy was to procure four 'Type 214'-class submarines with the local designation **'Katsonis' class**. The first boat, built by Howaldtswerke of Kiel, was launched in April 2004 prior to commissioning in 2006, and the other three are to be completed by the Skaramanga yard of Hellenic Shipyards. The four Greek boats are the **Katsonis**, **Papanilolis**, **Pipinos** and **Matrozos**.

Changes differentiating the 'Type 214' class from the 'Type 212A' class include the location of the diving planes on the forward part of the hull rather than the conning tower, more conventional control surfaces (horizontal and vertical elements rather than an X-configuration) at the stern, eight rather than six swim-out rather than water ram discharge bow tubes (including four fitted for Harpoon anti-ship missiles), a hull made of different materials for a greater diving depth, and slightly different electronics even though a similar Zeiss optronic periscope is used.

In December 2000, the South Korean defence ministry selected the 'Type 214' in preference to the French 'Scorpène' design (and the Russian offer of three 'Kilo'-class boats) to meet its 'KS-II' requirement for three submarines. The contract to build the new boats was awarded to Hyundai Heavy Industries rather than Daewoo Shipbuilding and Marine Engineering, which built South Korea's nine 'Chang Bogo' ('Type 1200' subclass of the 'Type 209' class) boats.

The boats are to be built with German technical assistance and are scheduled for completion in 2007, 2008 and 2009.

The advent of their 'Type 214' submarines, derived from the 'Type 209' design with the AIPS developed for the 'Type 212A', will transform the submarine capabilities of the Greek and South Korean navies.

SPECIFICATION	
'Type 214' class	**Performance:** speed 12 kts surfaced
Displacement: 1,700 tons surfaced;	and 20 kts dived
1,980 tons dived	**Diving depth:** 400 m (1,315 ft)
Dimensions: length 65 m	**Torpedo tubes:** eight 21-in (533-mm)
(213 ft 3 in); beam 6.3 m	tubes (all bow) for 16 STN Atlas
(20 ft 8 in); draught 6 m	torpedoes and Harpoon anti-ship
(19 ft 8 in)	missiles
Propulsion: two MTU 16V 396	**Electronics:** navigation radar, bow,
diesels delivering 6,320 kW	flank-array and towed-array sonars,
(8,475 shp) and one Siemens	ISUS 90 weapon-control system,
Permasyn electric motor delivering	ESM, and Circe torpedo decoy
unspecified power to one shaft	system
	Complement: 27

'Uzushio' class
Diesel attack submarine

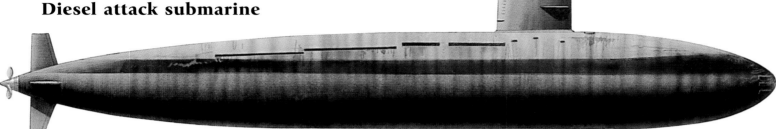

SPECIFICATION	
'Uzushio' class **Type:** Diesel-powered attack submarine **Displacement:** 1,850 tons standard surfaced and 3,600 tons dived **Dimensions:** length 72 m (236 ft 3 in); beam 9.90 m (32 ft 6 in); draught 7.50 m (24 ft 7 in) **Machinery:** two Kawasaki-MAN V8/V24-30 diesels driving one shaft delivering 2,685 kW (3,600 bhp) on	the surface and 5,369 kW (7,200 bhp) dived **Speed:** 12 kts surfaced and 20 kts dived **Diving depth:** 200 m (656 ft) normal **Torpedo tubes:** six 533-mm (21-in) amidships **Basic load:** 18 weapons, usually a mix of homing torpedoes **Complement:** 80

The revolutionary teardrop shape introduced by the US submarine **Albacore** *was a major influence on the design of Japan's first truly modern submarine, the* **Uzushio.**

The increase in Cold War tensions in the 1950s made it necessary for the US and its allies to allow former enemies Germany and Japan to rearm.

The US Navy's submarine stranglehold on the home islands was a major factor in Japan's defeat during World War II. The reborn Japanese navy, originally called the Maritime Safety Agency and latterly known as the Maritime Self-Defence Force, recognised that fact. As a result, its first priority was anti-submarine warfare.

ASW training

The best defence against submarines is often other submarines. The first MSDF boat was an ex-US 'Gato'-class vessel, followed in the late 1950s by a number of small coastal submarines. Five larger 'Oshio'-class boats followed in the late 1960s, the first Japanese fleet boats to sail since the war. They were conservative in design, and their primary function was to serve as targets for ASW training. Commissioned between 1971 and 1978, the seven boats of the

'Uzushio' class marked a great leap forward. Influenced strongly by American designs, the boats had an Albacore-type teardrop hull for maximum hydrodynamic efficiency. The bow sonar array meant that the torpedo tubes had to be located amidships, again following US Navy practice.

Double hull

Manufactured from NS-63 high-tensile steel, the 'Uzushios' were double-hulled, and had a

diving depth in excess of 200 m (656 ft). These incorporated a certain amount of automation, most notably in the provision of a kind of submarine auto-pilot, combining automatic depth and direction maintenance.

The 'Uzushios' were succeeded in production by the improved and enlarged 'Yuushio'-class, and were retired throughout the 1990s as they were replaced in service one for one by the 'Harushio'-class boats.

The 'Uzushio'-class submarine **Isoshio** *enters port. Commissioned in the 1970s, these boats were the foundation of Japan's modern submarine service.*

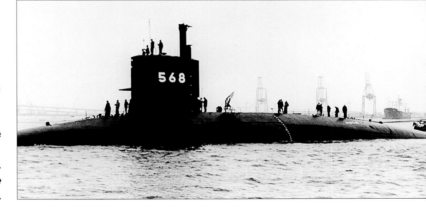

'Yuushio' class Diesel attack submarine

The 10 boats of the **'Yuushio' class** have provided the backbone of the Maritime Self-Defence Force's submarine strength since the 1980s. Essentially an enlarged version of the preceding teardrop 'Uzushio' class, the 'Yuushios' differ primarily in having a deeper diving capability.

The 'Uzushio'-class subs were decommissioned in the 1990s as the new 'Harushio' class was commissioned.

Bow sonar

Of double-hull construction, these boats follow the US Navy nuclear attack submarine practice of having a bow sonar array with the torpedo tubes moved to amidships and angled outwards. The first of the class, **Yuushio** (SS573), entered service in 1980 with the **Mochishio** (SS574), **Setoshio** (SS575), **Okishio** (SS576), **Nadashio** (SS577), **Hamashio** (SS578), **Akishio** (SS579),

Takeshio (SS580), **Yukishio** (SS581), and **Sachishio** (SS582) following at yearly intervals.

From the *Nadashio* onwards, the class was fitted to carry and fire the American Sub-Harpoon anti-ship missile, a capability which was retrofitted to all of the earlier boats except for the *Yuushio* itself. All the boats carry the Type 89 dual-purpose, active-passive torpedoes, which have a maximum speed of 55 kts (102 km/h; 63 mph)

and a maximum reduced speed range of 50 km (31 miles).

The electronics carried on the Yuushio-class are of the latest design, and include the ZQQ-5 bow sonar (a modified American BQS-4) and the ZQR-1 towed array (similar to the American BQR-15). *Yuushio* was removed from front-line service to become a training boat in 1996.

Last of the line

The last of the 'Yuushios' was

commissioned in 1989. By that time, the first three boats of the follow-on 'Harushio' class had been laid down, with the name-ship commissioning at the end of November 1990. *Harushio* was followed at yearly intervals by *Natsushio, Hayashio, Arashio, Wakashio, Fuyushio*, and by *Asashio* in 1997. As each entered service, one of the 'Uzushio'-class boats was paid off.

The 'Harushios' follow the same basic design as the 'Yuushios', but are slightly larger in all dimensions. More attention has been paid to reducing noise internally, and all have anechoic material applied to the outer surfaces. A stronger pressure hull means that operational diving depth has been increased to some 300 m (1,150 ft).

Asashio, the last of the class, was completed to a modified design. Increased systems automation has allowed crew to be reduced from 74 to 71.

Left: The second 'Yuushio'-class boat Mochishio *enters the US Pacific Fleet base as it makes a courtesy visit to Pearl Harbor in the mid-1990s.*

Below: Although influenced by US Navy practice, Japanese submarine designs were using mainly home-built systems and equipment by the time Harushio *was commissioned in 1990.*

SPECIFICATION	
'Yuushio' class	**Diving depth:** 275 m (900 ft) operational
Displacement: 2,200 tons standard surfaced and 2,730 tons dived	**Torpedo tubes:** six 533-mm (21-in) amidships
Dimensions: length 76 m (249 ft 4 in); beam 9.90 m (32 ft 6 in); draught 7.50 m (24 ft 7¼ in)	**Basic load:** 18–20 torpedoes and anti-ship missiles
Propulsion: two diesels delivering 2,535 kW (3,400 hp) to one electric motor driving one shaft	**Electronics:** one ZPS-6 surface-search radar, one ZQQ-5 bow sonar, one SQS-36(J) sonar, one ZQR-1 towed array, one ALR 3-6 ESM suite
Speed: 12 kts surfaced and 20 kts dived	**Complement:** 75

Left: Sailors prepare to moor as the Mochishio *approaches the dock.*

Below: Yuushio *conducts an emergency surfacing drill. The name ship of its class has been in use as a training submarine since 1996.*

'Oyashio' class Diesel attack submarine

The **Oyashio**, commissioned in 1998, was the first of five advanced diesel-powered patrol submarines to enter service with the Japan Maritime Self-Defence Force. The new submarines are examples of the changing face of Japanese military equipment acquisition since the establishment of the Self-Defence Forces in the 1950s.

The first generation of equipment was often second-hand and generally acquired from the United States. By 1960, however, Japanese industry was up and running after the devastation of World War II, and the second stage

Oyashio *is as capable as most nuclear boats. It is slower and has less endurance, but its diesel electric powerplant makes it quieter than a 'nuke'.*

saw American equipment or licence-built Japanese copies of American equipment installed in Japanese-built platforms.

All Japanese

From the late 1970s, an increasing proportion of JMSDF systems has been of Japanese origin. Even where those systems are based on state-of-the-art American or European designs, they have often been upgraded – at great cost – to be

more capable then the original. The 'Oyashio' class is equipped with Japanese-designed radar and electronics. Its sonar systems are based on American designs, but have been modified to suit Japanese requirements.

Outwardly, the 'Oyashios' have changed from preceding Japanese submarines. The revised outer casing makes them similar to British nuclear boats, while the fin is a more efficient hydrodynamic shape.

The new boats share the double hulls and anechoic coating of the previous class, but have been equipped with large flank sonar arrays, which may account for the increase in displacement over the 'Harushios'.

Future engines

Kawasaki Heavy Industries have been conducting experiments in using Sterling-Cycle air-independent powerplants and fuel cells, and at one stage these were planned for the later 'Oyashios'. It is now likely that such systems, which allow boats to operate submerged for extended periods, will make their appearance in the next class of Japanese submarines.

As the 'Oyashios' are completed, they will replace the older 'Yuushio' class boats. The Japanese Defense Agency expects that future world conditions will call for an operational total of 12–14 boats. Most of these will be of the 'Oyashio' class as current building plans call for as many as 10 boats to be in service by 2007 or 2008.

SPECIFICATION	
'Oyashio' class **Displacement:** 2,700 tons standard surfaced and 3,000 tons dived **Dimensions:** length 81.70 m (268 ft); beam 8.90 m (29 ft 3 in); draught 7.90 m (25 ft 11 in) **Propulsion:** two Kawasaki 12V25S diesels delivering 4,100 kW (5,520 hp) to two Fuji electric motors driving one shaft **Speed:** 12 kts surfaced and 20 kts dived **Diving depth:** 300 m (984 ft)	operational and 500 m (1,640 ft) maximum **Torpedo tubes:** six 533-mm (21-in) amidships **Basic load:** 20 Type 89 torpedoes and Harpoon anti-ship missiles **Electronics:** one ZPS-6 surface-search radar, one Hughes-Oki ZQQ-5B bow sonar, port and starboard flank sonar arrays, one ZQR-1 (BQR-15) towed array, one ZLR 7 ESM suite **Complement:** 69

Oyashio, commissioned in 1998, is the first Japanese submarine in nearly three decades to have a significantly different hull form and fin.

'Ula' class Patrol submarine

Since the deletion of the last six of the original 15 'Kobben'-class boats in the second half of the 1990s, the Norwegian navy operates just six submarines in the form of the boats of the **'Ula' class** with diesel-electric propulsion. The boats are named **Ula**, **Uredd**, **Utvaer**, **Uthaug**, **Utstein** and **Utsira**, all but the second of these names having been used for the boats of an earlier 'Ula' class (five British 'U'-class submarines bought from the UK in 1943–46, modernised in 1955–56 and deleted in the early 1960s).

The current 'Ula'-class submarines are intended primarily for coastal operations,

*The **Utsira** was the last of the six 'Ula'-class submarines to be completed and was commissioned in April 1992.*

and are therefore comparatively small in size and limited in their diving depth to some 250 m (820 ft).

German construction

The entire class was ordered from Thyssen Nordseewerke of Emden on 30 September 1982 in a joint Norwegian and West German programme known in the latter country as Project 210, but the option for another two boats of the class was not, in the event, exercised.

Although the boats were completed in the West German yard, they did incorporate a measure of Norwegian structural expertise inasmuch as sections of the pressure hulls were fabricated in a Norwegian facility and then shipped to Emden for inclusion into the otherwise German-built boats.

SPECIFICATION

SPECIFICATION	
'Ula' class	**Diving depth:** 250 m (820 ft)
Displacement: 1,040 tons surfaced; 1,150 tons dived	**Torpedo tubes:** eight 533-mm (21-in) tubes (all bow) for 14 DM2A3 Seehecht wire-guided active/passive-homing dual-role torpedoes
Dimensions: length 59 m (193 ft 7 in); beam 5.4 m (17 ft 9 in); draught 4.6 m (15 ft 1 in)	
Propulsion: two MTU 16V 396 SB83 diesels delivering 2,010 kW (2,695 shp) and one Siemens electric motor delivering 4,474 kW (6,000 shp) to one shaft	**Electronics:** one Type 1007 surface search and navigation radar, one passive flank-array sonar; one active/passive intercept, search and attack sonar, and one Sealion ESM system
Performance: speed 11 kts surfaced and 23 kts dived; range 9,250 km (5,750 miles) at 8 kts surfaced	**Complement:** 21

The boats were laid down between January 1987 and June 1990, then launched between July 1988 and November 1991, and finally commissioned into Norwegian service in the period between April 1989 and April 1992.

Though much of the hull and all of the propulsion machinery are German, the boats were completed with a mix of French, German and Norwegian systems. The basic command and weapon control systems are Norwegian (the torpedo fire-control system being the Kongsberg MSI-90U, which is being upgraded and modernized in 2000–05), while the sonars are of French and German origins. The Thomson-CSF low-frequency passive flank-array sonar is of French origin, and is based on piezoelectric polymer technology offering significantly reduced flow noise. The Atlas Elektronik CSU 83 medium-frequency active/passive

intercept, search and attack sonar, however, is of German origin. Another notable feature, designed to reduce the need to incorporate apertures in the pressure hull, is the use of Calzoni Trident modular non-penetrating masts, and the periscopes use Zeiss optics.

Eventful careers

Since entering service, the 'Ula'-class submarines have been found to suffer from noise problems with their machinery, which is a major handicap in submarine operations in which sound is the primary medium for discovering submerged boats. The submarines have undergone quite interesting careers to date. The *Ula*, for example, was damaged by a practice torpedo during the boat's trials in 1989, while the *Uredd* in March 1991 was damaged in a docking accident and then in February 1992 suffered a control room fire.

'Götland' class Patrol submarine

Resulting from a research and preliminary design contract placed with the Kockums yard of Malmö in October 1986 for a conventionally powered submarine to replace the obsolescent boats of the 'Sjöormen' class, the design of the boats of the **A19** or **'Götland' class** was derived from that of the A17 or

'Västergötland' class. The three boats of the class, namely the **Götland**, **Uppland** and **Halland**, were ordered from Kockums in March 1990, but another two projected units were not in the event procured. In September of the following year, before the first boat had been laid down, the programme was temporarily suspended to allow a reworking

The 'Götland'-class boats are fairly small, but offer excellent capabilities including a sizeable load of modern torpedoes and an extended underwater cruising capability.

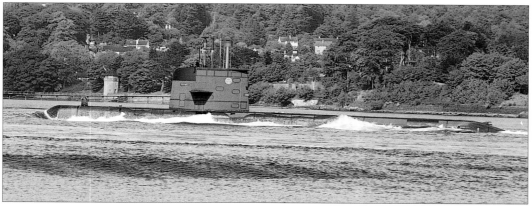

Above: Highly reliable boats, the 'Götlands' provide Sweden with effective coastal defence.

Above: The 'Götlands' are very quiet under the water, where their detectability is reduced by silent machinery and an anechoic outer covering.

Below: Commissioned in May 1997, the Uppland was the second of the three 'Götland'-class boats to be completed by the Kockums yard at Malmö.

to allow the incorporation of two such systems with volume left for the later addition of another two systems should this prove desirable. As it is, the boats can apparently cruise at a submerged speed of 5 kts for several weeks without recourse to snorting.

The boats were laid down in 1992–1994 and commissioned in 1996–97, the lengthening of the hull having resulted in a 200-ton increase in displacement. Another advanced feature of the design was the installation of a periscope with optronic sensors, and this unit is the only mast that penetrates through the pressure hull. The boats' underwater signature is being

of the design to incorporate – for the first time before the start of fabrication rather than as a retrofit – an AIPS (Air-Independent Propulsion System), using liquid oxygen and diesel fuel in a helium environment, for much enhanced submerged operating capability. The hull was lengthened by 7.5 m (24 ft 7 in)

SPECIFICATION

'Götland' class
Displacement: 1,240 tons surfaced; 1,494 tons dived
Dimensions: length 60.4 m (198 ft 2 in); beam 6.2 m (20 ft 4 in); draught 5.6 m (18 ft 4 in)
Propulsion: two Hedemora V12A-15-Ub diesels delivering 4,830 kW (6,480 shp), two Kockums V4-275R Mk 2 Stirling AIPS, and one Jeumont-Schneider electric motor delivering 1,350 kW (1,810 shp) to one shaft
Performance: speed 10 kts surfaced

and 20 kts dived
Torpedo tubes: four 533-mm (21-in) and two 400-mm (15.75-in) tubes (all bow) for 12 Tp 613 or Tp 62 wire-guided anti-ship and six Tp 432/451 wire-guided anti-submarine torpedoes
Electronics: one Scanter navigation radar, one CSU 90-2 passive search and attack sonar with bow and flank arrays, one IPS-19 torpedo fire-control system, and one Manta S ESM system
Complement: 25

further reduced by the application of anechoic coatings.

Torpedo armament

The torpedo tubes are all located in the bow, and comprise four 533-mm (21-in) tubes over two 400-mm (15.75-in) tubes. The larger units fire anti-ship torpedoes of the swim-out type in the form of the wire-guided Type 613 passive or (since 2000) Type 62 active/passive weapons: the former carries a 240-kg (529-lb) HE warhead to 20 km (12.4 miles) at 45 kts, while the latter carries a 250-kg (551-lb) HE warhead to 50 km (31.1 miles) at a speed of 20-50 kts. Twelve Tp 47 mines can be carried in place of the heavy torpedoes, which swim out to a predetermined position before laying themselves on the bottom. Another 48 mines can be carried by an external girdle. The smaller torpedo tubes can be tandem loaded with wire-guided Tp 432/451 active/passive ASW torpedoes, each able to carry a 45-kg (99-lb) HE warhead out to 20 km (12.4 miles) at 25 kts.

'Chang Bogo' class Patrol submarine

Up to the 1980s, the South Korean navy, faced with the threat of North Korean aggression through the agency of conventional submarines and small surface ships, concentrated its efforts on the deployment of ex-US surface warships and the development of its capability to operate more advanced vessels. The process began to bear fruit toward the end of the 1980s, when a number of more advanced vessels were ordered. Among the new types were the service's first submarines, which were of the West German Type 209 class in its Type 1200 subvariant, which was ordered as the **'Chang Bogo' class** with a diving depth of 250 m (820 ft).

The first order placed late in 1997 covered three boats, one to be completed by Howaldtswerke of Kiel in Germany and the other two by Daewoo at Okpo in South Korea from German-supplied kits. There followed additional three-boat orders placed in October 1989 and January 1994 for boats of South Korean construction, and the entire class comprises the **Chang Bogo**, **Yi Chon**, **Choi Muson**, **Pakui**, **Lee Jongmu**, **Jeongun**, **Lee Sunsin**, **Nadaeyong** and **Lee Okki**. The boats were laid between 1989 and 1997, launched between 1992 and 2000, and finally commissioned from 1993 to a final hand-over in 2001.

Turkish similarity

The South Korean boats are generally similar to Turkey's six 'Atilay'-class submarines, and emphasis is therefore placed on the installation of German sensors and weapons. Using the swim-out discharge method (resulting in reduced noise levels) from eight 533-mm (21-in) tubes all located in the bows, the latter comprise 14 SystemTechnik Nord (STN) SUT Mod 2 torpedoes, which are wire-guided weapons with active/passive homing and the ability to carry a 260-kg (573-lb) HE warhead out to a maximum range of 28 km (17.4 miles) at 23 kts or a shorter range of 12 km (7.6 mile) at a speed of 35 kts. The boats can also carry 28 tube-laid mines in place of the torpedoes.

The older boats are being upgraded from a time early in the 21st century, and although details are currently unclear, it is believed that the modernization will include a hull 'stretch' to the Type 1400 length of some 62 m (203 ft 5 in) with surfaced and submerged displacements of about 1,455 and 1,585 tons respectively, provision for tube-launched UGM-84 Harpoon missiles to enhance the boats' capabilities against surface ships, and possibly the addition of a towed-array sonar for a superior capability for the detection of submerged submarines.

SPECIFICATION	
'Chang Bogo' class **Displacement:** 1,100 tons surfaced; 1,285 tons dived **Dimensions:** length 56 m (183 ft 9 in); beam 6.2 m (20 ft 4 in); draught 5.5 m (18 ft) **Propulsion:** diesel-electric arrangement with four MTU 12V 396SE diesels delivering 2,840 kW (3,810 shp) and driving four alternators, and one electric motor delivering 3,425 kW (4,595 shp) to one shaft **Performance:** speed 11 kts	surfaced/snorting and 22 kts dived; endurance 13,900 km (8,635 miles) at 8 kts surfaced **Diving depth:** 250 m (820 ft) **Torpedo tubes:** eight 533-mm (21-in) tubes (all bow) for 14 SUT Mod 2 wire-guided active/passive-homing torpedoes or 28 mines **Electronics:** one navigation radar, one CSU 83 hull-mounted passive search and attack sonar, one ISUS 83 torpedo fire-control system, and one Argo ESM system **Complement:** 33

*The **Pakui** was completed by Daewoo on 3 February 1996, as the fourth of the South Korean navy's 'Chang Bogo'-class conventional submarines. The service plans to operate the boats as a trio attached to each of its three fleets, and further improvement of the boats may be based on an indigenous South Korean development of a US torpedo, the Northrop NP 37.*

'Santa Cruz' class (TR 1700) Attack submarine

Currently the most important submarines of the Argentine navy, the two **'Santa Cruz'-class** diesel-electric boats are the result of a chequered early history. In November 1977, the Argentine navy contracted with Thyssen Nordseewerke for the building of two **'TR 1700'** type submarines in West Germany and the provision of parts and supervision for the manufacture of four more boats in Argentina at the Astilleros Domecq Garcia facility in Buenos Aires.

As the Argentine navy's plan was originally conceived, the boats to be built in Argentina were to have been two more 'TR 1700' type submarines and two examples of the smaller 'TR 1400' type. In 1982, however, the contract details were finalized for a class of six 'TR 1700' type submarines and no 'TR 1400' type units.

The two boats built in West Germany are the **Santa Cruz** and **San Juan**, which were launched in September 1982 and June 1983, and commissioned in October 1984 and November 1985 respectively. There were problems with the four boats to be built in Argentina, however, for in 1996, when the initial pair of submarines, destined for completion as the *Santa Fe* and *Santiago del Estero*, were 52 and 30 per cent complete respectively, work ended. In February of that year, the dockyard was sold, and what had been completed of the two boats was cannibalized to aid in the maintenance of the two West German-built boats. The same fate befell the equipment

delivered from West Germany for the last two boats that were to have been built in Argentina but were not, in the event, even laid down.

The 'TR 1700' type was of notably advanced concept for its time, and offered both a high underwater speed and a considerable operational diving depth. The standard endurance is 30 days, but the maximum figure is believed to be 70 days. An automatic reloading system is provided for the torpedo tubes, this system performing the reloading of the torpedo tubes in just 50 seconds. The boats also have the capability to carry and land small parties of commando troops for special forces missions.

Both the *Santa Cruz* and *San Juan* are based at Mar del Plata, which is the home of the Argentine navy's small submarine force. Between September 1999 and 2001, the *Santa Cruz* received a mid-life update at a Brazilian yard, and an update is also planned for the *San Juan* at Puerto Belgrano in Argentina as and when the Argentine economy makes this feasible. The upgrade involves, among other things, the replacement of the submarine's main motors and the

The 'TR 1700' type submarine is still a highly effective design, and the achievement of the service's plan for six such boats would have given the Argentine navy a potent attack force by South American standards.

SPECIFICATION	
'Santa Cruz' class **Displacement:** 2,116 tons surfaced; 2,264 tons dived **Dimensions:** length 66 m (216 ft 6 in); beam 7.3 m (24 ft); draught 6.5 m (21 ft 4 in) **Propulsion:** four MTU 16V652 MB81 diesels delivering 5,000 kW (6,705 shp) and one Siemens Type 1HR4525 + 1HR4525 electric motor delivering 6,600 kW (8,850 hp) to one shaft **Performance:** speed 15 kts surfaced, 25 kts dived; endurance 22,250 km	(13,825 miles) at 8 kts surfaced **Diving depth:** 270 m (885 m) operational **Armament:** six 533-mm (21-in) tubes (all bow) for 22 SST-4 or Mk 37 wire-guided torpedoes, or 34 mines **Electronics:** one Calypso IV navigation radar, one Sinbads fire-control system, one Sea Sentry III ESM system, one CSU 3/4 active/passive search and attack sonar, and one DUUX 5 passive ranging sonar **Crew:** 29

updating of the sonar system's active/passive search and passive ranging units.

The torpedoes carried by the 'TR 1700' type submarines are the German SST-4 and US Mk 37 wire-guided types with swim-out

discharge. The former carries a 260-kg (573-lb) warhead to a distance of 12km or 28 km (7.46 miles or 17.4 miles) at 35 or 23 kts, and the latter delivers a 150-kg (330-lb) warhead to 8 km (4.97 miles) at 24 kts.

'Song' class Attack submarine

The **'Song' class** or **Type 039** is the latest and most advanced diesel-electric attack submarine type to have been designed and built by indigenous Chinese effort. Conceived as the successor to the Chinese navy's ageing force of obsolescent 'Ming'-class (Type 035) and wholly obsolete 'Romeo'-class (Type 033) submarines, which have constituted the core of the service's conventionally powered submarine arm for more than four decades, the 'Song' class is based in design terms on certain Western concepts. These include a low-drag hydrodynamically profiled hull and sail, new cylindrical bow-mounted sonars, a powerplant centred on the use

of four German MTU diesel engines (16V 396 units rather than the 12V493 units originally considered), and a new anti-submarine torpedo of Russian origin.

Another major enhancement contributing to the type's capability for offensive as well as defensive operations is the provision for an anti-ship missile capability. This is in the form of a tube-fired YJ-82 (submarine-launched version of the ship-launched C-801) missile, which can deliver its 165-kg (364-lb) warhead to a range of 40 km (24.9 miles) with the aid of an inertial platform and active radar terminal seeker.

In overall terms, the 'Song' class reveals a technological

standard generally similar to that of Western submarines built during the 1980s.

Pause for reflection

The first boat, **No. 320**, was laid down in 1991 and was launched on 25 May 1994 at the Wuhan Shipyard, but was not commissioned until June 1999 after the implementation of an exhaustive trials programme to assess the capabilities and, as it turned out, limitations of the design. It was at this trials stage that the Chinese navy postponed further construction to allow the rectification of serious performance and design problems, and thus create the initial full-production variant, known as the **Type 039G**. This

boat is characterized most obviously by a sail without the stepped-down forward section that in *No. 320* accommodates the bridge with the forward hydroplanes under it.

Production was resumed at the Wuhan Shipyard in 1995, and the first Type 039G boat was launched in November 1999 for commissioning during April 2001 as **No. 321**. By 2003 another three units had been completed.

Teardrop hull

Slightly shorter but beamier than the 'Ming'-class submarine it is designed to succeed, the 'Song'-class boat has a length/beam ratio of 8.91/1, which is slightly less than the

10/1 ratio of the 'Ming'-class submarines but of a decidedly superior hydrodynamic shape. The 'Song'-class submarine is propelled through the water by one large seven-bladed propeller, and the primary machinery is located on shock-absorbent mountings for reduced vibration and therefore minimized underwater noise radiation.

The 'stealthiness' of the design is further enhanced by the use of anechoic tiling similar to that of the Russian 'Kilo'-class submarine.

The 'Song'-class submarine has a multi-role combat and command system to provide all the data needed for control of the boat and the firing of torpedoes and/or missiles. The system may be an updated derivative of the combat and command system used in the 'Ming'-class submarines, and may be of a standard equivalent to that installed in Western submarines in the 1970s.

Mixed armament

The 'Song' class is armed primarily with anti-ship cruise missiles and torpedoes. As noted above, the YJ-82 missile is the submarine-launched variant of the C-801m launched underwater from the 533-mm (21-in) torpedo tubes. Boosted by a solid-propellant rocket until it has emerged from the water, whereupon the solid-propellant sustainer takes over, the missile approaches its target as a sea-skimmer and impacts under the guidance of its active radar seeker, the shaped-charge warhead being initiated by a delay-action impact fuse. The six 533-mm tubes, all located in the bows, have a maximum of 16 to 20 Yu-4 (SAET-60) passive homing and Yu-1 (Type 53-51) torpedoes, the total being reduced when the YJ-82 missile is shipped. As an alternative, the submarine can carry tube-launched mines.

Integrated sonar

The 'Song'-class submarine is fitted with an integrated sonar system comprising an active/passive medium-frequency spherical bow-mounted equipment and passive low-frequency reach arrays. The countermeasures suite comprises just the Type 921-A radar warning receiver.

The diesel-electric propulsion arrangement provided to power the 'Song'-class submarine comprises four MTU 16V396 SE diesel engines, four alternators, and one electric motor, the last powering a single shaft.

More units of the 'Song' class, probably to a standard improved to reflect current operational experience, may emerge in time.

SPECIFICATION	
'Song' (Type 039G) class	**Diving depth:** not available
Displacement: 1,700 tons surfaced; 2,250 tons dived	**Armament:** six 533-mm (21-in) tubes (all bow) for Yu-4 (SAET-60) and Yu-1 (Type 53-51) torpedoes, or mines, and YJ-82 anti-ship missiles
Dimensions: length 74.9 m (245 ft 9 in); beam 8.4 m (27 ft 6 in); draught 7.3 m (24 ft)	**Electronics:** one surface search and navigation radar, one Type 951-A ESM system, one active/passive search and attack bow sonar, and one passive search flank-array sonar
Propulsion: four MTU 16V396 SE diesels delivering 4,540 kW (6,090 shp) and one electric motor delivering power to one shaft	
Performance: speed 15 kts surfaced and 22 kts dived	**Crew:** 60

'Scorpene' class Attack submarine

The **'Scorpene' class** submarine was developed by DCN of France and Izar (formerly Bazán) of Spain, and the first two units were ordered by Chile to be constructed in France and Spain for commissioning in 2005 and 2006 as the **O'Higgins** and **Carrera**, replacing two 'Oberon'-class boats. The Malaysian navy placed a contract for two 'Scorpene'-class submarines in June 2002, the boats to enter service in 2007 and 2008 after construction in France and Spain. France and India also sign an agreement in October 2005 for the latter to build six 'Scorpene'-class boats at the state-owned Mazagon Docks in Bombay, with technical aid from the French DCN and Thales companies. The boats are to be completed in 2010–15 with SM.39 Exocet underwater-launched anti-ship missiles.

As ordered for the Chilean navy, the 'Scorpene'-class submarine will not have a towed-array sonar but will be equipped with flank-array sonar. The six 533-mm (21-in) bow torpedo tubes will in general be capable of launching German SUT torpedoes, F-17 Mod 2, Mk 48 or, in Chilean service, Black Shark 184 Mod 3 torpedoes, as well as the SM.39 Exocet anti-ship missile. The tubes possess a salvo launch capability, and use a positive-discharge system by air turbine pump. The submarine's weapon complement is 18 torpedoes and missiles, or 30 mines, and the handling and loading of weapons are automated.

Combat system

The SUBTICS combat management system, with up to six multi-function consoles and a central tactical table, is located with the platform-control facilities. SUBTICS comprises a command and tactical data-

The 'Scorpene'-class submarine offers exceptional capabilities, and can be enhanced, either in construction or during retrofit, with AIPS propulsion.

SPECIFICATION	
'Scorpene' class (Chilean standard)	(7,455 miles) at 8 kts surfaced
Displacement: 1,668 tons dived	**Diving depth:** 300+ m (985+ ft) operational
Dimensions: length 66.4 m (217 ft 10 in); beam 6.2 m (20 ft 4 in); draught 5.8 m (19 ft)	**Armament:** six 533-mm (21-in) tubes (all bow) for 18 Black Shark 184 Mod 3 torpedoes
Propulsion: four MTU 16V396 SE84 diesels delivering 2,240 kW (3,005 shp) and one Jeumont Schneider electric motor delivering 2,840 kW (3,810 hp) to one shaft	**Electronics:** one navigation radar, one SUBTICS fire-control system, one Argo AR 900 ESM system, and one active/passive search and attack hull sonar
Performance: speed 12 kts surfaced, 20 kts dived; endurance 12,000 km	**Crew:** 31

handling system, a weapon-control system and a suite of integrated acoustic sensors interfaced with the air/surface detection sensors and the navigation system.

Handling operations are effected in the control room. The boat has a high level of automation and system

surveillance, with automatic control of the rudders, hydroplanes and propulsion, full-time monitoring of the propulsion and platform installations, full-time centralized surveillance against hazards such as leaks, fires and noxious gases, and the checking of installations critical to

submerged safety. When submerged, the 'Scorpene'-class boat has low radiated noise levels, which improves the detection range of its own sensors and reduces risk of detection. These low noise levels are achieved by the use of very advanced hydrodynamics with an albacore bow shape, few external

projections, an optimized propeller, suspended decks, the location of equipment on elastic mountings wherever possible, and the use of double elastic mountings for the noisiest systems.

There is provision in the submarine's design for the incorporation of an air independent propulsion system.

'Harushio' class Attack submarine

Since its establishment in the 1950s, the Japanese navy (more formally designated the Japanese Maritime Self-Defence Force in accordance with the country's post-World War II pacifist constitution) has placed considerable emphasis on the development of a sizeable force of advanced submarines to provide a seaward capability for the destruction of possible maritime invasion forces.

After a number of single- or twin-boat classes, which enabled it to develop an initial capability and reacquaint itself with the technology of the time, the JMSDF adopted the 'Oshio' class as its first major submarine force, five such boats being commissioned in 1965–69. There followed seven 'Uzushio'-class boats in 1971–78, and then 10 'Yuushio'-class boats in 1978–88.

By the first half of the 1980s the 'Uzushio' class had become obsolescent, and the JMSDF started to plan a successor type. Just as the 'Yuushio' class had been a development of the 'Uzushio' class with improved electronics and a deeper diving capability, the new **'Harushio'**

class was schemed as an improved 'Yuushio' class with a towed-array sonar and improved noise-reduction features. Other features of the class include wireless antennae, an anechoic coating for the hull and sail, and a double hull.

The programme was approved in 1986, and the construction of one boat per year was authorized so that the **Harushio**, **Natsushio**, **Hayashio**, **Arashio**, **Wakashio**, **Fuyushio** and **Asashio** were commissioned in the period between November 1990 and March 1997. All of the boats were built at Kobe by Mitsubishi (four boats) and Kawasaki (three boats).

The *Asashio* was completed with a higher level of automation in the machinery and snorting control systems, increasing he displacement slightly and allowing the crew to be trimmed to 71. The boat also had a remote periscope viewer system. In 2001

The 'Harushio'-class submarines have distinct teardrop hulls with a lack of excrescences, and considerable operational diving depth.

the boat was also lengthened by 10 m (32 ft 10 in) to allow the retrofit of the Stirling air-

independent propulsion system, which was to be evaluated for use in later Japanese submarines.

Above: The 'Harushio'-class diesel-electric submarines are operated in the seaward defence role, and from 1998 have been complemented by the 'Oyashio'-class boats, of which a total of nine is planned for completion by 2006.

SPECIFICATION	
'Harushio' class	operational
Displacement: 2,450 tons surfaced; 2,750 tons dived	**Armament:** six 533-mm (21-in) tubes (all bow) for 20 Type 89 wire-guided active/passive homing and Type 80 anti-submarine torpedoes, and Harpoon anti-ship missiles
Dimensions: length 77 m (252 ft 7 in); beam 10 m (32 ft 10 in); draught 7.7 m (25 ft 3 in)	
Propulsion: two Kawasaki 12V25/25S diesels delivering 4,120 kW (5,525 shp) and two Fuji electric motors delivering ,5370 kW (7,200 shp) to one shaft	**Electronics:** one ZPS 6 surface search and navigation radar, one fire-control system, one ZLR 3-6 ESM system, one ZQQ 5B active/passive search and attack hull sonar, and one ZQR 1 passive search towed-array sonar
Performance: speed 12 kts surfaced and 20 kts dived	
Diving depth: 350 m (1,150 ft)	**Crew:** 75

'Anzac' class

Commissioned by the Royal Australian Navy in May 1996, HMAS Anzac was the first of its class, a capable frigate type with guided-missile frigate update capability.

In 1989, the Australian government contracted with Australian Marine Engineering Consolidated for the construction of 10 **'Anzac'-class** guided-missile frigates (eight and two ships for the Royal Australian and Royal New Zealand Navies respectively) based on the Meko 200 design prepared by Blohm & Voss of Germany. The design is of the modular type, allowing complete sections of the ships to be built in Newcastle in Australia and Whangerei in New Zealand for delivery to the Transfield Shipbuilding (now Tenix Defence Systems) yard at Williamstown in Australia for final assembly.

Originally to have been the Arrernte, HMAS Arunta is Australia's second 'Anzac'-class frigate. Capability for the Evolved Sea Sparrow SAM is retrofitted in the first two ships and built into the last six units.

The modular design also facilitates the retrofit of updated equipment, as a module can be removed and replaced by a new module fitted with the new equipment, which could include modern guided weapon types as well as advanced sensors.

The 'Anzac'-class ships differ from other Meko 200 frigates mainly in their single-shaft machinery, and in response to Australian army pressure the calibre of the main gun was increased from 76 to 127 mm (3 to 5 in).

The Australian ships, due for completion between May 1996 and March 2006, are HMAS **Anzac**, **Arunta**, **Warramunga**, **Stuart**, **Parramatta**, **Ballarat**, **Toowoomba** and **Perth**, while the New Zealand ships, commissioned in July 1997 and December 1999, are HMNZS **Te Kaha** and **Te Mana**.

SPECIFICATION

'Anzac' class
Displacement: 3,600 tons full load
Dimensions: length 118 m (387 ft 2 in); beam 14.8 m (48 ft 7 in); draught 4.35 m (14 ft 3 in)
Propulsion: CODOG with one General Electric LM2500 gas turbine delivering 22,495 kW (30,170 shp) and two MTU 12V 1163 TB83 diesels delivering 6,590 kW (8,840 shp) to one shaft
Performance: speed 27 kts; range 11,105 km (6,900 miles) at 18 kts
Armament: one 5-in (127-mm) gun, one octuple vertical-launch system for eight Sea Sparrow or Quadpack launcher for 32 Evolved Sea Sparrow SAMs, and two triple 324-mm (12.75-in) tubes for Mk 46 anti-submarine torpedoes
Electronics: SPS-49(V)8 ANZ air search radar, 9LV 453 TIR air/surface search radar, 9600 ARPA navigation radar, 9LV 453 fire-control radar, 9LV 453 Mk 3 combat data system, 9LV 453 optronic director, Sceptre A and PST-1720 Telegon 10 ESM, decoy launchers, SLQ-25A towed torpedo decoy, and Spherion B hull-mounted active sonar
Aircraft: one S-70B or SH-2G helicopter
Complement: 163

'Halifax' class FFG

In December 1977 the Canadian government decided to order an initial six out of a projected 20 helicopter-carrying frigates urgently needed to replace Canada's ageing force of ocean escort and anti-submarine frigates. The programme was then overtaken by a number of delays, and it was June 1983 before the contract for the first six ships was finally awarded to the St John Shipbuilding company of New Brunswick. Design of the **'Halifax'-class** ships was shared between St John and Paramax Electronics (now Loral Canada), and the building of three of the eventual 12 ships (including a second group of six ordered in December 1987) was entrusted to Marine Industries (now MIL-Davie) of Lauzon and Sorel, Quebec.

Laid down between March 1987 and April 1995 for launch between April 1988 and November 1995 and commissioning between June 1992 and September 1996, the 12 'Halifax'-class frigates are HMCS **Halifax**, **Vancouver**, **Ville de Québec**, **Toronto**, **Regina**, **Calgary**, **Montreal**, **Fredericton**, **Winnipeg**,

Charlottetown, **St John's** and **Ottawa**.

Considerable effort was placed in the design and construction phases of the programme on the enhancement of the ships' 'stealthiness', and for this reason the gas turbines are raft-mounted and there is a Dresball IR suppression system. Even so, trials of the first ships revealed a radiated noise level higher than anticipated, mainly at higher speeds, but these problems have been overcome and the ships are now regarded as notably quiet and stable in all sea conditions.

The ships have a full capability (a hangar as well as a flight platform and an Indal RAST handling system) over the stern for one large helicopter, which is currently the CH-124A anti-submarine or CH-124B HELTAS (HELicopter Towed-Array Support) version of the obsolescent Sikorsky S-61 Sea King.

Given the importance of an advanced anti-submarine capability to Canadian maritime operations, the ships are to be revised from 2006 with an ITAPSS (Integrated Towed Active/Passive Sonar System), and self-protection against air

Above: Seen in the form of HMCS Vancouver, the 'Halifax' class has only light gun armament (one 57-mm Bofors SAK Mk 2 mounting) but good anti-ship and anti-submarine capabilities.

Above: Resulting from a much-delayed programme and revealing a noise problem on trials, the 'Halifax' class of guided-missile frigates has matured as an excellent oceanic patrol type. This is HMCS Regina.

Below: The after part of the 'Halifax' class frigate is dominated by the hangar and flight platform for the embarked CH-124 Sea King helicopter. Over the hangar is located the radar-controlled Phalanx Mk 15 CIWS mounting with its 20-mm six-barrel cannon.

SPECIFICATION

'Halifax' class
Displacement: 4,770 tons full load
Dimensions: length 134.7 m (441 ft 1 in); beam 16.4 m (53 ft 10 in); draught 7.1 m (23 ft 2 in)
Propulsion: CODOG with two General Electric LM2500 gas turbines delivering 35,412 kW (47,494 shp) and one SEMT-Pielstick 20 PA6 V 280 diesel delivering 6,560 kW (8,800 shp) to two shafts
Performance: speed 29 kts; range 17,620 km (10,950 miles) at 13 kts
Armament: two quadruple launchers for eight Harpoon anti-ship missiles, Sea Sparrow SAM system, 57-mm gun, 20-mm Phalanx CIWS mounting, and two twin 324-mm (12.75-in) tubes for Mk 46 anti-submarine torpedoes
Electronics: SPS-49(V)5 air search radar, Sea Giraffe HC 150 air/surface search radar, Type 1007 navigation radar, two SPG-503 (STIR 1.8) fire-control radars, UYC-501 SHINPADS combat data system, Canews SLQ-501 and Ramses SLQ-503 ESM, decoy launchers, SLQ-25 towed torpedo decoy, SQS-510 hull-mounted active sonar, and SQR-501 CANTASS towed-array sonar
Aircraft: one CH-124 helicopter
Complement: 215 including 17 aircrew

attack is to be enhanced from 2004 by the retrofit of the Evolved Sea Sparrow SAM system in place of the current Mk 48 octuple vertical-launch system for 16 RIM-7P Sea Sparrow SAMs. The limitations of radar-based fire-control systems in the face of modern countermeasures were also reflected from 2002 by the retrofit of a Wescan 14 optronic fire-control capability.

While seven of the ships are deployed on Canada's Atlantic seaboard, the other five (in the form of the *Vancouver*, *Regina*, *Calgary*, *Winnipeg* and *Ottawa*) are based on the country's Pacific seaboard.

'Thetis' class Frigate

Requiring a successor to the 'Hvidbjørnen' class of obsolescent and relatively small frigates used for the patrol and fishery protection roles off Greenland and the Faeroe Islands as well as in the North Sea, the Danish government contracted with YARD of Glasgow in 1986 for a study to determine the parameters of the new class. This led to the award of a detailed design contract, completed in mid-1987, to Dwinger Marine Consultants. The design was of the StanFlex 3000 type, offering much commonality of concept and more limited commonality of components with the earlier StanFlex300 type, which had been ordered as the 'Flyvefisken' class of 14 multi-role large patrol/attack and minehunter/layer craft.

In October 1987 the Danish government ordered four examples of this **'Thetis' class** of frigate from Svenborg Vaerft. Laid down between October 1988 and January 1991 for commissioning between July 1991 and November 1992, the four ships are the **Thetis**, **Triton**, **Vaedderen** and **Hvidbjørnen**. The ships are based on a hull some 30 m (100 ft) longer than that of the 'Hvidbjørnen' class for improved sea-keeping and to provide the facility for the retrofit, as and when necessary, of additional armament and/or sensors. To this extent, the StanFlex concept is similar to the Meko concept pioneered by Blohm & Voss, as it permits the addition of new equipment built into standard-size containers.

Features of the design include a hull strengthened to allow operation in ice up to 1 m (3ft 4in) thick, and a double skin extends to a depth of 2 m (6ft 7in) below the waterline. Some consideration was also given to making the ships moderately 'stealthy', as evidenced by the location of the anchor equipment, bollards and winches below the upper deck. The ships have a full helicopter capability (hangar as well as a flight platform), and while the type currently embarked is a Westland Lynx light helicopter,

*The **Thetis** is the lead ship of a Danish class of four simple frigates optimized for the fishery and EEZ protection role, but the design has the capability for upgrade with more capable weapons and sensors. The **Thetis** differs from its three sisters in details of her stern, which is adapted for the towing of seismological noise generators and receivers.*

the platform has the size and strength to handle larger helicopters such as the Westland Sea King and Agusta/Westland Merlin. On each side of the hangar is accommodation for an inflatable rigid boarding craft handled by a dedicated crane.

The ships are optimized for the fishery and EEZ protection roles rather than high-intensity combat operations, and this made it feasible for the bridge and operations room to be combined as a single unit. The *Thetis* is used for seismological survey off Greenland and has a revised stern allowing the use of a towed-array sonar and a pneumatic noise gun. All four of the ships are to be upgraded with more modern air search radar and a SAM system.

SPECIFICATION	
'Thetis' class **Displacement:** 2,600 tons standard; 3,500 tons full load **Dimensions:** length 112.5 m (369 ft 1 in); beam 14.4 m (47 ft 3 in); draught 6 m (19 ft 8 in) **Propulsion:** three Burmeister & Wain diesels delivering 8,050 kW (10,800 shp) to one shaft **Performance:** speed 20 kts; range 15,770 km (9,800 miles) at 15.5 kts **Armament:** one 76-mm (3-in) gun, one or two 20-mm guns, and two depth charge rails	**Electronics:** AWS 6 air/surface search radar, Scanter Mil surface search radar, FR1505DA navigation radar, 9LV Mk 3 fire-control radar, 9LV 200 Mk 3 optronic director, Terma TDS combat data system, Cutlass ESM, Scorpion ECM, two Sea Gnat decoy launchers, C-Teck hull-mounted sonar, and TSM 2640 Salmon variable-depth sonar **Aircraft:** one Westland Lynx Mk 91 helicopter **Complement:** up to 72

'Jiangwei I and II' classes Guided missile frigates

The most modern elements in the frigate force operated by the navy of the People's Republic of China are the 12 **'Jiangwei'-class** guided missile frigates. These fall into two subclasses: the original **'Jiangwei I'-class** or **Type 053H2G** ships *(Anqing, Huainan, Huaibei* and *Tongling)* and the eight **'Jiangwei II'-class** or **Type 053H3** ships *(Jiaxin,*

Lianyungang, Sanming, Putian, Yichang, Yulin, Yuxi and one other).

The programme began in 1988 to replace the obsolete Type 053H1/2 ('Jianghu'-class) frigates.

The 'Jiangwei I' class marked a shift in Chinese naval thinking away from ships that operate close to shore and toward ocean-going warships. It is

closer to modern thinking, as it is a larger and more capable multi-role type. Even so, the 'Jiangwei I' class is obsolescent by comparison with the current frigates of the Western and Russian navies. In particular, the bulky launcher carrying six obsolete semi-active HQ-61B SAMs with manual reloading cannot deal with multiple air threats, but may be replaced by the HQ-7 SAM system based on an octuple launcher. Moreover, its sonar and helicopter are insufficient to cope with the threat of modern submarines.

With the same displacement, dimensions, propulsion and performance as the 'Jiangwei II' class, the 'Jiangwei I' class carries China's first-generation indigenous ZKJ-3A combat data system. Other systems include two JM-83H optronic directors for the 100-mm (3.94-in) DP main guns, SATCOM, digital communications and NH-900 datalink. The anti-ship missile

carried in two triple launchers is the indigenous YJ-1 (export C-801A). Close-range AA defence is dealt with by eight 37-mm guns in four twin mountings and the front and rear corners of the superstructure.

The air and surface search radars include the Type 360S (Chinese copy of Thomson-CSF DRBV 15) 2D unit, Type 363 surface search radar, and Type 517H-1 Knife Rest 2D long-range air search unit.

Four years after the end of the 'Jiangwei I' programme, the 'Jiangwei II' class entered production, eight ships being built for commissioning in 1998–2002. Improvements include four quadruple launchers for YJ-1 missiles, the HQ-7 (Chinese-made version of the French Crotale) SAM system, the redistribution of the AA guns, and updated fire-control radars. The ships serve with the East Sea and South Sea Fleets, and Pakistan may order two of the class.

SPECIFICATION

'Jiangwei II' class
Displacement: 2,250 tons full load
Dimensions: length 111.7 m (366 ft 6 in); beam 12.4 m (40 ft 8 in); draught 4.8 m (15 ft 9 in)
Propulsion: CODAD with two Type 18E 390 diesels delivering 17,900 kW (24,010 shp) to two shafts
Performance: speed 27 kts; endurance 7400 km (4,600 miles) at 18 kts
Armament: one twin 100-mm (3.94-in) gun, four twin 37-mm AA guns, two quadruple launchers for eight YJ-1 (C-801 or CSS-N-4 'Sardine') or C-802 anti-ship missiles, one HQ-7 octuple launcher for CSA-N-4 short-range SAMs, and two RBU

1200 five-tube anti-submarine rocket launchers
Electronics: one Type 517 air search radar, one Type 360 air/surface search radar, two RM-1290 navigation radars, one Type 343G SSM and 100-mm fire-control radar, one Castor II SAM fire-control radar, one Type 341G 37-mm fire-control radar, one JM-83H optronic director, one ZKJ-3C combat data system, one SR-210/Type 981-3/RWD-8 EW system, two Mk 36 SRBOC and two 26-barrel chaff and flare launchers, and one Type 5 active search and attack hull sonar
Aircraft: one Harbin Zhi-9A Zaitun helicopter
Crew: 170

'Floréal' class Guided missile frigate

The French navy's six **'Floréal'-class** ships are designed as *frégates de surveillance*, and are ocean-capable patrol vessels designed for service in the offshore area of any low-intensity combat theatre. As a result, and in an attempt to reduce building and operating

costs, the frigates were manufactured to merchant passenger rather than naval standards, and feature both stabilizers and air-conditioning, the latter allowing the ships to be based on French territories in regions such as the Antilles (one ship) and the Indian and Pacific

Oceans (two ships each). The last unit is retained at Brest in the north-west of France.

Pairs of the ships were ordered in January 1989, January 1990 and January 1991. Named after months of

the French revolutionary calendar, the **Floréal, Prairial, Nivôse, Ventôse, Vendémiaire** and **Germinal** were commissioned in 1992–94.

Trials revealed that the ships had the 50-day endurance

*F735 is the **Germinal**, which was commissioned in May 1994 as the last of the six 'Floréal'-class frigates. The ship is based at Brest, whereas the rest of the class is dispersed in French overseas territories.*

SPECIFICATION

'Floréal' class
Displacement: 2,600 tons standard; 2,950 tons full load
Dimensions: length 93.5 m (306 ft 9 in); beam 14 m (45 ft 11 in); draught 4.3 m (14 ft 1 in)
Propulsion: CODAD with four SEMT-Pielstick 6 PA6 L 280 diesels delivering 6,580 kW (8,825 shp) to two shafts
Performance: speed 20 kts; endurance 18,500 km (11,495 miles) at 15 kts
Armament: one 100-mm (3.94-in) Mod 68 CADAM DP gun, two 20-mm Giat cannon (replaceable by one or two Simbad twin launchers for Mistral short-range

SAMs), and two launchers for two MM.38 Exocet anti-ship missiles
Electronics: one DRBV 21A air/surface search radar, two DRBN 34A radars (one for navigation and the other for helicopter control), one Najir optronic director, one ARBR 17 or ARBG 1 Saigon ESM system, and one or two Dagaie Mk 2 chaff and flare launchers
Aircraft: one Eurocopter AS 565MA Panther helicopter with hangar facilities or one Eurocopter AS 332F Super Puma helicopter without hangar facilities
Crew: 86 plus 24 marines

anticipated and a greater range. Despite their comparatively short length, the ships handle well, and can operate their helicopters in conditions up to Sea State 5. The funnel design improves the air flow over the flight deck. The utility of the

ships in overseas deployments is improved by the provision of an aft hold for up to 100 tons of cargo, and for the embarkation of up to 24 marines.

A longer-range anti-ship capability is provided by two Exocet missiles: the MM.40

version was planned, but cost considerations dictated using shorter-range MM.38 weapons. The gun armament is a blend of medium and light weapons, and an effective short-range defence is provided by the optional installation of a launcher for

Mistral SAMs. The Super Puma helicopter is relatively large for a vessel of this type.

In 1998 Morocco ordered two similar vessels, commissioned in 2002–03 as the **Mohammed V** and **Hassan II** with the 76.2-mm (3-in) Otobreda Compact DP gun.

'Hydra' class (Meko 200HN) Guided missile frigate

Resulting from a procurement decision of April 1988, the Greek navy's four **'Hydra'-class** frigates are of the fin-stabilized **Meko 200HN** type related to the Portuguese 'Vasco da Gama' class, and are the **Hydra**, **Spetsai**, **Psara** and **Salamis**. The first was built by the design parent, Blohm + Voss, in Hamburg, and the other three by Hellenic Shipyards of Skaramanga in Greece in the period 1990–97, and were commissioned in 1992–98.

The ships are highly shock resistant, are stiff to ensure good fire-control and sensor capability, and possess great blast resistance. The hull is fabricated from high-tensile steel, and the ship is divided into 12 watertight sections functioning almost independently of each other and with the facility to transfer data to the Siemens Nautos naval automation system. The ship's battle management system is

the Thales Nederland (formerly Signaal) STACOS Mod 2. The weapons are a blend of Harpoon anti-ship and vertically launched Sea Sparrow surface-to-air missiles, 5-in (127-mm) Mk 45 DP and 20-mm CIWS guns, and 324-mm (12.75-in) Mk 46 Mod 5 anti-submarine torpedoes, the last launched from two Mk 32 triple units. Countermeasures include the SLQ-25 Nixie torpedo decoy and four Mk 36 Super RBOC chaff launchers, the latter working in conjunction with the Argo AR 700 ESM and Argo APECS radar jamming systems.

The Thales Nederland DA-08 FFT long-range air/surface radar has its antenna high on the main mast, while the Thales Nederland MW-08 medium-range air search radar's antenna is on the mast tower in the centre of the ship forward of the funnels, and the Thales Nederlands STIR fire-control radars have their conical

Each 'Hydra'-class ship has a side-by-side disposition of machinery spaces, with each engine pair exhausting via its own funnel.

antennae as one about halfway up the main mast facing the bow and the other on the mast tower facing the stern. The sonar is the Raytheon SQS-56 DE1160 system with hull-

mounted and variable-depth elements.

The 'Hydra'-class ships each have a twin-shaft propulsion arrangement powered by a CODAG system. Each shaft line

SPECIFICATION
'Hydra' class

'Hydra' class
Displacement: 2,710 tons light; 3,350 tons full load
Dimensions: length 117 m (383 ft 10 in); beam 14.8 m (48 ft 6 in); draught 6 m (19 ft 8 in)
Propulsion: CODOG with two LM 2500 gas turbines delivering 44,735 kW (60,000 shp) and two MTU 20V956 TB82 diesels delivering 7,770 kW (10,420 shp) to two shafts
Performance: speed 31 kts; endurance 7600 km (4,725 miles) at 16 kts
Armament: one 5-in (127-mm) DP gun, two 20-mm Phalanx CIWS mountings, two quadruple launchers for eight Harpoon anti-ship missiles, one Mk 48 Mod 2 vertical-launch system for 16 Sea

Sparrow short/medium-range SAMs, two 324-mm (12.75-in) triple Mk 32 tubes for Mk 46 anti-submarine torpedoes
Electronics: MW-08 air search radar, DA-08 air/surface search radar, Decca 2690 BT navigation radar, ARPA navigation radar, two STIR fire-control radars, one STACOS Mod 2 combat data system, one AR 700/Telegon 10/APECS II EW system, four Mk 36 SRBOC chaff and flare launchers, one SQS-56/DE 1160 sonar system with active hull and passive towed-array elements, and one SLQ-25 Nixie towed torpedo decoy
Aircraft: one Sikorsky S-70B-6 Aegean Hawk helicopter
Crew: 173 plus provision for 16 flag staff

comprises an MTU 20V956 TB82 diesel, a General Electric LM2500-30 gas turbine, a reduction gearbox with clutch coupling, and an SSS clutch driving an Escher Wyss controllable-pitch propeller. Control of the propulsion system is achieved via the Siemens Nautos system.

The Spetsai was completed in October 1996 as the first 'Hydra'-class frigate built in Greece, and some of the ship's prefabrication was undertaken in Germany.

'Brahmaputra' class Guided missile frigate

The Indian navy has a long association with ships derived from the original 'Leander' frigate class designed in the UK. In 1972–81, it commissioned six 'Broad-beam Leander'-class ships as its 'Nilgiri' class, and then in 1982–88 three

Yard of Calcutta, the three units are the **Brahmaputra**, **Betwa** and **Beas**.

Progress with the ships has been very slow: the first was laid down in 1989 but commissioned only in April 2000; the last unit was

completed in July 2005.

The hull is basically a lengthened version of the hull of the 'Godavari' class with a similar two-shaft propulsion system (though with Indian-

made steam turbines), but European and Indian electronics. It also has SS-N-25 rather than SS-N-2 anti-ship missiles and, when available, it is fitted with the Trishul SAM system.

Above: The hangar of the 'Brahmaputra'-class ships can house two medium helicopters with anti-ship missiles or anti-submarine torpedoes.

Below: Frigates of the 'Brahmaputra' class carry 16 SS-N-25 anti-ship missiles in four quadruple launchers on the forecastle, with the Trishul SAM system in a deckhouse abaft them.

SPECIFICATION	
'Brahmaputra' class **Displacement:** 4,450 tons full load **Dimensions:** length 126.5 m (415 ft); beam 14.5 m (47 ft 7 in); draught 4.5 m (14 ft 9 in) **Propulsion:** two Bhopal steam turbines delivering 22,370 kW (30,000 shp) to two shafts **Performance:** speed 27 kts; endurance 8,350 km (5,190 miles) at 12 kts **Armament:** one 76.2-mm (3-in) Otobreda Compact DP gun, four 30-mm AK-630 CIWS mountings, four quadruple launchers for 16 Kh-35 Uran (SS-N-25) anti-ship missiles, provision for one launcher for Trishul short-range SAMs, and two triple ILAS 3 324-mm (12.75-in) tubes for A 244S anti-submarine torpedoes	**Electronics:** LW-08/RAWL (PLN 517) air search radar, RAWS 03 (PFN 513) air/surface search radar, navigation and helicopter-control radar, three Seaguard 76.2-mm/30-mm fire-control radars, Aparna SSM fire-control radar, IPN-10 combat data system, INS-3 (Ajanta and TQN-2) EW system, two chaff and flare launchers, APSOH (Spherion) active search and attack hull sonar, Fathoms Oceanic variable-depth sonar, and one Graseby 738 towed torpedo decoy **Aircraft:** two Westland Sea King medium helicopters, or one Sea King and one HAL Chetak light helicopter **Crew:** 313 including air crew

'Godavari'-class ships with a longer and beamier hull for the embarkation of two Sea King helicopters. The vessels were also the first with a Western-designed hull to be fitted with Soviet weapons and sensors.

Finally, the Indian navy moved further along the evolutionary path with its three **Type 16A** or **'Brahmaputra'-class** frigates. Built by the Garden Reach Ship

'La Fayette' class Guided-missile frigate

Originally designated as *frégates légères* but reclassified in 1992 as *frégates type La Fayette*, the **'La Fayette' class** of multi-purpose frigates was ordered in July 1988 (first three) and September 1992 (last three, of which the final unit was later cancelled). All built by the DCN at Lorient, the ships were commissioned between March 1996 and October 2001 as the **La Fayette**, **Surcouf**, **Courbet**, **Aconit** (ex-**Jauréguiberry**) and **Guépratte**.

The ships were created to perform a number of missions, including crisis intervention and the seaward defence of France and its overseas territories. The ships can also be integrated into an intervention task force based on an aircraft carrier

Above: **Commissioned in 1997, the Surcouf was the second of the 'La Fayette' class of multi-role frigates to be completed. Note the 100-mm gun in raised position.**

Left: **The 'La Fayettes', this being Guépratte, are notable for their clean, protrusion-free lines designed to minimize radar reflectivity and so reduce vulnerability to detection.**

'Stealth' features

Each ship comprises about 70 modules, two of which are large propulsion modules housing the diesel engines. Many modules are prefabricated off-site and assembled on the building way. The design's other new feature is the emphasis placed on electromagnetic and acoustic 'stealthing'. The engines are mounted on suspended rafts to reduce noise, the sides of the hull and the superstructures are inclined at about 10°, an inclined bulwark forward shields the single gun mounting, the masts and superstructure are coated with radar-absorbent paint, the forecastle and quarterdeck have composite radar-absorbent cladding, and the 'cleanliness' of

---

SPECIFICATION

'La Fayette' class
Displacement: 3,700 tons full load
Dimensions: length 124.2 m (407 ft 6 in); beam 15.4 m (50 ft 6 in); draught 5.9 m (19 ft 4 in)
Propulsion: CODAD with four SEMT-Pielstick 12 PA6 V 280 STC diesels delivering 15,740 kW (21,110 shp) to four shafts
Performance: speed 25 kts; range 16,675 km (10,360 miles) at 12 kts
Armament: two quadruple launchers for MM.40 Exocet Block 2 SSMs, one octuple Crotale Naval CN 2 launcher for VT 1 SAMs (or EDIR launcher for eight V3 SAMs on *La Fayette*) (possibly to be replaced by a SAAM vertical-launch system for 16 Aster 15 SAMs), one 100-mm

(3.9-in) DP gun, and two 20-mm cannon
Electronics: one DRBV 15C Sea Tiger Mk 2 air/surface search radar, one Castor 2J gun fire-control radar, one Crotale SAM fire-control radar (possibly to be replaced by Arabel), two DRBN 34A navigation radars, one CTM radar/IR fire-control system, one TDS 90 VIGY optronic fire-control system, TAVITAC 2000 combat data system, ARBR 17 or 21 and ARBG 1 Saigon ESM systems, ARBB 33 ECM, and two Dagaie Mk 2 decoy launchers
Aircraft: one AS 565MA Panther or NH 90 helicopter
Complement: 163

---

and/or amphibious ships. The multiplicity of the tasks required, combined with the steady evolution of weapons and sensors, suggest a modular approach to construction in an effort to facilitate modifications and update, and also to cater for the requirements of the export market which, by a time early in the 21st century, comprised 15 ships (three to an improved **'Arriyad' class** standard for Saudi Arabia and six each for Singapore and Taiwan, the last of the **'Kang Ding' class**).

the superstructure is enhanced by concealing the ships' boats behind amidships doors.

The initial armament and sensor fit is optimized for overseas patrol, but there is provision for upgrade with an anti-submarine capability and more modern weapons and sensors, and the anti-air capability is being improved with a new SAM system.

'D'Estienne d'Orves' class
Guided-missile frigate

Above: Classed as an aviso, or coastal escort, the Commandant Blaison was one of the later 'D'Estienne d'Orves'-class frigates to enter service. All the class have Exocet capacity, though the weapons are not always shipped. The class is now being phased out of French service, in which nine survive, including this vessel, other vessels having been sold to Argentina (three 'Drummond' class) and Turkey (six 'Buruk' class).

Above: The 'D'Estienne d'Orves' class comprises small but useful coastal escorts. The type is being reduced in French service, six of the ships going to Turkey.

Designed for coastal escort, the 17 ships of the **'D'Estienne d'Orves' class** were commissioned between September 1976 and May 1984 as limited-capability corvettes that are now classified as light frigates. The ships can also be used for scouting missions, training and for overseas 'flag showing' duties, for which one officer and 17 men from the naval infantry can be accommodated. Since entering service, the type has been sold to the Argentine navy, whose three ships (the **Drummond**, **Guerrico** and **Granville**) included two that had originally been ordered by South Africa

but could not be delivered because of a UN arms embargo, and a third built for Argentina. The three saw service in the 1982 Falklands War, and in this campaign the *Guerrico* suffered the ignominy of being damaged by shore fire from small arms and antitank rocket-launchers during the Argentine seizure of South Georgia on 3 April; this required the vessel to be dry docked for three days for repairs to the hull and armament.

Rated as *avisos* by the French, the first of the class was laid down at Lorient Naval Dockyard in 1972 and commissioned into service in

'D'Estienne d'Orves' class
Ships in class: *D'Estienne d'Orves* (F781), *Amyot d'Inville* (F782), *Drogou* (F783), *Détroyat* (F784), *Jean Moulin* (F785), *Quartier Maître Anquetil* (F786), *Commandant de Pimodan* (F787), *Second Maître de Bihan* (F788), *Lieutenant de Vaisseau Le Henaff* (F789), *Lieutenant de Vaisseau Lavalle* (F790), *Commandant l'Herminier* (F791), *Premier Maître l'Her* (F792), *Commandant Blaison* (F793), *Enseigne de Vaisseau Jacoubet* (F794), *Commandant Ducuing* (F795), *Commandant Birot* (F796) and *Commandant Bouan* (F797).
Displacement: 1,175 tons standard; 1,250 tons or, later ships, 1,330 tons full load
Dimensions: length 80 m (262 ft 6 in); beam 10.3 m (33 ft 9½ in); draught 5.3 m (17 ft 4¾ in)
Propulsion: two SEMT-Pielstick 12PC2 V 400 diesels delivering 8,205 kW (11,000 shp) to two shafts or, in F791, two SEMT-

Pielstick 12 PA6 280 BTC diesels delivering 10,740kW (14,400 shp) to two shafts
Performance: speed 23.5 kts; range 8,350 km (5,190 miles) at 15 kts
Armament: (F781, F783, F786 and F787) two single launchers for MM.38 Exocet SSMs or (F792-F797) four single launchers for MM.40 Exocet SSMs, one Simbad twin launcher for Mistral short-range SAMs, one 100-mm (3.9-in) DP gun, two 20-mm AA guns, one 375-mm (14.76-in) Creusot Loire Mk 54 sextuple launcher for anti-submarine rockets (F789-F791), and four tubes for four L3 or L5 torpedoes
Electronics: one DRBV 51A air/surface search radar, one DRBC 32E gun fire-control radar, one DRBN 32 navigation radar, one Vega fire-control system, one Panda optronic director, ARBR 16 ESM, two Dagaie decoy launchers, and one DUBA 25 hull sonar
Complement: 108 with marines

1976. Six of the ships were sold to Turkey in October 2000 and delivered by July 2002 after refit at Brest. Two more of the 17 ships have been deleted from the French naval list, and of the remaining nine (six and three based at Brest and Toulon respectively), current plans call for their decommissioning from 2009 after a reprieve from the initial plan in which the first three would have been paid off in 1996 with the other 14 following at regular intervals up to 2004.

'Brandenburg' class Guided-missile frigate

The **'Brandenburg' class** of guided-missile frigates, otherwise designated as the **Type 123 class**, were designed as one-for-one replacements for the four elderly destroyers of the 'Hamburg' class, which were all decommissioned in the first half of the 1990s. The new frigates were originally to have been designated as the **'Deutschland' class**, and the ships were ordered in June 1989 from four German yards on the basis of a Blohm & Voss design selected in October of the previous year. The ships are the **Brandenburg** from Blohm & Voss of Hamburg, **Schleswig-Holstein** from Howaldtswerke of Kiel, **Bayern** from Thyssen

Nordseewerke of Emden, and **Mecklenburg-Vorpommern** from Bremer Vulkan/Thyssen. The ships were laid down in 1992–93, launched in 1992–95, and commissioned in 1994–96, and currently constitute the 6th Frigate Squadron based at Wilhelmshaven.

The design is a mixture of Blohm & Voss's now well-proved MEKO system of modular construction with improved serviceability features from the Type 122 or 'Bremen' class of eight smaller guided-missile frigates, with which the 'Brandenburg' class shares the

Above: Brandenburg, *lead ship of a four-strong class of general-purpose warships. The areas forward of the bridge carry the VLS for medium-range SAMs, a trainable launcher for short-range SAMs, and a 76-mm gun.*

Left: *Pending the advent of the three 'Sachsen' (Type 124) class of air-defence frigates, the 'Brandenburgs' are Germany's most advanced surface ships.*

propulsion arrangement. This, because of their greater size, results in a slight loss of speed in the 'Brandenburg' vessels. The ships are of all-steel construction and incorporate current 'stealth' thinking, fin stabilizers and provision for a task group commander and his staff. Each ship also possesses provision for one Rigid Inflatable Boat (RIB) to be used by boarding parties.

The main gun is sited on the forecastle, the two SAM systems are forward and aft on the superstructure, and there are two helicopters.

SPECIFICATION	
'Brandenburg' class	20-mm Rheinmetall AA guns (to be
Displacement: 4,900 tons full load	replaced by two 27-mm Mauser
Dimensions: length 138.9 m (455 ft	guns), and two 324-mm (12.75-in)
9 in); beam 16.7 m (54 ft 10 in);	Mk 32 twin tubes for Mk 46 (to be
draught 6.8 m (22 ft 4 in)	replaced by Mu 90 Impact) anti-
Propulsion: CODOG with two	submarine torpedoes
General Electric LM2500SA-ML	**Electronics:** LW-08 air search radar,
gas turbines delivering 38,025 kW	SMART 3D air/surface search radar,
(51,000 shp) and two MTU 20V	two STIR 180 fire-control radars,
956 TB92 diesels delivering 8,250	two Raypath navigation radars,
kW (11,065 shp) to two shafts	MWCS weapons control system
Performance: speed 29 kts; range	with a WBA optronic director, SATIR
7,400 km (4,600 miles) at 18 kts	combat data system, FL 1800S
Armament: two twin launchers for	ESM system, two SCLAR decoy
MM.38 Exocet anti-ship missiles,	launchers, DSQS-23BZ hull-
one VLS Mk 41 for 16 NATO Sea	mounted active sonar, LFASS
Sparrow medium-range SAMs, two	towed-array active sonar
Mk 49 21-cell launchers for RAM	**Aircraft:** two Lynx Mk 88 or Lynx
short-range SAMs, one 76-mm	Mk 88A helicopters
(3-in) OTO Melara DP gun, two	**Complement:** 218

'Bremen' class Guided-missile frigate

A German modification of the gas turbine-powered Dutch 'Kortenaer' design, the eight-ship **'Bremen' class**, also known as the **Type 122 class**, has replaced the deleted ships of two older types, namely the 'Fletcher' (Type 119) class of destroyers and the 'Köln' (Type 120) class of frigates. The hulls were mated with the propulsion plant in the five building yards, and the ships then towed to the yard of Bremer Vulkan for the installation of the electronic and weapon systems. The first order was placed in 1977, and the ship commissioned in May 1982.

Fin stabilizers and the US Prairie/Masker bubble system on the hull and propellers help to reduce radiated noise levels from the machinery. A complete NBC defence citadel system is also fitted. Two 21-round launchers for the RAM point-defence SAM, with passive radar/infra-red terminal homing, were retrofitted atop the hangar in 1993–96. Lynx Mk 88/88A helicopters are embarked, with a Bendix DASQ-18 active dunking sonar for use with Mk 46 homing torpedoes and Mk 54 depth charges. The Bear

*The **Emden** was the third of the 'Bremen'-class frigates to be completed. This general-purpose ship's primary ASW weapon is a pair of Lynx helicopters.*

Trap landing system enables flying in rough weather.

The eight ships are the **Bremen**, **Niedersachsen**, **Rheinland-Pfalz**, **Emden**, **Köln**, **Karlsruhe**, **Augsburg** and **Lübeck**. The ships will remain in front-line service well into the 21st century.

SPECIFICATION

'Bremen' or Type 122 class
Displacement: 2,900 tons standard; 3,680 tons full load
Dimensions: length 130 m (426 ft 6 in); beam 14.5 m (47 ft 7 in); draught 6.5 m (21 ft 4 in)
Propulsion: CODOG arrangement of two General Electric LM2500 gas turbines delivering 38,478 kW (51,600 shp) and two MTU 20V TB92 diesels delivering 7,755 kW (10,400 shp) to two shafts
Performance: speed 30 kts; endurance 7,400 km (4,600 miles) at 18 kts
Armament: two quadruple launchers for eight Harpoon anti-ship missiles, one Mk 29 octuple launcher for 16 RIM-7M Sea Sparrow SAMs, two 21-cell launchers for 42 RAM SAMs, one 76-mm (3-in) DP gun, and two twin Mk 32 324-mm (12.75-in) tubes for Mk 46 (later Mu 90) ASW torpedoes
Electronics: one TRS-3D/32 air/surface search radar, one 3RM20 navigation radar, one WM-25/STIR radar fire-control system, one WBA optronic director, one SATIR tactical data system, one FL1800S-II ESM/ECM system, four Mk 36 SRBOC decoy launchers, one SLQ-25 Nixie towed torpedo decoy, and one DSQS-21BZ (BO) bow-mounted active sonar
Aircraft: two Lynx Mk 88/88A ASW helicopters
Complement: 219

Based on the Dutch 'Kortenaer'-class design, the 'Bremen' class comprises eight multi-role frigates. Forward of the bridge are the 76-mm (3-in) gun and the launcher for Sea Sparrow medium-range SAMs, abaft the bridge are the two Harpoon anti-ship missiles, and at the stern are the helicopters and two RAM point-defence SAM launchers.

'Espora' class Guided-missile frigate

As part of the Argentine navy's modernization plans, a contract was signed for six missile-armed **Meko 140A16** ships, to be built to a light frigate design based on the Portuguese 'Joao Coutinho' class, and known locally as the **'Espora' class**. The programme was affected by Argentina's 1982 Falklands defeat and subsequent economic decline, so the lead ship **Espora** was commissioned only in July 1985, a trio comprising the **Rosales**, **Spiro** and **Parker** following in 1986, 1987 and 1990, and a final pair, the **Robinson** and **Gomez Roca**, in 2000 and 2002 respectively. The first three differ

Basically a scaled-down Meko 360 destroyer, the Meko 140 of the *'Espora' class is a light frigate optimized for the anti-ship/submarine roles. The first three ships were completed with only a platform (later enlarged to accommodate the AS 555 Fennec) for helicopter operations, while the last three were completed with a telescopic hangar of the type that is to be retrofitted to the earlier ships. The after gun mount is a Breda unit with two 40-mm Bofors guns, an identical unit being located immediately forward of the bridge behind and above the 76-mm (3-in) OTO-Melara DP gun.*

SPECIFICATION

'Espora' (Meko 140) class
Displacement: 1,470 tons standard; 1,700 tons full load
Dimensions: length 91.2 m (299 ft 2 in); beam 11.1 m (36 ft 5 in); draught 3.4 m (11 ft 2 in)
Propulsion: two SEMT-Pielstick diesels delivering 15,200 kW (20,385 shp) to two shafts
Performance: speed 27 kts; endurance 7,400 km (4,600 miles) at 18 kts
Armament: four container-launchers for MM.38 Exocet anti-ship missiles, one 76-mm (3-in) DP and two twin 40-mm AA guns, and two triple 324-mm (12.75-in) ILAS 3 tubes for 12 Whitehead A 244/S ASW torpedoes
Electronics: one DA-05 air/surface search radar, one TM1226 navigation radar, one WM-28 fire-control radar, one Lirod 8 optronic director, one WM-22/41 fire-control system, one SEWACO action information system, one RQN-3B/TQN-2X ESM/ECM system, and one ASO-4 hull-mounted search/attack sonar
Aircraft: one SA 319B Alouette III or AS 555 Fennec helicopter
Complement: 93

from the last three units in initially having only a helicopter landing platform amidships, whereas the others were completed with a telescopic hangar to allow the permanent carriage of a light helicopter.

The ships of the 'Espora' class replaced some of Argentina's ex-American destroyers of the World War II period, and though operated mainly in the offshore and fishery patrol tasks, the ships are equipped predominantly with ASW and anti-surface warfare weapon systems. The four MM.38 Exocet container-launchers shipped aft could be replaced by eight canisters for the lighter but longer-range MM.40 Exocet anti-ship missiles used on the four Meko 360 destroyers of the 'Almirante Brown' class.

Though designed primarily for service in coastal operations, the class forms a potentially capable offensive force for use in future naval operations.

The ships are all based at Puerto Belgrano, and the *Spiro* and *Rosales* joined the Coalition fleet during the Gulf War of 1990–91, but their primary role is nonetheless in Argentine waters.

Rosales *was built by AFNE of Rio Santiago, and although launched in 1983 was commissioned only in 1986 because of financial problems. The last two ships in the class may have different EW suites.*

'Sachsen' class Guided-missile frigate

The design of the **'Sachsen' class**, or **Type 124**, frigate is based on the 'Brandenburg', or Type 123, class but with enhanced 'stealth' features to deceive any opponent's radar and acoustic sensors. The ships were required as replacements for the German navy's ageing and, indeed, obsolete 'Lütjens' class of guided-missile destroyers in the air-defence role, and a memorandum of understanding was signed in 1993 between the German government and the Blohm & Voss, Royal Schelde and Bazán (now Izar) shipyards. The design that emerged is a joint German and Dutch project based on the use of a common primary anti-air warfare system using the Standard SM-2 and Evolved Sea Sparrow medium-range SAMs.

In June 1996 the German government contracted for three ships with an option on a fourth (to have been named the **Thüringen**), but this was not taken up. Thus the class comprises three ships, the **Sachsen**, **Hamburg** and

Above: The pyramidal tower abaft the pair of outward-canted funnels carries the antenna for the SMART L 3D air search radar. The Mk 41 VLS for the primary SAMs is located flush with the deck, forward of the bridge.

Right: Enhancing the 'stealthiness' of the design of the 'Sachsen' class are the replacement of vertical surfaces by inward- or outward-angled surfaces wherever possible, and the omission of other angles that could reflect electro-magnetic energy.

Hessen, which were built by Blohm & Voss of Hamburg, Howaldtswerke of Kiel and Thyssen Nordseewerke of Emden respectively. The ships were laid down in February 1999, September 2000 and July 2002, launched in December 1999, March 2002 and March 2003 and were commissioned in December 2003, December 2004 and December 2005.

The primary SAM armament is carried in the Mk 41 Vertical-Launch System forward of the bridge: this carries up to 32 Standard SM-2 missiles as well as Evolved Sea Sparrows in designated cells. Local defence

against air attack is entrusted to a pair of 21-cell launchers for RAM short-range SAMs, anti-ship capability is vested in Harpoon missiles, and anti-submarine capability in two helicopters and two tube mountings for lightweight torpedoes. Mounted round the top of the superstructure are the four antennae of the Thales APAR phased-array air/surface radar.

SPECIFICATION
'Sachsen' (Type 124) class
Displacement: 5,600 tons
Dimensions: length 143 m (469 ft 2 in); beam 17.4 m (57 ft 1 in); draught 4.4 m (14 ft 5 in)
Propulsion: CODAG arrangement with one gas turbine delivering 26,483 kW (35,514 shp) and two diesels delivering 15,009 kW (20,128 shp) to two shafts
Speed: 29 kts
Armament: two quadruple launchers for eight Harpoon anti-ship missiles, one Mk 41 VLS for 32 Standard SM-2 and Evolved Sea Sparrow SAMs, two launchers for 42 RAM SAMs, one 76-mm (3-in) DP gun, and two triple Mk 32 324-mm (12.75-in) tubes for Mu 90 torpedoes
Electronics: one SMART L 3D radar, one APAR air/surface search radar, one Sewaco FD action data system, one FL 1800S-II ESM/ECM system, one active attack sonar, and one active towed-array sonar
Aircraft: two NFH 90 or Lynx Mk 88A helicopters
Complement: 255

'Lupo' and 'Maestrale' classes Guided-missile frigates (FFG)

Built by CN Riuniti (now Fincantieri) naval shipbuilders, the four vessels of the **'Lupo' class** in the Italian navy were **Lupo**, **Sagittario**, **Perseo** and **Orsa**. In 2003 only the *Perseo* remained in service. The 'Lupos' were designed for the convoy escort role, with a capability for anti-surface warfare using SSMs if required. The hull is based on 14 watertight compartments and has fixed-fin stabilizers. To reduce the ship's complement, the machinery plant is highly automated and divided into four separate compartments housing the auxiliaries, gas turbine modules, reduction gearbox and the diesel alternator sets. A telescopic hangar houses one AB 212ASW helicopter that can double in the missile-armed surface strike role.

The 'Lupos' proved very popular in service, and the type was exported to Venezuela, Peru and Iraq in a modified form that

has a fixed-hangar structure and no reloads for the SAM launcher. The six Venezuelan ships are the **Mariscal Sucre**, **Almirante Brión**, **General Urdaneta**, **General Soublette**, **General Salom** and **Almirante Garcia**. The four Peruvian ships are the **Meliton Carvajal**, **Villavicencio**, **Montero** and **Mariategui**. The four Iraqi units were the **Hittin**, **Thi Qar**, **Al Yarmouk** and **Al Qadisiya**. Payment problems caused the cancellation of the order in 1990, following the UN sanctions placed on Saddam Hussein's regime in retaliation for its invasion of Kuwait. All four ships were placed in Italian naval service as fleet patrol ships and renamed **Artigliere**, **Aviere**, **Bersagliere** and **Granatiere** respectively.

Armament

The main anti-ship weapon carried on the Italian ships is

Perseo, *the third 'Lupo' frigate to enter service with the Italian navy is seen with its forward 76-mm gun at high elevation. A total of 18 'Lupos' were built.*

the Otomat Mk 2 missile, which has an Italian SMA active radar-homing seeker and a sea-skimming flight profile. The original Teseo launchers have been strengthened to take two missiles each. To use their over-the-horizon capabilities fully, the embarked helicopter is used for mid-course guidance.

'Maestrale' class

The eight-strong **'Maestrale' class** is essentially a stretched version of the 'Lupo' design a greater emphasis on ASW. The increase in length and beam over the earlier 'Lupos' was to provide for a fixed hangar installation and a variable-depth sonar (VDS) housing at the stern. The improvements have resulted in better seaworthiness and habitability, plus the room required to carry and operate a second light helicopter. However, to compensate for this the class carries 12 less SSMs, and because of the extra tonnage has suffered a speed reduction of around 3 kts. The

Raytheon VDS operates on the same frequencies as the hull sonar set and gives the vessels a valuable below-the-thermal-layer capability for use in the very difficult ASW conditions met in the Mediterranean. To enhance the ships' ASW operations further, the AB 212ASW helicopters carried are fitted with Bendix ASQ-13B active dunking sonars. The armament they carry is either the American Mk 46 homing torpedo or Mk 54 depth charge. The ship uses the Mk 46 torpedo as well. It is also fitted with two fixed tubes for the 25-km (15.5-mile) range Whitehead Motofides A184 533-mm (21-in) wire-guided torpedo beneath the helicopter pad aft. Capable of 36 kts, the A184 can be used against surface and sub-surface targets. In 1994, a decision was taken to modify the hull-mounted and VDS sonar to give the system better performance and a mine detection capability. A towed LF array may also be added.

SPECIFICATION

'Lupo' class (Italian navy)
Displacement: 2,208 tons standard and 2,525 tons full load
Dimensions: length 113.2 m (371 ft 4 in); beam 11.3 m (37 ft); draught 3.7 m (12 ft 1 in)
Propulsion: CODOG arrangement with two General Electric/FIAT LM 2500 gas turbines delivering 37,285 kW (50,000 shp) and two GMT diesels delivering 7,457 kW (10,000 shp) to two shafts
Speed: 35 kts
Armament: eight twin Teseo launchers for 16 Otomat Mk 2 SSMs, Mk 29 octuple launcher for RIM-7M Sea Sparrow or Aspide SAMs (eight reloads), 127-mm (5-in)

DP gun, two twin 40-mm Breda AA guns, and two triple Mk 32 324-mm (12.75-in) torpedo tubes with Mk 46 ASW torpedoes
Aircraft: one AB 212ASW helicopter
Electronics: RAN 10S air search radar, SPQ-2F surface search radar, SPS-702 air search/target indication radar, RTN 10X fire-control radar, two RTN 20X gun fire-control radars, Mk 95 SAM fire-control radar, SPN-748 navigation radar, IPN 20 combat data system, active and passive ESM systems, two SCLAR 20-tube chaff launchers, DE 1160B hull sonar, and SLQ-25 Nixie towed torpedo decoy
Complement: 185

Faster than most Western frigates of their generation (although slower than the 'Lupo' class), the 'Maestrale' vessels are comprehensively equipped with modern ASW technology including both a hull sonar and a towed variable-depth sonar. Several of these systems have been upgraded. The vessels are **Maestrale, Grecale, Libeccio, Scirocco, Aliseo, Euro, Espero** *and* **Zeffiro.**

'Lekiu' class Guided-missile frigate (FFG)

The **Jebat** is the flagship of the Royal Malaysian navy and was laid down five months after its sistership, the **Lekiu**. The **'Lekiu' class** were ordered in 1992, originally as corvettes but upgraded to light frigates. The pair were commissioned in August 1997.

Their main weapon is the latest MM.40 Block 2 version of the Exocet sea-skimming SSM, for which two four-cell launchers are located amidships between the radar masts. Range and bearing data are fed to the missile before launch, and terminal guidance is by active monopulse seeker head.

The ships' defensive system is the Seawolf SAM, which can engage incoming missiles as well as aircraft.

ASW equipment

Anti-submarine torpedoes, a full sonar suite and an ASW helicopter make these heavily

Although Lekiu *(30) is the nameship of the class,* Jebat *(29) is the senior ship and thus took the lower pennant number. These are the largest and most capable surface vessels in Malaysian service.*

armed ships for their size. Integration of the weapons systems did cause problems and the ships were eventually delivered to the Malaysian navy in 2000.

SPECIFICATION	
'Lekiu' class **Displacement:** 1,845 tons standard and 2,390 tons full load **Dimensions:** length 105.5 m (346 ft); beam 12.8 m (42 ft); draught 3.6 m (11 ft 10 in) **Propulsion:** CODAD arrangement with four MTU diesels delivering 24,500 kW (33,300 shp) to four shafts **Speed:** 28 kts **Armament:** eight MM.40 Exocet SSMs, one 16-cell VLS for Seawolf SAMs, one 57-mm Bofors gun, two MSI 30-mm guns, and two triple	B515 324-mm (12.75-in) tubes for Stingray ASW torpedoes **Electronics:** one DA08 air search radar, one Sea Giraffe surface search radar, one Racal Decca navigation radar, two Marconi 1802 fire-control radars, one Spherion hull sonar, Nautis F and Link Y combat data systems, Mentor and Scimitar ESM and ECM systems, one Sea Siren towed torpedo decoy, and two Super Barricade 12-barrel chaff launchers **Aircraft:** one Super Lynx Series 300 **Complement:** 146

'Karel Doorman' class Guided-missile frigate (FFG)

The Royal Netherlands navy's **'Karel Doorman' class** of multi-purpose frigates were commissioned between 1991 and 1995. The names were manipulated to make the **Van Speijk** the last to complete, although it retains its original pennant number. The seven other vessels in the class are **Karel Doorman**, **Willem Van der Zaan**, **Tjerk Hiddes**, **Van Amstel**, **Abraham Van der Hulst**, **Van Nes** and **Van Galen**. With surface-to-surface missiles, anti-aircraft missiles and anti-submarine torpedoes (plus an ASW helicopter), these are true multi-role warships. The design is intended to reduce the radar signature and infra-red signature and extensive NBC protection is provided to conduct operations in contaminated areas.

Frequent participants in NATO exercises, the Dutch frigates have also taken part in US Navy anti-drug operations in the

Caribbean and missions for the UN in the Mediterranean and Adriatic. They also contributed naval units to Operation Desert Storm in 1991.

Their main anti-ship weapon is the Block 1C Harpoon. The vertical launch system for the Sea Sparrow SAMs is similar to that on the Greek 'Meko' and Canadian 'Halifax' classes.

Possible future modifications include the addition of low frequency active sonar to the class. From 2007, the 20 Lynx helicopters will be replaced by NH 90 helicopters.

Modernization

Between January 1992 and mid-1994, the class underwent a series of modernizations. A new SEWACO (sensors, weapons and command systems) VIII(A) suite was installed and updated to VIII(B) standard by 1994. An APECS II electronic warfare system was also installed along

with a DSBV 61 towed array. Other new systems include the IRSCAN infra-red detector fitted onto the hanger roof. Fitted to the *Willem van der Zaan* for trials in 1993, it was then fitted across the class. This provides target data for the Goalkeeper 30-mm CIWS. In addition, the Mk 36 SRBOC launchers can disperse IR flares and chaff up

to 4 km (2.4 miles). An SHF satellite communications (SATCOM) system was fitted along with a Scout radar positioned on the bridge roof in 1997. Four ATAS (Active Towed Array Sonar) were trialled from 1998, and have been ordered for several vessels in the class. Other modifications provide better stealth protection.

SPECIFICATION	
'Karel Doorman' class Displacement: 3,320 tons full load **Dimensions:** length 122.3 m (401 ft 3 in); beam 14.4 m (47 ft 3 in); draught 4.3 m (14 ft 1 in) **Propulsion:** CODOG arrangement with two Rolls-Royce Spey gas turbines delivering 25,214 kW (33,800 shp) and two Stork diesel engines delivering 7,303 kW (9,790 shp) to two shafts **Speed:** 30 kts (gas turbines) and 21 kts (cruising diesels) **Armament:** two quadruple launchers for Harpoon SSMs, one Mk 48 VLS for 16 Sea Sparrow SAMs, one 76-mm (3-in) Mk 100 DP gun, one Goalkeeper 30-mm CIWS, two	20-mm AA guns, two twin Mk 32 torpedo tubes for Mk 46 lightweight ASW torpedoes **Electronics:** one SMART air and surface search radar, one Scout surface search radar, one LW08 air search radar, two STIR fire-control radars, one Racal Decca 1226 navigation radar, one DSBV 61 towed sonar (later ATAS), one PHS-36 hull sonar, APECS II ESM/ECM system, one SLQ-25 Nixie towed torpedo decoy, and two Mk 36 SRBOC 6-tube quad chaff launchers **Aircraft:** one SH-14D Lynx ASW helicopter **Complement:** 156

'Vasco da Gama' class (Meko 200) Guided missile frigate

Related in overall terms to the **'Meko 200'** frigates operated by the Australian, Greek, New Zealand and Turkish navies, the Portuguese navy's **'Vasco da Gama' class** of three guided missile frigates comprises the **Vasco da Gama**, **Alvares Cabral** and **Corte Real**. Ordered in July 1986 from a consortium of West German interests, the

*The **Alvares Cabral** was completed in May 1991 as the second of the Portuguese navy's three small but capable 'Vasco da Gama'-class frigates.*

ships were laid down by Blohm & Voss of Hamburg (first ship) and Howaldtswerke of Kiel (other two) in 1989, launched in 1989–90, and commissioned in

January, May and November 1991 as what are still Portugal's most capable surface ships. Portugal paid for 40 per cent of the programme, with other NATO countries (and especially the US with the CIWS, torpedo system and most of the missiles) contributing the rest.

The ships are built of steel and have stabilizers for reduced pitch and roll movement in a

seaway. Intended for the anti-submarine role, the vessels have a hangar and flight deck for two light helicopters whose operations are enhanced by the provision of a RAS system, and enhancement is possible through the addition of a towed-array sonar and a vertical-launch system for the Sea Sparrow SAM. The ships were all modernized in the early 2000s.

SPECIFICATION

'Vasco da Gama' class
Displacement: 2,700 tons standard; 3,300 tons full load
Dimensions: length 115.9 m (380 ft 4 in); beam 14.8 m (48 ft 9 in); draught 6.1 m (20 ft)
Propulsion: CODOG with two LM 2500 gas turbines delivering 39,515 kW (53,000 shp) and two MTU 12V1163 TB83 diesels delivering 6,590 kW (8,840 shp) to two shafts
Performance: speed 32 kts; endurance 9,100 km (5,655 miles) at 18 kts
Armament: 100-mm (3.94-in) Creusot-Loire CADAM DP gun, 20-mm Phalanx CIWS mounting, provision for two 20-mm cannon, two

quadruple launchers for eight Harpoon anti-ship missiles, octuple launcher for Sea Sparrow SAMs, and two 324-mm (12.75-in(triple tubes for Mk 46 anti-submarine torpedoes
Electronics: one MW-08 air search radar, one DA-08 surface search radar, one Type 1007 navigation radar, two STIR fire-control radars, one Sewaco combat data system, one Argo AR 700/APECS II EW system, two Mk 36 SRBOC chaff/flare launchers, one SQS-510(V) active hull sonar, and one SLQ-25 Nixie towed torpedo decoy
Aircraft: two Westland Super Lynx Mk 95 helicopters
Crew: 182 including 16 air crew and 16 flag staff

'Abukuma' class Guided missile frigate

The Japanese Maritime Self-Defence Force, as the Japanese navy is formally styled, does not use the classification 'frigate' for any of its warships, preferring instead the classification 'destroyer escort' that more accurately conveys their task in protecting merchant shipping and naval forces (in particular amphibious warfare groups) against surface ship and submarine attack. Only a limited air-defence capability is deemed necessary, as the ships of the JMSDF are constitutionally limited to operations in and around the Japanese home islands where, it is supposed, they would enjoy the tactical advantages of operating under friendly air cover.

In overall terms, the JMSDF has procured only modest numbers of destroyer escorts, its largest class having been the 'Chikugo' class, of which 11

units, each with a standard displacement of 1,500 tons, were commissioned in 1970–76 but then phased out of service from the 1990s, with the last paid off in 2002.

New class

However, from the mid-1980s it was appreciated that the JMSDF would require a class of larger and more capable destroyer escorts, and this led to the creation of the **'Abukuma' class**. Named **Abukuma**, **Jintsu**, **Ooyodo**, **Sendai**, **Chikuma** and **Tone** (names that had been used in World War II for cruisers), the six ships were ordered in pairs, laid down in 1988–91, launched in 1988–91, and commissioned in 1989–93. Complementing the other only three destroyer escorts in Japanese service (the *Ishikari* with a full-load displacement of 1,450 tons and

the related but slightly larger *Yuubari* and *Yuubetsu* with full-load displacements of 1,690 tons), the 'Abukuma'-class destroyer escorts are conventional in their construction, CODOG propulsion arrangement, armament and sensor fit. However, a measure of 'stealthiness' was built into the design by the inward sloping of the superstructure's flat

surfaces, and the rounding of the superstructure's corners.

Simple in concept

Though the flush-decked ship itself and its electronics are largely of Japanese manufacture, the propulsion arrangement combines British and Japanese engines, and the armament is of American and Italian origins. The substantial

SPECIFICATION

'Abukuma' class
Displacement: 2,000 tons standard; 2,550 tons full load
Dimensions: length 109 m (357 ft 7 in); beam 13.4 m (44 ft); draught 3.8 m (12 ft 6 in)
Propulsion: CODOG with two Rolls-Royce spey SM1A gas turbines delivering 19870 kW (26,650 shp) and two Mitsubishi S12U-MTK diesels delivering 4,475 kW (6,000 shp) to two shafts
Speed: 27 kts
Armament: one 76.2-mm (3-in) Otobreda Compact DP gun, one

20-mm Phalanx CIWS mounting, one octuple launcher for ASROC anti-submarine missiles, and two 324-mm (12.75-in) triple tubes for anti-submarine torpedoes
Electronics: one OPS-14C air search radar, one OPS-28C/D surface search radar, one Type 2-21 fire-control radar, one OYQ-6 combat data system, one EW system, two Mk 36 SRBOC chaff/flare launchers, and one OQS-8 hull-mounted active sonar
Aircraft: none
Crew: 120

pyramidal lattice mast carries the antennae for the OPS-14C air search radar and the OPS-28C or OPS-28D surface search radar, with the antenna of the Type 2-21 fire-control radar located above the bridge.

The armament layout is typical for Japanese destroyer escorts. From bow to stern, it comprises one 76.2-mm (3-in) Otobreda Compact dual-purpose gun on the forecastle with excellent fields of fire, the trainable and elevating Mk 112 octuple launcher for ASROC anti-submarine weapons between the two funnels, the two 324-mm (12.75-in) Type 68 triple tubes for Mk 46 Mod 5 NEARtip acoustic-homing anti-submarine torpedoes to each side of the after deckhouse, the two quadruple launchers for Harpoon long-range anti-ship missiles (firing laterally to port and starboard) above the after deckhouse, and the 20-mm Phalanx CIWS mounting over the stern, again with very good fields of fire like the Otobreda Compact DP gun on the forecastle. There is a satellite communications antenna in a comparatively small radome just forward of the Harpoon launchers, and volume and deck area have been left for the possible retrofit of SQR-19A towed-array sonar. There is no provision for a helicopter, and though it was believed at one time that the self-defence capability might be boosted by a launcher for the German/US RIM-116 RAM short-range SAM, this possibility has apparently been abandoned.

'Valour' class Guided missile frigate

Particular features of the **'Meko A-200' class** include a higher-than-average payload/displacement ratio, 'stealthy' design, advanced propulsion and combat systems with modular open architecture.

South Africa contracted in December 1999 for four such frigates. The four definite ships are the **Amatola**, **Isandlwana**, **Spioen Kop** and **Mendi** of the **'Valour' class**, and are of German construction. *Amatola* was delivered to South Africa in November 2003 for fitting out, *Isandlwana* arrived in March 2004, *Spioen Kop* in June 2004 and *Mendi* in early 2005.

'Stealth' design features include hull panels alternately angled to avoid large flat surfaces, the avoidance of right-angled corners, and the 'decluttering' of the decks and superstructure, the latter including the elimination of the bridge wings present on the original 'Meko' concept and the complete enclosure of the bridge. A reduction of about 75 per cent of the thermal signature has been achieved by elimination of the funnel, the hot exhaust gases being ducted through a horizontal system with sea water used to cool the exhaust gases before they are expelled just above the waterline.

The four 'Valour'-class frigates are optimized for the air-defence role, and will be equipped with Combat Management System and Navigation Subsystem made by African Defence Systems, which is also the segment manager for the ships' underwater systems, including the sonars and torpedoes. Created by Grintek, the ships' integrated Seacom communications system is based on dual redundant high-speed fibre-optic networks and a modular hardware and software architecture.

Armament

The primary armament is centred on two quadruple launchers for eight MM.40 Exocet anti-ship missiles, and two eight-cell vertical-launch systems for the Umkhonto SAM, which has a range of up to 12 km (7.5 miles), uses inertial mid-course and IR terminal guidance systems, and delivers a 23-kg (50.7-lb) warhead fitted with an active proximity fuse.

Existing 76.2-mm (3-in) Otobreda Compact guns will be transferred from offshore patrol vessels, these guns being accommodated in turrets for which Reutech has developed a new electric drive system replacing the original hydraulic system. The ships will also carry two 35-mm cannon in a 35DPG dual-purpose mounting: a Doppler radar and high-speed digital processing of the muzzle-velocity measurement provide compensating feedback to the fire-control computer, allowing the firing of 25-round bursts to destroy cruise and high-speed missiles at ranges of at least 2500 m and 1500 m (2,735 yards and 1,640 yards) respectively. The ships are equipped with the RTS 6400 optronic and radar tracking system developed by Reutech Systems: the radar's detection range is more than 25 km (15.5 miles) against fighter targets and more than 16 km (9.9 miles) against missile targets in poor weather. The dual-band thermal imaging sensor incorporates an eye-safe laser rangefinder.

The ships' propulsion is based on a CODAG-WARP (Combined Diesel and Gas turbine - Water Jet and Refined Propeller) arrangement. Two MTU 16V1163 TB93 diesels drive controllable-pitch propellers for a cruising speed of 20+ kts, and one LM 2500 gas turbine powers a waterjet propulsion system providing a maximum speed of 27+ kts.

Amatola, pictured on sea trials, is one of four 'Valour'-class frigates. Contracted in December 1999, the first unit was delivered for fitting out in autumn 2003.

SPECIFICATION

'Valour' class
Displacement: 3,445 tons full load
Dimensions: length 121 m (397 ft); beam 16.3 m (53 ft 7 in); draught 4.4 m (14 ft 5 in)
Propulsion: CODAG-WARP with one LM 2500 gas turbine delivering 19,995 kW (26,820 shp) to one waterjet and two MTU 16V1163 TB93 diesels delivering 12,000 kW (16,095 shp) to two shafts
Speed: 27+ kts
Armament: one 76.2-mm (3-in) Otobreda Compact DP gun, two 35-mm cannon in a twin mounting, two quadruple launchers for eight MM.40 Exocet anti-ship missiles, two 8-cell vertical-launch system for Umkhonto short-range SAMs, and two twin 324-mm (12.75-in) tubes for anti-submarine torpedoes
Electronics: one MRR air/surface search 3D radar, two Reutech ORT fire-control radars, one navigation radar, one helicopter control radar, two Reutech EORT optronic directors, one CMS combat data system, one Grintek EW system, two Grintek chaff/flare launchers, and one Kingklip active hull sonar
Aircraft: one Westland Super Lynx helicopter
Complement: 120

'Cheng Kung' class Guided-missile frigate

Based on the design of the USS *Ingraham* (the final unit of the US Navy's 'Oliver Hazard Perry', or 'FFG7', class of guided missile frigates), the Taiwanese navy's **'Cheng Kung'-class** frigates were ordered under the 'Kwang Hua 1' project and built by the China Shipbuilding Corporation at Kaohsiung. The first seven ships are the ***Cheng Kung, Cheng Ho, Chi Kuang, Yueh Fei, Tzu-I, Pan Chao*** and ***Chang Chien***, which were laid down in 1990–95 and commissioned in 1993–98. An eighth unit is the ***Tien Tan***, laid down in 2001 for completion in 2004. This was to have been the lead unit of another batch of ships that were then cancelled.

Like the American ships, the Taiwanese units have two closely spaced lattice masts placed comparatively well forward on the substantial single superstructure block. With the antenna for the Mk 92 fire-control radar in an almost spherical radome ahead of it, the fore mast carries the antenna of the SPS-49(V)5 or SPS-49A air search radar, while the taller main mast carries the antenna of the SPS-55 or Chang Bai surface search radar. The area between the masts had to

be strengthened to provide for the weight of the anti-ship missile fit, which comprises eight Hsiung Feng II missiles in two quadruple launchers: each carrying a 190-kg (419-lb) warhead to a range of 80 km (50 miles) with active radar and IR terminal guidance, these missiles may be replaced in due course by Harpoon missiles.

Helicopters

Although there is space for two helicopters, only one is normally embarked and handled with the aid of a RAST system. Mounted forward is a Mk 13 single-arm launcher for up to 40 SM-1MR Standard medium- range SAMs.

*The **Pan Chao** was built in Taiwan, as was the rest of the class, as the sixth of the eight 'Cheng Kung'-class guided missile frigates based on the 'FFG7' design.*

SPECIFICATION
'Cheng Kung' class

Displacement: 2,750 tons light; 4,105 tons full load
Dimensions: length 138.2 m (453 ft); beam 13.7 m (45 ft); draught 4.5 m (14 ft 10 in)
Propulsion: two LM 2500 gas turbines delivering 30,570 kW (41,000 shp) to two shafts
Performance: speed 29 kts; endurance 8,335 km (5,180 miles) at 20 kts
Armament: 76.2-mm (3-in) Otobreda Compact DP gun, two 40-mm Bofors AA guns, 20-mm Phalanx Mk 15 CIWS mounting, Mk 13 launcher for 40 SM-1MR Standard SAMs, two quadruple launchers for

eight Hsiung Feng II anti-ship missiles, and two triple 324-mm (12.75 in) tubes for Mk 46 anti-submarine torpedoes
Electronics: one SPS-49 air search radar, one SPS-55 surface search radar, one UD 417 STIR fire-control radar, one Mk 92 fire-control radar, one SYS-2 combat data system, one Chang Feng IV EW system, four Chang Feng 6 chaff/decoy launchers, one SQS-56/DE hull sonar, one SQR-18A(V)2 or ATAS towed array sonar, and one SLQ-25 Nixie towed torpedo decoy system
Aircraft: one Sikorsky S-70C(M) helicopter
Complement: 234

'Naresuan' class Guided-missile frigate

The newest frigate class to enter service with the Thai navy, the **Type 25T** or **'Naresuan' class** comprises a pair of ships, the ***Naresuan*** and ***Taksin***. Commissioned in December 1994 and September 1995 respectively, the ships were designed as a joint venture between the Thai navy and the China State Shipbuilding Corporation, and were conceived as cost-economical vessels for local defence purposes. The ships sailed for Thailand without electronic and weapon systems, which were installed locally. Though limited by the standards of the most

advanced Western navies, the 'Naresuan' class frigates are well suited to the needs and capabilities of the Thai navy, and offer a useful advance in operational capability in comparison with the service's preceding Chinese-built series, the four frigates of the Type 053 or 'Chao Phraya' class.

Though the weapons are mostly of American design, the AA battery comprises two twin Otobreda 40-mm guns made in China in a revised form firing 37-mm ammunition and controlled with the aid of an RTN-20 Dardo radar system, also made in China.

The after part of each ship has a helicopter installation, with the

operating platform complemented by a full hangar.

SPECIFICATION
'Naresuan' class

Displacement: 2,500 tons standard; 2,980 tons full load
Dimensions: length 120 m (393 ft 9 in); beam 13 m (42 ft 9 in); draught 3.8 m (12 ft 6 in)
Propulsion: CODOG with two LM 2500 gas turbines delivering 32,995 kW (44,250 shp) and two MTU 20V1163 TB83 diesels delivering 8,780 kW (11,775 shp) to two shafts
Performance: speed 32 kts; endurance 7,400 km (4,600 miles) at 18 kts
Armament: one 127-mm (5-in) DP gun, two twin 37-mm AA guns, two quadruple launchers for eight

Harpoon anti-ship missiles, one Mk 41 8-cell vertical launcher for Sea Sparrow medium-range SAMs, and two triple 324-mm (12.75-in) tubes for Mk 46 torpedoes
Electronics: one LW-08 air search radar, one Type 360 surface search radar, two SPS-64(V)5 navigation radars, two STIR fire-control radars, one Type 374G 37-mm gun fire-control radar, one JM-83H optical director, one Newton Beta EW system, four Type 945 GPJ chaff/flare launchers, and one SJD-7 hull sonar
Aircraft: one Kaman SH-2G Seasprite helicopter
Complement: 150

'Chao Phraya' class Guided missile frigate

In July 1988 the Thai ministry of defence contracted with the China State Shipbuilding Corporation for the construction and delivery of four frigates to a modified 'Jianghu' class design. The Chinese persuaded the Thais to accept ships with Chinese sensors and weapons.

The four **Type 053HT/HT(H)** or **'Chao Phraya' class** ships were commissioned in 1991–92 as the **Chao Phraya**, **Bangkapong**, **Kraburi** and **Saiburi**. The first two ships had the primary armament of four 100-mm (3.94-in) guns in two twin mountings fore and aft,

while the second two vessels had only two such guns in single mountings. The after gun mounting of the two later ships was removed to allow the incorporation of a helicopter platform (for one Bell Model 212 machine later replaced by a Kaman SH-2G Seasprite).

On arrival in Thailand, problems arising from the poor standard of Chinese shipbuilding were rectified and the damage control facilities were enhanced.

There is little of note about the ships, which are used mainly for training, with a monthly rotation to the Thai coast guard.

One of four simple 'Chao Phraya'-class frigates, the Bangkapong was the second unit to be completed and has twin 100-mm (3.94-in) open-backed gun mounts fore and aft.

SPECIFICATION

'Chao Phraya' class
Displacement: 1,676 tons standard; 1,924 tons full load
Dimensions: length 103.2 m (338 ft 6 in); beam 11.3 m (37 ft 2 in); draught 3.1 m (10 ft 3 in)
Propulsion: four MTU 20V1163 TB83 diesels delivering 21,940 kW (29,425 shp) to two shafts
Performance: speed 30 kts; endurance 4,040 miles (6500 km)
Armament: one single or one or two twin 100-mm (3.94-in) guns, four twin 37-mm AA guns, four twin launchers for eight C-801 anti-ship missiles, provision for one launcher for short-range SAMs, two Type 86

8-barrel anti-submarine mortars, and two depth charge racks
Electronics: one Type 354 air/surface search radar, one 352C surface search and fire-control radar, one Type 343 100-mm and one Type 341 37-mm gun fire-control radars, one Decca 1290 and one RA 71CA navigation radars, one combat data system, one Type 923(1) and Type 981(3) EW system, and two Type 945 chaff/flare launchers
Aircraft: one light helicopter on two ships
Complement: 168

'Yavuz' & 'Barbaros' classes Guided-missile frigates

The eight Turkish frigates of the **'Yavuz' class** and **'Barbaros'** class were completed in 1987–89 and 1995–2000 to **'Meko Type 200' class** and **'Modified Meko Type 200'** class standards respectively.

The first four ships, ordered in 1982 and completed with a full-load displacement of 2,919 tons and a CODAD propulsion arrangement of four MTU 20V1163 TB93 diesels delivering

22320 kW (29,935 shp) to two shafts for 27 kts, are the **Yavuz** built by Blohm + Voss, the **Turgutreis** built by Howaldtswerke, and the **Fatih** and **Yildirim** built in Gölcük's Izmit yard. The second four ships were ordered in pairs during 1990 and 1992, and were completed to an improved standard (including a CODOG propulsion arrangement for higher speed) as the **Barbaros**

and **Salihreis** by Blohm + Voss, and the **Orucreis** and **Kemalreis** by Gölcük's Kocaeli yard.

Armament fit

The ships are similar in their basic armament, although the Mk 29 octuple launcher abaft the funnel for Sea Sparrow medium-range SAMs was replaced in the first two 'Barbaros' class ships (and retrofitted in the second two) by the Mk 41 vertical-launch

system for Aspide (to be replaced by Evolved Sea Sparrow) SAMs. Other changes introduced in the 'Barbaros' class were a full command system, improved radars and a citadel providing NBC protection.

In both classes, the embarked helicopter is armed with Sea Skua light anti-ship missiles complementing the eight Harpoon missiles carried by the ships themselves.

SPECIFICATION

'Barbaros' class
Displacement: 3,380 tons full load
Dimensions: length 118 m (387 ft 1 in); beam 14.8 m (46 ft 8 in); draught 4.3 m (14 ft 2 in)
Propulsion: CODOG with two LM 2500 gas turbines delivering 44,735 kW (60,000 shp) and two MTU 20V1163 TB93 diesels delivering 8,780 kW (11,775 shp) to two shafts
Performance: speed 32 kts; endurance 4,725 miles (7600 km) at 18 kts
Armament: one 127-mm (5-in) gun, three 25-mm Sea Zenith CIWS mountings, eight Harpoon anti-ship missiles in two quadruple launchers, one launcher for 24

Aspide medium-range SAMs, and two triple 324-mm (12.75-in) tubes for Mk 46 anti-submarine torpedoes
Electronics: one AWS 9 3D air search radar, one AWS 6 Dolphin air/surface search radar, one or two STIR SAM fire-control radars, one TKMu SSM and gun fire-control radar, two CIWS fire-control radars, one Decca 2690 navigation radar, one STACOS combat data system, one Cutlass/Scorpion EW system, two Mk 36 SRBOC chaff/flare launchers, one SQS-56 hull sonar, and one SLQ-25 Nixie towed torpedo decoy
Aircraft: one Agusta (Bell) AB.212ASW helicopter
Complement: 187 plus 9 aircrew

Built in Germany, the Barbaros was completed as the first unit of the Turkish navy's 'Modified Meko Type 200' class of guided missile frigates.

'Neustrashimy' class Project 1154 Guided-missile frigate

Built by Yantar at Kaliningrad and commissioned in January 1993, the **Neustrashimy** is the sole unit of the **Project 1154 Jastreb** or **'Neustrashimy' class** of guided-missile frigates that were to have been four or more in number. The second ship was launched in 1991 but the hull was later scrapped to pay the yard's debts, and the third hull was launched incomplete in 1993 to clear space for the repair of Norwegian merchant ships, and was then abandoned.

Designed as a complement to the 'Krivak'-class or Project 1135 guided-missile frigate and successor to the 'Grisha'-class or Project 1124 light frigate, the ship is based on the 'Krivak III'-class vessel with slightly greater dimensions, more advanced sensors and weapons

The Neustrashimy has a very elegantly configured hull, the forward end's rake, flare and freeboard helping to reduce the amount of water and spray taken over the bows in heavy weather.

including full capability for an embarked helicopter. The design is optimized for operations against submarines and surface ships, and the escort of task forces and convoys.

The ship features a long hull with relatively great forward freeboard and an acutely raked stem reducing the chance of damage to the bow bulb by the anchors. The flare of the sides over the ship's forward end minimizes slamming and spray. The ship has bilge keels; fin stabilizers enhance seakeeping capabilities by reducing roll.

SPECIFICATION	
'Neustrashimy' class **Displacement:** 3,450 tons standard; 4,250 tons full load **Dimensions:** length 131.2 m (430 ft 5 in); beam 15.5 m (50 ft 10 in); draught 4.8 m (15 ft 9 in) **Propulsion:** COGAG arrangement with two gas turbines delivering 36,250 kW (48,620 shp) and two gas turbines delivering 18050 kW (24,210 shp) to two shafts **Performance:** speed 30 kts; endurance 8,350 km (5,190 miles) at 16 kts **Armament:** one 100-mm (3.9-in) gun, provision for four quadruple launchers for SS-N-25 anti-ship missiles, four octuple vertical-launch systems for SA-N-9 SAMs,	two CADS-N-1 combined 30-mm cannon and SA-N-11 short-range SAM systems, six 533-mm (21-in) tubes for SS-N-16 anti-submarine missiles and/or torpedoes, one RBU 12000 anti-submarine rocket launcher, and two mine rails **Electronics:** one 'Top Plate' 3D surveillance radar, two 'Palm Frond' navigation radars, one 'Cross Sword' SAM-control radar, one 'Kite Screech-B' SSM/gun-control radar, two 'Bell Crown' data-links, two 'Salt Pot' and four 'Box Bar' IFFs, eight ESM/ECM systems, and 10 chaff/decoy launchers **Aircraft:** one Kamov Ka-27 helicopter **Complement:** 210

Missile armament

The ship has a missile/torpedo launch system for six Vodopod-NK (SS-N-16 'Stallion') anti-submarine missiles or torpedoes, and is equipped for (but not with) four quadruple launchers for 16 Uran (SS-N-25 'Switchblade') anti-ship cruise missiles. The Klinok air-defence system comprises four octuple vertical-launch modules for SA-N-9 'Gauntlet' SAMs just abaft the 100-mm (3.9-in) AK-100 gun. Short-range air defence is entrusted to a Kortik/Kashtan gun/missile system: this

comprises a command system and two CADS-N-1 fire units, each with two 30-mm rotary cannon (600 rounds), an octuple launcher for 9M311 (SA-N-11 'Grison') SAMs, one 'Hot Flash' fire-control radar and a 'Hot Spot' optronic director.

Submarine combat

Defence against submarine attack comes from one RBU 12000 10-tube launcher installed on the raised deck abaft the four Klinok missile launchers to fire anti-submarine and anti-torpedo rockets. Longer-range offensive anti-submarine operations are entrusted to the single embarked helicopter, a Kamov Ka-27 'Helix' machine using an operating platform occupying the width of the deck at the stern with a hangar just forward of it in the rear superstructure block.

In the area forward of the bridge are three weapons, in the form of the 100-mm (3.9-in) gun, the four vertical launchers for SA-N-9 SAMs flush with the deck and the RBU 12000 rocket launcher.

'Cornwall' class (Type 22 Batch 3) Guided-missile frigate

The Type 22 class of guided-missile frigates was one of the larger construction programmes undertaken for the Royal Navy in the last quarter of the 20th century, and amounted to 16 ships in all. First came the four 'Broadsword', or Type 22, Batch 1-class ships, commissioned in 1979–81 and all sold to Brazil in 1995–97. Then came the six 'Boxer'-class or Type 22 Batch 2 ships commissioned in 1984–88 with a longer hull and the Type 2031Z towed-array sonar. Finally there came the four **'Cornwall'-class**, or **Type 22 Batch 3,** ships based on the hull and machinery of the Type 22 Batch 2 ships but with operational improvements.

Conceived as a successor to the 'Leander' class, and originally to have been procured by the Netherlands as well as the UK, the Type 22 frigate was schemed for the oceanic escort role with optimization for the anti-submarine task but with a potent short-range air-defence capability to cope with the developing threat of the sea-skimming anti-ship missile. The Type 22 Batch 3 ships were ordered at the end of 1982 to replace ships lost in the Falklands campaign of that year, and the opportunity was taken to create an improved Type 22 Batch 2 variant with improved command facilities (including officer in tactical command and flag accommodation within

provision for a maximum complement of 301), new anti-ship missile armament, the restoration of 4.5-in (114-mm) gun armament of the type lacking from the Batch 1 and 2 ships, and a new close-in weapons system mounting for last-ditch defence against attack aircraft and missiles.

The new weapons fit required a modification of the ships' layout to accommodate the medium-calibre gun on the forecastle and the two quadruple launchers for Harpoon anti-ship missiles athwartships in the position immediately abaft the wheelhouse, and the Goalkeeper CIWS above and behind the Harpoon launchers with good forward and lateral arcs of fire. The ships have the CACS-5 combat data system in place of the earlier vessels' CACS-1 systems. The Mk 8 mounting for the 4.5-in gun, fitted mainly for the shore bombardment role, is controlled by two GSA 8B Sea Archer optronic directors (TV and IR imaging and laser rangefinding) side-by-side above the bridge.

The ships were also the first Royal Navy units to be completed with 30-mm RARDEN short-range anti-aircraft and anti-FAC guns in DS 30B mountings in place of the 40-mm Bofors cannon that had been standard since World War II.

The Type 22 Batch 3 ships have a good balance of offensive weapons and electronics, and also have the habitability and seakeeping for extended operations. The ships can also embark senior officers and their staff and then operate in the command role.

Class of four

The four ships, with names beginning with C to differentiate them from the B-batch ships, were built by Yarrow (two), Cammell Laird and Swan Hunter respectively, and were completed as HMS **Cornwall**, **Cumberland**, **Campbeltown** and **Chatham** and commissioned in April 1988, June 1989, May 1989 and May 1990. Together with HMS *Sheffield*, which is the sole Batch 2 ship retained by the Royal Navy, the ships constitute the 2nd Frigate Squadron based at Devonport.

Helicopter facilities

The long-range anti-submarine helicopter facilities are large enough to carry and operate one Westland Sea King medium helicopter, but the standard complement is two Westland Lynx light helicopters. The ships are also being upgraded with Type 2050 hull-mounted search and attack sonar in place of the Type 2016 equipment, improved electronic warfare systems and an enhanced Sea Wolf short-range SAM capability with improved radar, an added optronic tracker and a new fuse for better low-altitude capability.

SPECIFICATION

'Cornwall' class
Displacement: 4,200 tons standard; 4,900 tons full load
Dimensions: length 148.1 m (485 ft 10 in); beam 14.8 m (48 ft 6 in); draught 6.4 m (21 ft)
Propulsion: COGOG arrangement with two Rolls-Royce Spey SM1A gas turbines delivering 21,995 kW (29,500 shp) and two Rolls-Royce Tyne RM3C gas turbines delivering 7,965 kW (10,680 shp) to two shafts
Performance: speed 30 kts; endurance 8,375 km (5,200 miles) at 18 kts
Armament: one 4.5-in (114-mm) guns, two quadruple launchers for Harpoon anti-ship missiles, two sextuple launchers for Sea Wolf

short-range SAMs, two 30-mm DP cannon, one 30-mm CIWS mounting, and two triple 12.75-in (324-mm) tubes for Stingray lightweight torpedoes
Electronics: one Type 967/968 air/surface search radar, one Type 2008 surface search radar, one Type 1008 navigation radar, two Type 911 SAM-control radars, two Sea Archer optronic directors, one UAT 1 ESM system, one Type 675(2) ECM system, four Sea Gnat decoy launchers, one CACS-5 combat data system, one Type 2050 hull sonar, and one Type 2031 towed-array sonar
Aircraft: one or two Westland Lynx HMA.Mk 3/8 helicopters
Complement: 250

Type 23 or 'Duke' class Guided-missile frigate (FFG)

Although the ships of the Type 22 or 'Broadsword', 'Boxer' and 'Cornwall' classes were clearly very effective anti-submarine warships, they were also very expensive. The Admiralty thus planned a lower-cost frigate with the Type 2031Z towed-array sonar rather than the Type 2050 hull-mounted active search/ attack sonar.

The result of this process is the **Type 23** or **'Duke' class** of frigate, the development of which then came to include the Type 2050 as well as the Type 2031Z sonar, one medium rather than two light helicopters, an enhanced general-purpose capability, and a two-ended Sea Wolf SAM system. By the time the design was being finalized, the vertical-launch version of this SAM system was nearing the trials stage, and was selected in preference to the earlier

A key feature of the 'Duke' class is the minimization of the ships' electro-magnetic signature through the shaping of the hull and superstructure.

GWS.25 lightweight launcher. Analysis of naval operations in the Falklands War also led to the introduction of upgraded fire precautions and enhanced damage control.

The class totals 16 ships, of which 12 and four respectively were built by Yarrow and Swan Hunter. Laid down in 1985–99, launched in 1987–2000 and commissioned in 1990–2002, these are the **Norfolk**, **Argyll**, **Lancaster**, **Marlborough**, **Iron Duke**, **Monmouth**, **Montrose**, **Westminster**, **Northumberland**, **Richmond**, **Somerset**, **Grafton**, **Sutherland**, **Kent**, **Portland** and **St Albans**.

The 'Duke'-class frigates are notably 'quiet'. Their acoustic, thermal and electro-magnetic signatures have all been reduced to the maximum degree possible.

Quiet operations

The Type 23 frigate is optimized for towed-array operations, so quietening of machinery was important and a unique combined diesel-electric and gas turbine (CODLAG) propulsion arrangement was selected with diesel-electric drive for quiet operations and Spey gas turbines for high speed. The CODLAG arrangement reduces gearbox noise, and the electric generators are above the waterline for a lowering of radiated noise.

Anti-noise, IR and electro-magnetic 'stealth' features were also incorporated to improve survivability, and include a flared hull with a bubble system to reduce radiated noise, and a superstructure with sloped surfaces and rounded corners.

The first ships were completed without their planned CACS-4 command system but its successor, the DNA 1 system, was retrofitted from 1995 onward and was later upgraded to DNA 5 standard. The first six ships had the UAF-1 ESM system, but later ships were completed with the UAT system, which was then retrofitted to the earlier ships. All the ships have Type 675(2) or Scorpion ECM.

*Right: HMS **Grafton** was built on the Clyde by Yarrow and commissioned in 1997. Evident are the 4.5-in gun and four of the eight Harpoon launchers.*

Upgrades

Upgrade programmes are to enhance the Sea Wolf system (upgraded missile fuse, improved radar and another optronic tracker), replace the Type 2031Z passive sonar with the Type 2087 active sonar, and introduce the Mk 8 Mod 1 gun, the Surface Ship Torpedo Defence system and, in seven of the ships, the CEC (Co-operative Engagement Capability) system.

*Above: HMS **Iron Duke**, named after the Duke of Wellington. The ship's after section is dominated by the hangar and large helicopter platform.*

SPECIFICATION

'Duke' (Type 23) class
Displacement: 3,500 tons standard; 4,200 tons full load
Dimensions: length 133 m (436 ft 4 in); beam 16.1 m (52 ft 10 in); draught 7.3 m (24 ft)
Propulsion: CODLAG with four 1510-kW (2,025-shp) Paxman Valenta 12CM diesel generators powering two GEC electric motors delivering 2,980 kW (4,000 shp) and two Rolls-Royce Spey SM1A or, from *Westminster*, RM1C gas turbines delivering 23,190 kW (31,100 shp) to two shafts
Performance: speed 28 kts; range 14,485 km (9,000 miles) at 15 kts
Armament: two quadruple launchers for eight Harpoon SSMs, two

GWS.26 VLS for 32 Sea Wolf SAMs, one 4.5-in (114-mm) Mk 8 DP gun, two DS 30B 30-mm AA guns, and two twin 12.75-in (324-mm) tubes for Stingray ASW torpedoes
Electronics: one Type 996(I) air/surface search radar, one Type 1008 surface search radar, one Type 1007 navigation radar, two Type 911 SAM fire-control radars, one GSA 8B/GPEOD optronic director, DNA combat data system, UAT and Type 675(2) ECM, four Sea Gnat 6-barrel decoy launchers, Type 2070 torpedo decoy, Type 2050 hull sonar and Type 2031Z towed-array sonar
Aircraft: one Lynx HMA.Mk 3/8 or Merlin HM.Mk 1 helicopter
Complement: 181

'Oliver Hazard Perry' class Guided-missile frigate (FFG)

At its peak numerically the largest warship class in the modern US Navy, the **'Oliver Hazard Perry' class** was designed to succeed the 'Knox' class of ocean escort frigates, and was therefore optimized for the anti-air warfare role with anti-submarine and anti-ship warfare as its secondary tactical tasks.

The class was criticized for the same failings as the 'Knox' class, namely a single propeller and a single main 'weapon' (one Mk 13 missile launcher).

On the other side of the coin, the ship benefits from a major degree of redundancy: the Mk 92 fire-control system has two channels (two guidance radars physically well separated from each other), and there are two extending 242-kW (325-shp) motor/propeller units to bring the ship home at 6 kts if it loses its main power.

Although the hull sonar is the SQS-56 short-range unit, the primary anti-submarine sonar onboard is the SQR-19 towed-array sonar.

Combat system

The Dutch Mk 92 fire-control system is part of a combat system well adapted to the task of defeating attacks by 'pop-up' weapons. The Italian 76-mm (3-in) gun was selected as superior to the US Navy's standard 5-in (127-mm) L/54 gun in the medium/short-range air-defence role.

Cost considerations meant that many of the early ships were not revised for the carriage of two LAMPS III multi-role helicopters in place of the original pair of LAMPS I machines. The ships have aluminium armour over their magazines, steel over the machinery, and Kevlar plastic armour over their vital electronic and command facilities.

The magazine for the Mk 13 launcher can take only Standard SAM and Harpoon anti-ship missiles, so the shipboard ASW capability is vested in Mk 46 torpedoes and LAMPS helicopters.

Many of the older ships have been transferred to US allies or

*The guided-missile frigate **USS** **McClusky** **(FFG-41)** manoeuvres at slow speed while training near San Diego, California. The original single hangar configuration was altered to two adjacent hangars. The two **SH-60B LAMPS III** helicopters normally deployed can carry **AGM-119B Penguin** anti-ship missiles in order to boost the ships' limited **ASuW** capabilities.*

SPECIFICATION

'Oliver Hazard Perry' class
Displacement: 2,769 tons standard; 3,638-4,100 tons full load
Dimensions: length 135.6 m (445 ft) in LAMPS I ships or 138.1 m (453 ft) in LAMPS III ships; beam 13.7 m (45 ft); draught 4.5 m (14 ft 10 in)
Propulsion: two General Electric LM2500 gas turbines delivering 29,830 kW (40,000 shp) to one shaft
Performance: speed 29 kts; range 8,370 km (5,200 miles) at 20 kts
Armament: one Mk 13 single-rail launcher for 36 Standard SM-1MR surface-to-air and four Harpoon anti-ship missiles, one 76-mm (3-in) Mk 75 DP gun, one 20-mm Mk 15

Phalanx CIWS, and two triple 12.75-in (324-mm) Mk 32 ASW tubes for 24 Mk 46 or Mk 50 ASW torpedoes
Electronics: one SPS-49(V)4 or 5 air search radar, one SPS-55 surface search radar, one STIR fire-control radar, one Mk 92 fire-control system, one URN-25 TACAN, one SLQ-32(V)2 ESM system, two Mk 36 SRBOC 6-barrel chaff launchers, one SQS-56 hull sonar, and (from *Underwood*) one SQR-19 towed-array sonar
Aircraft: two SH-2F Seasprite LAMPS I or SH-60B Sea Hawk LAMPS III helicopters
Complement: 176–200

are reserved for such transfer (seven including one for cannibalization to Turkey, four to Egypt and one each to Bahrain and Poland, with further transfers to Poland and Turkey made in 2002), and only 33 of the class survived in US Navy service at the beginning of the 21st century.

At its peak, the class consisted of the ***Oliver Hazard Perry, McInerney, Wadsworth, Duncan, Clark, George Philip, Samuel Eliot Morrison, John H. Sides, Estocin, Clifton Sprague, John A. Moore, Antrim, Flatley, Fahrion, Lewis B. Puller, Jack Williams, Copeland, Gallery, Mahlon S. Tisdale, Boone, Stephen W. Groves, Reid, Stark, John L. Hall, Jarrett, Aubrey Fitch, Underwood, Crommelin,***

Curts, Doyle, Halyburton, McClusky, Klakring, Thach, De Wert, Rentz, Nicholas, Vandegrift, Robert G. Bradley, Taylor, Gary, Carr, Hawes, Ford, Elrod, Simpson, Reuben James, Samuel B. Roberts, Kauffman, Rodney M. Davis and ***Ingraham***.

Further ships are Australia's six **'Adelaide'-class** units ***Adelaide, Canberra, Sydney, Darwin, Melbourne*** and ***Newcastle***; Spain's six locally built **'Santa Maria'-class** units ***Santa María, Victoria, Numancia, Reina Sofía*** (ex-***América***), ***Navarra*** and ***Canarias***; and Taiwan's eight locally built **'Cheng Kung'-class** units ***Cheng Kung, Cheng Ho, Chi Kuang, Yueh Fei, Tzu-I, Pan Chao, Chang Chien*** and ***Tien Tan***.

Though the object of much criticism, the 'Oliver Hazard Perry' class has proved very successful despite the steady growth of displacement, equipment and complement, and in service has also been revealed as notably sturdy. The lead ship of the class is illustrated.

'Almirante Brown' class
Guided-missile destroyer

Originally to have been a class of six, with four built in Argentina, the **Meko 360** design is based on the modularized systems concept in which each of the weapons and sensor systems is carried as a separate modular unit that can be interchanged with a replacement or newer system without the usual reconstruction

Right: The commissioning of the destroyers of the 'Almirante Brown' class – Sarandi is illustrated with an Alouette on the flight deck – into the Argentine navy represented a significant increase in the service's overall capabilities. Almirante Brown took part in operations in the Persian Gulf in 1990.

1983–84 as the **'Almirante Brown' class**. During the Falklands War, the ships were under construction, and the

Above: Argentina trimmed its 1978 Meko 360 order from six to four ships after deciding to order six smaller Meko 140 frigates (the locally built 'Espora' class) in 1979. All four Meko 360s are active and based at Puerto Belgrano. The vessels can also be used as flagships.

SPECIFICATION

'Almirante Brown' class
Displacement: 2,900 tons standard; 3,360 tons full load
Dimensions: length 125.9 m (413 ft 1 in); beam 14 m (46 ft); draught 5.8 m (19 ft)
Propulsion: Rolls-Royce COGOG with two Olympus TM3B delivering 37,280 kW (50,00 shp) and two Tyne RM1C delivering 7,380 kW (9,900 shp) to two shafts
Speed: 30.5 kts
Armament: two quadruple launchers for MM.40 Exocet SSMs, one Albatros octuple launcher for 24

Aspide SAMs, one 127-mm (5-in) DP gun, four twin 40-mm AA guns, two 20-mm guns, and two triple 324-mm (12.75-in) ILAS 3 tubes for 18 Whitehead A 244 anti-submarine torpedoes
Electronics: one DA-08A air/surface search radar, one ZW-06 navigation radar, one STIR fire-control radar, one AEG-Telefunken ECM suite, two SCLAR and two Dagaie decoy launchers, and one DSQS-21BZ active hull sonar
Aircraft: one or two AS 555 Fennec
Complement: 200

Note the forward quadruple launcher for Exocet anti-ship missiles on the port side of Heroina: the original weapons may be upgraded to MM.40 Block II standard.

that otherwise accompanies the modernization of a ship. The final agreement signed with the West German firms of Thyssen Rheinstahl and Blohm & Voss in December 1978 was for four ships to be built in West Germany. All four, the **Almirante Brown**, **La Argentina**, **Heroina** and **Sarandi**, were commissioned in

British Rolls-Royce Olympus and Tyne gas turbines were embargoed for a short time. In 1996 Fennec helicopters were delivered in order to improve the ASW capability and provide over the horizon SSM targeting for the 'Almirante Brown' class.

A near sister to Argentina's vessels is the Nigerian navy's **Aradu**, ordered in 1977 as the

world's first warship with modular construction. This differs from the Argentine vessels in having Otomat Mk 2 SSMs, a single Lynx Mk 89

helicopter and a CODOG propulsion system. Although its longterm future is uncertain, the *Arudu* remained the flagship of the Nigerian navy in 2006.

'Iroquois' class
Guided-missile destroyer

The Iroquois was commissioned in July 1972 and with its three sister ships is destined to serve on into the second decade of the 21st century as the major ASW platform of the Canadian navy. The design weight limit of the 'Iroquois' class has now been reached and the initial SAM armament of navalized AIM-7E Sparrows has been replaced by SM-2MR Standard missiles. A new class will supplement them from about 2010 to extend the capabilities of the 12 'Halifax'-class frigates.

Ordered in 1968 as anti-submarine destroyers, the four vessels of the **'Iroquois' class** comprise **Iroquois**, **Huron**, **Athabaskan** and **Algonquin** and are a revised version of the eight Tartar SAM-equipped 'Tribal' class of general-purpose frigates cancelled in 1963. They retain the same hull design, dimensions and basic characteristics of the 'Tribals' but have enhanced ASW features such as three sonars, a helicopter flight deck and hangarage for two licence-built CH-124A Sea King ASW helicopters: these can also carry 12.7-mm (0.5-in) machine-guns and ESM/FLIR equipment in

place of ASW gear. The weapons and sensor fit was a mixed bag with an Italian 127-mm (5-in) OTO Melara Compact gun, two four-rail launchers for the US Sea Sparrow SAM system that retracted into a deckhouse in the forward superstructure, Dutch and US electronics and a British ASW mortar. The last was the ubiquitous triple-barrelled Mk 10 Limbo weapon.

For a new class of proposed helicopter-carrying destroyers, the *Huron* tested a vertical-launch Sparrow system in 1982, but the class did not materialize, and in the TRUMP (TRibal class Update and Modernization

Project) in 1986 the ships were revised with a Mk 41 vertical-launch system (with 29 Standard SM-2MR medium/long-range SAMs in place of the Limbo installation). The electronics were also improved, yielding enhanced anti-aircraft and anti-submarine capabilities. The original main gun was replaced by a 76-mm (3-in) Super Rapid weapon from the same manufacturer and is

complemented by a single Mk 15 Phalanx installation.

ASW helicopters

For the embarked helicopters the ships can carry the active acoustic-homing Mk 44 and active/passive acoustic-homing Mk 46 torpedoes. The landing decks are fitted with the Beartrap system. The 'Iroquois' class are to remain in service until at least 2010.

SPECIFICATION

'Iroquois' class (early 2000s)
Displacement: 5,300 tons full load
Dimensions: length 129.84 m (426 ft); beam 15.24 m (50 ft); draught 4.72 m (15 ft 6 in)
Propulsion: COGOG with two Pratt & Whitney FT4A2 gas turbines delivering 37,280 kW (50,000 shp) and two Allison 570-KF gas turbines delivering 9,470 kW (12,700 shp), both to two shafts
Performance: speed 27 kts; range 8,370 km (5,200 miles) at 15 kts
Armament: one Mk 41 VLS for 29 Standard SM-2MR Block III SAMs, one 76-mm (3-in) Super Rapid DP

gun, one 20-mm Mk 15 Phalanx CIWS, and two triple Mk 32 324-mm (12.75-in) tubes for 12 Mk 46 anti-submarine torpedoes
Electronics: SPS-502 air search radar, SPQ-501 surface search radar, Pathfinder navigation radars, two SPG-501 fire-control radars, SLQ-501 CANEWS ESM system, Nulka ECM system, four Shield decoy launchers, SLQ-25 Nixie torpedo decoy, and two SQS-510 combined hull and variable-depth sonars
Aircraft: two CH-124A Sea King ASW helicopters
Complement: 255

'Luda' class Guided-missile destroyer

The first ocean-going warships built by communist China, the **'Luda I' class** or **Type 051** destroyers were derived from the earlier Soviet 'Neustrashimy' (NATO 'Tallinn') class, of which just a single example was built. The Chinese ships have two

Zhuhai is the sole 'Luda III' and is rumoured to have received a ballistic trajectory ASW weapon known as the CY-1 for launch from the modified rear missile launcher.

triple launchers for HY-2 (CSS-N-2 'Seersucker') or (in **Kaifeng** only) two quadruple launchers for C-802 (CSS-N-8 'Saccade') anti-ship missiles in place of the Soviet ship's torpedo tubes, but the design of their hull and also their armament and sensors compare poorly with those of contemporary destroyers and even with those of Taiwan's refitted ex-US ships.

Some 16 of the class were completed between 1971 and 1991 by three yards (Luda, Shanghai and Dalian), and one unit was scrapped after an explosion off Zanjiang in August 1978. The ships have possessed an underway replenishment capability since the early 1980s, but have poor command and control facilities. In 1987, **Jinan**

was refitted with a hangar and flight platform aft for two Z-9A helicopters, replacing the after gun mountings and the depth-charge throwers, to become the sole **'Luda II'-class** trials vessel.

China has made several attempts to obtain Western armament and electronics for these ships, but almost all of these failed. The sole exceptions are the French Crotale octuple launcher for the HQ-7 SAM (and associated radar) in *Kaifeng*, **Dalian** and **Xian**, and the Tavitac combat data system (complete with Vega fire-control system) in some ships. The sole **'Luda III'-class** ship **Zhuhai** was completed in 1991 with four twin launchers for YJ-1 (CSS-N-4 'Sardine') SSMs, two triple tubes for Mk 46 torpedoes and

much French electronic gear. CY-1 ASW missiles may be fitted

on the after set of missile launchers.

'Luhu' class Guided-missile destroyer

The design of the **Type 052** or **'Luhu'-class** destroyer was conceived during a time of Sino-American detente, and was therefore schemed with US weapons and equipment. The latter included General Electric LM2500 gas turbines that were, in the event, among the little US equipment exported to China. Helicopter facilities (flight platform and hangar) are located over the after part of the hull with a French helicopter-handling system.

American embargo

Following the 1989 embargo on the delivery of US military equipment to China in response to the Tianenmen Square massacre, the class was terminated at just the original pair of ships. The second is powered by gas turbines purchased from the Ukraine.

Ordered in 1985 but delayed by the greater priority afforded to the construction of ships ordered by Thailand, these ships are the **Harbin**, commissioned in July 1994, and the **Qingdao**, commissioned in March 1996.

By Chinese standards the two 'Luhu'-class destroyers are

*Qingdao **is the second 'Luhu' destroyer and, in the absence of the US gas turbines for which it was designed, was fitted with Ukrainian gas turbines.***

highly capable, with compact container launchers for two types of anti-ship missile (the YJ-8A (CSS-N-4 'Sardine') and C-802 (CSS-N-8 'Saccade'), a Crotale SAM launcher over the forward superstructure, a modern 100-mm (3.9-in) gun, and modern French electronics including radars, sonars and a combat data system.

'Georges Leygues' & 'Cassard' Guided-missile destroyers

Rated as anti-submarine frigates by the French navy, the seven ships of the **'Georges Leygues' class** were built at a leisurely rate. The first three units – **Georges Leygues**, **Dupleix** and **Montcalm** – were authorized in 1971 and commissioned in 1979, 1981 and 1982, respectively. Four more vessels: **Jean De Vienne**, **Primauguet**, **La Motte-Picquet** and **Latouche-Tréville** were completed and joined the fleet between 1984 and 1990.

The first two ships of the class were armed with sea-skimming Exocet anti-ship missiles of the MM.38 type, while the remaining vessels have the extended-range MM.40. Air defence is handled by an octuple Crotale Naval launcher on all vessels, and two Simbad twin launchers for

The two vessels of the 'Cassard' class – this is **Jean Bart** *– carry a Panther helicopter for third part missile targeting.*

The **Jean De Vienne's** *primary 100-mm (3.9-in) main gun armament is situated forward of the bridge, while the powerful DBRV 26A air-search radar is seen forward of the main mast.*

Mistral missiles may be carried in lieu of two 20-mm AA guns on the last four ships. Two Sadral sextuple SAM launchers for the Mistral SAM and two 30-mm Breda/Mauser guns were fitted to the first four ships in the class as an upgrade.

All the ships of the class carry a comprehensive sonar fit and are armed with L5 anti-submarine torpedoes launched from two fixed tubes.

The ships carry two Lynx Mk 4 helicopters armed with Mk 46 or Mu 90 anti-submarine torpedoes, except *Georges Leygues,* which carries no helicopters, its hangar being converted for training. The helicopters track and monitor submarine contacts.

'Cassard' class

The two units of the **'Cassard' class**, **Cassard** and **Jean Bart**, share the hull design but have diesel propulsion. As anti-aircraft frigates, they have forty SM-1MR Standard long-range SAMs. Fired from a Mk 13 launcher, these semi-active radar-homing missiles intercept targets to a range of 46 km (29 miles). The Standard missiles will be replaced during mid-life refits by Aster 30 missiles. Their primary anti-ship weapon is the MM.40 Exocet, and the vessels carry one AS 565MA Panther helicopter, for SSM targeting.

SPECIFICATION	
'Cassard' class **Displacement:** 5,000 tons full load **Dimensions:** length 139 m (456 ft); beam 14 m (45 ft 11 in); draught 6.5 m (21 m 3½ in) **Propulsion:** four SEMT-Pialstick V280 diesels delivering 32,214.2 kW (43,200 shp) to two shafts **Speed:** 29 kts **Endurance:** 15,186 km (9,436 miles) at 18 kts; 8,890 km (5,524 miles) at 24 kts **Armament:** eight MM.40 Exocet SSMs, one Mk 13 Mod 5 launcher for SM-1MR Standard SAMs (40 missiles), two Matra Sadral sextuple launchers for Mistral SAMs, one 100-mm (3.9-in) gun, and two 20-mm Oerlikon guns	**Defensive systems:** two 10-barrel chaff/flare launchers, Dassault LAD offboard decoys, Nixie towed torpedo decoy **Electronics:** Thomson-CSF DRBJ 11B and 3D air search radar, DRBV 26C air/surface search radar, Racal DRBN 34A navigation radar, Thomson-CSF DRBC 33A fire-control radar (guns), two Raytheon SPS-51C fire-control (missiles), Thomson-Sintra DUBA 25A hull-mounted active search and attack sonar (*Cassard*), DUBV 24C in *Jean Bart* **Aircraft:** one AS 565MA Panther helicopter **Complement:** 244

'Rajput' and 'Delhi' classes Guided-missile destroyers

The Indian Navy ordered five modified 'Kashin II'-class guided missile destroyers from the Soviet Union in the 1970s. Built at Nikolayev (now in Ukraine) between 1977 and 1986, the **'Rajput' class** was commissioned between 1980 and 1988. Their countermeasure suites were upgraded in 1993–94 but plans for further modernization with Ukrainian assistance have been shelved and the navy is now looking to Russia for improvements.

Indian press reports in 2002 indicated that one of the 'Rajputs' is being fitted with the Brahmos Indo-Russian missile for its first test-firings at sea. This 300-km (186-mile) range missile is designed to carry a nuclear warhead.

The primary anti-shipping ship weapon is the P-20M (SS-N-2D 'Styx'), a large subsonic infra-red homing missile with a range of 83 km (52 miles), it carries a 513-kg (1,131-lb) warhead. **Ranjit** and the **Ranvijay** are due

to be fitted with Uran (SS-N-25 'Switchblade') missiles after refit. The ships' Volna (SA-N-1 'Goa') SAMs have a range of 31.5 km (19.6 miles) and can engage aircraft at up to 22,860 m (75,000 ft).

All the 'Rajputs' are equipped with a twin 76-mm (3-in) gun forward, while four twin 30-mm weapons are carried by **Rajput**, **Rana** and *Ranjit*, and four six-barrel 30-mm CIWS mountings are fitted to **Ranvir** and *Ranvijay*.

'Delhi' class

The construction of the **'Delhi' class**, the largest warships yet built in India, was delayed by the collapse of the Soviet Union and the Black Sea naval yards being taken over by the newly independent Ukraine. **Delhi** was laid down in 1987 and launched in 1991 but was not commissioned for another six years. **Mysore** was commissioned in 1999 and **Mumbai** in 2001. These are very much multinational platforms, with Russian Kashmir SAMs, Canadian sonar mountings, Dutch radar, and French and Italian electronics systems.

Intended to serve as command ships for task forces, all three vessels have flag facilities and are designed to be able to operate in an NBC contaminated area. The 'Delhis' sport massive blast deflectors associated with the Moskit (SS-N-22 'Sunburn') anti-shipping missiles, which they may have been intended to carry. Instead, they are armed with Uran (SS-N-25 'Switchblade'), an active

SPECIFICATION

'Delhi' class
Displacement: 6,700 tons full load
Dimensions: length 163 m (534 ft 10 in); beam 17 m (55 ft 10 in); draught 6.5 m (21 ft 4 in)
Propulsion: two Zorya M36E gas turbines delivering 47,725 kW (64,000 shp) to two shafts
Speed: 32 kts
Endurance: 7242 km (4,500 miles) at 18 kts
Armament: 16 Uran (SS-N-25 'Switchblade') SSMs, two Kashmir (SA-N-7 'Gadfly') SAM launchers, one 100-mm (3.9-in) gun, four six-barrel 30-mm guns, five 533-mm

(21-in) torpedo tubes
Defensive systems: Bharat Ajanta EW suite, TQN-2 jammer, PK-2 decoy launchers
Electronics: 'Half Plate' air/surface and Bharat/Signaal surface search radars; 'Plank Shave' (SSM), 'Front Dome' (SAM), 'Kite Screech' (100-mm) and 'Bass Tilt' (30-mm) fire-control radars, Bharat hull-mounted sonar (*Delhi*, *Mysore*), Garden Reach hull-mounted active search VDS and towed array sonar (*Mumbai*)
Aircraft: one Sea King or two ALH
Complement: 360

Above: With its 'Half Plate' air search radar clearly visible at the top of its main mast, Delhi lies at anchor. Eight Uran missile launchers are visible below the bridge.

Below: The Rajput displays its Soviet heritage with a characteristic display of aerials and antennae. This class of ships normally deploy a single Ka-28 'Helix'.

radar-homing SSM with a range of 130 km (81 miles) and a 145-kg (320-lb) warhead. Four quadruple launchers are fitted, and the missiles can be launched at intervals of a few seconds.

The Kashmir SAM with which the Delhi class are equipped is

the export version of the Uragan (SA-N-7 'Gadfly'). This Mach-3 semi-active homing missile has a maximum range of 25 km (15.5 miles) against aircraft and about half that against missiles. It can sustain 23 g manoeuvres and carries a 70-kg (154-lb) warhead. The fire-control radars

can track 12 targets and illuminate and track six. There are reportedly plans to arm the 'Delhi' and 'Rajput' classes class with the Israeli Barak SAM, designed to kill sea-skimming

missiles, a task for which the 'Delhis' currently carry four six-barrel 30-mm gun systems. The 'Delhis' carry a single Sea King Mk 42 or two ALH helicopters for ASW.

'Audace' class Guided-missile destroyer

Both **Ardito** and **Audace** were laid down in 1968 and commissioned in 1972. Based on the previous 'Impavido' class, they are general purpose destroyers with anti-ship and anti-aircraft missiles plus anti-submarine torpedoes. They also carry a pair of torpedo-armed ASW helicopters, normally the AB 212ASW, although EH 101 operations can be supported.

When built, the **'Audace' class** deployed two 127-mm (5-in) guns in single turrets but

the 'B' turret has been replaced by an octuple Selenia Albatros launcher for the semi-active radar-homing Aspide point defence missile system; long-range threats are dealt with by SM-1MR Standard SAMs launched from a Mk 13 launcher.

Anti-ship weapon

The primary anti-ship weapon is the OTO Melara/Matra Teseo Mk 2 sea-skimming missile which has 180-km (112-mile) range, flies at a speed of Mach 0.9,

SPECIFICATION

'Audace' class
Displacement: 4,400 tons
Dimensions: length 136.6 m (448 ft 2½ in); beam 14.2 m (46 ft 7 in); draught 4.6 m (15 ft 1 in)
Propulsion: two turbines delivering 54,436 kW (73,000 shp) to two shafts
Speed: 34 kts
Endurance: 4828 km (3,000 miles) at 20 kts
Armament: four twin launchers for Teseo Mk 2 SSMs, Mk 13 launcher for SM-1MR Standard SAMs (40 carried), octuple Albatros launcher for Aspide SAMs, 127-mm (5-in) gun, three 76-mm (3-in) Compact

guns (*Ardito*), one (*Ardito*) or four (*Audace*) 76-mm Super Rapid guns, two triple 324-mm (12.75-in) tubes for Mk 46 ASW torpedoes
Defensive systems: two Breda 20-barrel chaff launchers, SLQ-25 Nixie towed torpedo decoy search/attack sonar
Electronics: SPS-52C and SPS-768 air search radars, SPS-774 air/surface search and SPQ-2D surface search radars, SPG-76 and SPG-51 fire-control radars, CWE 610 hull-mounted active
Aircraft: two AB 212ASW or EH 101 helicopters
Complement: 380

and carries a 210-kg (463-lb) warhead. Four twin launchers are carried amidships, two each angled to port and starboard. Gun armament comprises a single OTO Melara 127-mm DP weapon in a forward turret; this can engage aircraft to a range of 7 km (4.3 miles), or strike surface targets at a range of 23 km (14.3 miles). Both ships are equipped with four 76-mm (3-in) OTO Melara DP weapons;

Audace is armed with the Super Rapid version, while *Ardito* is fitted with a combination of Super Rapid and Compact guns of a similar calibre.

Ardito was modernized in 1988 and *Audace* in 1991, and stern torpedo tubes have been removed. Both ships have also added improved EW equipment, and these vessels were used for the first ship trials of the EH 101 helicopter in 1992.

Original plans for the 'Audace' class called for a total of five ships, although only two were built. **Ardito** *carries a single 76-mm Super Rapid gun (suitable for anti-missile work) and three slower-firing 76-mm Compact weapons.*

'De la Penne' class Guided-missile destroyer

The guided-missile destroyers **Animoso** and **Ardimentoso** were laid down in 1986 and 1988 respectively. They were launched in 1989 and 1991 and both commissioned in 1993. The previous year the Italian navy had decided to re-name both of the ships after Italian naval heroes of World War II. *Animoso* and *Ardimentoso* were thus renamed **Luigi Durand de la Penne** and **Francesco Mimbelli** respectively.

These multi-role destroyers have served in the Adriatic during NATO operations in Bosnia and in 2000 were fitted with the OTO Melara/Matra Milas anti-submarine system, which can launch a Mk 46 or Mu 90 torpedo out to a range of 55 km (34 miles). Their primary anti-ship weapon is the Teseo Mk 2, a sea-skimmer with a range of 180 km (112 miles) and a 210-kg (463-lb) warhead. The weapons are due to be replaced by the Teseo Mk 3, with radar/IR-homing to a range of 300 km (186 miles). The ships are also fitted with one OTO Melara 127-mm (5-in) main gun mounting forward (taken from the 'B' turrets of the 'Audace' class), and three OTO Melara Super Rapid 76-mm (3-in) DP guns as secondary armament. Six 324-mm (12.75-in) torpedo tubes are fitted to deploy further

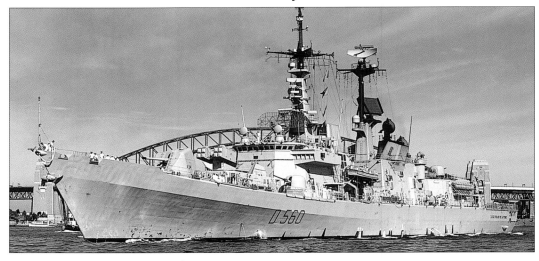

Mk 46 torpedoes with a 11-km (6.8-mile) range. The ships can also deploy either AB 212ASW, SH-3D Sea King or EH 101 helicopters for stand-off ASW missions.

Air defence weapons

For the air defence role, these DDGs are armed with a total of 40 SM-1MR Standard missiles, which are launched from a single-arm launcher. The vessels may be upgraded to carry the SM-2 Standard missile. For point-defence, a single Albatros Mk 2 octuple automatic-loading launcher is used to deploy the Aspide semi-active radar-homing SAM, of which 16 are carried. Aspide has a range of 13 km (8 miles) flying at a speed of Mach 2.5.

The **Luigi Durand de la Penne** *at Sydney. These ships are protected by Kevlar armour. Note the octuple Aspide launcher forward of the bridge.*

SPECIFICATION
'De la Penne' class

Displacement: 4,300 tons standard; 5,400 tons full load
Dimensions: length 147.7 m (484 ft 7 in); beam 16.1 m (52 ft 10 in); draught 8.6 m (28 ft 2½ in)
Propulsion: CODOG; two FIAT gas turbines delivering 40,267.8 kW (54,000 shp) plus two GMT diesels developing 9,395.8 kW (12,600 shp) to two shafts
Speed: 31 kts
Range: 12,964 km (8,056 miles) at 18 kts
Armament: four or eight OTO Teseo Mk 2 (two or four twin) SSMs, Mk 13 launcher for SM-1MR Standard SAMs, Albatros Mk 2 SAM launcher for Aspide SAMs, OTO Melara/Matra Milas anti-submarine missile launcher with Mk 46 Mod 5

or Mu 90 torpedoes, two triple B-515 324-mm (12.75-in) torpedo tubes with Mk 46 torpedoes, OTO Melara 127-mm (5-in) gun, three OTO Melara 76-mm (3-in) Super Rapid guns
Countermeasures: two CSEE Sagaie chaff launchers, one SLQ-25 Nixie anti-torpedo system
Electronics: SPS-52 long range air search radar, SPS-768 air search radar, SPS-774 air/surface search radar, SPS-702 surface search radar, four SPG-76 fire-control radars, two SPG-51G fire-control radars, SPN-748 navigation radar, DE 1164 low-frequency bow and variable depth sonar.
Aircraft: two AB 212ASW, SH-3D or EH 101 helicopters
Complement: 377

'Murasame' class Guided-missile destroyer

In the 1991 fiscal year, the Tokyo yard of Ishikawajima Harima Heavy Industries began work on nine **'Murasame'-class** ships officially designated as guided-missile destroyers for the JMSDF (Japanese Maritime Self-Defence Force). It is debatable whether these ships are really destroyers or large frigates, but there is no argument that they are escort ships and constitute a major component of the JMSDF. The first ship of the class, **Murasame (DD 101)** was laid down in 1993 and was commissioned in 1996.

The vessels of the 'Murasame' class are multi-purpose ships in which considerable effort was devoted in the design phase to the maximized automation of onboard systems wherever possible. This effort paid off in the reduction of the crew to 165 sailors, who thus enjoy the benefits of improved crew accommodation spaces. The ships are powered by four gas turbines for a maximum speed of 30 kts or more, and at a cruising speed of 18 kts the range is 8,350 km (5,190 miles).

US weapon systems

Under contract to Lockheed Martin of the US, Mitsubishi Heavy Industries assembled and tested the primary armament for the 'Murasame'-class ships, namely the Mk 41 Vertical-Launch System (VLS). Mounted below deck in the bows of the ship, this system is capable of launching several types of missile, though only the Vertical Launch Anti-Submarine Rocket (VL ASROC) is carried in the 'Murasame' class. The first eight ships of the class were each fitted with two eight-cell

modules, but in 1998 it was decided to double this capability to four modules on the ninth ship of the class, the **Ariake (DD 109)**.

A 16-cell Mk 48 VLS unit is located amidships, and this carries the RIM-7M Sea Sparrow surface-to-air missile. A 76-mm (3-in) OTO Melara Compact main gun is mounted forward of the VLS unit on the forecastle. Eight Harpoon anti-ship missiles are mounted amidships, as are six torpedo tubes, in the form of two triple units, to fire the Mk 46 Mod 5 anti-submarine torpedo. For self defence, two 20-mm Close-in Weapon Systems (CIWS) are mounted, one forward of the bridge and the other above the helicopter hangar.

With an aft landing pad and hangar, the 'Murasame'- class ships are each able to carry, house, maintain and operate a single SH-60J helicopter in the anti-submarine warfare role.

With new Japanese legislation directed against terrorism, the JMSDF has deployed ships in non-combat military support roles to the Indian Ocean. On 9 November 2001, the **Kirisame (DD 104)** was one of three JMSDF ships deployed, with the primary mission being to gather information and intelligence on routes to ferry supplies into the area.

In November 2002, Japanese Self-Defence Forces participated in Exercise Keen Sword 2003 in conjunction with US military forces. A number of JMSDF ships, including the *Ariake,* which was integrated into the USS *Kitty Hawk*'s carrier battle group, took part in this bilateral co-operation training exercise for regional conflict.

DD 109 is the **Ariake,** *themost formidably equipped of the Japanese Maritime Self-Defence Force's nine 'Murasame'-class destroyers.*

SPECIFICATION

'Murasame' class
Ships in class: *Murasame* (DD 101), *Harusame* (DD 102), *Yuudachi* (DD 103), *Kirisame* (DD 104), *Inazuma* (DD 105), *Samidare* (DD 106), *Ikazuchi* (DD 107), *Akebono* (DD 108) and *Ariake* (DD 109)
Displacement: 4,400 tons standard; 5,200 tons maximum
Dimensions: length 150.8 m (494 ft 9 in); beam 17 m (55 ft 9 in); draught 5.2 m (17 ft 1 in)
Propulsion: two General Electric LM2500 gas turbines delivering 64120 kW (86,000 shp) and two Rolls-Royce Spey SM1C gas turbines delivering 20130 kW (27,000 shp) to two shafts
Speed: 30+ kts
Armament: Mk 41 VLS for ASROC (two 8-cell modules on ships DD 101 to DD 108, four 8-cell modules on

Ariake), 16-cell Mk 48 VLS for RIM-7M Sea Sparrow SAMs, eight SSM-1B Harpoon SSMs, one 76-mm (3-in) OTO Melara Compact gun, two 20-mm Phalanx Mk 15 CIWS mountings, and two 324-mm (12.75-in) Mk 32 Mod 14 triple tubes for Mk 46 Mod 5 anti-submarine torpedoes
Electronics: OPS-28 surface search radar, OPS-24 3D air search radar, OPS-2 navigation radar, two Type 2-31 fire-control radars, URN-25 TACAN radio beacon, UPX-29 AIMS Mk XII IFF, OQS-5 hull-mounted active search sonar, OQR-1 (SQR-19) TACTASS towed-array passive search sonar, four SRBOC 6-barrel fixed Mk 36 Mod 12 chaff/flare decoys, and SLQ-25 Nixie towed decoy
Aircraft: one SH-60J Seahawk
Complement: 165

'Hatsuyuki' class Guided-missile destroyer

This 12-strong class of destroyers was authorized at the end of the 1970s for the

Japanese navy, or Japanese Maritime Self-Defence Force as it has styled itself since being

re-established in the 1950s. The gas turbine-powered 'Hatsuyuki' class was created as a multi-

purpose design incorporating a balanced anti-air, anti-ship and anti-submarine sensor and

SPECIFICATION

'Hatsuyuki' class

Ships in class: *Hatsuyuki* (DD 122), *Shirayuki* (DD 123), *Mineyuki* (DD 124), *Sawayuki* (DD 125), *Hamayuki* (DD 126), *Isoyuki* (DD 127), *Haruyuki* (DD 128), *Yamayuki* (DD 129), *Matsuyuki* (DD 130), *Setoyuki* (DD 131) and *Asayuki* (DD 132)

Displacement: 2,950 or, from DD 129, 3,050 tons standard; 3,700 or, from DD 129, 3,800 tons full load

Dimensions: length 130 m (426 ft 6 in); beam 13.6 m (44 ft 7 in); draught 4.2 m (13 ft 9 in) or, in DD 129-132, 4.4 m (14 ft 5 in)

Propulsion: COGOG with two Rolls-Royce Olympus TM3B gas turbines delivering 36,535 kW (49,000 shp) and two Rolls-Royce Tyne RM1C gas turbines delivering 7,380 kW (9,900 shp) to two shafts

Speed: 30 kts

Range: 12975 km (8,065 miles) at 20 kts

Armament: two quadruple Harpoon launchers, one Mk 29 Sea Sparrow SAM launcher, one Mk 112 octuple ASROC ASW torpedo launcher, one 76-mm (3-in) OTO Melara Compact gun, two Mk 15 20-mm Phalanx CIWS, two triple Type 68 324-mm (12.75-in) tubes for Mk 46 Mod 5 anti-submarine torpedoes

Electronics: OPS-14B air search radar, ORS-18 surface search radar, Type 2-12A SAM fire-control and Type 2-21/21A gun fire-control radars, OQS-4A (SQS-23) bow-mounted active search/attack sonar, OQR-1 TACTASS passive sonar in some, and Mk 36 SRBOC chaff/flare launchers

Aircraft: one SH-60J Seahawk

Complement: 195–200

The Asayuki *(DD 132) was the penultimate unit of the 'Hatsuyuki' class, and was built by Sumitomo, one of five shipyards involved in the building programme.*

fast-reacting anti-missile system was progressively fitted to the rest of the class during the 1990s. Other improvements include the Canadian Beartrap helicopter landing system and state-of-the-art ECM equipment to the last three ships of the class. The **Shimayuki** (**DD 133**) was converted to a training ship (**TV 35**) in 1999 and now has a lecture theatre added to the helicopter hangar.

The 'Hatsuyuki' class are capable all-round warships fitted with fin stabilizers. Their primary anti-ship armament is the Harpoon missile, which has a range of some 130 km (80 miles): flying just above the sea,

it delivers a 500-lb (227-kg) warhead at a speed of Mach 0.9. To attack submarines, the ships carry the widely used ASROC system that can drop a Mk 46 homing torpedo up to 9 km (6 miles) from the ship.

The 'Hatsuyuki'-class ships do not carry a long-range anti-aircraft weapon, built as they were to engage surface and sub-surface threats under cover of the US or Japanese air forces. Their Sea Sparrow SAMs have a range of 15 km (9 miles), while the CIWS is purely a point-defence system intended primarily for the engagement and destruction of anti-ship missiles.

armament fit. The first seven ships were built with weight-saving aluminium alloy for their bridge structures and other upperworks, but later vessels used steel, which led to a slight increase in displacement. The name-ship was laid down in March 1979, launched in November 1980 and commissioned in May 1982; the last of the class was laid down in 1984 and commissioned in 1987. In 1992 the **Shirayuki** (**DD 123**) became the first to be

fitted with the 20-mm Phalanx CIWS (Close-in Weapons System): this short-ranged but

The 'Hatsuyuki' destroyers, seen in the form of the Isoyuki *(DD 127), are optimized for the anti-ship and anti-submarine roles with Harpoon and ASROC.*

'Asagiri' class Guided-missile destroyer

The eight guided-missile destroyers of the **'Asagiri' class** were laid down between 1985 and 1988, and commissioned between 1988 and 1991. Like the destroyers of the preceding 'Hatsuyuki' class, they are intended primarily for the engagement of surface or sub-surface targets, although the ships do also carry a powerful suite of point-defence systems to defeat incoming missiles or aircraft. The ships' primary anti-ship weapon is the Harpoon medium-range surface-to-surface missile, and their main

Right: The **A**sagiri *(DD 151) is the name-ship of this eight-strong class of well-armed and well-equipped anti-ship and anti-submarine destroyers.*

SPECIFICATION

'Asagiri' class
Ships in class: *Asagiri* (DD 151), *Yamagiri* (DD 152), *Yuugiri* (DD 153), *Amagiri* (DD 154), *Hamagiri* (DD 155), *Setogiri* (DD 156), *Sawagiri* (DD 157) and *Umigiri* (DD 158)
Displacement: 3,500 tons standard; 4,200 tons full load
Dimensions: length 137 m (449 ft 6 in), beam 14.6 m (47 ft 11 in); draught 4.5 m (14 ft 9 in)
Propulsion: COGAG with four Rolls-Royce Spey SM1A gas turbines delivering 39,515 kW (53,000 shp) to two shafts
Speed: 30 kts
Armament: two quadruple Harpoon launchers, one Mk 29 Sea Sparrow SAM octuple launcher with 20 missiles, one octuple Mk 112

launcher for ASROC ASW rockets with Mk 46 Neartip torpedoes, one 76-mm (3-in) OTO Melara Compact gun, two Mk 15 20-mm Phalanx CIWS, two Type 68 324-mm (12.75-in) triple tubes for Mk 46 ASW torpedoes
Electronics: OPS-14C (or from DD 155 OPS-24) air search radar, OPS-28C (or DD 153-154 OPS-28Y) surface search radar, Type 2-22 gun fire-control radar, Type 2-12G (or from DD 155 Type 2-12E) SAM fire-control radar, OQS-4A hull-mounted active search/attack sonar, OQR-1 towed-array sonar, two SRBOC 6-barrel chaff/flare launchers, and one SLQ-51 Nixie or Type 4 towed anti-torpedo decoy
Aircraft: one SH-60J Seahawk
Complement: 220

Below: The original position of the main mast, just to the rear of the funnels for the large quantities of hot exhaust gases from the four gas turbines, was poor.

anti-submarine weapon is the Mk 46 Mod 5 Neartip lightweight homing torpedo delivered by the ship-launched ASROC rocket, torpedo tubes or by the ships' embarked helicopter. When first commissioned, the ships each carried one HSS-2B Sea King helicopter, but these have now been replaced by the SH-60J Seahawk.

The 'Asagiri' class destroyers suffered from a design fault: hot gases from the funnels

damaged the electronic systems on the main mast and also gave the ships a very pronounced IR signature. The main mast was therefore heightened and offset to port, the forward funnel was offset to port and the after funnel to starboard. This was undertaken on the last four as they were completing. These vessels also carry improved electronics including a data link to their helicopter, a system that was later retrofitted to the earlier ships.

The revision of the main mast and after funnel arrangement saw the former offset to port and the latter to starboard. Pictured is **Yuugiri** *(DD 153).*

'Haruna' and 'Shirane' class
Anti-submarine warfare destroyers

Shirane as completed in the early 1980s. The two 'Shirane'-class destroyers are distinguishable from the preceding 'Harunas' by their twin 'macks' – combined radar masts and smoke stacks.

The **'Haruna' class** and follow-on improved **'Shirane' class** were the world's first destroyer-sized warships designed to carry and operate three large Sea King-sized ASW helicopters. Both ship classes were completed with strong ASW armaments, though as built they were weaker than most contemporary Western designs in both anti-air and anti-surface warfare systems.

To help rectify these shortcomings, both classes were refitted in the late 1980s and early 1990s. The destroyers had 20-mm Phalanx CIWS and Sea Sparrow missile systems added to improve anti-aircraft and anti-missile point defence.

The 'Haruna' class,

comprising **Haruna** (DD 141) and **Hiei** (DD 142), were completed in 1973 and 1974. They have continuous superstructures. Their single combined radar mast and funnel (known as a 'mack') offset to port allow space for the third helicopter in the hangar.

Improved

The later 'Shirane'-class units, **Shirane** (DD 143) and **Kurama** (DD 144), were commissioned in 1980 and 1981 respectively. They have a broken superstructure with two 'macks', one offset to port atop the main superstructure forward, and the other atop the detached hangar aft. Larger than their predecessors, they were fitted

with towed-array sonars in the early 1990s.

Helicopters

For landing helicopters in bad weather, the ships are fitted with the Canadian Bear Trap haul-down system. To reduce their underwater radiated noise

levels from the main propulsion machinery they are equipped with the 'Masker' bubble-generating system. This forms a continuous curtain of minute air bubbles over the parts of the hull beneath the machinery spaces, with the bubbles acting as a sound-damping layer.

Haruna was completed in 1973. Its ability to carry three helicopters made it one of the most capable ASW destroyers of its time.

SPECIFICATION	
'Shirane' class **Displacement:** 5,200 tons standard and 6,800 tons full load **Dimensions:** length 158.8 m (521 ft); beam 17.5 m (57 ft 5 in); draught 5.3 m (17 ft 5 in) **Machinery**: geared steam turbines delivering 52,200 kW (70,000 shp) to two shafts **Speed:** 32 kts (59 km/h; 37 mph) **Aircraft:** three Mitsubishi-Sikorsky SH-60J Seahawk ASW helicopters **Armament:** one octuple ASROC Mk 112 ASW missile launcher (24 missiles carrying Mk 46 NEARTIP lightweight torpedoes); two triple	324-mm (12.75-in) Type 68 ASW torpedo tubes armed with Mk 46 Mod 5 NEARTIP ASW torpedoes); two single FMC 127-mm (5-in) DP guns; one octuple Sea Sparrow SAM launcher; two 20-mm Phalanx CIWS **Electronics:** one OPS-12 3D radar, one OPS-28 surface-search radar, OFS-2D navigation radar, Signaal WM-25 missile fire-control radar, two Type 72 gun fire-control radars, one ORN-6C TACAN, comprehensive ESM and counter-measures/decoy suite, OQS-101 bow-mounted sonar, SQR-18A passive towed-array sonar, and SQS-35(J) active/passive variable depth sonar

'Tachikaze' and 'Hatakaze' class Anti-air warfare destroyers

During the early 1970s, the Japanese Maritime Self-Defence Force needed to improve its medium-range area defence SAM capabilities, and thus laid down the three **'Tachikaze'-class** ships at three-yearly intervals from 1973. These vessels are the **Tachikaze** (DDG 168), **Asakaze** (DDG 169) and **Sawakaze** (DDG 170), which commissioned in 1976, 1979 and 1982 respectively.

Missile fit

Each ship carries one single-rail Mk 13 launcher for the Standard SM-1MR missile, allowing the ships to engage aircraft targets out to a range of nearly 50 km (31 miles). The altitude envelope of the SM-1MR enables aircraft and missiles to be intercepted at heights between 40 m (131 ft) and 18000 m (59,055 ft).

The two dual-purpose guns can also be used for air defence as well as for engaging surface targets, and surface attack capability was enhanced in the 1980s by the addition of Harpoon anti-ship missiles, fired from the Mk 13 launcher. All three ships received Phalanx CIWS at the same time.

These vessels were designed almost exclusively as anti-aircraft platforms. No helicopter facilities are provided, and the ASW armament is confined to ASROC missiles and Mk 46 self-defence torpedoes. In order to save on construction costs, the class adopted the propulsion plant and machinery of the 'Haruna' class of helicopter-carrying ASW destroyers.

Soon after the last of the 'Tachikazes' was completed, work started on the first of two slightly larger air-defence destroyers of the **'Hatakaze' class**. The **Hatakaze** (DDG 171) and the **Shimakaze** (DDG 172) were commissioned in 1986 and 1988 respectively.

They have a similar armaments fit to the preceding vessels, though their increased size – the 'Hatakazes' are eight

Above: The 'Tachikaze'-class destroyer Asakaze soon after its commissioning. The first two ships serve with the 64th DesDiv at Yokosuka; Sawakaze is part of the 62nd DesDiv at Sasebo.

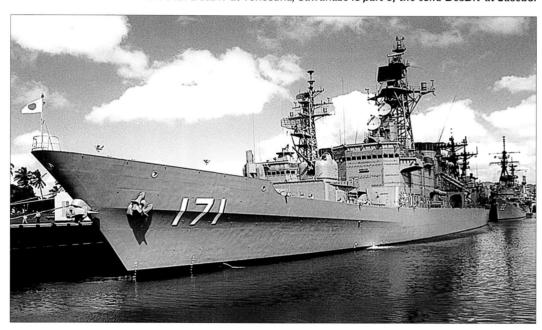

Above: Larger than the 'Tachikazes', Hatakaze is part of the 61st DesDiv at Yokosuka. Shimakaze is based at Maizuru with the 63rd DesDiv.

metres (26 feet) longer and displace about 700 tons more than the 'Tachikazes' – means that they can carry two quadruple Harpoon launchers, which frees magazine space for SAMs.

They also have platforms capable of accepting a single SH-60J Seahawk helicopter.

SPECIFICATION

'Tachikaze' class
Displacement: (DDG 168 and 169) 3,850 tons standard and 4,800 tons full load; (DDG 170) 3,950 tons standard and 4,800 tons full load
Dimensions: length 1430 m (469 ft 2 in); beam 14.3 m (46 ft 11 in); draught 4.6 m (15 ft 1 in)
Machinery: geared steam turbines delivering 52,200 kW (70,000 shp) to two shafts
Speed: 32 kts
Armament: single-rail Mk 13 launcher able to fire both Standard SM-1 MR and Harpoon missile (standard load 40 missiles); two single 127-mm (5-in) DP guns; two 20-mm (0.8-in)

Phalanx CIWS mountings; octuple ASROC ASW missile launcher (only DDG 170 carries reloads), and two triple Type 68 324-mm (12.75-in) ASW torpedo tubes with six Mk 46 Mod 5 torpedoes
Electronics: SPS-52B/C 3D radar, OPS-110 air-search radar, OPS-160 (OPS-28 in DDG 170) surface-search radar, two SPG-51C missile fire control radars, two Type 72 gun fire control radars, two SATCOM communications systems, comprehensive countermeasures suite, four Mk 36 Super RBOC chaff launchers, and OQS-3A hull sonar
Complement: 250–270

'Kongou' class Advanced anti-air warfare destroyer

For decades after the war, the primary focus of the Japanese Maritime Self-Defence Force was on anti-air and anti-submarine warfare. During the 1980s and 1990s, the increasing threat from China, together with the reduction of the US military presence in the region, forced Japan to take a more active military role in Asian waters.

For this, a new **'Kongou' class** of guided-missile destroyers was commissioned. These anti-aircraft vessels are the most capable of their type in the region.

AEGIS system

Based upon the US Navy's 'Arleigh Burke' class, the 'Kongous' have been built to mercantile instead of warship standards. They are bigger than the American ships, and carry an improved lightweight version of the AEGIS air defence system. AEGIS integrates weapons, radar and fire control into one system, capable of controlling a fleet battle above and below the surface.

First proposed in the JSDF's FY 87 programme, **Kongou** (DDG 173) was commissioned in 1993. It was followed by **Kirishima** (DDG 174) in 1995, **Myouko** (DDG 175) in 1996 and **Choukai** (DDG 176) in 1998. A difference between these vessels and the 'Burkes' is that the 'Kongous' have a longer flush deck at the stern, making it easier to handle helicopters up to the size of the SH-60J Seahawk or larger.

The long-range air defence capability of the 'Kongous' is seen as a national asset beyond their duty to protect the fleet. Though the National Defense Program Outline, or NDPO, has called for a slimming in

The 'Kongous' have a longer helicopter flight deck than the closely related 'Arleigh Burke' class, but like the American destroyers they have no permanent aircraft facilities.

The characteristic octagonal phased array antennae of the SPY-1 radar system identify the Kongou as an AEGIS-equipped vessel. There are four arrays, giving 360° coverage.

Japanese Self-Defence force levels, it has also called for an expansion in its counter-terrorism capabilities. To its cost, the world has learned that air defences are vital when defending against terrorist attacks.

SPECIFICATION

'Kongou' class
Displacement: 7,250 tons standard and 9,485 tons full load
Dimensions: length 1610 m (528 ft 3 in); beam 21 m (68 ft 10 in); draught 6.2 m (20 ft 4 in)
Machinery: four General Electric LM 2500 gas turbines delivering 76,210 kW (102,160 shp) to two shafts
Speed: 30 kts
Armament: two Mk 41 VLS launchers with 90 Standard SM-2MR SAMs and ASROC ASW missiles; two quad Harpoon launchers; one OTO-Melara 127-mm (5-in) compact DP gun; two Mk 15 Phalanx; two triple HOS 302 torpedo tubes with Mk 46 Mod 5 Neartip ASW torpedoes
Electronics: SPY-1D phased array air search 3-D system with four arrays; OPS 28 surface search, OPS-20 navigation radar, three SPG-62 fire-control radars; AEGIS combat data system, WSC-3 SATCOM; SQQ-28 helicopter datalink; comprehensive ESM/ECM/countermeasures suite; OQS 102 bow-mounted active sonar, OQR-2 passive towed array
Complement: 307

'Kara' class
Large anti-submarine ship

Built at the 61 Kommuna, Nikolayev North Shipyard between 1971 and 1977, the seven units of the **'Nikolayev' class** (known as the **'Kara' class** by NATO) were intended to boost the Soviet fleet's blue-water anti-submarine capability. Cruiser-sized ships, they were rated as BPKs (*Bolshoy Protivolodochnyy Korabl*, or large anti-submarine ship) by the Soviets, and were considered as destroyers by function.

The 'Kara' is an enlarged gas turbine-powered refinement of the steam-powered 'Kresta II' design, with improved anti-aircraft and anti-submarine capability. The class was commissioned between 1973 and 1980 for service primarily in

the Black Sea, as well as in the Mediterranean and the Pacific. Extensive command and control facilities meant that the 'Karas' often acted as hunter-killer task group leaders.

A single gas-turbine exhaust funnel dominated the large superstructure. On the ship's stern was a helicopter landing pad with a hangar partially recessed below the flight deck. To stow the ASW helicopter, the hanger roof hatch and doors had to be opened; the helicopter was pushed in and then lowered to the deck via an elevator.

Nuclear armed

The ship's Shtorm (SA-N-3 'Goblet') and Rastrub (SS-N-14 'Silex') ASW missiles have

Above: Although classed by some authorities as a destroyer thanks to its primary anti-submarine mission, the powerful 'Kara' class is cruiser-sized, and carries a heavy and versatile weapons mix.

Above: A 'Kara'-class cruiser underway shows the incredible clutter of search, navigation and fire-control radars together with missiles and guns. This appearance is characteristic of large Soviet navy warships commissioned in the 1970s and 1980s.

SPECIFICATION

'Kara' class
Type: large ASW ship
Displacement: 8,200 tons standard and 9,700 tons full load
Dimensions: length 173 m (567 ft 7¼ in); beam 18.60 m (61 ft); draught 6.70 m (22 ft)
Propulsion: COGAG gas turbine arrangement delivering 89,485 kW (120,000 shp) to two shafts
Speed: 34 kts
Aircraft: one Ka-27 'Helix' ASW helicopter
Armament: two quadruple Rastrub (SS-N-14 'Silex') ASW launchers with eight missiles, two twin Shtorm (SA-N-3 'Goblet') SAM launchers with 72 missiles (except in *Azov* which has one Shtorm system plus one Fort (SA-N-6 'Grumble') system with 24 missiles), two twin Osa-M (SA-N-4 'Gecko') SAM launchers with 40 missiles,

two twin 76-mm (3-in) DP guns, four 30-mm AK-630 six-barrel CIWS, two 12-barrel RBU 6000 ASW rocket launchers, two RBU 1000 ASW rocket launchers
Electronics: MR-700F Pobderezovik 'Flat Screen' 3D air search radar, one MR-310U Angara-M 'Head Net-C' 3D search radar, two 'Don Kay' or 'Palm Frond' navigation radars, two Grom 'Head Light-B' SA-N-3 and SS-N-14 fire-control radars, two MPZ-301 'Pop Group' SA-N-4 fire control radars, two 'Owl Screech' 76-mm fire-control radars, two 'Bass Tilt' CIWS fire control radars, 'High Pole-A' and 'High Pole-B' IFF; one 'Side Globe' ESM suite, one 'Bell' series or one 'Rum Tub' ECM suite, one MG-332 Titan-2T 'Bull Nose' hull mounted sonar, one MG-325 Vega 'Mare Tail' variable depth sonar
Complement: 525

---

secondary anti-ship capabilities, the former having a 25-kiloton nuclear warhead available in place of the normal 150-kg (331-lb) HE type. It is believed that at the height of the Cold War, all Soviet ships with dual-capable weapon systems had at least 25 per cent of their missiles equipped with nuclear warheads while at sea.

Nikolayev was transferred to the Ukraine after the fall of the USSR, and was scrapped in India in 1994. *Ochakov* went into reserve in the Pacific in the late 1990s. *Kerch* went into refit in the late 1990s, and is the only member of the class still to be

nominally in commission, serving as flagship of the Black Sea Fleet.

Test ship

Azov was the trials ship for the new generation SA-N-6 vertical-launch SAM and its associated 'Top Dome' fire control radar. She remained in the Black Sea after one Shtorm and 'Headlight' fire control radar combination had been replaced by the new systems. *Petropavlovsk* is in reserve in the Pacific, and is likely to be scrapped, a fate that *Tashkent* has already met. *Vladivostok* is in reserve in the Black Sea.

'Kirov' class Large guided-missile cruiser

In December 1977, the Baltic Shipyard in Leningrad launched the largest warship (other than aircraft carriers) built by any

nation since World War II. Commissioned into Soviet fleet service in 1980, **Kirov** was assigned the RKR (*Raketnyy*

Kreyser, or missile cruiser) designation by the Soviets and a CGN designation by the Americans. Planned initially to

find and engage enemy missile submarines, it became a much more capable warship when it was equipped with the long-

*The primary 'Kirov' mission in time of war would have been to destroy US Navy carrier battle groups with **Granit** nuclear-tipped missiles.*

*Frunze, renamed **Admiral Lazarev** in 1992, served with the Soviet Pacific Fleet. The comprehensive command and communications facilities it carries meant that it was often used as a fleet flagship.*

range P-700 Granit anti-ship missile. In appearance and firepower *Kirov* is more like a battlecruiser than a normal missile cruiser.

Nuclear/steam

Its powerplant is unique in being a combined nuclear and steam system. Two reactors are coupled to oil-fired boilers that superheat the steam produced in the reactor plant to increase the power output available during high-speed running.

Missile 'farm'

Most of the weapons systems are located forward of the massive superstructure. The stern is used to house machinery and a below-deck helicopter hangar, which accesses the flight deck via a lift. Up to five Kamov Ka-25 'Hormone' or Ka-27 'Helix'

The largest surface-action fighting ships built for any navy since World War II, the 'Kirov'-class battlecruisers carry heavy armament beneath the hatches on their foredeck. However, they are very expensive to crew and maintain, and have spent relatively short periods at sea.

helicopters can be accommodated in the hangar, though a normal complement is three.

The helicopters are a mix of ASW and missile-guidance/Elint variants. The latter provide target data for the main battery of 20 Granit (SS-N-19 'Shipwreck') Mach-2.5 anti-ship cruise missiles, located below decks forward in 45° angled launch tubes. Other weapons and systems vary from ship to ship.

Area air defence is provided by vertical launch Fort (SA-N-6) missiles, housed in 12 eight-round rotary launchers forward of the SS-N-19 bins. Close-in air defence is handled by a mix of Osa-M (SA-N-4 'Gecko') missiles, 30-mm CIWS

mountings and 130-mm (5-in) DP guns. The main ASW armament is a reloadable twin Rastrub (SS-N-14 'Silex') ASW missile-launcher with associated variable-depth low-frequency sonar aft and a low-frequency bow sonar. Later ships carry 10

SPECIFICATION

'Kirov' class
Type: Large guided-missile cruiser
Displacement: 24,300 tons standard and 26,500 tons full load
Dimensions: length 252 m (826 ft 10 in); beam 28.50 m (93 ft 6 in); draught 10 m (32 ft 10 in)
Propulsion: two KN-3 PWR reactors and two steam boilers providing 102900 kW (140,000 shp) to two shafts
Speed: 30 kts
Aircraft: three Ka-25 or Ka-27
Armament: 20 Granit (SS-N-19 'Shipwreck') SSM, 12 octuple Fort (SA-N-6 'Grumble') SAM launchers, two Kinshal (SA-N-9 'Gauntlet') octuple launchers with 128 missiles, two twin Osa-M (SA-N-4 'Gecko') SAM launchers with 40 missiles, two 130-mm (3.0 in) DP guns, six Kashtan (CADS-N-1) combined 30-mm AK 630/SA-N-11 'Grison'

gun/missile CIWS, one Rastrub (SS-N-14 'Silex') twin ASW launcher with 16 missiles, one 12-barrel RBU 6000 ASW rocket launcher, two six-barrel RBU 1000 ASW rocket launchers, two quintuple 533-mm (21-in) ASW torpedo tubes firing Type 40 torpedoes or Viyoga (SS-N-15 'Starfish') ASW missiles
Electronics: 'Top Pair' 3D radar, 'Top Steer' 3D radar, two 'Top Dome' SA-N-6 fire control, two 'Pop Group' SA-N-4 fire control, three 'Palm Frond' nav radars, 'Kite Screech' 130-mm fire control, two 'Eye Bowl' SS-N-14 fire control, four 'Bass Tilt' CIWS fire control, one 'Side Globe' ESM, 10 'Bell' series ECM, four 'Rum Tub' ECM, one Polinom low-frequency bow sonar, one 'Horse Tail' medium-frequency variable-depth sonar
Complement: 727

Vodopod (SS-N-16 'Stallion') torpedo-carrying missiles.

Flagships

The sheer size of the ships mean that they have plenty of space for a command, control and communications (C^3) outfit, and could serve as effective fleet flagships. One of their intended missions was to act as a task group command escort to the aircraft carriers being planned by the Soviet navy.

Five vessels were laid down between 1974 and 1989, but only four were completed. The first ships were named after heroes of the Bolshevik revolution, but with the end of the Communist state all have been renamed. *Admiral*

Ushakov (ex-*Kirov*) was inactive through most of the 1990s following a reactor accident, and has been cannibalized to provide parts. *Admiral Lazarev* (ex-*Frunze*) has been out of service for a decade, and is destined to be scrapped. The *Admiral Nakhimov* (ex-*Kalinin*) was refitted in 1994, but did not go to sea for more than three years

from 1997. The *Nakhimov* is the only 'Kirov' on the active list in late 2001. *Petr Veliky* was launched in 1989, but was not completed until 1998, and was laid up soon after completing sea trials. Lack of funds also meant that the fifth ship, the *Kuznetsov*, was scrapped before launch, the name being assigned to a carrier.

'Slava' class Missile cruiser

The Slava (now known as the Moskva) seen during the first foray into the Mediterranean in 1983. As with most large vessels, these powerful cruisers are too expensive for the cash-strapped Russian navy to keep in operation.

The first of the 'Kara' follow-on class was first seen outside the Black Sea in 1983. At first designated **BlackCom 1** by Western intelligence, and later known as the **'Krasina' class**, these powerful vessels are now known as the **'Slava' class** after the original name of the lead ship. *Slava* (now **Moskva**), was laid down at the Nikolayev Shipyard in 1976. Launched in 1979, *Slava* entered service in 1983 after extensive trials. By 1990, three of the class were in service, with a fourth under construction.

Surface action

Possibly designed as a less-expensive complement to the massive 'Kirov'-class battlecruisers, the 'Slavas' are primarily surface action vessels, designated RKR (*Raketnyy Kreyzer*, or missile cruiser). Their primary weapons are 16 P-500 Bazalt (SS-N-12 'Sandbox') anti-

ship missiles, although they possess great anti-aircraft and anti-submarine capability.

Design features

The hull appears to be an improved 'Kara' type with increased beam and length to accommodate new weapon systems, the larger size also enhancing stability and allowing the radar mast height to be increased. Twin funnels are fitted, venting the exhaust from the gas turbine propulsion system.

There have been reports that the 'Slavas' were built with large quantities of flammable material, and their damage control systems were poorly designed.

Initially it was believed that at least eight and as many as 20 cruisers were planned, replacing the 'Kynda' and 'Kresta' classes as they retired. However, with the Russian navy virtually bankrupt there were no funds available for such expensive

warships, and only four were laid down.

Moskva was in refit through most of the 1990s, returning to become flagship of the Black Sea Fleet. The second unit, **Marshal Ustinov**, commissioned in 1986, serves with the Northern fleet, though it has been in overhaul since the mid-1990s. **Varyag** (formerly the **Chervona Ukraina**) was commissioned into the Pacific Fleet in 1989. The fourth unit was launched in 1990 as the **Admiral Lobov**, but was transferred incomplete to the Ukrainian Navy. Renamed **Ukraina**, it was still incomplete in 2000, but if funds become available it is intended to serve as the Ukrainian fleet flagship.

The hull of Slava is dominated by the launch tubes for 16 Bazalt (SS-N-12 'Sandbox') missiles. These Mach-1.7 weapons are nuclear-capable, and have a range of more than 550 km (342 miles).

SPECIFICATION

Moskva (ex-*Slava*)
Type: Guided-missile cruiser
Displacement: 10,000 tons standard and 12,500 tons full load
Dimensions: length 186 m (610 ft 2½ in); beam 21.50 m (70 ft 6 in); draught 7.60 m (24 ft 11 in)
Propulsion: four main and two auxiliary gas turbines delivering 79,380 kW (108,000 shp) to two shafts
Speed: 32 kts
Aircraft: one Ka-27 'Helix' ASW helicopter.
Armament: eight twin Bazalt (SS-N-12 'Sandbox') SSM launchers, eight octuple Fort (SA-N-6 'Grumble') SAM launchers, two twin Osa-M (SA-N-4 'Gecko') SAM launchers with 36 missiles, one twin 130-mm (5-in) DP gun, six 30-mm AK-630 six-barrel CIWS mountings, two 12-barrel RBU

6000 ASW rocket-launchers, two quintuple 533-mm (21-in) ASW torpedo tubes
Electronics: one MR-800 Voshkod 'Top Pair' 3D Air Search radar, one MR-700 Fregat 'Top Steer' 3D Air/Surface Search radar, three 'Palm Frond' navigation radars, one Argument 'Front Door-C' SS-N-12 fire control radar, two MPZ-301 'Pop Group' SA-N-4 fire control radar, one Volna 'Top Dome' SA-N-6 fire control radar, one 'Kite Screech' 130-mm fire control radar, three 'Bass Tilt' CIWS for fire control radars, one 'Side Globe' ESM suite, one 'Punch Bowl' SATCOM, one MG-332 Tigan-2T 'Bull Horn' low-frequency hull mounted sonar, one Platina 'Mare Tail' variable-depth sonar
Complement: 480–520

'Sovremenny' class Destroyer

The **'Sovremenny' class**
(**Project 956 Sarych**) was
derived from the hull of the
previous 'Kresta II' cruisers, and
was intended to offer a surface-
strike capability and to provide
other warships with protection
against air and ship attack. As
such, the class was seen as a
specialist anti-shipping
complement to the 'Udaloy'
ASW cruiser.

A total of 20 vessels were
constructed at Zhadanov (later
North Yard), with another three
cancelled or aborted (up to 28
ships may have been planned).
The first, **Sovremenny**, was
laid down in 1977 and
commissioned in December
1980. From **Bespokoiny**
(commissioned February 1992)
onwards, the class was known
as the **Project 956A**, which
features improved weapons and
EW systems. Currently, there
are only four units in active
Russian service (three of Project
956A type), reduced from a total
of 17, with a single vessel
(**Bulny**) awaiting completion.

Surface warfare

Designated by the Soviets as
eskadrenny minonosets

(destroyer), the class was first
armed with the rocket/ramjet-
powered P-80 Zubr missile,
replaced on the Project 956A by
the longer-range P-270 Moskit.
The P-80 is a sea-skimming

*Above: Although they were designed to operate in concert with one
another, the 'Sovremenny' vessels are being sacrificed by the
Russian navy in favour of the 'Udaloy' class, which has a more
reliable propulsion system.*

*Above: The remnants of the 'Sovremenny' class serve with Russia's
Baltic Fleet (Nastoychivy and Bespokoiny), Northern Fleet
(Besstrashny) and Pacific Fleet (Burny).*

*Left: The 'Sovremenny' class introduced the telescopic helicopter
hangar to the Soviet navy, and was the first vessel to appear with
the fully automatic twin-barrel 130-mm AK-130 gun, which is
mounted fore and aft and provided with 2000 rounds. The guns can
fire 35-45 rds/min to a distance of 29.5 km (18 miles).*

weapon, with a low-altitude speed of Mach 2.2 and a 320-kg (705-lb) or 200-kT nuclear warhead. Both weapons carry the NATO designation SS-N-22 'Sunburn'. Air defence requirements are handled by the Mach-3 Uragan (SA-N-7 'Gadfly') missile system, with a range of 44 km (27 miles) and an altitude of 15,000 m (50,000 ft). A total of 44 missiles are carried for

launchers mounted on the raised decks fore and aft of the two islands. Project 956A ships introduced the Yozh (SA-N-12 'Grizzly'), using the same launcher.

In 2000–1, the Chinese navy received two Project 956A vessels (hulls 18 and 19), **Hangzhou** (ex-**Yekaterinburg**) and **Fuzhou** (ex-**Alexandr Nevsky**).

The 'Sovremenny' is comparable in size to the US Navy's 'Aegis' class, its the primary weapon being the Moskit anti-ship missile, for which two quadruple launchers are provided, one either side of the forward island.

SPECIFICATION	
Type 956 'Sovremenny' class	six-barrel 30-mm CIWS mountings,
Displacement: 6,600 tons standard	two RBU-1000 ASW rocket
and 7,940 tons full load	launchers with 48 rockets, two twin
Dimensions: length 156 m (511 ft	533-mm (21-in) ASW torpedo tubes
10 in); beam 17.3 m (56 ft 9 in);	and 30-50 mines
draught 6.5 m (21 ft 4 in)	**Electronics:** one 'Top Plate' 3D air
Machinery: two GTZA-674 turbo-	search radar, three 'Palm Frond'
pressurised steam turbines	surface search radars, one 'Band
delivering 73.13 MW (99,500 shp)	Stand' SSM fire-control radar, two
to two shafts	'Bass Tilt' CIWS fire-control radars,
Speed: 33 kts	one 'Kite Screech' 130-mm fire-
Aircraft: one Ka-27 'Helix-A' ASW	control radar, six 'Front Dome' SAM
helicopter	fire-control radars, two 'Bell Shroud'
Armament: two quadruple Zubr	and two 'Bell Squat' ECM systems,
(SS-N-22 'Sunburn') SSM launchers	two PK-2 and eight PK-10 decoy
(no reloads), two single Uragan	launchers, 'Bull Horn' and 'Whale
(SA-N-7 'Gadfly') SAM launchers (44	Tongue' hull sonars, two 'Light Bulb'
missiles), two twin AK-130 130-mm	TACAN
(5.12-in) DP guns, four AK-630	**Complement:** 296–344

'Udaloy' class ASW destroyer

The **'Udaloy I' class (Project 1155 Fregat)** were considered 'large ASW ships' (*bolshoy protivolodochny korabl*). The programme was initiated in 1972, and two ships, **Udaloy**

and **Vitse-Admiral Kulakov** were operational by early 1982. Based upon the 'Krivak' class, the 'Udaloy I' ships were long-range ASW platforms, with an underway replenishment

'Udaloy I' vessels may be seen as Soviet equivalents to the US 'Spruance'-class destroyers. The ASW emphasis on these ships means they have limited anti-surface and anti-air capabilities, but this was addressed in the design of the 'Udaloy II' class, which introduced hypersonic anti-ship missiles and combined gun/missile CIWS.

capability, to provide support for surface task forces. The series yielded 12 vessels. Seven ships remain in service, maintained partly at the expense of the 'Sovremenny' class.

The 'Udaloy I' class is armed with two quadruple launchers for the Rastrub (SS-N-14 'Silex') missile. A unique twin hangar system with associated helicopter flight deck is located aft for two Ka-27 'Helix-A' ASW helicopters. Additional ASW equipment comprises a Polinom ('Horse Jaw') active/passive search/attack sonar system. For air defence, the 'Udaloy I' ships

Above: Compared to its predecessors, the 'Krivak I' and 'Krivak II' classes, the 'Udaloy I' vessels offer facilities for helicopter operations, limited sonar capabilities and improved air defence systems.

Below: The Soviet navy intended to deploy two or three brigades of seven 'Udaloy I' and 'Udaloy II' ships before follow-on vessels were cancelled in the early 1990s.

Above: The 'Udaloy I' class are based with Russia's two principal fleets: the Northern Fleet (Severomorsk, Admiral Kharlamov and Admiral Levchenko) and the Pacific Fleet (Marshal Shaposhnikov, Admiral Panteleyev, Admiral Vinogradov and Admiral Tributs).

are fitted with eight six-round vertical launchers for the Klinok (SA-N-9 'Gauntlet') missile, of which 64 are carried. These can engage aerial targets at a range of up to 12 km (7.5 miles) and at altitudes as low as three metres and up to 12,192 m (10–40,000 ft).

Improved 'Udaloy'

A single follow-on vessel of the **'Udaloy II'** (**Project 115.I Fregat**) class was commissioned in 1995. This design was intended to provide more balanced capabilities, and as such introduced two

quadruple P-270 Moskit (SS-N-22 'Sunburn') anti-ship missile launchers in place of the Rastrub. For self-defence, two Kortik (CADS-N-1) combined gun/missile CIWS were added, each incorporating two six-barrel 30-mm guns and eight 9M87/9M88 (SA-N-11 'Grison') SAMs. A new twin 130-mm DP gun is also fitted, whilst ASW capability is maintained by Viyoga (SS-N-15 'Starfish') missiles. Although two more vessels were planned, only **Admiral Chabanenko** has entered Northern Fleet service.

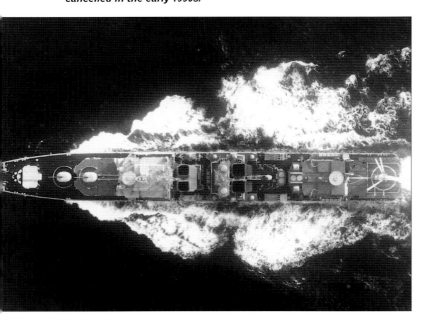

SPECIFICATION

Type 1155 'Udaloy I' class
Displacement: 6,700 tons standard and 8,500 tons full load
Dimensions: length 163.5 m (536 ft 5 in); beam 19.3 m (63 ft 4 in); draught 7.5 m (24 ft 7 in)
Machinery: COGAG; two M62 gas turbines developing 10 MW (13,600 shp); two M8KF gas turbines developing 40.8 MW (55,500 shp)
Speed: 29 kts
Aircraft: two Ka-27 'Helix-A' ASW helicopters
Armament: two quadruple Rastrub (SS-N-14 'Silex') ASW missile launchers (no reloads), eight Klinok (SA-N-9 'Gauntlet') SAM launchers (64 missiles), two 100-mm (3.9-in) DP guns, four AK-630 CIWS six-barrel 30-mm mountings, two RBU-6000 ASW rocket launchers,

two quadruple 533-mm (21-in) torpedo tubes and rails for 26 mines
Electronics: 'Strut Pair' air search radar, 'Top Plate' 3D air search radar, three 'Palm Frond' surface search radars, two 'Eye Bowl' SS-N-14 fire-control radars, two 'Cross Sword' SA-N-9 fire-control radars, 'Kite Screech' 100-mm fire-control radars, two 'Bass Tilt' CIWS fire-control radars, two 'Round House' TACAN, two 'Salt Pot' IFF, 'Fly Screen-B' and two 'Fly Spike-B' aircraft landing aids, two 'Bell Squat' jammers, two 'Foot Ball-B' and two 'Wine Glass' ESM/ECM, six 'Half Cup' laser warning aids, two PK-2 and 10 PK-10 decoy launchers, 'Horse Jaw' low-/medium-frequency bow sonar and one 'Mouse Tail' medium frequency variable-depth sonar
Complement: 220–249

'Alvaro de Bazán' class Destroyer

In the early 1980s, the Spanish Navy identified a need to develop a multi-role frigate for escort duties. In 1983, Spain decided to participate in the future NFR-90 Frigate initiative. The NFR-90 project would see eight NATO members trying to co-develop a common ship. However, this project was eventually abandoned in 1989, given the divergence of national requirements among the participating nations. This led Spain to develop its **F-100 class** of frigate. Its missions include protection of expeditionary forces, anti-submarine duties, long-range anti-aircraft defence and anti-missile protection. The vessels are also fitted with command facilities and can act as flagships.

Advanced design

The design of the F-100 emerged from Spain's desire to create a technologically advanced ship, which also featured a high degree of national industrial input. This would afford the Spanish navy a high degree of independence in the definition, selection and modification of the ship's weapons systems. In 1994, Spain signed an agreement with Germany and the Netherlands to co-develop the F-100. However, unlike NFR-90, this agreement only covered co-operation on the design of the ship itself, not its construction or associated weapons systems.

Four of the ships will enter service by 2006. The Spanish shipbuilder Izar will construct the entire class. The first vessel, **Alvaro de Bazán**, was launched in October 2000, and was commissioned in September 2002. The second ship, the **Almirante Don Juan de Borbón**, was launched in 2002, while **Blas de Lezo** was commissioned in 2004. The final ship, **Mendez Nuñez**, will be commissioned in 2006.

The ships' weapons will

As integrated onto the F-100, the Fire Scout UAV will feature a laser designator and range-finder, and surveillance equipment. It will be able to transmit real-time information to commanders on the ship. Alvaro de Bazán is illustrated.

feature the Lockheed Martin Naval Electronics SPY-1D Aegis system. Aegis is already in service with the US Navy. It controls the detection and engagement of hostile air, surface and submarine threats. The core of the Aegis system is the AN/UYK-43/44 computer system. This co-ordinates the processing capabilities of the system, and is linked to the ship's Weapon Control System (WCS) and Command and Decision System (C&D). Using a multi-function phased array AN/SPY-1 radar, Aegis can track hundreds of targets simultaneously, whilst providing fire control tracks. Northrop Grumman Norden Systems builds the Aegis AN/SPS-67 G/H band surface search radar. Furthermore, the vessel is fitted with the Link 11 secure tactical data system for communication with other naval assets.

F-100 weapons

The F-100's weapons system is reinforced with the Boeing Harpoon anti-ship missile. The Harpoon has a range of 120 km (75 miles), a 220-kg (485-lb) warhead and active radar and thermal guidance. The surface-to-air system is the Evolved Sea Sparrow Missile (ESSM), developed by a consortium led by Raytheon. Area air defence is provided by the Raytheon Standard SM-2MR missile, which is also linked to the Aegis system. SM-2MR has a range of 70 km (43 miles) and a speed of Mach 2.5. Additionally, the vessel is fitted with a 127-mm (5-in) United Defence Mk 45 gun for shore and anti-ship bombardment. Gun control is provided by the Dorna

radar/electro-optic fire control system. The Dorna system includes K-band radar as well as infra-red, TV and laser range-finding. A FABA Meroka 2B weapon system forms the Close-In Weapons System (CIWS), which features two 20-mm guns. Further anti-submarine/anti-shipping capabilities are provided via two Mk 32 twin torpedo launchers for Mk 46 lightweight torpedoes.

Detection

Submarine detection is provided by a Raytheon DE 1160 active and passive sonar system. The ships also carry two anti-ship mortars. The F-100's electronic countermeasures (ECM) suite includes four Sippican Hycor Mk 36 SRBOC chaff and decoy launchers, together with an

SLQ-25 Nixie acoustic torpedo countermeasures system.

The vessel was designed with a 26.4-m (86-ft 7-in) long flight deck, which can accommodate the Sikorsky SH-60B Seahawk LAMPS Mk III helicopter. The Spanish navy ordered six of the aircraft, which it designates HS.23, and the first was delivered in December 2001. The helicopters are fitted with Hellfire ASMs and FLIR. They can also deploy AN/SQQ-28 LAMPS III sonobuoys to aid submarine detection.

In August 2002, the Spanish Navy announced its intention to purchase the Northrop Grumman Fire Scout uninhabited rotorcraft. Fire Scout will improve the vessel's precision targeting capabilities, when guiding weapons during land attack missions.

Type 42 class Destroyer

The **Type 42** destroyer emerged from the cancelled Type 82, which yielded a single ship – HMS *Bristol* – in the 1960s. The Type 42 was developed as an air-defence and escort ship. Outfitted with Sea Dart missiles to deter air threats, it was smaller and cheaper than the Type 82.

The Type 42 is the Royal Navy's primary air defence platform, providing full area air defence coverage for other ships. The Type 42 also has a limited anti-shipping capability. Designed with the smallest possible hull, the Type 42 placed a heavy emphasis on automation to reduce the ship's complement and crew workload. The first vessel, **HMS Sheffield**, was launched in 1971, and the entire class was completed by 1985. Two ships, *Hercules* and *Santisima Trinidad*, were built for Argentina and both were in service by 1981.

Sub-classes

There were three sub-classes within the Type 42 series. **Batch 2** ships were similar to the original **Batch 1** vessels, but contained an improved sensor suite, including the Type 1022 long-range air search radar. **Batch 3**, often referred to as the 'Manchester' class – on account of the lead ship's name – have a stretched hull. This extra space allows for additional weapons systems and increases stability in bad weather. In addition, the Sea Dart missile system and Mk 8 gun could be spaced slightly further apart to improve their arcs of fire. To the rear, the extension allowed for

With the Type 42 continuing to perform the air defence role, a single ship of the class sails with each of the Royal Navy's three aircraft carriers on overseas deployments.

extra space on the flight deck.

The Type 42 saw active service during the Falklands War in 1982. The Argentine Navy also deployed its two Type 42 vessels, and the Royal Navy's ships were painted with a large black band surrounding their hulls to assist identification. Five of the Royal Navy's Type 42 vessels took part in the conflict: HMS *Coventry*, HMS *Sheffield*, HMS *Cardiff*, HMS *Exeter* and HMS *Glasgow* all provided fleet air defence to the task force aircraft carriers. *Sheffield* was lost to an Argentine Exocet missile on 4 May 1982 and, 20 days later, HMS *Coventry* was sunk, after being hit by three bombs.

Several lessons were learnt from the Type 42's experiences in the South Atlantic. Most importantly, the Royal Navy identified the need for a CIWS to protect the vessels against low-flying aircraft and sea-skimming missiles. To this end, a 20-mm gun system was installed, together with chaff decoys. The ships were also fitted with Type 996 radar, and an improved Sea Dart fusing and control system.

The Type 42, including HMS Exeter (D 89), will serve with the Royal Navy until 2006, after which the eleven remaining units will be decommissioned at six monthly intervals.

SPECIFICATION	
Type 42 class (Batch 1/2) **Displacement:** 3,500 tons standard; 4,100 tons full load **Dimensions:** length 125 m (412 ft) overall; beam 14.3 m (47 ft); draught 5.8 m (19 ft) **Machinery:** combined gas turbine or gas turbine (COGOG); two Rolls-Royce Olympus TM3B gas turbines delivering 37.3 MW (50,000 shp) and two Rolls-Royce Tyne RM1C gas turbines delivering 7.4 MW (19,900 shp) to two shafts **Speed:** 29 kts **Aircraft:** one Lynx HAS.Mk 3 or	HMA.Mk 8 **Armament:** one Sea Dart twin launcher (22 missiles), one Vickers 4.5-in (114-mm) gun, two or four Oerlikon 20-mm AA, two 20-mm Vulcan Phalanx CIWS, two twin 324-mm (12.75-in) Mk 3 torpedo tubes **Electronics:** Type 1022 air search radar, Type 996 air/surface search radar, Type 1007 and 1008 navigation radar, two Type 9091 fire-control radars, Type 2050 or 2016 hull-mounted sonar **Complement:** 253 (24 officers)

The Type 42 class fared much better during the 1990–91 Gulf War, when the ships' Lynx helicopters extended radar coverage. Furthermore, the Lynx deployed the Sea Skua anti-shipping missile and, flying from HMS *Gloucester* and **HMS Cardiff**, were successful in destroying several Iraqi small combat craft and AA batteries. HMS *Gloucester* scored a spectacular success when it detected and destroyed a hostile 'Silkworm' missile, which was targeting the battleship USS *Missouri*.

Following the end of the Gulf War, Type 42 ships have helped to enforce sea embargoes in the Gulf and the Adriatic during the war in Yugoslavia. **HMS Southampton** and **HMS Liverpool** assisted humanitarian operations in Montserrat and East Timor, while HMS *Glasgow* supported the UN peace-keeping force in East Timor.

Type 45 class Destroyer

The Royal Navy's Type 42 destroyers will eventually be replaced by the **Type 45**. The Type 45 ships will be the largest surface combatants to be operated by the Royal Navy since World War II. It is claimed that the class will provide an air defence capability 'several orders of magnitude' greater than that offered by the Type 42.

The Type 42 class was originally to be replaced by a joint Anglo-French-Italian project called 'Project Horizon'. However, this initiative was beset with delays. When the project stalled, the US Navy offered to lease to the Royal Navy five 'Ticonderoga'-class Aegis cruisers, but this offer was declined. In 1999, the Royal Navy decided to commence the development of the Type 45 class. It is expected that the first ship, **HMS Daring**, will enter service in 2007.

Several features will be incorporated into the Type 45, which were earmarked for the ill-fated Project Horizon. These include some of the internal architecture of the ship, and the Principal Anti-Aircraft Missile System (PAAMS). PAAMS will strengthen the Type 45's air defence capability, and will incorporate the Aster 30 missile, which has a range of 80 km (50 miles). The system can intercept super-agile missiles fitted with re-attack modes, together with the full envelope of current and anticipated air threats. Furthermore, the ship can engage missile threats operating either individually or in salvos. In addition to PAAMS, it is hoped that the Type 45 will eventually deploy Tomahawk cruise missiles.

Sensor suite

While Type 45 is expected to have cheaper operating overheads than Type 42, the cost of its individual spare parts could be slightly higher, although the ships will field a smaller complement of crew and officers. The ships will feature a comprehensive suite of sensors. An S1850M radar will provide wide-area, long-range search. This will be reinforced by an MFS-7000 bow-mounted sonar. Air defence combat management will be co-ordinated by the Sampson radar system, combining surveillance and tracking roles in a single system.

This can detect and track hostile aircraft or missiles while providing guidance for the ship's own weapons systems. The ship's sensors will be linked together by the Combat Management System (CMS), while communications with other vessels and satellite systems will be facilitated through the Fully Integrated Communications System (FICS).

Ship protection is provided by the Surface Ship Torpedo Defence System. Furthermore, the ship will embark a complement of 60 Royal Marine Commandos with a supporting aircraft. The flight deck will accommodate the Royal Navy's Merlin helicopter, although the ships will initially operate with Lynx. Type 45 will feature a revolutionary WR-21 advanced gas turbine engine which will afford significant cost savings. The engines will feature an Integrated Electric Propulsion System, which eliminates the gearbox and increases fuel efficiency.

Complement

The ship's interior has been designed with 'room for growth' as a major consideration. While the ship's complement will include around 190 crew, there will be the option to increase this to 235. This will permit the accommodation of specialist personnel, which will allow for an increased range of missions, such as humanitarian relief, to be performed. In total, six Type 45 vessels will be built. HMS *Daring* will be followed by **HMS Dauntless** and **HMS Diamond** in 2009. These original vessels will be followed by another three ships: **HMS Dragon**, **HMS Defender** and **HMS Duncan**.

The Navy may commission a further six ships, leading to total class of 12 units. The original production contract was placed with Marconi Electronic Systems (now BAE Systems) as the prime contractor. All of the vessels will be assembled and launched at BAE's facilities at Yarrow.

SPECIFICATION
Type 45 class
Displacement: 7,350 tons full load
Dimensions: length 152.4 m (462 ft 11 in) overall; beam 21.2 m (69 ft 7 in); draught 5.3 m (17 ft 5 in)
Machinery: Integrated Electric Propulsion; two Rolls-Royce WR-21 gas turbine alternators; two diesel generators; two motors
Speed: 29 kts
Aircraft: one Lynx HMA.Mk 8 or Merlin HM.Mk 1
Armament: two quadruple Harpoon launchers (optional), six A 50 vertical launchers for PAAMS (16 Aster 15 or 32 Aster 30 missiles), one Vickers 4.5-in (114-mm) gun, two 30-mm AA, two 20-mm Vulcan Phalanx CIWS
Electronics: Link 11/16/22, SATCOM, CEC, GSA 8/GPEOD weapons control, S1850M air/surface search radar, Sampson surveillance/fire-control radar, MFS-7000 bow-mounted sonar
Complement: 187

A computer graphic depicts the possible configuration of HMS Daring, the lead ship in the class, supporting the Merlin helicopter.

'Spruance' class
ASW destroyer

USS Comte de Grasse (DD 974) soon after commissioning in 1978. The Kaman SH-2D LAMPS I ASW helicopter has now been replaced by two Sikorsky SH-60B LAMPS III aircraft.

The 31 destroyers of the **'Spruance' class** were the first large US Navy warships to use all gas-turbine propulsion. In a break from traditional building techniques, the 'Spruances' were constructed by the modular assembly technique, whereby sections of the hull are built in various parts of the shipyard, then welded together on the slipway. **USS Spruance (DD 963)** was commissioned in September 1975, and the class continued into the early 1980s.

Much larger than previous American destroyers, they were built with future growth in mind. Their size and modular design allowed for easy installation of entire subsystems of weapons, equipment and sensors.

They were originally developed as anti-submarine (ASW) destroyers, to hunt down submarines in all weathers. However, 24 ships of this class were given significant anti-ship and land attack capabilities in the 1980s with the installation of a 61-cell Vertical Launch Missile System (VLS) capable of launching Tomahawk and Harpoon missiles.

SPECIFICATION	
'Spruance' class	torpedoes
Displacement: 8,200 tons full load	**Electronics:** one SPS-40E air-search radar, one SPS-55 surface- search radar, one SPG-60 fire-control radar, one SPQ-9A fire-control radar, one SLQ-32(V)2 ESM suite, two Mk 36 Super RBOC chaff launchers, one SQS-53 bow sonar, one SQR-19 towed sonar
Dimensions: length 171.70 m (563 ft 3 in); beam 16.80 m (55 ft 2 in); draught 8.80 m (29 ft)	
Machinery: four General Electric LM2500 gas turbines delivering 59655 kW (80,000 shp) to two shafts	
Speed: 33 kts	**Complement:** 320-350
Aircraft: Two SH-60B (SH-60R) Seahawk LAMPS III helicopters	
Armament: one Mk 41 vertical launch system for Tomahawk; 2 quad Harpoon launchers; 2 octuple Sea Sparrow SAM launchers (24 missiles); two Mk 15 Phalanx 20-mm CIWS; two 127-mm (5-in) DP guns; one octuple Mk 112 ASROC launcher; two triple 324-mm (12¾-in) Mk 32 ASW torpedo tubes with Mk 46	**'Kidd' class**
	Similar to early 'Spruance', except:
	Armament: includes two twin Mk 26 Standard SM-1 ER SAM/ASROC ASW missile launchers (50 Standard, 16 ASROC and 2 test missiles)
	Electronics: includes one SPS-48C 3D radar; one SPS-49 air search radar, two SPG-51D Standard fire control radars

Helicopters

As completed, the class carried two Kaman SH-2D/F Seasprite LAMPS Mk I helicopters, but the primary ASW weapon system is now the SH-60B LAMPS Mk III helicopter, which extends the range of the ship's weapons and sensors well beyond the horizon. The SH-60B is due to be replaced fleet-wide as the SH-60R by 2012. Secondary missions for the helicopters include gunfire spotting, over-the-horizon targeting, MEDEVAC, transport and SAR operations. In 1974 the government of Iran ordered six SAM-equipped versions of the 'Spruances' for service in the Persian Gulf and Indian Ocean.

The 'Spruances' are as large as a World War II cruiser, giving plenty of room for additional weapon systems and upgrades.

However, following the revolution in that country, two were cancelled in 1979 whilst the remaining four under construction were taken over by the US Navy as the **'Kidd' class**. These are powerfully armed general-purpose destroyers, and for some time were unofficially known in the US Navy as the 'Ayatollah'-class. The four ships were commissioned as the **USS Kidd (DDG 993)**, **USS Callaghan (DDG 994)**, **USS Scott (DDG 995)** and **USS Chandler (DDG 996)**.

'Ticonderoga' class AEGIS air defence cruiser

Envisaged as a minimum cost, advanced area-defence platform for construction in large numbers, the **'Ticonderoga' class** has evolved over the years into what is possibly the most advanced warship ever built. The design was based on the hull of

the cruiser-sized 'Spruance'-class destroyer. **USS Ticonderoga** was originally designated as a destroyer, but the design was redesignated as a cruiser in 1980 with the pennant number **CG 47**. The original number to be

constructed was 28, increased by the Reagan administration to 30, and then cut back to 27, and USS Ticonderoga was commissioned in 1983. The last of the class was the USS Port Royal, which entered service in 1994.

The 'Ticonderogas' were the first surface combatant ships equipped with the AEGIS Weapons System, the most sophisticated air defence system in the world. The heart of AEGIS is the SPY-1A radar. Two paired phased array radars

Based on the hull of the 'Spruance'-class destroyer, USS Ticonderoga and her sisters were criticized for being top-heavy. However, they have served with distinction in most American naval actions since 1983.

automatically detect and track air contacts to beyond 322 km (200 miles).

Air defence

AEGIS is designed to defeat attacking missiles by providing quick-reacting firepower and jamming resistance against any aerial threat faced by a US Navy Battle Group. The AEGIS system can control friendly aircraft as well as providing simultaneous surveillance, target-detection and target-tracking in a hemisphere over and around the ship. It also provides a unified command and control platform for all the vessels of a battle group.

The first five ships have two twin Mk 26 missile launchers, firing Standard SM2-MR missiles. These were designed to cope with saturation attacks

by high-performance aircraft as well as low-level and high-level air, surface- and sub-surface launched anti-ship missiles in heavy ECM environments.

From **USS Bunker Hill (CG 52)** onwards, the two Mk 26 launchers and their magazines have been replaced by two Mk 41 vertical launchers. The 127 VLS cells can be loaded with Standard, Harpoon, ASROC and Tomahawk missiles, giving later vessels the ability to engage targets above, on and below the surface.

The 'Ticonderoga'-class cruisers were built to support and protect Carrier Battle Groups and Amphibious Assault Groups, and to perform interdiction and escort missions. The class has served in most operations of recent decades, from the Lebanon in 1983 to the Tomahawk bombardment of Afghanistan in 2001.

A Tomahawk is launched against Afghanistan in October 2001. Cruise missiles give the 'Ticonderoga' class the ability to strike at targets hundreds of miles inland from the coast.

SPECIFICATION

'Ticonderoga' class
Displacement: 9,960 tons full load
Dimensions: length 172.80 m (566 ft ³/₄ in); beam 16.80 m (55 ft); draught 9.50 m (31 ft)
Propulsion: four General Electric LM2500 gas turbines delivering 59655 kW (80,000 shp) to two shafts
Speed: 30 kts
Aircraft: two Sikorsky SH-60B Seahawk LAMPS III (SH-60R) multi-role helicopters
Armament: Two Mk 41 VLS systems with Standard SM2-MR, Tomahawk and ASROC missiles; two quad Harpoon SSM launchers, (two twin Standard SM2-ER/ASROC SAM/ASW launchers with 68

Standard and 20 ASROC missiles in first five ships); two Mk 45 127-mm (5-in) DP guns; two Mk 15 20-mm Phalanx CIWS mountings; two triple 324-mm (123⁄4-in) Mk 32 ASW torpedo tube mountings with Mk 46 torpedoes
Electronics: Four SPY-1A AEGIS radar arrays (SPY-1B in last 15 ships); one SPS-49 air-search radar, one SPS-55 surface-search radar, one SPQ-9A gun fire control system, four SPG-62 Standard fire control/illuminator radars; one SLQ-32 ESM suite, four Mk 36 Super RBOC chaff launchers; one SQS-53 sonar, and one SQR-19 tactical towed-array sonar system
Complement: 364

'Arleigh Burke' class AEGIS general-purpose destroyer

The **'Arleigh Burke' class** of guided-missile destroyers was designed as a gas turbine-powered replacement for the 'Coontz'-class missile destroyers and the 'Leahy'- and 'Belknap'-classes of missile cruisers.

The design was intended to be a cheaper, less capable vessel than the 'Ticonderoga'-class cruiser, but has evolved into an extremely capable general purpose warship, incorporating advanced weaponry and systems.

Stealth ship

Arleigh Burke **(DDG 51)** was the first large US Navy vessel to incorporate stealth shaping techniques to reduce radar cross-section. Tasked with defending against Soviet aircraft, missiles and submarines, this potent destroyer is now used in high-threat areas to conduct anti-air, anti-submarine, anti-surface, and strike operations.

High-speed hull

A new hull profile improves seakeeping, permitting high speeds to be maintained in difficult sea states. The hull form is characterized by considerable flare and a 'V'-shape appearance at the waterline.

Built primarily from steel, the class has aluminium masts to reduce topweight. Kevlar armour is fitted over all vital machinery and operations room spaces. Surprisingly, it was the first US warship class to be fully equipped to operate in NBC environments, with the crew confined to a protected citadel located within the hull and superstructure.

The AN/SPY-1D Phased Array Radar incorporates advances in the detection capabilities of the AEGIS Weapons System, particularly in its resistance to enemy electronic countermeasures (ECM).

The AEGIS system is designed to counter all current and projected missile threats to the Navy's battle forces. A conventional, mechanically rotating radar 'sees' a target when the radar beam strikes that target once during each 360° rotation of the antenna. A separate tracking radar is then required to engage each target.

AEGIS radar

By contrast, the AEGIS system brings these functions together within one system. The four fixed arrays of the SPY-1D send out beams of electromagnetic energy in all directions simultaneously, providing a search and tracking capability for hundreds of targets at the same time. The SPY-1D and the Mark 99 Fire Control System allow them to guide vertically-launched Standard missiles to intercept hostile aircraft and missiles at long ranges. For

The USS **Arleigh Burke** *(DDG 51) was named after the US Navy's most aggressive and successful World War II destroyer commander.*

point defence, the ships are equipped with the Block 1 upgrade to the Phalanx CIWS.

The US Navy will have a force of 57 'Burke'-class destroyers in service by 2008. A criticism of the original design was that no hangar was provided for a helicopter, although the first 28 vessels do have flightdecks capable of handling a Sikorsky SH-60 helicopter.

The improved **'Flight IIA'** has a helicopter hangar, as well as an enlarged vertical launch system, a new 127-mm (5-in) gun and improved communications.

Commissioned in 1995, USS **Laboon** *(DDG 58) was the eighth ship in the 'Arleigh Burke' class. The ship launched Tomahawk missiles at air defense targets in Iraq on 3 September 1996. The* **Laboon** *thus became the first 'Arleigh Burke' class destroyer to engage in combat.*

SPECIFICATION

'Arleigh Burke' class
Displacement: 8,300 tons standard and 9,200 tons full load
Dimensions: length 142.10 m (466 ft); beam 18.30 m (60 ft); draught 7.60 m (25 ft)
Machinery: four General Electric LM2500 gas turbines delivering 78330 kW (105,000 shp) to two shafts
Speed: 32 kts (59 km/h; 37 mph)
Aircraft: helicopter landing pad only; two Sikorsky SH-60 LAMPS III (SH-60R) from DDG 79 onwards
Armament: two quadruple Harpoon SSM launchers (first 25 vessels); two Mk 41 vertical-launch missile systems (90 Standard SM-2MR, ASROC and Tomahawk SSM

missiles in first 25, 106 in remainder), one 127-mm (5-in) DP gun; two 20-mm Phalanx CIWS mountings; NATO Evolved Sea Sparrow in 'Flight IIA' only; two triple 324-mm (12¾-in) Mk 32 ASW torpedo tubes (Mk 46/50 torpedoes)
Electronics: two SPY-1D paired AEGIS radars, one SPS-67 surface-search radar, one SPS-64 navigation radar, three SPG-62 Standard fire control radars; one SLQ-32 ESM suite, two Mk 36 Super RBOC chaff launchers; one SQS-53C bow sonar, one SQR-19 towed array sonar
Complement: 303–327

'De Zeven Provincien' class Guided-missile destroyer (DDG)

Royal Schelde of Vlissingen is building four air-defence guided-missile destroyers of the **'De Zeven Provincien' class** for the Dutch navy, the first two with a command (flagship) capability as successors to the two 'Tromp'-class frigates and the second two without this capability as successors to the two 'Jacob van Heemskerck'-class frigates. Ordered in February 1995, **De Zeven Provincien** was commissioned in April 2002, the **Tromp** in March 2003, with **De Ruyter** launched in April 2002 for commissioning in 2004 and the **Evertsen** launched in 2003 and commissioned in 2005.

The ships are the result of a tripartite programme initiated by Germany, the Netherlands and Spain. Germany and Spain are responsible for building three 'Sachsen'- and four 'Alvaro de Bazán'-class frigates with much ship platform commonality with the 'De Zeven Provincien'-class ships. The design incorporates stealth features to minimize the radar, thermal, acoustic, electrical and magnetic signatures. Meanwhile insulation, redundancy in vital systems, compartmentalization, power distribution, and structural features that channel and retain blast and fragments all combine to offer enhanced survivability. And to provide NBC protection, the ship is subdivided into two main citadels and one sub-citadel.

Missile triad

The core of the ship's operational capability is the SEWACO XI combat data system developed by Thales Naval Nederland (originally Signaal). The shorter-range SAM system is the Evolved Sea Sparrow Missile (ESSM) developed by an international team led by Raytheon Missile Systems with semi-active radar guidance and vectoring of the rocket motor's thrust for greater manoeuvrability, range and speed. The medium-range SAM system is based on the Raytheon Standard Missile SM-2MR Block IIIA with a range of 70 km (43.5 miles), speed of Mach 2.5 and semi-active radar guidance. Both the ESSM and SM-2MR are launched from a 40-cell Mk 41 Vertical Launch System (VLS). The five octuple launchers are installed with the caps almost flush with the surface of the forecastle abaft the main gun. Expanded anti-ship capability is provided by the Harpoon missile system located on the raised deck immediately abaft the mast.

The ship's main gun is a 127-mm (5-in) Otobreda L/54 weapon, and last-ditch defence against anti-ship missiles is provided by two 30-mm Thales Naval Nederland Goalkeeper CIWS, one just forward of the mast and the other on the roof of the helicopter hangar. There are also two 20-mm Oerlikon cannon (to port and starboard of

Above: The mast carries four planar antennae for the APAR radar, and is flanked by satcom antennae in spherical radomes.

Below: Gas turbine and diesel gases from the CODOG machinery are vented via outward-canted funnels.

SPECIFICATION

'De Zeven Provincien' class
Displacement: 6,048 tons full load
Dimensions: length 144.2 m (473 ft); beam 18.8 m (61 ft 8 in); draught 5.2 m (17 ft 1 in)
Propulsion: CODOG with two Rolls-Royce Spey SM1C gas turbines delivering 38995 kW (52,300 shp) and two Stork-Wärtsilä 16V 26 ST diesels delivering 10140 kW (13,600 hp) to two shafts
Performance: speed 28 kts; range 9250 km (5,750 miles) at 18 kts
Armament: eight Harpoon anti-ship missiles, one 40-cell Mk 41 VLS for SM-2MR and ESSM SAMs, one

127-mm (5-in) gun, two 30-mm CIWS, two 20-mm cannon, and two twin 324-mm (12.75-in) Mk 32 launchers for Mk 46 anti-submarine torpedoes
Electronics: one SMART-L 3D radar, one APAR air/surface-search and fire-control radar, one Scout surface-search radar, one Sirius optronic director, one SEWACO XI combat data system, one Sabre ESM/ECM system, SBROC chaff launchers, and one DSQS-24C sonar
Aircraft: one Lynx or NFH 90 helicopter
Complement: 204

Large enough to accommodate an NFH 90, the hangar carries the SMART-L radar and one of the two CIWS. F802 is lead ship of the class.

the mast). Short-range anti-submarine defence is vested in two 324-mm (12.75-in) Mk 32 twin launchers (one on each side of the ship) for 24 Mk 46 Mod 5 torpedoes. Longer-range anti-submarine operations are entrusted to a single Lynx (to be succeeded by the larger NFH 90 from 2007) helicopter stowed in a hangar just forward of the flight platform (with a DCN Samahé handling system) located over the stern.

Advanced radar

The ship's radar suite is also supplied by Thales Naval Nederland. The SMART-L system above the hangar offers 3D air search, the APAR (Active Phased Array Radar) round the mast offers air/surface search and SM-2MR fire-control capability, and the Scout LPI (Low Probability of Intercept) radar on the front of the mast offers surface search. Other key Thales elements are the Sirius long-range IR search and track system above the bridge and the Mirador optronic surface surveillance system.

The sonar system is the STN Atlas Elektronik DSQS-24C bow-mounted active search and attack equipment.

As indicated by its character as a CODOG system, the ship's propulsion system has two independent elements. The two Rolls-Royce Spey SM1C gas turbine units each provide 19495 kW (26,150 shp) for high-speed operations, while the two Stork-Wärtsilä 16V 26 ST diesel engines each provide 5070 kW (6,800 shp) for economical cruising. The two gearboxes are installed in a separate transmission room, and the ship has two propellers of the controllable-pitch type, and two rudders that also provide roll stabilization.

'Okpo' class Guided-missile destroyer (DDG)

The South Korean navy is in the midst of a major shipbuilding programme within the context of its Korean Destroyer Experimental (KDX) effort. This is a three-stage programme based on three classes: the 3,800-ton KDX-1, 5,000-ton KDX-2 and 7,000-ton or more KDX-3 for service from 1998, 2004 and 2007–08 respectively. Each class is more ambitious than its predecessor in ship size, sensors and weapons. The KDX-1 programme yielded three destroyers of the **'Okpo' class** from which the KDX-2 and KDX-3 classes were evolved. The 'Okpo' ships marked the beginning of the South Korean

Above the helicopter hangar are, from forward, the SPS-49(V)5 air-search radar, one of the two STIR 180 fire-control radars, and one of the two 30-mm Goalkeeper CIWS. The Harpoon anti-ship missile launchers are abaft the funnels.

navy's transformation from a coastal to oceanic force.

Design of the 'Okpo' class was a somewhat slow process: the first ship was to have been laid down in 1992 but was in fact started in 1995. The primary task is the air-defence and anti-submarine escort of strike, anti-submarine and amphibious forces. As such, the ships of the 'Okpo' class (so named from the city in which Daewoo built the vessels) are multi-role combatants with advanced sensors and weapon systems. Originally to have comprised up to 10 units, the class was curtailed to just three units to allow concentration on the KDX-2 type. **Kwanggaeto the Great**, **Euljimundok** and **Yangmanchun** were thus commissioned in 1998, 1999 and 2000 respectively.

The ships are equipped for offensive operations in multi-threat environments, working either independently or as part of a combat group. For this reason, there is a high degree of integration and automation in the control and weapon systems to facilitate effective operation in any aspect of modern naval warfare.

Propulsion is entrusted to a CODOG arrangement of two gas turbines and two diesels for high combat speed combined with long cruising endurance, and as part of the integration of ship systems the propulsion control, electric plant control, damage control and fire detection consoles are located in the central control station.

The 30-mm Goalkeeper CIWS is for use against anti-ship missiles and, with Frangible Armour-Piercing Discarding Sabot ammunition, FACs.

The ships incorporate many items of sensor, weapon, fire-control and propulsion equipment of US and European origin. US input includes the Sea Sparrow short-range SAMs, Harpoon anti-ship missiles, anti-submarine torpedo system and air-search radar, while European input includes the 127-mm (5-in) gun, CIWS, Super Lynx helicopters and sensors such as the surface-search and fire-control radars, and the sonar. The hangar and flight platform support two helicopters.

SPECIFICATION

'Okpo' class
Displacement: 3,855 tons full load
Dimensions: length 135.4 m (444 ft 3 in); beam 14.2 m (46 ft 7 in); draught 4.2 m (13 ft 9 in)
Propulsion: CODOG; two General Electric GE LM2500 gas turbines delivering 43395 kW (58,200 shp) and two MTU 20V 956 TB92 diesels delivering 5960 kW (7,995 shp) to two shafts
Performance: speed 30 kts; range 7400 km (4,600 miles) at 18 kts
Armament: two quad launchers for Harpoon AShMs, one Mk 48 Mod 2 VLS for RIM-7P Sea Sparrow SAMs, one 127-mm (5-in) Otobreda gun,

two 30-mm Goalkeeper CIWS, and two triple 324-mm (12.75-in) Mk 32 launchers for Mk 46 ASW torpedoes
Electronics: one SPS-49(V)5 air-search, one MW-08 surface-search, one SPS-55M navigation, and two STIR 180 fire-control radars; one SSCS Mk 7 combat data system, one Argo ESM/ECM system, four Dagaie Mk 2 chaff launchers, one SLQ-25 Nixie torpedo decoy, one DSQS-21BZ hull-mounted active search sonar, and one Daewoo passive towed-array sonar
Aircraft: two Super Lynx helicopters
Complement: 170

'Luhai' class Guided-missile destroyer

The Chinese navy's **'Luhai' class** or **Type 051B** guided missile destroyer comprises just one ship, the **Shenzhen**. It was built by the Dalian Shipyard, which is the largest and most modern builder of warships in China. The ship was laid down in January 1996 and launched in October 1997, then finally commissioned in January 1999.

The ship is a follow-on from the two destroyers of the 'Luhu' or Type 052 class. A second unit of the 'Luhai' class was expected, but this has now apparently been cancelled in favour of the construction of more advanced types as the Chinese come successfully to grips with the integration of local technology with imported ideas and equipment adapted to suit Chinese requirements and local manufacture.

The *Shenzhen* is in essence a slightly scaled-up version of the 'Luhu' class units. The ship can readily be distinguished from its 'Luhu' class counterparts by the presence of a second funnel, the installation of two octuple, rather than quadruple, launchers for anti-ship missiles abaft the forward funnel, and the location of all four of the twin 37-mm AA gun mountings above the helicopter hangar. This last decision has left more deck area available in the space forward of the bridge, where there is a retractable autoloader for the HQ-7 SAM system based on the French Crotale short-range system and firing a missile known to West as the CSA-N-4. This has command to line of sight guidance, and a range of 13 km (8.1 miles) at Mach 2.4 with a 14-kg (30.9-lb) warhead. Other conceptual changes are a

*The **Shenzhen** of the 'Luhai' class is one of China's most modern destroyers, but has already been overtaken in production planning by the advent of more advanced ships.*

number of features designed to reduce the ship's electro-magnetic features and so enhance its 'stealthiness', and the incorporation into the basic design of the volume and deck area to allow for later enhancements and/or upgrades.

SPECIFICATION

'Luhai' class
Displacement: 4,920 tons standard; 6,495 tons full load
Dimensions: length 153 m (502 ft); beam 16.5 m (54 ft 2 in); draught 6 m (19 ft 8 in)
Propulsion: two geared steam turbines delivering about 44700 kW (59,950 shp) to two shafts
Performance: speed 30 kts; endurance 26000 km (16,155 miles) at 14 kts
Armament: one twin 100-mm (3.94-in) DP gun, four twin 37-mm AA guns, 16 YJ-82 (C-802) anti-ship missiles in two octuple launchers, one octuple launcher for 24 HQ-7 short-range SAMs, and two 324-mm (12.75-in) triple tubes for Yu-6

anti-submarine torpedoes
Electronics: one Type 517H-1 air search radar, one Type 381A 3D air search radar, one Type 360S air/surface search radar, one Type 343G 100-mm gun and anti-ship missile fire-control radar, two Type 347G 37-mm gun fire-control radars, one Type 345 SAM fire-control radar, two RM-1290 navigation radars, two OFD-630 optronic directors, one TAVITAC combat data system, one SRW210A ESM system, two Type 946 chaff/decoy launchers, and one DUBV 23 hull-mounted sonar
Aircraft: two Harbin Zhi-9C or Kamov Ka-28 'Helix' helicopters
Complement: 250

Steam propulsion

It was initially believed in the West that the ship was powered by a CODOG arrangement (as in the 'Luhu' class) with two gas turbines imported from Ukraine and two MTU diesel engines imported from Germany, but in fact the *Shenzhen* has steam propulsion with four boilers supplying steam to two sets of geared turbines powering two shafts.

The ship began trials in October 1998, later than planned as she suffered damage to her starboard side when alongside in a gale. Now the *Shenzhen* is part of the South Sea Fleet based at Zhanjiang.

'Horizon' class Guided-missile destroyer

The project that led eventually to the **'Horizon' class** of guided-missile destroyers was launched in 1993 as a joint programme between France, Italy and the UK, the last withdrawing in April 1999. Its aim was to develop and construct a new-generation destroyer optimized for the air-defence role but with significant anti-ship and anti-submarine capabilities so that the ships can undertake a range of missions: air defence as part of an aircraft carrier battle group, support of more lightly armed or indeed unarmed vessels, or detached operations as single units.

Initial pairs of 'Horizon'-class ships are scheduled to enter service with the French and Italian navies between 2006 and 2009. The French ships, laid down by the Direction des Constructions Navales at its Lorient yard for commissioning in 2006 and 2008, are the **Forbin** and **Chevalier Paul**, which will replace the *Suffren* and *Duquesne*, and a further two ships are planned as successors to the *Cassard* and *Jean Bart*. The Italian ships, laid down by Fincantieri at Riva Trigoso/Muggiano, are

scheduled for commissioning in 2007 and 2009, and differ from the French ships in details such as their Agusta/Westland EH.101 helicopter, armament details and certain of the electronic systems. Two more Italian ships are probable.

The core of the ships' air-defence capability is the PAAMS (Principal Anti-Air Missile System) using two variants of the Aster SAM for the medium- and long-range roles. Some 48 of these missiles will be accommodated in the Sylver A50 vertical-launch system flush-mounted on the forecastle. Target detection and acquisition are entrusted to the EMPAR radar located in the almost spherical radome mounted at the head of the pyramidal fore mast, which also carries the satellite communications antennae, an optronic director and the surface search radar. At the head of the other pyramidal mast (also carrying an optronic director or, in the case of the Italian ships, the other RTN-25X fire-control radar) and over the forward edge of the helicopter hangar is the DRBV 27 (S1850M) Astral air/surface

search radar. The Italian ships will each support a single optronic director on the after face of the fore mast.

While the French ships will carry MM.40 Exocet anti-ship missiles in four twin launchers, the Italian ships will use the Teseo Mk 2 system with eight Otomat Mk 3 missiles in two

The 'Horizon' class destroyer is optimized for the area air-defence role with a 48-cell vertical-launch system forward of the bridge for Aster-15 and -30 SAMs.

quadruple launchers. Both the French and Italian ships will carry a side-by-side pair of 76.2-mm (3-in) Otobreda Super Rapid gun mountings forward of the bridge, but the Italian ships will have a third such mounting above the hangar in place of the French ships' Sadral launcher for Mistral short-range SAMs.

'Horizon' class (French standard)
Displacement: 6,700 tons full load
Dimensions: length 150.6 m (494 ft 1 in); beam 19.9 m (65 ft 3 in); draught 4.8 m (15 ft 9 in)
Propulsion: CODOG with two LM 2500 gas turbines 42990 kW (57,660 shp) and two SEMT-Pielstick 12PA 6STC diesels delivering 7760 kW (10,410 shp) to two shafts
Performance: speed 29 kts; endurance 13,000 km (8,080 miles) at 18 kts
Armament: two 76.2-mm (3-in) Super Rapid DP guns, eight MM.40 Exocet anti-ship missiles in four twin launchers, one PAAMS(E) SAM system with six octuple Sylver A50 vertical-launch units for 48 Aster 15 medium-range and Aster 30 long-range SAMs, two

Sadral sextuple launchers for Mistral short-range SAMs, and two launchers for 12 MU 90 Impact anti-submarine torpedoes
Electronics: one DRBV 27 Astral air/surface search radar, one EMPAR surveillance and fire-control radar, one surface search radar, one NA 25 fire-control radar, navigation radar, two Vampir optronic directors, one CMS combat data system, one ACOM or SIC 21 follow-on command support system, one SIGEN EW system, two NGDS chaff/decoy launchers, one DUBV 23 hull-mounted sonar, and one SLAT torpedo decoy system
Aircraft: one NH-90 helicopter
Complement: 190 with accommodation for 230

Providing a close-range defence against small craft are two cannon, 20-mm GIAT and 25-mm Oerlikon weapons in the French and Italian ships respectively.

Between the shorter pyramidal masts will be a taller mast carrying the antennae for the EW warfare systems, which will be based on the SIGEN system in the French ships, but on the JANEWS system in the Italian ships. Both classes will use the French-developed SENIT 8 combat data system.

'Takanami' class Guided-missile destroyer

Though generally satisfied with the capabilities of its nine 'Murasame'-class destroyers commissioned between 1996 and 2002, the Japanese Maritime Self-Defence Force realized that these ships were limited in their air-defence and anti-submarine capabilities by their use of two different vertical-launch systems for 16 Sea Sparrow medium-range SAMs and 16 ASROC anti-submarine rockets. This class had its origins in the rising cost of the 'Kongou' class of guided missile destroyers, which are equipped with a lightweight version of the American AEGIS air-defence system using the SPY-1D 3D air search radar and the Standard Missile SM-2 SAM in 29- and 61-cell Mk 41 vertical launch systems (fore and aft): the provision of three fire-control systems offered the possibility of the simultaneous engagement of three targets.

Delayed programme

Delays in the US release of the AEGIS technology and the rising cost of the ships then led the Japanese government to curtail the 'Kongou' class at just four ships. This created a fleet air-defence shortfall, so the navy was authorized to procure a lower-cost substitute in the form of the 'Murasame'-class destroyers. Although the weapons fit is similar to that of the 'Asagiri' class, the missiles (Sea Sparrow SAMs and ASROC anti-submarine weapons) are stored in and fired from vertical-launch systems. The introduction of a number of 'stealth' features included a superstructure with rounded corners and inward-sloping faces, and a higher level of automation to reduce the manning requirements.

Further enhancement

Since it was clear that the 'Murasame'-class design could be improved further, the design was modified to the more capable 'Takanami'-class standard incorporating a 32-cell Mk 41 vertical-launch system, capable of handling both the Sea Sparrow and the RUM-139 vertical-launch development of the ASROC, in the area forward of the bridge. The opportunity was also taken to improve the missile fire-control system (two FCS 3 systems in place of the 'Murasame'-class ships' two Type 2-31 systems for the simultaneous engagement of two targets) and replace the OQS-5 low-frequency active search and attack hull sonar with a newer system.

The first two ships, to be built by Sumitomo and by Mitsubishi, were authorized in 1998 and commissioned in 2003 as the **Takanami** and **Oonami**. Two more ships, one being built by Ishikawajima Harima and the other by Mitsubishi were authorized in 2000 and 2001. The first was completed in 2005 as the **Sazanami**. A fifth unit will be completed in 2006.

Blocky superstructure

In common with other modern Japanese warships, the 'Takanami'-class destroyers have a very blocky superstructure arrangement (here characterized by a number of 'stealth' features) with a tall four-sided lattice mast abaft the bridge. On its forward face this mast carries many of the antennae for the electronic systems, including, from the bottom upward, the OPS-24 three-dimensional air-search radar, the SQQ-28 helicopter data-link, and the OPS-28D surface-search radar. Above the bridge and above the helicopter hangar are the antennae of the two FCS 3 fire-control radars.

The gun armament is limited to one 127-mm (5-in) Otobreda L/54 weapon (firing a 32-kg/70.5-lb shell to a range of 23 km/14.3 miles at the rate of 45 rounds per minute) in a turret on the forecastle, and two 20-mm Phalanx Mk 15 close-in weapon system mountings carried to provide a last-ditch defence capability against anti-ship missiles and aircraft at short range. These CIWS mountings are located forward of the bridge and above the rear of the helicopter hangar, both locations being comparatively high and thus providing the largest possible fields of fire for these quick-reaction weapons, which are capable of autonomous operation when firing at the rate of 3,000 20-mm rounds per minute to a maximum effective range of about 1510 m (1,650 yards).

The long-range anti-ship capability of the 'Takanami'-class destroyers is vested in eight SSM-1B radar-guided missiles. These were developed and manufactured in Japan, and are capable weapons each carrying a 225-kg (496-lb) warhead to 150 km (93.2 miles) at a high subsonic speed. The missiles are carried in two quadruple launchers, firing to port and starboard, in a location forward of the second funnel.

Three torpedo modes

The primary anti-submarine weapon remains the VL ASROC, used in conjunction with the OYQ-103 fire-control system and able to deliver its payload of one Mk 46 Mod 5 NEARtip acoustic-homing lightweight torpedo to a range of 10 km (6.2 miles). However, the ships embark a longer-range anti-submarine punch in their helicopter, the Sikorsky SH-60K Seahawk. This carries Mk 46 torpedoes out to a further range. Short-range self defence against submarine attack is entrusted to two triple 324-mm (12.75-in) Type 68 tubes, one on each beam, which also launch the Mk 46 Mod 5 torpedo, carrying a 44-kg (97-lb) warhead to a range of 11 km (6.8 miles) at a speed of 40 kts.

SPECIFICATION

'Takanami' class
Displacement: 4,605 tons standard; 5,150 tons full load
Dimensions: length 151 m (495 ft 5 in); beam 17.4 m (57 ft 1 in); draught 5.3 m (17 ft 5 in)
Propulsion: COGAG with two Rolls-Royce Spey SM1C gas turbines delivering 31040 kW (41,630 shp) and two LM 2500 gas turbines delivering 32020 kW (43,000 shp) to two shafts
Speed: 30 kts
Armament: one 127-mm (5-in) Otobreda gun, two 20-mm Phalanx Mk 15 CIWS mountings, eight SSM-1B anti-ship missiles in two quadruple launchers, one Mk 41 VLS for 32 Sea Sparrow medium-range SAMs and VL ASROC anti-submarine rockets, and two triple 324-mm (12.75-in) tube mountings for Type 68 anti-submarine torpedoes
Electronics: one OPS-24 3D surveillance radar, one OPS-28D surface search radar, two FCS 3 fire-control radars, one OPS-20 navigation radar, one OYQ-103 anti-submarine weapons fire-control system, one OYQ-7 combat data system, one NOLQ-2/3 EW system, four Mk 36 SRBOC chaff/decoy launchers, one active search and attack hull sonar, one OQR-1 towed-array passive sonar, and one SLQ-25 Nixie torpedo decoy
Aircraft: one Mitsubishi/Sikorsky SH-60J Seahawk helicopter
Complement: 175

'Ouragan' class Landing Ship Dock (TCD/LSD)

The **'Ouragan' class** of dock landing ship is used both for amphibious warfare and logistic transport by the French navy. They are fitted with a well dock some 120 m (393 ft 8½ in) in length with a stern gate measuring 14 m x 5.5 m (45 ft 11 in x 18 ft). The well dock can accommodate two 670-ton full load EDIC LCTs (carrying 11 light tanks, or 11 trucks or five LVTs) or 18 LCM6s (carrying 30 tons of cargo or vehicles). Above the well deck is a 36-m (79.4-ft) long six-section removable helicopter deck capable of operating one SA 321G Super Frelon heavy-lift helicopter or three SA 319B Alouette III utility helicopters. If required, a 90-m (295-ft 4-in) long temporary deck can also be fitted to stow cargo or vehicles, but its use reduces the number of landing craft carried, as half the well deck is taken up. If used with this extra deck as a logistic transport, the total cargo capacity of the vessel becomes some 1,500 tons. This can comprise either 18 Super Frelon or 80 Alouette III helicopters, or 120 AMX-10s or 84 light amphibious vehicles or 340 light utility vehicles or 12 50-ton barges. A typical load may comprise one 380-ton CDIC LCT, four 56-ton CTMs, 10 AMX-10RC armoured cars and 21 further vehicles, or a total of 150 to 170 vehicles (without landing craft). There is a permanent helicopter deck for up to four Super Frelons or 10 Alouette IIIs located next to the starboard bridge area. Two 35-ton capacity cranes handle the heavy equipment carried. Each of the two ships also has command and control facilities to operate as amphibious force flagships. They also carry an extensive

*The **Orage** has an enclosed flag bridge; it has served as a floating headquarters for France's nuclear test mission in the South Pacific.*

*Used for both amphibious warfare and as a logistic transport, **Ouragan** is capable of deploying and supporting half a battalion of marines (349 troops). In addition, a typical helicopter load comprises three or four Super Frelon or 10 Alouette III, although the former is today rarely carried and the Super Puma or Cougar (for CSAR operations) are more likely to be deployed.*

SPECIFICATION	
Names: *Ouragan* (L 9021) and *Orage* (L 9022)	**Troops:** 349 (14 officers plus 335 enlisted men) normal, 470 overload
Commissioned: L9021 1 June 1965; L9022 1 April 1968	**Cargo:** 1,500 tons as logistic transport; two LCTs, or up to 8 CTMs or 18 LCM6s; plus 3 LCVP
Displacement: 5,800 tons light; 8,500 tons full load	**Armament:** two Matra Simbad twin launchers for Mistral SAMs, four single 40-mm Bofors guns (two later replaced by Breda/Mauser 30-mm guns)
Dimensions: length 149 m (488 ft 10 in); beam 23 m (75 ft 6 in); draught 5.4 m (17 ft 8½ in)	
Propulsion: two diesels delivering 6413 kW (8,600 shp) to two shafts	**Electronics:** one DRBN 32 navigation radar, one DRBV 51A air/surface search radar, one SQS-17 sonar (L 9021)
Speed: 17 kts	
Complement: 211 (10 officers plus 201 enlisted men)	

range of repair and maintenance workshops to support the units embarked. Troop accommodation is provided for 349 men under normal conditions, although 470 can be carried for short distances.

Three LCVPs are carried as deck cargo.

Nuclear test role
The *Orage* (**L 9022**) was allotted to the French Pacific nuclear experimental centre as the logistic transport to and from France. It also served as the centre's floating headquarters, using a modular facility within the well deck area. In 1993, both vessels received two twin Simbad launchers for Mistral SAMs as well as new search radars.

Both the *Orage* and ***Ouragan*** (**L 9021**) have had service life extensions but will be replaced in 2005/6 by the two new 20,000-ton 'Mistral'-class LHDs.

'Foudre' class Landing Ship Dock (TCD/LSD)

Foudre has a 1450-m² (15,608 sq ft) flight deck, with two landing spots, one of which is fitted with a landing grid and a helicopter landing system.

For years the French navy's amphibious capability was based on two LSDs dating back to the 1960s, *Ouragan* and *Orage*. The French recognized the limitations of its ageing LSDs and ordered a new TCD (Transport de Chalands de Débarquement)/LSD in 1984. The ***Foudre*** (**L 9011**) was laid down at Brest in 1986, launched in 1988 and commissioned in 1990. A sistership was authorized in 1994: the ***Siroco*** (**L 9012**) was laid down that year, launched in 1996 and commissioned in 1998.

The **'Foudre' class** are designed to carry a mechanized battalion of France's Rapid Action Force (FAN), the new professional army that replaces the conscript force of the 20th century. The vessels can also act

Twin Simbad launchers for the Mistral IR-homing SAM provide the 'Foudre' class with air defence out to a range of 4 km (2.5 miles).

as logistics support ships. A typical load for these vessels consists of one CDIC (Chaland de Débarquement d'Infanterie et de Chars) – a 380-ton LCT of which the French built a pair to operate with the 'Foudre' class; four CTMs (Chalands de Transport de Matériel) – 56-ton LCMs; ten AMX-10RC armoured cars, and up to 50 other vehicles. Without the landing craft, the 'Foudre' class can carry up to 200 vehicles. The well dock measures 122 x 14 m (400 ft 4 in x 45 ft 11 in) and can accept a 400-ton ship. Cranes of 52-ton (*Foudre*) or 38-ton (*Siroco*) capacity handle heavy equipment.

In terms of personnel, the 'Foudre' class can accommodate 467 troops (plus 1,880 tons load) or 1,600 troops for an emergency situation. With 700 personnel embarked, the 'Foudre'-class LSD has an endurance of 30 days.

Both vessels carry comprehensive command and control facilities and medical provision includes two operating theatres and 47 beds. *Siroco* is designed to accommodate a modular field hospital.

Helicopter operations
There are two landing spots on the 1450-m² (15,608 sq ft) flight deck plus one on the removable rolling cover above the well deck. They can operate a pair of Super Frelons or four AS 332F Super Puma helicopters. The landing deck on *Siroco* is

extended aft as far as the lift, to give an increased area of 1740 m² (18,730 sq ft).

Foudre is due to receive the same anti-aircraft gun armament as the Siroco. Air defence against close-in threats and sea-skimming missiles is handled by a pair of Matra Simbad lightweight twin launchers for Mistral IR-homing missiles; these are located on either side of the bridge. Without the three Breda/Mauser 30-mm guns as

fitted to Siroco, Foudre relies on a single 40-mm Bofors gun forward of the bridge, and two GIAT 20F2 20-mm guns; both ships are also armed with two 12.7-mm (0.5-mm) machine-guns. In 1997, a Sagem optronic fire-control system was fitted to both vessels. A Dassault Electronique ESM/ECM system is due to be fitted. The two ships are based at Toulon and assigned to the FAN; Siroco was deployed to East Timor in 1999.

SPECIFICATION	
Names: Foudre (L 9011), Siroco (L 9012)	**Troops:** 467
Commissioned: L 9011 7 December 1990; L 9012 21 December 1998	**Cargo:** two CDIC or 10 CTM or one EDIC/CDIC and 4 CTMs
Displacement: 12,400 tons full load; 17,200 tons flooded	**Armament:** two Matra Simbad launchers for Mistral SAMs; Foudre has one 40-mm Bofors gun and two 20-mm AA guns, Siroco has three 30-mm Breda/Mauser AA guns
Dimensions: length 168 m (551 ft 2½ in); beam 23.5 m (77 ft 1 in); draught 5.2 m (17 ft), 9.2 m (30 ft 2½ in) flooded	**Electronics:** one DRBV 21A Mars air/surface search radar, one Racal Decca 2459 surface search radar, one Racal Decca RM 1229 navigation radar, one Sagem VIGU-105 gun fire control system, Syracuse SATCOM combat system
Propulsion: two SEMT-Pielstick V400 diesels delivering 15511 kW (20,800 shp) to two shafts	
Speed: 21 kts	
Complement: 215 (17 officers)	

'San Giorgio' class Amphibious Transport Dock (LPD)

San Marco, with medium trucks carried on the deck. The stern docking well, which can accept two LCMs, measures 20.5 by 7 m (67 ft 3 in by 23 ft). The 'San Giorgio'-class LPDs are based at Brindisi and are assigned to the Third Naval Division.

Capable of operating three SH-3D Sea King or EH 101 Merlin or five AB 212 helicopters from a carrier-type flight deck, the **'San Giorgio' class** LPDs each carry a battalion of Italian infantry. **San Giorgio** (**L 9892**) and **San Marco** (**L 9893**) have bow doors for amphibious landings but **San Giusto** (**L 9894**) does not. All three can ship two LCMs in the stern docking well. The San Giorgio and San Marco were laid down in 1985 and 1986 respectively while the larger San Giusto was not ordered until 1991. The first two ships were

launched in 1987 and thwn commissioned in 1987 and 1988. The San Giusto, launched in 1993 and commissioned in 1994, is some 300 tons heavier as a result of a longer island and increased accommodation. San Marco was funded by the Italian Ministry of Civil Protection and, although run by the Italian navy,

is specially fitted for disaster relief operations.

Modernization

From 1999, the ships' 20-mm guns were replaced by 25-mm Breda Oerlikon weapons, while the San Giorgio has had its 76-mm (3-in) gun removed, and its LCVP installation relocated from davits to a port-side sponson. The flight deck has been lengthened to allow simultaneous operations of two

EH 101s and two AB 212s, and the bow doors are also being removed. Similar modifications are planned for the San Marco.

Four landing spots are provided, and a 30-ton lift and two 40-ton travelling cranes are used to transport the 64.6-ton LCMs. A typical load includes a battalion of 400 personnel, plus 30–36 APCs or 30 medium tanks. A total of two (on davits) or three (on port side sponson) LCVPs can be carried.

San Giorgio and San Marco are seen at dock, with SH-3D and AB 212 helicopters embarked. Note the port side sponsons for LCVP carriage.

SPECIFICATION	
'San Giorgio' class	to two shafts
Names: San Giorgio (L 9892), San Marco (L 9893), San Giusto (L 9894)	**Speed:** 21 kts
	Complement: 163 (San Giusto); 196
Commissioned: L 9892 9 October 1987; L 9893 18 March 1988; L 9894 9 April 1994	**Troops:** 400
	Cargo: up to 36 APCs or 30 medium tanks with LCMs in docking well and two or three LCVPs; one LCPL
Displacement: 7,665 tons full load; (San Giusto) 7,950 tons	**Armament:** one OTO Melara 76-mm (3-in) gun, two Oerlikon 25-mm guns
Dimensions: length 133.3 m (437 ft 4 in), (San Giusto) 137 m (449 ft 6 in); beam 20.5 m (67 ft 3 in); draught 5.3 m (17 ft 5 in)	**Electronics:** one SPS-72 surface search radar, one SPN-748 navigation radar, one SPG-70 fire control radar
Propulsion: two diesels deliver 12,527.8 kW (16,800 shp)	

'Oosumi' class Amphibious transport dock/landing ship tank

*The **Shimokita** is the second of a planned four 'Oosumi'-class ships, which combine **LPD** and **LST** capabilities in a single hull with a stern docking well.*

The so-called LPD/LSTs of the Japanese **'Oosumi' class** look like aircraft carriers, the first to fly the rising sun naval emblem since 1945. With their stern docking wells and flight deck, the ships also resemble scaled-down US-type LHAs rather than the tank landing ships they purport to be. If this sounds like paranoia, Japan's ability to maintain secrecy over its naval projects was afeature of the first half of the 20th century.

The **Oosumi** was approved in 1990 but not laid down until December 1995. The initial drawings that were released showed a ship half the size of the one completed and resembling the Italian 'San Giorgio' class. Launched in 1996 and commissioned in 1998, it was followed by the **Shimokita** from the same yard, and a third unit, the **Kunisaki** is under construction at Hitachi's Maizuru yard, with a fourth unit planned.

SPECIFICATION	
'Oosumi' class **Displacement:** 8,900 tons standard **Dimensions:** length 178 m (584 ft); beam 25.8 m (84 ft 8 in); draught 6 m (19 ft 8 in) **Propulsion:** two Mitsui diesels delivering 20580 kW (27,600 shp) to two shafts **Speed:** 22 kts **Armament:** two Phalanx CIWS	**Electronics:** OPS-14C air search, OPS-28D surface search, and OPS-20 navigation radars **Military lift:** 330 troops, 10 Type 90 tanks or 1,400 tons of cargo, and two LCACs **Aircraft:** platform for two CH-47J Chinook helicopters **Complement:** 135

Designed for the movement of a full battalion of marines together with a tank company, the 'Oosumi'-class accords with the recent Japanese power-projection operations into the Indian Ocean and around the Pacific. Each ship's defensive armament is limited to a pair of Phalanx CIWS systems with a six-barrel rotary cannon, but the ships operate within a task force whose other ships provide primary protection.

'Rotterdam' & 'Galicia' classes Amphibious transport dock

This venture between Dutch and Spanish shipbuilders is known to the Dutch navy as the **'Rotterdam' class** and by the Spanish navy as the **'Galicia' class**. The **Rotterdam** and **Galicia** were both laid down in 1996, and were commissioned in 1997 and 1998 respectively. The **Castilla** was laid down in 1997 and commissioned in 2000. A second Dutch ship, the **Johan de Witt**, should enter service in 2007.

The ships of the class are designed to carry a battalion of marines and all its associated combat and support vehicles. Carrying a large docking well in the stern, the ships can operate their landing craft and helicopters in varying degrees of bad weather conditions. They carry extensive medical facilities including a treatment room, operating theatre and medical laboratory, and have already been used to help out during humanitarian emergencies. In addition to land forces and their kit, the ships are designed to carry additional naval ordnance (including up to 30 torpedoes) in their magazines to support a

*The **Rotterdam** was built at the Royal Schelde yard at Vlissingen, and provides capabilities for the delivery of a full battalion of marines with all necessary kit.*

task force operating at some distance from home ports.

The defensive armament differs between the Spanish and Dutch ships, each carrying indigenous CIWS mountings in the form of the Meroka and Goalkeeper, in addition to 20-mm cannon.

The 'Rotterdam' and 'Galicia' classes provide a large area over the stern for the operation of helicopters above the dock from which landing craft operate. The **Johan de Witt** *has a stronger helicopter deck than the* **Rotterdam** *on a hull that is longer and wider.*

SPECIFICATION	
'Rotterdam'/'Galicia' class **Displacement:** 12,750 tons standard; 16,750 tons ('Rotterdam') or 13,815 ('Galicia') full load **Dimensions:** length 166 m (544 ft 7 in) ('Rotterdam') and 160 m (524 ft 11 in) ('Galicia'); beam 25 m (82 ft); draught 5.9 m (19 ft 4 in) **Propulsion:** four diesel generators delivering current to two electric motors delivering 12170 kW (16,320 shp) to two shafts **Performance:** speed 19 kts; range	11125 km (6,910 miles) at 12 kts **Armament:** ('Rotterdam') two 30-mm Goalkeeper CIWS and four 20-mm cannon, and ('Galicia') two 20-mm Meroka CIWS **Electronics:** DA-08 air/surface and Scout surface search radars **Military lift:** 611 troops, 33 tanks or 170 APCs, and 6 LCVPs or 4 LCUs or LCMs **Aircraft:** six NH 90 or four EH 101 helicopters **Complement:** 113

'Ivan Rogov' class Amphibious transport dock

Designated *bol'shoy desantnyy korabl'* (BDK, or large landing craft) by the Soviets, the **Ivan Rogov** was launched in 1976 at the Kaliningrad shipyard. The vessel entered service in 1978 as the Soviets' largest amphibious warfare ship. A second unit, the **Aleksandr Nikolayev**, was laid down in 1979 and completed in 1983, and the third unit, laid down in 1985 and completed in 1990, is the **Mitrofan Moskalenko**. A fourth unit was not completed, and the first two were decommissioned in 1996 and 1997, one of them for possible overhaul and sale to Indonesia.

The ship can carry a reinforced Naval Infantry battalion landing team with all its APCs and other vehicles plus 10 PT-76 light amphibious tanks. An alternative load is a Naval Infantry tank battalion. The vessels were unique in Soviet amphibious ship design as they had both a well dock and a helicopter flight deck and hangar. This allowed the ship to perform not only the traditional role of over-the-beach assault by use of bow doors and ramp, but also the stand-off assault role using a mixture of helicopters, landing craft, air-cushion vehicles (ACVs) and amphibious vehicles.

Accessibility

The bow doors and internal ramp position provide access to a vehicle parking deck located in the lower forward part of the ship. Further vehicles can be accommodated in the midships area of the upper deck, access to this being by hydraulically operated ramps that lead from the bow doors and the docking well. The vehicle deck itself leads directly into the floodable well which is some 79 m (259 ft 2 in) long with a stern door some 13 m (42 ft 8 in) across. The well can accommodate either two pre-loaded 'Lebed'-

SPECIFICATION	
'Ivan Rogov' class **Displacement:** 8,260 tons standard; 14,060 tons full load **Dimensions:** length 157.5 m (516 ft 9 in); beam 24.5 m (80 ft 6 in); draught 6.5 m (21 ft 4 in) **Propulsion:** two gas turbines delivering 29820 kW (39,995 shp) to two shafts **Performance:** speed 19 kts; range 13900 km (8,635 miles) at 14 kts **Armament:** one twin launcher for 20 SA-N-4 'Gecko' SAMs, one twin 76.2-mm (3-in) DP gun, four 30-mm ADG-630 CIWS mountings, two SA-N-5 quadruple launchers, and two 122-mm (4.8-in) rocket launchers	**Electronics:** one 'Top Plate-A' 3D radar, two 'Don Kay' or 'Palm Frond' navigation radars, two 'Squeeze Box' optronic directors, one 'Owl Screech' 76.2-mm gun fire-control radar, one 'Pop Group' SA-N-4 missile fire-control radar, two 'Bass Tilt' CIWS fire-control radars, one 'Salt Pole-B' IFF system, three 'Bell Shroud' ESM systems, two 'Bell Squat' ECM systems, 20 decoy launchers, and one 'Mouse Tail' VDS **Military lift:** 522 troops, typically 20 MBTs or an equivalent volume of APCs and trucks, 2,500 tons of freight, and three ACVs or six LCMs **Aircraft:** four Ka-29 'Helix' helicopters **Complement:** 239

class ACVs and a 145-ton full load 'Ondatra'-class LCM, or three 'Gus'-class troop-carrying ACVs.

Two helicopter landing spots are provided, one forward and one aft above the well dock, each with its own flight control station. Both these spots have access to the massive block superstructure, in which a hangar could accommodate five Kamov Ka-25 'Hormone-C' utility

helicopters, which were subsequently replaced by four Ka-29 helicopters.

Accommodation for the embarked Naval Infantry is located within the superstructure block, which also includes vehicle and helicopter workshops. To starboard, immediately in front of the block, is a tall deck house, on top of which is mounted a 122-mm (4.8-in) rocket-launcher

system with two 20-round packs of launcher tubes, one to each side of a pedestal mounting that trains them in azimuth and elevation. The rockets are used to provide a saturation shore bombardment capability for the assault units. A twin 76.2-mm (3-in) DP gun turret is located on the forecastle, and a pop-up two-rail launcher bin units for SA-N-4 SAMs and four 30-mm CIWS

mountings are mounted on top of the main superstructure block to provide an air-defence capability. Extensive command, control and surveillance equipment is fitted for amphibious force flagship duties.

The two Pacific Fleet units have paid off, leaving only the *Mitrofan Moskalenko* in service with the Northern Fleet from the base at Severomorsk.

'Albion' class Landing platform dock (LPD)

The Royal Navy's two assault ships, HMS *Fearless* and HMS *Intrepid*, laid down in 1962, were due for deletion in 1981 as part of the Conservative government's decision to end the Royal Marines' amphibious capability. This ruling played a major role in the Argentine decision of the following year to invade the Falklands Islands. The two ships were reprieved and played a vital role in the liberation of the islands. It was another 10 years before a decision was taken to authorize replacements for what were, by the 1991 Gulf War, very elderly ships. Even then, the two **'Albion'-class** LPDs were not laid down until 1998 and 2000 respectively, by which time the *Intrepid* had been cannibalized to keep the *Fearless* operational.

Even then, the fire in the ship's engine room during November 2000, when the *Fearless* was operating off Sierra Leone, demonstrated the dangers in relying on a 40-year old ship. Keeping it in service was estimated to require another £2 million, so the *Fearless* was paid off in March 2002.

The £429 million replacement programme was accelerated after the events of 11 September 2001, and the requirement was altered to supply the capability for the mounting of more than one amphibious operation at a time. **HMS *Albion*** was launched in March 2001, but its in-service date of March 2002 slipped by a year. **HMS *Bulwark*** was launched in November 2001, but workers on it were transferred

to accelerate the completion of the *Albion*.

Much larger and more capable LPDs than the ships they are replacing, the 'Albion'-class units are part of a drive to modernize Britain's amphibious capability. They will serve alongside the new helicopter carrier HMS *Ocean* and the four 'Bay'-class landing ships (logistic) that are planned to replace the 'Sir Bedivere'-class LSLs. The extensive command and control systems aboard the 'Albion' class represent a great leap

forward for the Royal Navy and Marines.

One feature worthy of note is the diesel-electric propulsion system, the first to be used by a British surface warship. This requires only two-thirds the engineering complement of the older LPDs and, in overall terms, automation and new technology have reduced the manning requirement from 550 to 325. The four new LCU Mk 10 'ro-ro' landing craft operated by each 'Albion' are capable of carrying a Challenger 2 MBT.

Right: The two 'Albion'-class assault ships were built by BAE Systems (formerly Vickers) at Barrow-in-Furness, and were somewhat delayed by lack of skilled workers.

Below: HMS Albion and HMS Bulwark are Royal Navy ships that provide the Royal Marines with a quantum leap forward in their amphibious assault capabilities.

SPECIFICATION	
'Albion' class **Displacement:** 19,560 tons full load; 21,500 tons docked down **Dimensions:** length 176 m (577 ft 5 in); beam 29.9 m (98 ft 1 in); draught 6.7 m (22 ft) **Propulsion:** diesel generators powering two electric motors driving two shafts **Performance:** speed 20 kts; range 14825 km (9,210 miles) at 14 kts **Armament:** two 30-mm Goalkeeper CIWS mountings and two twin 20-mm AA guns	**Electronics:** one Type 996 air/surface-search, one surface search and two navigation radars, ADAWS 2000 combat data system, UAT-1/4 ESM system and eight Sea Gnat decoy launchers **Military lift:** 305 or overload 710 troops, six Challenger 2 tanks or 30 APCs, four LCUs and four LCVPs **Aircraft:** two/three medium helicopters **Complement:** 325

'Tarawa'-class Amphibious assault ships

The 'Tarawa'-class LHA ships were intended to combine the capabilities of the helicopter carrier (LPH), the amphibious transport dock (LPD), the command ship (LCC) and the amphibious cargo ship (LKA) in a single hull. The class was originally to have numbered nine, but as a result of the end of the Vietnam War and budgetary constraints, the eventual number built was five. The Ingalls shipyard built them by means of its multi-ship construction technique between 1971 and 1978.

The ship's sides are vertical for some two-thirds of their length in order to maximize the internal space available for cargo. A hanger 82 m (268 ft)

Above: The USS Belleau Wood photographed in 1987. The vessel was still equipped with a Mk 45 gun in the starboard bow position. The fully automatic 5-in weapon could fire once every three seconds, putting a 30-kg (66-lb) shell out to a range of 24,000 m (78,740 ft). Primarily intended for shore bombardment, the guns could also be used against aircraft.

Below: The USS Saipan is seen in comapny with the amphibious transport dock (LPD) ship USS Ponce (top) and the underway replenishment oiler USNS Patuxent (centre) during a simultaneous underway replenishment in September 2002.

long by 24 m (78 ft) wide, with a 6.1-m (20-ft) overhead, is located above a similarly sized well deck set into the stern. To port, the hangar is served by a side lift with an 18182-kg (40,085-lb) capacity and a larger 36364-kg (80,170-lb) capacity centreline lift at the stern. The docking well, vehicle deck, cargo holds and hangar deck are connected by a series of five elevators capable of carrying 1000-kg (2,205-lb) palletized loads. The three forward elevators serve the vehicle deck and use a conveyor belt system, while the aft two elevators (located at the other end of the belt) serve both the well deck, where an

overhead cargo-carrying monorail system takes the pallets onto the landing craft, and the hangar deck. An angled ramp from the hangar deck leads to the flight deck to allow direct loading of helicopters.

Vehicle accomodation

Forward of the docking well (and connected to it and the flight deck by ramps) are the vehicle decks. These normally

accommodate 160 tracked vehicles, artillery pieces and trucks as well as 40 AAV7A1 amphibious assault personnel carriers. The well deck can accommodate up to four LCUs or two LCUs and two LCM 8s or 17 LCM 6s. The four LCUs and eight of the AAV7A1s can be launched simultaneously from the well deck. The vessels normally carry two LCM 6s and two LCPLs stowed on deck for

launch by a large deck crane. The aircraft hangar has the capacity for 26 CH-46E Sea Knight or 19 CH-53D Sea Stallion/CH-53E Super Stallion helicopters, although the normal air group embarked tends to be either 12 CH-46Es, six CH-53D/Es, four AH-1W Super Cobra gunships and two UH-1N Twin Huey utility helicopters; or six CH-46Es, nine CH-53D/Es, four AH-1Ws and two UH-1Ns.

Below: The main function of an assault ship is to get troops ashore in the shortest possible time, with assault troops riding into battle within amphibious assault vehicles. Here an AAV7A1 Amphibious Assault Vehicle from the USS Nassau advances onto the beach during a mock invasion of Newfoundland. In the post Cold War era, such realistic training exercises improve the skills that may be called upon during a NATO-led peacekeeping support operation. The AAV is the heart of the Marine assault, 'Tarawa'-class vessels carrying up to 40 examples.

Below right: A US Navy LCAC (Landing Craft Air Cushion) of Assault Craft Unit Five delivers troops and cargo to the USS Peleliu during an amphibious exercise off the coast of Southern California.

Below left: Mainstay of the USMC's heavylift capability, a CH-53E Super Stallion lands on the deck of the USS Nassau off the coast of Nova Scotia. In service with five active duty units, the three-engined CH-53E variant is capable of externally lifting any USMC tactical jet or an LAV.

Both the AV-8 Harrier series and the OV-10 Bronco fixed-wing aircraft have also been operated, the former being a V/STOL close-support fighter and the latter a STOL observation/attack aircraft. An acclimatization and training room allows the US Marine battalion to exercise in a controlled environment.

To act as an amphibious squadron flagship, the LHA is fitted with the Tactical Amphibious Warfare Data System (TAWDS) to provide command and control over the group's aircraft, weapons, sensors and landing craft. The same satellite communications system and data links as fitted to the LCCs are carried. Two of the LHAs are assigned to the Atlantic fleets while the other three are with the Pacific fleets.

'GATOR NAVY': US AMPHIBIOUS ASSAULT

The five 'Tarawa'-class vessels form an important component of the US Navy's assault fleet, or 'Gator Navy'. These ships are now ageing, but to date only a single additional 'Wasp'-class ship has been ordered to replace the USS Tarawa. The latter may replace the USS Inchon in the specialist mine warfare role. Nocturnal operations are illustrated aboard the USS Nassau during the Combined Joint Task Force Exercise '96, with a CH-46 preparing for a night launch (below left) and a

USMC LAV (Light Armored Vehicle) backing onto a US Navy landing craft prior to amphibious operations from the ship's well deck (below right).

The 'Tarawa' class have also been active in military campaigns. Pictured bottom is an AV-8B taxiing aboard the USS Tarawa in the Persian Gulf in support of Operation Southern Watch, enforcing the No-Fly Zone over southern Iraq in December 1998.

'Whidbey Island' and 'Harpers Ferry' class Landing ships

Based on the 'Anchorage' class, the **'Whidbey Island' class** were replacements for the 'Thomaston'-class LSDs. The first 'Whidbey Island' vessel was laid down in 1981. In 1988 the class was enlarged from 8 to 12 units, the last four forming a sub-class (the **'Harpers Ferry'-class LSD-CV**s or Landing Ship Dock-Cargo Variant ships) with an enhanced cargo capacity. The **LSD 41** (Landing Ship Dock-41) programme replaced the eight ageing LSD 28-class ships that ended service during the 1980s.

Enter the hovercraft

The 'Whidbey Island' class were designed from the outset to operate LCAC (Landing Craft Air Cushion) hovercraft. These carry a 60-ton payload and travel at speeds in excess of 40 kts in calm conditions, enabling amphibious assaults to be made over greater distances and against a wide variety of beaches. The well deck measures 134.1 x 15.2 m (440 ft x 50 ft). It can accommodate four hovercraft, which is more than any other amphibious assault vessel.

The most obvious visual differences between the sub-classes are that the LSD-CVs have only one crane and that the forward Phalanx CIWS is mounted atop the bridge on LSD 41-48 but below and forward of the superstructure on the 'Harpers Ferry' class.

Ship self defence

USS *Whidbey Island* trialled the QRCC (Quick Reaction Combat Capability) system from June 1993. The combination of RIM-116A missiles, Phalanx CIWS and AN/SLQ-32 EW system was accorded a higher priority after the Iraqi Exocet attack against the USS *Stark* on 17 May 1987. Now designated the SSDS (Ship Self Defense System) it has been installed on all 'Whidbey Island'-class ships.

The 'Whidbey Island'-class ships are intended to land a battalion of US Marines via four LCAC hovercraft, 21 LCMs (Landing Craft Medium) or three LCUs (Landing Craft Utilities). Alternatively, the troops can be landed in 64 AAV7A1 amphibious tracked armoured personnel carriers. The LSD-CV cargo variants deploy fewer landing craft: two hovercraft, nine LCMs or one LCU. In addition to the anti-aircraft and anti-missile guns and missiles carried for active defence, extensive passive measures are available. A powerful ESM suite is complemented by chaff rockets capable of 'seducing' incoming missiles and AN/SLQ-49 chaff buoys that are effective for several hours in moderate sea conditions, producing a

*As well as having generous freight space, the 'Whidbey Island'-class **LSD**s also feature a potent self defence weapons system. This is **LSD 44**, the USS Gunston Hill.*

radar signature that is greater than that of the ship. The Nixie decoy system has a similar effect on torpedoes trying to target the ship.

The first two units cost over $300 million. The last four averaged $150 million per ship. 1996 figures quoted the annual operating cost of one of these vessels at approximately $20 million.

SPECIFICATION	
'Whidbey Island' class **Displacement:** 15,726 tons full load (LSD 41-48); 16,740 tons (LSD 49-52) **Dimensions:** length 185.8 m (609 ft 6 in); beam 25.6 m (84 ft); draught 6.3 m (20 ft 6 in) **Propulsion:** four diesel engines delivering 24608 kW (33,000 shp) to two shafts **Speed:** 22 kts **Range:** 8,000 nm (14816 km; 9,206 miles) at 18 kts (33 km/h; 20 mph) **Complement:** 22 officers and 391 enlisted personnel **Troops:** 402; surge capacity is 627 **Cargo:** 141.6 m³ (5,000 cu ft) available for general cargo plus 1161 m² (12,500 sq ft) for vehicles (including four pre-loaded	hovercraft in the well deck); LSD 49-52 have 1914 m³ (67,600 cu ft) space for cargo plus 1877 m² (20,200 sq ft) for motor transport but only two or three hovercraft **Armament:** two General Dynamics 20-mm six-barrelled Vulcan Phalanx Mk 15 guns; two 25-mm Mk 38 guns; eight or more 0.5-in (12.7-mm) machine-guns **Countermeasures:** four Loral Hycor SRBOC six-barrelled Mk 36 launchers, AN/SLQ-25 Nixie acoustic torpedo decoy, AN/SLQ-49 chaff buoys, AN/SLQ-32 radar warning/jammer/deception system **Electronics:** AN/SPS-67 surface search radar, AN/SPS-49 air search radar, AN/SPS-64 navigation radar **Aircraft:** two CH-53 Sea Stallions (platform only)

*A 'Whidbey Island'-class **LSD** disgorges an **LCAC** hovercraft from the well deck at the rear of the vessel. Stores can be seen stacked on the helo deck, which is normally used by **CH-53** helicopters.*

'Wasp' class Amphibious assault ship

The **'Wasp'-class** ships are the largest amphibious assault vessels in the world, providing the US Navy with an unrivalled ability to attack hostile shores. They are the first ships specifically designed to operate both the AV-8B Harrier II and LCAC hovercraft. The last three of the class to be completed have cost an average of $750 million each. The US plans for a 12-strong ARG (Amphibious Ready Group) to be deployed by 2010, when the first 'Tarawa'-class vessel will be 35-years-old.

The 'Wasp' class follows on from the 'Tarawa' class and its ships share the same hull and engineering plant. However, the bridge is two decks lower than the LHAs (Landing Helicopter Amphibious) and the command, control and communications centres are inside the hull, where they are less easy to disable. To facilitate landing and recovery operations, the ships can ballast some 15,000 tons of sea water for trimming.

Capable of embarking a 2,000-strong MEU (Marine Expeditionary Unit), the 'Wasp' class can land its troops on the beach from its own landing craft, or deliver them inland via helicopters (a manoeuvre known as 'vertical envelopment'). Each 'Wasp' class can accommodate up to three LCACs or twelve LCMs in the 81 x 15.2 m (267 x 50 ft) well deck. In total, 61 AAVs (Amphibious Assault Vehicles – the AAV7A1) can be shipped aboard, 40 stowed in the well deck and 21 in the upper vehicle storage area.

The flight deck has nine landing spots for helicopters and up to 42 CH-46 Sea Knights can be operated; the class can also deploy AH-1 SeaCobra attack helicopters or other transports

In addition to deploying a powerful air component, the 'Wasp'-class vessels can operate three LCAC hovercraft (pictured) or 12 LCM type landing craft.

such as the CH-53E Super Stallion, UH-1N Twin Huey or the SH-60B Seahawk. The 'Wasp' class can operate six to eight AV-8B Harrier IIs in the combat role, but can support up to 20. There are two aircraft elevators, one amidships on the port side, the other to starboard, abaft the 'island'. To pass through the Panama Canal, these have to be folded inboard.

Air wing

The composition of the air group depends on the mission. The 'Wasp' class can function as aircraft carriers, operating 20 AV-8Bs in the sea control role, plus six ASW helicopters. For amphibious assault, a typical group consists of six AV-8Bs, four AH-1W attack helicopters, 12 CH-46 Sea Knights, nine CH-53 Sea Stallions or Super Stallions and four UH-1N Twin Hueys. Alternatively, it can also operate 42 CH-46s.

The 'Wasp'-class ships are designed to carry a balanced force of combat vehicles, including five M1 Abrams main battle tanks, 25 AAV7A1 armoured personnel carriers, eight M198 155-mm self-propelled guns, 68 lorries as well as other support vehicles. Monorail trains deliver cargo from the storage areas to the well deck, which opens to the sea through gates in the stern.

Each ship features a 600-bed hospital and six operating theatres, thereby reducing an amphibious task force's

The USS Wasp (LHD 1) alongside the underway replenishment (UNREP) vessel USNS Supply during a deployment in support of Operation Enduring Freedom. Wasp's airwing includes AV-8B and CH-53 aircraft.

SPECIFICATION

'Wasp' class
Displacement: 41,150 tons
Dimensions: length 253.2 m (844 ft); beam 31.8 m (106 ft); draught 8.1 m (32 ft)
Propulsion: two geared steam turbines delivering 33849 kW (70,000 shp) to two shafts
Speed: 22 kts
Range: 9,500 nm (17594 km; 10,933 miles) at 18 kts (33 km/h; 20 mph)
Complement: 1,208 personnel
Troops: 1,894
Cargo: 2860 m³ (101,000 cu ft) for general stores plus 1858 m² (20,000 sq ft) for vehicles
Aircraft: number deployed depends on mission but can include AV-8B, AH-1W, CH-46, CH-53 and UH-1N
Armament: two Raytheon GMLS Mk 29 octuple SAM launchers for Sea Sparrow semi-active radar homing

missiles, two GDC Mk 49 RAM launchers for RIM-116A infra-red/radiation homing missiles, three General Dynamics 20-mm six-barrelled Vulcan Phalanx Mk 15 guns (only two on LHD 5-7), four 25-mm Mk 38 guns (three on LHD 5-7) and four 0.5-in (12.7-mm) machine-guns
Countermeasures: four or six Loral Hycor SRBOC 6-barrelled Mk 36 launchers, AN/SLQ-25 Nixie acoustic torpedo decoy, Sea Gnat missile decoy, AN/SLQ-49 chaff buoys, AN/SLQ-32 radar warning/ jammer/deception system
Electronics: one AN/SPS-52 or AN/SPS-48 (later vessels) air search radar, one AN/SPS-49 air search radar, one SPS-67 surface search radar, navigation and fire control radars, AN/URN 25 TACAN

dependence on medical facilities ashore.

The 'Wasp' class has been replacing the older LHAs since the mid-1990s. **USS Bataan** was built by pre-outfitting and modular construction techniques. Subassemblies were brought together to produce five hull and superstructure modules, which were then joined together on land. This construction technique meant that the ship was three-quarters complete on launch. *Bataan* is the first amphibious assault ship designed from the outset to accommodate female personnel, both in the crew and Marine contingent. Full accommodation for up to 450 female officers, enlisted personnel and troops is provided on the vessel.

'San Antonio' class Amphibious transport docks

The 12 ships of the **LPD 17** or **'San Antonio'** (**Landing Platform Dock**) **class** will eventually replace three classes of amphibious assault vessel: LPD 4s, LSD 36s and LSTs, as well as the LKA (already retired in 2002) – a total of 41 vessels. This will not only modernize an elderly amphibious assault fleet but deliver significant savings in life-cycle costs and personnel numbers. However, costs of the first three vessels are over-budget: the LPD 17 class will cost more than $800 million against an estimate of $617 million. This is despite numerous cost-saving measures, including the decision to adopt a commercial surface search radar (AN/SPS-73). The design process exploited virtual reality computer programmes, enabling many internal layouts to be tested without prototypes being built. Input from over 2,500 serving personnel is intended to produce a vessel truly designed for the men and women who will live onboard.

Mobility triad

Approved in 1993, construction of the LPD 17 was delayed by legal disputes over the award of contracts but the first of the class, **San Antonio**, was launched in 2003 and was commissioned in 2005.

The US Marine Corps has developed the concept of the 'mobility triad' and the LPD 17 class is the first assault ship designed to accommodate all three modes of transport: the MV-22 Osprey tiltrotor aircraft, the LCAC hovercraft and the AAV amphibious APC. It is thus capable of landing troops some 173 nm (320 km; 200 miles) inland, making 'littoral operations' far greater in scope than ever previously imagined. Two LCAC hovercraft or one LCU are embarked along with 14 AAVs. The well deck and stern layout are similar to that of the 'Wasp' class, but the superstructure is angled to reduce radar signature. A 24-bed hospital is included with two operating theatres and a casualty overflow capacity of 100 persons. Defensive weapons systems will include the SSDS that will be fitted once the vessels are completed.

The LPD 17 class ships deploy up to four CH-46 Sea Knight helicopters simultaneously or two MV-22 Ospreys. Four MV-22s can be spotted on deck and one more in the hanger. Alternatively the hanger can accommodate one CH-53E, two CH-46s or two UH-1s. With double the vehicle storage space of the old LPD 4 class, the LPD 17 class is also designed for maximum survivability: the combination of reduced radar profile and advanced computer systems to coordinate defensive weaponry is intended to allow the ship to operate alone if required, although it would normally be part of an amphibious ready group. *San Antonio* is the first US warship to be equipped with a fibre-optic Shipboard Wide Area Network (SWAN) that connects all ship systems, sensors and weapons, providing integrated real-time data to its combat command centre.

The LPD 17-class vessels have been designed with low-observable characteristics. An MV-22 Osprey can be seen on the flight deck in this illustration.

On 7 September 2002, about one year after the attack on the World Trade Center, Gordon England, Secretary of the Navy, announced that the fifth ship of the class would be named *New York*.

SPECIFICATION
'San Antonio' class
Displacement: 25,300 tons full load
Dimensions: length 208.4 m (684 ft); beam 31.9 m (105 ft), draught 7 m (23 ft)
Propulsion: four diesels delivering 29,828 kW (40,000 shp) to two shafts
Speed: 22 kts
Range: unknown
Complement: 32 officers and 465 enlisted personnel
Troops: 699 (surge capacity 800)
Cargo: 708 m³ (25,000 cu ft) cargo space below decks plus 2323 m² (25,000 sq ft) deck space for vehicles
Armament: Mk 41 VLS (Vertical Launch System) for two octuple Sea Sparrow systems and 64 missiles, two GDC Mk 31 RAM launchers, two Bushmaster Mk 46 30-mm close-in guns, two Mk 26 0.5-in (12.7-mm) machine guns
Countermeasures: four Mk 36 SRBOC launchers, Nulka rocket-launched hovering decoy system, AN/SLQ-25 Nixie acoustic homing torpedo decoy, AN/SLQ-32A radar warning/jamming/deception system
Electronics: AN/SPS-48 air-search radar, AN/SPS-73 surface-search radar, AN/SPQ-9 fire-control radar, navigation radars and sonar
Aircraft: two CH-53 Sea Stallions/Super Stallions or four CH-46 Sea Knights or two MV-22 Ospreys or four UH-1N Twin Hueys

'Mistral' class Amphibious assault ship

Ordered in 2000, the new **'Mistral' class** are amphibious assault ships classified as NTCD (*Nouvelles Transports de Chalands de Debarquement*). The first to be completed was the **Mistral** in 2004, while the **Tonnere** is due to complete in 2006. They will serve as pre-positioned command platforms and landing docks for amphibious operations, and will also undertake non-military tasks such as evacuation and humanitarian relief.

The two 'Mistral'-class ships are successors to the *Ouragan* and *Orage*. To control costs, the ships are being constructed to civil rather than naval standards, the forward sections and accommodation modules being built at St Nazaire by Chantiers de l'Atlantique, and the middle and aft sections (operations and payload) by DCN, which will combine its own sections with those delivered from St Nazaire. The ships will be outfitted as flagships for joint task force operations, and will include

Due to replace the two 'Ouragan'-class LSDs (landing ships dock) from 2005 and 2006, the pair of 'Mistral'-class LHDs (landing ships helicopter and dock) will transform the French navy's amphibious capabilities.

satellite communications as well as national and NATO data-link systems, the object being close co-operation with British, Dutch, Italian and Spanish vessels.

The 'Mistral'-class has a 'through-deck' design with two lifts (one astern and the other abaft the island) to connect the hangar deck with the flight deck, which will have spots for six

helicopters. The stern dock will be compatible with US LCAC (air-cushion landing craft) and a new class of LCM (Landing Craft Mechanized).

SPECIFICATION

'Mistral' class
Displacement: 20,670 tons full load
Dimensions: length 199 m (652 ft 11 in); beam 32 m (105 ft); draught 8 m (26 ft 3 in)
Propulsion: four diesel generators delivering 15210 kW (20,400 hp) to two podded propulsor units trainable though 360° and to one bow thruster
Performance: speed 19 kts; endurance 20400 km (12,675 miles) at 15 kts
Armament: two sextuple launchers

for Mistral short-range SAMs, two 30-mm cannon and four 0.5-in (12.7-mm) machine-guns
Electronics: one MRR 3D air/surface search radar, two Racal navigation radars, two optronic directors, and one SIC 21 command support system
Aircraft: up to 16 NH 90 or Cougar helicopters
Lift: 450 troops and 60 AFVs or 230 vehicles
Complement: 160

Each of the ships will have a complete 63-bed hospital, and provision for facilities erected from containerized field hospital units.

'Endurance' class Landing platform dock/landing ship tank

The lead unit of a four-ship class, the Endurance is a comparatively small but nonetheless capable LPD/LST type, and well suited to short- and medium-range operations in Far Eastern waters.

In the early 1990s the Republic of Singapore decided to press ahead with the creation of a modern amphibious assault capability, and in September 1994 ordered from the Banoi yard of Singapore Technologies Marine four **'Endurance'-class** vessels named **Endurance**, **Resolution**, **Persistence** and **Endeavour**. Laid down in 1997–98 and launched in 1998–2000 for completion between March 2000 and April 2001, these four units are combined LPD (landing platform dock) and LST (tank landing ship) vessels. Based at Changi, the ships constitute the Singapore navy's 191st Squadron.

The design is of a US roll-on/roll-off (drive-through) type with stern and bow ramps, the former a virtually full-width unit and the latter installed behind opening bow sections. Internally there is a single intermediate deck with vehicle movement between decks made possible by three hydraulic ramps.

The docking well is located in the after part of the design with the large helicopter deck above it. The docking well can accommodate four LCUs (Landing Craft Utility), and ship-to-shore movement is facilitated by the carriage in davits of four LCVPs (Landing Craft Vehicle and Personnel). The design has

hangar accommodation, forward of the helicopter deck, for two Super Puma medium-lift helicopters. On each side of the helicopter hangar door is a 25-ton capacity crane. Self-protection is entrusted to a pair

of twin launchers for Mistral short-range SAMs, and a 76.2-mm (3-in) Otobreda Super Compact gun forward of the bridge. The IAI Barak vertical-launch SAM system may be retrofitted in due course.

SPECIFICATION

'Endurance' class
Displacement: 8,500 tons full load
Dimensions: length 141 m (462 ft 3 in); beam 21 m (68 ft 11 in); draught 5 m (16 ft 5)
Propulsion: two Ruston 16RK 270 diesels delivering 8950 kW (12,000 hp) to two shafts
Performance: speed 15 kts; endurance 7440 km (4,625 miles) at 12 kts
Armament: two Simbad twin launchers for Mistral short-range SAMs, one 76.2-mm (3-in) Otobreda Super Rapid DP gun, and five 0.5-in (12.7-mm) machine-guns
Electronics: EL/M-2238 air/surface search radar, Type 1007 navigation radar, two Najir 2000 optronic directors, RAN 1101 EW system, and two Shield III chaff launchers
Aircraft: two Super Puma helicopters
Lift: 350 troops, or 18 tanks, or 20 vehicles or 4 LCVPs
Complement: 65

'Ocean' class Landing platform helicopter

The result of a programme launched in 1987 and then allowed to lapse until 1993, when an order was placed with Vickers Shipbuilding of Barrow-in-Furness as prime contractor to complete a hull built by Kvaerner at Govan on the River Clyde, **HMS Ocean** is an LPH (Landing Platform Helicopter). The ship was laid down in May 1994, launched in October 1995, sailed to Barrow under her own power in November 1996, and was commissioned in September 1998.

Providing the Royal Navy with a modern helicopter lift and assault capability, the Ocean is based on the design of the 'Invincible'-class light carrier with a completely revised superstructure and propulsion.

Assault role

As such, the ship can embark, support and operate a squadron of helicopters (assault transport or attack) and a complete Royal Marine commando with all its vehicles, weapons, ammunition and other equipment.

The ship is also large enough to carry up to 20 BAE Systems Harrier STOVL warplanes, although it does not embark the stores and other equipment necessary to support these fixed-wing warplanes.

Helicopter deck

The helicopter deck is large and strong enough to support six Boeing Chinook twin-rotor helicopters, and is marked with six landing and parking spots.

The twin 20-mm cannon mountings, designed for last-

ditch defence against aircraft and small craft, are often not shipped, and may be replaced by single 20-mm cannon.

HMS Ocean's ability to defend itself against anti-ship missiles is vested primarily in the Phalanx CIWS mountings.

SPECIFICATION

'Ocean' class
Displacement: 21,758 tons full load
Dimensions: length 203.4 m (667 ft 4 in); beam 34.4 m (112 ft 11 in); draught 6.6 m (21 ft 8 in)
Propulsion: two Crossley Pielstick 12 PC2 6V400 diesels delivering 13690 kW (18,360 hp) to two shafts
Performance: speed 19 kts; endurance 14805 km (9,200 miles) at 15 kts
Armament: four twin 20-mm cannon and three 20-mm Phalanx Mk 15 CIWS mountings
Electronics: one Type 996 air/surface search, two Type 1007 surface search/navigation radars, one ADAWS 2000 combat data system, one UAT EW system, and eight Sea Gnat decoy launchers
Aircraft: 12 Sea King HC.Mk 4 or Merlin helicopters, and six Lynx or Apache helicopters
Lift: up to 972 standard or 1,275 overload troops, 40 vehicles, and four LVCPs and two Griffon hovercraft
Complement: 285 plus 206 aircrew

Glossary

AA Anti-aircraft, as in 'anti-aircraft artillery' (AAA); air-to-air, as in 'air-to-air missile' (AAM).

ASM Anti-submarine missile; anti-submarine mortar (also air-to-surface missile, air-to-ship/anti-ship missile).

ASW Anti-submarine warfare.

Axial fire Gunfire ahead or astern, along the major axis of the vessel.

Battlecruiser The made-up designation for a hybrid warship armed like a battleship but sacrificing passive protection in the form of armour plate for speed.

Battleship Originally the biggest and most powerful ships of the fleet, mounting guns of usually 10 in (254 mm) or larger calibre (the biggest were those of the Japanese Yamato class, which were 18.1 in (460 mm), and heavily armoured. The word was derived from 'line-of-battle ships', the equivalent warships in the days of sailing navies.

Broadside The simultaneous firing of the guns located on the side (or front) of ship.

Bulkhead/Water-tight bulkhead A vertical partition employed to divide up a ship's internal space, both longitudinally and transversely. These partitions may be water-tight, in which case the openings in them to allow passage must be capable of being sealed, preferably by remote control.

Capital ship A term coined around 1910 to describe the most important naval assets, and group together battleships and battlecruisers (chiefly to give extra credibility to the latter); it was later extended to include monitors.

Carrier battle group A force designation coined during World War II; it was made up of one or more fleet aircraft carriers together with associated defensive elements – destroyers and cruisers – but often included battleships, which had by then largely been relegated to the shore bombardment role.

Corvette Originally a (French) sailing ship of war, too small to warrant a rate (and thus the equivalent of the British sloop); more recently, a warship smaller than a frigate or destroyer-escort.

Cruiser A warship, larger than a frigate or destroyer, much more heavily armed and often armoured to some degree, intended for independent action or to act as a scout for the battlefleet. Modern cruisers operate as defensive elements within carrier battle groups.

CVNX The latest generation of US Navy aircraft carriers that incorporate many new design features including a new nuclear reactor design (the A1B reactor), stealthier features to help reduce radar profile, electromagnetic catapults, advanced arresting gear, and reduced crewing requirements. The US Navy believes that with the addition of the most modern equipment and extensive use of automation they will be able to reduce the cost of future aircraft carriers.

DDG Guided missile destroyer.

Deck The continuous horizontal platforms, the equivalent of floors in a building, which separate a ship. Each has its proper name (though there is often duplication and some confusion); the orlop is the lowest, then the lower, main, upper, shelter, bridge and boat, though many passenger liners have many more, with names like promenade deck and hurricane deck.

Destroyer Originally torpedo-boat destroyer; a small warship of little more than 200 tons displacement, itself equipped to launch torpedoes, but also armed with light guns. By the end of Word War I, the first major conflict in which they played a serious role, they had grown to well over 1000 tons, and by the end of World War II, to over triple that. In more modern times, the type has largely disappeared, and been replaced by enlarged frigates.

Draught (also Draft) The measure of the depth of water required to float a ship, or how much she 'draws'.

Dreadnought The generic name given to a battleship modelled after HMS *Dreadnought*, the first with all-big-gun armament.

ECM Electronic Countermeasures; actions taken to confuse an enemy force's sensors.

Flotilla In the Royal Navy up to World War II, an organised unit of (usually eight) smaller warships – destroyers and submarines in particular, but also minesweepers and fast attack craft; cruisers and capital ships were grouped into squadrons, and squadrons and flotillas made up fleets – derived from the diminutive of the Spanish *flota*, fleet.

Forecastle Originally the superstructure erected at the bows of a ship to serve as a fighting platform, later the (raised) forward portion and the space beneath it, customarily used as crews' living quarters. Pronounced fo'c'sle.

Frigate Originally, fifth- or sixth rate ships carrying their guns on a single deck, employed as scouts, and the counterpart of the later cruiser. The term fell into disuse from the mid-1800s and was revived a century later to designate a small warship, between corvette and destroyer in size, used for convoy escort duties; later it became the generic term for smaller warships.

Horsepower A measure of the power produced by an engine; one horsepower = 550 foot/pounds per second ('the power required to raise 550 pounds through one foot in one second'). Various forms were and are used – brake horsepower (bhp) is the useable power delivered by an engine or motor as measured by a brake on its output shaft.

Keel The main longitudinal timber of a ship or boat, effectively her spine and certainly her strongest member.

Knot Internationally, the measure of a ship's speed – one nautical mile per hour.

Magazine Secure storage for explosives.

Masts Spars, mounted vertically or close to it employed to allow sails to be carried. Bigger ships had topmasts and even topgallant masts mounted above the lower mast. A secondary use was to provide a platform for lookouts and signal flags, and that continued, especially in warships, long after sails had been eliminated. Latterly masts acted as platforms for radio and radar antennae.

MGB/MTB Motor gun boat/motor torpedo boat.

Minesweeper A small ship, roughly the size of a trawler (many were, in fact, converted fishing boats originally) adapted and equipped to locate and neutralise submarine mines. Later supplemented by specialist minehunters.

NATO North Atlantic Treaty Organisation.

Nautical mile Internationally, the measure of distance at sea which has become standardised at 6080 ft (1852 m).

Periscope An optical device allowing an observer to change his plane of vision; it works by means of right prisms, or mirrors placed in parallel planes, which reflect incident rays at identical but opposed angles. At sea they were commonly used to allow submerged submarines a view of the surface, and also in gun turrets.

Propeller Properly speaking, the screw propeller; as essential to steam- and motor ships as their powerplant, the rotation of the screw propeller and the angle of its blades or vanes combine to generate thrust against the mass of water, which pushes the vessel through it.

Radar An acronym for Radio Direction and Range – a means of using electromagnetic radiation (in this case at the very top of the radio spectrum) to locate an object in space by bouncing signals off it and measuring the time elapsed before they return to the plane of the emitter, the orientation of the receiving antenna providing directional data.

Rudder A vertical board or fin hung on the centreline of the vessel at the stern post, originally (and still, in small boats) from simple hinges known as pintels, and connected either directly to the tiller or by ropes or chains to the steering wheel, which, when it is angled relative to the vessel's course, causes a change of direction.

Squadron In the Royal Navy, originally an organised unit of (usually eight) major warships – cruisers and capital ships, but in the US Navy (and the practice became widespread), an organised unit of ships of any type, from minesweepers upwards, the term having taken over from flotilla.

SAM Surface-to-air missile.

SSM Surface-to-surface missile.

SSN Nuclear-powered submarine.

Tonnage The load carrying capacity of a merchant ship or the displacement of a warship. In a merchant ship, tonnage (the term comes from 'tun' – a wine cask – the original standard cargo unit; 'ton' means not 2240lbs, but 100 cubic feet) may be calculated in a number of ways. Gross tonnage is the total internal volume of a ship's hull derived from a calculation based on her dimensions; net tonnage is the internal volume available for the loading of cargo (ie, the gross tonnage minus space allocated to crew accommodation, machinery, bunkerage etc). Deadweight tonnage is a measurement of the total weight of cargo, fuel and stores a vessel can carry when fully loaded.

Turret Armoured, rotating gun mounted on a ship's deck.

U-boat German submarine.

Index of Ships
Page numbers in *italics* refer to illustrations.

General Index Page numbers in *italics* refer to illustrations.